DATE DUE

Parenting
in
Contemporary
Society

SECOND EDITION

Tommie J. Hamner
University of Alabama

Pauline H. Turner
University of New Mexico

ALLYN and BACON
BOSTON LONDON TORONTO SYDNEY TOKYO SINGAPORE

Library of Congress Cataloging-in-Publication Data

Hamner, Tommie J., 1932-
    Parenting in contemporary society / Tommie J. Hamner, Pauline H.
Turner. -- 2nd ed.
        p.   cm.
    Includes bibliographical references.
    ISBN 0-13-648882-X
    1. Parenting. 2. Parenting--Study and teaching. 3. Family.
4. Child rearing. I. Turner, Pauline H., 1937-   . II. Title.
HQ755.8.H35 1990
649'.1--dc20   89-71061
                                                   CIP

Editorial/production supervision: Mary McDonald
Interior design: Karen Buck
Cover design: Photo Plus Art
Manufacturing buyer: Robert Anderson

Copyright © 1990 by Allyn and Bacon
A Division of Simon & Schuster, Inc.
160 Gould Street
Needham Heights, Massachusetts 02194

©1985, 1980, 1973, 1967 by Prentice-Hall, Inc.
A Division of Simon & Schuster
Englewood Cliffs, New Jersey 07632

Printed in the United States of America

10 9 8 7 6 5   95 94

ISBN 0-13-648882-X

Contents

**PART II
Parenting: Contemporary Variations**

Preface

This book was written to acquaint upper-level and graduate students with parenting in three major areas: (1) concepts, challenges, and changes; (2) contemporary variations; and (3) risks and alternatives. While it is specifically designed as material for students who will enter a profession requiring them to work with parents directly, the book also provides useful information in developing life skills. It is our hope, then, that this book will be helpful to students preparing for teaching, social work, other human service professions, health professions, and mental health professions—and to parents themselves. The second edition, we hope, is even better than the first. We have made significant revisions to all sections and have included new topics of interest. This book does not take a "cookbook" approach to parenting. We believe that there is no "recipe" for effective parenting behavior, but instead that there are a number of strategies, skills, insights, and resources that can assist parents. Therefore, the topics selected represent those we believe to be the most relevant contemporary issues facing both parents and the professionals who work with them. We have included classical and current research, but we have attempted to emphasize the practical application of research and the implications for parenting and parent education.

Part I, "Parenting: Concepts, Challenges, and Changes," consists of the first five chapters. The first chapter introduces the concept of parenting, traces historical views from biblical times to the present, addresses the need for parent education, and explores the determinants of parenting behavior. Chapters 2, 3, and 4 are companion chapters that discuss the changing nature of parenting throughout the life cycle, from infancy through old age, emphasizing the reciprocal nature of the parent/child relationship. Chapter 4 includes a section on communication throughout the life cycle. Developmental needs of parents, as well as those of children, at all stages of development are examined. Chapter 5 describes, compares, and evaluates the major contemporary strategies of parenting that many parents utilize to assist them in becoming more effective parents.

Part II, "Parenting: Contemporary Variations," is the unique feature of this book. Chapter 6 discusses parenting in diverse cultures and includes sections on socioeconomic differences, black families, Chicano families, and Native American families, with similarities and differences among cultures noted. Chapters 7 and 8 examine parenting in nontraditional families. The structural variations—single-parent and blended families—are examined in relationship to adjustment for both parents and children, and the life-style variations include dual-career families, mobile families (military, corporate, and migrant), cohabiting families, and homosexual families.

Part III, "Parenting: Risks and Alternatives," begins with Chapter 9, which addresses parenting in high-risk families with teenage parents or abusive parents. Parenting an exceptional child is the topic for Chapter 10. Because we believe that each type of exceptionality has different implications for parenting, relationships are discussed separately for children with physical handicaps, sensory impairments, mental handicaps, learning disabilities, emotional disturbance, and giftedness. A separate section on sibling relationships is included. Another unique section of the book is Chapter 11, which examines alternatives to biological parenthood, and includes adoptive parenthood, parenting via embryo technology (artificial insemination by donor, in-vitro fertilization, and surrogate mothers), and foster parenthood. The concluding chapter is devoted to child care, an extremely timely issue. It describes types of child care, addresses both infant care and children in self-care separately, identifies the components of quality care, discusses the effects of child care on children, and describes other preschool programs.

Keeping the book a manageable length was a monumental task for us. Some topics only scratch the surface, and we regret that space limitations prevented a more in-depth discussion. Other sections are necessarily limited by a current dearth of relevant research, particularly the sections on cohabiting parents, homosexual parents, and embryo technology. We hope that the inclusion of these topics will stimulate further research.

We are indebted to all of the members of our family who so patiently endured the writing of this second edition, which often resulted in a neglect of other family responsibilities. Pauline is especially grateful to her husband, David Hamilton, who provided encouragement and support every step of the way, and who did far more than his share of household duties to permit sufficient writing time.

Two problems perplexed us in the preparation of this book. The first was how to use a nonsexist pronoun in referring to the child. Rather than using either he/his or she/her exclusively, we chose to alternate the use of the masculine and feminine. We hope this practice reflects our desire to treat all children equally.

Finally, since there was no senior or junior author, we wondered how to resolve the issue of whose name should appear first. Since we are sisters from a closely knit family, we worked together on this book in an unusually cooperative way. Neither feels she did more than her share. Therefore, we have chosen to have our names appear in alphabetical order, coincidentally in order of our birth.

Tommie J. Hamner
Pauline H. Turner

1

Parenting in Perspective

A distinctive feature of our high-tech society is the growing recognition that parenthood can be a choice rather than an inevitable event. No previous generation has been as free to choose. Parallel to the development of this freedom has been the increasing realization of the necessity of choosing wisely. As the pressures and demands of the parenting role have become more complex, the decision to delay parenthood or to remain childless has become more realistic for some; for others it has become necessary to rely on formal and/or informal support systems once parenthood is assumed.

This book is aimed at assisting those students who are prospective parents and those who are already parents in exploring the concepts of parenting so that they might develop the skills necessary for effectiveness in their roles. In addition, the information should provide persons in, or desiring to enter, the helping professions with some suggestions for becoming more effective in working with parents.

A logical place to begin is to clarify the various concepts involved in the areas of parenting. We will then review what has occurred in the past, assess the present, and glimpse at the challenges for the future.

CONCEPTS OF PARENTING

Parenthood

To many, it would seem foolish to define the concept of parenthood. After all, it has been with us since Adam and Eve. But with the complexity of society and the many variant life-styles, the term *parenthood* has been expanded. Although in the past parenthood meant that a person was responsible for biologically reproducing a child, today many kinds of individuals can be called parents. The dictionary points out that a person is a parent if he or she has produced the offspring or has the legal status of a father or a mother. The term *parent* comes from the Latin word *parens*, meaning "give birth." The synonym for *parent* provided by the dictionary is *parenthood*.

Motivations for parenthood. Approximately 95 percent of the people who can become parents do so (Worthington & Buston, 1986). Economic contributions of children to the family may be ruled out, for children today are an economic liability rather than an asset. The estimated cost of rearing a child in an urban setting from birth to 18 years is about $75,000 and

1

could be as high as $250,000 if loss of income and a private college education are included (Edwards, 1981). Why, then, do so many individuals become parents? For some, pregnancy is planned—an overt decision is made. For others, while they plan sometime in the future to become parents, the pregnancy is an accident due to failure of, improper use of, or neglect to use contraceptives. Ignorance as to how and when contraception occurs also may be the reason for pregnancy.

Bigner (1979) pointed out two basic reasons why people become parents. The first explanation is theoretical. For example, Erikson's theory proposes that when an individual reaches adulthood, he or she feels a desire to care for others by having children and assuming the parenthood role. Even though some individuals can achieve this sense of generativity in other ways, such as teaching or engaging in social services, parenthood appears to be the primary vehicle.

The second explanation, that attitudes toward parenthood have significant early antecedents, is a more plausible one. These attitudes are present long before one is able to have children. The reasons individuals may verbalize regarding their desire for children are likely to be closely associated with the experiences they had as children. These psychological reasons may or may not be consciously known to the individual. Some of these reasons are as follows. *Fatalism* may serve as a reason if one believes that reproduction is the reason for his or her existence. This type of person, who believes that preventing conception is a sin, is motivated by religious beliefs. Another fatalistic motivation is to ensure the continuation of the family name after the parents are deceased. Of course, this can be achieved only if the child is a boy or if a girl maintains her maiden name after marriage. This reason for parenthood explains why some couples desire male over female children. *Altruism* also may serve as motivation for parenthood and may be a result of one's unselfish desire or need to express affection and concern, with children being the ideal persons to receive these feelings. This reason closely resembles Erikson's sense of generativity. *Narcissistic* motivations are those in which an individual believes that having children will reflect on his or her goodness and serve as

a concrete example of maturity, adequacy, and sexuality. Other reasons for parenthood are *instrumental* in nature. These include the expectation that children will achieve specific goals for the parent, such as obtaining a college education or being an outstanding athlete, as well as the belief that the parenting experience represents a second chance at life. Other instrumental reasons for assuming the parenthood role are to begin a marital relationship or to repair a troubled marriage. Although both of these reasons are invalid, they are still adhered to by large numbers of people.

Having children to appease one's parents or because all of one's friends have children represent an instrumental reason stated by some. Middle-aged people may indicate that they wish to be grandparents and want someone to look after them in old age. Some men view the fathering role as a source of power and a way to confirm their masculinity.

Social meanings of parenthood. In each society, predominant ideal roles exist, and the characteristics and functions of these roles are defined (Bigner, 1985). Individuals rarely question these roles; as the individuals grow and develop, the ideas tend to become so much a part of the personality that they shape one's thoughts, reactions, and behaviors. Parenthood is one of these ideal notions of our society. The cultural meanings of parenthood exert pressure on individuals, especially women, to assume this role. Bigner (1985) pointed out that there are six major classifications of the social meanings of parenthood:

1. Many individuals believe that it is their moral obligation to become parents. The source of this notion may be the Judeo-Christian belief based on the Old Testament, which says, "be fruitful and multiply."

2. Some see parenthood as a way of fulfilling a civic obligation, that is, continuation of government depends on replenishment of the population. If couples are financially and socially able to have children and do not, then they are believed to be selfish and irresponsible.

3. Becoming a parent is thought to be natural behavior. Conception is believed to be a natural result of intercourse; if individuals do not conceive, then some physical problem must be the reason.

4. Reproduction is thought to be a major way of achieving sexual identity by both males and females.

5. Children round out a marriage and make a family complete. Although evidence exists to indicate that birth of children decreases marital happiness and places stress on a marriage, this belief continues to be widely held. Many couples believe that the way to "save" a marriage is to have a child.

6. Individuals who want to have children are thought to be more mentally normal than those who desire to remain childless. For a woman, especially, bearing children fulfills a destiny. Childlessness by choice is seen as unnatural and abnormal.

Obviously these cultural pressures are greater for some people than for others. It is possible that socioeconomic status, membership in a minority group, education, and other factors mediate these pressures.

Transition to parenthood. From time to time throughout life, individuals enter a state of transition, moving from the developmental stage of childhood to adolescence, from youth to adult status, from single to married, from married to single, from a nonparent to a parent, and so on. Bridges (1980) viewed transition as a natural process with disorientation and reorientation as the turning points in the path of growth. The process is difficult. One must let go of an old situation, suffer the confusing nowhere of in-betweenness, and then finally launch forth again in a new way of life.

While Bridges did not write specifically about the transition to parenthood, in his work there are many implications that parallel the transition from nonparenthood to parenthood. To say the least, following the birth of a baby, life will never be the same. An old way of life must be ended and a new one begun. In early research on the process of becoming a parent, new parent-hood was conceptualized as a crisis (Wilkie & Ames, 1986). More recent research has viewed the addition of a baby to a couple's life as a transition rather than as a crisis.

Research on the transition to parenthood has centered around a number of issues: the stresses experienced by couples resulting from the birth of a child, the effect on the marital relationship and the functioning as a couple, how couples cope with the stresses of parenthood, the differences between men and women in experiencing and dealing with stress, and the infant's role in the degree of stress parents experience.

Ventura (1987) reported four categories of stress described by parents of infants 3 to 5 months of age: demands of parent, spouse, and worker roles; infant care; interactions with spouse; and interactions with family members. Both mothers and fathers reported stresses associated with multiple role demands: Mothers reported difficulties juggling parenting responsibilities with work and home responsibilities; fathers' concerns were primarily with career and work demands. Financial issues emerged as a common theme for many of the parents in the study. Parents reported stress due to infants' fussy behaviors in relation to feeding or soothing techniques. Mothers indicated feelings of guilt, helplessness, or anger when confronted with a fussy baby. Stress arose in relationship to the spouse. Men and women reported marital conflicts, lack of spousal support, and concerns about sexual relations. Finally, interactions with other family members and friends were the source of additional stress experiences reported by the new parents in this study.

McKim (1987) asked new parents to describe their concerns, problems, and needs. Infant illness was the most frequently reported problem throughout the first year. Infant crying, feeding, and nutrition concerns also were reported as problems. Parent-centered problems, such as role conflicts, were viewed as significant concerns. Working mothers and those with difficult infants were more likely to report problems than nonworking mothers and mothers with easy babies.

LaRossa (1983) reported that time was mentioned by parents as the most changed aspect of life following the birth of a baby. Parents complained about their lives being more hectic and that sleep time, television time, communication time, sex time, and even bathroom time were in short supply. This researcher hypothesized that physical time (which is quantitative) and social time (which is artifactual) must be differentiated, and the manner in which the new parents perceive time is of utmost importance. For example, if new parents perceive time fatalistically, then time is conceptualized as a scarce commodity, and parents find themselves suffering the inconveniences. But if time is perceived in a humanistic manner, then time is within one's power. He concluded that the transition to parenthood makes family members more aware of their schedules. What has been taken for granted can no longer be. The new parents are much more aware of the clock, which, in turn, makes them feel that they are constantly running out of time. The degree of commitment to performing certain tasks also is a factor in how new parents perceive time. An overcommitment to motherhood, "being consumed" by the baby and the house, would cause the new mother to feel overwhelmed by a lack of time. Worthington and Buston (1986) concluded that the addition of a new child demanded a new balance among work, home life, social life, and married life.

The effect of a new baby on the marital relationship and the differences between the perceptions of husbands and wives has received considerable attention. Much research has indicated that becoming a family is accompanied by change, much of it negative, in various aspects of family life and in men's and women's overall satisfaction with their marriage (Cowan et al., 1985). Considerable research summarized by Worthington and Buston (1986) reported that the impact of having children is more stressful for the wife than for the husband. Numerous studies have found that wives' marital satisfaction significantly declines immediately after the birth of a child, and that this dissatisfaction continues into the second year (Cowan et al., 1985; Waldron & Routh, 1981; Worthington & Buston, 1986).

Many couples experience increased marital conflicts (Waldron & Routh, 1981; Worthington & Buston, 1986). Disagreements about finances, sex, in-laws, career plans, household duties, and social life may occur. Couples who have established a balanced sense of power prior to the transition to parenthood will probably have fewer disagreements than those who have not.

Few studies have included the role of the infant in the transition to parenthood, but it has been assumed that the infant contributes equal stress to both parents. Infant crying, irritability, and colic have been linked to depression, helplessness, anger, exhaustion, and rejection of the infant (Isabella & Belsky, 1985; Wilkie & Ames, 1986). Clearly it is logical to assume that a passive, easy-to-soothe, cuddly baby elicits very different feelings and behaviors from parents than does a crying, difficult-to-satisfy baby. Interestingly, Wilkie and Ames found that infant crying had a greater effect on fathers than on mothers. Infant crying caused mothers to rate their infants more negatively, but crying did not affect mothers' feelings of adequacy. For fathers, however, infant crying was associated with greater anxiety, more concern about life-style changes, and rating themselves and their wives as low in potency.

Isabella and Belsky (1985) conducted an interesting study on the relationship of infant-parent attachment and the marital change during transition to parenthood. These researchers found that mothers of insecure infants experienced significantly greater declines in positive marital activities and sentiments and greater increases in negative marital activities and sentiments following the birth of their babies than did mothers of secure 1-year-old infants. This difference emerged between 3 and 9 months postpartum, the period during which the baby becomes increasingly social and generally positive in behavior. Another interesting finding of the study was that the mothers of insecure infants and mothers of secure infants differed in their marital appraisal prior to the birth of their babies. Mothers of secure babies based their prenatal marital satisfaction appraisals more on positive than on negative aspects of the marriage. The reverse was found for mothers of insecure infants. Although it was not a purpose of this study, support was provided for the contention that a positive marital relationship is important in the development of the infant.

Satisfactions with parenthood. As noted earlier, a large percentage of people desire to and do become parents. It can be assumed that those who deliberately decide to have children anticipate the rewards to outweigh the costs and the satisfactions to surpass the dissatisfactions, making the long, arduous, and challenging efforts of parenting personally worthwhile (Goetting, 1986). Nearly all Americans choose parenthood in spite of the continuous flow of evidence that suggests that the expected lofty satisfactions often remain unfulfilled.

A great deal of research has centered around the parent-child relationship, but there has not been consistent research attention to parental satisfaction. This is surprising since the issue of parental satisfaction is one of central importance to American society, as well as to the many individuals who invest a lifetime to parenting. Goetting (1986) provided an extensive review of this area, including research compiled from two national surveys that compared parental views in 1957 and 1976. While the 1976 parents were slightly but statistically significantly less positive toward parenthood and children than were the 1957 parents, parenting remained a central anchor of satisfaction for most parents. In the 1976 sample, 87 percent indicated that parenthood had provided them with a great deal or a lot of fulfillment. Only 4 percent reported little or very little satisfaction from the role. The variables investigated and the results of the research are identified in Box 1a.

In summary, the research seems to indicate that both mothers and fathers tend to emphasize the emotional benefits of parenthood, although mothers more often than fathers express satisfaction intrinsic to the parent-child relationship. The greatest dissatisfaction with parenthood tends to center around discipline, financial costs, the child's nonfamily adjustment, and the parents' loss of freedom.

Caution must be exercised when drawing conclusions regarding previous research on parental satisfaction because many of the findings have resulted from single studies that have not been replicated and have yielded conflicting results. Conceptual and methodological limitations also must be taken into consideration. These include a lack of standard conceptualization and measurement of parental satisfaction; the oversimplification of the concept of parental satisfaction; the use of convenience and biased samples; and the presentation of measurement items so that social desirability, which tends to inflate parental satisfaction, is a major problem. Further, few longitudinal studies have been conducted, and data analyses in many cases have not been sound.

Delayed parenthood. In the 1980s the baby boomers of the years 1947 to 1964 began having the babies they postponed in the 1970s. The first births to women 25 years and older more than doubled between 1970 and 1982. Among women aged 30 to 34, first births more than tripled in these 12 years (U.S. Bureau of the Census, 1987). With the help of contraceptives, women are delaying childbirth after marriage. The median interval between marriage and first birth for mothers older than 30 is now more than 5 years.

The trend for delayed childbearing is a response to recurrent recessions and the fierce competition in the job market as young people reach working ages. This trend also has coincided with the increase in women entering the work force and the new commitment to careers. Most delayed childbearers are white, highly educated, two-career couples. Even black college-educated women are twice as likely as their white counterparts to be mothers by age 25.

Parenting

The term *parenting,* which has become rather common, is one to which some object. Strict grammarians object because a noun has been made into a verb; others object because a social relationship is made to sound like a motor or technical skill—something that can be taught and practiced, that can be analyzed and improved—such as knitting or table manners. The concept of parenting has been defined as the process or the state of being a parent (Brooks, 1987; Morrison, 1978). Morrison defined parenting as "the process of developing and utilizing the knowledge and skills appropriate to planning for, creating, giving birth to, rearing, and/or providing care for offspring" (p. 23). Brooks pointed

BOX 1a SATISFACTIONS WITH PARENTHOOD

Variable	Findings
Gender of parent	Women may experience greater parental role fulfillment than men do, but they also perceive parenthood to be more restrictive and burdensome.
Educational attainment	This may be negatively correlated with parental satisfaction. The more educated tend to see both the positive and the negative aspects of parenthood than the less educated do. Parenthood does not appear to be the pivotal focus of life for the college educated as it is for the less educated.
Employment status	For women, preferred work or nonwork roles may influence the degree of satisfaction. If a woman achieves desired employment status, she may experience greater satisfaction with the maternal role than if she is unable to do so.
Premarital pregnancy	This has a negative effect on maternal but not paternal satisfaction. This effect is probably due to the fact that premarital pregnancy is nearly always unplanned and precipitates premature entry into parenthood. Since it is the mother who is more likely than the father to adopt parenthood as the pivotal role, she is more likely to be affected by premarital pregnancy than the father.
Single parenting	This yields greater satisfaction than marital parenting. Single fathering may be more rewarding than single mothering.
Age at parental onset	Older, more mature parents tend to report higher levels of parental satisfaction.
Gender of child	Research has yielded mixed results; therefore no conclusions may be reached.
Number of children	Mothers of small (one child) and large (four or more children) families report their maternal roles as more cogenial than mothers of intermediate-sized families do.
Type of role (traditional or modern)	Parents who view themselves in the traditional parental role may experience greater satisfaction than those who evaluate their adequacy in terms of the more modern role, which emphasizes interpersonal warmth and tolerance.
Family setting during parents' childhood development	Only maternal satisfaction may be positively related to family setting during childhood. For women, a happy childhood in which mothers are viewed as having been good disciplinarians and fathers as having been too lenient may contribute to parental satisfaction.
Social network and support	Some evidence indicates the strength of the social network is associated with maternal competence. Other research has shown emotional support from friends to be significantly related to maternal satisfaction. Some researchers have found no relationship of support network to maternal satisfaction of single mothers.
Stage in life cycle	The first stage of parenting, representing the transition from nonparenting, is probably the most intense in terms of both positive and negative effects. Parents report the greatest degree of satisfaction during the earliest stage of parenthood and the least satisfaction in the stages when children are adolescents and adults.

Source: Adapted from Goetting, A. (1986). Parental satisfaction. *Journal of Family Issues, 7*(1), 83–109.

out that parenting is a process that includes nourishing, protecting, and guiding the child through the course of development. In this process, parenting is a continuous series of interactions between parent and child, and these interactions change both. This process or state of being has been extended to actions performed by a variety of persons—parents, siblings, peers, relatives, teachers, friends, and others—that influence and guide the physical, social, emotional, and intellectual development of individuals. These actions result in a nurturing and caring relationship between human beings, whatever their age or kinship.

Mothering. While parenting has been defined as the process or state of being a parent, the processes of mothering and fathering have traditionally been somewhat different. Dictionaries have produced some interesting concepts of mothering, ranging from "the biological process of giving birth" to "exercising control over and responsibility for one's young." The phrase "exhibiting kindliness and affection" and vague references to "demonstrating the qualities of a mother" also appear. Mothering, then, may be viewed as simply possessing the biological and/or legal status of mother, the process of performing a social role, or engaging in behavior that facilitates the growth and development of one's children. Obviously each of these concepts has vastly different implications. In his examination of mothering, Schaffer (1977) pointed out that "there is nothing simple or straightforward about mothering" and emphasized that it is a complex pattern involving two individuals. He examined the concept of mothering from four principal perspectives: mothering as physical care, mothering as a set of attitudes, mothering as stimulation, and mothering as mutual dialogue.

However one chooses to conceptualize the term, it seems reasonable to assume that optimal mothering contributes to the optimal development of children. In a review of three studies involving home observations of mothers' interactions with their infants and toddlers, Moore (1977) pointed out that competent infants are likely to have mothers who are conscious of their part in providing for their children's intellectual

and social needs and who provide them with more than nurturant physical care.

The prevalent Madonna/child image implies that for some time there has existed a cultural ideal of a unique dyadic relationship between mother and child. For some this dyad has represented an instinctive drive or a biologically predestined relationship, with the implication that mothering was a "natural" phenomenon. Although this notion is currently rejected by most sociologists, psychologists, and biologists, there still remains a certain mystique with respect to the exclusiveness of the mother-child relationship. While pointing out that most female behavior in the human species is learned, LeMasters and DeFrain (1983) implied that the biological fact of female pregnancy and childbirth contributes to the greater emphasis on mothering as opposed to fathering. These authors and others (Bigner, 1985) stress the fact that mothering is the primary role for which females have been socialized. It appears, then, that mothering as one of life's roles remains significant for women and for their children, but our conceptions of mothering have changed in interesting ways.

Child-rearing manuals aimed at mothers in

America from 1913 to 1976 were examined by Weiss (1978). She noted a shift in emphasis on physical care to promoting cognitive and emotional growth, with manuals usually advocating practices to be administered solely by mothers. As the mother's perceived environmental influence on the child increased, so did she become the sole victim of attack when things went wrong in the child's development. And Heffner (1978) suggested that motherhood is a high-risk profession because of the universal guilt associated with it (which is based on the demand that the mother be omnipotent), the mother's feelings of anger, and her conflicts concerning the child's dependency and great need for maternal care.

LeMasters and DeFrain (1983) commented on the awesome responsibility of motherhood and the bitter attacks that have been made on the American mother since World War II. For example, Lundberg and Farnham (1947) stated the following:

The spawning of most neurosis in Western civilization is the home. The basis for it is laid in childhood, although it emerges strongly later, usually from adolescence until middle age, provoked by circumstances and conditions encountered in life. And, as we have pointed out, the principal agent in laying the groundwork for it is the mother. (p. 303)

While some contemporary writers might not be so harsh, the notion that a mother is the creator of all the emotional ills in her children is still subtly present in much of the literature. Caplan and Hall-McCorquodale (1985) argued that, despite the gains achieved through the women's movement during the past 15 years, the practice of many clinicians and members of the helping professions of blaming mothers for whatever goes wrong with their children still continues to be a problem.

In light of the women's liberation movement, the large number of mothers in the work force, and the increase in the number of single and adolescent mothers, one wonders why, if all this is so, we do not have a nation of neurotic children. Nevertheless, there is ample evidence to support the notion that the mother's role is a critical factor in the child's overall development, especially during the early years. One should be aware, however, that competence in children almost certainly has multiple causes (Moore, 1977) and that there appear to be few absolutes in mothering. Numerous genetic and environmental factors impinge on the mother-child relationship. Research, however, does suggest that there are certain behavioral and attitudinal traits of mothers and certain environmental conditions that mothers can provide to enhance the optimal development and competence of their children.

Research related to mothering. Much of the literature related to mothering and its effects on children has emphasized mothering during infancy, especially the process of attachment. The work of Klaus and Kennell (1976) described the development of attachment from mother to infant. They stated the following:

This original mother-infant bond is the wellspring for all the infant's subsequent attachments and is the formative relationship in the course of which the child develops a sense of himself. Throughout his lifetime the strength and character of this attachment will influence the quality of all future bonds to other individuals. (pp. 1–2)

They contended that the following are the principles that govern the mother's attachment to her infant: close skin-to-skin contact with the infant for the first 45–60 minutes immediately following birth; the infant's response to the mother by some signal, such as body or eye movement; witness of the birth process by mothers in a state of alertness; and the difficulty a mother has attaching herself to an infant when she is under stress.

The healthy bonding process of mothers to infants seems to make possible a healthy attachment of infant to mother. In some of the classic studies on attachment, it was considered axiomatic that an infant became optimally attached to only one person at a time (the concept of monotropy) and that person was usually the mother. The literature emphasized the dangers of separation of mother and infant, especially during the last half of the first year, when the attachment process was paramount in the child's development. There was disagreement as to the extent of harm a child would experience as a result of prolonged separation and whether this harm would be temporary or permanent. As infant day care became a necessity, one of the primary criticisms was that placing an infant in day care would interrupt the attachment process, and some authors equated it with the devastating effects of prolonged or total separation. Subsequent studies, however, examined other factors, such as the time and duration of separation, the quality of care received by the child, and the possibilities of multiple attachments (Ainsworth, 1973; Caldwell, Wright, Honig, & Tannebaum, 1970; Lamb, 1976a, 1976b, 1977). Caldwell and her associates (1970) found essentially no differences in child-mother and mother-child attachment patterns between home-reared and day-care infants. Recently the issue of the impact of early and prolonged out-of-the-home infant care on infant-mother attachment has resurfaced (*U.S. News and World Report,* 1987; *Wall Street Journal,* 1987). Some researchers are once again contending that out-of-home care of more than 20 hours per week is related to insecure attachment, but there is lack of consensus among experts regarding this issue.

Much of the emphasis on the mother-child interaction during infancy and early childhood has focused on the nurturant and control functions of the mothering role. Tolan and Tomasini (1977) affirmed Ainsworth's claims by their findings that mothers of 12-month-old infants rated as "secure" were significantly more sensitive, more accepting, more expressive of affect, and less angry than mothers of "insecure" toddlers. It has been concluded that consistent and prompt maternal responding to the crying of infants is associated with a reduction in the frequency and duration of their crying in later quarters of that year (Bell & Ainsworth, 1972).

Cognitive development seems to be related to several aspects of mothering during the earliest periods of childhood. For example, Bradley, Caldwell, and Elardo (1977) found that provision of appropriate play materials in the home was the variable most highly related to IQ, and avoidance of restriction and punishment, variety in daily stimulation, and organization of the environment were other related variables. Parks and Smeriglio (1986) found a relationship between parenting knowledge and the quality of stimulation in the home for low socioeconomic mothers.

Clarke-Stewart (1977) pointed out in her review of research that maternal speech directed to the infant following his or her babbling, such as smiling, touching, and feeding, tends to increase vocal behavior. In general, the more the mother and the infant interact actively, the higher the infant's IQ or developmental score is likely to be. Stimulating maternal behavior, such

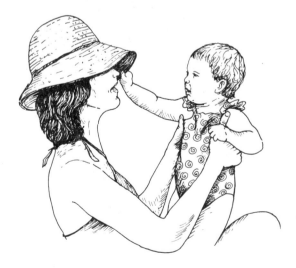

as looking at, talking to, and playing with the baby, has been shown to be related to optimal cognitive development (Clarke-Stewart, 1977). Quality time and variety of maternal stimulation appear to be as important as, or more important than, quantity.

When one examines the literature related to mothering in the preschool period, increased emphasis is placed on the control aspect of the role, with nurturance continuing to be a significant variable. Especially in the area of cognitive development, maternal stimulation continues to emerge as an important factor as well. Clarke-Stewart (1977) stated the following:

Children's exploration of the environment and lack of anxiety in new places and their willingness to play with novel objects is facilitated by an interesting environment and the presence of a nonrestrictive mother with whom they have interacted frequently. (p. 27)

The following mothering characteristics seem to be related to the child's intellectual ability: The mother is sensitive, warm, and loving toward the child; she is accepting of his behavior in general and allows exploration and expression; she uses reasoning and inductive discipline when controlling the child's behavior; she uses more elaborate language and teaching strategies; and she encourages the child's development and stimulates his growth (Clarke-Stewart, 1977).

Mothers who are warm but set firm limits, emphasize the dos rather than the don'ts, treat their children with respect, and encourage independent behavior tend to produce mature and competent social behavior in their children. By contrast, parents who are punitive, hostile, and aggressive tend to provide a model of aggression for their children, who, in turn, produce the same sorts of behaviors and are more socially immature and dependent.

BOX 1b POSITIVE CHARACTERISTICS OF MOTHERING

Infancy/Toddlerhood

Healthy bonding
Nurturance
Acceptance
Sensitivity
Consistent and prompt responsivity
Provision of appropriate play materials
Avoidance of restriction and punishment
High degree of verbal and physical interaction

Preschool

Nurturance
Acceptance
Sensitivity
Allowance of exploration/expression
Reasoning and inductive discipline
Use of elaborated language and teaching strategies
Setting limits

School Age

Nurturance but not restrictiveness
Stimulation but not directiveness
Responsiveness but not control

Mothering, while it is likely to be an 18- to 21-year commitment, appears to be reduced gradually in its impact as children reach middle childhood and approach adolescence. Chapters 2, 3, and 4 will discuss in detail how the parenting role changes as the child gets older. That is not to say that mothers stop influencing their children once the children are 6 years old. In most cases, however, the pattern of interaction that becomes established during the early years, especially with respect to nurturance and attitudes toward control, is likely to remain similar in the later years of childhood. Given similar circumstances, an accepting, warm mother is not likely to turn into a hostile, punitive shrew. That, plus the emergence of the child into a larger culture, tends to reduce the direct impact of mothering.

However, there are many studies related to the effects of maternal behavior on the child's academic achievement during the school years. It appears that the intellectual development of boys continues to be positively related to a close mother-son relationship throughout childhood, but the same does not hold true for girls. Further, the mother's (and father's) demands for achievement of both their sons and their daughters consistently predict success in school in the traditional sense. However, it appears that the most effective pattern of parental behavior for facilitating success in academic settings that require self-initiated, independent, and innovative work would be one that is nurturant but not restrictive, stimulating but not directive, and responsive but not controlling (Clarke-Stewart, 1977).

The reciprocal nature of mothering. Perhaps the single most important point regarding mothering is that maternal behaviors at every age level of the child are affected by the child's behavior and temperament—in other words, the relationship is always reciprocal. The child-rearing manuals and attacks on mothers mentioned earlier in this section failed miserably at considering the notion that a child plays a major role in the kind of mothering he or she receives. Infants differ from the moment of birth, as demonstrated when they were observed in hospital nurseries before environmental influences become so apparent (Brazelton, 1969; Chess & Thomas,

1973). Some cry a lot; others cry little. Some are easy to soothe; others are difficult. Some eat and sleep well; others seem to demonstrate rhythmicity only with great effort. Picture the mother of an "easy" baby who cries little, sleeps soundly, is socially responsive, and generally thrives. If she is awakened only once a night to feed and manages to get her chores done while the baby is sleeping, it appears obvious that she will have energy and enthusiasm for mothering and will interact with her baby in generally positive ways. Compare that picture to one of a mother who is awakened at midnight, 2:00 A.M., and 4:00 A.M. for feedings. Even after feeding, the baby continues to cry. Rocking, walking, singing, and patting do not seem to help. She becomes anxious and communicates that anxiety to her infant through her tone of voice, rigid body, and facial expressions. A vicious circle is set in motion, and her maternal behaviors will be far from enthusiastic and energetic.

Infant responsiveness as well as maternal perceptions and expectations of infant behavior appear to interact to influence maternal behavior. For example, Campbell (1977) noted that mothers who rated their babies as "difficult" at 3 months vocalized to them less, were less responsive to their cries, and looked at them less. Further, maternal perceptions of infant temperament influence maternal behavior in ways that do not lead to optimal mothering.

The point here is that it is often difficult to determine whose behavior is shaping whose. We believe firmly that maternal behaviors are critical in promoting the optimal development of children, but we believe just as firmly that children themselves play an equally critical role in determining their own destiny, especially in eliciting certain behaviors from their mothers.

One final point should be made. Every reference to mothering or maternal behaviors in this section need not apply to only the biological or adoptive mother. Grandmothers, babysitters, child-care workers, nurses, and friends can all be effective "mothers." It would seem that all the variables of maternal behavior apply to both full-time and employed mothers and to the substitute caregivers as well.

Schaffer (1977) pointed out that a mother's love for her child is not necessarily inevitable.

He cited several possible conditions that are likely to affect mothering, including personality factors, such as depression, anxiety, mental illness, and simply insensitivity; environmental conditions, such as poverty, unemployment, and poor health; hormonal influences that occur in conjunction with childbirth; ignorance or lack of factual information concerning development and behavior of children; and, most important, the mother's own developmental history of being mothered herself.

Other researchers (Cox et al., 1985) have noted the importance of mothers' own mothering in the quality of mother-infant relationships. It was found that mothers who had a high interaction pattern with their infants were those who reported satisfying relationships with their mothers. A history of disadvantage in the mothers' backgrounds was associated with less adequate and sensitive care of infants.

It is appropriate to destroy the motherhood myth that all normal women instinctively want, need, and will enjoy having children and that they are psychologically, mentally, and technically equipped to rear them. Probably the most important variable in mothering is the desire to be a mother and the satisfaction derived from it. The choice is available to most women and should be exercised. Further, Heffner (1978) contended that many women who are engaged in mothering do not value highly what they are doing, and it is abundantly clear to them that no one else values it either. If mothering is to achieve the status it deserves, mothers must be mothers by choice and not by cultural compulsion or accident. They must be provided with the tools needed to meet the responsibility with which they have been charged. They must be provided with an understanding of child development and emotional assistance that enables them to accept their own feelings and guide the behavior of their children in constructive ways.

Fathering.   Traditionally, *fathering* has been referred to in the context of being a biological contributor to the formation of a human organism. Even today dictionaries use *father* as a figurative definition for *creator* or *originator*. Only since about 1975 has the term appeared in the literature in the context of the more direct psy-chological and physical role a man enacts in the rearing of his children. Since that time the discussion of fathering has become popular.

In the traditional perspective, fathers cared for their children primarily by succeeding in their careers or occupational roles so that their families were cared for and their wives could devote their time and energies to care of the home and the children. As such, fathers have been exemplified as distant and even cold to their children, stern and even punitive, respected, and sometimes feared.

In the psychoanalytic movement, fathers had no direct and caring role for infants and young children. "Freud clearly regarded the father as the parent who incites children (especially boys) to incorporate the prohibitions, rules, principles, and values of society" (Lynn, 1974, p. 103). But he was seen as a supreme authority rather than as a caregiver.

From a traditional sociological point of view, Parsons and Bales (1955) described the father's role in the family as being "instrumental." He was responsible for and encouraged the family's relationships with the outside world. He usually expressed explicit child-rearing values and goals, among which were education, moral and personal values, and safety. However, his direct role in the implementation of these values and goals, as manifested in child-rearing experiences, was minimal. Mothers, on the other hand, were seen as "expressive," being the givers of love and care. Margaret Mead once said, "Fathers are a biological necessity, but a social accident."

In the 1960s the literature included emphasis on the role of fathers in contributing to the psychosocial development of their children. For the first time fathers were seen as being important in child rearing. Three of the major child-development outcomes that were emphasized in relationship to fathering were sex-role development, academic performance, and moral development (Fein, 1978). Studying father-absent families became the mode for assessing these and other variables. From the bulk of the literature in this area, it appears that father absence has its greatest effects on male children. If the father is absent, especially before the son is 4 or 5 years old, the boy tends to be less aggressive and more dependent on his mother (Clarke-Stewart, 1977). Biller's review (1974) suggested that children without fathers had significantly more difficulty in academic achievement and in moral development and behavior.

Lynn (1974) reached several conclusions concerning fathering based on father absence from all types of studies. He stated that children generally view their father, more than their mother, as instrumentally nurturant, punitive, strong, powerful, and fearsome. Further, he noted that there is an association between the father's nurturance and his boy's masculinity; that fathers exert a more direct influence on the specific occupational choices of their sons than of their daughters; and that unloving, punitive, and authoritarian fathers tend to produce withdrawn, anxious, and dejected children of both sexes. Father-absent boys have been found to have lower scores on maximum guilt, internal moral judgment, acceptance of blame, moral values, and conformity to rules and higher scores on overt aggression (Hoffman, 1971).

It is important to point out that results based on the variable of father absence alone should be viewed with caution. In many instances of father presence, the father is functionally absent or ineffectual. Further, other variables—such as the power of social-class differences, the additional stress placed on the family as a result of the loss of the father, and the reason for the father's absence—might be more important factors affecting the child's development than father absence per se (Fein, 1978). Father substitutes in the form of male family members or friends may alleviate some of the negative effects of father absence.

An emerging perspective on fathering discussed by Fein (1978) emphasized the notion that men are psychologically able to participate in the full range of parenting behaviors and the benefits that would be derived by both parents and children if fathers took active roles in child care and child rearing. From this perspective, fathering, like mothering, must be viewed as a complex interactive process occurring between at least two people and influenced by a variety of genetic and environmental factors.

Recent research has examined the father's experience in childbirth, the father's role in infancy, the development of bonds between young children and their fathers, fathers in nontraditional roles, and the effects of parenting experiences on fathers. Some of these studies have utilized observation of fathers in both naturalistic and laboratory settings, which much of the earlier research did not include.

An important change that has occurred in our society, and one that recently has received attention in the literature, is the father's preparation for childbirth and his participation in labor

and delivery. A stimulating book by Phillips and Anzalone (1978) included a collection of memories recounted by fathers 1 to 15 years after being present at the birth of one or more of their children. The "fathers reported themselves to be profoundly affected by the birth of their infants and to experience great feelings of satisfaction with themselves for sharing in the birth experience" (p. 145). The possibility that men's involvement in the birth process positively affected later relationships with their wives and infants was supported by Fein (1978) based on interviews within his sample. Keller, Hildebrandt, and Richards (1985) investigated the amount of contact hours fathers had with their newborns during the mother's hospital stay. Their results indicated that fathers who received extended postpartum hospital contact with their infants engaged in greater amounts of *en face* behavior and vocalization with their infants when observed 6 weeks after birth. Further, these fathers had higher self-esteem scores following the births compared to those fathers who received traditional amounts of contact.

The long-term effects of preparation for childbirth and participation in labor and delivery on paternal attitudes and behavior have yet to be established. Only future longitudinal studies that include observations of fathers interacting with their children in naturalistic settings will provide these insights. The available evidence strongly suggests that there are at least significant short-term advantages for the father and the child as well as for the mother.

Another recent area of interest has been the father's role in infancy. Parke and Sawin (1976) reported that fathers were just as involved with their infants as mothers were and were just as nurturant (that is, touching, holding, kissing, and vocalizing); in fact, in some situations they were more nurturant. They did, however, find that mothers assumed a greater caretaking role for their infants, but fathers demonstrated capability and competence in caretaking activities. Fathers seem to have different kinds of experiences with their infants than mothers do. For example, fathers have been shown to elicit more positive responses from infants in a play situation than mothers do (Lamb, 1977). In addition, the father's role as playmate appears to increase

in the period from 15 to 30 months, so that by the latter age the father is a more frequent playmate (Clarke-Stewart, 1978). Other studies seem to indicate that fathers make themselves especially salient in the lives of their sons from the beginning of the second year of life, which may lead the boys to interact with their fathers preferentially, thereby facilitating the identification process.

Since the early 1970s differences in maternal and paternal roles and behavior appear to have diminished. However, fathers still demonstrate differences in their treatment of boys and girls, particularly beyond the stage of infancy. As long as these differences occur, we can probably expect a father to influence his son's development in the preschool and childhood years to a somewhat greater extent than he does his daughter's. The direct impact of the father as a model of achievement for his son becomes evident during the school years. More indirectly, the father's acceptance of his daughter and his harmonious relationship with his wife appear to facilitate girls' achievement and cognitive development (Clarke-Stewart, 1977). However, it appears that, as roles become more androgynous, fathers will influence their children's behavior in much the same way as mothers do; that is, that there will be more clearly defined paternal behaviors that tend to promote social competence, academic achievement, sex-role development, and mature moral behaviors in children. Most certainly the myth of the father as "the other partner" who exerts little influence over his children's overall development will be destroyed.

A group of researchers (Zeidler, Nardine, Scolare, & Mich, 1987) asked college students about dissatisfaction with their parents as they were growing up. Of the subjects, 80 percent responded that they would have wanted some kind of change in their family when they were growing up. This dissatisfaction was especially apparent for the fathers. It was evident that, for the most part, fathers were identified with respondents' dissatisfaction. Fathers were viewed as not providing for the emotional needs of their children and criticized for a lack of attention or interest in their families and children. Even those young adults who stated that they wanted no change rated their parents relatively low. This

---

BOX 1c   POSITIVE CHARACTERISTICS OF FATHERING

Infancy/Toddlerhood

Nurturance
Caretaking
Playing with child

Preschool

High degree of interaction
Engaging the child in play
Warmth, nurturance
Strength
Protection
Limit setting

School Age

Acceptance
Model for achievement, sex-role, and moral development

---

finding may indicate a general dissatisfaction with parents that lasts beyond childhood, since 40 percent of the sample were over 25 years of age.

The reciprocal nature of fathering.   We should stress here that, like maternal behaviors, paternal behaviors must be viewed in the context of reciprocity; that is, at every age level, the child's behavior influences the father's behavior. It has been noted that the paternal variables most closely associated with children's intellectual competence (specifically, interacting longer with the child, expecting early dependence, being able to engage the child in play, and rating the child high on competence) are most likely to be the result of the child's own competence (Clarke-Stewart, 1978).

It can no longer be said with any degree of conviction that fathers are the "forgotten contributors to child development" (Lamb, 1975). First it seems clear that fathers do not, and have not in the past, necessarily taken a back seat to mothers in exerting a positive and powerful influence over their children—their influence has simply been less visible. Research indicates that children develop best when their fathers (as well

as their mothers) combine warmth and nurturance with strength, protection, and specified limits. The combination of providing discipline with warm affection seems to facilitate creativity, independence, generosity, and sensitivity. It can be concluded that fathers are undeniably playing an important role in child development from infancy on through childhood.

When summarizing results from a number of studies, Hamilton (1977) concluded that the father's influence not only is more than negligible but also at times exceeds that of the mother, especially in such areas of behavior as sex-role learning, development of quantitative skills, and choice of an occupation.

The fatherhood myth is as ripe for destruction as the motherhood myth is. No longer can we afford to neglect the recognition of the impact of the father on his children's development, given the opportunity to do so and the prestige for fathering. We can liberate men from their traditional instrumental role and reward them for being expressive, toward both their wives and their children. We can integrate fathers not only into the role of child care but also into the role of child rearing, which means more than changing diapers and chauffeuring. We can share both the joys and griefs of child rearing between men and women so that fathers are no longer second-class citizens as parents. We can strive for a new perspective that emphasizes equal parenting. The assessment of fathering in the future must be made within a context in which the father and child are operating, that is, the family system and the larger social system, and through examining emergent conceptions of parenting in general.

Similarities and differences between parenting and other roles.   Parenthood is one of the most significant roles in our society and one that a large percentage of the population will assume. There are some unique features of the parenthood role that distinguish it from other adult roles (Bigner, 1979, 1985).

First, women experience greater cultural pressures to assume the role of parent than men do. Early in life girls begin to be oversocialized toward parenthood. They are encouraged, and sometimes coerced, to play with certain toys, such as dolls, and to engage in household-type activities. Thus girls grow up to believe that adult status and fulfillment come from motherhood and child-rearing duties. Boys, on the other hand, are socialized toward occupational roles outside the home rather than for fatherhood, and they are provided with toys that stimulate action and aggression.

Second, the parenthood role is not always voluntarily assumed, as are other adult roles. A certain degree of freedom exists in selecting an occupation, becoming a spouse, or serving in leadership roles. Even though individuals technically do have a choice of becoming a parent, a variety of personal, religious, or moral reasons may preclude the use of contraceptives or other forms of birth control.

Third, the role of parenthood is irrevocable. Once one decides that a pregnancy is to be continued and birth occurs, it is difficult to abandon the commitment to be a parent. Although a child may be placed for adoption, this alternative is not psychologically easy, and it is not a widely socially acceptable practice. One can quit a job or even become an ex-spouse much more easily than one can give up the responsibility of parenthood.

Fourth, preparation for parenthood is poor as compared to preparation for other roles. Illustrations of this phenomenon include the paucity of educational experiences or training for parenthood through the educational system, the limited amount of preparation for parenting during pregnancy, the minimal guidance provided by the culture for successful parenting, and the abrupt transition to parenthood.

Fifth, parenthood is a developmental role—parents develop as the child develops. The developmental needs and changes occurring in the parent affect parenting behavior. Further, methods and techniques of guiding the child and providing for her needs change as the child develops. Coping with a 2-year-old is obviously very different from guiding an adolescent. The changing nature of parenting is discussed in subsequent chapters.

The characteristics of the contemporary parent role can be summarized as follows (LeMasters & DeFrain, 1983):

1. The parenthood role is ambiguous. The traditional unidirectional model of socialization stresses the primary role of the parent as teacher of the child, instilling the values, attitudes, and behavioral traits that are considered appropriate or essential for effective functioning as a future adult. The flow of information is from parent to child. Now the parent-child relationship is viewed as a dynamic, interactional relationship in which each participant affects the other—a bidirectional model of interaction. Because the parent-child relationship is very complex, specific criteria for parenthood cannot be defined, and ambiguity of the role may result in confusion and frustration.

2. The parenthood role is not adequately delimited. Parents are expected to succeed and have been blamed for many ills of society.

3. Parents are not adequately prepared for their roles. As noted earlier, the educational system does not include enough training in parenthood, and children do not learn to be parents by being appropriately parented.

4. There is a romantic notion about parenthood. The social meanings of parenthood in our society generate many myths so that people grow up believing that parenthood is fun, fulfilling, and a desirable role.

5. Parents have complete responsibility for their children as they are growing up but only partial authority over them. Day-care personnel, church workers, teachers, and many others are given responsibilities for rearing children, yet parents are legally and socially accountable for their development and behavior.

6. Standards for parent role performance are too high. Parental performance is judged by professionals rather than by peers.

7. Parents are victims of an inadequate social science. The science of parenthood is clearly in its infancy. While specific aspects of the parent-child relationship have been researched and a great deal of information has been provided, there have been no consolidation of parent theories and no organization of research findings into a comprehensive science.

8. Parents do not choose their children. Even though heredity plays a significant role in determining development and behavior, parents have little or no choice as to how the genes arrange themselves: "What you see is what you get." Parents cannot return a child once he or she is born.

9. No traditional model exists for contemporary parents to follow. Families and the environment are vastly different from that experienced by one's own family; therefore today's parents are without a model to imitate.

10. The role of parenthood does not have a high priority in our society. A lack of government, professional, and social support of day care, as well as work practices that do not support parents, illustrates this phenomenon.

11. Other roles assumed by parents are not always compatible with parenthood. For example, the dual roles of wife and mother often produce conflict.

12. Parenthood is one of the few roles from which an individual cannot honorably withdraw.

13. Parents cannot rear children in their own image but must rear them to be different and better. With rapid societal changes, children cannot be reared as their own parents were. Most parents, too, wish for their children a better life than they had.

Thus it can easily be seen that the parenthood role differs significantly from other adult roles. It also is obvious that individuals grow up in great need of being adequately prepared to assume the one role that they are most likely to assume—parenthood.

Determinants of parenting behavior. Traditionally, determinants of parenting behavior have been examined in isolation from one another and in a single direction. For example, during the 1960s considerable attention was focused on differencces in child-rearing patterns among low- and middle-class families, the implication being that socioeconomic status per se could account for a large portion of the variance. In a similar manner, scarcely a single study considered the role the child plays in influencing parental behaviors. The major point is that numerous factors affect parenting behaviors, not the least of which is the child, and the factors interact in different ways for different families. This statement implies, then, that parenting behaviors are the result of a complex network that is not yet clearly understood, especially with regard to the relative impact each dimension has on the child.

Family of origin. "If adults are to be tender, loving, and caring human beings, they must be tenderly loved and cared for in their earliest years, from the moment they are born" (Hoopes, 1974, p. 54). This statement clearly underscores the important influence of one's family of origin on one's own parenting behavior. Many theorists suggest than a person's early relationships with parents are significant in subsequently shaping the kinds of relationships established with his or her own children (Cox et al., 1985).

There are numerous animal and human studies to document the fact that the primary affectional bond between infant and parent affects future affectional bonds—to peers, sexual partners, spouses, and finally to one's own children. A recent study on levels of mother-child interaction lends additional support. In a sample of low-birth-weight infants and their mothers, high-interacting mothers reported more satisfying relationships with their own mothers than did the low-interacting mothers (Cox et al., 1985).

Everyone has been parented—some by biological parents, others by adoptive parents, some by relatives and friends, and a less fortunate few by institutional staff. The quality of parenting received in the formative years is unquestionably reflected in the quality of parenting a person later demonstrates. For example, research indicates that mothers' perceptions of nurturant experiences in their childhood are strongly associated with secure versus anxious patterns of attachment in their infants. Other intergenerational influences found to affect parenting behaviors are as follows: Women's delight in their children, their investment in their children, their sensitivity to their children's individual needs, and their acceptance of their children were significantly predicted by their perception of their own mothers' intrusiveness, the support they received from their fathers in adolescence, their fathers' sensitivity, and their mothers' level of psychological health (Cox et al., 1985).

For fathers, the perception of their own fathers' intrusiveness and the quality of their current marriage were important predictors for succcessful adaptation to parenthood. For both men and women, perception of a relationship with the same-sexed parent that supported individuality and independence was a major predictor of successful adaptation to the parenthood role.

It was important also that women perceived their fathers as sensitive to them and supportive during adolescence. Thus for mothers it appears that their perceptions of the relationships with both parents are important in predicting the quality of mother-infant interactions. These researchers concluded that aspects of the relationships with one's parents during childhood and adolescence can predict the qualities of relationships established with one's own children.

Another area where parenting practices may reflect intergenerational influences is child abuse. It has been documented that abusive parents are likely to have been abused themselves as children. Although it cannot be said that this is the only factor that contributes to child abuse, it appears to be a significant one.

There are other factors in one's family of origin that appear to affect subsequent parenting behaviors: family constellation; ordinal position; and, most certainly, genetic factors relating to physical and mental health. While volumes could be written about these factors, suffice it to say that the number of children in one's own family, one's birth order in that family, and the genetic predisposition to certain physical and mental characteristics will be among the factors that influence a parent's behavior with regard to his or her own children.

Unfortunately, family of origin is not modifiable. We cannot now change the conditions under which we came into and grew up in this world. We *can*, however, change some of our attitudes about these conditions.

Personality patterns.   One's personality development results from hereditary and environmental forces from the moment of conception. Earlier experiences perhaps have a more profound effect than later ones, but personality continues to develop throughout the life cycle. It is reasonable to assume that parents begin their roles with unique personalities. Some are soft-spoken, others shout with little provocation; some are adaptable, others are more rigid; some are expressive, others are reticent. Yet parents with very different personalities have been shown to be equally successful in rearing children.

Personality patterns doubtlessly exert a strong influence on the kinds of parental behaviors one demonstrates. How much noise a person can tolerate or how fastidious she is will affect how restrictive that parent is about certain aspects of her child's behavior. How aggressive the parent is will have an influence on how aggressive her child becomes. How the parent handles her own stress will provide a model for handling stress for her children.

There are many personality patterns that can be described within the broad framework of "normal." And, no doubt, children manifest many of their parents' traits, whether by genetic predisposition, modeling, or other environmental factors. What is important to remember is that there is no one optimal personality pattern for a parent. Parents will continue through the ages to *be* different people and therefore to *behave* in different ways toward their children. It seems that, in the long run, parents with different personality patterns—so long as they are not neurotic or psychotic—can be effective in the parenting role. If, however, parents' personality patterns are sufficiently deviant as to result in overindulgence, rejection, coldness, lack of encouragement and reward, or neglect and abuse, then the end result most certainly can be devastating for children.

It is important to emphasize once again that not only parents' but also children's personalities are to be considered. Children demonstrate differences in temperament and personality at least from the moment of birth. These differences contribute to the reciprocal relationship between parent and child throughout the child-rearing years. Furthermore, the personality pattern of one child in the family can affect parenting behavior, not only toward that child but also toward siblings.

Finally, the personality pattern of one parent affects the behavior of the other parent. There are differences in the behavior of both the mother and the father toward their infants in triadic and dyadic situations. Whatever the reason for these differences, it is safe to assume that the mother and the father influence each other in significant ways. Further, as more children are added to the family and as personalities become more variable, relationships become far more complex because different dyadic and triadic interactions affect other family members—for example, the mother-father interaction affects each of the children and the mother-child interaction affects the father and other children. It will take much more research to delineate more clearly how the personality patterns of all family members interact to affect parenting behaviors, but the research to date indicates that the process is a complex one.

Culture. When examining the role of culture in determining parenting behaviors, we find that the relevant literature is vast, almost overwhelming, and fixated on the conclusion that certain discrete variables in one's culture may be said to exert an extraordinarily strong influence. The factors mentioned in this section are clearly interdependent among themselves and with other factors. The role of culture will be explored in greater detail in Chapter 6.

1. *Social class.* In literature perhaps the most salient aspect of culture as it relates to parenting is social class. The myth of the deprived child

was born in the 1960s with the advent of federal programs for children of low-income families, but since that time many of the generalizations that were made have been found to be exaggerated. Poverty does not necessarily imply deprivation. And further, variation within socioeconomic groups may be greater than that among groups. It is apparent, however, that the poor have fewer resources to assist them in parenting, and socioeconomic status inevitably is related to certain parenting behaviors.

2. *Ethnicity and religion.* Aside from social class, parents' ethnicity and religion are factors that impinge on parenting behaviors. These variables, alone or in combination, play a role in the kinds of activities the family engages in, the limits set and the controls placed on children's behavior, and the set of expectations that parents hold for their children. Some of these will be discussed in more detail later. Not only do cultural and religious values affect parental behaviors, but also, in many cases, stereotyping, discrimination, and prejudice against certain minority groups complicate the child-rearing process.

3. *Peer values.* Closely associated with social class, religion, and ethnicity is the peer value system, which influences attitudes toward parenting and personal expectations of children's behavior. With the decline of the extended family, increasing numbers of parents are being influenced in their parental attitudes and behavior by their peers. All too often a mother initiates toilet training, weans her baby, or uses corporal punishment because all her friends are doing it. Similarly, a father may play golf with the boys instead of going on a family outing because that is more acceptable to his peer group. This is not to say that the influence of the adult's peer group is always negative; surely peer groups provide models of positive parenting behaviors as well. Although parents generally are not as easily influenced by their peers as children are, most of them prefer not to be conspicuously different.

4. *Other cultural influences.* Other factors in the larger culture influence how parents behave. Some evidence indicates that parents' level of education in general, knowledge of child development or training in parenting skills, education for childbirth, and father involvement in labor and delivery contribute to more positive behaviors. While these factors alone cannot guarantee an effective parent, we believe that future research will indicate that they are significant. This means that the larger culture must undergo a number of changes in order to make these experiences possible for all parents.

A final aspect of culture that should be considered is the family itself. Variables such as the family structure (one parent or two parents, nuclear family or extended), life-style, number and birth order of children, parents' ages and age and sex of each child obviously affect parental behaviors. Since parenting in nontraditional families will be discussed in Chapters 7 and 8, we will not treat the subject of single parents, adolescent parents, or homosexual parents here. But even in the traditional family, parents have been shown to interact with their children differentially based on sex, age, birth order, and number of children. Fathers appear to differentiate between the sexes to a much greater degree than mothers do. And, unquestionably, as the child gets older, parenting behaviors change in response to the child's needs as well as to the parent's. Chapters 2, 3, and 4 will explore this phenomenon more fully.

A study by Wilson (1977) produced some interesting results concerning parents' ages. She observed that among mothers aged 15 to 36, maternal age was one of the two variables that predisposed mothers to positive nurturant caregiving 4 weeks following delivery. The results from her sample substantiated the conclusion that older mothers have a better-developed capacity to provide nurturant care to a dependent infant. Taken together, a multiplicity of influences properly labeled as cultural interact in a complex way to affect parental behaviors.

Mass media. While the mass media are most certainly cultural, we have treated them separately because we feel that they have a powerful effect on parenting. Approximately 99 percent of American homes have at least one television, a greater percentage than those having refrigerators and indoor plumbing, and many families have more than one set. The number of families with videocassette recorders is increasing daily. It is not our intent, however, to present evidence concerning the effects of television and video on children. There are numerous studies that may be reviewed on that topic. We do believe, however, that the various forms of the mass media, especially television and videocassette recorders, have a definite impact on parents and how they interact with their children.

LeMasters and DeFrain (1983) stated the following: "Parents and children are so immersed in messages from the mass media that they are scarcely aware of it" (p. 11). These authors were referring primarily to television but also included movies, advertising, and other media. They further noted that today's adults are the first generation reared under the influence of television. It does appear that the media frequently espouse values that conflict with parental values, especially in the areas of sex, drugs, violence, materialism, and hedonism (LeMasters & DeFrain, 1983). On the one hand, parental values probably are shaped partially by mass media, but, on the other hand, conflicting values often result in negative parent-child interactions.

For example, as a result of advertising, children are prompted to ask for more and more. Parents, wanting to be "good" parents, are inclined to give them more and more—and, if they are unable to, they may even feel guilty. In a similar vein, mass media carry the subtle message to children that "times have changed" and that some of the values being taught by their parents are old-fashioned.

One of the most significant effects of television and video on parenting is the amount of time they consume in many families, resulting in a presumably decreased amount of time spent in interaction with children. Furthermore, television-watching parents provide the model for television-watching children. Bronfenbrenner (1971) stated: "Turning on the television set can turn off the process that transforms children into people" (p. 158).

Evidence from several studies indicated that mothers who watch television at least 3½ hours a day are likely to have children who watch a lot of television. Conversely, mothers who watch television no more than 1 hour a day are likely to have children who watch little. A similar relationship exists between fathers' and children's viewing. Some evidence indicates that the amount of time children spend watching television and the programs they watch are among the major sources of friction and argument in a family.

All too often parents use the television or VCR as a babysitter, especially for preschool children. It enables them to get the child "out of their hair" while attending to household or social functions. There is ample evidence to show that the majority of parents do not monitor their children's viewing of television programs, and if they do it is in terms of total amount of time spent as opposed to specific programming. If parents were at least viewing programs with their children, opportunities for interpretation and explanation of events would present themselves. While Bronfenbrenner (1978) recommended that television personnel take a new approach in programming, little positive change has occurred. He proposed that, instead of portraying families as farce, fairy tale, or psychiatric orgy—as is the usual approach—television should focus on the circumstances in which families live out their lives. What the environment is like for children and youth in America—where the children are, what they are doing, and what places and people are available to them—should be documented. Naturalistic situations and human happenings that show children and their caretakers in circumstances allowing them to realize their potential would be more educational. With increased technology there is greater opportunity for both parents and children to view a wide variety of subject matter. Some information, obviously, is educational and expands knowledge, but a disproportionate amount portrays unrealistic family patterns, violence, and even pornography. Many experts are concerned that children are growing up to accept these situations as a way of life, so it appears that parents must be more effective in monitoring the media available to their children. Further, there is a need for effective control of the accessibility of videocassettes to children.

Parents are influenced, too, by other forms of mass media, particularly newspapers, magazines, pamphlets, and books, many of which contain material related to child rearing. It is hardly possible today to pick up a newspaper or buy a women's magazine without noticing at least one reference to parenting. Ann Landers has been the sole parent educator for many. With this deluge of information, much of it contradictory and confusing, parental behaviors have been significantly affected.

We wish to emphasize again that we do not take the view that the influences of the mass media are all negative. For example, some television programs provide materials that guide parents in skills to practice with their children. Although the evidence is not conclusive, there are preliminary indications that the use of nonbroadcast materials to be used in conjunction with instructional television can lead to increased learning. Television is the medium through which most parents in this country can be reached. It is sad to observe the underutilization for increasing effective parenting. It would be quite interesting to see what effects a media blitz on parent education would have on parenting behaviors.

Other forms of mass media (movies, for example) also may offer the parent insight into the nature of children's behavior and provide a model of effective interaction. Most certainly we would not discourage the distribution of printed materials to parents. For many, they are the major source of information on parenting, and the written word is gospel. What we should realize is that these materials do have an impact on parental behaviors, and often what is reported in the media is distorted or taken out of context. Even in the professional literature there is no common agreement as to what constitutes a "good" parent and no recipes for successful parenting. It seems to us that parents need assistance in interpreting what they read and in applying it in their own lives.

Historically, printed materials have reflected the middle-class pattern of child rearing. Some attempts have been made in recent years to provide more appropriate materials for the undereducated—materials with more pictures and fewer words. But printed materials probably will continue to be more effective with the educated, middle-class parent.

It seems reasonable to conclude, then, that all the mass media have an impact on parenting behaviors, but the exact nature of the influence varies among parents, depending on their exposure to other sources and the degree of credibility they associate with the media.

In summarizing the determinants of parenting behavior, the main point to make is that they are numerous. A parent's relationship with a given child may be influenced by her family of origin; her personality and the personalities of her spouse and all of her children; the aspects of the culture relating to social class, ethnicity, religion, peer value system, education for parenting, and family variables; and the mass media. While some of these determinants are modifiable, others are obviously inflexible, and the various factors operate together in an extremely complex manner.

Parent Education

The concept of parent education has existed for a long time. The term was used in this country as early as the 1920s. Recently, parent education has been used to include a variety of experiences to assist persons who are already parents to be more effective in their roles as well as to educate individuals who plan to be parents in the near or distant future.

There is greater consensus concerning what parenthood is than whether it requires any special training. Parenthood is viewed by some as a profession, which may be defined as an occupation requiring special education or training. While the assumption that once a child is born the mother miraculously knows how to care for him has been widely accepted, mothers have actually received training in their own homes throughout the ages.

In the Victorian age one would not have been confronted with multiple decisions related to parenthood, with the question of whether to become a parent, and with the multiple ways by which one could become a parent. For most people, once marriage occurred, parenthood followed. Admiration and respect were earned by parents if a child was born every year or so for several years. After conception, decisions about pregnancy and childbirth were made based on the experience of previous generations. Once a child was born, infant-care routines that had been practiced for generations most often were adopted with little thought or discussion. In the absence of information on child rearing from books, television, or other forms of media, parents simply did the "natural" thing, and the "natural" thing was what one had observed or remembered from being parented in one's own home (Biehler, 1976).

Today many mothers are combining parenthood with other roles and are unable to teach

---

BOX 1d DETERMINANTS OF PARENTING BEHAVIOR

Family of Origin
Personality Patterns
    Of parents
    Of children
Culture
    Social class
    Ethnicity
    Religion
    Peer value system
    Education
    Family structure
Mass Media
    Television
    Videocassettes
    Books, pamphlets, articles

or demonstrate effective parenting skills to their children. LeMasters and DeFrain (1983) stated the following:

It is usually assumed in our society that people have to be trained for difficult roles: most business firms would not consider turning a sales clerk loose on the customers without some formal training; the armed forces would scarcely send a raw recruit into combat without extensive and intensive training; most states now require a course in driver's education before high school students can acquire a driver's license. Even dog owners often go to school to learn how to treat their pets properly. This is not true of American parents. (pp. 75–76)

Although it will be some time—and maybe never—before all persons receive formalized training for parenthood, the view that this role requires training is widely held by professionals working with families and by many parents themselves.

Part of the problem in training for parenthood is the necessity of developing a set of competencies or coming to agreement about what constitutes an effective parent. There is no doubt that individuals with a wide variety of personalities; value systems; interests; abilities; and physical, social, emotional, and intellectual charcteristics can be effective parents. Further, parents from varying educational and socioeconomic levels may be equally effective. Although consensus may never be reached as to what an effective parent is and no recipe for rearing a child be developed, there is much that can be gained from research to assist parents in their tasks.

HISTORICAL VIEWS

Parenting began as Adam and Eve produced Cain and Abel and commenced their child rearing. Parent education soon followed, as they served as models for those sons in the development of their parenting skills. The prehistoric cave woman no doubt instructed her daughter in how to care for her newborn infant. Several thousand years later, parent education was hailed as an entirely new approach and showed signs of being the most significant educational reform in the 1970s. Some experts (Schlossman, 1976; White, 1975) stated that parent education would be the clarion call of reformers in the 1980s and 1990s. Unfortunately, parent education in the 1980s was not the significant force that these experts predicted, because many programs suffered the ax of the Reagan administration. The concepts of parenting, parent education, and parent involvement were revived in the 1970s, but there has been a concern for parenting and parent education throughout the ages.

As early as the time of Plato and Aristotle (300 B.C.), advice was being given to parents. Plato, in his desire for a better society, recommended that children be taken away from their parents and raised by state-appointed personnel in order to avoid inconsistency and the risk of incompetent parents. The sexes were to have the same general education, but boys needed more severe instruction. However, Plato's student Aristotle felt that the inconsistencies of the family system would enhance individualism, which would assist in delivering Greece out of its troubles.

These two recurring themes are evident in the philosophies of child experts throughout recorded history. It is interesting to note the recycling of ideas from the past, but it is perhaps unsettling to realize that many of the techniques assumed to be demonstrative of our modern, scientific society are really revivals of age-old treatments used by others (McCulloch, 1984).

During the fourth through the fourteenth centuries, the Dark Ages, child-management techniques exemplified the philosophy of the Church—that children were born sinful and wicked. Parenting doctrines were based on the Bible, especially Proverbs. Slowly the overall attitude concerning children changed; beginning in the twelfth century and continuing until the seventeenth century, the notion about the wicked and sinful nature of the child changed to one of children as innocent (Aries, 1962). This reversal in attitude was a process that evolved over five centuries. It was during this Renaissance that children began to be depicted as children rather than as miniature adults, since they were thought of as separate from adults (Biehler, 1976).

During the seventeenth and eighteenth centuries, John Locke and Jean Jacques Rousseau contributed to the attitudes about children. Reminiscent of Aristotle, Locke emphasized individuality in the education of children. He described the child as a blank slate to be written on by experience. Therefore he advocated patience, praise, and encouraging curiosity. As noted by Biehler (1976), the advice is as appropriate now as it was then. Rousseau's emphasis was on the natural goodness of children. Education was to be based on careful observation of children, never coercing them to learn things as yet beyond them. He advocated some compromise between spoiling the child and impeding his development of individuality, again echoing Aristotle and Plato (Biehler, 1976).

In the United States during the eighteenth century, children were still disciplined sternly. The church and the state actually worked together to manage child behavior according to the strict interpretation of the Bible. Many clergymen delivered from their pulpits sermons that were concerned with family matters and the "obligations and opportunities of parents" (Groves & Groves, 1928, p. 175). Parents were monitored to be sure that they complied with the accepted parenting code. Fathers were seen as better disciplinarians than mothers since they possessed greater wisdom and authority. The role of the mother was to give birth to, care for, and feed infants. After these first few months, child management was taken over by the father. Even though the child was under the mother's influence for such a short time, the father would have to severely correct the wickedness caused by the mother's overindulgence (Cable, 1975). Parents believed it was important for children to conform to religious doctrine. To facilitate moral instruction children often were in attendance at public hangings, and clergymen used "hellfire and brimstone" tactics that caused anxiety in the young. The children were constantly reminded that they might die in the night and live in the eternal fire (Cable, 1975).

The Modern Era

The nineteenth century, the beginning of the modern era, brought a change in the attitudes of American parents toward their children. As part of the Industrial Revolution, families began to migrate to the cities and leave the rural life of the colonies. For the first time since the colonial period, large numbers of fathers were away from home during the day (Cable, 1975; Karpowitz, 1980), and pamphlets and books on parent management were abundant. These were directed to mothers, and mothers began to be accepted as the true rulers of the home, those most responsible for the rearing of children (Schlossman, 1983). Other innovations included the first self-help parent groups (which increased in the 1880s and out of which grew the PTA). During the latter part of the nineteenth century, mothers' disciplinary techniques became more permissive, but they were encouraged to shield their children from the hazards of the ''outside'' world and to protect their innocence. Embodying the Victorian philosophy, mothers and children were isolated from the real world and fathers were expected to cope.

At the turn of the twentieth century, many ''experts'' in the area of child study began to appear, and the first permissive era of child rearing was over—a laissez-faire attitude toward rearing children was unpopular (Cable, 1975). The ideas of the parent-education movement for this period were described by Schlossman (1983):

We thus see in early twentieth century parent education, as embodied in the work of the PTA, an intriguing balance of perspective between private domestic responsibility and public political activity, and a reliance on religion and maternal instinct, versus a reliance on science and formal instruction. . . .It is important to recognize the existence of this balance and these tensions in the theory and practice of parent education in the pre–World War I era. (p. 10)

During the decade of the 1920s, dramatic changes took place in the professional and public attitudes toward child-care practices. The parent-education movement, transformed into a ''well-organized social movement'' (Schloss-man, 1976, p. 10), reached millions of people for the first time. Many programs and publications appeared, reflecting a new interest in the scientific aspect of child-care and parenting skills. The impact of science was noted by the disappearance of references to the Diety in the literature. Whereas mothers of the late Victorian era had put their faith in the Bible, the mothers of the 1920s relied on scientific information on nutrition and good habits to help them solve child-rearing problems (Cable, 1975). The vigorous interest in parent education during the 1920s was affected by the breaking down of the social and moral codes that had guided the behavior of the middle class for generations.

Further, there was great confidence in the ability of science to solve problems in all aspects of life (Schlossman, 1983). As the movement grew and as parenthood brought increasing frustration, the number of parent-education organizations increased. Between the 1930s and the 1970s, contemporary parenting programs emerged. As more and more research was conducted, programs were developed by such experts as Skinner, Spock, Ginott, and Dreikurs. Many concepts from these experts form the foundation for present parenting strategies.

A Rebirth

In the 1960s and 1970s, a renewed interest in parenting, combined with social and cultural changes in society, early intervention research, certain political movements (women's movement, civil rights movement, and others), federal legislation, and increased interest of parents themselves served as the impetus for parent education. A proliferation of programs emerged during these years. Many of the programs of the 1960s and 1970s were totally or partially funded by the federal government and during the Reagan administration were discontinued due to lack of financial and ideological support. Since the early 1980s there has been a major movement toward the development of family-support programs, which take a broad approach to parent education by focusing on the whole aspect of family life (Powell, 1986). Many of these programs emphasize the development of support systems for families rather than try to change what may be perceived as deficits in family functioning. Helping families to prevent problems rather than to repair damaged parent-child relations has been a priority.

The Future

A number of experts recently indicated that parent education in the 1980s and 1990s is warranted more than ever (Powell, 1986; Roehl, Herr, & Applehaus, 1985; Seckinger & Day, 1986). The reasons include the challenging, complex, and continuous tasks associated with the parenthood role; the lack of preparation for the role; the limited knowledge about growth and development and needs of children; the increase in the number of teenage parents; the changing structure and functions of the American family; women as major wage earners of the family; the reduction of the amount of time parents can devote to parenting; and the many myths and misconceptions that exist about parenthood.

Despite the long history of parent education and the recent emphasis on increasing parenting effectiveness, the value of parent programs continues to be questioned by many policy makers, funding agencies, and even some of parents the programs wish to serve. Powell (1986) reviewed research on the effects of parent education on both children and parents. Studies have indicated strong short-term effects on children. For example, children's IQs have been examined most frequently and have been found to increase as an apparent result of parental participation. There also have been positive relationships between children's school achievement and parent involvement. The longer and more extensive the parental involvement, the longer the gains have been maintained. Parent programs have been found to increase infant responsiveness to parent behavior.

Program effects on parents have not been studied to the degree that child effects have been. There is, however, evidence of immediate positive effects on maternal behavior, parental competencies in reading infant cues, use of positive and facilitative language interactions with the child, open and flexible child-rearing attitudes, and parental roles as educators.

Families' economic and life circumstances also have been found to be more positive, in both short- and long-term follow-up of programs. Impoverished mothers involved in the Yale Child Welfare Project were found 10 years later to be more self-supporting, have more education, and have smaller families than mothers not involved in the program (Seitz, Rosenbaum, & Apfel, 1985).

While there is not convincing evidence that one particular program is significantly more effective than another, some research has found that parents involved in a program utilizing a personal-meaning approach demonstrated more effective learning and retention than did parents involved in a traditional approach (Hills & Knowles, 1987; Powell, 1986). The personal-meaning approach utilized techniques designed to help parents see the relevance of skills (potential for meeting important needs) and the awareness of feelings associated with the application of skills. These researchers noted that in the follow-up of many parent-education programs, a lack of transfer of skills taught in programs to actual family situations was found, even though the increased skills in paper-and-pencil tests were noted. They emphasized that parent educators should use teaching strategies that create opportunities for parents to bring their experiences and concerns into all phases of learning the skills. Parents should be asked to describe their understanding of a concept and encouraged to develop their own wording and judgment when implementing a skill.

Studies of 28 different parent-training programs found no relationship between the content of the curriculum and the degree of program impact on children's cognitive skills. Efforts to compare the effectiveness of programs that focused on child-management skills have failed to identify a superior model. In addition some researchers have failed to find a relationship between program effectiveness and the degree of structure (Powell, 1986). These findings cannot be interpreted to mean, however, that curriculum content is unimportant or that any parent-education model will work with any population, but it does seem to imply that the most important attributes of a parent program are not clearly indicated. The process of implementing a program and the personality and skills of the leader are probably as important as the content. Seckinger and Day (1986) emphasized that when developing parent programs educators must respect the family values and traditions as well as the talents of individual family members.

It appears from the available research that many approaches to parent education can be effective. Roehl, Herr, and Applehaus (1985) proposed creative approaches to utilizing a variety of settings in delivering information on parenting. They suggested that commuting time could be a convenient period to share information, yet it is drastically underutilized. Commuting for many parents is a time when there are minimal distractions. Daily radio programs and cassette series also could be utilized when parents are driving to and from work. Printed materials and learning packets may be helpful for passengers riding in a train, on a bus, in a van, on a subway, or in a carpool.

Employee-assistance programs provide another vehicle for parent education. Information can be shared at lunch or before and after work hours. Other parent-education modes can be successfully utilized in the work place—for example, computer programs, videotapes, cassettes, movies, lectures, slide presentations, and discussions. The parent educator also might serve as a resource person at the work site where employees schedule appointments to discuss particular child-rearing problems on a one-to-one basis.

Parent education also could be provided as a consumer service in children's specialty shops, department stores, and supermarkets. Churches, family housing areas, and neighborhood groups are other avenues for reaching parents. Many of the same materials and delivery systems used in other locations can be made available for parents to use at home. These may be mailed to parents or checked out from a central location.

It is apparent that creative and innovative approaches to disseminate parenting information can significantly increase the number of parents reached. Several investigators (Powell, 1986; Tingey, Boyd, & Casto, 1987) have emphasized the need for parent-education programs to offer a wide variety of services from which parents can choose. Since families differ considerably, they should be able to choose those services most beneficial to them.

SUMMARY

Concepts of parenthood, parenting, and parent education have existed since biblical times. Both mothers and fathers have been shown to contribute significantly to the development of their children, but the interpretations of their roles have changed significantly, thereby bringing change in both the form and the content of parent education.

The beginning of the modern era of parent education has been placed at the beginning of the nineteenth century, when publications on child rearing began to appear and when organizations emphasizing education and support for parents emerged. The twentieth century saw the major impetus for parent education in the 1920s and the 1960s. The complex technological and rapidly changing society of the final decade of the century necessitates continual support for parents.

The need for education for parenting in contemporary society is supported by the prevalence of myths about parenthood and children, by the changing nature of the family itself, and by the lack of sufficient and reliable guidelines for effective parenting. Even though education for parenthood appears to be a necessity, it is important to understand that parenting behaviors result from a complex network of variables that includes family of origin, personality patterns, culture, ethnicity, religion, and the mass media.

REFERENCES

AINSWORTH, M. (1973). The development of infant-mother attachment. In B. Caldwell & H. Ricciuti (Eds.), *Review of child development research* (3), 1–94. Chicago: University of Chicago Press.

ARIES, P. (1962). *Centuries of childhood: A social history of family life.* R. Baldick, trans. New York: Knopf. (Originally published, 1960.)

BELL, S., & AINSWORTH, M. (1972). Infant crying and maternal responsiveness. *Child Development, 43,* 1171–1190.

BIEHLER, R. F. (1976). *Child development: An introduction.* Boston: Houghton Mifflin.

BIGNER, J. (1979). *Parent-child relations*. New York: Macmillan.

BIGNER, J. (1985). *Parent-child relations* (2d ed). New York: Macmillan.

BILLER, H. (1974). *Paternal deprivation*. Lexington, MA: D. C. Heath.

BRADLEY, R., CALDWELL, B., & ELARDO, R. (1977). Home environment, social status, and mental test performance. *Journal of Educational Psychology, 69*(6), 697–701.

BRAZELTON, T. B. (1969). *Infants and mothers: Differences in development*. New York: Dell.

BRIDGES, W. (1980). *Transitions*. Reading, MA: Addison-Wesley.

BRONFENBRENNER, U. (1971). Who cares for America's children? *Young Children, 26*(3), 157–163.

BRONFENBRENNER, U. (1978). Who needs parent education? *Teachers College Record, 4,* 767–787.

BROOKS, J. (1987). *The process of parenting* (2d ed.). Palo Alto, CA: Mayfield.

CABLE, M. (1975). *The little darlings: A history of child rearing in America*. New York: Scribner's.

CALDWELL, B., WRIGHT, C. M., HONIG, A., & TANNEBAUM, J. (1970). Infant day care and attachment. *American Journal of Orthopsychiatry, 40,* 397–412.

CAMPBELL, S. B. (1977, March). Maternal and infant behavior in normal, high risk, and "difficult" babies. Paper presented at the biennial meeting of the Society for Research in Child Development, New Orleans.

CAPLAN, P., & HALL-McCORQUODALE, I. (1985). The scapegoating of mothers: A call for change. *American Journal of Orthopsychiatry, 55*(4), 610–613.

CHESS, S., & THOMAS, A. (1973). Temperament in the normal infant. In J. Westman (Ed.), *Individual differences in children* (pp. 83–103). New York: Wiley.

CLARKE-STEWART, A. (1977). *Child care in the family: A review of research and some propositions for policy*. New York: Academic.

CLARKE-STEWART, A. (1978). And daddy makes three: Father's impact on mother and young child. *Child Development, 49*(2), 466–578.

COWAN, C., COWAN P., HEMING, G., GARRETT, E., COYSH, W., CURTIS-BOLES, H., & BOLES, A. (1985). Transitions to parenthood. *Journal of Family Issues, 6*(4), 451–481.

COX, M., OWEN, M., LEWIS, J., RIEDEL, C., SCALF-McIVER, L., & SUSTER, A. (1985). Intergenerational influences on the parent-infant relationship in the transition to parenthood. *Journal of Family Issues, 6*(4), 543–564.

EDWARDS, C.S. (1981, Winter). User's guide to USDA estimates of the cost of raising a child: Part II. *Family Economics Review,* pp. 19–31.

FEIN, R. (1978). Research in fathering: Social policy and an emergent perspective. *Journal of Social Issues, 34*(1), 122–136.

GOETTING, A. (1986). Parental satisfaction. *Journal of Family Issues, 7*(1), 83–109.

GROVES, E. R., & GROVES, G. H. (1928). *Parents and children*. Philadelphia: J. B. Lippincott.

HAMILTON, M. (1977). *Father's influence on children*. Chicago: Nelson-Hall.

HEFFNER, E. (1978). *Mothering: The emotional experience of motherhood after Freud and feminism*. New York: Doubleday.

HILLS, M., & KNOWLES, D. (1987). Providing for personal meaning in parent education programs. *Family Relations, 36*(2), 158–162.

HOFFMAN, M. (1971). Father absence and conscience development. *Developmental Psychology, 4,* 400–406.

HOOPES, M. (1974). Touch me! Touch me not! *Family Perspective, 9*(1), 54.

ISABELLA, R., & BELSKY, J. (1985). Marital change during the transition to parenthood and security of infant-parent attachment. *Journal of Family Issues, 6*(4), 505–522.

KARPOWITZ, D. (1980). A conceptualization of the American family. In M. Fine (Ed.), *Handbook on parent education* (pp. 27–48). New York: Academic.

KELLER, W., HILDEBRANDT, K., & RICHARDS, M. (1985). Effects of extended father-infant contact during the newborn period. *Infant Behavior and Development, 8*(3), 337–350.

KLAUS, M., & KENNELL, J. (1976). *Maternal-infant bonding*. St. Louis: C. V. Mosby.

LAMB, M. (1975). Fathers: Forgotten contributors to child development. *Human Development, 18,* 245–266.

LAMB, M. (1976a). Effects of stress and cohort on mother and father infant interaction. *Developmental Psychology, 12*(5), 435–443.

LAMB, M. (1976b). Twelve-month-old infants and their parents. *Developmental Psychology, 12,* 237–244.

LAMB, M. (1977). Father-infant and mother-infant interaction in the first year of life. *Child Development, 48,* 167–181.

LaROSSA, R. (1983). The transition of parenthood and the social reality of time. *Journal of Marriage and the Family, 45*(3), 579–589.

LeMASTERS, E., & DeFRAIN, J. (1983). *Parents in contemporary America*. Homewood, IL: Dorsey.

LUNDBERG, F., & FARNHAM, M. A. (1947). *Modern woman: The lost sex*. New York: Grossett & Dunlap.

LYNN, D. (1974). *The father: His role in child development*. Monterey, CA: Brooks/Cole.

McCULLOCH, J. (1984). *The history of parent education*. Unpublished manuscript.

McKIM, M. (1987). Transition to what? New parents' problems in the first year. *Family Relations, 36*(1), 22–25.

MOORE, S. (1977). Mother-child interactions and competence in infants and toddlers. *Young Children, 32*(3), 64–69.

MORRISON, G. S. (1978). *Parent involvement in the home, school, and community*. Columbus, OH: Chas. E. Merrill.

PARKE, R., & SAWIN, D. (1976). The father's role in infancy: A reevaluation. *The Family Coordinator, 25*(4), 365–371.

PARKS, P., & SMERIGLIO, V. (1986). Relationships among parenting knowledge, quality of stimulation in the home and infant development. *Family Relations, 35,* 411–416.

PARSONS, T., & BALES, R. F. (1955). *Family, socialization, and the interaction process.* Glencoe, IL: The Free Press.

PHILLIPS, C., & ANZALONE, J. (1978). *Fathering: Participation in labor and birth.* St. Louis: Mosby.

POWELL, D. (1986). Parent education and support programs. *Young Children, 41,* 47–53.

ROEHL, J., HERR, J., & APPLEHAUS, D. (1985). Parenting education—now more than ever. *Lifelong Learning, 9,* 20–22, 27.

SCHAFFER, F. (1977). *Mothering.* Cambridge, MA: Harvard University Press.

SCHLOSSMAN, S. (1976). Before home start: Notes toward a history of parent education. *Harvard Educational Review, 46*(3), 436–467.

SCHLOSSMAN, S. L. (1983). The formation era in American parent education: Overview and interpretation. In R. Haskins & D. Adams (Eds.), *Parent education and public policy* (pp. 7–36). Norwood, NJ: Ablex.

SECKINGER, D., & DAY, M. (1986). Parenting education: The way we were. *Lifelong Learning, 10,* 8–10, 23.

SEITZ, V., ROSENBAUM, L., & APFEL, N. (1985). Effects of family support intervention: A ten-year follow-up. *Child Development, 56*(2), 376–391.

TINGEY, C., BOYD, R., & CASTO, G. (1987). Parental involvement in early intervention: Becoming a parent-plus. *Early Child Development and Care, 27,* 91–105.

TOLAN, W., & TOMASINI, L. (1977). Mothers of ''secure'' vs. ''insecure'' babies differ themselves nine months later. Paper presented at the biennial meeting of the Society for Research in Child Development, New Orleans.

U.S. Bureau of the Census (1987). *Statistical abstract of the U.S.: 1988* (10th ed.). Washington, DC: U.S. Department of Commerce.

U.S. News and World Report (1987, May 4). Second thoughts about infant day care, pp. 73–74.

VENTURA, J. (1987). The stresses of parenthood re-examined. *Family Relations, 36*(1), 26–69.

WALDRON, H., & ROUTH, D. (1981). The effect of the first child on the marital relationship. *Journal of Marriage and the Family, 43*(4), 785–788.

Wall Street Journal (1987, March 5). Day care for infants is challenged by research on psychological risks, p. 3.

WEISS, N. P. (1978). The mother-child dyad revisited: Perceptions of mothers and children in twentieth century child-rearing manuals. *Journal of Social Issues, 34*(2), 29–45.

WHITE, B. (1975). *The first three years of life.* Englewood Cliffs, NJ: Prentice-Hall.

WILKIE, C., & AMES, E. (1986). The relationship of infant crying to parental stress in the transition of parenthood. *Journal of Marriage and the Family, 48*(3), 545–550.

WILSON, A. (1977). A predictive analysis of early parental attachment behavior. Paper presented at the biennial meeting of the Society for Research in Child Development, New Orleans.

WORTHINGTON, E., & BUSTON, B. (1986). The marriage relationship during the transition to parenthood. *Journal of Family Issues, 7*(4), 443–473.

ZEIDLER, A., NARDINE, F., SCOLARE, C., & MICH, P. (1987, April). Adult perceptions of parent-child relations: Implications for families as educators. Paper presented at the Annual Meeting of the American Educational Research Association, Washington, DC.

2

The Changing Nature of Parenting: Infancy and Early Childhood

The role of parent is one of several adult roles achieved by a large percentage of men and women in society today. Unlike other roles, however, parenting has unique features that were described in Chapter 1 in arguing for the need for education for parenting. In light of these features, it is no wonder that parents feel confused and even overwhelmed, particularly with the birth of the first child. Further, professionals traditionally have studied the effects of inadequate parenting on the development of the child and have ignored the significance of the interaction between the parent and the child within the context of the contributions that each makes to the other in shaping behavior.

There are a number of factors that have an impact on the specific nature of the parent's role. We have previously pointed out the characteristics of, and differences between, mothering and fathering. However, it appears that contemporary parents are becoming more androgynous, thereby minimizing many of the traditional differences between the roles of mothers and fathers. Fathers classified as androgynous have been found to carry out more child-care tasks and interact more with their children than fathers rated as masculine. Other studies have indicated that fathers who participate more extensively in child rearing also are more nurturant and sensitive.

Another factor that impinges on the parenting role is the birth of siblings. As more children are added to the family, the character of parent-child relationships may be altered. In fact, the birth of a sibling may represent a developmental crisis for the family. The interactions of pregnant mothers and their first-born children were observed both before and after the delivery of the second child. There was a consistent decrease in the expression of warmth on the part of both mothers and children after the birth of a sibling (Taylor & Kogan, 1973).

Family size, too, affects parenting style. It has been noted that in larger families child rearing becomes more rule-ridden and less individualized, with corporal punishment being more common and less investment of resources occurring. Children in smaller families tend to have higher IQs and greater academic achievement and occupational performance, whereas children from larger families are at greater risk for delinquency and alcoholism (Wagner, Schubert, & Schubert, 1985).

The stuctural makeup of the family is still

another condition that affects the parenting role. Children reared in intact nuclear families are likely to have different relationships with their parents than children reared in extended families or in single-parent families. As children develop from infancy through adolescence, the changes in their developmental characteristics bring about changes in the parenting role.

PARENTS AND INFANTS

Parents as Caregivers

The term *caregiver* has recently been used in the literature to refer to the person or persons responsible for providing the care of the infant or young child. Its use implies that males are as capable of giving care as females are and that persons other than biological parents are frequently significant caregivers. Most recent research indicates that infants may attach and adapt to more than one significant caregiver, as long as the number remains small and those persons are consistent in the kind of care they provide. Of particular interest has been the role of the father as caregiver and the infant's interactions with him.

Fathers appear to be capable of nurturant behavior toward their infants and are strongly interested in them, although they engage in less caretaking and more play with them than mothers do (Gearing, 1978). However, Power (1985) examined mother-infant and father-infant play for the predominant kinds of play and for the individual differences in play style. Both the content and the style of play varied with infant age at 7, 10, and 13 months. Mothers were more responsive than fathers to infant cues of interest and attention and at 13 months were more successful in influencing infant behavior.

Nevertheless, the traditional, noninvolved "breadwinner" image of the father is changing into a new, more actively involved father who is willing to assume some caretaking responsibility for his children soon after birth. It has been speculated that the combination of a playful father and a talkative mother might provide the greatest facilitation of cognitive development (Clarke-Stewart, 1978).

It is our position that a number of people can be effective caregivers for infants—mothers, fathers, grandparents, child-care workers, older siblings, and friends. It is on the parents, however, that we wish to focus here. While caregiving by the parents may be supplemented by others in cases where neither parent devotes full time to the care of the infant, we want to emphasize the quality as opposed to the quantity of caregiving activities. The kind of parent-child transaction that seems to promote competence has less to do with the amount of time a parent spends with a child than with the quality of the transactions, which, after all, may consume relatively little time in the course of a day. Further, studies of day-care versus home-reared infants have suggested that supplemental caregiving in a day-care center does not interfere with the healthy attachment process between infants and their mothers. Therefore we will consider the parents as primary caregivers of their infants, whether the infant receives supplemental care or not (Caldwell, Wright, Honig, & Tannebaum, 1970).

In most cases when an infant is born, her needs for mothering are in excess of the mother's need for the child. This fact necessitates reduction of a woman's, and many times a man's, involvement in nonfamily interests and social roles. With the decline of the extended family, most young parents today have little physical or emotional support for the awesome task that faces them. They are prepared poorly, at best, to cope with the strain of the sudden demands that they find. The infant is helpless and dependent on caregivers for all her needs. Her parents assume the roles of protectors and providers. Parents, who are accustomed to freedom, suddenly find themselves unable to go shopping, visit friends, or take a weekend trip without considerable preparation and adaptation. Further, during the first few months, the infant's capabilities are unfolding so rapidly that parents' behavior must undergo continual change to meet the baby's needs.

Initial caregiving has been defined as the provision of life support and protection by Bell (1974). He pointed out that the pregnancy, the infant's physical appearance, the helpless thrashing movements, as well as the fact that the infant's sensory and motor system matches that of the mother, all contribute to maintaining the caregiving system.

Three major factors appear to determine relationships between parents and infants: (1) the quality of the parents' own early experiences—the care each received as a child; (2) the conditions of the present situation—family stability or marital discord, job security, health, degree of stress in daily lives, and so on; and (3) the characteristics of the infant himself (Naylor, 1970). Parental attitudes and accuracy of perceptions about the baby's characteristics and needs were additional influences cited by Willemsen (1979). Other studies have shown that the infant's behavior is related to the mother's and the father's expectations, for example, what they believe the infant can do.

When we examine the parent-infant relationship from the perspective of what the infants themselves contribute, it is clear that infants differ from the beginning in their responses to the environment. Brazelton's delightful book *Infants and Mothers: Differences in Development* (1969) described the normal developmental paths of three very different infants as well as the different ways in which they affected their environments. His portraits of Daniel, Louis, and Laura illustrated that normal babies differ from the beginning in their level of activity, their adaptability, their biological rhythmicity, and their general responsiveness to their environments.

In her study of the stresses of first-time parenthood between the third and fifth postpartum months, Ventura (1987) found that the infants' fussy behavior in relation to feeding or soothing techniques was the major stress reported by 35 percent of the mothers in her sample and 20 percent of the fathers. Mothers reported feeling guilty, helpless, or angry when caring for their fussy infants. In another study, fathers were found to experience *more* stress than mothers did when they had a crying baby, even though new parenthood, overall, had a greater impact on women than on men, both negatively and positively (Wilkie & Ames, 1986).

Another study that examined mother-infant interactions suggested that the more difficult the child was temperamentally, the less responsive the mother was (Milliones, 1978). The author

noted that child temperament seems to represent most cogently the infant's effect on the caregiver.

Babies contribute to the parent-child interaction in four ways: (1) by their state of awareness—that is, whether they are asleep, awake, drowsy, or alert; (2) by the types of signaling they employ through vocalizing, touching, or looking; (3) by the amount of attention they seek; and (4) by the extent of responsiveness they demonstrate (Willemsen, 1979).

It seems obvious, then, that the infant is no mere passive recipient of stimulation who is controlled by the adults in her environment but is an active participant in her own development, and her unique manner of participation is a critical factor in the kind of parenting behaviors she receives. Easy caregiving, however, lays the foundation for social interactions, reciprocal communication and signaling, and the development of special skills during the period of infancy.

Establishing Basic Trust

Erik Erikson (1963) described the stages of the life cycle and the psychosocial development of the ego. Erikson conceived of each stage as being marked by an issue or a "crisis" to connote an emphasis in the individual's life. The first of these stages, occurring from birth to about 1 year, is defined as trust versus mistrust. The degree to which the child comes to trust the world, other people, and himself depends to a considerable extent on the quality of care that he receives. The infant whose needs are met when they arise; whose discomforts are quickly removed; and who is cuddled, fondled, played with, and talked to develops a sense of the world as a safe place to be and of people as helpful and dependable.

When, however, the care is inconsistent, inadequate, and rejecting, it fosters a basic mistrust, an attitude of fear and suspicion on the part of the infant toward the world in general and toward people in particular that will carry through to later stages of development. Erikson did not believe, however, that the problem of basic trust versus mistrust was resolved once and for all during the first year of life; rather it arises

again at each successive stage of development. If basic needs are not met, the child feels somehow empty, cheated, at a loss, and ill at ease with others and with himself.

On examining Piaget's description of the growth of intelligence during the period of infancy, it becomes even more clear that the environment does not mold the child's behavior by simply imposing itself on a passive infant. Rather the infant seeks contact with her environment; she searches for environmental events to happen and seeks increased levels of stimulation and excitation. The infant interprets events in her environment and gives them meaning and consequently produces specific behaviors (Piaget, 1952).

These descriptions of developmental characteristics have important implications for parenting during the period of infancy. First, it is important to elaborate on ways that a sense of basic trust can be fostered. The newborn comes equipped with one major means of communicating with others in the environment—crying. At first parents must infer what the infant is attempting to communicate with his cries. They check his diapers, feed him, change his positions, rock him, or do whatever it takes to relieve his distress. In essence parents are at the mercy of the infant's cries (Bell, 1974).

It is not long, however, until parents begin to distinguish a hunger cry from a distress cry and can attend to these with less trial-and-error behavior. There has been some controversy concerning how much attention should be given and how quickly parents should respond to infant crying.

Infants who have an early history of delay on the part of the mother in responding to crying tend later to cry for longer periods than do infants with a history of less delay (Bell & Ainsworth, 1972). In other words Bell and Ainsworth concluded that the consistency and promptness of maternal response during the first 3 months (or its absence) affects the pattern of later infant crying. Moreover, they found that infants whose cries had been neither ignored nor responded to with undue delay developed modes of communication other than crying. Thus a baby whose experience has been that his mother responds to his signals with consistency and promptness learns to expect that signaling—and, later, communication—is effectual—and not merely that there will be a response to crying. (Fathers were not involved in this study, but we assume that these conclusions would apply to them as well.)

While there are those who are still convinced that if a mother or a father attends to crying, then the infant will be reinforced and thus cry more, we believe that Bell's and Ainsworth's conclusions are valid. Prompt attention to crying during the early months is one way of facilitating the basic trust that Erikson believes to be so important.

Equally important as prompt, consistent attention to the infant's needs is the maintenance of an orderly, predictable environment. The infant at birth does not view herself as a separate entity from others in the environment. In fact, at first, everyone and everything is an extension of herself. A critical task of the period of infancy is to develop a sense of self and of others as separate from self. This task is related in a complex way to establishing a sense of basic trust.

In the beginning much of the infant's world is bound to his physiological needs. If he is fed when he is hungry, changed when he is wet, helped to sleep or rest when he is tired, and cared for by the same few people whom he eventually comes to recognize as significant, then his day-to-day environment becomes predictable, orderly, and consistent. He comes to know that certain things happen at particular times and that familiar people come when he needs them. He learns to recognize, too, the particular patterns of responses of his special caregivers—their tones of voice, their odors, and the way their bodies feel when he is held close. All of these consistent, predictable subtleties help him to learn who he is and that he can depend on others for his safety.

Trust is built also from the child's own behavior, that is, he begins to view himself as competent by his ability to act on his environment and his success in eliciting certain responses from his caregivers. If, however, the infant is cared for by a number of different people; if there is no predictability in her feeding, sleeping, or being played with; and especially if she is neglected or abused, then her sense of basic trust in herself as competent and in others as dependable will be impeded.

Developing Reciprocity

At this point it should be obvious that the parent-infant system is reciprocal in nature, with the behavior and characteristics of one influencing the behavior and characteristics of the other. Since much more has been written about mother-infant reciprocity than father-infant, we will focus on the mother-infant dyad. However, we want to emphasize that we believe the same sort of reciprocity can be developed between a father and his infant and between any other caregiver and an infant.

Reciprocity has been defined as a parallel waxing and waning of each partner's level of arousal, the degree of positive or negative involvement at given points during interaction (Brazelton, Koslowski, & Main, 1974). An example of this type of behavior was called "ping-pong"—I do something, you do something—by Gordon (1976). Escalona (1973) noted that either mother or baby could start a chain reaction of mutual gazing, vocalizing, or peek-a-boo. These three viewpoints refer to the reciprocal nature of parent-child interactions.

Mother-infant reciprocity appears not to be a phenomenon brought about solely by good mothering but rather by a process of mutual adaptation between mother and child (Thrift, 1976). Both learn to recognize cues, signals, or patterns of specific behaviors and characteristics of each other in numerous situations. This sort of mutual adaptation begins in the prelinguistic phase and, in time, allows each partner to communicate to the other her involvement in the interaction.

In keeping with Brazelton's notion of level of arousal, both mother and infant contribute to the maintenance of an optimal level. Sensitive mothers provide appropriately timed stimulation for their infants; that is, they watch for cues of responsiveness from the infant—whether she is alert or drowsy, what stimuli she is attending to, and what signals she is sending. These mothers reduce or stop stimulation, when appropriate, to allow the infant a brief period to withdraw and reestablish equilibrium. By the same token, babies seek stimulation when they desire it, they create or prolong pleasant situations, and they avert their gaze or turn their heads when stimulation is too overwhelming. Thus, the two partners work together to regulate the level of arousal.

Five kinds of experiences that a mother offers her infant in a period of interaction were summarized by Brazelton (1974):

1. Reduction of interfering activity.
2. Setting the stage for a period of interaction by bringing the baby to a more alert, receptive stage.
3. Creating an atmosphere of expectancy for further interaction through her behavior.
4. Acceleration of the baby's attention to receive and send messages.
5. Allowing for reciprocity with sensitivity to the baby's signals, giving him time to respond with his own behavior, as well as time to digest and recover from the activation her cues establish.

In other words, the mother does not bombard her infant with stimulation, does not talk away at the baby, and does not wait for the child always to initiate interaction with her. The balance is consistent with the needs of each member of the dyad.

The development of reciprocity during the first 6 months of life facilitates the infant's learning to separate herself from others in her environment. The infant learns which behavior patterns represent "Mother" and thereby can distinguish her from others in the environment. Reciprocity fosters a sense of competence in that the child learns that she can influence how others behave toward her. During the last half of the first year, the infant's behaviors signal a preference for certain types of responsiveness instead of generalized responsiveness. She begins to anticipate her mother's actions in response to her own. The youngster initiates interactive sequences or alters interaction the mother has initiated, in order to better suit her own needs and devices (Thrift, 1976). The development of a system of communication is determined to a large extent by the manner in which the mother has responded to the infant's signals in the earlier months.

It appears that the development of reciprocity in the early months and the maintenance of reciprocal relationships in later months are both critical to healthy development. It is clear that both mother and infant either facilitate or impede this progress. The following barriers to reciprocity were noted by Thrift (1976): a mother who ignores the wishes and moods of her baby as having validity, a mother who attempts to teach or train her baby to live up to some developmental standard and thereby lacks spontaneity in play, a mother who seldom gives her baby a chance to initiate interactions, and a baby who is unresponsive.

Infant Stimulation

Only within the last decade or two has attention been given to any aspect of infant care other than caring for physical needs. The influence of Piaget, the development of infant day-care centers, and the convincing research concerning the importance of the first 2 years of life have led to much more emphasis on optimal experiences during the period of infancy.

It is now clear that infants exhibit curiosity and active participation in learning experiences. They develop significant motor, social, and cognitive skills that have strong implications for healthy development throughout their lives. As a result the kinds of stimulation that parents provide during this period appear to be crucial.

Parents provide stimulation in two ways: by structuring the environment to facilitate sensorimotor activities and by interacting directly with their infants. There is an abundance of research relating to the sensory equipment of infants and their preferences in attending to certain types of stimuli. For the sake of brevity, we will attempt to summarize and interpret results in a practical way that relates to parenting.

It is now known that infants can see from the moment of birth but their focus and coordination are immature. Visual stimulation should consist of bright colors, light and dark contrasts (stripes, bull's-eye patterns, and geometric shapes), objects that move, and contoured surfaces. Although familiarity is important in the early months, within 5 or 6 months infants seem to prefer attending to moderately discrepant or complex stimuli. The human face is a favorite object for attention; it is contoured, it moves, and it talks. Close face-to-face gazing and vocalizing provide an opportunity for significant visual, auditory, and even tactile stimulation. Frequent changes in position—from back to stomach, from crib to pallet, and from infant seat to swing—provide infants with different vantage points of vision and the variation they seek. Instead of Mother Goose wallpaper that the infant has to look at for 3 to 6 years, we recommend the use of pictures, posters, mobiles, and collages that can be changed frequently as the infant seeks novelty and variation.

For auditory stimulation, vocalizing (imitating coos and babbles, talking, singing) is of utmost importance. The amount and the type of language used in the home during the period of infancy has been shown to be a critical factor in the child's intellectual development. Exposure to music (all types), daily sounds in and out of the house, and reading to the baby all help to provide auditory stimulation. It should be emphasized, however, that control of noise and distraction is necessary. Infants who are bombarded with noise (constant television, radio, shouting, and general commotion) learn to tune out the distractions and may have difficulty later in auditory discrimination and attention.

Of all the types of sensory stimulation, tactile stimulation seems to be the most important for healthy development. The sense of touch is the most highly developed sense at birth, having functioned prenatally longer than the other senses. Holding, cuddling, stroking, rocking, and movement have been shown to be essential. Other forms include massaging and bathing. Caregivers can provide these kinds of stimulation during feeding, changing, and other routine activities. Mothers who prop bottles or who put their babies to bed with a bottle not only are

depriving them of a sense of warmth and closeness but also are depriving them of critical visual, auditory, and tactile stimulation. Toys that have varied textures (soft, slick, flexible, and rigid) also provide diverse tactile experiences. Variations in flavors and textures of foods provide stimulation for taste and smell.

Eye-hand coordination can be enhanced by crib toys and cradle gyms; by encouraging participation in feeding; by placing toys slightly out of reach when infants are old enough to move their bodies in an effort to retrieve them; and by providing objects that can be banged, thrown, or dumped and filled.

If the parent creates an interesting, stimulating environment, much of the infant's learning will be self-initiated. However, the parent's role does not end there. Gordon (1976) noted that today's view is that the parent is the primary teacher of the child, beginning in infancy. Aside from providing the learning environment, parents model behavior and engage in direct instruction. The five *P*s Gordon described are the following: (1) provision of the learning environment; (2) predictability; (3) ping-pong; (4) persistence—permitting and encouraging the child to stay interested in an activity; and (5) avoiding being the professor—talking, followed by talking, followed by more talking. The four *R*s listed by Gordon were responsiveness, reasoning, rationality, and reading. He emphasized that warmth (tender, loving care) is necessary for the five *P*s and the four *R*s to work.

The sensitive caregiver encourages action cycles with the infant by observing her moods, knowing what is interesting to her and learning what her skills are, giving her a chance to practice the familiar, and then challenging her to extend her skills in new directions with moderately

---

BOX 2a WAYS TO PROVIDE INFANT STIMULATION

Visual—bright colors, light/dark contrasts, movement, contour, facial expressions
Auditory—talking/singing, reading, rattles, music, household sounds
Tactile—holding/cuddling, stroking, rocking, bathing, textured toys
Eye-hand coordination—crib toys, mobiles, holding toys about 7 inches away

novel materials and behaviors (Cooper, 1976).

It is important, then, to balance the infant's day with self-initiated, independent activities for which the parent has set the stage and interactive games or exchanges. An effort should be made to keep these interactions spontaneous, fun, and consistent with the needs of both parent and child, striving for high mutuality. Mastery-related behavior of infants during their second year is related to maternal style in play; infants whose mothers are supportive of their autonomy display greater task-oriented persistence and competence during play than do infants of more controlling mothers (Frodi, Bridges, & Grolnick, 1985).

In conclusion, infant stimulation needs to be varied, appropriately timed, linked to the infant's actions, and presented in a context of basic trust, remembering always that quality of stimulation is more important than quantity (Cooper, 1976). We believe that if this task is accomplished, along with establishing basic trust and developing reciprocity, the infant will have the best possible start in life.

Myths About Infants

A number of cultural myths believed to interfere with optimal development of a nurturant relationship between the caregiver and the infant were discussed by Aaronson (1978). To refute these myths, she summarized the following facts:

1. The infant is not helpless.
2. The infant is capable of acting, reacting, and learning from birth.
3. The infant will be enabled to respond in more consistent and predictable ways if the caregiver's responses are consistent and predictable.
4. Over and above the survival needs, an infant needs the emotional gratification of exercising some control over the environment.
5. The infant is capable of shaping the behavior of the caregiver even while the latter shapes his.
6. Crying and other vocal sounds, eye-to-eye contact, facial expression, and body contact are the earliest forms of communication, with the repertoire gradually increasing in variety and complexity.

7. The infant's language learning stems from language hearing and early vocalizations, bolstered by much encouragement and many expressions of approval.
8. The infant has the capacity to adjust and adapt gradually to family needs as his own abilities and self-control increase.
9. As a human being, the infant has psychological needs over and above the physical ones, can experience loneliness, and needs human interaction—to be held, touched, cuddled, fondled, stroked; to hear human sounds; and to feel another warm body next to his.

PARENTS AND TODDLERS

The Parents' Roles As Protectors

"It is necessary to realize that each period of parent/child interaction is capable of altering the status of a child, so that during the subsequent period of interaction the child stimulates the parent in a different fashion, or reacts differently to parent behavior" (Bell, 1974, p. 12). In turn, parents discover that previous behaviors are no longer appropriate, and they are faced with finding new ways of guiding and interacting with the child.

As the child becomes mobile, the role of the parent gradually takes on the new dimension of protector. The once dependent, "helpless" child is transformed into an active, tireless, and curious toddler. Suddenly she can see the top of the table, reach the magazines or ashtrays, flush toys down the toilet, drink from the pet's bowl, and perform a host of other activities that are fascinating to her growing curiosity. These behaviors are related to the fact that the toddler no longer needs hands to assist with locomotion and is free to feel and touch things that are attractive. First-time parents (and grandparents who have forgotten) are astonished at the ingenuity toddlers employ to satisfy their curiosity.

A sensitive period for the development of social and cognitive competence was postulated by White and Watts (1973). They suggested that the 10- to 18-month period is critical, basically because of the child's increasing locomotor facility. The child during this period will develop in such a way as to produce a vigorous, secure, loving, and healthy social being, or else she will take other paths. However, mother-infant interactions in the home from the precrawling through the walking stages were observed by Banks (1979). Coding from narrative records included infant behaviors that were believed to be stress-provoking and maternal reactions indicating stress. Comparisons of precrawling, crawling, and walking stages showed no consistent increase in these behaviors. Patterns of mother-child interaction were consistent throughout the age span. Based on her findings, Banks concluded that there is not a critical period for the development of harmonious, productive mother-child relationships, as White and Watts predicted, but instead that basic patterns of mother-child relationships develop early in infancy and represent continuity instead of discontinuity. It should be noted, however, that Banks's sample was very small, and caution must be used in the interpretation of her findings.

As protectors, parents must provide the safest possible environment for toddlers to exercise their growing autonomy and increased capacity for learning. The house and yard must now be accident-proofed. Glass, nails, and other sharp objects outdoors should be discarded; fences and gates need to be secure; and outdoor equipment should be safe and in good repair. In the bathroom all medicines should be locked and glass objects put out of the reach or put away entirely. In the kitchen breakable items should be removed from lower cabinets, and all detergents, bleaches, and cleaning supplies should be stored in an inaccessible place. Many parents find that specifying a low cabinet especially for toddlers with metal or plastic utensils that they can bang and stack relieves parents and children of much tension. If parents are consistently firm about restricting the child to one special cabinet, he soon learns to leave the others alone.

The rest of the house (living room, bedrooms, and so on) should be accessible to the child to expand her space and possibilities for learning experiences. However, for a time everyone will be happier if breakable, fragile, or precious items are put away. In addition, it frequently is necessary to put safety devices in electrical outlets and put gates across entrances and exits to stairways. The argument from some is, ''But he has to learn sometime.'' Yes, he has to, and he will. Obviously, parents cannot be expected to put away every lamp, get rid of all their plants, and eat off paper plates until their child gets older. Our point is that there will still be plenty of ''no's'' around that are necessary, and the child will have ample opportunity to learn that there

are some things that are not meant for him without inviting temptation with other things that can easily be put away.

No matter how carefully parents accident-proof the house and yard, the precocious toddler always finds that one button under the carpet that she can swallow or climbs up on the kitchen cabinet and gets the aspirin bottle on the top shelf. This means that, in addition to taking all the necessary precautions, parents must keep a constant watchful eye on the toddler's whereabouts and provide maximum supervision (as distinguished from interference) at all times.

For many parents the transition from caregiver (which does not cease altogether) to protector is a difficult one. First, they are not prepared for the safety measures they must take, and many learn through unfortunate experiences. Accidental poisoning is one of the leading causes of death during the first 2 years of life. Second, parents find that the care of a toddler is physically exhausting, so that they have little energy left to devote to social activities or to attending to the needs of their spouses. And finally, they find themselves being irritable at having to play the role of a police officer, and they long for the days when they could put the young baby in the crib or in the highchair and he would stay there. To compound the problem, if there are older siblings, conflict frequently develops over the toddler "getting into and messing up" their things. This appears to be a stage, then, when co-parenting is particularly essential and when both parents need to allow time to be together away from the child (or children).

Coping with Growing Autonomy

More difficult for parents perhaps than fulfilling the role of protector is coping effectively with the child's growing autonomy. The years from 1 to 3 comprise for the child a declaration of independence (Brazelton, 1974). Stage 2 in Erikson's theory of psychosocial development was described as autonomy versus shame and doubt. The child takes pride in her new accomplishments of walking and climbing, opening and closing, dropping, pushing and pulling, and holding on and letting go. She wants to do

everything for herself, from turning off the light switch to flushing the toilet.

If parents recognize the young child's need to do what he is capable of doing at his own pace and in his own time, then the toddler develops a sense that he is able to control his muscles, his impulses, himself, and, not insignificantly, his environment.

This is easy to say but much more difficult to do. The phrase "Me do it" is familiar to most parents who have experienced the endless patience required to let the child dress herself in the morning, pour her own milk, or put away her toys. Erikson believes, however, that if caregivers are impatient and do for the child what he is capable of doing himself, they reinforce a sense of shame and doubt. When caregiving is consistently overprotecting or critical or harsh and unthinking, the child develops an excessive sense of doubt about his abilities to control his world and himself and shame with respect to other people.

The growing sense of autonomy in toddlers often is coupled with open negativism toward the parents. With toddlers' "no's," they establish themselves as separate from their parents. They learn what parents expect of them and how parents will act in response to them. As Brazelton (1974) put it, the negativism quickly becomes a first line of defense in order to stall for time—time for inner decision and evaluation. It is logical to assume that the number of "no's" the child uses is related to the number of "no's" the parents use. Furthermore, parents should be careful to avoid setting themselves up for a "no" from the child by phrasing statements in the form of a choice rather than an expectation. For example, if a parent expects the toddler to go to bed, she should not say, "Do you want to go to bed now?" Instead she should say, "It's bedtime." That is not to say that, by being positive with the child, the parent can eliminate negativism. It does appear, however, that positive techniques of guidance do *reduce* negativism.

There is no question that once children become mobile parents must set firm limits and enforce them consistently in a loving manner. Either extreme in the setting of limits at this stage will interfere with healthy development. The most important limits have to do with the child's own safety and well-being—he does not go into the street, he does not eat the pet food, he does not climb on objects that are not sturdy or safe, he does not touch hot objects. The newfound freedom of the toddler carries with it potential danger, making the setting and maintenance of limits necessary. The purpose of external control (aside from safety) at this point is to make it possible for the child to know how and when to control himself. Erikson (1963) believed that a lasting sense of good will and pride derive from a sense of self-control without loss of self-esteem.

More severe forms of negativism are manifested by toddlers in their frequent temper tantrums, which occur normally because wishes or desires for independence are thwarted. They are perpetuated by the parents who either force a contest of wills or give in to toddlers' desires. Neither technique is appropriate. Contests of wills may be avoided by making expectations simple, clear, and consistent. When children test these expectations, parents can assist cooperation by reinforcing verbal requests by physical contact (taking the child by the hand and leading her in the desired direction), modeling the expected behavior for the child, and offering legitimate choices so that she can exercise her independence—what kind of juice she wants, which book she wants to read, or which skirt she wants to wear. If all this fails and a tantrum ensues anyway, then the worst possible behavior is for the parent to give in to the child's wishes, if it is clear that those wishes are inconsistent with the limits the parent already has set. Consistent failure to pay attention to tantrum behavior usually serves to reduce it in normal, healthy children. Parents fail to reinforce it not only by not giving in but also by withdrawing attention from the tantrum and refusing to allow the child to harm himself, others, or property. It may be necessary to remove the child from the immediate environment in order to remove reinforcing agents.

As part of a larger study, Schoggen (1963) reported an analysis of 18 specimen records available for 3 mother-toddler pairs, the shortest of the 18 covering over 11 hours. He found that from 49 percent to 61 percent of the interactions were initiated by the behavior of the child. Furthermore, the most frequent goal of the mothers in all but one of the 18 records was that of getting the toddler to cease his demands on her (to quit bothering her, not to question her further, to leave her alone, not to press a request, and/or not to attack).

Toddler behavior often invokes maternal anger, which in the long run may result in negative child outcomes. Crockenberg (1985) found that maternal anger resulted in more frequent self-concern on the part of the child and angry defiance toward others. Further, more frequent maternal anger was associated with more frequent nonempathic responses when toddlers were bystanders to the distress of others.

From the foregoing, it should be recognized that the growing sense of autonomy in the toddler, while it is a necessary stage of healthy development, may be extremely frustrating for both parent and child. Parents need to recognize what is considered normal behavior for the child and not allow themselves to be threatened by the child's negativism. At the same time they need to set firm limits, consistently maintain them, and apply mild punishment when necessary in a loving, reasonable manner. Appropriate techniques of guidance are those that allow the child choice of action and emphasize the positive rather than the negative. Opportunities for positive interaction and patience in providing independence training in self-help skills also are important. Parents should recognize an appropriate balance between too little and too much autonomy and facilitate self-control without causing the child to lose her self-esteem.

Providing Learning Experiences

Self-help skills. The first area in which a parent can provide learning experiences for the toddler is in self-help skills. Even before toddlers begin to walk, they indicate a readiness to feed themselves. They can handle finger foods, and they like to try to spoon foods into their mouths, often with the result that less ends up in the mouth than on the face, in the hair, and on the highchair tray. However, the wise parent picks up the infant's cues that he is ready, even though his coordination may not be equal to his desire for independence. Some parents find it easy to give the baby a spoon or a piece of finger food and alternate feeding him with his own attempts. This gets the job done and allows the child to be involved in the interaction and practice his rudimentary skills. Later, when he is old enough to eat at the table with the family and to eat family food, the parent can gradually reduce assistance but keep a watchful eye to help when it is needed. There is no need for a parent to go into orbit over a mess of peas on the floor or applesauce in the hair. The child himself can help clean the table, the floor, and himself when the meal is over.

Somewhat later the child repeats her "Me do it" in connection with dressing. A compromise may be reached between parent and child by allowing the child to do simple things such as pulling up her pants, putting on her socks, and zipping her jacket after the parent has gotten the zipper on the track. Simple clothing that the child can manipulate (large buttons, no straps to cross or pull over the shoulders, and shoes that do not need to be tied or buckled) make the task easier for the child and save the parent a lot of frustration. Pants that can be pulled up and down are especially important during the toilet-training phase. No one can expect a young child who waits until the very last minute to wait even longer until her belt is unbuckled or her straps are unsnapped.

Toilet training in the United States perhaps has caused parents more frustration than any other single experience of child rearing. The degree of attention it receives in the literature varies with changing attitudes of the culture, which have come full circle from rigid to laissez-faire to permissive and all the way around again. However, in our present society there is no urgency in accomplishing toilet training; we can wait for the child to learn at his own pace. We are emphasizing "developing strong individuals who make their own choices in childhood, as preparation for an adulthood frought with choices. To treat toilet training differently from all of the child's other tasks places undue emphasis on it" (Brazelton, 1974, pp. 143–144). Because this area has caused so much parental frustration, it often serves as a basis for conflict between parent and child that is not resolved easily. If we view the toilet-training process as

an important learning experience for the child rather than a contest of wills, then perhaps conflict can be minimized.

The child indicates to his caregiver that he is ready for assistance in learning to control his bodily functions first by demonstrating regularity in bowel movements and later in frequency of urination, followed by the child's understanding that dirty or wet pants are related to an act that he himself has performed. Finally, language skills to communicate the need to go to the bathroom signal the readiness for transition from diapers to training pants, at least during waking hours. If parents are alert to these cues, assist the child by providing simple clothing and accessibility to toileting facilities, and have infinite patience, the process will proceed smoothly (but perhaps not quickly by parental standards). A positive, reinforcing, patient attitude on the part of the parent will help the child to gain a sense of autonomy, while a critical, harsh, and impatient attitude will promote a sense of doubt and shame and a loss of self-esteem.

Brazelton (1974) believes that the developmental step of toileting should be treated like all others, such as feeding oneself or making choices about clothing, so that parents should wait for the children to learn at their own pace. If it is treated differently from the child's other tasks, then undue emphasis is placed on it. If it becomes a focus for attention, the child may use it for rebellion and negativism, and the child's determined strength will usually win. After all, urinating and defecating at the appropriate time and place is the *one* thing a parent cannot force the child to do. Constipation, wetting pants after being removed from the toilet, denying the need and then demonstrating it, or hiding in a corner to produce a bowel movement may be signals of too much parental control.

Further, Brazelton (1974) feels that the child's motivation and autonomy are of primary importance to any real success in toilet training. Viewing toilet training as a learning experience within the context of acceptance, the child will get pleasure and excitement from mastering each step herself.

Social and intellectual learning. Aside from utilizing independence in self-help skills as learning experiences for the toddler, there seem to be four other areas of learning that are critical during this period: the acquisition of social skills, language, the development of curiosity, and the formation of the roots of intelligence. In the first area toddlers should be exposed to interactions with other children their own age. Frequently parents choose to place toddlers in a play group or a child-care center at this time so that they can learn such rudimentary skills as waiting one's turn, sharing toys and equipment, delaying gratification, and getting along well in groups. Vandell (1979) compared mother-son and father-son interactions of toddlers who were completely home-reared with the parent-child interactions of male toddlers who were participants in a daily 3-hour play group. She found that the play-group toddlers proportionally became more active in their parent-child interactions and also became more responsive to the interaction initiations of their parents. Further, the parents of the play-group children became significantly less dominant. Her study would appear to suggest that, besides facilitating the development of certain social skills, a group experience may have positive implications for parent-child interactions, at least insofar as male children are concerned.

Children who do not have play-group, nursery school, or day-care experience at the toddler stage need the opportunity to interact with their peers. Parents frequently can encourage neighborhood gatherings or associations with children of other friends. It should be emphasized, however, that toddlers frequently treat their peers as objects rather than as persons, especially in the beginning stages of association. The "Me do it" phrase mentioned earlier in this section is indicative of the egocentric nature of the young child. The "No, mine" protest that is familiar to all of us further emphasizes the immaturity of the toddler's understanding of social interaction. And the toddler's grabbing, pulling, biting, hitting, and so forth are in part due to egocentricity and in part due to lack of language skills that older children use when cooperating in play.

The learning of appropriate social skills requires a patient adult who recognizes the child's immature level of development and therefore does not place too many demands on her to "be nice" or to "share the toys" or to wait too long. The wise parent or teacher duplicates toys and activities to minimize conflict over any special one; uses distraction and offers alternatives; and, most important, models appropriate social behavior for the child.

An extremely important event in the life of the toddler is the rapid development of language. From 18 months to 3 years, the average vocabulary of a child jumps from approximately 20–22 words to 900 words. Naturally, the child understands far more words than he uses. The parent's role in language development includes labeling familiar objects and events; expanding on the child's telegraphic speech; reinforcing language attempts; and, most important, modeling. Numerous studies have indicated that a child's language development is correlated closely with the quantity and quality of language used in the home. Further, children learn early language from adults, not from other children. The degree to which a parent talks *with* the child; asks questions as well as answers hundreds of *why*s, *what*s, and *how*s; reads to the child; and considers language as a valued tool for intellectual development relate to early language facility in the child.

The development of curiosity and the formation of the roots of intelligence during the toddler stage are related closely to language development. Even before the toddler has the language to ask questions, she demonstrates her curiosity by using the senses of touch, taste, smell, vision, and hearing. These senses, coupled with the ability for independent locomotion, provide important cues about her expanded world and assist her in the formation of rudimentary concepts related to color, shape, size, weight, distance, and causality. As she acquires greater language facility, she is able to expand her concepts by attaching labels to them.

In order to provide the child with optimal intellectual development and satisfaction of curiosity, parents need to provide a variety of objects and experiences in a safe environment. Ample space in and around the house for the child to explore and experiment; rotation of toys and books; and excursions to the supermarket, the shopping center, the library, the zoo, and numerous other interesting places provide invaluable learning experiences. Parents need to be careful to avoid structured, didactic "lessons" that have preconceived expectations for performance and to encourage spontaneous, natural learning experiences where the child is able to draw from the experience a wide variety of learning, based on his own interests and motivations. For example, a toddler with a coffee can full of objects from around the house will spend hours filling the can, dumping it, filling it again, and so on. From this experience he is learning something about size, shape, weight, color, and cause-and-effect relationships. With the parent's verbal interaction, he is also learning that a particular word stands for a particular object. Besides, he is having much more fun than a toddler whose mother is trying to teach him the alphabet or how to use the computer.

Put another way, the most important learning experiences for the toddler are those that are intellectual in nature and those of discovery. The role of the parent in discovery learning essentially is to structure the environment so that discovery can occur—that is, the parent provides the materials and the experiences and interacts with the child both verbally and physically when appropriate. As in earlier infancy, there should be a balance between self-initiated and self-sustained activity by the child as well as parent-child interaction. In this way the child controls much of her own learning within a framework provided by the parent.

PROGRAMS FOR PARENTS OF INFANTS AND TODDLERS

Since formal parent education is a relatively new phenomenon, there is no consensus about the form it should take or the timing that is most effective. It seems, however, that parent-education programs for parents of very young children would be particularly important for two reasons. First, it is believed by some that a person is most motivated when he or she *is* a parent as opposed to before he or she becomes a parent. Further, parents should be more realistically oriented to some of the problems of parenthood than potential parents are and thus will reap

more benefits from a program that is directed toward their current needs. Second, the emphasis that has been placed on the importance of environmental experiences in the early years and their implications for the child's further development would seem to suggest the need for early intervention and support for parents. In fact, it has been said of parent-education programs that "the earlier, the better; the longer, the better; the more consistent, the better" (Gordon, Guinagh, & Jester, 1977, p. 116).

The consensus of early parental support and education in a formal way was evident as early as 1968 when 36 Parent-Child Development Centers, funded by the federal government, were established for low-income parents and their children under 3 years of age. These programs combined home visits with center-based programs and comprehensive services to parents. A number of other home-based infant-education programs were established during the 1970s, with the primary target for education being the parent rather than the child. Home Start, a downward extension of Head Start, was one example.

Research conducted on the effectiveness of these programs generally indicated success. The evaluation of Home Start parents indicated that after the program they were more involved with their children through verbal interaction; they allowed their children to engage in more household tasks; they provided more books and read more to their children; and they engaged in more thought-provoking question-and-answer sessions with their children (Morrison, 1978).

Gordon and his associates concluded that a home-visitor/parent-education program, applied early and/or consistently over the first 3 years of the child's life, produces long-term effects on the intellectual performance of children from low-income homes (Gordon, Hanes, Lamme, Schlenker, & Barnett, 1975).

Since 1980 little federal support has existed for parent education. Most of the programs of the late 1960s and 1970s no longer exist. However, the notion of early support is currently attested to by the prevalence of classes for new parents offered by hospitals and birthing centers. These classes most often emphasize the practical aspects of parenting, such as feeding, bathing, soothing, and health-related issues. Although discussion of these daily routines may be useful to first-time parents, more in-depth exposure to the psychological aspects of parenting would be desirable. Existing programs normally are limited to the first few days after birth or, at best, to the first few weeks, and they seldom are led by psychologists or child-development specialists. Most parents who participate are middle class.

It has been noted that " . . . parents of infants view their situation as being qualitatively different from that of parents with older children" (McKim, 1987, p. 25). Therefore programs for these parents need to be especially designed, targeted, and advertised. McKim's sample of parents with children under 12 months of age were most interested in such topics as role conflict, anxiety, depression, alternate care, developmental expectations, infant stimulation, crying, nightwaking, and nutrition.

There are several impediments to the success of education and support programs for parents of infants. The first is the reluctance of parents to admit to nonmedical concerns or problems with their babies. This reluctance is compounded by the lack of specialized training of well-intentioned social-service and health professionals who imply that "nothing is wrong" to parents who do seek help. Second, even if individual or group sessions for parents are available, they often do not accommodate working parents or make provisions for including care of infants. Parent group sessions seem to be more effective when the infants participate in a concurrent but separate program (McKim, 1987). Finally, parents who most need help are not receiving it. The lack of time, energy, motivation, and resources frequently prevent single parents, families with handicapped babies, working parents, and parents of "difficult" babies from participating in programs or seeking support services.

Further, parents of different socioeconomic levels may have different needs. It has been found that socioeconomic status (SES) is an important variable in the relationship between parenting knowledge and quality of stimulation in the home. Low SES mothers' perceptions about the influences of infant caregiving practices on infants' well-being were directly related to high quality of the home environment, and

quality of stimulation in the home was, in turn, directly related to infants' performance on the Griffiths Mental Development Scale (Parks & Smeriglio, 1986). These results suggest that parenting education groups for low-income parents should emphasize the importance of caregiving practices for specific developmental outcomes.

As children develop from infants to toddlers, the support needs of parents change, and the emphasis of programs must reflect this change. For example, program content should include such topics as toilet training, behavior problems, ways of coping with growing autonomy, management techniques, and training in self-help skills. Even though for many parents toddlerhood presents special challenges, few programs currently focus on this particular developmental period.

In summary, the following issues need to be considered in developing programs for parents of infants and toddlers: (1) training professionals to be sensitive to and skillful in counseling about daily issues and adjustments of parents of young infants; (2) designing long-term programs that emphasize the psychological aspects of parenting children during the first 3 years of life; (3) considering the particular needs of parents of different socioeconomic levels in developing program content; (4) designing programs that have immediate relevance for age-related development; and (5) utilizing delivery systems, such as television, that reach a broader range of parents, particularly those who are the most in need.

PARENTS AND PRESCHOOL CHILDREN

The Parents' Roles As Nurturers

Nurturance is defined by *Webster's* (1979) as "affectionate care and attention"; and to nurture is "to educate or to further the development of. . . ." These definitions aptly describe the chief role that parents assume as their children move into the preschool period. It is now clear that nurturance can be provided by both mothers and fathers. While the child's environment still must remain safe and protective, preschool children do not need the constant watchful eye

of parents that was so necessary for a toddler. To discover the optimal amount of supervision without interference, assistance without indulgence, and warmth and love without suffocation is difficult for many parents. They find that their need to be needed is still very strong, and some find it difficult to meet that need in a way that is healthy for both themselves and their children.

It is at this point that many mothers immerse themselves in the parenting role. Young children are loud, intrusive, and demanding of their parents' attention, time, and energy. Adults find themselves constantly interrupted in conversations, visited by their children in the bathroom, and irritable at the consistent elevated noise level and disarray of the house. Further, the preschool child seems to alternate between behavioral extremes—that is, there are phases of cooperative, compliant behavior that alternate with phases of resistant, negative behavior, coupled with emotional extremes of shyness and aggressiveness. These inconsistent behaviors puzzle many parents and often cause them to question their methods of discipline, which may result in vacillation between freedom and control.

Broadly interpreted, nurturance may be seen as the psychological process of emotional gratification and meeting emotional needs through words, actions, and physical touch, for example,

warmth (Bigner, 1979). It is likely that a child's perception of the emotional climate that exists within the home is of far greater consequence in healthy development than the specific behaviors of the parents. Further, consistency in the kind of discipline utilized by parents seems to be more influential in facilitating healthy development than the specific type of discipline used. However, if parents have not agreed already on the goals and values they have for their children, it is critical that some agreement be reached at this point. Children can adjust to differences in the behavior of parents (Daddy spanks, Mommy does not; Daddy reads to me, Mommy bathes me). They find it much more difficult to adjust to conflicts in long-term goals and values. It is a plus if parents are similar in the way they handle particular situations, but it is not a necessity. Each parent is different and will interact with the child in ways that are unique to his or her own style, but consistency in making and enforcing rules and a common agreement as to whether discipline will be permissive, authoritative (democratic), or authoritarian will offer the young child the consistency that is vital to her growing sense of competence. Gordon (1976) has stated: "Children need to know that behavior allowed today will not lead to punishment tomorrow; behavior approved by mom is also approved by dad. They need the comfort that parents do not operate from whim, but from some sense of consistency, both within the individual parent and between the parents'' (p. 176).

A strong love relationship between the parents at this time facilitates their roles as nurturers of their children. Respect for each other and respect for their children as individuals creates a positive emotional climate in the home. Furthermore, love and respect of parents for each other is an effective tool for facilitation of the identification process in the late preschool period.

One major consideration in providing nurturance is knowing how to establish limits and achieve responsible behavior in young children without threatening their sense of autonomy and initiative.

Discipline versus Punishment

One of the major concerns that parents of young children face is how much or how little to ''discipline'' their children. Unfortunately, in our society the terms *discipline* and *punishment* are used synonymously. The phrase ''What that child needs is discipline'' usually means that the child needs punishment, most often physical in nature. In fact, however, the term *discipline* derives from the stem word *disciple,* meaning ''one who leads or guides others.'' When the word is used in its exact context, then, a discipline system should imply a broad positive system of guidance of the young child, with the particular methods of punishment utilized being only a minor aspect of that system. While punishment may be of limited value in consistently influencing rule-related behavior of children, nonpunitive techniques have a greater impact on children who have begun to master language (Toner, 1986).

Three prototypes of adult control that are referred to frequently in the literature as discipline systems were described by Baumrind (1966). Box 2b summarizes the characteristics of these systems.

Baumrind and others have emphasized that

BOX 2b   PROTOTYPES OF PARENTAL CONTROL

Type	Parental Characteristics
Permissive	Nonpunitive, accepting, and affirmative Allows self-regulation of activities by child Avoids exercising control Obedience to externally defined standards not valued Consults child on family decisions Exerts few demands on child for household responsibility and orderly behavior Uses reason and manipulation rather than power
Authoritarian	Uses set standard of conduct (absolute, theologically motivated) to control and shape child Values obedience Uses punitive, forceful measures Restricts autonomy Curbs child's self-will
Authoritative	Rational, issue-oriented Values both autonomous self-will and conformity Firm control coupled with some freedom Encourages verbal give and take Uses reason, power, reinforcement in shaping behavior

Source: Baumrind, D. (1966). Effects of authoritative parental control on child behavior. *Child Development, 37*(4), 887–907.

the effects of punitiveness on the part of the parent are difficult to differentiate from the effects of rejection, which are nearly always detrimental. However, mild punishment administered by a parent who is loved and respected may have beneficial side effects, but a clear distinction must be made between punishment that is just, deserved, and administered in a warm, loving environment and punishment that is harsh, unjust, and administered in a restrictive, rejecting environment. It appears that it probably is impossible as well as undesirable to see a child through the preschool period without utilizing some form of punishment. It would seem, however, that some thought should be given to the form that punishment takes, the frequency with which it is used as a means of control, and the context in which it is administered. Alternatives to the use of punishment include appeals of reason tailored to children's cognitive levels, exposure to rule-following models, provision of rewards for rule-following behavior, and provision of guidelines for resisting temptation (Toner, 1986).

Guidelines for the use of punishment. Before punishment is administered the child should know clearly what the expectations for his behavior are and what consequences will occur if these expectations are not met. When the parent deems it advisable to administer punishment for a given act, several conditions should be met. First, the punishment should follow the act immediately. If a mother, for example, says, "Wait until your father gets home; he will spank you," then two significant things are happening to the child—first, he is learning to fear his father and dread his coming home, and, second, he really is being punished all day because he has to live with the threat until his father comes home. Furthermore, punishment has been shown to be more effective at suppressing children's rule-breaking behavior when it is administered without delay (Toner, 1986).

Second, the punishment needs to be deserved and understood. Often there are extenuating circumstances that cause misbehavior. The parent needs to take the time to determine what the circumstances surrounding the misdeed were in order to decide if, in fact, mild punishment is warranted. Children are affected negatively by punishment that they perceive as unfair far longer than they are affected by punishment that they believe they deserve. Further, children need to know exactly for what they are being punished, particularly in the case of preschool children whose memories are short and whose conceptions of right and wrong are different from adults because of their premoral characteristics (Kohlberg, 1975). An explanation of the misbehavior and the punishment, accompanied by a suggestion of a more acceptable act, will in the long run be more effective and more humane.

Third, the punishment needs to be related to the act. If, for example, the preschool child colors on the wall, perhaps the most effective punishment would be to have her scrub it off and have the crayons put away for a while. Or if she continues to be aggressive in a hostile way to a friend, she should be deprived of the opportunity to play with that friend for a brief period of time. In this way the child associates the punishment with the act and is likely to have a clearer understanding of the forbidden behavior. On the other hand, if global punishments such as spanking, sending the child to her room, or not allowing television watching are used for *all* forms of misbehavior, the child has more difficulty learning appropriate forms of behavior.

Finally, the punishment should be administered within a context of love and respect. Parents should attempt to remain as objective as possible and refrain from venting their own anger at the child's expense. One of the major disadvantages of spanking or other forms of corporal punishment is that normally they serve as a vehicle for the release of parental feelings as opposed to helping the child learn appropriate behavior. But even more distastefully, the parent is modeling aggressive, angry behavior for the child and is, in effect, telling him that it is all right for a person to hit another person when he becomes angry. If the parent remains calm and focuses on the behavior of the child instead of the child himself, then the child's self-respect is not damaged in the process of facilitating acceptable behavior.

It has been pointed out that "parents' perceptions of desirable child behavior are important because these perceptions influence their objectives in childrearing as well as the discipline techniques they employ to attain these objectives" (Brown, 1979, p. 68). Based on his observations of parents' discipline in public places, Brown concluded that parents' self-esteem is partly dependent on the behavior of their children, and, if the child does not "fit in," especially in public, the parents' presentation of themselves as good and adequate parents is threatened. He found that restrictive discipline techniques were the most common sort used in public, probably as an effort to obtain quicker results. Brown concluded that until parents' self-esteem becomes less dependent on the behavior of their children, they will hesitate to use those autonomy-granting discipline techniques that are integral to parent-effectiveness programs because they take much longer to implement.

For a person to behave autonomously, she must accept responsibility for her own behavior, which in turn requires that she believe that the world is orderly and susceptible to rational mastery (Baumrind, 1966). The child needs to know that she has or can develop the necessary skills to manage her own affairs.

The frequency with which punishment is used as a form of control also is of primary importance. If parents use it judiciously and concentrate on achieving compliance with their standards by using reason, power, and external reinforcement, it may be possible to obtain obedience and self-correction without stimulating self-punitive reactions (Baumrind, 1966). It should be considered, however, that children often influence parental behavior as strongly as parents influence children's behavior. Some researchers have suggested that assertive, irritable children may "train" their parents to use upper-limit controls of physical punishment, hence producing a positive correlation between punishment and aggression.

When Baumrind was gathering her 1966 data, she found a few parents who departed from her three models described earlier in this section (Baumrind, 1971). These "harmonious" parents, she noted, almost never exercised control, but they seemed to have control in the sense that the child generally took pains to intuit what the parent wanted and to do it. The home atmosphere was characterized by harmony, equanimity, and rationality, and the parents focused on developing principles for resolving differences and for right living. The parents were egalitarian and valued honesty, harmony, justice, and rationality in human relations. These values took precedence over power, achievement, control, and order. Both parents encouraged independence and individuality and took pains to enrich the child's environment. Baumrind found that the female children of these parents were extraordinarily bright, achievement-oriented, friendly, and independent. By contrast the male children were cooperative but submissive, lacked achievement orientation, and exhibited dependency. These results must be viewed with caution since the sample was extremely small and was very homogeneous. It is interesting to note, however, that this particular parenting style suggested differential effects on male and female children.

Inductive discipline.   The use of inductive discipline, which focuses on encouraging the young child to take into account the potential effects of his behavior on other people and himself when making decisions about what he will and will not do, was discussed by Brophy (1977). The inductive parent emphasizes process goals, stressing the "how" rather than the "what" of behavior. This procedure is in contrast to the parent telling the child that certain behaviors are good and others are bad, which is more likely to produce unnecessary feelings of guilt and shame. Brophy stated: "A parent who wants to get children to voluntarily change some behavior pattern should concentrate on showing them why their present behavior pattern is inappropriate, showing them how to act instead, and projecting the expectation that they will change in the desired direction" (p. 312). Parents who use inductive, rational disciplinary techniques often have children who are less likely to violate prohibitions than other children are (Toner, 1986).

Natural and logical consequences.   Similarly, Rudolf Dreikurs is noted for his approach to discipline through the use of natural and logical consequences (Dreikurs & Grey, 1968). Natural consequences for those that occur naturally from behavior; for example, the child who refuses to eat goes hungry. Logical consequences are those that are designed by the parent to express the reality of the social order, not of the person; for example, a child who is disturbing the rest of the family at mealtime is given the choice to settle down or to leave the table.

Some advantages of using natural and logical consequences rather than relying on reward and punishment were pointed out by Dinkmeyer and McKay (1976). First, it holds children, not their parents, responsible for the children's behavior; second, it allows children to make their own decisions about what courses of action are appropriate; and, third, it permits children to learn from the (impersonal) natural or social order of events rather than forces them to comply with the wishes of other persons. When parents apply natural and logical consequences, the consequences must be sensible and logically related to the behavior, and children must see them as logical. In addition, choices are essential. Alternatives are proposed by the parent, and the parent accepts the child's decision. Then the child makes a choice without external pressure. The parent should be both firm and kind, with firmness referring to following through with the behavior and kindness referring to the tone of voice and manner in which choices are given to the child. Finally, the parent must separate the deeds from the doer; that is, the parent's action must be based on respect for the child as a person, separate from her deeds.

It appears difficult for many parents to use natural and logical consequences, first, because parents do not like to see their children suffer from some of the consequences, and, second, because they become discouraged if they do not see changes in the child's behavior right away. Encouragement is implicit in this approach, and, if the parent is patient and consistent, children will learn to accept responsibility for their own behavior in a way that conveys mutual respect and avoids power struggles.

Self-concept

It appears that one of the most significant results of nurturance during the preschool period is the building of a healthy self-concept in young children. Self-concept is believed to be intimately related to the individual's interactions with significant others in his social world. Based on significant research, we can make three assumptions concerning the development of the self-concept: first, the self-concept is learned; second, the self-concept is learned early within the socialization process of the family; and, third, the self-concept is a powerful determinant of behavior.

Early beginnings. The current literature suggests that the first step in self-awareness during the period of infancy is both affective and cognitive. The infant has experiences that help her to learn that she is separate and distinct from the objects in her environment. As people and more objects are introduced, she develops an awareness of others and a sense of basic trust that has been discussed in an earlier section. As an active, curious, striving individual, she develops a sense of competence about her ability to effect changes in the environment and in the behavior of others. These views of the infant support the notion that self-concept begins to be learned in the period of infancy within the context of the family. The preschool period, then, seems to be a critical time for the validation of these early impressions that the child has in regard to herself.

Sears (1970) suggested that warmth in both early and middle childhood was a significant correlate of good self-concept at the latter time. Coopersmith (1967) found that parental acceptance and respect for the child, coupled with a limit-setting democratic parenting style, resulted in children with high self-esteem, while lack of affection, regard, and the use of severe punishment resulted in lower self-esteem. Further, he concluded that parents of children with high self-esteem are concerned with and attentive to their children, that they structure the world of their children along the lines they believe to be appropriate, and that they permit relatively great freedom within the structure they have established. Other studies have supported Coopersmith's findings.

Aspects of self-concept. Traditionally the two aspects of the child's self-concept that have been emphasized are a sense of belonging and a feeling of worth. While these are no doubt critical to the child's overall feeling of self-esteem, the more recent examination of the child's perceived behavioral competencies is consistent with the view of the child as an active participant in her overall development. It appears that the young child's ability to interact successfully with her environment is a vital aspect of her development of a positive sense of self-worth.

A relationship has been established between parenting practices and the young child's competence. Baumrind (1967) compared three groups of nursery school children and their families. A group that was self-reliant, assertive, self-controlled, buoyant, and affiliative (Pattern I) was compared with a withdrawn, discontented, and distrustful group (Pattern II) and also with a group considered lacking in self-control, lacking in self-reliance, and tending to retreat from novel situations (Pattern III).

Her results indicated that parents of the first group were consistent, loving, conscientious, and secure in the handling of their children. These parents balanced high nurturance with high control and high demands with clear communication about what was required of the child. Parents of Pattern II children were less nurturant and involved with their children; they exerted firm control and used power freely but offered little support or affection. Parents of Pattern III children were significantly less controlling and more ineffective in managing their households.

They were relatively warm toward their children but noncontrolling.

Baumrind concluded that the parents of the most competent and mature boys and girls notably were firm, loving, demanding, and understanding. Parents of disaffiliative children were firm, punitive, and unaffectionate. Mothers of dependent, immature children lacked control and were moderately loving; fathers of these children were ambivalent and lax. Further examination of the same data revealed that parental acceptance and warmth were not enough to promote prosocial and competent behavior in children. Rather, there appeared to be an interaction between parental warmth and control. Box 2c summarizes parental behaviors that appear to promote positive self-concepts.

It has been stated that a widely prevalent belief is that the development of the concept of the mother and the concept of self (child) are based on early social relations between mother and child (Davids, 1973). This research employed several projective and objective techniques to assess the child's self-concept and the concept the child had of the mother. For both black and white preschool children, there was significant positive association between young children's concepts of themselves and of their mothers. Consistent with other researchers, Davids concluded that the most significant influences on one's self-esteem are found within the family and the home setting.

BOX 2c PARENTING BEHAVIORS THAT PROMOTE POSITIVE SELF-CONCEPTS

Demonstrates warmth, acceptance, and respect for child

Demonstrates concern and attentiveness to child

Structures child's environment according to beliefs about appropriateness for child

Permits child freedom within established structure

Provides environment for successful interaction

Demonstrates consistently love, conscientiousness, and security in handling child

Balances high nurturance with high control and high demands

Shows clarity of expectations of the child

Exhibits firmness in making demands and demonstrates understanding

Possesses own positive self-concept

Another study (Flynn, 1979) cited evidence for a modest relationship between parental self-concept and the child's self-concept. Flynn noted that previous available data did not reveal the interrelationship of the variables with the parent's attitude toward the use of authority. His study found that fathers of girls and mothers of girls advocated significantly more control than fathers of boys and mothers of boys. Fathers of girls rated their children significantly higher than fathers of boys. All intercorrelations of variables were higher for boys than for girls, especially between the child's self-concept and marital satisfaction, the parent's use of authority, the father's concept of the child, and the father's self-concept. The strongest relationship was between the boy's self-concept and his mother's use of authority, especially her use of punishment, which suggests that boys may benefit from less freedom and more control. It appeared that both mothers and fathers who were satisfied with their marriages tended to advocate the use of more control with their sons. Flynn concluded that children may benefit from a moderate amount of control but suffer from too much or too little. It also is evident that parenting styles have differential effects on boys' and girls' attitudes about themselves.

Self-concept as a determinant of behavior. There is abundant evidence that a child's self-concept is a powerful determinant of his behavior. For example, there seems to be a positive relationship between high self-concept and achievement in school, even in kindergarten (McCandless, 1967; Ozehasky, 1967). Children with high self-esteem are more likely to be expressive, happy, and relatively free of anxiety. Children and adults with poor self-concepts, when compared to those with positive self-concepts, are more anxious and less well adjusted, less popular, less effective in groups, less honest about themselves, less curious, and more defensive (McCandless, 1967).

The resultant behavior of successful image-building shows up in the child's ever increasing awareness of his own autonomy. He shows more self-direction in his behavior. He has a clearer notion of his goals and how to achieve them. If he does not succeed in reaching his goals, he more easily modifies them or the method by which he intended to reach them. (Hawkes, 1968, p. 336)

Correlates of self-concept. It seems, then, that the conditions that appear necessary for the development of a positive self-concept (a sense of belonging, a feeling of worth, and a sense of competence) are the following: parental acceptance toward the child; a democratic parenting style that sets clearly defined limits but allows unrestricted freedom within these limits; opportunities for the child to construct his own knowledge of himself and others; and, finally, a reciprocal parent-child relationship that is permeated with mutual respect. The child who has come to value himself under these conditions has a firm base from which to venture forth and try his hand at new learnings. During the preschool period the child begins to judge his self-worth partly on the basis of his competence with adults. This sense of competence has considerable implications for his later adjustment and achievement.

Developing a Sense of Initiative

Erikson (1963) described the third stage in psychosocial development as initiative versus guilt. This stage has its beginning in the latter part of the third year after the child has attained a proficiency in walking and feeding himself. Basic motor skills and bowel control have become relatively automatic. The child's attention, no longer needed to develop and control these activities, is now free to add a new dimension to his newly achieved muscular autonomy. He now directs his attention away from his own bodily functions and toward increasing participation in his social environment, largely the basic family but also, to some extent, other adults and peers.

The young child at this stage thus can initiate motor activities of various sorts on her own and no longer merely responds to or imitates the actions of others. The same holds true for her language and fantasy activities. Whether the child will leave this stage with a sense of initiative far outbalancing a sense of guilt depends to a considerable extent on how her parents respond to her self-initiated activities. Children who are given freedom, opportunity, and encouragement to initiate motor play, to ask questions, and to engage in fantasy play activities will have their sense of initiative reinforced.

On the other hand, conscience is beginning to develop, and the child begins to understand the difference between right and wrong and pleasing and displeasing his parents. If he thinks that his motor activity is bad or dangerous, that his questions are a nuisance, and that his play is silly or a waste of time, then he may develop a sense of guilt over self-initiated activities in general that will persist through later life stages.

Further, the child of this age becomes increasingly aware of a sex difference between mother and father figures and learns that he or she is "like" the parent of the same sex. This early awareness forms the basis of the child's first identification. The perception of similarity causes the child to consign to himself similar privileges and strivings to the like-sex parent. According to Freud, the basis is established for the Oedipus complex, which is exemplified by the child's love for the opposite-sex parent and his rivalry with the same-sex parent. Fantasies of displacing the same-sex parent may arouse a deep sense of guilt.

Erikson (1963) described the solution to the Oedipus complex as one of mutual regulation between the child and the family: "Where the child, now so ready to over-manipulate himself, can gradually develop a sense of moral responsibility, where he can gain some insight into the institutions, functions, and roles which will permit his responsible participation, he will find pleasurable accomplishment in wielding tools and weapons, in manipulating meaningful toys . . . and in caring for younger children" (p. 256).

Children who are encouraged, or at least allowed, to explore their environment tend to become eager and carefree about initiating such exploration, whereas children who are overprotected from or punished for such exploration of their environment tend to become inhibited (Brophy, 1977). If parents consistently are harsh, young children may develop strong guilt feelings and inhibitions, becoming very dependent and unable to take new initiatives without experiencing anxiety.

Implications of initiative. The implications of these contentions for parents seem obvious. First, preschool children will need the space, the opportunity, and the tools for initiating motor activity. Outdoor space and equipment for climbing, swinging, riding, jumping, and simply running and shouting will allow children to use new capacities and develop skills. As skills are developed and practiced, the child gains a sense of self-confidence and competence and extends these skills into more elaborate forms of play that frequently include fantasy (for example, the tricycle becomes the fire engine and the climbing structure becomes the firehouse). Initiative can be further reinforced by allowing children space and opportunity indoors to engage in both fantasy and real-life activities. Parents who are overly fastidious about keeping the house in order frequently restrict children to such a degree that they are unable to initiate activities for fear of displeasing parents. Impatient parents often do not allow the child to assume the initiative in routine household chores because their expectations far exceed the child's skills.

Second, intellectual initiative can be fostered by parents' both answering and asking questions. The *whos*, *whats*, *whys*, and *hows* of the child may seem endless, but the patient responses of parents encourage further exploration and curiosity—and result in the child's valuing the pursuit of knowledge. Questions from parents that encourage the child to think on higher cognitive levels, such as problem-solving and inference questions, lay the foundation for future intellectual curiosity.

Finally, providing play materials that encourage fantasy and imagination allows the child to try out a range of life roles and to come to grips with reality. The testing of roles indicates that the child is attempting to identify with her own appropriate role and should not be viewed by the parent as silly or inappropriate behavior. Fantasy also is a vehicle for the expression of feelings and conflicts that the young child needs to work out.

Preschool sexuality. Overtones of sexuality may be one of the most difficult aspects of initiative with which parents deal. Many mothers

do not know how to respond to their child's curiosity about her own or the parent's body or to their children's statements of intention to marry them when they grow up. Most children have only the faintest notion of what *marry* means, and the statement does not imply that children lust after their parents in the adult sense of the word (Brophy, 1977). If these behaviors are seen as normal and naïve and are not over-reacted to by parents, then a strong sense of guilt will not be produced. Acceptance of the child's level of understanding, role modeling, explanations of reality, and a strong love relationship between parents usually serve to resolve the Oedipus complex and facilitate identification.

When commenting on the stage of initiative versus guilt, Brophy (1977) supported the idea that children who resolve the conflict successfully will learn to control their behavior and respect social conventions and moral responsibilities. At the same time they will not lose their psychological freedom to assume initiatives and the responsibilities that come with them. Conversely, children who fail to resolve this conflict suc-

cessfully will tend to emerge with overly strong and inflexible consciences that inhibit them from taking initiative in ambiguous situations where they are not sure that they are safe from disapproval.

Providing Learning Experiences

The influx of compensatory education for preschool children and the emphasis on the first 6 years of life as being critical for learning experiences that determine later development have led many parents to be concerned about providing materials and opportunities for learning during the early years. In a delightful and enlightening article, Edward Zigler (1980–1981) stated that overemphasis on training the intellect has led to a distorted view of parental tasks and an erroneous view of children. He believes that we have lost sight of the child as a whole person and that we must help parents relearn that a full and rich relationship with their child will lead to optimal development in all spheres—social, emotional, and intellectual.

Viewed in that way, much of what we have already discussed in this section—methods of discipline, the building of a healthy self-concept, and developing initiative—can hardly be separated from providing optimal learning experiences. It is axiomatic that a child who is nurtured, who is given freedom to explore and initiate, and who feels good about herself as a person and a family member will be inspired to learn in keeping with her potential. It was further pointed out that the young child learns from every event in which she participates—her peers, her play, and her everyday interaction with her environment, especially if her parents are responsive to her interests and inquiries (Zigler, 1980–1981). Further support for this notion was found in a study of the relationship between paternal child-rearing practices, sex-role preference, and intellectual functioning in 4-year-old boys (Radin, 1972). She found that boys' IQ was positively correlated with paternal nurturance and negatively correlated with paternal restrictiveness. So it seems that warmth, nurturance, and responsiveness are necessary prerequisites for effective learning experiences during the preschool years.

Rutter (1985) concluded that environmental effects on IQ are relatively modest within the normal range of environments, but the effects of markedly disadvantageous circumstances are substantial. However, he, too, contended that cognitive development is influenced by direct effects on cognition and by indirect effects through alterations in self-concept, aspirations, attitudes toward learning, and styles of interaction with other people.

Creating a learning environment. Besides providing a positive social and emotional climate that facilitates the natural learning process, parents might want to consider a few other factors. Measures of specific environmental processes in the home have been found to be more strongly associated with cognitive development than measures of social status were (Bradley, Caldwell, & Elardo, 1977). Of the socioeconomic variables examined, however, the educational level of parents demonstrated the strongest relationship to children's IQ. Fathers' education

evidenced the strongest relationship to young boys' IQ, whereas mothers' education showed the highest correlation with young girls' IQ. An examination of environmental factors indicated that providing appropriate play materials was more highly related to IQ than any other factor. Avoidance of restriction and punishment and organization of the environment seemed to show a much less pronounced association with mental ability for males than for females. Avoidance of restriction and punishment appeared less strongly associated with IQ for blacks than for whites, whereas variety in daily stimulation appeared less strongly associated with IQ for whites than for blacks.

There are several interesting points to be considered from the results of this study. First, it appears that mental test performance for females is related to a wider variety of environmental inputs than for males. These results may indicate that females are more influenced by environmental events than males are during the first few years of life. An alternative explanation (Bradley et al., 1977) is that mothers tend to be more sensitive and effective when interacting with young girls than with young boys. Further, environmental quality seems to be more strongly associated with IQ among whites than among blacks; more specifically, the correlations between the environmental variables and IQ were somewhat lower for blacks than for whites. For these reasons, and those discussed previously in relation to self-concept, it is extremely difficult to recommend specific guidelines that are generalizable to both sexes and all ethnic and socioeconomic classes.

Assuming that the provision of appropriate play materials and variety in daily stimulation could be two environmental variables that are important in facilitating cognitive development, what kind of advice can be given to parents in order for them to provide these experiences?

Appropriate play materials. The provision of appropriate play materials is an important consideration, partly because parents want to provide toys that stimulate learning and partly because, over a period of time, toys represent a real investment. For this reason toys during the

---

BOX 2d   GUIDELINES FOR TOY SELECTION

Appropriate to child's developmental level—challenging but not frustrating
Versatile—variety of uses (Lego, blocks, Tinker Toys)
Durable—outlast child's desire to play with them
Encourage active participation rather than passive observation
Aesthetically pleasing
Safe

Source: Hulls, J. (1977). Toys: Get the most for your money. In *Conference proceedings: Between grown-ups and kids.* Austin, TX: Southwest Educational Development Laboratory.

---

preschool period should be selected with care. Basic guidelines for toy selection, as recommended by Hulls (1977), are summarized in Box 2d.

If parents follow these basic guidelines and do not succumb to the persuasive advertising of the media, toys can provide valuable learning experiences for young children. It should be remembered, however, that the best toys in life are free. Common household items such as pots and pans, measuring spoons and cups, coffee cans filled with odds and ends, nesting cans or boxes, blocks made from milk cartons or cigar boxes, and plastic bottles with screw-on caps provide hours of creative play in which children can extend and elaborate on their skills. It cannot be overemphasized that optimal learning can occur in the home without a big investment in "educational" toys. Almost any toy can "teach" if parents take the time to use it to arouse the child's interest and curiosity and if it provides for social interaction between parent and child (Zigler, 1981).

Play and learning. Although toys are the tools for the child's play and play is a major vehicle for learning during the preschool years, it should be remembered that young children like to "mess and manipulate." They learn about their physical world by touching, examining, testing, exploring, evaluating, and imagining. Raw materials such as sand, dirt, water, paints, clay, and even mud allow children sensory experiences that are vital for the formation of basic concepts about their world that facilitate later academic learning. Experience with pets and plants helps them to understand growing and living things. Cooking experiences lay the foundation for scientific concepts. And short trips away from home (to museums, parks, shopping centers, farms, libraries, airports, and concerts) help them to understand how their culture operates.

Information about children beginning at 3 months of age, again at 3 years of age, and again at 6 years of age was gathered by Gordon (1976). He found the most important provision of learning experience to be out-of-home experience—the planning and use by the family of the environment outside the home for learning, such as the short trips mentioned above. Gordon further found that the presence of reading material in the home at age 6 related positively to Stanford-Binet scores, especially for male children. If the parent makes an issue out of reading itself, it seems to have a positive effect on female children.

Perhaps the most important ingredient for learning experiences is people. A loving, caring adult who is available to the child to answer her questions, to engage her in imagination and fantasy, to introduce her to new words and ideas, and to pick up on her cues of curiosity cannot be replaced by dozens of toys or daily field trips. The adult who structures the environment so that learning will occur; who allows the child freedom and encouragement for exploration; and who interacts with her in a warm, accepting manner will provide the most important learning experiences of all.

PROGRAMS FOR PARENTS OF PRESCHOOL CHILDREN

Parent involvement and/or parent education was a requirement of the federally funded preschool programs in the late 1960s and 1970s. More than any other Great Society program of the Johnson administration, Head Start translated the parent-participation principle into specific guidelines. Exploring Parenting is a formalized parent-education program that is still used with parents of preschool children in Head Start programs, in conjunction with other forms of parent participation and involvement (U.S. Department of Health, Education and Welfare, 1978). Since Head Start was the only early intervention program to survive the federal budget cuts of the 1980s, few formalized parent-education programs for parents of young children currently exist. However, a few nursery schools and day-care centers provide some form of parent support or education in conjunction with their children's program. These efforts tend to be more common among nonprofit programs, those serving largely low-income parents, and university-based laboratory programs. Further, the efforts tend to be directed toward one-shot speakers or workshops led by community professionals rather than toward a series of formalized instruction for parents.

Unfortunately, little empirical research has been conducted on the effectiveness of parent education, with a few exceptions. For example, Head Start parents cited numerous benefits, both personal and parental, as a result of their involvement (Zigler & Valentine, 1979). Other program evaluations in the 1970s indicated at least short-term effectiveness regarding the child's performance on standardized measures; parent attitudes; and, less often, parent behaviors. However, few definitive answers have been provided regarding the best method of delivery, the role of the parent educator, how to reach the parents who are most in need, and whether efforts have had lasting effects on parents and their children.

Conventional wisdom implies that parents of all races, all socioeconomic levels, all ages, and both genders can profit from support and education, especially during their children's early years, but programs obviously need to be designed individually. Powell (1986) stated that "There is no convincing evidence that one particular program is significantly more effective than another" (p. 49). Further, he concluded that perhaps the primary functions of a parent-education curriculum are to stimulate parents to more closely examine their relationship with their children and to encourage interaction among parents. Therefore, few generalizations can be made regarding the content of such efforts. However, the trend in the 1980s was toward broad-based family-support programs that emphasized support rather than intervention.

The most common vehicles of delivery for education for parents of preschool children in the 1980s have been preschool/day-care settings and churches. Clearly other agencies (hospitals and social-service agencies) also are involved, but parents are more likely to participate in such programs if they have established some social relationship with other participating parents.

The following guidelines may be useful in developing support/education programs for parents of young children:

1. Assess the demographic characteristics of the parent population (age, level of eduation, number of children, socioeconomic status, marital status, and so on). Programs for middle-class parents may not be effective with low-income parents; programs for two-parent families may be ill-suited for single parents.

2. Utilize parent input, if possible, when determining content so that it has relevance for the population it is designed to serve. Participation is likely to be greater if parents are involved in the decision making.

3. Plan programs around the convenience of parents (in a day-care setting, a potluck supper at closing time followed by a program is likely to draw greater participation than a later event).

4. Provide child care and transportation, if necessary, and keep the program brief.

5. Plan programs where sessions can be either

discrete or serial. Working parents are reluctant to make long-term commitments.

6. Avoid "patronizing" parents. Accept and emphasize parents' roles as primary educators of their own children.

7. Utilize a variety of methods of delivery—speakers, discussion leaders, peer-led support groups, reading material, video and television, and so forth.

8. Be flexible in both program content and format of presentation.

9. Offer information within a supportive context rather than in a threatening one. Strive to view parents as partners.

Because the early childhood years are so important for laying the foundation for later development and because parenting today is so complex, careful, well-planned programs that support and enhance parents' roles are essential.

DEVELOPMENTAL NEEDS OF PARENTS

Erikson (1963) described the seventh stage in his theory of psychosocial development as generativity versus self-absorption. *Generativity* is defined as the interest in establishing and guiding the next generation, or a sense of caring for others or becoming involved with creative production. Erikson believes that people are "triggered" by physical, psychological, and social stimuli to develop this sense of generativity. The parenting role is one of the major vehicles for facilitating a sense of generativity, and it allows parents to manifest what Erikson believes is an inborn desire to teach.

With the birth of their first child, most parents begin to develop their sense of generativity as their infant begins to develop a sense of basic trust. Mature first-time parents are probably better able to mesh their needs with those of the infant than younger, less mature parents are. Other factors, such as marital status, economic condition, career involvement, and availability of support systems, also affect the developmental needs of parents of infants and determine how effectively these needs are fulfilled.

The transition to the birth of their first child, in any event, represents a significant change in the life-style of most mothers and fathers and for some may even constitute a major crisis. Roles and relationships that precede parenthood often are altered. Time and resources have to be reallocated. The demands of the infant result in less leisure time for the parents and the juggling of multiple responsibilities. Several research studies have suggested that a decline in marital satisfaction may begin shortly after the birth of the first child and continue to decline throughout the child-rearing years, with the decline being greater for women than for men (Waldron & Routh, 1981; Worthington & Buston, 1986). If this is so then it appears that the obligations and responsibilities of parenting for many families take precedence over those related to the marriage. This, in turn, would suggest that having children is a detriment to the marriage relationship rather than a support for it (Bigner, 1979). In spite of these potential stresses, there usually is a mutual interdependence of the infant's needs and the parents' needs to be needed, so that each serves as a source of stimulation for development and socialization of the other.

Adjustment to later-born infants in some ways is easier for parents. They feel more secure in their parenting skills and less anxious about the baby's development and often are more relaxed in their interactions. On the other hand, multiple children may present special problems to parents, such as sibling rivalry, searching for quality child care, and lack of time and energy to meet the needs of each child. With the birth of each subsequent child, parents are faced with a new adjustment. The extent of these adjustments depends on a number of factors, such as the spacing between children, whether the mother is employed, the support systems available to the family, and the father's participation in child care and work at home. Further, parents must meet the developmental needs of their children at different stages of development while taking into account their own needs.

When the child becomes a toddler, it is more difficult for parents to include him in adult activities and sometimes more difficult to obtain reliable babysitters. However, recognizing the importance of early experiences, parents often neglect their own personal needs for privacy, for socializing with other adults, and for developing interests outside the family. Their developing sense of generativity, then, is confined solely to the process of parenting, as opposed to including other activities that contribute to becoming a fully functioning human being. Traditionally this has been truer for mothers than for fathers. However, in families where both parents are employed and share somewhat equally in child-rearing responsibilities, there hardly seems to be enough time for either parent to meet the children's needs, the spouse's needs, and one's own personal needs. The end result for parents often is fatigue, a sense of isolation from their peer group, and growing dissatisfaction with the marriage relationship.

Throughout the preschool years, the issues of child care, balancing work and family demands, and maintenance of self continue to loom large for parents. The research on marital satisfaction serves as an indication that adults need to be aware of the stresses that begin during the child-bearing years (Bigner, 1979). This awareness can assist parents in making an effort to meet their own personal needs and in maintaining the marriage relationship. It seems that our culture has made many parents feel entirely responsible for their children's behavior and development, and if they do not create a child-centered family and sacrifice their own needs, they feel as if they are bad or inadequate parents.

It has been emphasized throughout this chapter that parent-child relationships are reciprocal. No doubt parents face many responsibilities and challenges in providing the best possible environment for their children; in turn, children can and should assume their share of responsibility to the family. If each family member is viewed as having rights and status, then adults need not always sacrifice their own needs for those of their young children. When they do, they find that their overall relationship with their children gets worse instead of better. Children quickly learn to depend totally on their parents for everything, and parents, in turn, come to experience hostility toward their children for being unable to fend for themselves.

The theories of Rossi (1968), Galinsky (1980), and Rhodes (1977) desribed in Van Hoose and Worth's book *Adulthood in the Life Cycle* (1982) conceptualize the changing role demands of par-

ents. During the child-rearing stages, the individual developmental needs of both parents and children are intermeshed. According to Rossi there is an anticipatory stage for prospective parents during pregnancy corresponding to the engagement period in marriage, which prepares the couple for the responsibilities of parenting. Galinsky referred to this time as the parental image-making stage, in which the idealistic concepts of parenthood are based on how parents would have liked to have been treated by their own parents.

After the birth, parents experience a honeymoon stage (Rossi, 1968) during which they see the child as a real person, and after initial adjustment to the infant a plateau stage begins, during which parents exercise their full responsibilities. Galinsky called this the nurturing stage, with the parents' major task being to form an attachment with the infant. In yet another view, Rhodes (1977) identified the childbearing years as being marked by the developmental crisis of replenishment versus turning inward, which concerns the couple's ability to give to their children and to each other. Each parent at this time needs support from his or her spouse.

When children are preschoolers, parents may question their own ability as parents; they see inconsistencies between ideals and reality—the concept of a "perfect" parent comes into question. Galinsky (1980) labeled this as the authority stage.

The evidence, then, suggests that parents as well as children are in a critical stage in the life cycle. Predictable crises of adult life were creatively described by Sheehy in *Passages* (1976). These crises seem to be intensified when parents neglect their own developmental needs. To minimize some of the stresses of parenting during the early years, parents need to balance their needs with those of their children—for example, by taking occasional trips alone as well as with the children, interacting socially with adult friends as well as families that include children, developing interests or hobbies with peers outside the family, and making some household rules that ensure a degree of privacy. These arrangements not only strengthen personal and marital development but also foster a sense of autonomy and initiative in the children.

SUMMARY

Parenting infants, toddlers, and preschool children is a challenging task. During the first 6 years of life, a child evolves from a "helpless" infant who cannot turn over in his crib to a curious toddler emptying every available drawer and cabinet, and, finally, to an intrusive preschooler who asks questions constantly and has endless energy. To be sure, parents are the most influential people in the lives of these children, and early parental influences will be felt for many years to come.

On the other hand, parents assume the parental function rather abruptly, and their role changes from caregiver to protector to nurturer in a remarkably short time. The reciprocal interaction between parents and children that has been established will remain fairly consistent throughout the parenting years as parents and children continually respond to one another's needs and behaviors. And parents will experience developmental changes equal in importance to those of their children.

REFERENCES

AARONSON, M. (1978). Infant nurturance and early learning: Myths and realities. *Child Welfare, 57*(3), 165–173.

BANKS, E. (1979). Mother-child interaction and competence in the first two years of life: Is there a critical period? *Child Study Journal, 9*(2), 93–107.

BAUMRIND, D. (1966). Effects of authoritative parental control on child behavior. *Child Development, 37*(4), 887–907.

BAUMRIND, D. (1967). Child care practices anteceding three patterns of preschool behavior. *Genetic Psychology Monographs, 75,* 43–88.

BAUMRIND, D. (1971). Harmonious parents and their preschool children. *Developmental Psychology, 4*(1), 99–102.

BELL, R. (1974). Contributions of human infants to caregiving and social interaction. In M. Lewis & L. Rosenblum (Eds.), *The effect of the infant on its caregiver* (pp. 1–19). New York: Wiley.

BELL, S. M., & AINSWORTH, M. D. (1972). Infant crying and maternal responsiveness. *Child Development, 43,* 1171–1190.

BIGNER, J. L. (1979). *Parent-child relationships.* New York: Macmillan.

BRADLEY, R., CALDWELL, B., & ELARDO, R. (1977). Home environment, social status, and mental test performance. *Journal of Educational Psychology, 69*(6), 697–701.

BRAZELTON, T. B. (1969). *Infants and mothers: Differences in development.* New York: Dell.

BRAZELTON, T. B. (1974). *Toddlers and parents: A declaration of independence.* New York: Dell.

BRAZELTON, T. B., KOSLOWSKI, B., & MAIN, M. (1974). The origins of reciprocity: The early mother-infant interaction. In M. Lewis & L. Rosenblum (Eds.), *The effect of the infant on its caregiver* (pp. 49–76). New York: Wiley.

BROPHY, J. (1977). *Child development and socialization.* Chicago: Science Research Associates.

BROWN, B. (1979). Parents' discipline of their children in public places. *The Family Coordinator, 28*(1), 67–71.

CALDWELL, B., WRIGHT, C. M., HONIG, A., & TANNEBAUM, J. (1970). Infant day care and attachment. *American Journal of Orthopsychiatry, 40,* 397–412.

CLARKE-STEWART, A. (1978). And daddy makes three: Father's impact on mother and young child. *Child Development, 49*(2), 466–478.

COOPER, C. (1976). Competent infants and their caregivers. In M. Cohen (Ed.), *Understanding and nurturing infant development* (pp. 20–32). Washington, DC: Association for Childhood Educational International.

COOPERSMITH, S. (1967). *The antecedents of self-esteem.* San Francisco: W. H. Freeman.

CROCKENBERG, S. (1985). Toddlers' reactions to maternal anger. *Merrill-Palmer Quarterly, 31*(4), 361–373.

DAVIDS, A. (1973). Self-concept and mother-concept in black and white preschool children. *Child Psychiatry and Human Development, 4*(1), 30–43.

DINKMEYER, D., & MCKAY, G. (1976). *Parents' handbook* (A part of the complete STEP Program). Circle Pines, MN: American Guidance Service.

DREIKURS, R., & GREY, I. (1968). *A new approach to discipline: Logical consequences.* New York: Hawthorne.

ERIKSON, E. (1963). *Childhood and society.* New York: Norton.

ESCALONA, S. (1973). Basic modes of social interaction: Their emergence and patterning during the first two years of life. *Merrill-Palmer Quarterly, 19,* 205–232.

FLYNN, T. M. (1979). Parental attitudes and the preschool child's self concept. *Child Study Journal, 9*(1), 69–79.

FRODI, A., BRIDGES, L., & GROLNICK, W. (1985). Correlates of mastery-related behavior: A short-term longitudinal study of infants in their second year. *Child Development, 56*(5), 1291–1298.

GALINSKY, E. (1980). *Between generations: The six stages of parenthood.* New York: Times Books.

GEARING, J. (1978). Facilitating the birth process and father-child bonding. *The Counseling Psychologist, 7*(4), 53–55.

GORDON, I. (1976, March). Parenting, teaching and child development. *Young Children,* pp. 173–183.

GORDON I., GUINAGH, B., & JESTER, R. (1977). The Florida parent education infant and toddler programs. In M.

Day & R. Parker (Eds.), *The preschool in action* (pp. 19–127). Boston: Allyn & Bacon.

GORDON, I., HANES, M., LAMME, L., SCHLENKER, P., & BARNETT, H. (1975). *Research report of parent oriented home-based early childhood education programs.* Gainesville: Institute for Development of Human Resources, College of Education, University of Florida.

HAWKES, G. (1968). Building self-image in preschoolers. In J. L. Frost (Ed.), *Early childhood education rediscovered: Readings* (pp. 333–335). New York: Holt, Rinehart & Winston.

HULLS, J. (1977). Toys: Get the most for your money. In *Conference proceedings: Between grown-ups and kids.* Austin, TX: Southwest Education Development Laboratory.

KOHLBERG, L. (1975). The cognitive developmental approach to moral education. *Phi Delta Kappan, 56*(10), 670–677.

MCCANDLESS, B. (1967). *Children: Behavior and development.* New York: Holt, Rinehart & Winston.

MCKIM, M. (1987). Transition to what? New parents' problems in the first year. *Family Relations, 36,* 22–25.

MILLIONES, J. (1978). Relationship between perceived child temperament and maternal behaviors. *Child Development, 49,* 1255–1257.

MORRISON, G. S. (1978). *Parent involvement in the home, school, and community.* Columbus, OH: Chas. E. Merrill.

NAYLOR, A. (1970). Some determinants of parent-infant relationships. In L. Dittman (Ed.), *What we can learn from infants* (pp. 25–48). Washington, DC: NAEYC.

OZEHASKY, R. (1967). Children's self concept and kindergarten achievement. Unpublished doctoral dissertation, St. John's University.

PARKS, P., & SMERIGLIO, V. (1986). Relationships among parenting knowledge, quality of stimulation in the home and infant development. *Family Relations, 35,* 411–416.

PIAGET, J. (1952). *The origins of intelligence in children.* M. Cook, trans. New York: Norton.

POWER, T. (1985). Mother- and father-infant play: A developmental analysis. *Child Development, 56*(6), 1514–1524.

POWELL, D. (1986). Parent education and support programs. *Young Children, 41,* 47–53.

RADIN, N. (1972). Father-child interaction and the intellectual functioning of four-year-old boys. *Developmental Psychology, 6*(2), 353–361.

RHODES, S. (1977). A developmental approach to the life cycle of the family. *Social Casework, 58,* 301–311.

ROSSI, A. S. (1968). Transition to parenthood. *Journal of Marriage and the Family, 30,* 26–39.

RUTTER, M. (1985). Family and school influences on cognitive development. *Journal of Child Psychology & Psychiatry & Applied Disciplines, 26*(5), 683–704.

SCHOGGEN, P. (1963). Environmental forces in the everyday lives of children. In R. G. Barker (Ed.), *The stream of behavior: Explorations of its structure and content* (pp. 42–69). New York: Appleton-Century-Crofts.

SEARS, R. (1970). Relation of early socialization experiences to self concepts and gender role in middle childhood. *Child Development, 41,* 267–289.

SHEEHY, G. (1976). *Passages.* New York: Bantam.

TAYLOR, M., & KOGAN, K. (1973). Effects of birth of a sibling on mother-child interactions. *Child Psychiatry and Human Development, 4*(1), 53–59.

THRIFT, J. (1976). Reciprocal interactions between infants and their mothers. In M. Cohen (Ed.), *Understanding and nurturing infant development* (pp. 33–36). Washington, DC: ACEI.

TONER, I. (1986). Punitive and non-punitive discipline and subsequent rule-following in young children. *Child Care Quarterly, 15*(1), 27–37.

U.S. Department of Health, Education and Welfare (1978). *Exploring Parenting.* Washington, DC: U.S. Government Printing Office.

VANDELL, D. (1979). Effects of a playgroup experience on mother-son and father-son interaction. *Developmental Psychology, 15*(4), 379–385.

VAN HOOSE, W. H., & WORTH, M. R. (1982). *Adulthood in the life cycle.* Dubuque, IA: Brown.

VENTURA, J. (1987). The stresses of parenthood reexamined. *Family Relations, 36*(1), 26–29.

WAGNER, M., SCHUBERT, H., & SCHUBERT, D. (1985). Family size effects: A review. *Journal of Genetic Psychology, 146*(1), 65–78.

WALDRON, H., & ROUTH, D. (1981). The effect of the first child on the marital relationship. *Journal of Marriage and the Family, 43*(4), 785–788.

Webster's New Collegiate Dictionary. (1979). Springfield, MA: Merriam.

WHITE, B., & WATTS, J. (1973). *Experience and environment: Major influences on the development of the young child.* Englewood Cliffs, NJ: Prentice-Hall.

WILKIE, C., & AMES, E. (1986). The relationship of infant crying to parental stress in the transition to parenthood. *Journal of Marriage and the Family, 48*(3), 545–550.

WILLEMSEN, E. (1979). *Understanding infancy.* San Francisco: Freeman.

WORTHINGTON, E., & BUSTON, B. (1986). The marriage relationship during the transition to parenthood. *Journal of Family Issues, 7*(4), 443–473.

ZIGLER, E. (1980/81). On growing up, learning and loving. In H. E. Fitzgerald (Ed.), *Human Development, Annual Editions.* Guilford, CT: Dushkin Publishing Group.

ZIGLER, E., & VALENTINE, J. (1979). *Head Start: A legacy of the War on Poverty.* New York: Free Press.

3

The Changing Nature of Parenting: Middle Childhood and Adolescence

The transition of a child from total physical and psychological dependency to self-sufficiency and independence occurs gradually. Starting school, however, is an early major step in the process. Patterns of interaction established during the early years continue to influence children as they progress in school. The reason is twofold: Many of the behaviors of children have already been shaped, and the same child continues to interact with the same parents. While we are emphasizing the developmental relationship that occurs between parent and child and the reciprocal nature of that relationship, it is nevertheless safe to assert that, once patterns of family interaction are established, they tend to persist. Change occurs gradually as family members change (Strommen, McKinney, & Fitzgerald, 1977).

The general pattern of stabilization that occurs during the school years makes this period critical. From observations during middle childhood, one can predict with moderate accuracy what the young adult will be like. Personality develops during the school-age years in important ways. It has been noted (Strommen et al., 1977) that personality attributes stabilize into something similar to their adult form somewhere between the ages of 6 and 10. In addition, a wide range of competencies develops rapidly.

Middle childhood, then, is a period of active development involving expansion and integration of social, affective, and cognitive phenomena (Bryant, 1985).

PARENTS AND SCHOOL-AGE CHILDREN

The Parents' Roles As Encouragers

As a child develops from infant to toddler to preschooler to school age, the parent's role changes from caregiver; to protector; to nurturer; and, finally, to encourager. With growing competencies and an emerging sense of individuality, the child gradually decreases conformity to parents and increases conformity to peers (Berndt, 1979).

In fact, with conformity to peers, antisocial behavior increases greatly between the third and ninth grades and then begins to decline. Specifically, Berndt (1979) found that, up to the third grade, children usually sided with their parents against their peers, causing parent conformity to be greater than peer conformity. However, peer influence increased greatly between the third and sixth grades, but this did not seem to increase parent-peer conflict. But when peer conformity reached its peak in the ninth grade, the opposition of parents and peers was stronger than at any other age. Berndt also noted a sex difference: School-age girls showed less conformity than boys did on antisocial behavior and more conformity than boys did to parents on neutral behavior.

School offers children alternative sources of rewards and evaluations while simultaneously adding pressure that may increase anxiety, due to the evaluative relationship that develops between children, teachers, and peers (Felker, 1974). Because this is so, children must develop a system for dealing with occasional incompetencies, failures, and rejection by friends. Thus the role of the parent as encourager becomes crucial. Further, encouragement appears to be the most corrective influence on behavior during this period. Although nurturance still is a necessary ingredient in the parent-child relationship, it is normally manifested in different ways. It is sometimes difficult for a mother to accept the fact that her child no longer wants to be kissed good-bye in the presence of friends or for a father to understand why his son would rather play softball with the neighborhood gang than go on a family picnic. The nurturance that is expressed, then, may be more in a psychological than in a physical form.

It is true, however, that some parental attitudes and practices will carry over into the school-age years. Certain forms of punishment, feelings of love and affection, reasoning, and decision making are among the attitudes and practices that are likely to continue, perhaps in a different form or to a different degree. But as interaction between parent and child becomes more psychological and less physical and as children are exposed to a wider range of significant other people and experiences, the parent finds himself in the encouraging role more and more frequently. The necessity for this should become obvious in the following sections.

Discipline

In Chapter 2 we differentiated between discipline and punishment. If discipline is viewed in its broadest context of positive guidance, then it becomes obvious that the discipline system gradually changes as children reach school age and as parents' own needs change.

Parents continue to serve as strong models and reinforcing agents for their children's behaviors, but the range of behaviors and attitudes to which children are exposed on entering school becomes far greater. Children may begin to question the values their parents hold and become far more inclined to model behaviors of their peers, or, occasionally, other adults whom they admire. Parents may find themselves utilizing different consequences for behavior simply because they are either more effective or more suited to the child's developmental level. For example, withholding privileges becomes a common technique for achieving desired behavior for many parents, whereas isolation for undesirable behavior may become less common. Reasoning and explanation may be used more frequently simply because the parent believes the child of school age is more capable of responding to such techniques than the toddler or the preschooler. The use of natural and logical consequences, as described in Chapter 2, seems to be especially effective in achieving acceptable behavior, particularly if the parent has established an early pattern of utilizing the techniques.

Hoffman (1970) differentiated three major categories of child-rearing practices and their effects on children. These categories, which seem especially applicable to school-age children, are summarized in Box 3a. Hoffman contended that both power assertion and love withdrawal techniques are punitive in nature. Further, power assertion is not associated with positive conscience development, while induction, at least for mothers and children, shows a positive relationship with conscience development. Parents who use love withdrawal techniques will likely produce more anxious children who are more susceptible to adult influence than other children are (Strommen et al., 1977). Realistically, most parents will probably use a combination of the above three categories. However, a prevailing attitude of induction appears to be, in the long run, far more effective in producing psychologically healthy children.

In interviews conducted with 44 fifth-grade children and their parents, children were asked

---

BOX 3a TYPES OF CHILD-REARING PRACTICES

Power Assertion

Attempts to control children by exercising power of a superior nature, either physical or control of resources (spanking, deprivation of privileges/objects, grounding, withholding meals, or threats of punishment)

Love Withdrawal

Direct expression of anger and/or disapproval without use of power; love is conditional on child's behavior

Induction

Provision of reasons or explanations to describe desirable behavior; emphasis of impact of behavior on self and others

Source: Hoffman, M. L. (1970). Moral development. In P. Mussen (Ed.), *Carmichael's manual of child psychology,* vol. 2 (3d ed.). New York: Wiley.

---

to describe the discipline practices of both parents (Zussman, 1978). Responses were coded as power assertion, love withdrawal, or induction. The results indicated that boys received more love withdrawal and more power assertion than did girls, who were likely to receive more induction techniques. As parental education increased, the use of power assertion decreased for boys. As family size increased, parents appeared to be employing more sex-differentiated discipline, since boys from larger families reported greater use of power assertion and girls from these families reported greater use of induction with fewer power assertion techniques.

Correlations between parents' behaviors and children's attributes are already evident before children reach school age, particularly in such areas as achievement motivation, anxiety, and dependence. Differences among children of permissive, authoritative (democratic), and authoritarian parents also are evident. These relationships continue to exist throughout the period of middle childhood (Strommen et al., 1977).

Authoritative discipline tends to foster in children what has been called instrumental competence (Baumrind, 1978). For example, children demonstrate other-oriented rule-following tendencies that enable them to cooperate altruistically with peers and comply with authori-

ty while at the same time demonstrating individualistic, autonomous tendencies. This, in turn, enables the individual to take personal responsibility for his own life, to reject normative rules when they threaten the common good, and to be an agent of personal change.

Baumrind also contended that instrumental competence in school-age children includes the attributes of social responsibility, independence, achievement orientation, vigor, objectivity, and self-control. Since the school-age child is entering Piaget's stage of concrete operations, she now can empathize and assume the roles of others. For this reason Baumrind asserted that social approval and disapproval as well as inductive discipline methods are particularly appropriate, since they tend to facilitate role taking and the child's ability to make inferences about how others feel. Emphasizing the child's responsibility for the welfare of others appears to foster prosocial behavior partly because of the reinforcing effect of having produced a positive effect on others.

An interesting recent study (Amato & Ochiltree, 1986) found that certain forms of child competence are related more strongly to family structure resources (parental income, occupation, and education), while other forms of competence are more strongly related to family process resources (parental help, time, and attention). Specifically, reading ability in elementary school children was related to both sets of resources, whereas self-esteem was more strongly related to family process resources—that is, interpersonal relationships within the family—than to family structure resources. Parent helping, talking, and time were generally associated with children's self-esteem, and correlations for fathers were as consistently high as correlations for mothers.

Discipline techniques parents often use that tend to be self-defeating have been described by Ginott (1969). They include *threats* (invitations to repeat a forbidden act only challenge the child's autonomy), *bribes* (they seldom inspire the child toward continual efforts), *promises* (may build up unrealistic expectations, as they do not account for situational factors), *sarcasm* (invites counterattacks), and *provoking lies* (the child feels he is not allowed to tell the truth for fear of punishment). Ginott further emphasized that limits should tell the child clearly what constitutes acceptable conduct and what substitute will be accepted. Set limits on undesirable acts but allow the child to speak out about what he feels. Ginott contended that limits imposed in this fashion, without violence or excessive anger, preserve the self-respect of both the parent and the child.

Some of the common problems that parents face with school-age children are identified in Box 3b. If these problems can be faced factually, realistically, and unemotionally with reasonable, firm limits imposed that are understood by the child, then nagging and power struggles can be avoided. Even if children cannot have a choice in the solution to a problem, they can have a voice in its solution.

Some parents have particular difficulty responding to the child's questions regarding sex. Sex education is a lifelong process, and obviously the groundwork is laid during the period of infancy and early childhood with the parents' attitudes toward their own sexuality and their body language, gestures, and verbal responses to the child's early questions. Again, if relaxed communication can be achieved without moralizing or making the child feel that her questions are "dirty" or silly, then the child's sex education can proceed smoothly. Factual answers geared to the child's level of understanding appear to be best.

Many parents want their children to receive the bulk of their sex education at home but preclude this possibility because they do not create a comfortable climate in which the child can ask questions. Exactly what parents say and how they say it will vary, depending on what is comfortable for them and the level of understanding of the child. Many parents find pamphlets or books to be helpful. There are several excellent ones available at local book stores or from a physician's office.

In summary, discipline during the school-age years seems more effective if it is inductive, is encouraging rather than punitive, and includes limits that are reasonable and understood. Promoting mutual respect while gradually encouraging greater independence and self-discipline are important goals at this time. Finally, studies have indicated the importance of consistent discipline. For example, Sawin and Parke (1979) examined interagent discipline practices of first- and second-grade boys. When boys received inconsistent discipline in the form of approval from one agent (adult) and disapproval from another,

---

BOX 3b COMMON PROBLEMS OF PARENTS OF SCHOOL-AGE CHILDREN

Lying	Television
Stealing	Bedtime
Rudeness	Allowance
Irresponsibility	Sex education
Homework	Drugs

significantly higher levels of hitting behavior resulted. The researchers noticed that when inconsistent discipline was used, boys either (1) appeared quite disconcerted by the conflicting cues and behaved in a cautious and inhibited manner, or (2) appeared annoyed, and even angry, at the conflicting cues, and then their hitting became more vigorous and continued for longer periods of time. Sawin and Parke concluded that children who receive consistent feedback from socializing agents are able to form reliable expectations about the consequences of their behavior and therefore modify the behavior accordingly.

Developing a Sense of Industry

The fourth stage in Erikson's theory of psychosocial development is industry versus inferiority and spans the school-age period, from approximately 6 through 11 years of age. The school-age child shows unceasing energy toward investing all possible efforts in producing. On the other hand, there is a pull toward an earlier level of lesser production. Because he still is a child,

there are fears of inferiority that he tries to overcome by diligently engaging in opportunities to learn by doing. He works incessantly on expanding bodily, muscular, and perceptive skills as well as on expanding knowledge of the world around him. A concern with how things are made, how they work, and what they do predominates. It is the age of collections, long-term projects, and "making a mess." The child's peers become far more significant to him at this phase, and he tries to relate to and communicate with them. He feels a strong need for a sense of accomplishment and will ward off failure at almost any price. Acceptance by his peers is critical for his ego development.

The sense of competence at this stage is the sense of oneself as capable and able to do meaningful tasks. It includes taking on tasks and projects because of a basic interest in doing them and in working to complete them to achieve satisfaction from the results. When the child's use of her expanding skills and competencies meets with success, when she receives support and approval from parents, peers, and teachers, then she will develop a sense of industry. But if there are

repeated experiences of failure and disapproval, then the sense of inferiority will predominate.

Erikson believes that many of the attitudes toward work and work habits that are exhibited later in life are formed during this period. It is important that both teachers and parents provide many opportunities for the child to succeed at a variety of work experiences. Since children are striving to accomplish a sense of industry, they are work-oriented. Attention should be given, both at home and at school, to the establishment of positive work habits—doing one's best, appropriate standards for work attempted, and so on.

Play continues to be important. Most pursuits are segregated by sex. Children begin to see their families as representatives of society and begin to measure them against other representatives. The Oedipal complex is resolved, and the child forms relationships with other adults—teachers, relatives, family friends, and recreational leaders. Therefore social institutions other than the family come to play a central role in the child's development. Thus the achievement of a sense of industry does not depend solely on the caretaking efforts of the parents.

During the sense-of-industry stage, the child becomes capable of deductive reasoning and of playing and learning by rules. New words and ideas are learned from peers and are tried out at home. Children begin to compare their own homes with those of their peers. The assumption that adults are not very bright becomes apparent (Strommen et al., 1977). This phenomenon in children has been referred to as cognitive conceit, and it develops when children use the new reasoning skills at their command and catch adults in errors of reasoning or fact (Elkind, 1970). If parents see the child's behavior as being silly, then a sense of inferiority may be established.

Building a Healthy Self-concept

The discussion in Chapter 2 pointed out the three basic dimensions of self-concept: a sense of belonging (that is, the individual perceives himself as part of a group and is accepted and valued by the other members of that group); a sense of worth (that is, the individual perceives himself as a "good" or worthy person); and a sense of competence (that is, the individual perceives that he is successful at doing things well) (Coopersmith, 1967; Felker, 1974; Gordon, 1971). We have further noted that parenting style and the quality of interactions between parents and children are significantly related to the child's development of a healthy self-concept.

Sex differences in the development of self-concept have been noted in the literature. For example, Amato (1986) found a strong negative association between marital conflict of parents and self-esteem among elementary school girls but not among boys. This finding conflicts with previous work that suggests that boys succumb more easily than girls do to psychological stress. Further, for school-age females marital conflict was associated with a poor relationship with the father, even though daughters indicated that they desired more time with their fathers, suggesting that it was the father who was withdrawing from the relationship. Only when girls had a good relationship with *one* parent did it buffer the effects of marital conflict, but not when either a good or a poor relationship with *both* parents existed. These provocative findings, among others, suggest the importance of recognizing potential differences in the impact of familial relationships on male and female children.

Children's perceptions of parents. One related factor not previously mentioned is the child's perception of parental attitudes and behavior, more fully recognized by the school-age years. There may be a difference between *actual* parental attitudes and characteristics and how they are *perceived* by children. In an effort to support the work of Coopersmith (1967) and Sears (1970), Graybill (1978) assessed the behaviors of mothers from the perspective of the children themselves. The children ranged in age from 7 to 15 years. Those children who perceived their mothers as using psychological pressure techniques to discipline them ("If I loved her, I'd do what she wants me to do") had low self-esteem. Children who perceived their mothers as accepting and nurturing ("She gives me a lot of care and attention") had high self-esteem. Further, the latter group of children did not report drastic forms of punishment.

BOX 3c OTHER FACTORS RELATED TO SELF-CONCEPT DURING SCHOOL YEARS

Physical appearance (body image)
Anxiety level
Competence (especially academic)
Peer acceptance
Size of family
Ordinal position

Sources: Felker, D. (1974). *Building positive self concepts.* Minneapolis: Burgess; and Sears, R. (1970). Relation of early socialization experiences to self-concepts and gender role in middle childhood. *Child Development, 41,* 267–289.

Similarly, Dickstein and Posner (1978) assessed the quality of the parent-child relationship through a questionnaire given to children between 8 and 11 years of age. The child's view of the quality of the parent-child relationship with the parent of the same sex seemed to be associated with high self-esteem.

To support the belief that the individual's perception of events is a more salient determinant of attitudes and behavior than are external objective events themselves, Rahner (1980) assessed the perceived parental acceptance/rejection of 316 children in third grade through sixth grade. She concluded that rejected children the world over, in comparison to accepted children, are more hostile, aggressive, and dependent and have more impaired feelings of self-esteem and self-adequacy. She reported that 27 percent of the children have behavior personality dispositions that were accounted for by their perceptions of parental acceptance scores.

It seems obvious, then, that parental attitudes and behaviors, the quality of the parent-child relationship, and the child's perceptions of these begin very early to have a strong impact on how the child views herself. Dickstein and Posner (1978) stated: "The school age child's sense of worth is still very much a reflection of the success of his interactions with others and should, therefore, be greatly influenced by his interactions with those most crucial to his survival and well being: his parents" (p. 273). Other factors related to self-concept during the school years are summarized in Box 3c.

Self-concept and academic achievement. Is self-concept important? If one accepts Felker's (1974) contention that self-concept determines an individual's actions in various situations, then obviously a positive self-concept *is* important. Most parents particularly want their children to do well in school. There has been much discussion concerning the relationship between self-concept and academic achievement. Which is the cause of the other is not always clear, however. Felker (1974) stated unequivocally that positive self-concept is related to high academic achievement during the school-age years. He contended that low self-concept and low academic achievement interact and feed back negatively on each other, with this phenomenon being more significant for males than for females. Since parental acceptance seems to be a relevant factor in the child's self-concept, this dimension of parent behavior should be related to the child's academic performance.

The perception of fourth- and fifth-grade children's acceptance or rejection by their parents was assessed by Starkey (1980). Those children who perceived their parents as more accepting tended to obtain higher scores on standardized achievement tests as well as higher grade-point averages. However, sex differences did appear. For girls, perceived parental warmth was significantly correlated with composite achievement test scores and with specific scores in mathematics but not in reading. For boys, perceived parental warmth was associated with all three sets of scores. For girls, but not for boys, perceived warmth was correlated with IQ scores. In general, the more rejecting children perceived their parents to be, the greater the decrease in academic performance.

One cannot overlook, however, the role the child plays in the view of herself. Children will behave in ways consistent with the ways they see themselves. If a child feels she is worthless, she will expect others to treat her as worthless (Felker, 1974). Since children cannot be viewed as simply mirror images of external events but as active, striving, learning individuals, self-esteem, then, represents the child's unique organization of her own genetic makeup, the evaluations made of her by significant adults, and the feedback she receives from her world. There seems to be a downward trend in self-concept as children enter school due to the increased sources of evaluations by teachers and peers, but by fifth grade the trend climbs upward. Since, however, the school-age child is more independent and increasingly in charge of herself, more and more evaluations of behavior are self-evaluation, and a larger percentage of her rewards will be self-rewards. It seems important, then, for parents to help children identify their strengths and reward themselves for those while minimizing negative evaluations of weaknesses.

In summary, the role of the parent in developing a healthy self-concept during middle childhood, just as in infancy and early childhood, remains crucial. The same parental characteristics and behaviors that were mentioned in Chapter 2 in relation to early childhood also are important in middle childhood.

Providing Learning Experiences

Even though the school-age child is now in the structured learning environment of school, the home continues to be an important learning laboratory. When describing the growing sense of industry earlier in this chapter, we stated that the school-age child is concerned with how things are made, how they work, and what they do. Further, the child works to expand both his body skills and his perceptual skills. The role that parents play in structuring the home environment to permit these capacities to develop and in assisting and encouraging the child to pursue relevant out-of-home, out-of-school activities is extremely important. Therefore we will discuss learning activities during middle childhood from two perspectives: (1) those that occur out of the home and out of the school (commonly labeled as extracurricular activities) and (2) those that occur mostly in the home or with the family.

The importance of play during middle childhood cannot be overemphasized, as it provides the child with situations where she can test herself, work out feelings, experiment with roles, learn rules and expectations, and develop and practice skills that will be important for adult life in society. Many of these goals are achieved by play involving peers or by team efforts. Games of strategy are associated with the complexity of the social organization, and games of chance are associated with the stress on responsibility and anxiety about achievement (Strommen et al., 1977). One school-age child lamented the fact that she never had time just to read a good book because she was so busy with school and extracurricular activities. However, school-age children also need time to play by themselves or just "mess around," as they sometimes describe their activity.

Peer relationships begin to take on new dimensions and increased emphasis during the school years. Children begin actively to seek out others of their own age as they attempt to gain access to their new social world. Only peers can provide them with effective models of how to behave among other children. Further, peers provide direct reinforcement to each other, both positive and negative, of which most parents are aware. Through group interaction, modeling, and reinforcement, group norms are established. Most children strive to establish status in the group and to meet its expectations.

Out-of-home learning experiences. Aside from peer-group interaction within the normal course of a school day, children have an opportunity to achieve group status as well as to broaden their scope of learning through organized out-of-home activities. These usually fall into the following categories: sports (football, baseball,

basketball, gymnastics, swimming, tennis, soccer, and so forth); music/dance/drama/crafts; Cub Scouts, Boy Scouts, Brownies, Girl Scouts, or Campfire Girls; church activities; and camps.

Clearly there are both advantages and disadvantages to children being involved with such activities. The advantages are relatively obvious: Children begin to associate and identify with unrelated adults that are important socializing agents for them; children extend their peer interactions beyond the classroom and are frequently exposed to children from a variety of cultural backgrounds; children can spend time with other children who share their interests; children learn to develop a team spirit; children can develop and practice their growing bodily and perceptual skills within the context of a group setting; children can learn to play by rules and how to be a good winner and a good loser; children can establish status in the group; and children can expend energies in playing.

The disadvantages may not be quite so obvious to parents. First, many parents fall into the "more is better" trap or the "my child is busier than your child" syndrome when planning for the child's out-of-home activities. In their desire to develop well-rounded children, some parents overenroll their children in "classes" so that there is little time left for meaningful interaction or for children to pursue other interests.

The second major disadvantage is that parents may actually coerce children to be involved in an activity simply because the parents themselves enjoy it. A typical example is the "jock" father who almost literally forces his son into sports. When children are not genuinely interested in an activity, the activity will not provide effective learning experiences for them.

Finally, the competitive aspect of organized sports may overshadow their inherent learning potential. We have attended Little League baseball games that could compare to the stress and tension of the World Series. The desire to win superseded any effort to help children develop and refine skills or to teach the rules of cooperation. Further, the models presented by both coaches and parents were ones of competition and aggression rather than of cooperation. Parents need to examine the competitive aspects of such organized groups and identify the potential for positive development that accompanies them.

While it is not our intention to minimize the importance of extracurricular activities for the school-age child, we do wish to encourage parents to follow the guidelines in Box 3d. If these guidelines are followed, out-of-home activities can provide a source of valuable learning for the child.

In-home learning activities. Two types of family activities that can provide valuable learning experiences for school-age children are those that are planned and organized and those that are unplanned or spontaneous. Organized activities include vacations; camping, picnicking, or hiking; going out to dinner, parks, the movies, or cultural events; attending sports events or amusement parks; and shopping. Naturally, these activities offer a wide range of learning experiences for the child. They give families opportunities to share common interests, to be together away from a usually hectic home schedule, and to share new experiences. Often it is difficult to plan such activities so that every family member enjoys them equally. As children reach middle childhood, they develop new interests and an increasing sense of individuality. Therefore organized activities should be planned with the interests of each family member in mind. The favorite activity of individual children might be combined or alternated. Or perhaps some family members might engage in activities together while the rest of the family participates in another activity.

Equally as important as organized activities are those that occur spontaneously in the home, such as games, hobbies, family projects, and reading or talking together. Unplanned and unorganized leisure time with children may yield the fondest memories for children as well as stimulating learning. It has been said that there is math in the bathroom and science in the sink, and parents who take advantage of these opportunities stimulate learning in the home for their children.

Frequently public schools will prepare materials that can be used in the home to support academic performance. A case in point includes two examples from Albuquerque, New Mexico. The public school system distributes a calendar each month during the academic year to parents of school-age children with a suggested activity each day that parents can do with their children. It may be as simple as "Take a walk with your child and listen for different sounds" or as complicated as a science experiment. In addition, the curriculum center for the public school system prepared summer math activities for elementary school children. These were inserted as a separate page in the daily newspaper and designed so that students could have fun with mathematics and keep their skills sharpened in preparation for the next school term.

There is no consensus among experts on the issue of the role parents should play in the child's "homework." Clearly a child's homework is his responsibility, not his parents. If one subscribes to the use of natural consequences, then the child who does not complete his homework assignments will suffer the natural consequences of not doing well in school. A "hands-off-the-homework" approach is difficult for many parents who see their role as assisting the child in his learning experiences. Probably the more sensible and effective approach is to encourage and assist

---

BOX 3d GUIDELINES FOR CHOOSING OUT-OF-HOME ACTIVITIES FOR SCHOOL-AGE CHILDREN

Examine alternatives carefully. Consider time commitment, competitive aspects, and characteristics of participating adults.

Determine child's interest and "fit" between activity and developmental level.

Give encouragement and guidance as child selects his or her own activities.

Select judiciously; do not overcommit child's time.

Help child select activities in which he or she can be successful.

when necessary but refuse to assume responsibility for its completion. How does one accomplish this? First, parents can create a home environment that is conducive to study; a quiet time and place for children to work; a flexible schedule to allow enough time for work; resources (newspapers, books, magazines, dictionaries, encyclopedias) to assist in completion of assignments; encouragement and assistance in areas in which the child seems to be having problems; and elimination of nagging.

It is critical that parents and teachers establish a partnership relationship if the child is to receive maximum benefit from school. If the child is having learning difficulties, on the advice of the teacher parents may need to secure tutoring for the child in some academic area. By working together, realistic expectations can be determined and a plan of action initiated.

One issue that commonly divides parents and their school-age children is television viewing—when, how often, and what kind. Clearly how television influences children is an issue that has attracted much attention in recent years. Studies indicate that effects of television watching are evident in children's play and fantasy behavior as well as in everyday behavior and personal interactions (Fairchild & Erwin, 1977; Friedrich & Stein, 1973). However, mediating factors such as personality characteristics, IQ, and social class begin to interact with television viewing during the preschool period and continue to do so into school age (Strommen et al., 1977). Although some of the child's behaviors that appear to be related to television are negative, that is, aggression or sex-role stereotypes or standards (Miller & Reeves, 1975), others may be positive. For example, Atkin and Gantz (1975) found that those children from kindergarten through fifth grade who watched news shows had greater knowledge of political events, were more likely to discuss news events with others, were more interested in public affairs, and were more likely to seek additional information about what they saw.

A somewhat unique approach to children and television was taken by Abelman (1986), who examined the impact of patterns of parental discipline and interactions on children's acquisition and potential modeling of prosocial TV portray-

als. He argued that the television portrays a fairly equal amount of prosocial and antisocial behaviors, but beyond the use of explicitly stated rules and practices regarding television, parents fail to deal with other forms of social interaction that might affect children's learning of specific behaviors. He found that parents who use inductive discipline techniques had children who seemed to be the most affected by prosocial television content and the least affected by antisocial fare. On the other hand, parents who were high in power assertion and love withdrawal techniques had children who appeared least affected by prosocial and most affected by antisocial television content. Therefore parental discipline styles may be an important mediator, affecting not necessarily what children watch but what they get from TV programming.

Obviously television viewing is associated with both negative and positive characteristics in children. If the child demonstrates media addiction—that is, if other activities are excluded for the purpose of watching television—then personal maladjustments may occur. Media addiction has been associated with neurosis, strong feelings of rejection, and personal insecurity. Whether these personality difficulties are the *result* of media addiction or whether they are already present is not clear.

Whatever rules parents make about television watching should be reasonable and enforceable. For example, it is rather difficult for a parent to forbid television viewing when there is no adult present to enforce such a rule. It probably is a good idea for parents to be thoroughly familiar with the content of programs before setting limits on the types of programs they allow their children to watch. Avoiding viewing stimulating programs just prior to bedtime will help the child relax. Clearly the solution to the television problem is not a simple one. Parents and children need to develop mutual reasonable solutions and avoid power struggles over the issue. It seems apparent, however, that parents who are addicted to television will produce children who are television addicts.

One of the major criticisms of too much television viewing is that it reduces the level of conversation within the family. Surely one of the most valuable learning experiences for children is conversation with other family members. Most conversation is spontaneous, centering around specific interests or activities that occur at a given moment. One child whose parents had designated the evening meal as the specific time for conversation in the family felt so frustrated that conversation became less frequent. Parents should value spontaneous moments to such an extent that enough time is left in organizing individual and family schedules to preserve them.

In summary, the school-age years continue to be an important stage during which learning experiences outside the school play a crucial role in the child's development. Parents can enhance learning by creating a home environment that is conducive to learning, by helping the child select extracurricular activities that promote overall adjustment and development, and by helping the child achieve a mix of peer and family activities that is acceptable to both parents and children.

PROGRAMS FOR PARENTS OF SCHOOL-AGE CHILDREN

The older the child, the fewer the programs that exist for parents. Therefore parent-education programs for those with infants and preschool children are far more numerous than programs for those with school-age children. As a society we have assumed that parents with young children need more support and assistance than those with older children. We also have assumed that parent behaviors and attitudes are resistant to change, and therefore we should focus on early parental behavior. Although a variety of agencies—including churches, mental-health clinics, and family-counseling agencies—have made sporadic attempts at education for parents of school-age children, the most consistent efforts have been through the public education system.

Parent Involvement in the Schools

Efforts to involve parents in school programs are not new. Since the founding of the National Congress of Mothers in 1897, which became the PTA in 1924, attempts to create a link between home and school have been evident. A variety of approaches have been used, including parent-teacher conferences, involving parents in fundraising and open houses, and utilizing parents as volunteers in the classroom and as tutors either at home or in the school. These activities have been most successful with middle-class mothers, with little involvement of fathers or working-class parents, except for Chapter 1 programs (see below). It has been assumed that this kind of involvement contributes to greater adjustment and achievement of children and improved attitudes on the part of parents (Kagan, 1984).

Even so, parent involvement in the schools has left much to be desired, often reaching the point of hostility between parents and school personnel. Currently a few successful home-school partnerships have been reported (Johnston & Slotnik, 1985), but parents and teachers for the most part remain independent socializers of children. It is not unusual for teachers to complain that parents have little interest in their children, leaving the business of childrearing to the schools, and, on the other hand, resenting parents' intrusion into the classroom. Parents, too, may insist that teachers are poorly prepared and assert their perceived parental rights to determine school curricula. Of course the success with which these issues are resolved varies from teacher to teacher, school to school, and district to district. The rebirth of the ''back to basics'' movement of the 1980s, however, has resulted in state legislation allowing home education and a greater proportion of parents educating their children at home because of dissatisfaction with both the content of public school curricula and the degree of parental input into curriculum decision making. The issue of parental versus institutional rights in public education is far from resolved. Professionals and parents alike are renewing their interest in finding ways to work together for the benefit of children, as evidenced, for example, by the first National Institute for Parent Involvement in Education, held in 1987, which was entitled ''Home/School Partnerships for Student Success.''

Chapter I Programs

Title I, now known as Chapter I, programs in the public schools serve low-income children, and a major objective of such programs has been parent involvement. There are four major capacities in which parents have been involved: (1) as observers or learners, (2) as participants in school activities, (3) as volunteers in the classroom, and (4) as participants on school advisory committees. The major purpose of involving parents as observers or learners is to teach parents, to increase understanding of themselves, their children, or the school program. These efforts have been most successful when parents perceived that the information offered was vital to learning, to their child's interests, or when the programs were aimed specifically at parent interests and needs (Nebgen, 1979).

A lesser degree of involvement has occurred when parents were participants in school activities that are peripheral to the classroom, such as supervising after-school clubs, producing newsletters, and assisting in the school library. Research has shown that children in Chapter I programs with high parent involvement in these types of activities make significant achievement gains, but variables other than parent involvement may have accounted for the improvement. Parents, however, have reported increased self-esteem and a better understanding of school programs (Nebgen, 1979).

The use of parents as volunteers in the classroom has been minimal in Chapter I programs. In those instances in which it has occurred, parents have reported improved self-image and a greater understanding of the curriculum and the teacher's problems. There are no data available on the relationship between this type of involvement and children's achievement (Nebgen, 1979).

In general there has been a low level of involvement of parents in school advisory committees of Chapter I programs. Often administrators have not encouraged participation at this level, and confusion has existed over role responsibilities. The effects of such participation, where it has occurred, on student achievement, on the school program, and on the parents themselves have not been definitively shown by the research (Nebgen, 1979).

It seems clear that further research is needed to determine what types and degrees of parent involvement are most effective and under what conditions. Multiple outcomes—adjustment and achievement of the child, attitudes and behavior of the parent, and impact on the school program—need to be assessed.

Parent Education via the Child's School

In some instances the school has been a vehicle for the delivery of more formalized parent education, although this practice is not commonplace. Several school districts have provided STEP or PET classes to parents (see Chapter 5), with moderate success (Johnson & Brown, 1986). One district with which we are familiar sponsors a yearly mini–parent conference on a Saturday, which includes a keynote speaker and a variety of workshops led by community professionals. Other school districts offer similar programs using different contemporary strategies or a combination of more than one. These programs represent more of an attempt to meet the needs of parents in the community than to empirically test the effectiveness of such programs as it relates to the child's behavior and achievement in the school setting. As with efforts toward achieving parental involvement in school programs, most participating parents have been middle class.

Another unique program that was initiated as a collaborative effort between a public school district and a university is the Parent Center located in Albuquerque, New Mexico. The center was initially funded by a training grant and a model programs grant from the Bureau of Education for the Handicapped. The training component includes training both regular and special education teachers of school-age exceptional children to work more effectively with parents. In addition parents are trained to work more effectively with school personnel. Assistance to teachers in designing and implementing parent-education programs is provided by the center on request from both parents and teachers. The center is currently using parents to conduct many of their parent-education programs.

The second component of the program was to develop a mirror model of parent involvement, a comprehensive package that would be readily available to schools. The model examines parent strengths as well as parent needs. The model includes parents teaching other parents, parents as classroom volunteers, and parents as members of advisory boards (R. Kroth, personal communication, November 14, 1980).

Even though education and support programs for parents whose children are in middle childhood are not numerous and research regarding the effectiveness of such programs is scarce, increased efforts should be made in this direction. The complexity of parenting in contemporary society suggests that parents are in need of such services. For example, drug use by school-age children is becoming a greater problem, early sexual activity is a concern for many parents, and the lack of accessibility to programs that provide before- and after-school supervision for children creates problems for working parents. Therefore creative ways to reach parents and program content that focuses on current issues and concerns need to be developed.

DEVELOPMENTAL NEEDS OF PARENTS

The sense of generativity that was described in Chapter 2 continues to develop for parents as their children move from the preschool period into middle childhood. However, the need to care for others or to become involved with creative production may begin to be fulfilled in new or different ways. As children enter school and are absent from the home for large parts of the day and as they are developing a wider range of interests outside the home, mothers who have not already done so may return to school, obtain a job, or resume leisure activities after a long absence. These opportunities enable them to blend their parenting role with other roles that are related to developing a sense of generativity. However, as more women with very young children are entering the work force or continuing with their education, the stereotype of the mother who stays home with her children until at least school age is rapidly disappearing. In any case many parents do find that middle childhood, with its decreasing demands on physical care, allows them an opportunity for a wider variety of experiences to meet their developmental needs, whether they are employed outside the home or not. Socializing with other adults, time

for privacy, and developing interests outside the family become a little easier. Fatigue may be somewhat alleviated as children begin to contribute to household responsibilities.

However, several problems confront parents at this time. The first is the changing nature of the guidance that parents give children, which becomes less physical and more psychological. Parents identify with the disappointments their children feel when they fail at a task or are rejected by their peers. Often the pain is greater for the parents than it is for the children. Encouragement in the face of pain may be difficult for parents. Further, as children develop skills of logic and reason, parents have to find new ways of discipline that are effective. As Rhodes (1977) put it, the developmental task for the parent at this time is individuation versus pseudomutual organization. Parents, especially mothers, may be ambivalent toward the child's increasing self-sufficiency. If parents feel that peers, school, and other community relations detract from them, they may behave in ways that curtail children's activities outside the family. On the other hand, Galinsky (1980) described the latency stage in children as corresponding to a parental interpretive stage, in which the expanding social environment of the child causes the parent to assess his or her own perceptions with reality. The interpretive stage begins with parents evaluating their own beginning years of parenthood, revising their theories of child rearing, and then forming images of the future.

Nevertheless, one of the biggest problems parents face when their children enter school is that of "letting go" to some degree. While nurturance is still an important ingredient in the parent-child relationship, it is difficult for parents to accept the growing influence of peers and other adults. Their need to be needed is still quite strong (Bigner, 1979). If, however, parents can develop outside interests while their children are expressing a growing need for individuality and peer relationships, letting go becomes somewhat easier. We remember the traumatic experience of leaving our children alone for the first time without a sitter. Of course, most children are ready for this experience before their parents are. We also remember the first time our children spent the night with friends or the first time they went to a movie without us. These experiences are part of the process of letting go and are necessary milestones in the lives of both parents and children. Parents who fail to encourage the child to develop independence and form new relationships contribute to poorly adjusted children and unhappiness for themselves.

Finally, parents may be preoccupied at this time with the direction their lives are taking. Are they satisfied with their jobs? Do they want more education? Is their marital satisfaction diminishing? Glick and Norton (1973) reported that the average length of marriage before divorce is 7.2 years. This means that for many parents the beginning of the period of middle childhood or just prior is a critical period for maladjustment in marriage. Further, if the mother does return to work or school at this time, she may experience role strain that contributes to marital dissatisfaction. If parents can positively evaluate the direction their lives are taking, share the responsibilities of parenting and maintaining the household, and develop interests outside the family, then this role strain can be reduced. In addition, if they capitalize on the decreasing demands their children are making upon them, middle childhood can offer a period of satisfaction.

Again it is important to emphasize the reciprocal character of the parent-child relationship during middle childhood. There seems to be a natural dovetailing of the developmental needs of school-age children and the developmental needs of parents at this time. Just as children are beginning to strive for greater independence and are moving toward stronger peer relationships, parents are beginning to reevaluate their lives and develop new interests. If equal attention is given to the needs of both children and parents, then the developmental tasks of all family members can be met with minimal stress. Both parents and children play a crucial role in the resolution of psychosocial crises, and the behavior of one member continues to influence the behavior of another. It seems that a mutually satisfying resolution of establishing a sense of industry for the child and a sense of generativity for the parent results in an easier transition for both during the stages of preadolescence and adolescence.

SIBLING RELATIONSHIPS

Interactions between parents and children are affected by a variety of factors, including the number and the spacing of children in the family. While considerable attention has been given to spousal and parent-child relationships, little has been directed toward sibling relationships. We include a brief discussion here because we believe that the presence or absence of siblings and their relationships to one another have a significant impact on parent-child relationships.

Presence versus Absence of Siblings

Some research has been conducted regarding the comparison of only children to those with siblings. In general the research has suggested that these two groups of children are little different with respect to personality characteristics; however, only children tend to demonstrate greater achievement motivation than children with siblings (Polit & Falbo, 1987). The differences are more pronounced when "onlies" are compared to later-borns and to children from large families. The difference can be explained by the nature and amount of parental interactions with their children, that is, ". . . heightened parental attention may presumably lead to both greater expectations for performance and more opportunities to witness and reward achievements" (Polit & Falbo, 1987, p. 319). It seems, then, that the parent-child relationship plays a more powerful role in the development of achievement motivation and personal adjustment than it does in building character, sociability, and personal control.

Berndt and Bulleit (1985) observed 3- to 5-year-olds both at home and in preschool to assess interactions among siblings and consistency in interactions with siblings and peers. At home preschoolers with older siblings were the recipients of both more aggressive and more prosocial behaviors than those without older siblings were. On the other hand, preschoolers with younger siblings were more dominant in their interactions and displayed certain types of verbal behavior less often than preschoolers without younger siblings did. Indicators of sibling status, however, were not strongly related to behaviors at preschool, but children who were more aggressive toward siblings and those who were more often onlookers or unoccupied at home showed similar behaviors with peers.

Developmental Tasks of Siblings

The average family of the late 1980s has approximately two children. Therefore most children have an average of one sibling, and because of increased mobility, children have little access to other children in their kin network. The result is that children form close relationships with their siblings, especially if they are the same gender, and these ties tend to be enduring.

Goetting (1986) described the developmental tasks of siblings over the life cycle. She contended that from childhood through old age, one of the primary roles of siblings is to provide companionship and emotional support. The intensity of the sibling relationship decreases in early and middle adulthood, only to intensify again in old age.

During middle childhood and adolescence, siblings, particularly oldest daughters, contribute to the care of younger children. This is especially true in large families, single-parent families, and low-income families. In some families where the parent lacks involvement and commitment or where the parent is incapacitated, older daughters may adopt a surrogate-parent role. However, caretaking styles of siblings differ from parental caretaking styles. Delegated caretaking may serve as anticipatory socialization for parenthood, but, at the same time, may cause hostility in the older child and may be less effective than parental caretaking (Goetting, 1986).

Provision for aid and direct services among siblings is another role that occurs from childhood through old age, though the form changes over time. During childhood and adolescence, siblings often form coalitions for dealing with parents or as compensation for parental inadequacies. During adulthood siblings may share clothes, lend money, help each other during illness or crises, or provide babysitting services. During old age siblings may support one another in financial affairs, making decisions, home care, and shopping. It is interesting that the sibling bond often becomes reactivated during the adult

years when siblings cooperate in the care of elderly parents and often ultimately dismantling the family home. In old age siblings often reminisce together because they have similar life histories. For some, sibling rivalry may not be resolved until old age (Goetting, 1986).

Sibling Rivalry

Much has been written about sibling rivalry and the ways for parents to cope with it. The frequency and intensity of sibling rivalry will vary across families. Closely spaced siblings (less than 5 years apart), especially those of the same gender, tend to be more rivalrous than those with 5 or more years between them. The role of the parents, however, is a key one. While it is true that the vast majority of siblings will, at some time in their lives, experience rivalry, there are several things that parents can do to minimize it.

First, parents need to treat each child as an individual, encouraging and supporting the unique interests and skills each demonstrates. Some children do well academically, others do not; some children are interested in sports, others are not; some children have talent in music and the arts, others do not. Therefore expectations for children's performance will be different for each child. Second, parents should avoid even subtle references of comparison among children. The more parents compare children, the more competitive they will become with one another and the more intense sibling rivalry will become. Third, parents should organize their time so that the needs of each child can be met. This does not mean that each child will necessarily receive *equal* time, for often one child requires more time than another because of her age or her personality characteristics. However, special time for each child, according to her needs, is essential. Third, parents should respect each child's wishes to have her own possessions protected from siblings. Children need to own something before they can share it, and children who are continually forced to share their possessions with younger siblings do not develop attitudes of generosity. Finally, when siblings become old enough to settle their own disputes, parents should avoid intervening. Parents who intervene in their children's daily disputes often find themselves in the permanent role of police officer and deny their children opportunities to learn problem-solving skills.

It seems apparent that sibling relationships constitute a significant aspect of family life and may be as important as the parent-child relationship itself. Just as children are affected by their parents and siblings, so are parents affected by their children, individually and collectively.

PARENTS AND PREADOLESCENTS

The Unstable Role of Parents

Preadolescence is a period of transition between childhood and adolescence, roughly spanning the years between 9 and 13 and fifth or sixth grade through eighth grade. Donald Eichhorn (as reported by Moss, 1969) aptly labeled this growth stage as "transescence," beginning in late childhood prior to the onset of puberty and extending through the early stages of adolescence.

This transition period is the one about which the least is known. As early as 1944 Fritz Redl pointed out the neglect of this developmental stage by researchers—probably due to the fact that it tended to be both puzzling and disappointing for parents (Redl, 1944). More than 40 years later there continues to be little information on the preadolescent stage and limited advice to parents about it. One thing is clear—the role parents play during this period of development is crucial but confusing and sometimes unstable. When discussing the "push-pull" nature of preadolescence, Williams and Stith (1980) stated: "While [the children] are pushing away from the family, they still need the pull of the family to give security and to allow them to try out new ways of acting and relating" (p. 111).

Preadolescence was described by Redl (1944) as a period when the well-knit pattern of a child's personality is broken up or loosened so that adolescent changes can be built into it and modified into the personality of an adult, that is, the purpose of the phase is not improvement but temporary disorganization. It is a universal phenomenon, according to Redl, for preadolescents to decrease their identity with adult society and establish a strong identification with a group of peers. Therefore it is not easy to live with children of this age. They are not *really* children, even though they still appear to be so physically; they are not adolescents because most are not yet maturing sexually. Yet parents may find it difficult to accept behavior that exemplifies the urge to become self-directive, and children are trying to meet the expectations of both parents and peers without offending either.

It appears, then, that the role of parents during this stage is one that vacillates between encourager and counselor. Obviously, because peer identification is paramount, preadolescents still need the encouragement from their parents that was so necessary during middle childhood. Loyalty to gangs is evident, but rejection by the peer group can threaten the self-concept. It can, in fact, cause the preadolescent's world to disintegrate. Team sports are popular at this time, and those children who do not excel in these areas need encouragement from parents to pursue other activities that will facilitate acceptance by the peer group.

Awkwardness, restlessness, and laziness are common characteristics of preadolescents as a result of rapid and uneven growth. Accompanying behaviors may include excessive criticism, unpredictability, rebellion, and lack of cooperation in the home setting (Jenkins & Shacter, 1975). These on-and-off behaviors may result in rejection of adult standards, and they make the parenting role a difficult one. In addition to encouragement, parents need to understand the physical and emotional changes that are about to come and understand and accept peer group pressure. Counseling the child, without undue pressure, in the move toward greater independence and increased responsibility is a role that parents will begin to assume and one that will flourish as the child moves into adolescence. Condemnation for the child's choice of friends (inevitably, ones who are rejected by the parents), nagging about keeping appointed meal times and failure to do chores, and "talking down" as one might do to a younger child are nonproductive forms of parental behavior. Warmth; affection; a sense of fairness; and, most of all, a sense of humor and being a good sport are necessary in order for parents to survive.

The following preadolescent behaviors that

are likely to cause parent-child conflict were pointed out by Redl (1944) and continue to be relevant: return to infantile habits (nail biting, finger drumming, or speech problems), fantasy and wild daydreams, distrust and suspicion of adult standards, lack of consideration of adult feelings, disobeying the rules of time and space, and lack of submission to parent-accepted manners. His advice was for parents to avoid two common mistakes: defeatism or tough-guy stubbornness. The answer seems to lie somewhere in between.

Developing a Sense of Industry and an Initial Sense of Identity

Earlier we discussed the fourth stage in Erikson's (1963) theory of psychosocial development— industry versus inferiority. The early preadolescent is still in the latter part of this stage, using expanding bodily, muscular, and perceptive skills. The peer group has become far more significant now than during the early part of middle childhood, and social institutions outside the family have played a central role in the child's development. Therefore she or he has already partially developed either a sense of competence based on successful experiences or a sense of inferiority based on repeated failures and/or lack of support.

One way of furthering the more mature sense of industry during this phase is skillful planning of school and recreational programs and ac-tivities in the home. These should provide a mix of activities that facilitate a sense of competence in producing and that facilitate acceptance by the peer group (see Box 3e).

The older preadolescent will be moving toward Erikson's fifth psychosocial stage, identity versus role diffusion. Since this stage will be discussed fully in the following section, it will be discussed only briefly at this point. One obvious change that occurs when children begin to develop an initial sense of identity is that parents become representatives of the value system of adult society versus the child, and the child no longer wishes to live within the confines of the adult value system. Children will begin to question, even ridicule, family values that they have previously accepted. Give them the means, and they will create a totally utopian society.

The transition to developing a healthy sense of identity at adolescence will be easier if a sense of industry has developed smoothly. Parents, then, may see inconsistent demands made by their children as they make this transition, for example, contempt for members of the opposite sex on one occasion and lengthy discussion about members of the opposite sex with like-sex peers, usually behind closed doors, on another occasion; a preoccupation with comic books or collections one day and never-ending discussion about adult values the next day.

There is a wide range of individual differences in the maturity level of preadolescents. One has only to observe a sixth- or seventh-grade class-

---

BOX 3e RECOMMENDED RECREATIONAL ACTIVITIES FOR PREADOLESCENTS

Team games and sports
Picnics, hikes, movie/snack parties
Social dancing/folk dancing
Tennis, archery, Ping-Pong,
    swimming, riding
Band/orchestra

Hobbies/collections
Table games
Books/records
Sets (chemistry, airplanes/cars/trucks,
    construction, crafts)

Source: Williams, J., & Stith, M. (1980). *Middle childhood: Behavior and development.* New York: Macmillan.

room to notice the astounding differences in physical, social, and emotional development. Just prior to adolescence, differences between boys and girls become especially apparent. Because of this phenomenon, it is difficult to make generalizations. Suffice it to say that there is a need to both finalize a sense of industry and to begin developing a sense of identity.

Transition from Adult Code to Peer Code

The preceding discussion suggests that preadolescence represents a transition from the adult code of the parent to the peer code—a transition from dependence to independence, which will ultimately lead the child at adolescence into identity formation. The group phenomenon, or clique and gang formation, during preadolescence is essential to the child's later functioning as a citizen in society. However, the more the "gang" character is subversive of certain adult standards, the more thoroughly it is enjoyed by the child. In many cases, then, the peer code may be diametrically opposed to the adult code. Some examples include the values of cleanliness, good grades in school, obedience to adults, dress codes and hairstyles, and dirty jokes and/or language. What is labeled "good" or "bad" behavior by

parents may be labeled exactly the opposite by peers. Often the peer group behavior or code is unspoken but nevertheless strongly implied.

Few studies have focused on the extent to which preadolescents comply with peer versus parent wishes. An exception was research by Thompson (1985), which found that, overall, 9- to 11-year-olds were more parent- than peer-compliant. In values of long-term significance, preadolescents were particularly parent-compliant, but in situations related to use of free time they were peer-compliant. There were age trends in the direction of peer compliance, with boys demonstrating the greatest change over the 2-year span. However, the vast majority of children reported closeness to their parents. Perhaps greater degrees of peer compliance would be found in families where closeness is minimal or absent.

However, the change from adult code to peer code is not an easy process for a child, and it may be accompanied by conflict. While the preadolescent wants and needs to be admired and respected by his friends, he is still loyal to his family and does not want to be misunderstood by them or make them unhappy. On the other hand, if he pleases his parents and they accept him, he may run the risk of being called a "sissy" or a "coward" by his friends.

If a serious conflict develops between the two sets of standards, preadolescents may develop what Redl (1944) called "social hysteria"—they will overdo their loyalty to one of the two behavior standards. To prevent social hysteria Redl advised parents to avoid counterhysterics; interpret the cause of the behavior and judge how much and in what way to interfere rather than fight the behavior itself; create an appropriate setting for the early expression of troublesome behavior; avoid places where preadolescents are hypersensitive; and, if in doubt, make a diagnostic check-up, that is, seek professional advice. These techniques may ease the transition from adult code to peer code and make the process less painful for child and parent alike.

Developmental Needs of Parents

While preadolescents are experiencing conflicts between loyalty to parents and loyalty to peers, parents may be experiencing a similar conflict between loyalty to their children and loyalty to their spouse, careers, and own needs. Because children at this age are so acutely involved with their peers and group activities and are not yet old enough to drive, often the demands on parents for chauffeuring, chaperoning, and entertaining children's friends can become quite burdensome.

If the parent reorganized his or her life either before or when children become school age to include more emphasis on the career, educational pursuit, or social and cultural contacts outside the family, then conflicts will likely occur when demands from opposing sources become too numerous. Although it is important for parents to assist the child in finalizing a sense of industry and in beginning to develop a sense of identity, it is equally important for parents to attend to their own needs. Often a compromise between the needs of parents and the needs of their children must be reached. The growing independence of the child can be used by the parent to continue to develop a broader sense of generativity, as discussed in the preceding section.

The marital dissatisfaction that may have been experienced a few years earlier when the child entered school might now be in a recovery period as parents adjust to role changes within the family. If this is so parents who are happy with each other will find it easier to provide appropriate adult models for their children who are questioning adult standards. They will also be less inclined to be threatened by the child's erratic and inconsiderate behavior. Measures to increase and/or maintain marital satisfaction, then, seem to be especially beneficial at this time.

Perhaps the most difficult adjustment that parents must make is that of understanding and accepting the child's rejection of adult standards and her loyalty to peers. While most parents *want* their children to be independent, they wish it could be done less painfully. They wish they could impart the wisdom of experience to their children. Parents may feel guilty because they think that they have failed—otherwise the child would not reject them. The child, in turn, may feel guilty because she does love her parents but cannot bear to lose face with her friends. The resolution of this crisis is an important factor in parent-child relationships at this time. A satisfactory resolution will determine, to some extent, how parents deal with the so-called mid-life crisis, to be discussed in the next section.

PARENTS AND ADOLESCENTS

Many parents in Western society dread their children's approaching adolescence; at best they experience some degree of confusion in parenting an individual who is neither a child nor an adult. The notion that parent-adolescent conflict is inevitable has contributed to the uncertainties of parents and their general lack of enthusiasm for this stage of development. Because of the biological, cognitive, and psychosocial changes that occur in adolescence and because of the rapid social changes occurring in our society, the concept of a generation gap between parents and children is widespread. There are anthropological and sociological studies, however, indicating that adolescence itself does not universally represent a period of polarization and social difficulties. In fact, even in the United States it has been suggested that many adolescents feel respect and fondness for their parents; have value systems consistent with them; talk openly about special concerns and problems; and seek guidance on such issues as morality, education, career, and marriage (Richardson, Abramowitz, Asp, & Petersen, 1986; Sebald, 1986).

There seems to be little consensus in our society, then, on the degree of conflict that occurs between adolescents and their parents and to what extent conflict is dependent on parenting behaviors, changes in adolescents' behaviors, or social changes. It seems reasonable to assume, however, that as children reach puberty significant biological and cognitive changes affect behavior in such a way that parents themselves must make significant adjustments to their parenting roles.

The Parents' Roles As Counselors

In order to understand the changing parental role, it is important to understand what is happening to the adolescent. First, there are obvious physical and hormonal changes that occur at puberty that affect adolescent behavior. A teenager can ''go into orbit'' over a few extra pounds or hair that is too curly, too straight, or too short. The psychosocial development of a sense of identity, which will be discussed in the next section, has important implications for adolescent behavior, especially when the idealism of the teenager is incompatible with the pragmatism of the parent. And finally, significant

changes in cognitive development, often misunderstood by parents, help to explain adolescent behavior.

In a delightful manner Elkind (1978) attempted to show that early adolescent behavior attributed by parents to bad manners derives instead from intellectual immaturity. The characteristics he described are summarized in Box 3f. Because of the developmental characteristics of adolescents, which often result in behaviors that are confusing and irritating, parents must once again change their roles. While caregiving, nurturance, and encouragement continue to be important aspects of parental behavior, the primary role of the parent becomes that of counselor. An effective counselor has established positive communication with the counseled, and this aspect of the parent-child relationship is perhaps the single most important ingredient. The specifics of communication in general, and parent-child communication in particular, will be discussed in Chapter 4. However, since communication is so important during adolescence, it deserves emphasis at this point.

Communication with one's adolescent begins in the cradle. Parents begin to communicate with their infants by responding to a variety of behaviors, such as touching of genitals or even crying. The parent's tone of voice, facial expression, and specific answers to a preschooler's questions further influence the direction a com-

---

BOX 3f ADOLESCENT CHARACTERISTICS

Pseudostupidity

Appear stupid because they are too bright; capacity to conceive variety of alternatives not yet accompanied by assigning priorities in deciding appropriate choice.

Imaginary Audience Behavior

Think everyone around them equally preoccupied with adolescent's behavior/appearance and thereby become exceedingly self-conscious in presence of audience.

Personal Fable

Belief of being special and not subject to natural laws pertaining to others; and belief that own unique feelings and needs are incomprehensible to parents.

Source: Elkind, D. (1978). Understanding the young adolescent. *Adolescence, 13*(40), 127–134.

munication system will take. Tolerance of others' opinions and acceptance of school-age children's feelings and attitudes assist in keeping channels of communication open. In short, by the time a child reaches adolescence, the communications system in the family can already be described as open or closed, determining how comfortable the teenager will feel in discussing openly her other concerns and problems with the parents.

The family's communication system is important in influencing adolescents' willingness to disclose themselves (sharing personal information about themselves with others). Disclosure, despite risk, and openness to positive feedback have been established as two aspects of the relationship between parents and teenagers (Klos & Paddock, 1978). Disclosure by adolescents has been associated with positive feelings toward parents and highly correlated with adolescents' perceptions of their parents as warm, affectionate, and nurturant (Klos & Paddock, 1978; Snalk & Rothblum, 1979). In addition both disclosure and openness to feedback were significantly related to the adolescent's perceiving her parents as casual and easygoing instead of strict and punitive (Klos & Paddock, 1978).

Self-concept appears to have an effect on communication patterns within the family. It has been suggested that those adolescents who have poor self-concepts perceive communicaiton with their parents as significantly more nonconstructive than do adolescents with better self-concepts. Also, mothers' own self-concepts seem to significantly influence daughters' perceived communication with their parents, but the same does not appear to apply for fathers and children (Flora, 1978).

Two recent studies by Gecas and Schwalbe (1986) and Hoelter and Harper (1987) emphasized the parent-adolescent relationship and self-concept. The first examined perceptions of parental behavior as reported by parents and perceptions as reported by adolescents themselves. Adolescent self-esteem was more strongly related to the adolescents' perceptions of parental behavior (control, support, and participation) than it was to parental reports of their behavior, with perceptions of fathers' behavior being more consequential than perceptions of mothers' behavior, especially for boys. Girls'

self-esteem was not affected by the degree of parental control but was more related to support and participation. On the other hand, boys' self-esteem was highly related to parental control, especially by the father. The second study also found that family support exerted the most influence on adolescents' self-esteem as well as on their son/daughter identity. The findings were applicable for both girls and boys.

Adolescents' perception of their parents as warm, affectionate, committed, and supportive appear to be related to the absence of disturbance and/or delinquent behavior as well. When these perceptions are absent, depression among adolescents is more prevalent (Blatt, Wein, Chevron, & Quinlan, 1979) and delinquency is more common (Smith & Walters, 1978). It has been suggested, in fact, that disturbance occurs less as a consequence of misfortune, hurt, and/or pathogenic influence than from the omission of positive resources (Kagel, White, & Coyne, 1978). Fathers as well as mothers have influence on adolescent behaviors.

An interesting study concerning the perception of male adolescents' feelings of whether they were understood by their fathers was conducted by Roll and Millen (1978). The boys who felt understood perceived that the time spent with their fathers was pleasurable, with shared common interests, as opposed to conflictual and consisting of activities that were forced and unwanted, as perceived by boys who felt misunderstood. Understood boys viewed their fathers' administration of discipline as being reasonable, whereas misunderstood boys saw their fathers as being irrational and unfair, with fear of punishment acting as a barrier to developing a close relationship. Finally, understood boys felt that their fathers' encouragement of their independence increased the closeness between father and son, but misunderstood boys felt that continual conflict between their mothers and fathers contributed to the deterioration of the father-son relationship.

At adolescence *parental power* that is based on coercion is not enforceable and cannot be legitimized (Baumrind, 1978). In fact, the greater the degree of parental power and authority, the greater the conflict between parent and child (Ellis, 1977). Treatment of adolescents that is harsh, arbitrary, and exploitative is strongly associated with antisocial rather than prosocial aggression. Punitive approaches to discipline (including verbal and physical abuse and unreasonable deprivation of privileges) are associated with low expressions of guilt and an external orientation to transgression and noncompliance (Baumrind, 1978).

Peer influence. Inevitably in adolescence occasions will arise when parents and children will disagree about what is appropriate behavior. Because of the adolescent's desire to establish a sense of identity and increasing degrees of independence, peers will exert more influence than in the past. When parents and peers are in agreement, a particular behavior in question is most likely to occur. If, however, parents and peers disagree, their respective influence varies with the issue involved and with the sex of the child.

Sebald (1986) found that teenagers turned to different social sets, not necessarily in conflict with one another, for different issues, questions, and needs. For example, in matters of finances, education, and career plans, adolescents seek advice or counsel from their parents. For the specifics of their social life (dress, dating, drinking, social events, and joining clubs) they clearly want to be attuned to the standards of their peers. These data denote equally important dual reference groups for teenagers. Since Sebald's study was longitudinal, he found some striking changes over time, especially in gender differences. For example, in the 1970s girls showed greater parent orientation and less peer orientation, while the reverse was true for boys. However, by the 1980s girls exceeded the boys in peer orientation.

Based on the evidence presented above, it appears that the parental role of counselor is characterized by allowing increasing independence by maintaining an atmosphere of warmth, affection, support, and understanding; by maintaining a positive communication system that involves self-disclosure and openness to feedback by both parents and adolescents; by limiting parental power and authority based on coercion; and by recognizing the influence of peers. If these conditions exist, adolescents who have previously internalized the values of their families and the larger society will, in most instances, continue to accept as legitimate the standards for behavior set by their parents.

Developing a Sense of Identity

The fifth stage in Erikson's (1963) theory of psychosocial development is identity versus role confusion, which corresponds to adolescence. As the adolescent matures physiologically, he experiences new feelings, sensations, and desires; and as he matures mentally, he develops a multitude of ways of looking at and thinking about the world (Elkind, 1970). Adolescents, in their crucial task of searching for identity formation, might be described as impatient idealists who believe there is little difficulty in realizing an imagined ideal. They become capable of constructing theories and philosophies designed to bring the varied and conflicting aspects of society into a harmonious whole.

By ego identity Erikson meant that, under a variety of circumstances, an individual's mind has a certain recognizable quality or character all its own, but in a certain measure it can be shared thoroughly with others (Coles, 1970). The adolescent's effort to formulate an identity involves the ego's ability to integrate the demands of the libido, the abilities she has developed from natural capacities, and the numerous opportunities offered by available social roles (Bernard, 1981). Further, adolescence may be seen as a time when all the crises of the previous stages are relived, and those of future stages are rehearsed, as the individual integrates previously acquired identifications with future aspirations into a cohesive ego identity. In Erikson's view, then, adolescence is a socially authorized delay of adulthood in which the individual has time to integrate herself into adulthood.

Adolescent identity strivings may result in the assumption of nonconforming roles, membership in cliques, adoption of faddish signs and styles that mark one as an "in-grouper," and/or experimenting with diverse ideologies. In addition, the sexual identity is rehearsed and tested during a period of first courtships. The final task for the adolescent is to bring together all the things he has learned about himself and to integrate all the images into a whole that makes sense as well as shows continuity with the past while preparing for the future. Erikson's discussion of identity, then, focuses on work, sex-role identity and sexuality, and ideology (Klos & Paddock, 1978).

If a child reaches adolescence with a sense of trust, autonomy, initiative, and industry, then her chances of arriving at a meaningful sense of identity are greatly enhanced. Preparation for a successful adolescence and the attainment of an integrated psychosocial identity must, therefore, begin in childhood. On the other hand, failure to attain a sense of personal identity results in identity or role confusion, which has been associated with severe emotional upheavals and delinquency.

Several investigators have reported evidence of the relationship between successful resolution of the identity crisis and overall psychological adjustment. Specifically, more high-identity older adolescents tend to have open life-styles, score significantly higher in internal control, show less vulnerability to fluctuation in self-esteem, and demonstrate less anxiety than their low-identity counterparts do. Further, studies have indicated that there are differences in the cognitive characteristics and academic performance of low- and high-identity adolescents (Bernard, 1981). Those individuals with high identity did significantly better on measures of learning and perseverance and had higher grade-point averages.

Questions have been raised concerning the differences between male and female adolescents in their evolution toward identity formation. It seems that the process of identity formation in males reflects the cultural expectations of autonomy and personality differentiation. For females, on the other hand, the process reflects the cultural expectation of establishing an intimacy relationship (Josselson, Greenberger, & McConochie, 1977; Matteson, 1975). Further, experiencing a crisis seems to be adaptive for males and maladaptive for females (Bernard, 1981). Therefore the literature suggests the existence of traditional sex-role stereotypes in identity formation, which may mean that a sense of identity and a sense of intimacy are more clearly differentiated for males than for females. One exception in the literature is Orlofsky's study

(1977), which found that for both males and females an androgynous orientation was conducive to identity achievement and self-esteem. Supporting the importance of parents' roles, fairly consistent results have been found in studies relating to the parent-child relationship and its effect on identity formation in adolescence (Bernard, 1981). There seems to be a negative relationship between ego identity and parent-child problems, particularly in mother-daughter relationships. Warm, supportive parents who use consistent rule enforcement seem to produce high-identity adolescents who are independent and self-directed. It therefore appears that the nature and quality of the parent-child relationship is an important factor in how the adolescent resolves the identity crisis.

Finally, the social milieu seems to affect the development of a sense of personal identity. When rapid social and technological changes occur that affect traditional values, the adolescent may have difficulty finding continuity between what he or she has learned or experienced as a child and what he or she is experiencing as an adolescent. The search for causes that give life meaning and direction may result in activism, cultism, or other forms of behavior that are confusing to parents (Elkind, 1970). Another interesting notion is that the present need for longer periods of education for adolescents may limit their experiences with the outside world and cause them to remain economically dependent on parents at a stage when they want to be independent and work out their own identity.

The task of identity formation may be difficult for adolescents and trying for parents, but it is doubtlessly an essential task if the individual is ultimately to function as a decision-making adult.

The Prevention and Resolution of Conflict

The degree of parent-adolescent conflict ranges from absence or near absence to extreme integenerational hostility, with few societies experiencing an intense struggle. At least three variables appear to affect the extent of conflict (Ellis, 1977): Conflict is greater in periods of rapid social change, it is greater where there is delay in granting adult status to adolescents, and it is greater when there is a high degree of parental power and authority. These variables help to explain the range of conflict among societies and, to a lesser degree, among families in our own society. Even if adolescents accept the dominant values and culture, they often are not allowed to enter the society in a responsible way and are exposed to contradictory expectations and demands from adults (Ellis, 1977). Thus conflict results.

Further, there is evidence to suggest that teenagers in the United States today experience more situations of stress and crises than did teens in the past, and many adolescents choose maladaptive behaviors in the adjustment process. When situational crises are combined with developmental crises during adolescence, the stress and conflict may become intense. Evidence of adolescent stress is manifested in the increasing rates of teenage suicide, eating disorders, drug use, pregnancy, and runaways.

Adolescent rebellion. Traditionally conflict between parents and adolescents has been attributed to adolescent rebellion. There is no consensus on how universal this rebellion is, but the phenomenon in our society has been attributed to the following variety of factors: restriction and postponement of sexual expression, confusion about the adolescent's economic role, the necessity to make life choices that may be conflicting, impending departure from the family, the failure of schools to fulfill the adolescent's needs, the difficulty in choosing a life occupation, authoritarian child rearing, excessive dominance of one parent, extremely restrictive or permissive parental practices, and discord between parents (Clemens & Rust, 1979). The present section will focus on those variables that are directly related to parents' attitudes and behaviors.

Two major aspects of parent behavior seem to be related to adolescent rebellion and to the degree of conflict between adolescents and their parents—the level of parental interest and involvement with teenagers and the types and degree of parental control used. Peterson (1977) compared parent-teen relationships in studies conducted 8 years apart. He concluded that during those years there was an increase in both parental interest (the degree of concern or regard parents have for their children) and parental control (attempts to modify or direct their children in accordance with predetermined standards of conduct). Consistently the mother was seen to display greater interest and control than the father, regardless of the child's sex. Further, results of of the second study showed a greater difference in the levels of interest in and control over boys than girls compared to 8 years earlier. Clearly these two aspects of the parent-adolescent relationship change over time and are probably related to such societal variables as greater sexual permissiveness and the increased availability of drugs.

Baumrind (1978) contended that low parental interest and involvement, even more than parental harshness, at early adolescence may be associated with negative outcomes and low self-esteem. Rejecting and neglecting attitudes by parents have been associated with delinquency, and parents who have difficulty controlling their adolescents have been shown to be less likely to take an interest in their children's activities. In fact, fathers of adolescent boys who were on probation showed a significantly higher degree of hostile detachment than did fathers of normal, well-behaved boys (Robinson, 1978). It seems that active interest and involvement in adolescent activities, then, is crucial in reducing and solving conflicts. Simple attitudes and behaviors, such as knowing the names of the teenager's friends; being interested (not nosy) in where they go and what they do; welcoming friends into the home; and participating in school, athletic, and social events facilitate the teenager's perception of parental interest and involvement.

We have previously discussed the merits of the democratic style of child rearing in terms of its effects on children. However, in adolescence it appears even more critical for parents to be warm, accepting, nurturant, supportive, and autonomy-granting. It has been noted that the acceptance dimension of parent-child relationships in adolescence is a key antecedent to socialization and empathy, two aspects of moral development. In fact, acceptance appears to supersede other variables in the parent-child interaction. Further, a high degree of control seems to represent a counterproductive influence on adolescents' moral character development (Hower & Edwards, 1979). That is not to say that limits are not clearly defined and maintained, but that the democratic process involves joint decision making, respect for the opinions of teenagers, and a lack of unjustified control by parents (Ellis, 1977). Parents who have difficulty controlling their adolescents have been shown to be less likely to use praise and encouragement and more likely to be inconsistent in setting and enforcing rules and limits (Robinson, 1978). Excessive permissiveness *or* excessive control by parents has been shown to be related to adolescent rebellion and deviance and thus to conflict. Almost twice as many dissatisfied as satisfied teens in the Clemens and Rust study (1979) reported that their parents were authoritarian. Further, adolescents whose parents did not normally use hostile psychological control techniques and who were more accepting tended to display higher achievement motivation. Firm limits seem to be more important for boys than girls in relation to achievement motivation (Nuttall & Nuttall, 1976). Finally, adolescent rebellion has been found to be the product of a home thought to be patriarchal and unhappy, patriarchal and very restrictive, or patriarchal and extremely permissive. The least rebellion was found in homes where one parent had slight authority over the other but did not usurp the power of the other (Balswick & Macrides, 1975).

Adolescents' perceptions of parents. It should be emphasized at this point that the teenager's perceptions of the parents' attitudes and behaviors are equally as important as the actual attitudes and behaviors. Several studies have shown that there may be discrepancies between what actually occurs and the teenager's perceptions as well as discrepancies between reported perceptions of the parents and reported perceptions of adolescents (Coleman, George, & Holt, 1977; Hamid & Wyllie, 1980; Robinson, 1978).

For example, Callan and Noller (1987) videotaped a family triad (mother, father, and their 12-year-old adolescent) in two discussion/communication segments. Immediately following the taping each family member rated each of the two other members as well as him or herself on scales of dominance, friendliness, anxie-

ty, and involvement. Results indicated that adolescents rated their parents as more anxious, less involved, and less dominant than parents rated themselves. It was suggested that adolescents possibly overestimate negative features of family life, whereas parents overestimate socially desirable aspects. However, adolescents and parents did not differ in their perceptions of friendliness. There were complex interactions between sex of the child, parents' level of marital quality, and perceptions of family interaction, suggesting the need for further research into these relationships.

In general adolescents tend to perceive lower levels of intimacy and independence, greater differences in characteristics, and slightly higher levels of conflict with their parents than parents themselves perceive. If teens approve of the way they are being reared and their perceptions are consistent with those of their parents, then rebellion is less likely to occur (Clemens & Rust, 1979). It may be important, then, for parents and adolescents to communicate the perceptions each has concerning the parent-child relationship.

One aspect of parent-adolescent conflict that cannot be overlooked is the differential relationships that occur with sex of the parent and sex of the child. Traditionally mothers have been more active participants in child rearing for both boys and girls than fathers have. We have already emphasized the importance of fathers in active child rearing, and this importance extends into adolescence. A study of depression in adolescent females revealed that the least vulnerability to depression existed when there was consistent paternal love, low conflict, and paternal dominance. In fact, the father's consistency was more important than the mother's consistency (Schwarz & Zuroff, 1979).

Several studies have indicated that relationships with the father are crucial for the healthy development of both adolescent boys and girls. Boys who receive less than adequate affection from fathers are less secure, less self-confident, and more distant from their fathers. A recent study examined the retrospective attitudes of normal male and female college students toward their parents. The results indicated that 41 percent reported that their emotional needs were unmet in childhood. Dissatisfaction with parental nurturing was high, but it was significantly higher for fathers (Zeidler, Nardine, Scolare, & Mich, 1987).

Smith (1983) found that mothers in his study tended to exert more control over their adolescents than the fathers did, and children demonstrated greater resistance to maternal attempts at control than to paternal attempts. It was suggested that adolescents may hold sex-role conceptions that define a high level of attempted control as more appropriate for men than for women. Further, it was found that adolescent compliance was minimized, but emotional acceptance of parents maximized when persuasion techniques without the use of commands were used. On the other hand, commands were more likely than persuasion to result in expressions of resentment by teenagers but also more likely to result in compliance.

When stress and conflict occur, the use of defense mechanisms inevitably follows. Erikson (1963) contended that males are psychologically oriented toward the external world and females are oriented internally. Studies of defense mechanisms used by younger and older adolescents show that males tend to use more "turning against the object" and "projection" techniques, whereas females use more "turning against the self," "intellectualizing," and "rationalizing" techniques. Cramer (1979) suggested that males, then, begin to externalize conflict, relying on projection and/or direct, overt aggression as defensive reactions, and that females rely on defenses that internalize the conflict, primarily through directing aggression inward. An understanding of these possible sex differences in reaction to conflict can be helpful to parents in resolving conflict.

There are several areas in which conflict is likely to occur between parents and adolescents. Some have to do with differences in attitudes relating to assuming responsibility, curfews, financial arrangements, use of the car, academic performance, tidiness, dress and grooming, choice of friends, and so on. While these differences can become real issues of conflict, they are easier to resolve than larger issues of morality or ideology. Obviously, joint decision making regarding traits and behaviors that are relevant to sharing the same roof is necessary. Mutual understanding and respect between parents and children, reasonable and consistent rule enforcement, and an interest and involvement in the teenagers' activities will facilitate resolution of minor differences and minimize conflict. However, two problems that currently cause much greater conflict between adolescents and their parents are sexual activity and the use of drugs and/or alcohol.

Adolescent sexuality. Parental influence on adolescent sexual behavior is presumed to begin in early childhood, but the effect of the parent-child relationship is not entirely clear. While a poor parent-child relationship has been suggested as being linked to incidence of sexual intercourse, no evidence exists to show that a good parent-child relationship inhibits it (Walters & Walters, 1980). One aspect of a positive relationship is openness in communication. Almost all parents and their teenage children agree that teenagers should get full and accurate information concerning sex, contraceptives, teenage pregnancy, and abortion, and that this information should come from parents. Further, both teenagers and parents are in favor of more open discussions concerning these topics (Family Planning Perspectives, 1979). Nevertheless, many studies have noted that most parents do not discuss sexual topics with their children. In their 10-year review, Walters & Walters (1980) indicated that discussions of sexuality in the home seems to be related to the postponement of sexual activity and to the responsible use of contraceptives. Specifically, as the number of sex topics discussed by parents increased, the likelihood for engaging in intercourse decreased.

A more recent study by Moore, Peterson, and Furstenberg (1986), however, suggests that the relationship between communication and sexual activity is more complicated. These researchers found that parental discussion/communication was associated with less frequent early initiation of sexual activity only for females of parents with traditional values. Communication seemed to have little impact on children of both sexes of parents with nontraditional beliefs. Further, they suggested that the topic of sex is raised with sons in traditional families only after sons become sexually active, and therefore it serves to delay sex only for daughters. Finally, parents did not express their attitudes as readily or as explicitly to their sons as to their daughters, since only 17 percent of all sons in the study, as opposed to 67 percent of all daughters, reported discussing sex with either parent. Therefore it could be concluded that the effects of family communication on adolescent sexuality depend on the gender of the child and on the parental beliefs and value systems.

Newcomer and Udry (1987) investigated the relationship of parental marital status on the initiation of sexual activity by adolescents. Their data were collected at two time periods, 2 years apart. Results indicated that boys whose parents had divorced during the 2-year time period were more likely than other boys or girls to have initiated sexual activity. However, girls being reared by mothers only were more likely at both time periods to be sexually active. Therefore family disruption was the important variable for boys, whereas the state of maternal single parenthood was more significant for girls.

Both research and conventional wisdom suggest that adolescent nonmarital sexual activity began to increase sharply in the 1960s and still remains at a high level. This increase has been attributed to a variety of sociological, psychological, and biological variables (see Box 3g).

It has been reported that approximately 20 percent of single, sexually active women have never used contraceptives, but 40 percent always use them. The reasons given for failure to use

---

BOX 3g   VARIABLES RELATED TO ADOLESCENT SEXUAL ACTIVITY

Social

Low level of religious orientation
Permissive societal social norms
Poverty and racism
Migration
Single-parent families
Peer group pressure

Psychological

Use of drugs/alcohol
Poor educational achievement
Permissive parental attitude
Poor communication with parents
Risk-taking attitudes
Going steady, being in love
Low self-esteem, desire for affection, social criticism, passivity/dependence (females)
Aggression, high degree of interpersonal skills with opposite sex (males)

Biological

Older than 16
Early puberty

Source: Chilman, C. (1980, November). Social and psychological research concerning adolescent child-bearing: 1970–1980. *Journal of Marriage and the Family,* pp. 793–805.

contraceptives were numerous, including ignorance; religious beliefs; and sporadic, noncommitted relationships. (Chilman, 1980).

It appears, then, that there are many variables related to adolescent sexual activity, and some of them vary by sex. Further, some are outside the control of parents. While it is not completely clear what the direct influence of parents is on teenage sexual activity, it does seem clear that a positive parent-child relationship—particularly open communication and full and accurate information from parents about sex, contraceptives, pregnancy, and so forth—facilitate responsible sexual behavior in adolescents.

Adolescent drug use. "In contemporary western society perhaps no other behavior distinguishes between different generations as dramatically as the use of illicit drugs" (Kandel, 1978, p. 374). For the American population marijuana use begins in the early teens, peaks at ages 18–24, and decreases sharply thereafter (Kandel, 1978). Adolescent drug use has been related to three sets of factors: the personality characteristics of the adolescent, parental socialization, and peer group activity. Each set of factors has an independent relationship to drug use. In terms of the first set, drug users spend less time on school work, are more likely to skip school, and are less likely to get good grades (cause or effect?). Further, they are more involved in nonconforming acts, less likely to attend religious services, more likely to hold radical political beliefs, participate in more minor and major types of delinquent acts, and are more likely to be depressed and dissatisfied with themselves (Kandel, 1978). Finally, psychological distress is a significant precursor to greater drug involvement (Huba, Newcomb, & Bentler, 1986).

In addition, tolerance of deviance, irresponsibility, internal lack of control, interpersonal aggression, and cognitive style of receptivity and change are other adolescent personality factors related to drug use (Brook, Gordon, & Brook, 1980; Brook, Lukoff, & Whiteman, 1978). It is difficult to determine just how and to what extent these characteristics cause drug use and how and to what extent they are the result of it. It

has been pointed out that the use of drugs by adolescents may be secondary to other problems involving the whole family, and that drug abuse should be considered a family problem since the adolescent is part of a dysfunctional family system (Gantman, 1978). Family characteristics associated with drug use are the degree of parental affection, concern, and involvement, but little correlation has been found between drug use and parental discipline or control (Hundleby & Mercer, 1987).

Several studies have compared parent-child interactions in families with drug users and nonusers. Marijuana use seems to be influenced by the amount of structure the family provides for the adolescent (the emphasis on rules), and the adolescent's acceptance of these rules. Further, more assertive mothers have been shown to have a fewer number of marijuana-using children (Brook, Lukoff, & Whiteman, 1978). Another study indicated that families with nonusers were significantly more accurate in their perceptions of family members toward each other, engaged in more decision-making processes, produced significantly more positive communications, and allowed more freedom for members to express themselves. In addition, there was more cooperation, more equal participation, clarity of communication, and sensitivity to each other (Gantman, 1978).

Miller (1976) noted that adolescent male drug use seems to be more related to environmental variables such as experimentation, curiosity, and group conformity, whereas females are more affected by parent-child relationships and self-image attitudes. The female "present" drug users in the Miller study perceived their mothers as being less loving, more rejecting, neglecting, demanding, less rewarding, and more punishing than female "never" users. These same relationships did not apply between females and fathers. Female "never" users saw their relationships with both parents as being more loved and less rejected, demanded of, neglected, and protected than did male subjects. The users had poor self-images and regarded their environment as aggressive and hostile. Male users did not share these characteristics. On the other hand, a study by Brook and associates (1980) indicated

that differences in paternal handling do account for some of the variance in daughters' behavior. They found that fathers who are affectionate and child-centered and whose daughters identify with them are less likely to have marijuana-using daughters.

It appears, then, that both fathers and mothers have a significant and individual effect on adolescent drug use, perhaps in varying ways and degrees to sons and daughters. Baumrind (1978) contended that adolescent drug use was less common in traditional families where parents both discipline their children and spend much time with them and for whom religion plays an ongoing part in family and community life.

A third set of factors related to drug use is peer activity. Several studies have suggested that the strongest predictor of drug use is the extent to which one's friends consume drugs (Hundleby & Mercer, 1987). Marijuana use by the adolescent's best friend is one of the most important predictions of initiation into marijuana use by a prior nonuser, and use of other illicit drugs by one's friends is a major predictor of initiation into those illicit drugs among prior marijuana users (Kandel, 1978). Further, drug-using adolescents are more likely to interact frequently with their friends and to be distant from their parents than nonusers are.

However, it should not be inferred that high peer group interaction necessarily means rejection of parents and entrance into the drug subculture. The use or nonuse of drugs is more strongly related to a negative orientation to parents than to the strength of integration in a peer subgroup. When most of their friends are marijuana users, adolescents are more likely to be drug users themselves, even if they are not highly involved in an extensive network of peers, and adolescents in marijuana-using peer groups are also extensive users of illicit drugs. However, despite high involvement with their age-mates, adolescents in non-drug-using groups do not exhibit the estrangement from parents that characterizes adolescents in drug-using groups (Kandel, 1978).

It appears, then, that adolescent personality attributes, parental attitudes and behaviors, and peer activity have an independent impact on drug use. Thus use may occur in the face of any one set of factors but is compounded by the interaction of all three.

Most drug prevention programs have focused on the negative consequences of ingesting drugs. However, the study by Huba, Newcomb, and Bentler (1986) found that the knowledge, or even the experience, of a negative reaction is not sufficient to decrease drug use. Therefore more broadly based programs that combine information with a focus on resisting peer influences and decreasing psychological distress are needed.

Since the 1970s the concern about adolescents' use of alcohol has increased. Barnes, Farrell, and Cairns (1986) found that adolescents' drinking patterns, under certain conditions, reflect the drinking patterns of their parents. Abstaining mothers are more likely to have abstaining children than are mothers who drink moderately or heavily. Likewise, mothers who drink heavily have teenagers with the highest rate of drinking. Interestingly, however, abstaining mothers also were found to have high rates of heavy-drinking adolescents, suggesting that in a sociocultural context where drinking is a normative behavior, both extremes of maternal models of drinking may have negative effects on the behavior of teenagers. Equally important to the modeling function, parental support and nurturance are key factors in preventing alcohol abuse.

PROGRAMS FOR PARENTS OF ADOLESCENTS

Given the difficulties that many parents face at this particular stage in the life cycle, it is ironic that so few formalized parent-education programs exist specifically for parents of adolescents. It is true that most of the contemporary strategies of parenting described in Chapter 5 can be used with adolescents as well as with younger children. However, the majority of programs that use these strategies involve parents of children younger than adolescents. It is our contention that parents of adolescents are in critical need of some form of education, whether it be discussion groups, development of skills in behavior management, or an emphasis on maintaining positive communication.

Much of what currently exists for parents of adolescents is therapeutic in nature. Clinics sponsor parent-adolescent counseling sessions *after* the child is in trouble; mental-health agencies require parents and teenagers to participate in drug abuse programs *after* the child's achievement begins to lag. There seems to be very little preventive parent education available anywhere. Parents do have a rather wide selection of printed materials to choose from regarding the characteristics of adolescence and suggestions for positive

parent-adolescent interaction—newspaper articles, paperbacks, popular magazines, and so on. But there seems to be a void in support groups, discussion groups, and in preparing parents for the changes that will occur in their own lives and those of their children when they reach adolescence.

Programs for parents of normal adolescents should focus on the biological and psychological changes occurring at this stage of development and ways to facilitate healthy development. Helping parents to fulfill more effectively their roles as counselors by, for example, practicing communication skills and developing a balance between freedom and responsibility for their children would seem to be helpful. Talking with other parents about current teenage trends in music, dress, and leisure activities may help parents to be more accepting. Making an effort to get acquainted with the parents of children's friends can provide a support network. Clearly there is a need for programs that are preventive in nature if parents are to facilitate successfully their offspring's transition from child to adult.

DEVELOPMENTAL NEEDS OF PARENTS

Until recently little emphasis has been placed on adult development in the sociological and psychological literature. The crucial events of one's life were assumed to occur from birth through adolescence, virtually ending with the establishment of a sense of identity in late adolescence or early adulthood. After that a period of stabilization was believed to set in, characterized by relatively uneventful changes. While earlier theorists such as Erikson, Havighurst, and Duvall described developmental changes or tasks throughout the life cycle, the concept of adult developmental crises was not emphasized. Recently, however, emphasis has been placed on adult development, beginning with marriage and proceeding through death (Cook, 1983; Van Hoose & Worth, 1982; Walsh, 1983; Whitbourne & Weinstock, 1979). From the standpoint of parenting, these perspectives clearly indicate that significant changes occur in parents from the time their children are born until they "leave the nest" and that developmental crises occur for adults as well as for children.

Parents with teenagers have recently been described as approaching a time in their lives that may be as crucial as adolescence itself, quite apart from the fact that they are parents of teenagers. This period has been aptly termed "middlescence" by Gerald Nachman (1979). Normally it occurs between the ages of 35 and 45, with women experiencing it somewhat earlier than men (Levinson, Darrow, Klein, Levinson, & McKee,1979; Sheehy, 1976). The mid-life transition is the turning point between earlier and later periods of stability (Levinson et al., 1979). It is the "deadline decade" in which men and women take a serious look at what they are and what they want to be—the gap between the ideal and the realized self—preoccupied with the realization that it is a last-ditch effort to close this gap. In other words it is an authenticity or affirmation crisis, not completely unlike the identity crisis that the adolescent herself is experiencing. Preceding the transition to a period of restabilization in middle adulthood, there is a sense of constraint and oppression. For men and women who are employed, constraint and oppression may be experienced in work and, for both, perhaps, in the marriage and/or in other relationships. It is compounded by a feeling of bodily decline ("I'm not as attractive and appealing as I once was"), a recognition of one's mortality, a sense of aging, and a feeling that time is running out. These feelings are verified by the existence in novelty shops of materials to celebrate an "Over the Hill" party on one's fortieth birthday.

At the same time adolescent children are occupying their parents' time and thoughts less and less. Parents, particularly the mother, may be searching for something to fill the gap. Often the father in the mid-life crisis who has neglected spending time with his child or children over the years begins to feel a sense of guilt. Rossi (1968) has described the period before the children leave home as the disengagement-termination stage; Rhodes (1977) has called the developmental crisis for parents at this time companionship versus isolation; and Galinsky (1980) has referred to this period as the interdependent stage. These

theorists stress the idea that parents must reinvest in each other as companions, that parents' authority over their children must be redefined, and that there must be a gradual shift toward the child's financial and emotional independence.

When adolescents begin to leave home, somewhere between the ages of 16 and 22, parents may experience the "empty-nest" syndrome (Duvall, 1977), and mothers and fathers may react to it in very different ways. During this departure stage (Galinsky, 1980), both parents must evaluate their experiences and review their own strengths and weaknesses, followed by the formation of an adult-adult relationship with their children. Thus the developmental crisis of regrouping versus binding or expulsion occurs (Rhodes, 1977).

It is difficult to make generalizations concerning both the timing and the intensity of the mid-life crisis. If there are several children in the family, the crisis may be delayed for those parents still actively rearing younger children. This may be especially true for women who experience a significant portion of their rewards from mothering. The intensity of the mid-life crisis may be affected by the degree to which the marital relationship is satisfying and "the goodness of fit between the life structure and the self" (Levinson et al., 1979, p. 289).

Another factor that may be related to the timing and intensity of the crisis is the structure of the family. In nontraditional families (for example, single-parent families, blended families, stepfamilies, or families that began when the parents were themselves teens) the nature of the mid-life crisis may be quite different, since it is compounded by a host of other variables. If a single mother has had custody of her children for several years, she may have experienced the need for authenticity and affirmation much sooner than the "deadline decade." The noncustodial father may have separated himself from his child or children physically and/or psychologically long before they became teenagers so that the "empty-nest" syndrome is not one with which he must cope. Parents in blended families have already experienced a reorganization process that may well ward off much of the stereotypic adjustment described as necessary in traditional nuclear families. Parents of teenagers who were teens themselves when their children were born may be in an entirely different stage of development than older parents. It is probably safe to assume that these families have experienced, over time, a higher degree of stress and a quest for identity that may be quite dissimilar from other families' experience.

Many parents, however, are experiencing a kind of identity crisis themselves at nearly the same time their teenagers are searching for a sense of identity. Much of the literature concerning parent-adolescent conflict has failed to recognize the implications of such a phenomenon.

Again we emphasize that there is a reciprocal relationship that is developmental in nature between parent and child at every stage. We must consider to what extent the developmental needs of parents affect, either positively or negatively, the parent-teen relationship, as well as to what extent teens contribute to the socialization of their parents. Peters (1985) addressed specific areas in which adolescents affect and change attitudes and behaviors of their parents. This approach departs from the view of the child as the socializee and the parents as the socialization agents, which implies a marked status difference between the superior parent and the subordinate child. Rather it argues for a bidirectional or reciprocal nature of socialization. Peters found that considerable influence of adolescents on both mothers and fathers occurred in the areas of sports, personal care, and leisure activities. Further, notable changes were reported by parents in attitudes toward youth, sexuality, minorities, and handicapped individuals: 81 percent reported some additudinal changes, 60 percent reported change in participation levels, and 56 percent reported behavioral change. Peters concluded that these changes are not minor or incidental in our society but are marked, constituting resocialization of parents at this stage of the life cycle.

It has been pointed out that the crises experienced by adults make it possible to effect changes in personality. A woman may become more assertive; a man may become more nurturant; and, more important, both men and women may come to love themselves more, that is, to learn to value those things in the self formerly devalued (Levinson et al., 1979; Sheehy, 1976). The end result of the mid-life crisis need not, then, have negative implications. Parents do have more time for self-development when their children are adolescents. More meaningful personal relationships can be developed; more creative endeavors can be demonstrated; greater participation in social and cultural activities can become possible. If parents take advantage of these alternatives, they provide their teenagers as well as themselves with an opportunity for a healthy growth process. It is unfortunate that initially teenagers are generally insensitive to and intolerant of the developmental needs of their parents. It is inconceivable to them that parents share many romantic fantasies similar to their own. But when adolescents observe their parents reorganizing their life structure in a healthy way, the impact on their own growth process is phenomenal.

In summary, parents of adolescents demonstrate developmental needs that may be equal in importance to the developmental needs of adolescents. The interaction of parents and their children at this stage of development is influenced to a great degree by the needs of both and by the manner in which each seeks to satisfy his or her needs. If parents complete the development of a sense of generativity at this time and successfully regroup themselves, they will be able to move into their later years with a sense of integrity rather than a sense of despair.

SUMMARY

Parenting is a complex reciprocal relationship that manifests developmental change by all the individuals who are involved in the process. During the school years children become exposed to a diverse social milieu, and their broader experiences necessitate adaptive parental patterns. Encouragement seems to be a crucial parental characteristic as children develop a sense of industry and a healthy self-concept. The vacillating, unstable behavior of preadolescents may cause parents some confusion as they attempt to demonstrate patience and understanding.

As adolescence ensues, the prevention and

resolution of conflict becomes a primary task. Peer pressure may create differences over minor issues related to dress, punctuality, or assuming responsibility, but some parents experience especially grave concern over adolescent sexuality and/or drug and alcohol use. Positive communication, with parents assuming the role of counselor, seems to be a necessary ingredient to a solution.

Parents themselves have significant developmental needs as their children progress through latency and puberty, and recognition of these needs may offset some of the conflict that characterizes this period.

REFERENCES

ABELMAN, R. (1986). Children's awareness of television's prosocial fare. *Journal of Family Issues, 7*(1), 51–66.

AMATO, P. (1986). Marital conflict, the parent-child relationship, and child self-esteem. *Family Relations, 35,* 403–410.

AMATO, P., & OCHILTREE, G. (1986). Family resources and the development of child competence. *Journal of Marriage and the Family, 48*(1), 47–55.

ATKIN, C., & GANTZ, W. (1975). The role of television news in the political socialization of children. Paper presented at the annual meeting of the International Communication Association, Chicago.

BALSWICK, J., & MACRIDES, C. (1975). Parental stimulus for adolescent rebellion. *Adolescence, 10,* 253–266.

BARNES, G., FARRELL, M., & CAIRNS, A. (1986). Parental socialization factors and adolescent drinking behaviors. *Journal of Marriage and the Family, 48*(1), 27–35.

BAUMRIND, D. (1978). Parental disciplinary patterns and social competence in children. *Youth and Society, 9*(3), 239–276.

BERNARD, H. (1981). Identity formation during late adolescence: A review of some empirical findings. *Adolescence, 16*(62), 349–358.

BERNDT, T. (1979). Developmental changes in conformity to peers and parents. *Developmental Psychology 15*(6), 608–616.

BERNDT, T., & BULLEIT, T. (1985). Effects of siblings on preschoolers' behavior at home and at school. *Developmental Psychology, 21*(5), 761–767.

BIGNER, J. (1979). *Parent-child relationships.* New York: Macmillan.

BLATT, S., WEIN, S., CHEVRON, E., & QUINLAN, D. (1979). Parental representations and depression in normal young adults. *Journal of Abnormal Psychology, 88*(4), 388–397.

BROOK, J., GORDON, A., & BROOK, D. (1980). Perceived paternal relationships, adolescent personality, and female marijuana use. *Journal of Psychology, 105,* 277–285.

BROOK, J., LUKOFF, I., & WHITEMAN, M. (1978). Family socialization and adolescent personality and their association with adolescent use of marijuana. *Journal of Genetic Psychology, 133,* 261–271.

BRYANT, B. (1985). The neighborhood walk: Sources of support in middle childhood. *Monographs of the Society for Research in Child Development, 50*(3), 1–122.

CALLAN, V., & NOLLER, P. (1987). Perceptions of communicative relationships in families with adolescents. *Journal of Marriage and the Family, 48*(4), 805–812.

CHILMAN, C. (1980, November). Social and psychological research concerning adolescent childbearing: 1970–1980. *Journal of Marriage and the Family,* pp. 793–805.

CLEMENS, P., & RUST, J. (1979). Factors in adolescent rebellious feelings. *Adolescence, 14*(53), 159–173.

COLEMAN, J., GEORGE, R., & HOLT, G. (1977). Adolescents and their parents: A study of attitudes. *Journal of Genetic Psychology, 130,* 239–245.

COLES, R. (1970). *Erik H. Erikson: The growth of his work.* Boston: Little, Brown.

COOK, A. (1983). *Contemporary perspectives on adult development and aging.* New York: Macmillan.

COOPERSMITH, S. (1967). *The antecedents of self-esteem.* San Francisco: Freeman.

CRAMER, P. (1979). Defense mechanisms in adolescence. *Developmental Psychology, 15*(4), 476–477.

DICKSTEIN, E., & POSNER, J. (1978). Self-esteem and relationship with parents. *Journal of Genetic Psychology, 133,* 273–276.

DUVALL, E. (1977). *Marriage and family development* (5th ed.). Philadelphia: Lippincott.

ELKIND, D. (1970, April 5). Erikson's eight ages of man. *New York Times Magazine,* pp. 25–28.

ELKIND, D. (1978). Understanding the young adolescent. *Adolescence, 13*(40), 127–134.

ELLIS, G. (1977). Parent-adolescent conflict in the United States: Some societal and parental antecedents. *Family Perspectives, 11*(2), 13–25.

ERIKSON, E. (1963). *Childhood and society.* New York: Norton.

FAIRCHILD, L., & ERWIN, W. (1977). Physical punishment by parent figures as a model of aggressive behavior in children. *Journal of Genetic Psychology, 130,* 279–284.

Family Planning Perspectives (1979). *11*(3), 200–201.

FELKER, D. (1974). *Building positive self-concepts.* Minneapolis: Burgess.

FLORA, R. (1978, February). The effect of self concept upon adolescents' communication with parents. *Journal of School Health,* pp. 100–102.

FRIEDRICH, L., & STEIN, A. (1973). Aggressive and prosocial programs and the natural behavior of preschool children. *Monographs of the Society for Research in Child Development, 38* (Serial No. 151), pp. 1–64.

GALINSKY, E. (1980). *Between generations.* New York: Times Books.

GANTMAN, C. (1978). Family interaction patterns among families with normal, disturbed, and drug abusing adolescents. *Journal of Youth and Adolescence, 7*(4), 429–440.

GECAS, V., & SCHWALBE, M. (1986). Parental behavior and adolescent self-esteem. *Journal of Marriage and the Family, 48*(1), 37–46.

GINOTT, H. (1969). *Between parent and teenager.* New York: Macmillan.

GLICK, P., & NORTON, A. (1973). Perspectives on the recent upturn in divorce and remarriage. *Demography, 10,* 301–314.

GOETTING, A. (1986). The developmental tasks of siblingship over the life cycle. *Journal of Marriage and the Family, 48*(4), 703–714.

GORDON, I. (1971). The beginning of the self: The problem of the nurturing environment. In R. Anderson (Ed.), *As the twig is bent: Readings in early childhood education* (pp. 138–144). Boston: Houghton Mifflin.

GRAYBILL, D. (1978). Relationships of maternal child-rearing behavior to children's self-esteem. *Journal of Psychology, 100,* 45–47.

HAMID, P., & WYLLIE, A. (1980). What generation gap? *Adolescence, 15*(58), 385–391.

HOELTER, J., & HARPER, L. (1987). Structural and interpersonal family influences on adolescent self-conception. *Journal of Marriage and the Family, 49*(1), 129–139.

HOFFMAN, M. (1970). Moral development. In P. Mussen (Ed.), *Carmichael's manual of child psychology* (Vol. 2, 3d ed., pp. 261–359). New York: Wiley.

HOWER, J., & EDWARDS, K. (1979). The relationship between moral character and adolescents' perception of parent behavior. *Journal of Genetic Psychology, 135,* 23–32.

HUBA, G., NEWCOMB, M., & BENTLER, P. (1986). Adverse drug experiences and drug use behavior. *Journal of Pediatric Psychology, 11*(2), 203–219.

HUNDLEBY, J., & MERCER, G. (1987). Family and friends as social environments and their relationships to young adolescents' use of alcohol, tobacco, and marijuana. *Journal of Marriage and the Family, 49*(1), 151–164.

JENKINS, G., & SHACTER, H. (1975). *These are your children.* Glenview, IL: Scott, Foresman.

JOHNSON, M., & BROWN, D. (1986). Use of Systematic Training for Effective Parenting (STEP) with elementary school parents. *The School Counselor, 34,* 100–104.

JOHNSTON, M., & SLOTNIK, J. (1985). parent participation in the schools: Are the benefits worth the burdens? *Phi Delta Kappan, 66,* 430–433.

JOSSELSON, R., GREENBERGER, E., & McCONOCHIE, D. (1977). Phenomenological aspects of psychosocial maturity in adolescence, Part II. Girls. *Journal of Youth and Adolescence, 6*(2), 145–167.

KAGAN, S. (1984). Parent involvement research: A field in search of itself. IRE Report No. 8. Boston: Institute for Responsive Education.

KAGEL, S., WHITE, R., & COYNE, J. (1978). Father-absent and father-present families of disturbed and non-disturbed adolescents. *American Journal of Orthopsychiatry, 48*(2), 342–352.

KANDEL, D. (1978). On variations in adolescent subcultures. *Youth and Society, 9,* 373–384.

KLOS, D., & PADDOCK, J. (1978). Relationship status: Scales for assessing the vitality of late adolescents' relationships with their parents. *Journal of Youth and Adolescence, 7*(4), 353–368.

LEVINSON, D., DARROW C., KLEIN, E., LEVINSON, M., & McKEE, B. (1979). Stages of adulthood. In P. Rose (Ed.), *Socialization and the life cycle* (pp. 306–309). New York: St. Martin's.

MATTESON, D. (1975). *Adolescence today: Sex roles and the search for identity.* Homewood, IL: Dorsey.

MILLER, B. (1976). Student drug use: Attitudinal, parental relations, and sex differences—A pilot study. *International Journal of Addictions, 11*(6), 1077–1084.

MILLER, M., & REEVES, B. (1975). Children's occupational sex-role stereotypes: The linkage between television content and perception. Paper presented at the annual meeting of the International Communication Association, Chicago.

MOORE, K., PETERSON, J., & FURSTENBERG, F. (1986). Parental attitudes and the occurrence of early sexual activity. *Journal of Marriage and the Family, 48*(4), 777–782.

MOSS, T. (1969). *Middle school.* Boston: Houghton Mifflin.

NACHMAN, G. (1979). The menopause that refreshes. In P. Rose (Ed.), *Socialization and the life cycle* (pp. 279–293). New York: St. Martin's.

NEBGEN, M. (1979). Parent involvement in Title I programs. *Educational Forum, 43*(2), 165–173.

NEWCOMER, S., & UDRY, R. (1987). Premarital status effects on adolescent sexuality. *Journal of Marriage and the Family, 49*(2), 235–240.

NUTTALL, E., & NUTTALL, R. (1976). Parent-child relationships and effective academic motivation. *Journal of Psychology, 94,* 127–133.

ORLOFSKY, J. (1977). Sex-role orientation, identity formation, and self esteem in college men and women. *Sex Roles, 3*(6), 561–575.

PETERS, J. (1985). Adolescents as socialization agents to parents. *Adolescence, 20*(80), 921–931.

PETERSON, E. (1977, April). Changes in the adolescent-parent relationship according to sex role. (ERIC Document Reproduction Service No. ED 144 907).

POLIT, D., & FALBO, T. (1987). Only children: A quantitative review. *Journal of Marriage and the Family, 49*(2), 309–326.

RAHNER, E. (1980). Perceived parental acceptance-rejection and children's reported personality and behavioral dispositions: An intercultural test. *Behavior Science Research, 1,* 81–88.

REDL, F. (1944). Pre-adolescents—What makes them tick? *Child Study, 21,* 44–48, 58–59.

RHODES, S. (1977). A developmental approach to the life cycle of the family. *Social Casework, 58,* 301–311.

RICHARDSON, R., ABRAMOWITZ, R., ASP, C., & PETERSEN, A. (1986). Parent-child relationships in early adolescence: Effects of family structure. *Journal of Marriage and the Family, 48*(4), 805–812.

ROBINSON, P. (1978). Parents of ''beyond control'' adolescents. *Adolescence, 13*(49), 109–119.

ROLL, S., & MILLEN, L. (1978). Adolescent males' feeling of being understood by their fathers as revealed through clinical interviews. *Adolescence, 13*(49), 83–94.

ROSSI, A. (1968). Transition to parenthood. *Journal of Marriage and the Family, 30,* 26–39.

SAWIN, D., & PARKE, R. (1979). Inconsistent discipline of aggression in young boys. *Journal of Experimental Child Psychology, 28,* 528–538.

SCHWARTZ, J., & ZUROFF, D. (1979). Family structure and depression in female college students: Effects of parental conflict, decision-making, power, and inconsistency of love. *Journal of Abnormal Psychology, 88*(4), 398–406.

SEARS, R. (1970). Relation of early socialization experiences to self concepts and gender role in middle childhood. *Child Development, 41,* 267–289.

SEBALD, H. (1986). Adolescents' shifting orientation toward parents and peers. *Journal of Marriage and the Family, 48*(1), 5–13.

SHEEHY, G. (1976). *Passages.* New York: Bantam.

SMITH, R., & WALTERS, J. (1978). Delinquent and nondelinquent males' perceptions of their fathers. *Adolescence, 13*(49), 21–28.

SMITH, T. (1983). Adolescent reactions to attempted parental control and influence techniques. *Journal of Marriage and the Family, 45*(3), 533–542.

SNALK, D., & ROTHBLUM, E. (1979). Self-disclosure among adolescents in relation to parental affection and control patterns. *Adolescence, 14*(54), 333–340.

STARKEY, S. (1980). The relationship between parental acceptance-rejection and the performance of fourth and fifth graders. *Behavior Science Research, 1,* 67–80.

STROMMEN, E., McKINNEY, J., & FITZGERALD, H. (1977). *Developmental psychology: The school-aged child.* Homewood, IL: Dorsey.

THOMPSON, D. (1985). Parent-peer compliance in a group of preadolescent youth. *Adolescence, 25*(79), 501–508.

VAN HOOSE, W., & WORTH, M. (1982). *Adulthood in the life cycle.* Dubuque, IA: William Brown.

WALSH, P. (1983). *Growing through time: An introduction to adult development.* Monterey, CA: Brooks/Cole.

WALTERS, J., & WALTERS, L. (1980, November). Parent-child relationships: A review, 1970–1979. *Journal of Marriage and the Family,* pp. 807–822.

WHITBOURNE, S., & WEINSTOCK, C. (1979). *Adult development: The differentiation of experiences.* New York: Holt, Rinehart & Winston.

WILLIAMS, J., & STITH, M. (1980). *Middle childhood: Behavior and development* (2d ed.). New York: Macmillan.

ZEIDLER, A., NARDINE, F., SCOLARE, C., & MICH, P. (1987, April). Adult perceptions of parent-child relations: Implications for families as educators. Paper presented at the annual meeting of the American Education Research Association, Washington, DC.

ZUSSMAN, J. (1978). Relationship of demographic factors to parental discipline techniques. *Developmental Psychology, 4*(6), 685–686.

4

The Changing Nature
of Parenting:
Later Life

The traditional concept of the role of parenthood has spanned the period from the birth of the first child through the adolescent period of the last child. Parenting, then, has been thought of as a 20 to 30 year commitment. Family relations research has consistently identified the stage when young adult children leave home as the "launching" stage and has referred to parents as experiencing the "empty-nest" syndrome after the departure of children from the home. Put another way, the period of childbearing is considered the expansion phase for families, and following the maturity of all children, the family is said to be in the contracting stage.

Recent social changes, however, have contributed to a somewhat expanded conception of parenthood. These changes have resulted in children remaining in the parental home longer and for some, returning to live, at least for a brief period. Further, grandparents have become more numerous because of greater longevity, and the roles of many grandparents have been altered as a result of divorce. Finally, greater longevity has also contributed to increased responsibility of middle-aged adults in providing assistance and care to their elderly parents. All of these phenomena have significant impact on the changing nature of parenting, both for parents and children. This chapter examines parenting in later life, grandparenting, elderly parent caring, and communication throughout the life cycle.

PARENTS AND ADULT CHILDREN

In this country it has been the practice for young adults to be launched, or to leave the parental home, in their late teens or early twenties to establish homes of their own or to attend college. However, in the 1980s more young adults were living with their parents than at any other time since 1940, when the aftermath of the Depression resulted in a high unemployment rate, thus prohibiting young people from becoming financially independent. Specifically, in 1984, 37 percent of persons 18 to 29 years (18 million) were residing with their parents, representing a larger proportion of sons than daughters. Fifteen million of these were between the ages of 18 and 24, and 3 million were between 25 and 29. The two major reasons for this phenomenon appear to be prolonged schooling and family disruption (Glick & Lin, 1986).

These young adults residing with parents consisted primarily of those who had never been married. For the remaining few who had ever been married, about half had their spouses living with them; the other half were separated, divorced, or widowed. Approximately two thirds of this population were employed, and the employment rate was higher for women than for men. For those who had never been married, the major proportion were attending school. For women who had been previously married, two thirds had young children residing with them. However, surprisingly, the proportion of previously married men living with parents was consistently higher than that for women (Glick & Lin, 1986).

Based on the above data, it seems that the 1980s marked for many families a period when the launching stage was postponed or when the child-rearing stage was resumed after a brief empty-nest period. This phenomenon has been referred to as "the cluttered nest." Interestingly there is an inverse relationship between the extent to which young adults live with their parents and the birthrate of the preceding decade or two. The tendency toward having smaller families seems to be simultaneous with the tendency for young adults to remain in or return to the parental home, and these trends are likely to continue. Further, economic conditions affect the availability of employment, and when unemployment is high, young adults are more likely to live with their parents. Finally, the availability of financial-aid programs in colleges and universities determines to some extent living arrangements of college students. A recent study found that the average payment by parents to adult children was $3,755 per year, *not* including college costs, and that approximately 500,000 adult children are currently receiving such financial assistance ("Grown children . . . ," 1989). The typical family at the turn of the century is likely to consist of parents and adult children rather than parents and young children.

Parenting Young Adult Children

While recent attention has been given to adult development, little has been given to parenting young adult children. Adult children are considered to be those 18 years of age or older, married or single, living in or out of the parental home. The time at which "young adult children" cease to be young is clearly debatable. For convenience's sake children referred to here are those between 18 and 29 years of age. In this country "coming of age" is not noted by any particular rite of passage, but becoming eligible to vote—and, for men, becoming eligible for the draft—signify in our society legal status as an adult. By law parents are no longer responsible for their offspring after their eighteenth birthdays. According to Bernard (1975), "In the name of tidiness, . . . motherhood ought to end when children leave home" (p. 133). However, the truth is that for many, parenting continues for years to come. There are few norms governing familial relationships in adulthood, and research has not yet identified the special bonds that occur between parents and their grown children (Thompson & Walker, 1984). Therefore our remarks will have little empirical support.

Adult children living at home. The most typical adult child who resides at home is one who is continuing his schooling at a college or university or at a vocational school within commuting distance of the parental home. There are, however, young adults who are not in school who continue to live at home, most of whom are employed or seeking employment. In either case parents are faced with the task of interacting with offspring whom they have little control over and who generally have a different life-style from that of their parents. The rules and regulations that governed the period of adolescence and the nature of interactions are no longer appropriate, but daily proximity forces intrusion of one life-style on the other. The need for independence among young adults is widely known, but the need for independence of middle-aged parents often is ignored (Thompson & Walker, 1984).

The major issue in households with adult children seems to be lack of privacy. (See Box 4a for other issues.) Unless the living quarters are spacious, neither parents nor children can maintain independent, private lives. Coming and going, entertaining friends, use of leisure time, and even eating habits must be subjected

---

BOX 4a ISSUES IN PARENTING LIVE-IN ADULT CHILDREN

Life-style Differences

Listening to music
Coming and going privately
Entertaining friends
Using leisure time
Eating and dressing

Division of Labor

Doing the laundry
Preparing the meals
Maintaining the household

Economic Issues

Providing financial support
Providing room and board

Rules and Regulations

Curfews
Use of car and other family
  possessions
Use of alcohol/drugs

---

on other members of the family. Young and older adults often differ significantly in their choice of music, food, and clothing, and their schedules of sleeping, working, studying, and eating may not coincide. Therefore compromises must be made.

The pattern of aid between generations has been the focus of some research, which suggests that there is a shift in the pattern as parent and child grow older. In the early years and continuing through the child's young adult stage, the flow of material assistance is from the parent to the child. This pattern reverses as the young generation reaches middle age and the parent becomes elderly. The same pattern persists in the provision of nonmaterial aid.

The issue of the division of labor may then arise. For example, do parents continue to do laundry for their adult children? Do they prepare meals for them? Buy their clothes? Are adult children expected to participate in the maintenance of the home? If so, how and to what extent? The fact that more male than female adult children live with their parents suggests than sons continue to rely on their parents, especially their mothers, to perform stereotyped gender-related activities. However, we suspect that whether the child is in school or is employed, or both, and whether the parents are employed determines to some extent the expectations parents have of their children.

The related issue of financial aid raises similar conflicts. Does the adult child pay rent? Does she contribute to the purchase of food? Does she pay for her own health and car insurance? Has she begun a savings account? What kind of financial assistance does she get from her parents, if any? Again, financial issues seem to be related to whether the young adult is employed or is in school and on the economic status of the parents. Many parents, if they are willing and able, subsidize their children's room and board as well as their tuition and books as long as they are actively pursuing an education. Some parents place a time limit on these kinds of subsidies. On the other hand, most parents expect some financial contribution from their live-in children if they are employed full-time. And most young adults desire to form their own homes independently once they become financially self-sufficient. However, moving out of the parental home may result only in returning later, only to move out once more. This is not an uncommon occurrence due to the fluctuating economic status of young adults.

Finally, the issue of rules and regulations

looms large for many families with adult children at home. To what extent do parents have a right to know where their children are, when they will be home, and whom they are with? Should parents set down rules about dress, socializing with friends, use of parents' possessions, and the use of alcohol and drugs? Most parents feel the need to apply rules that make their own lives more comfortable, yet they feel guilty that they are not accepting their child's level of maturity and sense of responsibility. Creating an atmosphere of peaceful coexistence while maintaining mutual respect is often difficult. There actually is no secret solution to solving this dilemma. Each party must be sensitive to the feelings and expectations of the other, and, no doubt, compromises must be made by all.

Using Erikson's framework, most parents of young adult children are completing their stage of generativity and moving toward the final stage of integrity versus despair. At the same time their offspring are seeking to achieve a sense of intimacy, beginning to think about establishing their own homes and families. Unlike the developmental reciprocity between parents of younger children (generativity stage) and the children themselves (initiative and industry stages), this period of the life cycle does not lend itself well to complementarity. As a result the conflicts previously discussed would not seem surprising. In fact, a recent study found that 42 percent of the middle-aged parents surveyed reported serious conflicts with at least one of their resident adult children (Clemens & Axelson, 1985). However, caution is warranted in generalizing their results because the sample was small and not representative.

Adult children living away from home. Aldous (1985) pointed out that when children leave home to establish financial independence and to begin their own families, parental solicitude does not stop. In other words there is no such thing as a "postparental" period. However, relationships between parents and their adult children are perhaps less stressful once children leave the parental home permanently, because the conflicts that arise from attempting to mesh two different life-styles are absent. Nevertheless, children may still be dependent on parents economically and/or emotionally. Parents, too, may have difficulty in resolving their emotional dependency on their children. Rarely has parent-child attachment been studied when children reach adulthood; it has been speculated that emotional dependencies are more balanced in adulthood than in early parent-child relationships when the child is more dependent on the parent (Thompson & Walker, 1984). Still later an imbalance may occur in the other direction as aging parents become more dependent—physically, economically, and psychologically—on their mature children

The nature of the relationships between parents and their adult children depends to some extent on the marital status of the parent(s) and the marital and parental status of the children. In general, parents and daughters are more involved with each other's lives than parents and sons are. However, parents show greater solicitude for their divorced adult children who have children than for other children. They are more likely to provide child care for these grandchildren, to give comfort to their own divorced children, and to help them with housework. On the other hand, parents are more likely to provide financial aid and help with transportation to their unmarried children. Overall there appears to be greater intimacy of parents with adult daughters who have made them grandparents. In addition to these variables, geographic proximity significantly affects the frequency of contact between the generations (Aldous, 1985).

Sources of conflict surround the degree of communication between parents and children (telephoning, visiting, or writing); the exchange of aid, goods, and services; economic dependency; and concern about life-style. These issues are similar to those that arise with live-in adult children, but they tend to be far less intense. Rosenmayr (1978) noted that the transfer of aid is never really symmetrical; it is transferred from parent to child. Only by grown children transferring to their own children is there any balancing of material and emotional investment.

In the Thompson and Walker (1984) study, two generations of mother-daughter relationships were examined. Most of the youngest generation of daughters (who were university students) were single. The investigators found, not surprisingly, that nonreciprocity existed in the transfer of aid: The mothers were essentially the givers, and the daughters were the receivers. They concluded that these young adult women could invest only upward to their parents—neither horizontally to their husbands nor downward to their children. Marital status of parents, too, seems to be a factor. Adams (1986) reported greater closeness and reciprocity of aid between mothers and their young adult daughters when the mothers were widowed as opposed to married. Hill (1970) suggested that it is the family member in the nonreciprocating position (receiving but not giving help) who avoids contact with kin; the nonreciprocated giver (giving but not receiving help) does not.

Finally, proximity of parents to their adult children is clearly a pivotal factor. Geographical distance affects the frequency and type of communication, the exchange of aid, the degree of independence, and the differences that may arise over conflict in life-style.

In sum, it seems apparent that relationships between mature adults and their adult children, whether the children are living at home or not, are complex and little understood. While we suspect that there is great diversity in the degree and extent of contact and in the transfer of aid, goods, and services, few generalizations can be made, and few guidelines can be established. Therefore it appears that an interesting and promising area of research would be the relationships between parents and their adult children.

GRANDPARENTING

Although there is little theoretical foundation for the dynamics of grandparenthood, the topic has recently stimulated interest in both the scholarly and the popular areas. Our perceptions about grandparents have changed radically over the years. The perception of grandmother, for example, in the late 1800s was one of a kindly, elderly, somewhat frail, gray-haired woman sitting in a rocking chair by the fire. Today grand-

mothers range in age from their thirties to their hundreds, and the "typical" grandmother is a middle-aged active woman, most likely dressed for work or a tennis game (Bengston, 1985). Hagested (1985) echoed the fact that there is no uniform, consistent picture of grandparents; rather there is great heterogeneity and diversity.

Several social changes have contributed to these broader perceptions and renewed interest. First, greater longevity is permitting a longer period of grandparenthood. Further, smaller, more closely spaced families have resulted in little overlap between the cycles of parenting and grandparenting so that the two roles are more sharply differentiated. Third, geographic mobility of young families makes it difficult for some grandparents to assume active roles. And, finally, the high divorce rate has altered grandparents' relationships with their grandchildren (Hagested, 1985).

Grandparents are more prevalent today than ever before. More than three fourths of people over the age of 65 are grandparents, and nearly half of these will become great-grandparents. Yet, expectations for grandparents vary considerably, and the role of grandparent is ambiguous, tenuous, and without clear norms. The rights and responsibilities of grandparents are not well articulated (Hagested, 1985). It has been noted that grandparenthood is not self-initiated or voluntary, as most other adult roles are. Therefore the transition into the role may be more difficult for some (Hagested & Lang, 1986). Specifically Bengston (1985) found that the transition to grandmotherhood was more easily accepted if it was perceived as occurring "on time" rather than "early."

Functions and Styles of Grandparenthood

It has been suggested that there are four symbolic dimensions of grandparenthood: "being there" (the presence of grandparents during family transitions and disruptions); serving as the "national guard" or the "family watchdog" (the family's militia to protect and give care when needed); as arbitrators (negotiating between parents and children in issues relating to family continuity); and as active participants in the family's social construction of its history (Bengston, 1985). It is this last dimension that has been emphasized by many researchers as being the most crucial; that is, grandparents tie the present to the past as well as to the future and thereby provide the crucial links between generations.

McCready (1985) cited a study that described five grandparenting styles (see Box 4b). In his own research he created somewhat different typologies based on these five. He combined the "formal" and "distant" typologies and characterized these grandparents' attitudes as wishing grandchildren to have good manners, be neat and clean, and have self-control. The "fun seekers" had more of a qualitative interest and wanted grandchildren to get along well with other children, to be considerate of other people, and to be interested in how and why things happen. McCready's "surrogate parent" wanted the grandchildren to try hard, obey their parents, be good students, and act in sex-appropriate ways. The "reservoir of family wisdom" types wanted children to be honest, to be responsible, and to have good sense. He found both ethnic and gender differences in the popula-

tion he studied—for example, males were more likely to demonstrate characteristics of the formal and distant type, whereas females were more affect-oriented.

Using a similar framework Cherlin and Furstenberg (1985) failed to find the "fun seeker" type in their sample of grandparents, but it was emphasized that all grandchildren in the sample were teenagers. Like the styles of parenting, the styles of grandparenting change as grandparents and grandchildren age. They found, instead, frequent reciprocal patterns of exchange of services between these teens and their grandparents. Further, one quarter of their grandparents fit the *detached* type; one quarter were characterized as *passive*; and half were considered as being *active,* which consisted of three subtypes of *influential, supportive,* and *authoritative.* The detached grandparents were older, lived further away, and had lower frequencies of contact with their grandchildren. Further, they were more likely to admit that the family was not close. About half of the passive, supportive, and authoritative grandparents had seen their grandchildren about once a week or more over the past few months. The influential grandparents had almost daily contact with their grandchildren and

---

BOX 4b   FIVE STYLES OF GRANDPARENTING

Style	Characteristics
The "Formal"	Follows proper and prescribed roles for grandparents; perceives clear lines between parenting and grandparenting; gives little advice.
The "Fun Seeker"	Relationship is informal and playful; focuses on mutual satisfaction; is source of leisure activity for grandchildren.
The "Distant Figure"	Emerges from the shadows on holidays and special rituals; distant and remote.
The "Surrogate Parent"	Daily contact with grandchildren; assumes actual caretaking responsibilities.
The "Reservoir of Family Wisdom"	Relationship is authoritarian and patricentered; lines of authority are distinct; grandfather is often the dispenser of special skills and resources.

Source: McCready, W. (1985). Styles of grandparenting among white ethnics. In V. Bengston & J. Robertson (Eds.), *Grandparenthood* (pp. 49–60). Beverly Hills: Sage.

were closely tied to them. They were least likely to say the family was not close.

Overall the grandparents who had very frequent contact and who were younger demonstrated greater amounts of parentlike behavior. Levels of authority over grandchildren were influenced by race (blacks scored significantly higher on the authority scale than others) and marital status of the middle generation (grandparents of children not living with two parents were somewhat higher on authority).

Cherlin and Furstenberg (1985) concluded that passive grandparents best fit the popular American image of the American grandparent—the loving older person who sees the grandchildren fairly often and who is ready to provide help in a crisis but under ordinary circumstances practices the "norm of noninterference." They also described a life course for grandparenting: Early on, grandparents offer substantial assistance in the form of babysitting and gifts and seek leisure-oriented fun from their grandchildren. With development, patterns of assistance may continue, but they are transformed into direct exchange of services between grandparents and grandchildren. As grandchildren enter adolescence, "fun seeking" is superseded by mutual assistance, advice giving, and discussion of problems, or it is superseded by a passive grandparental style.

Variables Related to Grandparenting

Several variables have been identified that seem to affect the style of grandparenting (see Box 4c). The first of these is *gender*. Women outlive men by about 8 years, so that the oldest member of a family lineage is likely to be female. Therefore most grandfathers are likely to be married, and a greater proportion of grandmothers are likely to be widowed. For example, in 1979, 67 percent of men 75 years and older were living with a spouse, whereas only 21 percent of women this age were (Hagested, 1985). Perhaps that is the reason that grandmothers have been studied in more depth than grandfathers have. Further, several researchers have referred to women as being the "kin-keepers," bringing family members together. A grandmother has been named "secretary of the interior," whereas a grandfather is more aptly described as an "ambassador" or a "foreign minister." These labels have grown out of research, albeit limited, that has found gender differences in grandparent behavior, but, in addition, the quality of the grandparent-grandchild relationship most often reflects the work of a kin-keeper in the middle—the mother.

Hagested (1985) found grandmothers to have a wider spectrum of influence with grandchildren than grandfathers did. Their relationships included concerns about friends and family interaction and distinction between grandsons and granddaughters. Nevertheless, for both grandmothers and grandfathers, links to a same-sexed child stood out. The highest level of involvement seems to be from grandmother to mother to daughter, and then from grandfather to father to son.

Grandfathers have been found to talk about and emphasize different things with grandchildren than grandmothers do. Specifically, men tended to emphasize task-oriented involvement outside the family, and women tended to emphasize interpersonal dynamics and the quality of ties in the family. Race relations, social policy, and sex-roles seemed to be "sore spot" discussion topics with grandfathers; among females conflict typically occurred over how to relate within the family. Reverse socialization was noted, too, as grandchildren enlightened both their parents and their grandparents on social issues, involvement in work and education, and changing styles in dress and grooming (Hagested, 1985). It has been further noted that grandmothers saw continuing the family line as the most important feature of grandparenthood, whereas grandfathers cited being able to help grandchildren as most important. The majority of both grandmothers and grandfathers reported that their lives had changed for the better as a result of grandparenthood (cited in Hagested & Lang, 1986).

An interesting study conducted by Thompson and Walker (1987) examined the extent to which mothers are mediators between grandmothers and their young adult granddaughters. They noted that the strongest and most enduring bonds are those through the maternal lines. They found that the degree of access and con-

---

BOX 4c VARIABLES RELATED TO GRANDPARENTING

Gender of grandparent and grandchildren
Kin position (maternal versus paternal)
Geographic distance
Ethnicity
Divorce

---

tact between grandparents and granddaughters determined the need for mediation on the part of the middle generation; that is, if granddaughters had less than monthly contact with their grandmothers, they tended to adopt their mothers' feelings for the older generation. On the other hand, with greater contact granddaughters derived their feelings of closeness with grandmothers from three sources: a direct relationship with the grandmother, feelings mediated by the mother, and feelings for the mother that overflowed to the grandmother.

Grandmothers in this study tended to express their closeness to the granddaughter as part of a global family feeling; that is, they could not separate their feelings for the granddaughter from those for the daughter (mother). In addition there was more influence of the mother as mediator when the granddaughters were young. Finally, the grandfather-grandchild bond was found to be more remote; grandfathers had less contact with and felt less close to their grandchildren than grandmothers did. However, *kin position* (maternal versus paternal) was a stronger predictor of closeness than was gender of the grandparent (Thompson & Walker, 1987).

A second factor that influences grandparent-grandchild relationships is the *geographic distance* separating them. Proximity has been cited as one of the strongest predictors of the grandparent-grandchild relationship. In fact, grandmothers indicated that the extent to which becoming a grandmother affected them depended on the geographic distance between them and their grandchildren. Women are more likely to feel that grandparents and grandchildren should live close to one another and have daily involvement (Hagested & Lang, 1986).

Ethnicity is another factor related to grandparenting style. Bengston (1985) reported an especially distinctive style for Mexican-American grandparents. First, they had more children, grandchildren, and great-grandchildren as potential sources of support. Second, they reported higher frequencies of contact with their grandchildren, and their expectations of intergenerational assistance differed. Two thirds of the Mexican-Americans wanted to live in the same neighborhood with their adult children as opposed to one third of the blacks and one fifth of the Anglos. If something happened and they could not live alone, half the Mexican-Americans wanted to live with their children and grandchildren, whereas only 10 percent of blacks and 4 percent of Anglos expressed this desire. Overall, blacks in this study were similar to Anglos on other dimensions except one: 47 percent of the blacks, as opposed to 8 percent of the Anglos, indicated that they had reared at least one nonbiological child and grandchild ("fictive kin").

Cherlin and Furstenberg (1985) reported that 63 percent of the black grandparents in their study were in the categories of either authoritative or influential, both being styles that are substantially similar to parental authority. Only 26 percent of the Anglo grandparents and one third of the nonwhites fell into these two categories. On the other hand, only 8 percent of blacks were classified as passive. Even though there is a higher percentage of single parents among blacks, which might suggest the need for a more authoritative grandparent role, the tendency for passivity held up almost equally in two-parent homes.

Finally, family disruption, especially the *divorce* of adult children, has been found to have substantial, often profound, effects on grandparents. Divorce may alter the normative, voluntaristic nature of the grandparent role, and the nature, type, and amount of interaction may either significantly increase (if the caretaking role is assumed) or decrease (in the case of paternal grandparents where maternal custody has been awarded). Divorced daughters get more grandparental help than any others. Further, custodial grandparents (usually maternal) develop closer ties with their grandchildren than noncustodial or paternal grandparents who lose access by their sons' divorces (Robertson, Tice, & Loeb, 1985). It has, in fact, been suggested that the adult child's need for parental attention as reflected by his or her marital and parental status constitutes part of the explanation for intergenerational contacts (Aldous, 1985). The down side of that phenomenon, then, is reflected in the experience of the paternal grandparents. At the time of this writing, however, 49 states had passed grandparent visitation statutes, and federal legislation calling for uniform law in all 50 was pending in order to protect and promote grandparent visitation.

Grandparents: A Potpourri

It is easy to see that grandparents come in all ages, represent all vocations, have few to many grandchildren and possibly great-grandchildren, have varied frequencies of contact with their grandchildren, and demonstrate a wide variety of grandparenting styles. For these reasons few generalizations can be accurately made. Grandparenthood has been variously described as parenthood one step removed, as a second chance, and as a reliving of parenthood.

Whatever grandparenthood represents, an individual's expectations are, no doubt, derived from his own parents and grandparents (Hagested & Lang, 1986). Maintaining a sense of family continuity may be the most significant role of grandparents, who are crucial as transmitters of culture and history and are functionally necessary to ensure adequate socialization of the young. Younger generations, then, socialize elders by needing, receiving, and incorporating their knowledge and experiences into their life space (Robertson et al., 1985).

The visibility of grandparenthood has been facilitated by the proclamation of Grandparents Day (the first Sunday after Labor Day), by the establishment in the 1980s of the Foundation for Grandparenting and its newsletter, and by state statutes regarding the rights and responsibilities of grandparents. Intergenerational programs reflect the recognition of the importance of grandparents for children. However, family policy that emphasizes intergenerational interdependence rather than an age-segregated society is needed (Robertson et al., 1985).

In sum, the literature on grandparenting repeatedly stresses the changing perceptions of grandparenthood and the heterogeneity among grandparents. Yet the norms for grandparent behavior are ambiguous at best, and the rights and responsibilities are poorly articulated. There are symbolic dimensions of grandparenthood as well as different styles and typologies of grandparenting.

Grandparents differ on a number of dimensions by gender; by kin position; by geographic distance from grandchildren; by ethnicity; and by experiences of family disruption, especially divorce. Nevertheless, most grandparents view their lives as being enriched by having grandchildren.

The immediate future is likely to see more in-depth research on grandparenthood, more intergenerational programs, and more social policy related to the preservation of intergenerational contacts. As more people become grandparents and live longer to enjoy the role, grandparenting will once again come of age.

CARING FOR ELDERLY PARENTS

The final stage in Erikson's stages of psychosocial development occurs when individuals approach old age. This stage, integrity versus despair, represents a time in which people reflect on their lives—hopefully with a sense of satisfaction. It is at this point in the life cycle for most extended families that child-rearing and parenting demands decrease or cease and caring for elderly parents increases. Some sociologists have maintained that there is, in fact, a role reversal as the middle-aged adult child becomes "parent" to her own parents when the burden of care shifts to the middle generation. Other sociologists have maintained that the role-reversal model is far too simplistic to explain the relationships between adult children and their aging parents, and still others suggest that role reversal is pathological.

Clearly a shift in dependency needs occurs. In fact, the years between 40 and 60, in which people often find themselves coping simultaneously with the demands of both children and their own parents, have been referred to as the "sandwich generation" (Schwartz, 1979). Because parent care almost always is provided by a daughter (and to a lesser extent by a daughter-in-law) (Brody, Johnsen, Fulcomer, & Lang, 1983; DeWit, Wister, & Burch, 1988; Lang & Brody, 1983; Leigh, 1982; Stoller, 1983), women in this sandwich generation have been referred to as "women in the middle" (Brody, 1981; Noelker & Wallace, 1985). These "women in the middle" are more likely to provide care to their mothers, so that both the givers and the receivers of this care are overrepresented by women.

Brody (1981) stated that ". . . to an extent unprecedented in history, roles as caregiving daughters and daughters-in-law to dependent older people have been added to their traditional roles as wives, homemakers, mothers and grandmothers" (p. 471), and we might add the additional contemporary role of worker to the list. Further, recent evidence suggests that, in spite of increased labor force participation by women, few significant changes in the household division of labor have occurred. Rather than a redivision of domestic tasks between husband and wife, the length of the wife's work week has increased, and daughters respond to the needs of their impaired elderly parents by allocating less time to leisure (Stoller, 1983).

Several demographic trends have been cited as reasons for this relatively new role: The decreased birthrate has resulted in fewer children to provide elderly care; as people are living longer, the population of elderly people has increased, especially those who live into their eighties and nineties; and geographic mobility has resulted in fewer adult children living near their elderly parents, who consequently assume most or all of the responsibilities of care.

Cicerelli (1981) conceptualized parent care from a life-span perspective, likening it to child rearing. In the early part of the life span, parents provide the necessities for the child's survival—food, clothing, shelter, love, and guidance. During this time there is an imbalance in the exchange of help in favor of the child, often resulting in parental sacrifices. The child, hopefully, develops the basic attachment that provides the foundation for later relationships. When the child reaches young adulthood, the exchange of help becomes more balanced, especially if the young adults have children of their own. Middle-aged parents may provide babysitting, help with finances, and so forth, and young adults may assist their parents with transportation, household and yard maintenance, and so forth. In the latter part of the life span, the exchange of help often shifts in favor of the elderly parent, when parent caring is essential for survival of the elderly. Viewed this way parent caring and child rearing become intricately related.

Several investigators, however, have noted demographic trends that threaten to disrupt this cycle of caregiving. First, the increasing number of women in the work force limits the resources (time and energy) that middle-aged adults may need to invest in elderly care. Second, since elderly parents are living longer, they are more apt to have chronic health conditions that require more intensive care. Third, divergent family forms (divorce/single parenting, remarriage, cohabitation, gay marriages, and so on) may disrupt the helping relationships between adult children and their parents (Cicerelli, 1981; Dewit et al., 1988; Lang & Brody, 1983). Finally, geographic mobility alters the form of communication and the kind of assistance given.

In spite of these demographic changes, most of the data suggest that both the ideology and the practice of familial responsibility for the elderly persist. Older people still tend to live near (but rarely with) at least one child, interact frequently with their children, and are often involved in exchange of mutual aid with their adult children. The notion that older people are alienated from their children, then, appears to be a myth (DeWit et al., 1988; Shannas, 1979; Stoller, 1983). However, ". . . the intergenerational type of caregiving reflects the prevalent

norm of parents and adult children, as well as the greater likelihood of intergenerational conflict when multiple generations share a household'' (Noelker & Wallace, 1985, p. 24).

An interesting study by Brody and her associates (1983) included members of three-generation matrilines—a middle-aged mother, her elderly mother, and her young adult daughter. They found that attitudes toward egalitarian gender roles (in child care and in parent care) became progressively stronger among women of each successive younger generation. However, a substantial majority of *each* generation endorsed shared roles. When asked whether grown children should help their elderly parents, the youngest generation and then the middle generation agreed more strongly than the oldest generation. In addition the youngest generation emphatically felt that grandchildren should provide help to their grandparents. Finally, the elderly people, themselves, were the most receptive to the use of formal services, whereas the youngest generation was the least receptive. The authors concluded that values connected with family care of elderly parents have not eroded, even among women who overwhelmingly support nontraditional roles for both sexes.

Types of Parent Care

A number of studies have examined the types of assistance and aid given to elderly parents by

their adult children as well as the degree of contact between them. However, most have failed to differentiate among contact, aid, and intimacy, assuming that the quantity of interaction is the same as the quality and that material exchange is the same as emotional exchange. However, evidence suggests that contact does not necessarily imply intimacy and that family members can feel close to one another without frequent contact, although some contact may be necessary to maintain intimacy. In fact, one study found that aid and contact did not predict intimacy at all (Walker & Thompson, 1983).

Most elders are involved in some type of exchange assistance within the familial network, and most often the exchange is reciprocated in some way. It has been suggested that the exchange of aid is a better indicator of the mutual involvement of the generations in one another's lives than is the frequency of contact, especially if the exchanges are voluntary (Lee & Ellithorpe, 1982). Lang and Brody (1983) found that middle-aged daughters provided an average of about 8.5 hours each week of help to their mothers. Nearly one third helped with food shopping; one fourth provided transportation; and about 20 percent provided assistance with laundry, cooking, or housework. Relatively few of the elderly mothers required assistance with personal care.

A recent report indicates that relatively few older Americans are financially dependent on their children. Less than one million elderly parents receive regular financial support from their adult children; support payments average $1,484 per year, considerably less than the average financial assistance provided by middle-aged parents to their adult children. Although daughters are more likely to provide services to elderly parents, sons are more likely to provide financial assistance. Surprisingly, fewer than 10 percent of elderly parents receiving help live in nursing homes, while 83 percent live in private homes ("Grown children . . . ," 1989).

Living arrangement was the most important variable in predicting the amount of help provided—those daughters who shared households with their mothers provided eight times more help than those who lived separately did (28.5 hours versus 3.5 hours). Older daughters provided more help than younger daughters; separated and divorced daughters provided three times more help than did married daughters (19 hours versus 6 hours). Contrary to the findings of Stoller (1983), nonworking women provided nearly twice as much help as working women did (12.3 hours versus 6.2 hours).

Other studies have examined the types and frequency of contacts between adults and their elderly parents. While some studies have minimized the significance of geographic distance as a factor in the degree of overall contact, other studies have found it to be the strongest predictor (Cicerelli, 1981; DeWit et al., 1988; Leigh, 1982). It does appear that, in general, there is at least a moderate level of contact between most elderly people and their adult children. When distance prohibits certain types of contact (for example, face-to-face), other types of contact seem to be substituted (for example, overnight visits, writing, or phoning). Therefore most researchers agree that distance places limits on proximal aid and contact, but distal aid and contact may counteract these limits.

Is contact between elderly parents and their adult children related to intimacy? An interesting study cited by Walker and Thompson (1983) found that contact was associated positively with intimacy only when moderate distances existed between elderly parents and children. Specifically, when the two generations lived in the same city *or* when they lived more than 250 miles apart, contact was unrelated to affection. How-

ever, if family members lived outside the city but less than 250 miles apart, contact was related positively to affection. The conclusion reached was that physical proximity imposes and great distance limits the frequency of contact, but affection determines the frequency of contact at moderate distances.

Variables Related to Aid and Contact

Obviously the frequency and type of aid and contact provided by middle-aged children to their parents varies. Stoller (1983) elicited information from 532 subjects on assistance to elders with preparing food, shopping, managing personal finances, doing light to heavy chores, filling out applications, making appointments, doing laundry, and providing personal care. She found that contact and aid were higher when elders exhibited greater limitations; higher for daughters than for sons; lower when the older parent had a living spouse; lower when the adult child was married; and lower when sons were employed, but not when daughters were employed.

Specifically she noted that even though there was somewhat greater assistance by sons when the daughters and daughters-in-law were most heavily involved with early child care, sons tended to turn over the responsibilities to their wives and/or sisters once the demands of child care began to decrease. Further, married adult children provided approximately 20 hours per month less help time than unmarried children did. Finally, when sons were employed, they reported approximately 20 hours per month less help time than nonemployed sons; but for daughters, employment resulted in no significant time reduction.

It has been concluded that the feeling of closeness and the enjoyment of keeping in touch are significant influences in these kinship interactions. Even though a sense of obligation and an exchange of aid also play roles, most intergenerational contact seems to be by choice rather than by expectation (Leigh, 1982).

Qualitative Aspects of Parent Care

Several researchers have examined the affective impact of interactions between adult children

---

**BOX 4d   VARIABLES RELATED TO AID AND CONTACT
BETWEEN THE ELDERLY AND THEIR CHILDREN**

Degree of limitation of the elder
Gender of the children
Marital status of the elder
Marital status of the children
Employment of the children
Geographic distance between the elder and the children
Living arrangements

---

and their parents. Specifically, Cicerelli (1983) has developed a path model to describe adult children's attachment to their parents. According to this model, attachment to one's parents endures throughout the life span and is expressed by the extent to which children maintain proximity to and contact with their parents. He found that these feelings of attachment not only predicted present behavior but also had a significant influence on the commitment for future help. In addition a sense of filial obligation tended to increase the adult child's attachment behaviors. Apparently, adult children increase their attachment behaviors to their parents in later life as the first signs of decline begin to appear and at a point before actual help may be needed.

Houser and Berkman (1984) noted that the provision of emotional support by adult children is more important than financial support. Further, they found that the filial behavior (as demonstrated by various activities and behaviors) of the adult child did not significantly affect the elder's satisfaction with her relationship with her children; rather it was the *perception* of the general quality of contact with her children and her belief that they would provide for her future needs. This finding underscored the relative unimportance of actual quantity of parent-child contact as opposed to the perception of quality. Cicerelli (1983) concluded that affectional closeness between the generations represents a purely volitional aspect among the factors associated with interaction.

Another issue related to intergenerational interaction is the effect of aid and contact on the psychological well-being and morale of older persons. Interestingly, most research indicates the absence of a correlation between interactions with adult children and feelings of well-being among the elderly (Lee & Ellithorpe, 1982). Some investigators have argued that because of the imbalance in the exchange of aid (more flowing *from* the adult child *to* the older parent), low morale and depression result. Stoller (1985) found that the impact of helping others had a significant positive impact on older people. Further, the inability of elders to reciprocate rather than the need for assistance (dependency) undermined the morale of the older persons. However, other studies have failed to support a positive relationship between the frequency of the interaction and the morale (Lee & Ellithorpe, 1982), and imbalances in aid exchange do not seem to have negative consequences for either partner's perception of attachment (Walker & Thompson, 1984).

Problems of Parent Care

Caring for an aging parent can result in stress and strain for the adult children providing the care. Cicerelli (1983) found that 52 percent of his population reported some degree of strain, with one third reporting substantial strain. This included exhaustion and feelings that the elderly parent was not satisfied no matter what the children did. To a lesser extent the children felt tied down and had to give up social and recreational activities. But for most the total amount of strain was not great. Nearly three fourths of the adult children reported some degree of negative feelings toward the parent, including frustration, irritation, impatience, and guilt, with about half reporting substantial negative feelings. Personal strain and negative feelings, however, seemed to be more strongly related to the perceived parental dependency than to the actual amount of help provided.

The caregiving arrangement where two generations share the same household seems to be particularly fragile and vulnerable to disruption. In the Noelker and Wallace sample (1985), caregivers who were married with dependent children experienced greater health deterioration, more family disruption, and more elder-caregiver conflict than did unmarried children caring for a live-in parent. The married adult children with both spouse and dependent children reported the highest level of family disruption. While the caregivers, for the most part, reported commitment to their roles, which more viewed as permanent, multiple role demands contributed to stress. However, Suitor and Pillemer (1988) conducted a study of elderly parents who had an adult child residing with them. They found an unexpectedly low rate of parent-child conflict—64 percent reported no disagreements within the last year. The parents' health and dependency were less related to conflict than social structural variables. For example, conflict was lower when the resident child was older and when the parent and the child had the same or a similar marital status. According to Kochakian (1988), adult children should be encouraged to admit ambivalence and negative emotions as a way of avoiding the emotional burden of guilt. Further, he emphasized that aging parents do not need perfect children, just "good enough" children.

In sum, caring for elderly parents is a common phenomenon in contemporary society, despite the increase of women in the workforce, geographical mobility, the declining birthrate, and divergent family structures. Most elderly people desire to remain independent for as long as possible, and therefore few share the same households with their adult children. Nevertheless, for most families, contact is maintained in various forms, and aid and assistance are exchanged between generations.

There are few norms to guide relationships between these two generations of adults, but it does appear that attachment to one another is sustained throughout the family life cycle. Perceptions of the qualitative aspects of these relationships seem to be more significant than the frequency of contact and assistance. Stress and strain of at least a moderate level may result for adult caregivers, and the inability of elders to reciprocate may result in lower morale. Although these relationships may be likened to parenting, most research indicates that role reversal should be avoided. Adult day-care and recreational programs in senior-citizen centers provide some assistance in elder care, but most agree that these services are inadequate to meet the need.

COMMUNICATION THROUGHOUT THE LIFE CYCLE

Because communication is such an important ingredient in family relationships and because of its relevance to the changing nature of parenting, it seems appropriate to single it out here for special emphasis. Communication is the process by which there is an exchange of verbal and nonverbal cues from sender to receiver. It involves accurately expressing one's own ideas and feelings to someone else and listening to and understanding the ideas and feelings of others. Since communication is a two-way process, it involves both a sender and a receiver who alternate roles; that is, the sender of the message becomes the receiver when a response is given by the initial receiver. Most communication efforts are face-to-face interactions through which two parties try to establish and maintain a more satisfying relationship. It is these face-to-face interactions between parents and children throughout the life cycle that this section will emphasize.

Communication is both verbal and nonverbal. The choice of words, tone of voice, and inflections employed communicate messages verbally between individuals. Equally important, however, are the nonverbal aspects of posture, body movements, facial expressions, and dress modes that communicate messages between two people. When verbal and nonverbal aspects of communication are not consistent with each other, the result is a mixed message. However, messages may be solely verbal or nonverbal as well as a combination of both.

One of the reasons that communication breakdowns occur is that the message received may not be identical to the message sent. This may occur because of the inconsistency between verbal and nonverbal cues or because of the values, beliefs, expectations, or past experiences of the two parties concerned. Because effective communication is so important in maintaining positive relationships, it is necessary to examine communication systems and to develop certain skills that facilitate clear, accurate messages between the sender and receiver.

Communication is probably the most important parenting skill, providing the foundation for the parent-child relationship. Ironically, it is also the most difficult to learn and to use consistently (Wagonseller & McDowell, 1979). Many factors contribute to the degree of effective communication that parents are able to achieve with their children—for example, the kind of communication system they had with their own parents, the degree to which openness in relationships is valued, their perception of their parenting roles and the type of discipline they employ, and their conscious or unconscious expectations of their children. Because of the influence of these and many other subtle factors, parents often are unaware of potential breakdowns in communication with their children until it is too late. We will emphasize in this section that communication begins with the birth of a child and continues until death. The foundation for effective communication gradually builds as parents speak and act in specific ways with their children as they develop from infancy through adulthood. It has been said that two principles that lay the groundwork for effective communication are positive support and constructive criticism (Ginott, 1965; Wagonseller & McDowell, 1979). Positive support includes the verbal and nonverbal language of acceptance without excessive qualifying statements—''I'm glad you cleaned your room, *but* you forgot to hang up your clothes.'' Constructive criticism has as its purpose to state in a positive way what has to be done and avoid the typical 12 roadblocks to communication (see Figure 4-1).

While Gordon (1975) emphasized that these typical 12 categories are common responses of parents, he pointed out the destructive influence they have on parent-child relationships and stressed other, more positive approaches that tend to build self-esteem and strengthen relationships (refer to Chapter 5, PET). Parents often wonder why a young child does not ask questions about sex, why a school-age child is unable to verbalize her anger, why an adolescent refuses to discuss peer conflicts with them, or why an adult child fails to call often. These parents fail to realize that an open communication system between parent and child begins in infancy and continues throughout the child's development. It cannot occur simply at the time when the parent feels that it is appropriate to discuss a specific matter.

Parent-Child Communication

Infancy. Evidence supports the importance of early parental behaviors in beginning to establish positive communication—frequently talking to the baby, reinforcing his efforts to communicate, providing words and labels for the child, and reflecting the child's feelings. While acquisition of language is an extremely complex process, it appears that modeling is one important factor. As the caregiver meets the infant's physical needs, talking to the child even though he does not understand the specific message stimulates growth of language. Responding immediately and consistently to the child's cues, such as crying or fussing, communicates to the child that his efforts are receiving attention. Parents soon learn that the baby is trying to communicate through various sounds and body language.

Perhaps one of the best ways to encourage language development during the infancy stage is to reinforce babbling. During this early stage of language development, parents can respond by mimicking the child, smiling, or talking back to her. Once the child begins to say real words, parents then need to enunciate clearly and refrain from using baby talk. Further, communication is facilitated if the child is encouraged to use language for expressing her needs.

Providing labels for objects through reading

FIGURE 4-1   Typical Roadblocks to Communication

1. Ordering, directing, commanding
2. Warning, admonishing, threatening
3. Exhorting, moralizing, preaching
4. Advising, giving solutions or suggestions
5. Lecturing, teaching, giving logical arguments
6. Judging, criticizing, disagreeing, or blaming
7. Praising, agreeing
8. Name-calling, ridiculing, shaming
9. Interpreting, analyzing, diagnosing
10. Reassuring, sympathizing, consoling, or supporting
11. Probing, questioning, interrogating
12. Withdrawing, distracting, humoring, directing

Source: Gordon, T. (1975). *Parent effectiveness training.* New York: New American Library.

picture books or by naming objects as they are presented to the child are important during this stage. Even labeling the child's feelings, such as anger or frustration, provides the foundation for later verbalizations of feelings by the child.

Attitudes of the parents toward the verbalization or expression of feelings in other ways are communicated even during infancy. An infant quickly learns that it is either all right or not all right to whine or express anger. A toddler soon realizes either that a tantrum gets what he wants or that some other more acceptable form of communication is necessary. What is important during these early months and years is to convey to the child that it is all right to have feelings, and that words stand not only for objects, but also thoughts and feelings.

Parents, then, set the stage for communication when their children are still infants and toddlers. They communicate acceptance of needs and feelings by their response to the child's expression of these; they indicate that they value language as a tool for problem solving when they fail to reinforce tantrum behavior; and they place a value on the communication process when they encourage and extend the child's language efforts. On the other hand, parents may communicate negative attitudes toward communication very early when they scold the child for repeating a "bathroom" or slang word or if the child asks the parent its meaning. Repeated experiences of this type say to the child that "we do not discuss these matters" and begin to create a barrier between parent and child.

The preschool years. Early childhood is particularly critical for promoting an open communication system, as the preschool child has the foundation for language and begins to express a wide variety of feelings in a verbal manner. Therefore it is important for the significant adults (parents and teachers) in the child's life to continue stimulating language development, to convey an accepting attitude toward feelings, and to assist the child in expressing feelings appropriately.

A continuation of language stimulation may be accomplished in a number of ways. The preschool child needs to have a wide variety of books read to him. Reading to the child and discussing the book with him not only assist in the development of many cognitive skills but also provide a time when parent and child can develop a warm, close bond. This sharing time communicates to the child that he is important and that the parent has time to listen. Continuing to promote development of vocabulary and other verbal skills is important. Children frequently exhibit incorrect word usage and grammar. It is wise at this stage not to make an issue of correct grammar. Simply repeating the phrase in the correct manner provides the appropriate model and does not belittle the child.

Taking time to really listen to the young child is a way to facilitate effective communication. Often parents respond to a child by saying "Uhhmh" or "Okay" without really hearing what has been said. Children recognize quickly that parents really are not listening. Repeated negative reinforcement in the form of not listening will lead eventually to a child's feeling that it is useless to talk.

During the preschool years (about 4 years of age), the peak age for questioning emerges. Children will ask the same question repeatedly. "Why" seems to be their favorite word. Children ask questions for many reasons—to get attention, to obtain additional information, or simply to be sure that their thinking is correct. It seems important for adults to respond to children's questions truthfully, patiently, and in a manner the children can understand. Children resist long lectures, being preached to, talked at, and criticized (Ginott, 1965).

Most children during the preschool period will begin to ask questions regarding sex differences and reproduction, especially if the young child has been exposed to older children or if a birth occurs in her own family. Many parents find these questions uncomfortable because they wonder if the child is old enough to understand, or how much they should say, or just what words to use. If parents respond to these questions with accurate answers in simple terms and with a tone of voice and body language that do not communicate disapproval, then young children are likely to continue to view their parents as adults whom they can trust to provide information and to participate in communication. On the other hand, adults who put the child off to a later time,

imply that the subject is dirty, or give the child false information will soon have children who stop asking questions.

Parents need to be alert to hidden meanings in the child's conversation during this stage of development. A child who says "Do you want to go outdoors with me?" may really be saying "I don't feel comfortable about going out there with all those children." It is important to help the child put the feelings into words. The adult may reflect the child's feelings by saying "You don't feel comfortable about asking them if you can play." Children during the preschool years experience both positive and negative feelings and are usually very open in expressing them. However, it is easy during these years for adults to convey that only positive feelings should be expressed. Feelings of anger, frustration, hostility, and jealousy are equally as legitimate as those of love, affection, and joy. Indicating to the child that it is all right to have these feelings and helping him express them constructively build self-esteem and facilitate communication.

Communication should preserve the child's, as well as the adult's, self-respect (Ginott, 1965). Children need help in putting their feelings into words and also in interpreting the feelings and actions of others. Adults can assist by verbal descriptions, such as "Timmy is crying because he didn't want his mother to leave."

A common mistake of adults during these early years is conveying the traditional stereotypical attitude that males should not express feelings. Saying "Big boys don't cry" tells boys that feelings of hurt should not be expressed. On the other hand, boys sometimes learn that openly expressing feelings of affection is not desirable either. It does appear critical during these years to help both boys and girls learn that feelings should be expressed constructively, regardless of sex, and to provide appropriate avenues for expression. Reading books and talking about pictures that portray individuals experiencing and expressing feelings seem to be helpful, as well as discussing the feelings of people in certain situations. Providing a variety of experiences to talk about stimulates communication.

Modeling of adults continues to be important during the preschool years. When adults express their own feelings (for example, anger) to the child in appropriate ways, an example is set for the child to follow. Other effective techniques of communication—such as maintaining eye contact by stooping to the child's level; establishing body contact by, say, placing a hand on her shoulder while talking; and using a calm, soft voice in speaking—should be practiced and exercised during this developmental stage.

It is not too soon for families to engage in family discussions where everyone can have a say. Children need to learn early that they are important family members who can participate in decisions that affect their lives. Planning together encourages consideration for others, as communication is a two-way process. Children need help in respecting and appreciating the viewpoints and feelings of others. A good motto might be ''Everyone can have a say even if he cannot have his way.''

In summary, during the preschool years, adults should provide experiences that promote language development; portray a warm, accepting attitude toward the child's feelings; utilize active listening to discover the hidden meaning of the child's verbalizations; share these hidden meanings; provide an appropriate model; and guide the child in appropriate expressions of feelings. This approach not only encourages the child to communicate but also provides him with skills to use in communication.

The school-age years.   Once the child starts school, her language skills are greatly expanded through formalized learning in the communication arts. Opportunities for communicating with a wider variety of people (other adults, teachers, and peers) are afforded and increased avenues of expression are provided. The child can then utilize the written form of communication as well as verbal expression. Adults cannot assume, however, that children understand all the words they use.

Parent-child communication during the school years also is expanded. Not only are family matters important, but also school work, teachers, peers, and leisure and extracurricular activities become topics of conversations between parents and children. Since children spend less time in direct contact with their parents, it is important for effective communication to occur. Parents communicate an interest in children by listening to their concerns relating to the expanded world. The listening techniques demonstrated during the preschool years should be utilized. Responding to children's questions by providing appropriate information and encouraging children to talk continue to be important. These are the years when the principles outlined in the strategies discussed in Chapter 5 may be utilized even more effectively.

Many communications between parents and children during these years are directly related to the developmental characteristics of children. Children talk back and accuse parents of unfairness; they forget chores; they fail to show up on time for dinner; they undertake projects enthusiastically by getting materials laid out and then have to be prodded to finish the project or clean up the mess. Many school-age children resist taking a bath, will not keep their rooms clean, and are not interested in social niceties. During the fourth, fifth, and sixth grades, problem behavior during the school-age years reaches its peak. Teasing, discourtesy, scuffling, rebelliousness, carelessness, untidiness, and disobedience are typical. Some children are frequently irritable, easily offended, and often discouraged. Even though family values have been internalized, children begin to drop identification with adult authority and establish strong bonds of identity with a group of peers. All these developmental problems put a strain on parent-child communication. Parents have to be particularly careful to avoid being totally negative and utilizing destructive criticism. Children's self-concepts are sensitive during the school-age years as they see themselves more realistically in comparison to their peers. Utilizing some of the principles set forth in Faber and Mazlish's (1980) strategy for effective communication appears to be particularly appropriate. Ginott (1965), on whose work Faber and Mazlish's strategy was based (see Chapter 5), advocated the following effective techniques: responding to the relationship rather than to the event itself, utilizing praise appropriately, and using constructive criticism.

In summary, parents should recognize the developmental problems that are likely to affect communication during the school-age years, demonstrate a sincere interest in the child's expanded world, and utilize the techniques of effective communication that have already been outlined. Active listening; sharing hidden meanings; and communicating acceptance of feelings, touch, and so on are still important tools for parent-child communication.

Adolescence.   Communication, or the lack of it, between parents and teenagers probably has

been one of the most widely publicized areas of conflict during the adolescent years. These years often present communication breakdowns for both adolescents and parents. However, the basis for effective communication between parent and child during adolescence has already been developed, and it is unlikely that effective communication can occur at this time if it has not been established. If the parents have been so rigidly authoritarian in their child rearing and have not encouraged their children to express feelings during the preschool and school-age years, it is unlikely that children will suddenly do so as adolescents (Albrecht, 1972). Some parents have been so immersed in their own activities or concerns that they have failed to demonstrate a sincere interest in their children's world. Therefore it is not unusual to get a simple "Okay" from a teenager who is asked "How did things go today?"

The point is that effective communication between parents and teenagers is largely dependent on the degree of healthy communication previously established. Even then, new barriers to effective communication emerge as teenagers seek to establish a sense of identity and as parents are struggling with their own developmental crises (see Chapter 3). Often teenagers who previously have been very open with their parents become more reticent about their activities, especially those that involve members of the opposite sex. What many parents fail to realize is that children may be very comfortable discussing issues that are general in nature (for example, venereal disease, sexuality, and reproduction), but when those issues become personalized, they then become more private and less open to discussion with parents. It seems important for parents to recognize teenagers' rights to private thoughts, feelings, and behaviors but at the same time to provide a sounding board for them to test these on.

Several criteria for effective communication with adolescents were outlined by Albrecht (1972). First, parents must recognize that communication is a two-way process, not merely a matter of establishing their own opinions and getting their own way with their children. Another factor that contributes to effective communication with adolescents is an awareness of what is occurring in the adolescent culture—current activities of interest, heroes, music, modes of dress, and even teenage "lingo." Awareness also means being sensitive to nuances of behavior—tone of voice, statements made, and questions asked—that may indicate that things are not going too well. Encouraging adolescents to express their feelings and accepting those that are expressed communicate an awareness of others so necessary for communication. Adolescents, however, often have very intense feelings, and this intensity may make parents withdraw or fail in their efforts to communicate. While parents cannot prevent children from feeling pain, hurt, frustration, confusion, and anguish, they can communicate feelings of empathy. The art of listening was emphasized by Albrecht as a necessary criterion for effective parent-adolescent communication. Active listening, listening with the third ear, or reading between the lines—or whatever it may be called—becomes an even more crucial tool for effective communication during the adolescent years. Just hearing adolescents out without being judgmental appears to be important in conveying a feeling of worthiness.

Being honest and leveling with teenagers was the final criterion described by Albrecht for communicating effectively. Trying to protect children from the realities faced by the family can only hinder communication efforts. Adolescents recognize both strengths and weaknesses of parents, no matter how hard parents try to conceal them. Openness in discussion and sincere negotiations are more effective approaches. Sometimes parents and adolescents have to call a truce and simply agree to disagree. When this situation occurs, it may be necessary for parents and teenagers to contract to work on an issue. The only agreement necessary is an agreement on the procedure. When a contract is to occur, first, identify the issue; second, secure the intention of both parent(s) and child to work on it; third, reach a procedural consensus; fourth, engage in complete self-disclosure by all parties; and, finally, proceed with an I'm OK, You're OK orientation (Miller, Nunnally, & Wackman, 1975). This procedure preserves the integrity of both the parent and the child and allows effective communication to continue in the face of disagreement.

Perhaps the most useful and in-depth guidelines for parents to help ease the communication barrier between themselves and their teenagers were discussed by Ginott (1969). These are summarized in Box 4e. While some of these suggestions may appear controversial, Ginott's explanations and examples are valid, sensible, and worthy of consideration.

In summary, communication is an issue that looms large in parent-adolescent relationships. If the foundation for open, effective communication has been built in the early years, barriers to communication are not likely to be insurmountable. Parents need to recognize the reciprocal nature of communication, be aware of the teen's special culture, encourage acceptance of feelings, engage in appropriate listening techniques, and be honest. The use of negotiation and formal contracts may facilitate communication.

Later Life

Parents and adult children. When children become adults, communication with their parents often improves, especially if the adult children no longer live in the parental home. Many of the adolescent sources of conflict have been resolved, and children and parents can communicate in a more mature, mutual fashion. Parents have normally reached the stage where they have resolved issues surrounding mid-life crises, and children have established a sense of identity and perhaps a sense of intimacy.

If children are living in the parental home, issues involved in communication may be those related to life-style, division of responsibilities, and/or finances. Parents may find themselves in frequent negotiation and compromise. It may be difficult for them to realize and accept that their children are really grown-up now, and that the nature of their relationship must move toward a peer relationship rather than a parent-child relationship. Children, too, may find it so comfortable to have their parents continue doing things for them that they have not moved toward more responsible adult behavior. "Letting go," then, is a reciprocal phenomenon.

Adult children who live near, rather than with, their parents may have fewer communication problems with them by virtue of their increased independence. These children usually stay in touch with their parents and perhaps participate in a mutual exchange of aid. Still, parents may not have fully accepted their adult

---

BOX 4e   GUIDELINES FOR COMMUNICATING WITH ADOLESCENTS

1. Accept the restlessness, loneliness, and discontent expressed by the adolescent.
2. Preserve the uniqueness teenagers may feel about themselves and their problems by not always providing "instant understanding"; for example, "I know exactly how you feel. I was your age once."
3. Differentiate between acceptance and approval, between tolerance and sanction.
4. Avoid emulating the language and conduct of a teenager.
5. Do not collect thorns; that is, do not ferret out unpleasant facts about the teen's conduct and track down small defects in his character.
6. Do not step on corns (see Chapter 3, regarding preadolescents); that is, avoid talking about areas in which the teenager is overly sensitive.
7. Do not invite dependence, as dependency creates hostility.
8. Do not hurry to correct facts, as a teenager often responds to corrections with obstinacy; for example, "My father is *always* right."
9. Do not violate the teen's privacy; by providing privacy, a parent demonstrates respect.
10. Avoid clichés and preaching, especially "when I was your age . . ."
11. Do not talk in chapters; that is, do not lecture, preach, teach, or pontificate.
12. Do not label the teenager in his presence, as children tend to live up to roles cast for them by their parents.
13. Do not use reverse psychology.
14. Do not send contradictory messages. To avoid conflict, a statement should carry one message: a clear prohibition, a gracious permission, or an open choice.
15. Do not futurize; focus on dealing with the present rather than preparing for the future.

Source: Ginott, H. (1969). *Between parent and teenager.* New York: Macmillan.

---

status and may be viewed by their children as interfering with their lives.

When adult children marry, parents may feel that the mate who has been selected is not really "good enough": A father tends to feel that no man is good enough for his daughter, and a mother tends to feel that no woman is good enough for her son. In-law relationships often present one of the biggest dilemmas for young married couples—for example, whose house should they visit for holidays and special occasions? Mutual understanding and effective communication in the resolution of these issues are important.

Further, young adults are faced with a number of fairly important decisions, such as continuing school, vocational choices, financial planning for the future, and living arrangements. Most adult children fail to appreciate unsolicited advice from parents. The role of parents, then, is to be available for counsel if requested. Knowing that parents can be used as resources often provides a sense of comfort and security for young adults, but noninterference is essential if good relationships are to be maintained.

Effective communication during this period is the result of, first, parental attitudes that reflect the maturity of children and, second, a continuation of appropriate techniques established earlier. Interpersonal distrust, defensive behavior, and alienation result in barriers to communication. Such techniques as evaluation, control, superiority, and certainty tend to close lines of communication. On the other hand, active listening, self- and other-awareness, self-disclosure, and sometimes negotiation are skills that keep lines of communication open.

Elderly caring. As with adult children, communication with elderly parents seems to proceed more smoothly when the two generations do not share the same household. It has been documented that, given good health, most elderly people choose to live independently of their children. Even so, middle-aged children and grandchildren who live nearby are generally in frequent contact and often assist with the provision of goods and services. When the elderly are physically and mentally fit, few communication problems with their adult children are likely to arise. However, as health begins to fail, as the older person becomes more dependent, and as the demands on the middle generation increase, poor communication may lead to a tense, often intolerable, relationship.

As elderly people reach Erikson's final stage, integrity versus despair, what Erikson calls the virtue of wisdom embodies all eight stages of development. According to Erikson (cited in Evans, 1967), if a person lives long enough, she faces a renewal of infantile tendencies—a certain childlike quality if she is lucky and senile childishness if she is not. It is this senile childishness that middle-aged children may find frustrating. In a sense, an adult caregiver may find herself faced with trying to communicate with an elder who behaves much like a child. Erikson pointed out that one cannot be very wise if she still tries to capture in old age what she did or did not have as a youth.

On the other hand, the elderly have a very special role in recapturing memories of the past for their children, grandchildren, and great-grandchildren. Being able to share these memories helps them to develop a sense of integrity about their lives and prevents loneliness and despair. Patience, acceptance, and even indulgence, much as with young children, prevents alienation. And, once again, effective techniques of communication help to keep the relationship strong.

In sum, the foundation for positive human relationships is the development and maintenance of effective communication. The vast array of literature on the subject and the prevalence of training programs indicate the need for understanding and developing communication skills.

Communication is a life-long process, beginning in the cradle and ending in the grave. Parents who have established good communication with their children continue to communicate with them effectively as adults. In addition, the same skills that they used with their children serve them well in communicating with their elderly parents.

SUMMARY

Parenting is a process that begins with the birth of the first child and continues through the maturity of all children in the family. As children develop from one major stage to the next, their needs and behavioral characteristics change. Similarly, as parents progress through the stages of adulthood, their developmental needs change, as well. Throughout the life cycle the process of parenting is a reciprocal one. Each child affects the behavior of each parent, and each parent affects the behavior of each child so that multidimensional relationships occur. When children are young, they are dependent on parents. As they approach adulthood, dependency needs become more balanced, and patterns of aid become more reciprocal. As parents approach later life, needs change so that elderly parents become more dependent on their children. In a sense, the process of parenting has come full circle.

An intervening stage in this process, for most families, is that of grandparenting. There is great heterogeneity and diversity in today's grandparents, and their rights and responsibilities are not well articulated. Because grandparenthood is not self-initiated or voluntary, it differs from parenthood and other adult roles. But for many, it represents an opportunity to relive parenthood, or to have a second chance. Like parenting adult children and elderly parent caring, grandparenting has few norms to guide relationships.

Throughout the life cycle, the single most important variable in parent-child relationships is the development and maintenance of effective communication. Children begin to learn communication skills or the lack of them very early in their relationships with parents. If parents develop and model an effective communication system with their children, the overall parent-child relationship is likely to thrive. Communication is an integral feature of the changing nature of parenting.

REFERENCES

ADAMS, B. (1986). The middle-class adult and his widowed or still-married mother. *Social Problems, 16,* 50–59.

ALBRECHT, M. (1972). *Parents and teenagers: Getting through to each other.* New York: Parents Magazine Press.

ALDOUS, J. (1985). Parent-adult child relations as affected by the grandparent status. In V. Bengston & J. Robertson (Eds.), *Grandparenthood* (pp. 117–132). Beverly Hills: Sage.

BENGSTON, V. (1985). Diversity and symbolism in grandparental roles. In V. Bengston & J. Robertson (Eds.), *Grandparenthood* (pp. 11–25). Beverly Hills: Sage.

BERNARD, J. (1975). *Women, wives, mothers.* Chicago: Adeline.

BRODY, E. (1981). Women in the middle and family help to older people. *The Gerontologist, 21,* 471–480.

BRODY, E., JOHNSEN, P., FULCOMER, M., & LANG, A. (1983). Women's changing roles and help to elderly parents: Attitudes of three generations of women. *Journal of Gerontology, 38*(5), 597–607.

CHERLIN, A., & FURSTENBERG, F. (1985). Styles and strategies of grandparenting. In V. Bengson & J. Robertson (Eds.), *Grandparenthood* (pp. 97–116). Beverly Hills: Sage.

CICERELLI, V. (1981). *Helping elderly parents: The role of adult children.* Boston: Auburn House.

CICERELLI, V. (1983). Adult children and their elderly parents. In T. H. Brubaker (Ed.), *Family relationships in later life* (pp. 31–47). Beverly Hills: Sage.

CLEMENS, A., & AXELSON, L. (1985). The not-so-empty nest: The return of the fledgling adult. *Family Relations, 34*(2), 259–264.

DEWIT, D., WISTER, A., & BURCH, T. Physical distance and social contact between elders and their adult children. *Research on Aging, 10*(1), 56–79.

EVANS, R. (1967). *Dialogue with Erik Erikson.* New York: Harper & Row.

FABER, A., & MAZLISH, E. (1980). *How to talk so kids will listen & how to listen so kids will talk.* New York: Avon.

GINOTT, H. (1965). *Between parent and child.* New York: Macmillan.

GINOTT, H. (1969). *Between parent and teenager.* New York: Macmillan.

GLICK, P., & LIN, S. (1986). More young adults are living with their parents: Who are they? *Journal of Marriage and the Family, 48*(1), 107–112.

GORDON, T. (1975). *Parent effectiveness training.* New York: New American Library.

"Grown children carrying more load." (1989, March 4). *Albuquerque Journal,* p. C10.

HAGESTED, G. (1985). Continuity and connectedness. In V. Bengston & J. Robertson (Eds.), *Grandparenthood* (pp. 31–48). Beverly Hills: Sage.

HAGESTED, G., & LANG, M. (1986). The transition to grandparenthood. *Journal of Family Issues, 7*(2), 115–130.

HILL, R. (1970). *Family development in three generations.* Cambridge, MA: Schenkman.

HOUSER, B., & BERKMAN, S. (1984). Aging parent/mature child relationships. *Journal of Marriage and the Family, 46*(2), 295–299.

KOCHAKIAN, M. (1988, July 18). Aging parents don't need 'perfect' children. *Albuquerque Journal,* p. A4.

LANG, A., & BRODY, E. (1983). Characteristics of middle-aged daughters and help to their elderly parents. *Journal of Marriage and the Family, 45*(1), 193–202.

LEIGH, G. (1982). Kinship interaction over the life span. *Journal of Marriage and the Family, 44*(1), 197–208.

LEE, G., & ELLITHORPE, E. (1982). Intergenerational exchange and subjective well-being among the elderly. *Journal of Marriage and the Family, 44*(1), 217–244.

MCCREADY, W. (1985). Styles of grandparenting among white ethnics. In V. Bengston & J. Robertson (Eds.), *Grandparenthood* (pp. 49–60). Beverly Hills: Sage.

MILLER, S., NUNNALLY, E., & WACKMAN, D. (1975). *Alive and aware: Improving communication in relationships.* Minneapolis: Interpersonal Communication Programs.

NOELKER, L., & WALLACE, R. (1985). The organization of family care for impaired elderly. *Journal of Family Issues, 6*(1), 23–44.

ROBERTSON, J., TICE, C., & LOEB, L. (1985). Grandparenthood: From knowledge to programs and policy. In V. Bengston & J. Robertson (Eds.), *Grandparenthood* (pp. 211–224). Beverly Hills: Sage.

ROSENMAYR, L. (1978). A view of multigenerational relations in the family. Paper presented at the 9th World Congress of Sociology, Uppsala, Sweden.

SCHWARTZ, A. (1979). Psychological dependency: An emphasis on the later years. In P. Ragan (Ed.), *Aging parents* (pp. 116–125). Los Angeles: University of Southern California Press.

SHANNAS, E. (1979). The family as a social support system in old age. *The Gerontologist, 19*(2), 169–179.

STOLLER, E. (1983). Parental caregiving by adult children. *Journal of Marriage and the Family, 45*(4), 851–858.

STOLLER, E. (1985). Exchange patterns in the informal support networks of the elderly: The impact of reciprocity on morale. *Journal of Marriage and the Family, 47*(2), 335–342.

SUITOR, J., & PILLEMER, K. (1988). Explaining intergenerational conflict when adult children and elderly parents live together. *Journal of Marriage and the Family, 50*(4), 1037–1047.

THOMPSON, L., & WALKER, A. (1984). Mothers and daughters: Aid patterns and attachment. *Journal of Marriage and the Family, 46*(2), 313–322.

THOMPSON, L., & WALKER, A. (1987). Mothers as mediators of intimacy between grandmothers and their young adult granddaughters. *Family Relations, 36*(1), 72–77.

WAGONSELLER, B., & MCDOWELL, R. (1979). *You and your child.* Champaign, IL: Research Press.

WALKER, A., & THOMPSON, L. (1983). Intimacy and intergenerational aid and contact among mothers and daughters. *Journal of Marriage and the Family, 45*(4), 841–849.

5

Becoming a More Effective Parent: Contemporary Strategies

Because of the eagerness of parents for support and guidance in rearing their children, a number of strategies for child rearing have evolved to help parents become more effective. Most have been reflective of the social nature of our society at the time and therefore have been discarded as they have become inappropriate or inconsistent with prevailing attitudes and practices. Many strategies have been introduced to parents simply by the publication of books designed specifically for them. Others have been more formalized in the sense that they have been "taught" to parents by professionals. More recently, strategies have been developed in kits or books intended to be taught to parents in the workshop format over a specified period of time, usually no longer than 6 to 8 weeks.

This chapter discusses contemporary strategies for parenting, some of which have been widely used over a period of time and others that are relatively recent. It is interesting to note that recent strategies represent combined concepts of the earlier strategies. The earlier strategies include the following:

1. Parent Effectiveness Training—developed by Dr. Thomas Gordon.

2. Systematic Training for Effective Parenting (STEP)—developed by Dr. Don Dinkmeyer and Dr. Gary McKay based on the work of Dr. Rudolf Dreikurs and Dr. Alfred Adler.
3. Transactional Analysis—originally developed as a therapeutic technique by Dr. Eric Berne and refined as a parenting strategy by Dr. Thomas Harris, Ms. Dorothy Babcock, and Dr. Terry Keepers.
4. Behavior Modification—based on the work of Dr. B. F. Skinner and applied to parenting by numerous psychologists and educators.

The more recent strategies include the following:

1. Active Parenting—developed by Dr. Michael Popkin based on ideas proposed by Dr. Alfred Adler, Dr. Rudolf Dreikurs, and Dr. Carl Rogers.
2. How to Talk So Kids Will Listen—developed by Ms. Adele Fabish and Ms. Elaine Mazlish based on work of Dr. Haim Ginott.
3. Living with 10- to 15-Year-Olds—developed by Gayle Dorman, Dick Geldof, and Bill Scarborough; a curriculum for parents and

professionals who work with young adolescents.

4. Responsive Parenting—developed by Saf Lerman; a series of nine pamphlets and videocassettes designed for parents, which form the core of the program.

5. Assertive Discipline—developed by Lee and Marlene Canter based on their earlier success with this model in school classroom management.

Since it is not possible to provide an in-depth description of each strategy, only the most salient aspects will be discussed. Relevant research will be included when available. Finally, a brief comparison and evaluation of the above strategies will conclude the chapter.

PARENT EFFECTIVENESS TRAINING

The first Parent Effectiveness Training (PET) class was organized in 1962 in Pasadena, California, by Dr. Thomas Gordon and consisted of 17 parents. By now, however, PET has reached over 400,000 parents in thousands of communities in the United States and abroad (Doherty & Ryder, 1980; Gordon, 1975). The program consists of eight weekly 3-hour classes taught by instructors who have participated in a 5½-day training program in methods and concepts led by Dr. Gordon and his staff. For the first few years classes were taught without a book, but Dr. Gordon published *Parent Effectiveness Training* in 1975 and *PET in Action* in 1976. As a result of requests from school administrators wanting to apply PET to teachers, Dr. Gordon published *Teacher Effectiveness Training* in 1975.

Expansion of the PET movement included training programs for supervisors, managers, and executives in organizations (businesses, industry, hospitals, and government agencies) called Leadership Effectiveness Training (LET). Finally, Youth Effectiveness Training (YET) was designed as a course for children in trouble, as well as for youth organizations such as Boys Clubs, Girls Clubs, Y.M.C.A., Y.W.C.A., and Girl and Boy Scouts.

Parent Effectiveness Training is based on a theory of human relationships believed to be applicable to all relationships between people, not only to the parent-child relationship. It includes a specific set of skills to be applied in these relationships. The basic principles of PET may be summarized as follows:

1. The inconsistency principle—Gordon "explodes the myth" that parents must be consistent or else they will harm their children. He emphasizes that the range of acceptable versus unacceptable behaviors will vary depending on parents' own moods, the child in question, and the given situation. Further, he contends that rather than creating a consistent "united front," each parent is free to take his separate stance in response to a particular behavior of the child. Recognition of these human inconsistencies serves to diminish guilt and anxiety in parents.

2. The problem ownership principle—Gordon believes that child behaviors fall into three categories: (a) behaviors that are unacceptable to the parent because they interfere with the parent's rights or prevent the parent from having his needs met (the parent owns the problem); (b) behaviors that indicate the child's needs are not being met or that she is unhappy, frustrated, or in trouble (the child owns the problem); and (c) behaviors that cause neither parent nor child a problem (the no-problem area). The contention is that differentiation of problem ownership is critical because a different set of skills is used in each case. When the parent owns the problem, he uses "confrontation skills" in its solution; when the child owns the problem, the parent uses "helping skills" in its solution (Gordon, 1975, 1976).

With these basic principles as fundamental to the theory, the PET method is based on skills that facilitate effective communication: counseling skills, confrontation skills, and problem-solving skills. The first skill is learning to use language to demonstrate acceptance. Gordon emphasizes the danger of false acceptance, pretending to accept the child's behavior when actually feeling angry or frustrated. He attempts to help parents understand that they will feel

both accepting and unaccepting of their children, and that acceptance of children must be demonstrated. Acceptance may be demonstrated by not intervening in a child's activities; by saying nothing (passive listening); or by the use of simple "door-openers" that encourage the child to say more—for example, "I see," "Really," "You don't say," and "Tell me about it."

Active Listening

However, a more important skill (a counseling skill) to keep communication open is what Gordon describes as active listening, in which the receiver is as actively involved in the communication process as the sender. The receiver tries to understand what the sender is feeling or what her message means. Then the receiver puts his understanding into his own words (codes) and feeds it back for the sender's verification. Gordon believes that active listening has several benefits, which are identified in Box 5a.

Gordon believes that active listening is a method for putting to work a set of basic attitudes. He identified the following attitudes that are necessary for the parent to be an active lis-

tener: (1) wanting to hear what the child has to say; (2) genuinely wanting to be helpful with the child's particular problem at the time; (3) being able to accept the child's feelings even if they are different from the parent's; (4) having a deep feeling of trust in the child's capacity to handle his feelings, to work through them, and to find solutions to his problems; (5) appreciating that feelings are transitory rather than permanent; and (6) seeing the child as someone separate from the parent, thereby permitting the child to have his own feelings. Examples of active listening may be found in Dr. Gordon's books (1975, 1976).

I-messages

Equally important to listening effectively to children is talking effectively to them. Most parents use ineffective methods of communicating, such as sending a "solution message" or a "put-down message." Gordon's emphasis on "I-messages" (a confrontation skill) rather than on "you-messages" helps parents to understand that, if they give the child a statement of fact about how the parent is feeling in a given situation, they

---

BOX 5a   BENEFITS OF ACTIVE LISTENING

Fosters a catharsis for troublesome feelings.

Helps children become less afraid of negative feelings.

Promotes a relationship of warmth between parent and child.

Facilitates problem solving by the child.

Influences the child to be more willing to listen to parent's thoughts and ideas.

"Keeps the ball" with the child; the child begins to analyze his own problem, eventually arriving at a solution.

Source: Gordon, T. (1975). *Parent effectiveness training.* New York: New American Library.

---

are less likely to be met with resistance and rebellion. For example, when a child has a messy room, a "you-message" might be: "You are so lazy; this room is a mess." An alternative "I-message" might be: "I get frustrated when I'm trying to keep the house clean and I see that you haven't done your share." The second alternative avoids implying that the child is "bad" and places the responsibility with the child for modifying his behavior. "I-messages" have three components: (1) a statement of feeling; (2) a non-judgmental description of the child's behavior; and (3) a description of the tangible effects of the child's behavior on the parent. Gordon suggests using active listening when the child owns the

problem and "I-messages" when the parent owns the problem.

No-Lose Method of Conflict Resolution

Another important concept in Gordon's PET strategy is the "no-lose" method of conflict resolution (a problem-solving skill). Normally parents tend to think of conflict resolution in terms of someone's winning and someone's losing, which inevitably involves a power struggle between parents and children. If the parent decides on the solution to a problem and influences the child to accept it, either by persuasion or by power and authority, then the parent wins (the

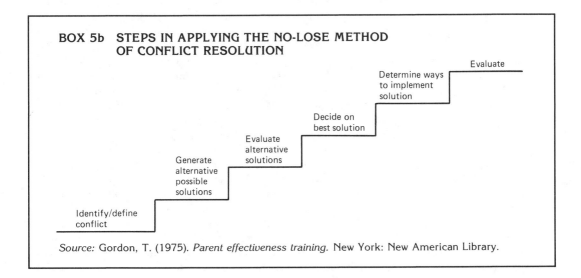

BOX 5b   STEPS IN APPLYING THE NO-LOSE METHOD OF CONFLICT RESOLUTION

Identify/define conflict

Generate alternative possible solutions

Evaluate alternative solutions

Decide on best solution

Determine ways to implement solution

Evaluate

Source: Gordon, T. (1975). *Parent effectiveness training.* New York: New American Library.

authoritarian method). On the other hand, if the child determines the solution and uses her power to persuade the parent to give in, then the child wins (the permissive method). Gordon contends that a more effective method of resolving conflict is based on the reduction of the power differential between parents and children, a "no-power," "no-lose" approach in which the solution to a problem is acceptable to both. See Box 5b for steps in applying the no-lose method of conflict resolution. When a conflict-of-needs situation occurs, both parent and child offer possible solutions, which they critically evaluate in order to arrive at a final solution. This method is effective because the child is motivated to carry out the solution, there is a greater chance of arriving at a high-quality solution, the child's thinking skills are utilized, less hostility occurs, there is less need for enforcement, and children are treated with respect.

In summary, Gordon emphasizes helping children become responsible through parents' creating an atmosphere of acceptance, respect, and consideration. Implicit in Gordon's strategy is the belief that children are capable problem solvers, particularly in an environment where effective communication prevails and power struggles are reduced.

Evaluation of PET

Even though PET has achieved a certain measure of acceptance by both parents and professionals, reservations about the program have been expressed. Four major criticisms were cited by Doherty and Ryder (1980):

1. PET tends to technologize the parent-child relationship; that is, it is presented as a parent-training program comparable to any other job-training program. It views effective parenting as an identifiable set of techniques that can be applied in a unidirectional fashion by the parents to the child.
2. PET makes harsh and unwarranted judgments about parents. Derogation and blaming of parents is a consistent theme.
3. PET presents a simplistic formula for handling all parent-child problems; that is, it is seen as a universal strategy for families in

all cultures and for children in all developmental levels. The proscription on the use of parental power is not differentiated for 2-year-olds and adolescents. Further, the implication is that if a skill does not work, then the parent has used it ineffectively or inappropriately.
4. PET is based on questionable assumptions about family dynamics; that is, PET fails to take into account the reciprocal relationship between parents and children. Since the emphasis is on a parent-child dyad, no attention is given to multiadic relationships.

These investigators further described potential hazards of PET as follows: There may be an increase in covert manipulation by the PET parent as she uses powerful communication techniques and controls the child without his knowledge; parents may come to mistrust their own capabilities and increase their dependence on the program; parents may experience unnecessary guilt if they fail to use the program faithfully; and there may be unnecessary family division unless both parents participate in, and are committed to, PET.

While these criticisms and potential hazards seem to us to be somewhat harsh, it certainly is true that there may be merit in considering some of the questions raised. It seems unwise to rely totally on a strategy that focuses almost entirely on the acquisition of skills without requisite feelings and attitudes. Although Gordon does address the attitudes and feelings of parents, he seems to assume that one can learn the skills and acquire the accompanying attitudes in the process. One other precaution seems necessary: Empirical research concerning the long-term effectiveness of PET is minimal.

One recent study was conducted by Hills and Knowles (1987). Mothers who were graduates of PET, Behavior Modification, and Adlerian programs were compared to control mothers 12 months later as they worked with their children on a task and discussed problem situations. Parents who had been trained in PET and Behavior Modification were judged to provide for independence of the child within a warm climate when compared to a control group. No significant differences were found for other comparisons. This study provided some support for the transfer and retention of certain skills. However, these authors concluded that parents may need additional theoretical understanding of concepts in programs and may need a post-training phase to deliberately provide for transfer and integration of skills.

A review of the literature (Rinn & Markle, 1977) noted that most research conducted has been unpublished, limited in scope, and inadequate in design. Some studies have shown significant gains in parental acceptance of their children's behaviors, whereas others have failed to show any change. However, because of many methodological factors, generalizations concerning PET's effectiveness are difficult to make. One study did produce encouraging results (Mitchell & McManis, 1977). Changes in authoritarian attitudes toward child rearing were examined in three groups of women: those who enrolled in a PET course, those who read Gordon's book but were not enrolled, and those who had neither of the above experiences. Those enrolled in PET showed significantly greater changes toward more liberal child-rearing attitudes than did those who read the book or those with no exposure. Further, parents in both the course group and the book group showed greater change than nonparents, suggesting that attitude changes are facilitated by the relevant background experience of being a parent. Since this study involved only middle-class females, the results are limited. Future research to determine the effectiveness of PET should include adequate control groups, efforts to assess both outcome and process variables, and appropriate statistical methods and follow-up.

SYSTEMATIC TRAINING FOR EFFECTIVE PARENTING

The development of Systematic Training for Effective Parenting (STEP) actually dates to almost 60 years ago when Alfred Adler, a psychiatrist, conducted open family-counseling sessions in Vienna. The sessions were open to the public as well as being designed to help the family in question. These groups were closed in the mid-1930s by Austrian fascists. Some of Adler's students

came to the United States and established family centers based on Adler's principles. Perhaps Adler's best-known student was Rudolph Dreikurs, who opened child guidance and Family Education Association centers in Chicago. Parent education study groups used Dreikurs's books *The Challenge of Parenthood* and *Children: The Challenge.* Two individuals who studied with Dreikurs, Don. Dinkmeyer and Gary McKay, in 1973 published *Raising a Responsible Child* and in 1976 published a comprehensive package of parent education materials called Systematic Training for Effective Parenting (STEP), based on Adlerian principles (Dinkmeyer, 1979).

Both Adler and Dreikurs advocated a democratic family atmosphere, which focused on encouragement, mutual respect, discipline that is consistent with behavior, firm limits, offering choices, making suggestions, and joint decision-making by parents and children (Hinkle, Arnold, Croake, & Keller, 1980). Their emphasis is on producing a socially responsible child (the basic requirements for which are enumerated in Box 5c).

The STEP kit, available in both English and Spanish, includes a detailed leader's manual, an introductory cassette tape, invitational brochures, a parent's handbook, five cassettes that cover each session, discussion guide cards, posters, charts, certificates of participation, and a carrying case. Nine sessions, lasting from 1½ to 2 hours weekly, are recommended to be conducted with about 12 group members. Each session is devoted to a specific topic in which a concept is presented and parents listen to tape-recorded examples of situations and solutions.

The Goals of Misbehavior

Implicit in the Adlerian approach to understanding behavior is the notion that behavior is purposive and best understood in terms of its social consequences (Dinkmeyer, 1979). Dreikurs expanded on this notion by identifying the four goals of misbehavior: attention getting, power, revenge, and display of inadequacy. Since misbehavior serves a purpose, it is best understood by observing the consequences—observing the parent's reaction to the misbehavior. The child's response to the parent's attempts at correction

---

BOX 5c   BASIC REQUIREMENTS FOR PRODUCING SOCIALLY RESPONSIBLE CHILDREN

Democratic relationships based on mutual respect; a feeling that the child deserves to be treated with both firmness and kindness.

Encouragement that communicates respect, love, support, and valuing the child as a person.

The use of natural and logical consequences to replace reward and punishment, which enables the child to develop responsibility, self-discipline, and judgment.

A basic understanding of human behavior that helps parents to maintain a consistent approach to human relationships.

Source: Dinkmeyer, D., & McKay, G. (1973). *Raising a responsible child* (p. 14). New York: Simon & Schuster.

---

serve to reveal the purpose of the misbehavior, which usually stems from the child's major goal in life—to belong. "Misbehaving children are discouraged; they do not believe they can belong in useful ways. Therefore, they seek to belong through misbehavior" (Dinkmeyer & McKay, 1976, p. 8).

Dreikurs's four categories of misbehavior are seen as "goals" in the sense that the misbehavior achieves something for the child. The first goal, attention, is almost universal in young children. If children cannot gain attention in constructive ways, they will seek it in destructive ways, especially if they feel that they can belong only by receiving attention. When this occurs, STEP advises parents to either ignore the misbehavior or pay attention to it in ways the child does not expect.

The second goal is power. Children who seek power may feel that they are important only when they are the boss. When children seek power, STEP recommends that parents refrain from getting angry and disengage themselves from the power struggle. If the struggle for power continues, children may alter their desire and pursue the third goal.

Revenge is a goal that children pursue when they feel they must hurt others as they believe they have been hurt. The child finds a place by being cruel and disliked. Parents need to realize that vengeful behavior stems from discouragement, and they should avoid retaliation.

Remaining calm and showing good will are necessary to improve the parent-child relationship.

When children continue a war of revenge with their parents, they may sometimes give up and seek to be excused for their misbehavior by displaying the fourth goal, inadequacy. These children are extremely discouraged and have given up hope of succeeding. Normally parents, too, feel despair, and children will respond to parents passively or fail to respond at all. When displays of inadequacy occur, parents need to eliminate criticism and focus on the child's strengths and assets, encouraging any efforts to improve.

Since children usually are unaware of their goals, their behavior and intentions toward their parents will change only if parents change their approaches. Before parents can change, it is important for them to understand more about their children and themselves. For example, STEP emphasizes that emotions are based on beliefs, and children learn to use their emotions to achieve one or more of the four goals. Often, beliefs are faulty because interpretations of experiences are inaccurate. Factors that contribute to beliefs are family atmosphere and values, sex roles played by parents, family constellation, and parents' attitudes and behavior toward children. The last factor is a significant one. STEP differentiates between "good" parents, who are so involved with their children that they believe they must do everything for them, and "responsible" parents, who give their children choices and let them experience the results of their decisions.

Reflective Listening

Like PET, STEP emphasizes both the receptive and the expressive aspects of communication in effective, responsible parenting. Reflective listening (similiar to PET's active listening) involves analyzing a child's "feeling" message and putting the feeling word into a response. For example, *C*: "I'll sure be glad when school's out," and *P*: "You seem to be saying you're bored with school" (Dinkmeyer & McKay, 1976, p. 50). Closed responses deny children a right to their feelings by demonstrating the listener's unwillingness to accept and understand; on the other hand, open responses acknowledge the child's right to his or her feelings by demonstrating that the listener both accepts and understands the feeling and the message.

The expressive aspects of communication that are emphasized in STEP are the following: (1) problem ownership, (2) "I-messages," and (3) exploring alternatives. Since the first two concepts have been discussed in the previous section, only the third will be explored here. There are times when reflective listening and "I-messages" do not solve problems; that is, children need help in considering various courses of action. This process should not be confused with giving advice. STEP outlines the process of exploring alternatives (see Box 5d).

In addition STEP emphasizes the importance of friendly conversation in a calm atmosphere in the face of conflict; avoiding sarcasm, ridicule, pressure, and labels that indicate lack of confidence; and communicating faith in the child through words, gestures, and tone of voice.

Natural and Logical Consequences

A key element in the STEP approach is the utilization of natural and logical consequences as an alternative to reward and punishment. Natural consequences are those that occur naturally as a result of behavior. For example, a child who refuses to eat goes hungry or a child who refuses to wear mittens gets cold hands (Dinkmeyer & McKay, 1976, p. 72.) Logical consequences are those that are imposed as a result of behavior but logically related to the behavior. They express the reality of the social order and acknowledge mutual rights and mutual respect. For example, a child who does not put her dirty clothes in the hamper by wash time must wash them herself. "The purpose of allowing natural consequences to occur and of designing logical consequences is to encourage children to make responsible decisions, not to force their submission" (Dinkmeyer & McKay, 1976, p. 73). Several principles are given in STEP to guide the use of natural and logical consequences (see Box 5e).

There are three steps in applying consequences: (1) provide choices and accept the child's decision; (2) as a consequence is followed through, assure the child that there will be an opportunity to change the decision later; and (3) if the child repeats the misbehavior, extend the

---

BOX 5d   EXPLORING ALTERNATIVES

Use reflective listening to understand and clarify the child's feelings.

Explore alternatives through brainstorming.

Assist the child in choosing a solution.

Discuss probable results of the decision.

Obtain commitment for the course of action.

Plan a time for evaluation.

Source: Dinkmeyer, D., & McKay, G. (1976). *Parent's handbook.* Circle Pines, MN: American Guidance Service, pp. 57–58.

**BOX 5e   PRINCIPLES FOR USING NATURAL
AND LOGICAL CONSEQUENCES**

Understand the child's goals, behavior, and emotions.

Be both firm and kind.

Do not try to be a *good* parent, but a *responsible* one.

Become more consistent in your actions.

Separate the deed from the doer.

Encourage independence.

Avoid pity.

Refuse to be overconcerned about what other people think.

Recognize who owns the problem.

Talk less, act more.

Refuse to fight or give in.

Let all children share responsibility.

Source: Dinkmeyer, D., & McKay, G. (1976). *Parent's handbook.* Circle Pines, MN: American Guidance Service, pp. 57–58.

---

time that must elapse before the child may try again.

STEP points out that there are some major differences between applying logical consequences and punishment. First, logical consequences express the impersonal reality of the social order, whereas punishment expresses the power of personal authority. Second, logical consequences are logically related to misbehavior, whereas punishment rarely is. Third, logical consequences imply no element of moral judgment, whereas punishment tells the child he is bad. Fourth, logical consequences focus on present and future behavior, whereas punishment focuses on what is past. Fifth, logical consequences are based on good will, and punishment is associated with threats or retaliation. Finally, logical consequences permit choice, whereas punishment demands obedience (Dinkmeyer & McKay, 1976). STEP includes excellent examples of applying logical consequences in common situations.

The Family Meeting

The final component of democratic family relationships outlined in STEP is the family meeting.

There is a regulariy scheduled meeting of all family members where beliefs, values, wishes, complaints, plans, questions, and suggestions are discussed. All members participate as equals in the family meeting, the goals of which are communication and agreements. If suggested guidelines for family meetings are met, then they can provide a resource for solving problems, giving encouragement, and planning family recreation.

Other STEP Programs

Since the publication of STEP, Dinkmeyer and McKay have developed several other programs. STEP/Teen (1983) was designed for parents of junior high and high school youth. The format of the program is similar to that of STEP in that it brings parents together in a structured framework of group discussions led by a leader, readings are assigned, recordings dramatizing true-to-life teen parent situations are used, and activities with the goal of changing negative family behavior are provided. The guide for parents focuses on topics of the weekly meetings and provides exercises to do at home. Box 5f provides topics included for discussions.

The Next STEP (Dinkmeyer, McKay, Dink-

meyer, Dinkmeyer, & McKay, 1987) was designed as a follow-up to STEP and has the goal of enhancing parental skills learned in STEP and STEP/Teen. Like the two earlier programs, this one is designed to show parents how to help children learn to be responsible, but the focus is on parents' needs and rights and on helping parents change their own behavior. The program is implemented in six sessions. The parents' handbook, *The Effective Parent*, provides reading material and activities for implementing concepts. Two features have been added that are not included in STEP and STEP/Teen. One is the opportunity for parents at each session to present a problem they are having in implementing their STEP skills at home. Using a seven-step

---

BOX 5f TOPICS IN STEP/Teen

Understanding your teenager and yourself
Personality development
Emotions—a source of support and frustration
Encouragement—building your teen's self esteem
Communication—expressing your feelings and exploring alternatives
Communication—listening
Discipline—the development of responsibility
Descipline—selecting the appropriate approach
The family meeting
Special challenges

BOX 5g   TOPICS INCLUDED IN THE NEXT STEP

Stress—How irrational beliefs cause stress
             Signs of stress in children
             Relaxation techniques for relieving stress
Asserting your rights as a parent
Building your self esteem
Choosing more realistic beliefs
Viewing situations positively

process, the group analyzes the problem and offers suggestions for solving it. The second addition to this program is the video medium. These cassettes demonstrate how a problem-solving group works and models effective family meetings. Topics included in the Next STEP are found in Box 5g.

Another program designed by Dinkmeyer, McKay, and Dinkmeyer (1980), although not for parents, applies the STEP concepts to teachers. Systematic Training for Effective Teaching (STET) is a program for teachers who want practical ways of dealing with motivation, encouragement, communication, discipline, group leadership, students with special needs, and parental involvement. It is designed for teachers of children in kindergarten through junior high school but also can be adapted for high school teachers.

Research Relating to the Adlerian Approach

Systematic research relating to the effects of parent eduation using the Adlerian approach, and STEP specifically, has been sparse. There is inconsistent evidence concerning its potential value in the lives of children whose parents have been trained. However, Gary McKay conducted research on STEP and found that mothers who participated in the STEP study group perceived their children's behavior as significantly more positive than the mothers in the no-treatment control group, as measured by their ratings on the Adlerian Parental Assessment of Child Behavior Scale (Dinkmeyer, 1979).

Another study compared an experimental group of 26 parents who had participated in a STEP program to a control group of 24 parents who had expressed a willingness to participate but had not yet attended the group sessions (Summerlin & Ward, 1978). The parents who participated in the STEP program showed differences in attitudes, as measured by the Parent Attitude Survey (PAS), from parents who had not yet participated. It was concluded that the STEP program accounted for the differences in parental attitudes, including the areas of acceptance of the child's behavior and trust for the child. Further, the children of parents who had participated in STEP showed differences two months later in self-concept as compared to children whose parents had not yet participated. Specifically, children whose parents had participated perceived themselves as being more accepted by their peer group and as being more capable of helping others in a social situation.

In a study conducted by Williams, Omizo, and Abrams (1984) it was found that learning-disabled students of parents completing a STEP program became more internally controlled. Further, parents expressed significantly more positive attitudes toward their children than parents in a control group did.

Jackson and Brown (1986) compared parents' attitudes toward their children, children's perceptions of their parents' functioning, and improvement of children's self-concept of parents completing the STEP program with a control group. It was found that the STEP parents differed significantly from the control parents on trust. Differences approached significance on causation, but no significant changes or trends were observed on confidence, acceptance, or understanding. No significant differences were found between the children of the STEP and control groups on self-concept and perceptions of parental functioning. Thus the authors concluded that the study provided modest support that participation in an Adlerian-based parent education program can positively influence parents' attitudes toward their children.

From a broader perspective, the effectiveness of Adlerian parent-study groups in facilitating democratic parental attitudes and behavior toward children and the relationship of these attitudes and behavior to children's self-esteem was assessed by Hinkle and his associates (1980). The sample included 74 participating parents and 50 nonparticipating parents. Results indicated that participating parents developed more democratic attitudes, especially during the first 4 weeks of participation, whereas the attitudes of nonparticipating parents remained basically the same. Further, the participating parents began to record changes in their children's behavior in the expected direction after the fifth week of group participation. Finally, children of participating parents showed significant increases in self-esteem over an 8-week period.

Few investigators have attempted to compare the relative effects of one strategy for parent education to another. However, an interesting comparison of the Adlerian approach, the behavioral approach, and a no-treatment control condition was conducted by an elementary school counselor and a professor of counselor education (Frazier & Matthes, 1975). Eighteen parents participated in Adlerian groups, 17 participated in behavioral groups, and 25 parents constituted the no-treatment control groups. Results indicated that parents in the Adlerian program were less restrictive in their attitude toward children's freedom than parents in either of the other two groups, and parents in the behavioral parent-education program were less restrictive than those in the control group. Further, Adlerian parents were more inclined to use logical consequences and discipline in line with the child's misbehavior than those in the control group. The behavioral parents were more likely to be inconsistent in relation to their children, and did not

play or talk with children as frequently as those parents in either of the other two groups. Finally, there were no significant differences among parents in the three groups as to show they perceived the behavior of their children.

A study comparing Adlerian, PET, and Behavior Modification techniques was reported by Hills and Knowles (1987). This study was discussed under the evaluation of PET. No significant differences were found in the graduates of the Adlerian program, the other two programs, and a control group.

Because of the limited research available, faulty design, and failure to follow-up parents and children over a period of time who have participated in Adlerian parent-education programs, including STEP, it is impossible to state unequivocally that the approach effects specific lasting changes in the parent-child relationship. It does appear, however, that parents' attitudes and behaviors become more democratic, at least during the process of such a program. Changes in children's behavior are more difficult to document. It may be assumed that it is the parents themselves who change, at least temporarily, in that they become less restrictive and less bothered by children's misbehavior, thereby leading to greater satisfaction for themselves as well as for their children.

TRANSACTIONAL ANALYSIS

The method of transactional analysis as therapeutic treatment was developed by Dr. Eric Berne, a psychiatrist. He published in 1961 a book entitled *Transactional Analysis in Psychotherapy* and, in 1964, a sequel called *Games People Play,* which was planned so that it could be read and understood independently (Berne, 1964). In 1967 another psychiatrist who had studied for 10 years with Berne, Dr. Thomas Harris, published a book called *I'm OK—You're OK,* which was revised and reprinted several times. Since 1970 thousands of professionals (psychiatrists, psychologists, teachers, social workers, and nurses) have been trained in transactional analysis (TA), and Dr. Harris has founded the Institute for Transactional Analysis in Sacramento, California. While transactional analysis was originally a system of individual and social psychiatry and was used largely in group settings, Harris emphasized that people do not have to be "sick" to benefit from it (Harris, 1973).

Harris's central focus has been on the notion that all persons can become transactional analysts. He has conducted TA sessions with preadolesents/adolescents and their parents and with the retarded. He recommends TA especially for victims of child abuse and their parents, adopted children, and children and parents who are experiencing separation or divorce. He pointed out that the best way to help children is to help their parents, with the emphasis being on what parents can achieve so that the nature of the transactions between parents and children will change, followed by a change in children. Another effective application of TA has been a teaching program for expectant parents in Sacramento, where it was found that an understanding of TA early in the pregnancy helps the couple to understand the source of new, rather complicated, not-all-positive feelings (Harris, 1973).

Definition of Terms

In order to understand the process of TA, it is necessary to understand the terms. A *transaction* is a stimulus piece of communication by one person and its accompanying response by another. The response, then, becomes the new stimulus for a response by the first person, and so on until the interchange ends. The purpose of the analysis of this transaction is to determine which part of each person's ego state generates each stimulus and each response in interaction with others. In the view of Berne and Harris, every individual is multinatured—each one has three parts: a Parent, an Adult, and a Child. All people demonstrate abrupt changes from one state to another, as evidenced by manner, appearance, words, and gestures. These states of being are not roles but psychological realities, which are produced by playback of recorded data of events in the past, involving real people, real places, real times, real decisions, and real feelings (Harris, 1973).

The Parent state is a large collection of record-

FIGURE 5-1   The Personality

Source: Harris, T. *I'm OK—You're OK: A Practical Guide to Transactional Analysis,* p. 18. Copyright © 1967, 1968, 1969 by Thomas A. Harris, M.D. Reprinted by permission of Harper & Row, Publishers, Inc.

ings of unquestioned or imposed events perceived by a person during his or her first five years of life. The recordings include all the admonitions, rules, and laws that children see and hear from their own parents. Included are all the "no's" and "don'ts" as well as the pleasures and delights. These events are recorded as truths and provide rules for living. While most Parent data derive directly from one's own parents, there are other sources, such as television, siblings, or other authority figures. Verbal clues to the Parent state are evaluative words such as *stupid, lazy, ridiculous,* and *naughty,* and other words such as *should, ought, always,* and *never.* Gestures, such as finger-pointing, head-wagging, and a horrified look, provide additional clues to the Parent state.

The Child state recording is made simultaneously with the Parent. It is a recording of internal events, the responses of the child to what she sees and hears. The body of data that the child records is characterized by seeing, hearing, feeling, and understanding, but most of the reactions are feelings. The heightened emotional states of our being—creativity, intuition, spontaneous drives, and enjoyment—are all part of the child state. Verbal clues include *I wish, I want, I don't care, I guess, better, best,* and *mine.* Gestures include crying, throwing tantrums, pouting, whining, and giggling.

The data for the Adult state accumulate as a result of the child's ability to find out for himself what is different about life from the "taught concepts" of his Parent and the "felt concepts" of his Child. The Adult dimension develops a "thought concept" of life based on data gathering and data processing. In other words the Adult mediates between the Parent and the Child and evaluates in a nonjudgmental fashion. The Adult state, then, processes information from the Parent, the Child, and itself in dealing with the reality of the moment at hand. The basic vocabulary of the Adult consists of words that indicate Adult data processing, such as *why, what, when, where, who, how, probably,* and *possibly.* The Adult face in a transaction is one that is straightforward and consists of movement of the face and eyes, as well as the body.

Once individuals begin to recognize which aspect of their personalities is generating a stimulus or a response in a given transaction, then the process of analysis has begun. The basic premise of TA is that when the stimulus and response of individuals on the Parent-Adult-Child (P-A-C) transactional diagram parallel or form complementary lines, communication proceeds smoothly. But once the transactions become crossed or uncomplementary, conflicts occur and communication stops. Complemen-

tary transactions (Figure 5-2) include parent-parent, child-child, adult-adult, parent-child, child-adult, and adult-parent. Crossed transactions (Figure 5-3) include adult-to-adult responded to by parent-to-child, child-to-parent responded to by adult-to-adult, adult-to-adult responded to by parent-to-child, and parent-to-child responded to by parent-to-child (Harris, 1973).

Four Life Positions

Basic also to TA is an understanding of the Four Life Positions as set forth by Harris (1973):

1. *I'm Not OK—You're OK:* The position that occurs first and is the universal position of early childhood.

2. *I'm Not OK—You're Not OK:* An unfortunate position that develops from the first position for those children whose "strokes" stop, that is, they are treated punitively.

3. *I'm OK—You're Not OK:* May also result from the first position when "stroke deprivation" occurs, because the child may develop the attitude that, since there are no OK people, there are no OK strokes.

4. *I'm OK—You're OK:* The most desirable position, a conscious and verbal one based on thought and faith, not on feelings. Harris contends that children are helped to be in position four by repeated exposure to situations in which they can prove to themselves their own worth and the worth of

FIGURE 5-2 Complementary Transactions

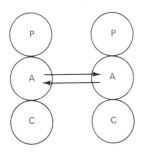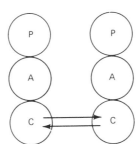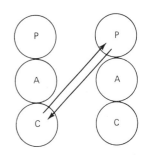

Source: Harris, T. *I'm OK—You're OK: A Practical Guide to Transactional Analysis,* pp. 71–72, 77. Copyright © 1967, 1968, 1969 by Thomas A. Harris, M.D. Reprinted by permission of Harper & Row, Publishers, Inc.

FIGURE 5-3   Crossed Transactions

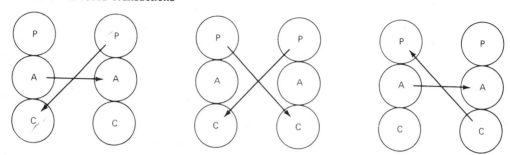

Source: Harris, T. *I'm OK—You're OK: A Practical Guide to Transactional Analysis*, pp. 83, 86, 88. Copyright © 1967, 1968, 1969 by Thomas A. Harris, M.D. Reprinted by permission of Harper & Row, Publishers, Inc.

others. "Strokes" consist of physical strokes (patting, hugging, and caressing) and psychological strokes (recognition and approval).

Using a TA framework, Babcock and Keepers published *Raising Kids OK* in 1976 (reprinted in 1977) in conjunction with courses they taught entitled "TA and Kids." They combined the behavior analysis tools of TA set forth by Berne and Harris with organized information on child development and communication. They have revised and expanded the work of professionals who used TA as a therapeutic approach and have made it applicable to all families and children. Using TA as a basic strategy for communication between parents and children, Babcock and Keepers discussed parenting from infancy through adolescence and described development from birth to death (Babcock & Keepers, 1977).

Evaluation of TA

Although much research on TA in general exists, little, if any, has been specifically aimed at determining the effectiveness as a parent-education strategy. One recent study (Anderson & Nuttall, 1987) evaluated the specific communication skills included in PET, STEP, and TA. Responsive listening, firmness statements, reaching consensus and compromise, and positive acceptance were the PET skills evaluated. Allowing children to experience logical and natural consequences of their actions was the STEP skill assessed; and evaluation of parental behavior in terms of three ego states (parent, adult, and child) was utilized. Further, parents who had children in three different age groups (preschool, schoolage, and adolescence) were compared.

The results showed a significant improvement in parents' self-reported skills following the training. Improvement was consistent across all three parenting groups, with no significant interactions between parents' reported skill changes and parenting stages. A majority of parents reported positive changes in their child's level of cooperation and the quality of communication shared with the parent. These findings supported the notion that communication skills can be taught successfully regardless of specific parenting tasks, which may vary from one parenting stage to another. Although parents in each stage significantly improved on measures of parenting skills, children's behavior change varied by age. Adolescents were significantly less likely to have changed their level of cooperation, demand, and acceptance of family rules than were preschool or school-age children.

When evaluating the techniques of teaching the parents, the participants identified peer group discussion as the most favored activity. It appeared that the opportunity to express personal feelings and receive support in implementing skills was an especially valued aspect of these parents' training experiences.

TA encourages the parent to develop his or her Adult state consistently so that children can have an appropriate model for developing their own Adult ego states. The strategy also encourages teaching children from an early age the language of TA and helping them to recognize which ego state they are using in an interaction. Instructional tools to facilitate this process include three books by Dr. Alvyn Freed: *TA for Kids, TA for Tots,* and *TA for Teens.* These volumes have been reprinted numerous times, and thousands of copies have been sold to parents and teachers. The books are designed to help children get acquainted with themselves and understand and get along better with others, to introduce TA language, and to spread knowledge of TA principles. The long-term effectiveness of TA as a strategy for parent education and of attempts to teach TA to children, however, remains to be seen.

BEHAVIOR MODIFICATION

Parenting strategies that emphasize changing a child's behavior through the use of reinforcements (rewards), punishments, and modeling are referred to as behavior modification, or social learning approaches. The notion of conditioning a person to behave in certain ways by the application of consequences immediately following the behavior in question was developed by Dr. B. F. Skinner of Harvard University and was initially called operant conditioning. Skinner contended that behavior could be shaped, modified, or extinguished by a contingent system of rewards and punishments. Basic to the notion of operant conditioning is the belief that if one desires that a

particular behavior increase in occurrence, then that behavior (or the semblance of it) must be reinforced or rewarded immediately after it occurs. Conversely, if one desires to eliminate or extinguish a behavior, then one must withdraw any reinforcement and/or apply punishment immediately after the behavior occurs. Behavior (or misbehavior), then, is simply the result of the degree to which it has been either reinforced or punished in one's life experiences. Little attention is given to the feelings, motives, and causes of the person demonstrating the behavior (Skinner, 1953). Later several theorists expanded on the concept of operant conditioning to include the importance of modeling (imitating the behavior of others, especially those that are significant) in explaining why people behave the way they do. Now social learning theory focuses on rewards, punishment, and modeling.

Reinforcement

It is important at this point to emphasize several aspects of social learning theory. First, there are several forms that reinforcement may take. It may be in the form of a material reward, such as food, treats, toys, or money. It may simply be a form of social reinforcement, such as praise, a hug, a smile, or an affectionate gesture, or it may be indirect in nature, such as rewarding through tokens, points, or gold stars that may be "saved up" to "trade in" later for a material reward or a desired activity.

It is important to note that basic to success

Material Reinforcement   Social Reinforcement   Indirect Reinforcement

in behavior modification is selecting a reinforcement that is truly rewarding to the child in question. For example, some children respond positively to food (ice cream, candy, gum, and the like), whereas others might respond more readily to praise or physical contact. Older children who can delay gratification might profit from an indirect system of rewards. Further, it is often more effective in changing behavior to simultaneously reward positive behavior while withdrawing rewards from, or punishing, negative behavior. For example, hitting another child is a behavior that is incompatible with cooperative behavior, such as using words to express feelings or desires. When the adult is focusing on eliminating hitting behavior, she is simultaneously rewarding cooperative behavior (Roedell, Slaby, & Robinson, 1977; Sheppard, Shank, & Wilson, 1973).

Most behaviorists recommend a contingency system of rewards for modifying behavior. At first a reward is given immediately following each successful act. Gradually the frequency of rewards is diminished and rewards are given intermittently until the desired behavior is reached. The exact contingency schedule to be implemented will depend upon the particular child and the behavior in question. Behaviorists contend that, once the behavior becomes firmly established, it is "self-rewarding" and will not need

continuous reinforcement to persist. If punishment is used to extinguish undesirable behavior, it must be administered immediately, and the parent must be certain that the punishment itself is not, in reality, rewarding for the child. For example, a child who receives the undivided attention of an adult in the process of being punished may actually perceive the attention as rewarding.

Shaping and Modeling

In some instances children may be unable to demonstrate the desired behavior. For example, a parent may wish that a child ask for a cracker instead of pointing. The parent, then, must "shape" the asking behavior by breaking it down and rewarding each step gradually until the desired behavior is reached—first rewarding any sound; then, rewarding an approximation of the word; and, finally, rewarding only the correct word itself.

An important aspect of learning, especially for young children, is modeling, or imitating the behavior of others. Children observe and imitate the behavior of their parents, other significant adults such as relatives or teachers, siblings, peers, and even television characters. It has been found that children imitate the behavior of others even when there is no reward given for the behavior. However, children are more likely to

---

BOX 5h   STEPS IN APPLYING BEHAVIOR MODIFICATION

Determine the desired behavior to be reinforced or extinguished in specific rather than general terms; for example, extinguish hitting, not aggression.

Gather baseline data over a period of time to determine how frequently the behavior occurs.

Select the reward and/or punishment to be used, being sure it is appropriate for the child.

Develop a contingency schedule; that is, the rate at which consequences will be applied for a given period of time.

Implement the program consistently.

Evaluate results by gathering postdata; that is, determine rate of behavior *after program completion.*

Source: Sheppard, W., Shank, S., & Wilson, D. (1973) *Teaching social behavior to young children.* Champaign, IL: Research Press.

imitate models that are warm, nurturant, powerful, and significant to them in some way. Adults often unconsciously serve as models for undesirable behavior. For example, adults who use corporal punishment with children are modeling violence and aggression for children (Roedell et al., 1977).

Behavior-Modification Programs

Several packaged programs for parents have been developed using behavior-modification techniques. One of the first was a kit called *Child Management: A Program for Parents*, developed in 1966 by J. M. Smith and D. E. Smith. A more recent program is called *The Art of Parenting* by Wagonseller, Burnett, Selzberg, and Burnett (1980). It is composed of three major areas—behavior management, communication, and assertion training—and contains a leader's guide, five tapes, five filmstrips, and five parent manuals.

A similar program called *Managing Behavior: A Parent Involvement Program* was developed by Dr. Richard McDowell in 1974 and revised in 1978. The program was developed to gain parental involvement in the child's educational process by introducing parents to techniques in behavior management and having them conduct a management project with their preschool or elementary-age children. The kit includes three filmstrips that sequentially present the concepts of behavior management; a Parent Log, which is a workbook containing exercises, activities, and materials to use in conducting the behavior management project; and a trainer's manual. The program is designed to be presented in a workshop format of three primary meetings and one or more follow-up meetings. McDowell has tested several aspects of the *Managing Behavior* program (1969). His results indicated that the program was successful in teaching parents factual knowledge about behavior modification and in assisting parents in modifying the behavior of their children.

Research Related to Behavior Modification

An interesting study conducted by Pinsker and Geoffray (1981) compared the effects of a behavior-modification parent-training group, a PET program, and a control group. Since behavior modification focuses on direct behavior change and PET focuses on the development of communication skills to reduce inappropriate child behavior, it was hypothesized that the two parent-training programs would produce differential effects. Results indicated that the behavior-modification program resulted in a significant decrease in problem behaviors, whereas the other two groups indicated nonsignificant changes but a trend toward a decrease in perception of problem behaviors. The PET group, however, showed significantly greater family cohesion and less conflict during the follow-up than either of the other two groups. Behavior observations also revealed that the PET groups had increased significantly the level of positive parental communication. While differences in level of parental control among the three groups were not significant, there was a definite trend for the behavior modification groups to increase parental control and for the PET groups to decrease parental control. The authors concluded that both techniques were useful in attaining certain goals, but the goals differed from one strategy to another.

Calvert and McMahon (1987) evaluated five components of a behavioral-training program (attends, rewards, ignoring, commands, time out) and three methods of introducing the skill to the child in these five areas. The methods assessed were parent training only, parent training plus verbal rationale, and parent training plus verbal rationale and demonstration. With the exception of two conditions (ignoring in all three groups and time out in the parent only and parent plus rationale and demonstration groups), all parenting skills, the methods of introduction, and the overall program were rated in the upper half of the positive range.

In the evaluation of the usefulness of the individual technique, ignoring was rated as significantly less useful than all other techniques. Time out was rated as significantly less useful than commands were. The difficulty of using the techniques also was evaluated. It was found that parents rated ignoring significantly more difficult to use than all other techniques. Time out was rated more difficult than rewards, commands, and attends; and commands and attends were considered more difficult than rewards. It was thus easier for parents to use techniques increasing positive behaviors than techniques to extinguish inappropriate behaviors.

In a review of more than 70 studies relating to training parents to use behavior modification techniques, O'Dell (1974) summarized the advantages of such an approach:

1. Unskilled persons can learn behavior modification techniques and implement them after only a short training period.
2. Parents can be taught in groups with a minimum of professional leadership.
3. The model does not assume that the child is "sick" or that parents are ineffective.
4. Many childhood behaviors are susceptible to treatment through behavior-management techniques.

O'Dell further summarized many studies that reported success in modifying child behaviors. He contended that there appears to be no class of overt behaviors that parents cannot be trained to modify. However, data are lacking on whether the parent's behavior changes generally and persists over a period of time as a result of training. Most studies have focused on the implementation phase and the immediate success in changing the child's behavior.

Because behavior modification is a vigorous and prestigious approach, Cagan (1980) contended that it must be critically examined and evaluated as a parent-education strategy. She examined more than a dozen behavior-modification books and manuals written specifically for parents and drew the following conclusions. First, if the techniques and theoretical perspective on which they are built become the sole or primary source for understanding and interacting with children, then serious problems will arise. For example, much of the punishment applied and the consistently rigid reinforcement that is advocated demonstrate an insensitivity toward the child as a person with needs, feelings, and rights. "The parent, as controller of the all-powerful environment, becomes supreme, while the child fades from view" (Cagan, 1980, p. 43).

Further, she contended that consistency in parent behavior is elevated into a fundamental principle of family life, and in the demand for order and predictability, there is little room for spontaneity, flexibility, or responsiveness. In addition the assumption is made that the parents' desires for their children are automatically legitimate, and the parent "becomes the controller of goodies" (Cagan, 1980, p. 46). In other words the distressing aspect of the strategy is the calculated nature of the parent's response. Cagan contended that by relying solely on behavior-management techniques the parent is not engaged with the child in any meaningful way; he or she is offering praise, disapproval, or silence not as a reflection of how the parent feels but as a part of a prearranged program designed to achieve certain ends.

It is easy to see that behavior-modification strategies are vastly different from any of the strategies previously discussed. The major focus is on changing the child's behavior with control by the parent being increased. Parent and/or child attitudes are irrelevant to the goals of the program. It is important, however, for parents to change their behavior to such a degree that they are successful in implementing the contingent system of rewards and punishments consistently throughout the period such a strategy is used. Behavior management techniques can be quite successful in changing behavior. It does appear, however, that these techniques might be more effectively combined with other parenting skills that are less restrictive in nature.

ACTIVE PARENTING

Active Parenting, a video-based parent-education program, was published in 1983 by Dr. Michael Popkin. The complete program kit includes videotapes, a leader's guide, a handbook and action guide, a promotion packet, promotional brochures, and announcement posters. Workshops to train Active Parenting leaders in building skills in parent-education and small-group leadership are conducted regularly in several locations across the country. Since its beginning, leaders have taken the program not only to locations throughout the United States but also to foreign countries, including Japan and Canada, and to several military Support Centers in Europe (Popkin, 1986).

Concepts included in the Active Parenting program are based on ideas proposed by Alfred Adler, Rudolf Dreikurs, and Carl Rogers. Since many of these concepts, included in PET and STEP, have been discussed earlier, they will not be discussed here. Concepts and parenting skills, in 40 vignettes, are presented in six 2-hour sessions. Box 5i lists the topics included in these sessions.

Active Parenting also publishes a newsletter through which interested persons may keep up with the activities of leaders and the director; locations of workshops; materials offered by Active Parenting, Inc.; and the other resources that may be utilized in parent education.

HOW TO TALK SO KIDS WILL LISTEN

This program is a unique parent-education program because it is a self-contained course designed to be used and administered by parents themselves. Any motivated person can serve as the chairperson, or the leadership role can be shared. No one needs special training, as the chairperson merely has to read simple directions, distribute materials, and operate the cassette player. It is a seven-session multimedia approach for use by a group of 6–12 parents who get together and discuss the problems of typical families. The program was designed by Adele Faber and Elaine Mazlish (1980), each a parent of three children, and it is based on 10 years of their experiences with parent-guidance groups led by Haim Ginott.

The kit includes a framework for each meet-

BOX 5i *ACTIVE PARENTING:* TOPICS

The Active Parent	Styles of parenting
	What kind of children do we want to raise?
	"Freedom within limits"
	Family enrichment activities
Understanding Your Child	The ABCs of behavior
	Four goals of misbehavior
	Parenting and anger
	Developing self-esteem
Instilling Courage	Avoiding discouragement
	Four methods of encouragement
	The encouragement circle exercise
Developing Responsibility	Who owns the problem?
	"I"-messages
	Natural and logical consequences
	Mutual respect
Winning Cooperation	Avoiding communication blocks
	Active communication
	Listening for feelings
	Expressing love
The Democratic Family in Action	The family council meeting
	Handling parents in a group
	Emphasizing the family unit
	Raising a "we" generation

Source: Popkin, M. (1983). *Active Parenting.* Atlanta: Active Parenting.

BOX 5j *HOW TO TALK SO KIDS WILL LISTEN:* TOPICS

Helping children deal with their feelings
Engaging cooperation
Providing alternatives to punishment
Encouraging autonomy
Using praise effectively
Freeing children from playing roles

---

ing, and the authors conduct each session on tape. Parents have their own workbooks and two books by the authors [*How to Talk So Kids Will Listen & Listen So Kids Will Talk* (Faber & Mazlish, 1980) and *Liberated Parents: Liberated Children* (Faber & Mazlish, 1974)] are required for each participant. Discussions and role-playing are incorporated. Box 5j lists the topics included, each of which will be discussed briefly.

Helping Children Deal with their Feelings

Constant denial of children's feelings confuses and outrages them. Common means of denying children's feelings are the following: *denial* (C: "Mommy, I'm sleepy." M: "You can't be sleepy, you just got up from your nap."), *being philosophical* (C: "Mommy, Jane won't play with me." M: "Well, that's just the way things go; you'll just have to learn to accept it."), *defense of the other person* (C: "The teacher picks on me." M: "Well, I'm sure she has a reason for it."), *pity* (C: "Dad, I cut my finger." D: "Oh, you poor baby; let me kiss it."), or *being an amateur psychologist* (C: "I'm so upset because John doesn't understand me." M: "Have you considered the fact that you are expecting John to be like your father?").

On the other hand, adults can demonstrate

Engaging Cooperation: Writing a Note.

acceptance of children's feelings by giving empathic responses ("It sure seems as though you're angry about the way that was handled") and by demonstrating an attitude of compassion. To help children to manage their feelings, adults should listen with full attention; acknowledge the child's feelings with a word or two ("Oh," "Mmmm," or "I see"); give feelings a name ("That really hurts"); or give children their wishes in fantasy ("If I were a fairy godmother, I would wave my magic wand and a new bike would appear").

Engaging Cooperation

Problems occur when there is a conflict between a parent's and a child's needs. Faber and Mazlish identified inappropriate methods commonly used by parents that deter cooperation. These are found in Box 5k. Instead of these techniques, five skills for engaging cooperation of children are *describing, giving information, saying it*

with a word, talking about your feelings, and *writing a note.*

Providing Alternatives to Punishment

Punishment can lead to feelings of hate, revenge, guilt, defiance, unworthiness, or self-pity. It usually deprives the child of a very important inner process of facing his own behavior, as it serves as a distraction. Several alternatives to punishment can be found in Box 5l.

Encouraging Autonomy

Autonomy can be encouraged in a variety of ways: *letting children make choices* ("Would you like to play indoors or outdoors?"), *showing respect for a child's struggle* ("Gee, it is really tough to learn long division."), *not asking too many questions* ("Welcome home" instead of "Where did you go? What did you do?"), *not rushing to answer questions* ("That's an interesting question. What do

---

BOX 5k   INAPPROPRIATE METHODS THAT DETER COOPERATION

Method	Example
Blaming and accusing	"Look at the dirty footprints you put on my clean kitchen floor. You never consider how hard I work."
Name calling	"You are the sloppiest person. Just look at your room!"
Threats	"If you don't start doing your share around here, I'm going to cut your allowance."
Commands	"Take the garbage out this minute, and no back talk, young man."
Lecturing and moralizing	"Now, do you think that was a nice thing to say about your friend? You should learn to treat your friends the way you want to be treated."
Warnings	"Don't step off the sidewalk. You'll get hit by a car."
Martyrdom statements	"Why are you doing this to me, as hard as I work?"
Comparisons	"Why can't you try as hard in school as your sister does?"
Sarcasm	"You knew you had to get up early, but you were so smart and stayed up until midnight."
Prophecy	"If you continue in the same manner, you'll never amount to anything."

Source: Adapted from Faber, A., & Mazlish, E. (1980). *How to Talk So Kids Will Listen.* New York: Avon.

you think?''), *encouraging children to use sources outside the home* (''I'll bet the public library has information on that. I'll take you there.''), *not taking away hope* (''That should be an interesting experience. Why don't you tell me more about how you see it.'').

Using Praise Effectively

Ginott believed that often the most well-meaning praise could bring about unexpected reactions. For example, praise can lead to doubt of the praiser (for example, you look awful but someone tells you how nice you look), can lead to immediate denial (''I know I look awful''), can be viewed as a threat (''I probably won't look good the next time, either''), can cause one to focus on her weaknesses (''I'm not really that attractive''), can create anxiety and interfere with activity (''I'll never be able to do that well again''), or can be seen as manipulation (''I wonder what she wants of me.'').

Instead of using praise, Faber and Mazlish recommend that the adult describe with ap-preciation what she feels or sees (''Your room looks so clean. I see that you've put everything away, vacuumed, and made your bed. It's such a pleasure to see how attractive your room looks.'') In this way the child is able to praise herself (''I really did a good job of getting my room clean.'')

Freeing Children From Playing Roles

When adults label children's behavior (bossy, bully, dumb, and the like), children gradually begin to fulfill the role. Labeling children is not always done verbally; children infer how parents feel about them—through a look, a tone of voice, or a question such as, ''Are you sure?'' To free children from playing roles, suggestions for parents are found in Box 5m.

Faber and Mazlish (1987) have developed an additional program for parents, Siblings Without Rivalry. In this program parents are taught how to help children deal with their feelings about each other, how to keep children separate and unequal, how to assist siblings in roles, what to

---

BOX 5l ALTERNATIVES TO PUNISHMENT

Alternative	Example
Point out ways to be helpful	"It would be extremely helpful if you would put dirty clothes in the hamper."
Express strong disapproval without attacking child's character	"I don't like dirty clothes left in the bathroom. Other people have to use it, too."
State your expectations	"I expect all clothes that need to be washed to be placed in the hamper."
Show how to make amends	"What this floor needs is a mopping to get up those muddy footprints."
Give a choice	"Jane, you can borrow my sweater and put it back in my closet, or you can give up the privilege of wearing my clothes."
Take action	"Jane, you must wear your own clothes until you can be considerate by placing mine back in their proper place."
Allow child to experience the consequences of her misbehavior	"I'm sorry, Jane, but you may not wear my sweater; I need to know that it will be where I left it."

Source: Adapted from Faber, A., & Mazlish, E. (1980). *How to Talk So Kids Will Listen.* New York: Avon.

BOX 5m   FREEING CHILDREN FROM PLAYING ROLES

Technique	Example
Look for opportunities to show the child a new picture of herself	"You have taken such good care of that book, it looks almost new."
Put children in situations where they see themselves differently	"While I am at the meeting, I'm putting you in charge of dinner."
Let children overhear you say something positive about them	"Sam, did you know that your son organized the garage today?"
Model the behavior you would like to see	"As hard as I tried, I couldn't beat you. Congratulations on your win."
Be a storehouse for the child's special moments	"I remember when you were just 4 and you learned to tie your shoes."
When child behaves according to the old label, state your feelings/expectations	"I expect you to put my things away when you are finished using them."

Source: Adapted from Faber, A., & Mazlish, E. (1980). *How to Talk So Kids Will Listen.* New York: Avon.

---

do when kids fight, and how to use problem-solving techniques. These two programs, based on the ideas of Haim Ginott, are relatively inexpensive and appear to be more appropriate for middle-class parents since parents must have the resources and motivation to implement the program. The material can be easily understood by middle-class parents and includes many cartoon-type drawings to illustrate concepts. However, research relating to the effectiveness of these strategies is unavailable.

LIVING WITH 10- TO 15-YEAR-OLDS

One of the few programs especially designed for pre- and early adolescence, Living with 10- to 15-Year-Olds was developed by Gayle Dorman,

---

BOX 5n   CURRICULUM FOR LIVING WITH 10- TO 15-YEAR-OLDS

Living with 10- to 15-Year-Olds	Focuses on understanding teenage children and skills that can improve parent-child relationships/family life with young adolescents; establishing rules and limits; problem areas
Parents and Young Adolescents: Talking About Sex	Healthy adolescent development, emphasizing puberty/sexuality; skills for educating young adolescents about sex
Risk-Taking Behavior and Young Adolescents	Risk-taking as part of normal development; ways to channel young people's desire for independence
Understanding Early Adolescence: An Overview	Understanding normal, healthy early adolescent development

Source: Dorman, G., Geldof, D., & Scarborough, B. (1982). *Living with 10- to 15-Year-Olds.* Chapel Hill, NC: Center for Early Adolescence.

Dick Geldof, and Bill Scarborough (1982) through the Center for Early Adolescence at the University of North Carolina at Chapel Hill. It is designed in a workshop format for approximately 20 hours of group discussion. It appears to be appropriate for professionals in a number of community agencies who wish to assist parents of young adolescents. Materials include goal-oriented curricula, three books, suggested reading lists, handout materials to be duplicated for participants, information on developing and managing a conference, publicity materials, and training techniques for group leaders. The curriculum focuses on four topics (see Box 5n).

RESPONSIVE PARENTING

This program, designed by Saf Lerman (1984), may be used by professionals working with individual parents or groups of parents. The kit includes a leader's manual, a participant's packet (set of nine booklets), charts highlighting major concepts in sessions, three audio cassettes consisting of vignettes to promote discussion, certificates of participation, and publicity materials. The nine pamphlets are the core of the program, and each one serves as the topic for a session. Pamphlet 1, "Helping Children As They Grow," takes a positive look at parenting through the ages and stages of childhood. It includes a discussion of letting children know they are loved, balancing parental and child needs, parenting from stage to stage, and a list of additional resources about topics discussed in the pamphlet.

Pamphlet 2, "Helping Children Help Themselves," is a guide to positive discipline. It includes information on the components of discipline, negative methods and why they will not work, positive approaches to discipline, positive techniques for dealing with common problems, and additional resources on these topics.

"Helping Siblings Get Along Together" is the title of Pamphlet 3. Ways to help children resolve conflicts and value each family member, preparing children for a new baby, dealing with sibling quarrels and jealousy, and encouraging good feelings among siblings are included, as well as additional resources.

Pamphlet 4 discusses "Using Role Reversal with Children" as a tool for helping parents and children understand the other person's point of view. A discussion of how to get children to play specific adult roles and specific examples and situations are included. This pamphlet, too, has a section of additional resources that parents might find helpful on the subject.

"Building a Child's Positive Self-image" is explored in Pamphlet 5. What parents can say and do to strengthen children's confidence and personal esteem, how to praise children (basically Ginott's ideas), other ways to build self-esteem, how to criticize constructively, why and how to stop casting children in negative roles, how to begin showing children appreciation and acceptance, and additional resources comprise the information in this pamphlet.

Pamphlet 6, "Sharing Sex Information with Children," explores how parents can help foster in children the development of a healthy attitude about sexuality. It includes information about sex that is appropriate for young children and adolescents, other issues relating to sex, and additional resources that parents may wish to utilize.

"Helping Children Understand and Express Feelings" is the topic of Pamphlet 7. Helping children deal with feelings relating to divorce and remarriage are discussed. Additional resources on the topic also are included.

Pamphlet 8, "Helping Children Handle Fear," provides information on guiding children through typical fears and helping them understand death as a part of life. Additional resources also are provided.

Pamphlet 9 is entitled "Building Independence and Cooperation in Children." How to raise children to be self-reliant and to work well with others are discussed. Information on guiding children to act independently, to think independently, and to avoid serious mistakes is included. Gaining children's cooperation also is discussed, and a list of additional resources is provided.

Responsive Parenting may be used by individual parents or it may serve as the basis for group discussion for a number of parents. The topics lend themselves best to parents of school-age and preadolescent children. No research evaluating the effects of this strategy has been located.

ASSERTIVE DISCIPLINE

This strategy was developed by Lee Canter, a family-child counselor, and Marlene Canter, a teacher. Originally their ideas were aimed at educators to help with discipline in the classroom when they wrote *Assertive Discipline: A Take Charge Approach for Today's Educator* (Canter & Canter, 1976). Based on their successful training workshops for educators that implemented this approach, *Assertive Discipline for Parents* (Canter & Canter, 1985) was developed. Since then workshops for parents have been conducted across the country.

The Canters define *discipline* as "corrective action designed to help teach children more appropriate behavior." Under no circumstances, they claim, should discipline violate the physical or emotional well-being of children. They feel that assertive discipline is warranted when other approaches have failed to work. They believe that a parent needs to take charge in problem situations and let children know that the parent is the "boss." The message that a parent should get across is that he loves the child too much to let her misbehave; therefore problem behavior must stop. Further, they feel that it is equally important for parents to provide their children with direct and positive feedback when they change the problem behavior. These strategists recognize that many parents are reluctant to "come on strong" with their children, and most do not know how to take charge.

Before parents are taught to implement an assertive discipline plan, the typical inappropriate responses that many parents use are discussed (see Box 5o). Nonassertive responses are inappropriate because parents are not stating clearly what they want the child to do or they are not reinforcing their words with actions. These responses, then, communicate to the child that parents do not "mean business." Hostile responses usually result in negative feelings between parent and child and communicate to the child that the parent is out of control.

Once parents have learned to recognize inappropriate responses, they are ready to learn how to put an assertive discipline plan into action. The assertive discipline plan has three basic steps: communicate assertively, back up words with action, and lay down the law.

Communicating Assertively

It is suggested that parents begin with step one; if the severity of the child's behavior warrants it, parents should continue with steps two and three. Suggestions for communicating assertively can be found in Box 5p. Praise is the most useful positive reinforcer ("I like the way you cleaned your room."). Use "super praise," accomplished first by praising the child and then by praising her in front of another adult. Utilize nonverbal praise (smile, hug, pat on back). It is suggested that a parent praise a child at least three times a day. If the child is having a particularly hard day, the parent should find something that the child has done right and tell her how much she liked it.

Backing Up Words with Actions

In order to implement step two, the parent must acquire three skills: how to use disciplinary consequences for inappropriate behavior, how to handle "testing" behavior of children, and how to provide positive support when the parent "catches" the child being good. After the parent tells the child assertively what is wanted, the parent must decide how she is going to back up her words if the child does not listen. Send her to her room? Take away her TV privileges? The more prepared the parent is, the easier it will be to help the child stop inappropriate behavior. Consequences should consist of something that is undesirable but not physically or psychologically harmful to the child. A 4- or 5-year-old child may feel that being sent to her room for 5 minutes is unpleasant, but an adolescent probably would not. The most common disciplinary consequences that parents have successfully utilized include the following: separation, taking away privileges, forcing compliance prior to granting a privilege, grounding, and physical constraint. (*Note:* the inclusion of these consequences does *not* imply our recommendation of

---

BOX 5o   INAPPROPRIATE RESPONSES OF PARENTS

Type	Example
Nonassertive responses	
Statements of fact	"You're misbehaving."
Questions	"Why did you do that?"
Begging and pleading	"Please try to be quiet."
Repeated demanding, not following through	"Turn off the TV and get your homework done."
Ignoring	N/A
Hostile responses	
Verbal put-downs	"You are so sloppy."
Unrealistic threats	"You've had it, kid, if you do that again."
Severe punishment	"You can't leave your room for a week."
Physical punishment	Beating, shoving, pulling hair, and so forth

Source: Adapted from Canter, L., & Canter, M. (1985). *Assertive discipline for parents.* New York: Harper & Row.

---

their use). Whenever possible the consequences should be logically related to the misbehavior. For example, if a 10-year-old damages a parent's tool, he should not be allowed to use the tool for 2 weeks; if a 9-year-old willfully breaks his brother's toy, he should use his allowance to replace it.

Consequences should be clearly articulated to the child and provided as a choice, placing the responsibility where it belongs—with the child. Providing a choice allows the child to learn the logical consequences of her actions and the re-sponsibility for her own behavior. Consequences should be imposed immediately when the child has refused to listen. The parent should provide the consequence every time the child chooses to misbehave, in a matter-of-fact, nonhostile manner. Consistency is the key to backing up words with actions. If parents find that the disciplinary consequence does not work, they should change it. Once the child has experienced the consequence he or she has chosen, the issue is over and it is time to move on. Parents should not harbor anger or resentment but should display

---

BOX 5p   SUGGESTIONS FOR COMMUNICATING ASSERTIVELY

Technique	Example
Address child with direct, assertive statements	"You must take out the garbage immediately."
Use appropriate nonverbal techniques	Calm, firm tone of voice, eye contact, hand gestures, physical contact
Use the "broken record" technique	Repeat the same thing over and over.

Source: Adapted from Canter, L., & Canter, M. (1985). *Assertive discipline for parents.* New York: Harper & Row.

confidence that the child has the ability to improve her behavior.

"Testing" behavior (crying, being defiant, and so on) occurs when children test their parents to see if they mean business. Parents who back down when tested are, in effect, teaching the child that he can get his way if he gets upset or angry enough. Thus children learn to use tantrums and fights, knowing that parents will eventually back down. When children test, the parent needs to respond assertively. It is helpful if parents anticipate at what times children will test so that they can be prepared to stand their ground—for example: "You will go to your room and you will stay there no matter how long you cry." When children test, parents should stay calm and speak assertively. If children argue, parents should use the "broken record" approach.

The child who responds to parental assertions by saying "So what, who cares?" or "I don't care if you do that" is demonstrating another form of testing behavior or manipulation. He has learned that this kind of response often sidetracks his parents from dealing with him effectively. If the same disciplinary technique used for three times fails to work, a "tougher" one should be applied.

A final skill involved in step two is providing positive support when parents catch children being good. Equally important to planning what should be done when children fail to listen is planning what to do when the child responds positively. Praise alone may not be sufficient motivation for changing children's behavior. Additional motivators such as special privileges and special rewards may be needed. These must be given immediately after the desired behavior and may continue for a period of time as reinforcement.

Laying Down the Law

Using steps one (communicating assertively) and two (backing up words with actions) will be effective in solving most problem behaviors. However, there are times when step three must be used. In order to lay down the law, three skills must be learned: setting up a systematic assertive discipline plan, using a "parent-saver" technique when all else fails, and conducting a "lay-down-the-law" session. Each of these will be discussed briefly.

First, a systematic assertive discipline plan is written and developed by both parents and children. This plan includes the specific behaviors that parents want changed, the consequences that will be provided for misbehavior, the reinforcement to be used for positive behavior, and ways to monitor the child's actions. This plan is needed when parents reach the conclusion that nothing has worked in trying to change the child's behavior. Parents feel frustrated, overwhelmed, and at a loss to know what to do next. It is a confidence builder for the parent in that he is prepared and is better able to respond in a consistently assertive manner.

The systematic discipline plan, developed collaboratively by both parents, will discourage children from playing the old "divide and conquer" game. Included in the plan is a listing of the specific behaviors the child is to change, what limits will be set, what parents' responses to misbehavior will be, whether the behavior will be monitored, and how parents will respond when they "catch the child being good."

The second skill in step three involves using "parent-saver" techniques. The first technique involves establishing a discipline hierarchy, ranking disciplinary consequences in order of severity. If the child continues to misbehave, she will receive increasingly severe consequences. For example—the first time, the child is warned; the second time, the child is required to spend 15 minutes in her room; the third time, the time is extended to 30 minutes in her room; and the fourth time it is extended to 1 hour in her room. A discipline hierarchy should contain only three or four consequences, beginning with a minor one and progressing to more severe consequences. It is helpful if parents keep track of misbehavior by recording each infraction on a chalkboard or poster in a strategic location, using a check mark. Each day the child starts with a clean slate.

Another technique is the use of a positive contract, an agreement between parent and child that states, "When you do what I want, in return I will provide you with something you want."

BOX 5q   SKILLS TO USE IN "LAYING DOWN THE LAW"

Set up a systematic assertive discipline plan
Learn "parent-saver" techniques
   Discipline hierarchy
   Positive contract
   Marble mania
Conduct a "lay-down-the-law" session

Source: Adapted from Canter, L., & Canter, M. (1985). *Assertive discipline for parents.* New York: Harper & Row.

A positive contract helps parents plan reinforcement and positive support. The contract must include what parents expect the child to do and what rewards she will receive for her behavior. Rewards should not be too expensive or too time consuming, such as a large toy or a trip. The amount of time it takes to earn the reward will vary with age of child—the younger the child, the shorter the time. For older children, the contract should be written. The contract should be in effect for a specific period of time and then evaluated to determine if it should be renewed or changed.

Finally, using marble mania can be effective if more than one child is involved. When any one child behaves as he has been told, a marble is put in a common jar. When the marbles reach a predetermined level, all the children earn the reward they want. Bonus marbles are provided for each day in which no child misbehaves. The success of marble mania is partly due to the peer pressure that is fostered. Parents should make sure that children earn a large amount of marbles each day in the initial stages of this approach. Further, marbles should never be removed when children misbehave; they deserve what they have earned. The marbles should be counted at the end of each day.

The final skill in "laying down the law" is to conduct a lay-down-the-law session, which is a "no-nonsense" approach asserting parental authority. The parent demands that the child change his problem behavior. Parents should meet with the child only when both parents are calm; they should never confront the child when upset or right after a major fight. No siblings should be present unless two or more children are involved in the misbehavior. There should be no distractions when the meeting is held. Parents should state their demands, looking the child in the eye, in a calm, firm way. The consequence that will occur in the case of noncompliance should be clearly stated. Describe to the child how his behavior will be monitored. Posting the assertive discipline plan for all to see will add additional impact to verbal statements and serve as a reminder to the child. Parents are cautioned about the "0-0-2-4-5-5-5 syndrome"

when the child's behavior improves for a few days, but gradually the old problems reappear, and soon the child is behaving as badly as ever. This syndrome occurs when inconsistent limits have been developed.

The Canters emphasize that when both parents are in the home, it is essential that they work as a team to implement this program.

Research Related to Assertive Discipline

No research could be located evaluating the effectiveness of assertive discipline as a parenting strategy. While incorporating some positive techniques from other strategies (reinforcement for "good" behavior, utilizing choices, selecting logical consequences, and developing a contract), the emphasis seems to be on a more authoritarian approach. Because the strategy incorporates aspects of several other strategies—STEP, PET, and behavior modification—it is difficult to generalize from results related to any single strategy.

However, there is no question that assertive discipline is an extremely popular approach in school classroom management across the country. In many school systems, all teachers are expected to use this approach and receive in-service training in implementing it. Nevertheless, there is little research related to its success in schools. According to Gartrell (1987) the model has become popular with schools because " . . . it provides a method for the teacher to 'assertively take control of the classroom' " (p. 10), and administrators propose it because it is a consistent approach that all teachers can implement to control problem behavior. Even though the model stresses a reward system for appropriate behavior, it is the intervention procedures that make it popular as well as controversial.

Among the criticisms of the approach made by Gartrell (1987) and Hitz (1988) are the following:

1. The model does not facilitate the development of a positive self-concept, especially for young children, 4 to 8 years.
2. Desirable behavior is forced through power assertion techniques rather than through developing responsible behavior rooted in ethical purposes. It appears that children learn only that behavior is good because it is rewarded or bad because it is punished.
3. Positive attitudes toward schoolwork and oneself are inhibited. The atmosphere seems to be one where the attention is focused on who gets his name placed on the chalkboard rather than on academics. The fear and stigma of public punishment cannot be overestimated. As adults, our recollections of school often are those of only a negative nature.
4. The approach tends to turn teachers into managing technicians rather than to assist them in the development of problem-solving guidance techniques or professional judgment in altering curriculum. It overlooks the fact that appropriate curriculum and methods often prevent discipline problems.
5. While positive reinforcement is recommended in the model, it is often ineffective and can be coercive and manipulative.

Although these criticisms may seem harsh, there are no data to date to refute them. Both Gartrell and Hitz emphasize the need for further research.

COMPARISON AND EVALUATION OF CONTEMPORARY STRATEGIES

Similarities

The strategies for parenting described in this chapter share several similarities and some differences, which are summarized in Box 5r. The most obvious similarity is the emphasis on a democratic relationship between parents and children, with the child's needs and feelings respected as being valid and as being highly correlated with behavior. Only in the case of behavior modification—and, to an extent, assertive discipline—are power assertion techniques emphasized. Punitive techniques (shouting, threatening, ridiculing, shaming, and physical punishment) are not advocated, whereas inductive techniques, encouragement, and developing self-control are emphasized (Bigner, 1985; Brooks, 1987). Parenting behaviors are mani-

BOX 5r SIMILARITIES AND DIFFERENCES AMONG STRATEGIES

	Strategy							
Situation	STEP	PET	TA	Behavior Modification	Active Parenting	How to Talk So Kids Will Listen	Responsive Parenting	Assertive Discipline
Minimizes use of parental power and emphasizes democratic relationships.	×	×	+	0	×	+	×	0
Warmth, nurturance, and acceptance are manifested by parent.	+	×	+	0	×	+	+	0
Limits are implemented.	×	+	0	N/A	×	+	+	×
Communication is emphasized.	×	×	×	+*	×	×	+	0**
Parents learn causes of children's behavior.	×	×	×	0	×	+	+	0
Raising a responsible child is a major goal.	×	×	+	0	×	×	+	×-0***
Emphasizes changing child's behavior.	×	+	+	×	×	×	+	×
Uses explicit reward/ punishment to change child's behavior.	0	0	+	×	0	+	+	×
Emphasizes use of punishment.	0	0	0	×	0	0	+	×
Emphasizes use of praise.	0	+	+	×	×	×	×	×

× = Strongly
+ = Moderately
0 = Little or not at all
N/A = not applicable
* = Language is used as a technique of behavior management
** = Emphasis on parent communicating
*** = Authors' claim may not be accurate

fested in a context of warmth, nurturance, and acceptance in all strategies, again with the exception of behavior-modification techniques, and most strategies recommend imposing certain limits.

Communication is seen as the major com-ponent of a positive parent-child relationship in most strategies. PET emphasizes "I-messages" and active listening; STEP encourages reflective listening and open responses; TA emphasizes analyzing a communication transaction; as-sertive discipline emphasizes assertive communication. Active Parenting emphasizes active listening, avoiding communication blocks, and "I"-messages. In How to Talk So Kids Will Listen, the emphasis is on what the parent says rather than on listening to the child. Behavior-modification techniques also emphasize communication but in a different way—specific language is used as reinforcement or punishment to manage behavior.

Identifying the causes of children's behavior is emphasized in all strategies except behavior modification and assertive discipline. STEP, especially, emphasizes that all misbehavior has a goal that is based on faulty beliefs, and parents need to understand the beliefs and identify the goals before they can effectively deal with the behavior. PET emphasizes the concept of problem ownership in dealing with misbehavior, which facilitates the understanding of both parents' and children's behavior. TA emphasizes developing understanding of ego states of personality in improving relationships. Active Parenting, a combination of STEP and PET concepts, emphasizes problem ownership and goals of misbehavior to understand both the parent's and child's behavior. In assertive discipline no concern for the cause of children's behavior is demonstrated, but parents decide what specific behavior they want to change.

Finally, most strategies have as their goal the raising of a responsible child. Goals that are implicit in most of the strategies are helping parents and children resolve conflict in ways that assist children in becoming more responsible, providing choices, promoting decision making, being consistent in demands, and emphasizing the needs of parents as well as children. Further, modeling of responsible behavior for the child is advocated as a way to foster responsibility in children.

Differences

The major difference among the strategies seems to be the degree of emphasis given to various principles (Brooks, 1987). STEP, behavior-modification techniques, and assertive discipline stress changing the child's behavior, but the mechanism for doing so is different in each strategy. Behavior-modification techniques and assertive discipline use explicit rewards and punishments to change behavior. These techniques, then, call for a more active parent role in controlling children's behavior. STEP, on the other hand, focuses on changing children's behavior by the use of natural and logical consequences. Even though other strategies focus less on changing children's behavior, these changes are believed to occur as a result of problem-solving sessions or changes in communication techniques.

The use of parental power is the technique that separates behavior modification and assertive discipline techniques from the remaining strategies. While other strategies seek to reduce the power of the parent and to create a more egalitarian relationship, behavior modification and assertive discipline enhance the parent as the powerful authority figure. Further, these two strategies forcefully employ the use of punishment more than other strategies.

Finally, most strategies advocate the use of praise, but the way in which it is used varies. STEP differentiates between praise and encouragement and recommends the use of only the latter. It is contended that praise focuses only on the outward manifestation of a specific behavior (the product), whereas encouragement focuses on the child's motives and efforts (the process). TA considers praise to be a form of stroking, a "warm fuzzy." PET prefers an appreciative "I-message" to praise. Praise is considered by behavior modification strategists to be an effective reinforcer for behavior in many instances. However, it must be used only as specified in the contingency schedule rather than spontaneously or inconsistently. How to Talk So Kids Will Listen focuses on the kind of praise that builds a positive self-image—praising efforts rather than children's personalities. Active Parenting stresses the instilling of courage by providing encouragement and avoiding discouragement.

Obviously, these similarities and differences in approach result in slightly differing parental behavior in certain situations and in similar parental behavior in other situations. Examples of parental behavior by strategy for selected situations are given in Box 5s.

BOX 5s PARENTAL BEHAVIOR IN GIVEN SITUATIONS BY SELECTED STRATEGIES

	Strategy		
Situation	*STEP*	*PET*	*TA*
Child does not clean room by agreed-on time	I-message; logical consequence; family meeting	I-message; no-lose method of conflict resolution	Achieves complementary transaction
Child forgets to take gym clothes to school	Natural consequence	Active listening	Achieves complementary transaction
Child complains about a particular teacher	Reflective listening	Active listening	Achieves complementary transaction
Children argue about assigned chores	Family meeting	No-lose method of conflict resolution	Achieves complementary transaction
Preschool child colors on the wall	Logical consequence	I-message	Achieves complementary transaction
Child does poorly in school	Identifies goal; logical consequence	Active listening	Achieves complementary transaction
Child comes home on time for dinner after several instances of being late	Encourages	Positive I-message	Gives a warm fuzzy

	Strategy		
Behavior Modification	*Active Parenting*	*How to Talk So Kids Will Listen*	*Assertive Discipline*
Administers punishment or withholds reinforcement	I-message; logical consequence; family meeting	Expresses strong disapproval; engages cooperation	States assertively that child is to clean room; uses "broken record"; applies disciplinary consequence
Gives reinforcement when child remembers	Natural consequence	Encourages autonomy and assumption of responsibility	Consequence stipulated by school; no action by parent
No action	Active communication	Feedback techniques—helps child cope with negative feelings	No action
Ignores	Family meeting	Includes children in decisions about chores	Communicates assertively; reinforces words with action; "lays down the law"
Administers punishment	Logical consequence; I-message	Expresses strong disapproval	Communicates assertively; reinforces words with action; "lays down the law"; uses parent-saver technique
Rewards when child does well	Identifies goal; logical consequence	Encourages responsibility for action; expresses strong disapproval	Establishes discipline hierarchy; utilizes positive contract; tries marble mania
Rewards	Encourages; I-message	Encourages efforts; builds on strengths; praises	Applies positive reinforcement, such as praise, especially in the presence of others

Strengths and Limitations

It appears that each of the strategies previously described has unique strengths and limitations. In general the skills described in the strategies are relatively simple for parents to learn. If parents apply them over a period of time with success and see that they actually cause either their children or themselves to change behavior, then they are likely to become encouraged and develop a more positive relationship with their children.

Further, being trained in a specific strategy of parenting may give parents some concrete ideas of how to deal with specific problems in the parent-child relationship. As we have already mentioned, parents are now more isolated from sources of support in parenting than they once were, and many of them are eager for sources of ideas and advice.

Finally, most of the strategies take into account the parents' feelings as well as the children's. Becoming aware of one's own anger, discouragement, satisfaction, needs, desires, and concerns may be the first step in becoming a more effective parent. And improving communication between parents and children can be mutually satisfying to both.

One must recognize, however, that strategies for parenting have limitations, both individually and collectively. First, most strategies do not account for either age or sex differences in children. Most research indicates that there are subtle differences in behavior of boys and girls and differences in the ways both mothers and fathers interact with each sex. Further, while the strategies make some attempt to differentiate between application of methods for younger children and teenagers, a precise differentiation is absent (Brooks, 1987). The impression one gets is that the strategists assume that all parenting behaviors are applicable equally to all age groups. Obviously one cannot engage in active listening with an infant. Parents need a bit more guidance in understanding the effects of both sex and the developmental level of children in their application of specific methods or skills. Hills and Knowles (1987) pointed out that many programs need teaching strategies that provide opportunities for parents to bring their experiences and concerns into all phases of learning the skills.

This would promote transfer of skills taught to actual family situations. They suggested that parents should be asked to describe their understanding of a concept and then to use their own judgment and words in implementing the skill.

Another assumption that seems to be made by strategists is that a given strategy is applicable equally to all cultures and socioeconomic classes. Therefore strategies fail to take into account variation in cultural attitudes and values and complex issues related to poverty. In fact, most strategies are oriented to the white middle class. One cannot help but wonder how motivated parents on an Indian reservation would be to learn and implement some of the skills set forth in strategies that ignore the preservation of their cultural heritage—or how it would be possible in the ecological context of poverty for mothers or fathers to practice "I-messages," reflective listening, or a rigid behavior-management program.

A glaring deficiency in all strategies is the assumption that, if parents learn and use the techniques accurately, then all parent-child relationships will be positive. Each strategist seems to think she or he has all the answers. Some attempts have been made to combine various aspects of several strategies, but few have been made to help parents evaluate aspects of strategies and select those techniques that appear most appropriate and most successful for them. In short there a few qualifiers placed on the effectiveness of skills described in each strategy.

Griffore (1980) emphasized that parents would probably benefit more from a basic, adequate knowledge of child development than from "glib guidelines." He contended that contemporary strategies are little more than cookbook approaches even though they are based on theoretical or philosophical perspectives. Further, a parent who relies on a single overall framework might achieve consistency in his or her relationships with children, but the chances are that a single approach will not serve the parent adequately in all respects. Further, the expectation that the specifically prescribed behaviors for parents will result in predictable behavior in children fails to consider the complex nature of the parent-child relationship and other variables that undoubtedly affect that relationship. Therefore Griffore recommended that more emphasis be placed on putting into the hands of parents child development literature that is understandable.

The program Living With 10- to 15-Year-Olds focuses on the normal growth and development of children in this age span and how parents can improve relationships with their children. The emphasis, then, is on helping parents understand the child rather than trying to change the child's behavior. When specific strategies are used, then, parents need to understand what their limitations are, what the qualifiers might be, and the undesirable as well as the desirable results of such techniques.

Lest we appear too negative, let us hasten to add that we believe there is some value in teaching specific skills to parents. At the same time, one must strive to develop in parents attitudes that are consistent with the techniques being used, and knowledge and understanding of child development and behavior. However, since we do not believe that any one strategy is a panacea for parent-child relationships, it seems wise to take a more eclectic approach in parent education. We should provide parents with a broad base from which to function and allow them more freedom to choose from a number of strategies with whose methods the parents feel more comfortable and which seem to be successful for them and their children.

SUMMARY

In an effort to assist parents in becoming more effective in a rapidly changing society, a number of professionals have developed strategies of parent education. Some of the strategies have been developed and packaged so that parents participate in structured training sessions over a given period of time, whereas others are simply outlined in reading and video materials so that parents can be self-taught. All strategies are allegedly designed for "normal" parents and children, providing support rather than crisis intervention.

Contemporary strategies share several similarities, and each has its strengths and weaknesses. Unfortunately, little research exists that tests the long-term effects of change in either parents' or children's behavior as a result of parent training utilizing a particular strategy. Therefore the effectiveness of these contemporary strategies must be assumed rather than known. Nevertheless, the availability of such resources for parents seems to be a positive force in today's society.

REFERENCES

ANDERSON, S., & NUTTALL, P. (1987). Parent communication training across three stages of childrearing. *Family Relations, 36*(1), 40–44.

BABCOCK, D., & KEEPERS, T. (1977). *Raising kids OK.* New York: Avon.

BERNE, E. (1964). *Games people play.* New York: Grove Press.

BIGNER, J. (1985). *Parent-child relationships* (2d ed.). New York: Macmillan.

BROOKS, J. B. (1987). *The process of parenting* (2d ed.). Palo Alto, CA: Mayfield.

CAGAN, E. (1980, January/February). The positive parent: Raising children the scientific way. *Social Policy,* pp. 40–48.

CALVERT, S., & MCMAHON, R. (1987). The treatment acceptability of a behavioral parent training program and its components. *Behavior Therapy, 2,* 165–179.

CANTER, L., & CANTER, M. (1976). *Assertive discipline: A take-charge approach for today's educator.* Seal Beach, CA: Canter & Associates.

CANTER, L., & CANTER, M. (1985). *Assertive discipline for parents* (rev. ed.). New York: Harper & Row.

DINKMEYER, D. (1979). A comprehensive and systematic approach to parent education. *Journal of Family Therapy, 7*(2), 46–50.

DINKMEYER, D., & MCKAY, G. (1973). *Raising a responsible child.* New York: Simon & Schuster.

DINKMEYER, D., & MCKAY, G. (1976). *Parents' handbook* (A part of the complete STEP Program). Circle Pines, MN: American Guidance Service.

DINKMEYER, D., & MCKAY, G. (1983). *STEP/Teen: Systematic training for effective parenting of teens.* Circle Pines, MN: American Guidance Service.

DINKMEYER, D., MCKAY, G., & DINKMEYER, D. (1980). *STET.* Circle Pines, MN: American Guidance Service.

DINKMEYER, D., MCKAY, G., DINKMEYER, D., DINKMEYER, J., & MCKAY, J. (1987). *The next STEP.* Circle Pines, MN: American Guidance Service.

DOHERTY, W., & RYDER, R. (1980, October). Parent effectiveness training (PET): Criticisms and caveats. *Journal of Marital and Family Therapy,* pp. 409–419.

DORMAN, G., GELDOF, D., & SCARBOROUGH, B. (1982). *Living with 10- to 15-year-olds.* Chapel Hill, NC: Center for Early Adolescence.

FABER, A., & MAZLISH, E. (1974). *Liberated parents, liberated children.* New York: Avon.

FABER, A., & MAZLISH, E. (1980). *How to talk so kids will listen & listen so kids will talk.* New York: Avon.

FABER, A., & MAZLISH, E. (1987). *Siblings without rivalry.* New York: Negotiation Institute.

FRAZIER, R., & MATTHES, W. (1975, October). Parent education: A comparison of Adlerian and behavioral approaches. *Elementary School Guidance and Counseling,* pp. 31–38.

GARTRELL, D. (1987). Assertive discipline: Unhealthy for children and other living things. *Young Children, 42*(2), 10–11.

GORDON, T. (1975). *Parent effectiveness training.* New York: New American Library.

GORDON, T. (1976). *P.E.T. in action.* New York: Bantam.

GRIFFORE, R. (1980, Spring). Toward the use of child development research in informed parenting. *Journal of Clinical Child Psychology,* 48–57.

HARRIS, T. (1969). *I'm OK—You're OK.* New York: Harper & Row.

HARRIS, T. (1973). *I'm OK—You're OK.* New York: Avon.

HILLS, M., & KNOWLES, D. (1987). Providing for personal meaning in parent education programs. *Family Relations, 36*(2), 158–162.

HINKLE, D., ARNOLD, C., CROAKE, J., & KELLER, J. (1980). Adlerian parent education: Changes in parents' attitudes and behaviors, and children's self-esteem. *American Journal of Family Therapy, 8*(1), 32–43.

HITZ, R. (1988). Assertive discipline: A response to Lee Canter. *Young Children, 43*(2), 25–26.

JACKSON, M., & BROWN, D. (1986). Use of Systematic Training for Effective Parenting (STEP) with elementary school parents. *School Counselor, 34,* 100–105.

LERMAN, S. (1984). *Responsive parenting.* Circle Pines, MN: American Guidance Service.

MCDOWELL, R. (1969). Parent counseling: An experiment in behavior modification. *Kansas Studies in Education, 19*(3), 16–19.

MCDOWELL, R. (1978). *Managing behavior: A parent involvement program.* Torrence, CA: Winch and Associates.

MITCHELL. J., & MCMANIS, A. (1977). Parent effectiveness training: A review. *Psychological Reports, 41,* 215–218.

O'DELL, S. (1974). Training parents in behavior modification: A review. *Psychological Bulletin, 81*(7), 418–433.

PINSKER, R., & GEOFFRAY, K. (1981). A comparison of parent effectiveness training and behavior modification parent training. *Family Relations, 30,* 61–68.

POPKIN, M. (1983). *Active Parenting.* Atlanta: Active Parenting.

POPKIN, M. (1986). *Active Parenting, 2*(1), newsletter.

RINN, R., & MARKLE, A. (1977). Parent effectiveness training: A review. *Psychological Reports, 58,* 301–311.

ROEDELL, W., SLABY, R., & ROBINSON, H. (1977). *Social development in young children.* Monterey, CA: Brooks/Cole.

SHEPPARD, W., SHANK, S., & WILSON, D. (1973). *Teaching social behavior to young children.* Champaign, IL: Research Press.

SKINNER, B. F. (1953). *Science and human behavior.* New York: Macmillan.

SMITH, J. M., & SMITH, D. E. (1966). *Child management: A program for parents.* Ann Arbor, MI: Ann Arbor Publishers.

SUMMERLIN, M. L., & WARD, G. R. (1978). The effect of parental participation in a parent group on a child's self-concept. *Journal of Psychology, 100,* 227–232.

WAGONSELLER, B., BURNETT, M., SELZBERG, B., & BURNETT, J. (1980). *The art of parenting.* Champaign, IL: Research Press.

WILLIAMS, R., OMIZO, M., & ABRAMS, B. (1984). Effects of STEP on parental attitudes and locus of control of their learning disabled children. *School Counselor, 32,* 126–133.

6

Parenting
in Diverse Cultures

The term *culture* refers to the sum total of the attainments and learned behavior patterns of a specific people, regarded as expressing a traditional way of life. The behavioral patterns of a given culture are believed to be transmitted from one generation to the next, subject to gradual and continuous modification. In this country many diverse groups exist that manifest distinct behavioral patterns and can be clearly designated as subcultures. These include ethnic groups, religious groups, socioeconomic classes, and geographical populations. In most subcultures certain aspects of the life-style deviate to some extent from that of the dominant culture. However, it is important to note that subcultures within the United States are probably similar in more ways than they are different. Socioeconomic differences are included in the following discussion of cultural diversity because poor families may display cultural behavior patterns that deviate from expectations implicit in the larger middle-class culture (Henderson, 1980). Class differences exist in all racial minority groups and are believed to be a more fundamental barrier than race to structural integration into American society (Staples, 1988).

SOCIOECONOMIC DIFFERENCES IN PARENTING

A serious contemporary concern is the growing number of children in the United States, especially younger ones, who live in poverty. The proportion of children living in poverty has increased steadily since 1975 and dramatically since 1981 (Miller & Coulter, 1984). Currently 20 percent of all dependent children (under age 18) and 25 percent of children under the age of 6 live in families below the poverty line. Of all children under 18 in 1984, half of the blacks, one third of the Hispanics, and 17 percent of the whites were poor (Aldous, 1986). The three groups of families significantly represented in the poverty population are single-parent families, black families, and families with preschool children. Yet nearly half of the families with an unemployed breadwinner receive no government support in the form of AFDC or unemployment compensation (Moen, 1983).

Of all AFDC recipients, two thirds are mothers and children only. AFDC mothers of all ages seem to prefer to live independently, and a larger proportion of teen mothers live alone than with their extended families. However, ethnic differences exist. Blacks are more likely to form extended households for mutual support when economic resources are low or unstable than Anglos or Hispanics are, and AFDC blacks are much less likely than the other two groups to have a father or stepfather in the house (Scheirer, 1983). Rank (1987) asserted that most female heads of household will not marry their way off public assistance. The chances of a marriage dissolving are almost twice as high as the chances of a marriage occurring among female welfare recipients. We should emphasize, however, that it is the conditions of poverty, not welfare programs *per se*, that lead to marital disruption. The combination of marital disruption and poverty result in considerable risk for children.

Even when two parents are available, economic loss by way of unemployment has multiple consequences in terms of the health status, life-style, interpersonal relationships, and feelings of self-worth of family members. During the Great Depression parental behavior was an important link between economic misfortune and the experiences of children. Financial loss increased the temperamental behaviors of fathers (but not mothers), which, in turn, increased their punitive actions. This behavior increased the likelihood of temper tantrums in children, which resulted in more punishment—a vicious circle (Moen, 1983).

Demographically, income and education are directly related to the age at first marriage and are inversely related to the average number of children ever born. Divorce varies inversely with family income (more divorces occur in lower-income families), but the likelihood of remarriage appears to be greater as income increases (Norton, 1983). A complex set of factors, then, may account for differences in parental styles.

For several decades researchers have been investigating differences in parenting practices among lower, middle, and upper socioeconomic classes. Particularly in the 1960s, in conjunction with the federal government's War on Poverty, there was a multitude of research on children from low socioeconomic status families and how best to help them. One of the difficulties of these studies was that socioeconomic status was often

confounded with ethnicity or minority group membership. Nevertheless, the picture that emerged, and subsequently the services that were provided, assumed a generalized image of poor families and poor children. Specifically the emphasis was on the detrimental effects of early experiences of "deprived" children. The terms *progressive retardation* and *cumulative cultural deficit* were commonly used to describe what would ultimately happen to poor children in an academic setting if intervention did not occur. Programs were designed to assist poor children in "catching up" so that they could match middle-class standards. Little attention was given to the strengths of poor families, and indeed poor children were assumed to be lacking in cognitive and affective strengths altogether.

Much of the research in the 1960s has been criticized for its biases, assumptions, and faulty methodology. The current perception is that social-class groups are not homogeneous and that social-class levels differ from one section of the country to another. Some researchers contend that there is as much variation in child-rearing patterns within a given social class as there is between social classes. It has been concluded that assertions on the effects of social class on child development represent probabilities, not inevitabilities (Clarke-Stewart, 1977). It does seem appropriate, however, to mention some of the studies that brought considerable attention to social-class differences.

Mother-Child Interaction

Hess and Shipman (1965, 1967) examined mother-child interactions with emphasis on discipline techniques and language patterns. They found lower-class mothers to be less "instructive" and more "imperative" in their control systems and their children to be poorer at conceptualization and classification. Their research did not, however, find the differences in maternal teaching styles between lower- and middle-class mothers to be in a consistent direction. Other researchers, however, have obtained consistent findings (Brophy, 1970). Similarly, middle-class mothers have been found to be less physically intrusive (as well as more instructive) and to be better able to discern the child's individual needs, whereas lower-class mothers were more critical, controlling, restrictive, and less sensitive to the child's cues (Bee, Van Egeren, Streissguth, Nyman, & Leckie, 1969).

These and other studies emphasized, then, that the way in which lower-class mothers interacted with their young children was consistently different from that of middle-class mothers. Specifically, middle-class mothers gave more reinforcement to children's behavior and responses and were far less controlling, and these behaviors were reflected in their language patterns and those of their children. It must be remembered, however, that most of these studies were experimental; mother-child pairs were observed in a controlled, experimental situation where lower-class mothers are less likely to feel comfortable.

Clarke-Stewart (1977) summarized a number of studies relating to socioeconomic class and parental acts that supported few significant differences related to socioeconomic status in maternal responsiveness, affection, or amount of talk directed to infants during the first six months of life. In fact, mothers with less education and income have been observed to touch and hold their infants more, to smile and look at them more, than middle-class parents have. However, the quality of vocal interaction between mothers and middle-class infants appears to be superior. She did note, however, that while the typical behavior of parents in different socioeconomic groups may not differ during the infancy period, other conditions associated with socioeconomic status (poverty, father absence, health, and nutrition) may have important consequences for the infant's development.

During later infancy and toddlerhood, however, attitudes of middle-class mothers appeared to be more positive and accepting, manifested by differences in behavior, the most consistently noted being the degree and quality of verbal interaction. Further, these mothers played more often with their children, were more affectionate, less likely to punish physically, and were less controlling.

During the preschool period the trends observed earlier were extended. In general parents of higher socioeconomic status rated higher on measures of adult-initiated interaction in the areas of affection, intellectual stimulation, and companionship. They exerted less strictness and control, being more likely to explain, request, and consult than to coax, command, or threaten.

At school age, middle-class parents have demonstrated higher expectations concerning achievement for their children; they talk and read to children more and tend to stress goals for their children such as curiosity, consideration, and self-control rather than obedience, neatness, and cleanliness.

An interesting recent study (Heffer & Kelly, 1987) compared attitudes of low- and high-income Anglo and black mothers toward the acceptability of five different kinds of parental behaviors in response to children's problem behavior: positive reinforcement, response cost (reprimand plus loss of privileges), time-out (10 minutes), spanking, and medication.

Response cost was perceived as highly acceptable by black and Anglo mothers of both income levels. Lower-SES mothers evaluated time-out as significantly less acceptable than positive reinforcement and response cost and equal in acceptability to spanking and medication. Middle-SES mothers viewed time-out, response cost, and positive reinforcement as equally acceptable and as significantly more acceptable than spanking and medication. Nevertheless, a majority of low-SES mothers rated spanking as more than moderately acceptable, and more than half of both low-SES and black mothers rated medication as moderately acceptable. Less labor-intensive techniques seem to be favored by low-SES mothers. Whether the expressed preferences of the mothers in the study are translated into practice is not known.

Very little regarding social-class differences and fathering behavior is noted in the literature. Perhaps this is due to the fact that, traditionally, lower-class fathers frequently were not present in the home, and if they were, possibly they interacted little with their children.

One study attempted to determine whether earlier established social-class differences continue to exist in the current social context in light of the social change that has occurred over the past 15 to 20 years, controlling for racial/ethnic differences (Harmon & Kogan, 1980). When these researchers analyzed play sessions of lower-, middle-, and upper-class white mothers and their preschool children, they found no differences among them on the variables of attention, praise, or control. They conceded, then, that social class was not a variable that could be used to predict differences in interaction between mothers and young children in their sample. They asserted that more refined methodology in gathering data might have altered the results of earlier studies, and that social changes over time might have eliminated earlier differences in child-rearing practices between lower- and middle-class parents.

In summary, it has been reported that upper-class mothers tend to be more tolerant of their children's aggression, that they more adequately meet their babies' physical needs, and they encourage more interaction than other mothers. However, working-class mothers reportedly hold their infants for longer periods of time, primarily as a means of prohibiting them from crawling around and getting into things. Further, working-class mothers have been reported as less confident that they could influence their child's development and to feel more powerless, overwhelmed, and helpless. Further, it appears that economically disadvantaged mothers project their own sense of powerlessness onto their daughters more than their sons, whereas they are more likely to praise their sons' simple accomplishments. However, upper-class mothers have been found to be more likely to criticize incompetent behavior in their daughters than their sons. These findings have often been cited as the basis for the closer relationship between social characteristics and cognitive achievement for females (Rogers, 1977).

Differences in Value Systems

For some time there has been the assumption that there are significant differences in socialization values between working-class and professional families. Working-class families have tended to stress more traditional social values, specifically obedience, whereas professional families have stressed independence, tolerance, and social concern. An interesting point has been made that these socioeconomic status differences in child rearing are based on differences in belief

systems. Beliefs are constructed on the basis of experiences with one's own children, the parents' own experiences as children, cultural assumptions, and access to expert opinion (McGillicuddy-DeLisi, 1980). However, other researchers have contended that blue-collar parents value conformity in children over self-reliance basically because the adult workers in this population are more closely supervised in their jobs (Ellis, Lee, & Petersen, 1978).

In keeping with the assumed traditional values of lower-class families, female children from these families have been reported to be more traditional in their sex-role orientation. It has been pointed out that lower-class families evidence considerable sex segregation, with the men being the providers and the women caring for the home and the children. Families tend to be larger, child care is more demanding, and lower incomes place restrictions on child-care alternatives. Women reared in these conditions are presumed to be less well prepared to compete in the job market, and thereby accept the traditional role as wife and mother. One study, however, found that when childhood relationships of women with their fathers were perceived as being less than "good," women tended to reject traditional sex roles, independently of socioeconomic status. However, social class had a pronounced effect on women who reported good childhood relationships with their fathers. For such women the lower the socioeconomic background, the more traditional these sex-role orientations were (McBroom, 1981).

Occupational and Educational Aspirations

Another area in which social-class differences have been reported is that of occupational and educational aspirations. Research findings have consistently shown that level of aspiration or level of expectation of children is positively related to the social class of the parent. However, there appear to be sex differences as well as ethnic differences. A recent study examined the range of aspirations of lower- and middle-class parents for their preschool children. They found that the lower the social-class position, the higher the percentage of respondents with a wide range of aspirations. Further, lower-class parents reached a peak of aspirations as high as middle-class parents, which seemed to suggest a built-in potential for mobility (Rodman & Voydanoff, 1978). While these findings were somewhat inconsistent with other studies indicating lower levels of aspiration for lower-social-class members, one must consider how and why parents may modify the aspirations they have for their children. The children in the study were 2½ to 5 years of age. Clearly, as children get older, their characteristics and performance affect the aspirations their parents may have for them. However, lower-class parents may also be influenced in their aspirations by lack of resources. "Social class provides differential access to power and resources and thus leads to differences in behavior and achievement" (Rodman & Voydanoff, 1978, p. 341). The researchers believe that their findings do not lend support to policies and programs that focus on the inadequacies of lower-class families and the need to change their values or raise their level of aspirations. Rather they suggest that mobility should be encouraged by providing greater opportunities and helping to establish a belief that their aspirations are within reach.

Time Devoted to Children

We have discussed thus far the differences in parenting attitudes, beliefs, and practices between lower- and middle-class families. Another difference among these groups that might relate to outcomes is quantity of time devoted to children. Several years ago it was reported that on a per-child basis, higher-class mothers allocated between 2½ and 3 times as much of their non-labor market time to their preschool children as low-status mothers did (Hill & Stafford, 1974). These researchers conducted a later study and found the following results: Women with at least some college education spend slightly more than 2 hours per week more on child care with children 0–3 years than women with less than a high school education; the time allocated to child care decreases as the child ages, but the decrease is much more pronounced in groups where the mother has relatively low educational attainment. Further, they found that college-

educated women reduce their personal care time (for example, sleep) and their passive leisure time (for example, television) in order to care for children and avoid excessively large reductions in market hours. In fact, the researchers asserted that, regardless of personal circumstances, college-educated women manage to care for their children at reasonably high levels in the form of direct child care and more goods produced through housework, even if labor force participation is great. It also appears that sheer quantity of time spent with children was not the only difference between better- and less-educated mothers. College-educated mothers provided a wider variety of care than less-educated mothers, including playing, reading, talking, and direct helping. In addition they spent almost twice as much time in travel that was child-related than did less-educated mothers. The researchers concluded that there are, then, substantial differences in both the quantity and quality of care time of preschool children among less-educated and more-educated mothers (Hill & Stafford, 1980).

Differences in Cognitive Performance of Children

Despite the confusing and often contradictory results of research concerning socioeconomic differences in parenting, many researchers contend that differences persist. For example, lower-class Anglo mothers talk less to their infants, are less likely to encourage cognitive development, and are more intrusive and autocratic with their discipline. Specifically, one study reported that the number of prohibitions issued by lower-class mothers to their children was one every 5 minutes, whereas middle-class mothers issued prohibitions on the average of once every 10 minutes (Kagan, 1977). Further, there continues to be a positive relationship between the child's social class and a variety of indices of cognitive functioning, including IQ or achievement test scores, grades in school, richness of vocabulary and memory, and inferential abilities (Kagan, 1977).

One possible relationship to cognitive performance may be that middle-class children are more likely to believe that effort results in success and lack of effort results in failure, whereas lower-class children are more likely to relate success and failure to chance or benevolent and malevolent social forces. Kagan (1977) stated that psychological experiences within the family account for these lower expectations of success on cognitive problems and less motivation to perform well. In fact, he stated, "A family's social class is associated with the degree of risk for biological and psychological deficits at birth, specific practices toward the child, projection of parental views of self onto the child, and, finally, the child's identification with his class" (p. 49).

In summary, it is safe to say that differences in parenting between lower- and middle-class parents exist. Some of these differences have been fairly consistent, others have not. It seems important, however, to recognize that generalizations have often been made without controlling for such factors as ethnicity and geographic location and that the methodology employed in gathering data may have been less than flawless. It is not clear how much of the difference among parenting behavior is the direct result of income and how much is related to other factors, such as education, health status, and biological differences. What can be concluded is that consistent

differences have been observed among different social-class levels, but that socioeconomic status *by itself* probably accounts for a relatively small proportion of the variance in children's behaviors and abilities (Clarke-Stewart, 1977). Further, conditions associated with poverty, such as slum neighborhoods, inferior employment, poor health, unstable marriages, and high birthrates, serve to devastate the child's well-being as much as specific parenting behaviors.

Finally, there appear to be "within-class" differences that might be equally significant to "between-class" differences. Clearly, lower-class parents lack resources in parenting equal to those of middle- and upper-class parents—financial, educational, psychological, and medical resources. And this lack of resources surely has some impact on the way in which they interact with their children.

PARENTING IN BLACK FAMILIES

In 1985 there were approximately 9 million black families and 29 million black people in the United States. More than 80 percent of these resided in metropolitan areas, most living in the inner-city sections of the largest cities (U.S. Bureau of the Census, 1986). According to some

researchers black people in America have been sufficiently isolated that they have participated in a distinctive culture. This isolation is particularly true of poor blacks. They tend to belong to all-black churches, volunteer organizations, and information groups. Thus, the major portion of their social interaction is with other black people in their neighborhood. This is true even though they attend school, work, and shop alongside whites. The tendency to live, study, work, and socialize together is reinforced by housing, school, and employment practices. The tendency to have dual or even several social systems or structural arrangements for access to, and receiving, resources and for enforcing laws has reinforced the development and continuance of a distinct black culture. This isolation is also due to the fact that black people enjoy being together and feel more comfortable with each other (Hale, 1980, Hale-Benson, 1986; Peters, 1978).

Demographics

There have been enormous changes among blacks over the past two decades: a rise of the black underclass, a rise of the black middle class (37 percent of blacks are classified as middle class), and the demise of the stable black blue-collar working class. Social scientists have emphasized the underclass, manifested by increased unemployment, poverty, and female-headed families. Black poverty was dramatically reduced between 1959 and 1979 by the combination of an expanding economy, greater educational opportunity, more government programs for the poor, and the enforcement of civil rights and affirmative action. Since 1979, however, these trends have been reversed. In 1983 black families had an annual income that was $818 lower than in 1980—a larger decline than for any other population group, and by 1985 black poverty had again reached unprecedented levels (Billingsley, 1988; Crawley, 1988; Staples, 1988).

The exceptionally high rate of unemployment for blacks and their relatively low level of education account for the fact that their median household income is approximately 56 percent of whites' and 79 percent of Hispanics'. Black males have three times the rate of unemployment

as white males do. At the present time the median family income for blacks is almost exactly equivalent to what it was in 1967 (U.S. Bureau of the Census, 1986). To make matters worse, the rising percentage of female-headed households with children under 18 has resulted in nearly 65 percent of these families living below the poverty line (Aldous, 1986). Although black women make a much greater contribution to the economic standing of their families than white women do, even when both groups are married to working husbands, black women earn less than white men, white women, and black men (Billingsley, 1988).

It has been said that even though the depressed status of black families is visible in every income level, the hardest hit have been black two-parent families in which one parent is employed and the other cares for the children. Between 1980 and 1984 these families experienced an average disposable income loss of more than $2,000 per year. Even when blacks utilize an opportunity such as higher education, they incur loss, as manifested by a 1982 comparison of average annual income yielded by 4 years of college. For white males the figure was $28,745; for black males it was $18,829; for white females it was $17,596; and for black females it was $16,183 (Crawley, 1988).

Traditionally, blacks have begun their childbearing much earlier than other ethnic groups; they continue their childbearing longer and have a higher average number of children ever born than whites or Hispanics do. Further, black females are more likely to divorce than whites or Hispanics and are less likely to remarry than Anglos. Separation and divorce occur at younger ages for blacks than for other groups, and the period of separation before divorce is longer (Norton, 1983). Even so, black families are represented by great diversity in life-style. In their struggle for equality and justice, blacks have survived by living in a variety of family forms—two-parent households, common-law marriages, extended families, male-headed families, and female-headed families (Crawley, 1988).

Since the 1970s, however, there has been a dramatic increase in both teenage pregnancies and out-of-wedlock births among blacks of all social classes. Nearly 60 percent of all black babies are born out of wedlock; 30 percent are born to teenagers, and 89 percent of those teens are unmarried (Staples, 1988). Illegitimacy rates among blacks are four times higher than among whites, even though out-of-wedlock births in the white population have tripled.

Diverse Viewpoints of the Black Family

Black families have immense differentiation in terms of cultural values and regional differences (Staples, 1988). Several viewpoints of the black family have been held by social scientists and have influenced research, policy, and programs. Until 1965–1970 the major image of black families, particularly of poor black families, was one of pathology and deviance. Most of these ideas developed because researchers failed to distinguish between factors of culture and class in family life-styles. For many years it was believed that family structure determined social achievement.

Amuzie Chimezie (cited in Hale-Benson, 1986) believes that black culture theorists are divided broadly into two categories—negative and affirmative. Negative theorists deny the existence of a black culture and attribute differences to class position; degree of poverty; and attendant social pathologies, that is, the *cultural deviant* approach.

In 1965 Daniel Patrick Moynihan published a report, *The Negro Family: The Case for National Action*. Moynihan's position was that slavery had destroyed African cultures and family patterns. The efforts of black males to protect and support their families were undermined so that the men were not authority figures in black families; therefore a matriarchal family emerged. The bond between the mother and the child became the most durable and meaningful feature of black family life. The black male did not have an opportunity to become acculturated to the dominant nuclear family form. Massive migration of blacks to northern cities prior to World War I and later to inner-city sections of large cities in the country only created more difficulties as black men were thrown into highly competitive and racially discriminating situations. The family

structure was further weakened, and desertion and divorce, sexual promiscuity, illegitimacy, crime, delinquency, and welfare dependency were thought to be characteristic of black families.

Other writers, such as Frazier (1939) and Rainwater (1966), also contributed to the idea that black families were unstable, structurally weak, socially disorganized, and handicapped in performing essential family functions. In addition, black families were said to be seriously deficient in necessary resources and competencies. It was felt that the extremely persistent negative conditions in which black families lived caused them to resort to adaptive strategies that produced expressive and violent behavior within the family as well as tendencies toward depression and a sense of fatalism. These attitudes were perpetuated from one generation to another. The idea of a cycle of poverty was a prevalent one in the 1960s. Those persons who still hold to the viewpoint that black families in general are deviant and pathological feel that the situation is growing steadily worse since the number of black divorces, out-of-wedlock births, and unemployed are increasing (Frazier, 1939; McQueen, 1979; Moynihan, 1965; Rainwater, 1966; Staples & Mirandé, 1980).

The affirmative theorists subscribe to at least four different viewpoints. The first is the African Heritage theory, which is based on the assumption that certain African traits have been retained by blacks and are evidenced in kinship patterns, marriage, sexuality, childrearing, and so forth (Hale-Benson, 1986; Staples & Mirandé, 1980). This viewpoint is sometimes referred to as the *cultural variant* approach and views black families as culturally unique units.

The affirmative New World Experience theory explains distinctiveness in terms of the experiences of blacks in America rather than African traditions. The Biculturation theory views black culture as composed of black and white elements in that black children are socialized in both Afro-American and Euro-American culture. However, there is lack of consensus about the importance of each culture to them.

The Eclectic theory recognizes a distinctive black culture and attempts to identify the salient

---

**BOX 6a   AFRICAN TRAITS OF BLACK FAMILIES:
THE CULTURAL VARIANT APPROACH**

Funerals

Magical practices

Folklore

Dance

Song

Wearing of kerchiefs, scarves

Motor habits—walking, speaking, dancing, burden carrying, and so on

Hairdressing—wrapping, braiding, cornrowing

Respect for elderly

Source: Hale-Benson, J. (1986). *Black children: Their roots, culture, and learning styles.* Provo, UT: Brigham Young University Press.

---

factors that are theoretically responsible for its cultural elements. These theorists believe that certain aspects of black culture are African retentions and others arise from American experience. They emphasize that many factors influence and affect black ways of life (Hale-Benson, 1986). Finally, some subscribe to the *cultural equivalent* approach, in which black families are seen as legitimate if they adhere to the white, middle-class life-style.

If one subscribes to the African Heritage theory, then one would contend that the development and behavioral styles of black children differ as a result of growing up in a distinct culture. Hale-Benson (1986) pointed out a number of characteristics peculiar to the black culture that have roots in West Africa, which have resulted in the emergence of a distinct language system and particular behavioral characteristics. Apparently the aspects of African culture that have survived and have been transmitted have occurred without conscious effort and so subtly that they are not thought of as Africanisms but may influence the manner in which black children are parented (see Box 6a).

Functions of Black Families

Black families are varied and complex. Depending on socioeconomic status, some families are adaptable and stable and are effective socializers of their children; others are marginal, operating close to their limits. Black families who live in poverty have few resources and may demonstrate some of the negative characteristics that have been attributed to them. On the other hand, many families are resilient and resourceful, even in the absence of adequate financial resources (Rashid, 1985).

Many people believe that the major function of Afro-American parents is to transmit the cultural heritage of Africa and African America to their children, often in the form of accounts of the struggles, achievements, and defeats of black heroes. Hale-Benson (1986) described the process of bicultural socialization that often occurs, whereby both the aspects of African heritage and the realities of America are integral aspects. When rearing children black parents may have to resolve basic conflicts between European and African views, often being forced to ignore white child-rearing norms that are irrelevant to the existing situation of their children.

Rashid (1985) identified the following four areas that distinguish the behavior of blacks among family members and within the broader context of community: (1) respect—the recognition of seniority and submission to those in authority; (2) restraint—balancing the rights of individuals with the needs and requirements of the group; (3) responsibility—the sense of duty or obligation to kin; and (4) reciprocity—the notion that good deeds will be reciprocated either in the short- or long-term. Upward mobility does not erase the sense of reciprocal obligation to kin. Rashid concluded, then, that the extended family is a cultural rather than an economic phenomenon.

Characteristics of Black Culture That Affect Parenting

Because of the emphasis on affective, interpersonal relations and the emotional, people-oriented characteristics of black people, children are likely to grow up to be feeling- and people-oriented and more proficient in nonverbal communication skills than white children are. White children are more likely to be object-oriented as they have had numerous opportunities to manipulate objects and to discover their properties and relationships. Black families are usually larger than white families, and babies are subjected to considerable human interaction with people of all ages. For example, Hale-Benson (1986) found that black families have more daily visitors than white families have. Box 6b summarizes the characteristics of black culture that affect parenting.

A few plastic toys picked up at the grocery store may constitute a baby's play materials, but most black babies are redirected when they try to reach for an object. They are encouraged to feel or to rub the holder's face. A game of "rubbing each other's face" ensues. Babies are thus inhibited from exploring and manipulating objects. Infants and young children often sleep with their parents. There is a rhythm of sleeping and eating, with each activity being of short duration and the pattern repeated frequently.

Toilet training is begun early and is stringent, largely due to the fact that the baby has been held so much of the time and the mother has been constantly and directly involved in the process. This pattern is in startling contrast to that ex-perienced by white infants where, after many months of paying no attention to wet and soiled diapers, the mother suddenly interferes and begins the toilet-training process.

Verbal communication is minimal in many black homes. There are, however, abundant forms of other types of communication, such as looking deeply into the child's eyes and caressing the baby. Looking into the eyes is used by the mother to impress a point on the child. When black school children refuse to look at their teachers, they may be trying to sever an intense level of communication that is typically shared by black people. Or, the child may feel that it is disrespectful to an authority figure to look her in the eye.

Black mothers and children frequently utilize a pattern of verbal communication where the mother echoes the words and tone of voice used by the child. Further, black mothers give directions for household tasks in a distinctive manner that is like the call-and-response patterns found in black music. Few words are used, and instructions are broken down into small units with brief directions for each task. Frequently, children and adults in the black culture engage in a verbal contest where there is rhythmical volleying of words. The child is encouraged to be spontaneous and assertive in her language and to develop a unique style. Children are taught early to participate with language. This is observed by the child when she attends religious services. Thus when the child starts to school she must adjust to an entirely different language exchange (Hale-Benson, 1986).

Black babies tend to be more physically ad-

BOX 6b   CHARACTERISTICS OF BLACK CULTURE THAT AFFECT CHILD REARING

Feeling orientation
People orientation
Proficiency in nonverbal communication skills
High degree of human interaction
Biculturation
Multiple environmental stimuli

vanced at birth than white babies are, and they continue the edge during the first year. One explanation is that black mothers handle their babies more and in a different manner from white mothers. For example, black babies are massaged frequently in order to shape their appearance. They tend to be motorically precocious, being more active and having a higher energy level than white babies.

Black homes generally have a high noise level as a result of large numbers of people, television, stereo music, and a number of activities occurring simultaneously. This tendency for the black home environment to provide an abundance of stimulation, intensity, and variation has been viewed by some as overstimulation, thought to be a handicap, resulting in the child's learning to "tune out" critical stimuli. Others feel that this abundantly stimulating atmosphere creates children who have an increased behavioral vibrancy and affinity for stimulus change. Hale-Benson (1986) explained that the typical classroom may seem dull and unstimulating to black children, who are less able than white children to tolerate monotony in academic task presentations.

Cultural specific values of black families have been found in such areas as discipline, expectations regarding age- and sex-appropriate responsibilities, kin network, and awareness of racism. There is special emphasis in child rearing on respect for authority figures; strict discipline; a high value on a variety of responses, abilities, and talents; open receptivity to multiple environmental stimuli, and expression of emotions by both males and females (Rashid, 1985).

A survey of black and white grandmothers was conducted to determine whether the above Afro-centric orientation to child rearing and other values between the two groups differed significantly. Support for most of the characteristics previously presented was found. Further, after-school activities for black and white children differed considerably. For example, the black children were more likely to perform household tasks; the white children listened to the radio or engaged in free play more frequently. Black parents assign household responsibilities based on age. At mealtime there was greater flexibility concerning who ate together in black families than in white ones (Hale-Benson, 1986).

Many writers have emphasized that black families utilize corporal punishment more than white families. In the Hale-Benson (1986) study the white and black families differed significantly in their attitudes toward and practices of discipline. Corporal punishment was used more frequently in black families, and black children were expected to be obedient. They were most often punished for being disrespectful to their elders, disobeying adults or older siblings, being irresponsible with money, and not fighting back when assaulted. They were more likely to be punished for irresponsibility with money than for other property offenses, such as soiling clothes. The confrontation/aggression orientation is encouraged in black families whereas white children are socialized not to fight.

When Bartz and Levine (1978) compared child-rearing attitudes and behaviors of low-income black, Anglo, and Chicano parents, they found that black parents differed from Anglo and Chicano parents on five factors, but did not differ in their basic orientation toward child rearing. These researchers concluded that black parents in their study believed in the value of strictness, expected early assumption of responsibility by the child for his own bodily functions and personal feelings, expected that the child's time would be used wisely and not wasted, and encouraged the child's involvement in decision making. Further, these parents expressed concern and care for their children while closely monitoring the child's behavior to assure development of specific goals, such as obedience and achievement. This combination of a high level of support, open communication, and demands for maturity are indicative of an authoritative parental role.

It seems that black parents are able to articulate more what they do not want children to do as occupations—such as hard, menial labor or domestic work—than the specific occupations they aspire to for their children. Black parents have been found to express the importance of education, viewing education as a means of upward mobility. Many black parents tell their children to be successful, but do not know how to assist them in implementing the mechanisms to achieve success (Hale-Benson, 1986).

Black Mothers

A strong bond seems to exist between black mothers and their children. Black heritage emphasizes that children represent the continuity of life, and the mother role is highly valued. While some researchers have described the black family structure as matriarchal with a domineering, pathological female as head, others have described the black mother as strong, particularly in the sense that she has been able to maintain the dual role of wage earner and manager of a household (Hale-Benson, 1986).

The great majority of black mothers work, with more than 70 percent of all black families having dual wage earners. Black wives often work when by white standards they would not. Black women perceive that "being a good provider" is an essential aspect of being a successful mother. They, more than white mothers, feel that working mothers can have a strong relationship with their children. Therefore most black women want to work outside the home and desire to continue working after marriage and the birth of their children. Black children are more likely than white children to see both parents as effective in fulfilling two roles—providing for food, clothing, and shelter and providing emotional support, warmth, and patience (Harrison & Minor, 1978).

The increasing out-of-wedlock birthrate may suggest that more young, black women desire to achieve the status of parenthood without getting involved in the marital role. Even though most blacks do not view childbearing outside of marriage as socially desirable, long-term shame and stigma are uncommon. In addition, black females have a more restricted field of marriage eligibles and often marry less-educated men. One study found that divorced women had higher levels of life satisfaction than did married women, and widowed black women demonstrated the highest level of satisfaction of all (Ball & Robbins, 1986). However, parenthood may not bring all that women hope for as evidenced by the surprising results of another recent study that indicated that blacks who were *not* parents reported greater satisfaction than those who *were*, contradicting other studies (Broman, 1988). The

accessibility and assistance of the kin network is particularly important to black single mothers, especially if they are young and/or poor.

A recent study compared low-income black teenage mothers, black adult mothers, and white mothers. Results indicated that willingness to report child-rearing problems and seeking help from extended family members were important predictors for black teen mothers in the quality of their parenting. Black mothers of all ages more often turn to kin and friends only, rather than professionals, for help with parenting (Stevens, 1988).

One of the prevailing stereotypes associated with black families prior to the 1970s was that black families were largely matriarchal in structure. One of the reasons this myth persisted was because much research on black families was limited to studies of poor black families. It is now the consensus that matriarchy is a hoax; it is more attributable to social class than to race (Rubin, 1978). Concern was expressed for the psychological consequences of the matriarchal orientation and the implications for the child's learning of sex attitudes toward marriage and child rearing.

Even though much has been written about the matriarchal theme in black families and its consequences, in reality the egalitarian family pattern is common. Although there is controversy regarding how prevalent the egalitarian pattern is, it does appear to be the norm for middle-class black families (Cromwell & Cromwell, 1978; Rubin, 1978). Cromwell and Cromwell concluded that ethnic membership alone is not sufficient to explain the differences in husbands' and wives' perceptions concerning dominance in conflict situations. Categorial labeling of family structure based on membership in an ethnic group is unwarranted and inappropriate.

Black Fathers

Black fathers have been neglected in the research on black families, probably because they have not been as accessible as white fathers and have been perceived as being less significant persons to their families. Frequently black fathers have been depicted as ineffectual and viewed only in relation to their abilities to contribute to the economic support of the family (Price-Bonham & Skeen, 1979).

Recent research found that marriage was associated with the lowest levels of satisfaction for black men, and better health and higher income were the only variables associated with high satisfaction (Ball & Robbins, 1986). For those married males, however, there is generally support for their wives' right or inclination to work. In that sense, they take a less stereotypical view of the "female role" than do white men. Black husbands rate their wives higher than do white husbands on having the knowledge and experience to hold a job (Harrison & Minor, 1978).

Black males may interpret fatherhood in several ways. Children may be viewed as a means of confirming masculinity but, at the same time, as an economic burden. Some evidence indicates that many black fathers relate to their children based on the quality of their relationship with their own mothers. For example, being reared in a matriarchal home itself deters them from being actively involved with their children. Moreover, socioeconomic status and education are factors that importantly affect the quality of parenting. A large percentage of low-income black families are headed by females, with the biological father being absent. Other adult males often serve as role models and may perform some parenting functions. Even if the father is present, "externally adapted" fathers frequently do not accept the responsibilities of parenthood and early child rearing, and thus they have little influence with their sons until they enter the male peer group (Rubin, 1978).

On the other hand, the "acculturated" black male is more likely to accept his responsibility as a father. Black married men have been reported as performing ably in a nurturing role. In fact, black middle-class men have been found to participate more in child rearing than white middle-class fathers do. When there are two parents in a black middle-class family, the father is likely to play a predominant role, and the child is more likely to develop a greater primary identification with the father than in middle-class white families. Actually, black and white middle-class intact families where fathers are employed are more similar than different in their attitudes toward father roles (Price-Bonham & Skeen, 1979).

When black and white married, middle-class, employed fathers with two or more children were compared, the following similarities and differences were noted (Price-Bonham & Skeen, 1979). Black fathers tended to be different demographically from the white fathers. They had more children and had more of them at home, were older, had been married longer, had wives with lower job status and educational levels, and were more often church members and attenders than white fathers were. Black fathers also came from larger families who had lower social status and who used more corporal punishment than did white fathers. The black fathers also stated that their fathers had not played a major role in child rearing. Black fathers viewed themselves as less strict than the white fathers, used ignoring as a discipline technique less, and talked with their children less than did the white fathers. It was more important to the black fathers that their children "be like me" than it was to the white fathers.

These researchers found that black and white fathers did not differ in their use of spanking, withdrawing privileges, isolating the child, or use of reasoning as disciplinary techniques. Nor did the fathers differ in the importance attributed to the child's liking, respecting, and obeying the father. Both the black and the white fathers listed the same three "best things" about being a father: someone to love and love me, someone to take care of me in my old age, and children make me feel respectable. Both listed the same items as "worst thing" about being a father—too much responsibility and problems with discipline. Both groups of fathers had similar feelings about how their ideas of parenthood and life goals had changed after the children were born. The black and the white fathers gave the same sources of information about parenthood—trial and error, parents, books or articles, friends, family doctor, television, classes, and so forth.

There were a few differences in the two groups' expectations of the father's role. The black fathers felt it was more important to provide the children with spending money, help them develop athletically, and assist the children with homework than the white fathers did. As a result of these data, the researchers concluded that middle-class, employed black and white fathers who lived in intact families were more similar than different in their functioning as parents, even though they differed in demographics.

Rearing Black Children

As in any culture, male and female black children are reared differently. By the age of 3, most black children are no longer treated as babies. Many assume responsibility for the care of younger siblings. For males the peer group is more important in the socialization process than for females. Male children are socialized into the peer group earlier and more completely than are females.

An important rite of passage into manhood by black males is that of "playing the dozens," a verbal duel in which two black males make derogatory comments about each other's family. Onlooking peers urge each on. The skills of each player are appreciated and judged by the peer group. To master this game the boy has to control his emotions so that he can think quickly and counter with an even more clever remark about a family member of his opponent. Learning to control one's emotions is an important aspect of socialization of the black male (Hale-Benson, 1986). London and Devore (1988) contended that black urban youth have developed other ritualized games, such as "ribbin'," "jivin'," and "shuckin'," to cope with the stresses and strains of their environment.

Black girls are usually given responsibility for the care of younger siblings and the household at an early age. Daughters are expected to be independent and capable of shouldering family responsibilities very early. Acceleration of development has been found to be the only attitudinal dimension on which black mothers of every class are stronger advocates than white mothers (Bartz & Levine, 1978). This emphasis helps to develop a strong motherhood orientation. Girls are not expected to have jobs outside the home until adolescence. The most frequent

jobs for younger black girls are often babysitting or other domestic duties. In many black families there is a strong emphasis on personal uniqueness. Girls are taught to develop their own style, sexuality, and personal distinctiveness. What one does and how it is done are both viewed as important. Personal attributes are considered more important than status or office.

The peer group exerts a strong influence on both black boys and girls. The peer group is critical for the continuation of the socialization process begun by the parents. It is a much more significant influence in families where the father is absent or unemployed and/or the matriarchal structure is the pattern. Identification with the peer group is achieved earlier and more completely for boys than girls. For both sexes it is a significant influence during the teen years. Boys, particularly, affiliate with informal gangs and are likely to be dependent on and influenced by them greatly. Concepts of womanhood and manhood are learned from the peer group. Friends are viewed as the source of rewards, both material and nonmaterial. In many families, dating has begun by age 12, as well as a heavy commitment to a peer group of the same sex. By adolescence an intensely sexual, frequently exploitative, web of informal social relations may have developed between the sexes.

The male peer group is a place where masculinity can be achieved. Female peer relationships are more stable and durable than those of the male. They are less dependent on the peer group. For children from the few remaining matriarchal families, the peer group takes on special significance. Girls depend on the peer group to evaluate their ability to manipulate males. By the late teens these girls may have already become disillusioned toward males. Boys may be further alienated from the family by the peer group. They often reject female dominance and turn to ways of expressing virility and manliness. They enter street life and are further socialized into a system that is hostile to women and weakness (Rubin, 1978).

The education of black children has received considerable attention by black scholars. For example, the major thrust of Hale-Benson's (1986) work is to offer an alternative approach to conceptualizing the behavioral styles of black children and to lay the foundation for devising educational strategies that complement black culture. She pointed out that Afro-American males are at the greatest disadvantage in the feminine orientation of most elementary classrooms. She cited a study that found that teachers tend to favor certain types of children, in the following order: white females, white males, black females, and black males. The students they identified as having the least potential as learners were black males. The behaviors they valued most were demonstrated by white females, and those valued least were demonstrated by black males.

Differential levels of education for blacks and whites were evident in a 1984 study conducted by the National Alliance of Black School Educators. They found that 28 percent of Afro-American high school students drop out before graduation; 75 percent of white high school seniors go to college, whereas only 20 percent of blacks enroll in college. Further, only 12 percent of black students who start college finish, and only 4 percent of these complete a graduate program (cited in Hale-Benson, 1986). Clearly the educational system has not yet found ways to encourage and assist black students, on the whole, to achieve even moderate levels of education.

Resources for Black Families

A number of researchers have pointed out that one of the strengths of black families is the extensive support system provided by a network of relatives, friends, and neighbors (Crawley, 1988; Rashid, 1985). This system provides emotional support and economic supplements, better enabling the family to handle adverse external forces. Since the majority of both black men and black women work, this support system is even more important. The kin network has been vitally important as a coping strategy for large numbers of black families. The extended network is a more salient structure for black than for white families. Blacks see more of their kin other than their parents than do white families. More whites have living parents than blacks do. Aunts frequently become mother substitutes in black families (McAdoo, 1978).

Even though many blacks are reared in nuclear families, a large number still receive instrumental or task-oriented help from a significant adult other than the parents. The unmarried, divorced, or widowed are most often integrated intimately into the extended kin network. Some of the services provided by this expanded network system include assistance with finances; help in making important decisions; assistance in planning and carrying out special occasions; providing clothing, food, furniture, and transportation to various places. Usually help is extended in the areas of greatest need. Among poor blacks the extended family assists in the socialization of children (McAdoo, 1978).

Some evidence indicates that kinship networks are declining (Staples & Mirandé, 1980). Statistics reveal that the average household size among blacks is declining. Young black women giving birth out of wedlock are more likely now to move into their own households rather than staying with their families. In addition, greater numbers of divorced or widowed men and women who can support themselves are living by themselves.

The extended family also can be a liability for the black family. In some instances it can deter upward mobility. Once a black family has achieved a higher status, the family may be expected to provide help for other extended family members. Thus the family may have to limit professional and social upward mobility to some extent due to the necessity of providing physical and financial resources to members of the wider family. In order for poorer blacks to be upwardly mobile, they may find it necessary to cut themselves off from their families. While they may still visit with the family on special occasions, they must separate themselves from the draining process of assisting in meeting the everyday needs of their extended families (McAdoo, 1978; Staples & Mirandé, 1980).

It is felt by some experts that, if the welfare of black children in this country were to be significantly enhanced, a national commitment would have to be made to full employment, a guaranteed minimum income, a comprehensive program of child development, meaningful education, decent housing, a restructuring of the health-care system, and reconsideration of foster child placements. Further, this commitment would have to be translated into public policies and comprehensive programs at the national level. Most of these ideas did not receive support during the 1980s. Instead, existing programs were eliminated or funding was cut to such an extent that survival is questionable.

In sum, varying viewpoints of black families in the United States are represented by the cultural deviant, cultural equivalent, and cultural variant approaches. Despite the lack of agreement among these approaches, it seems clear that black families are characterized by a number of behavior patterns and traditions that are significantly related to child-rearing practices.

There is considerable evidence to refute the persistent image of the black family as being matriarchal. Egalitarianism in family roles seems to be more common than once believed, especially among middle-class blacks. Nevertheless, black mothers seem to be especially close to their children, and the differences in child-rearing patterns for male and female children seem to be especially visible. The network of relatives, friends, and neighbors who provide a support system for black families is seen as being a particular strength, but some believe that it has been a factor in limiting upward mobility.

Clearly it can be concluded that many black families have been the victims of racism, poverty, and limited education, which accounts for many of the stereotypes that have held sway, and both future research and new programs are needed to completely replace these attitudes.

Future Research Needs

It has been suggested that future research on black families should move in at least three directions—toward research utilizing new theories about black families, research that will fill the knowledge void relative to black families, and research that implements action approaches. Unifying the developmental approach with the culturally variant perspective would appear to provide a sensitive way to study these families. This approach would facilitate the process of defining the special family forms found in black families. Systematically studying black families

in a variety of settings appears warranted. Many questions still need to be answered concerning black single-parent families, the extended family structure, and the informal adoption practices and results. Further, updating the demographic information about black families is very important.

PARENTING IN CHICANO FAMILIES*

The principal origins of Hispanic persons in the United States are Mexico, Puerto Rico, and Cuba, and the descendant population of all three groups is scattered widely. High immigration rates and birthrates increased the nation's Hispanic population by 34 percent in the 1980s. In 1988 Hispanics in the United States totaled 19.4 million, representing an increase of 5 million since the 1980 census. Hispanics are concentrated in nine states, led by California and Texas ("Education of Hispanics," 1988). Census data have often failed to distinguish the three Hispanic populations from one another by identifying an Hispanic as one with a Spanish origin, Spanish surname, and/or one who uses the Spanish language. However, it has been pointed out that Hispanics of Mexican descent (Chicanos) are considerably different on a number of characteristics from non-Mexican Hispanics.

In 1988 there were 12.1 million Mexican-Americans, representing the largest Hispanic subgroup in this country ("Education of Hispanics," 1988). More than 85 percent of Mexican-Americans live in three regions: Pacific, Mountain, and West South Central (Buriel & Cardoza, 1988). While recent data suggest that Hispanics, especially those between the ages of 25 and 34, are getting much closer to non-Hispanics in completing high school and college ("Education of Hispanics," 1988), data reported in 1980 indicated that Mexican-Americans (both males and females) complete fewer years of formal education and are less likely to graduate from high school than other Hispanics. Further, they are considerably lower on the occupational

---

*The terms *Mexican-American* and *Chicano* will be used interchangeably to refer to persons of Mexican descent who reside in the United States.

scale than other Hispanics, with Chicanos having higher percentages of manual laborers and farmers. Median incomes of Mexican-American women are lower than those of all other non-Mexican Hispanic women; and Chicano men earn less than Cuban men (U.S. Bureau of the Census, 1980). It has been said, however, that Mexican-Americans represent the nation's second-largest and most rapidly growing ethnic group. Because of the differences among Chicanos and other Hispanics and because of the large number of Mexican-Americans in this country, we have chosen to limit our discussion to parenting in Chicano families.

Demographics

There are a number of demographic characteristics that differentiate the Chicano family from the dominant Anglo family in the United States. The first is its high fertility rate. Mexican-Americans have the highest fertility rate of any major ethnic and racial group in the United States (Jorgensen & Adams, 1988). The average

Anglo family consists of approximately three persons, whereas the average Chicano family is slightly more than four. Attitudes and normative beliefs (what others think one should do) of significant others, combined with motivation to comply with those reference groups, have a relationship to whether Chicanas will or will not have more children. Those with lower incomes, less education, lower parity, and of the Catholic faith are more influenced in fertility by their normative beliefs. Further, evidence suggests that the church's influence on the fertility of Chicanas is considerably less than might be expected (Jorgensen & Adams, 1988).

According to the 1980 census data, 81 percent of Chicano children under 18 lived with both parents in intact families, a figure considerably higher than the population in general. Chicanos were about as likely to be married as other groups, but they were less likely to be divorced. In fact only 15 percent of Mexican-American families were headed by females. However, for Hispanics as a whole, the proportion of families maintained by married couples

dropped from 74 percent in 1982 to 70 percent in 1988 ("Education for Hispanics," 1988). While specific data for Chicano families were not available at the time of this writing, one would suppose that the percentage of female-headed households in this group also has probably increased slightly.

The income of Hispanics, as a group, is slightly higher than that of blacks but considerably lower than that of Anglos. Mexican-Americans earn less than other Hispanic groups. Approximately one quarter of these families are below the poverty line, as compared to 11 percent of all families (U.S. Bureau of the Census, 1986).

Roles of Family Members

For a number of years the Chicano family was described as rigid and patriarchal, with male dominance ingrained as a cultural trait. The traditional concept of *machismo* described the Mexican-American father as the unquestioned authority—the "lord and master" of the household. However, because it has been asserted that, in fact, the Chicano male has feelings of inadequacy, inferiority, and rejection of authority, "machismo" was thus compensation for powerlessness (Mirandé, 1979; Staples & Mirandé, 1980). The macho male subscribed to a double standard, expecting his wife to be submissive and faithful. An extension of machismo was believed to be manifested by violence toward the spouse and children when they did not accept their subordinate position or when they questioned the authority of the husband (Mirandé, 1977).

The traditional machismo male was viewed as a strict disciplinarian who demanded complete respect, deference, and obedience from his wife and from his children (Mirandé, 1979). Social scientists contended that the rigid, male-dominated structure was detrimental to the development of children. The father was viewed as being distant and remote, especially in his relationships with male children, and especially after children were about 10 years of age. Discipline was believed to be harsh, engendering fear of the father, poor communication, and ultimately parent-child violence. Passivity and dependence were said to develop in children. The mother, however, was depicted as being self-sacrificing and

saintly, albeit weak. Further, an orientation toward the present, the here-and-now, prevailed over a future-oriented outlook. It was long asserted that the Mexican-American culture propagated the subordination of women, impeding individual achievement, engendering passivity and dependence, stifling normal personality development, and giving rise to incestuous feelings among siblings (Mirandé, 1977). In short, the conclusion was that the Chicano culture stressed fatalism and resignation, in contrast to the Anglo culture's emphasis on achievement and control of the environment (Mirandé, 1977).

A Redefinition

It seems clear that the preceding descriptions of Chicano family life have presented a negative, stereotypical, even pathological view, with little optimism for the ultimate fate of Mexican-American children. That image persisted for some time, but, beginning in the late 1970s, a number of researchers began to challenge it. First, earlier researchers may have been guilty of using the dominant family structure as a yardstick by which to measure "deviant" family patterns in minority groups, failing to be sensitive to other cultural or ethnic systems. Second, many recent researchers have contended that earlier research was based on persistent traditional stereotypes rather than on convincing empirical evidence. Even when differences from the traditional images were found, they were attributed to the Chicano family's acculturation or modernization, as if an acculturated family was somehow "more correct." Or data that did not fit the picture were ignored, discarded, or considered irrelevant (Mirandé, 1977; Zinn, 1979). In fact, one writer concluded that the works he reviewed on Mexican-American culture and family life constituted an exercise in social science fiction and presented a distorted view of Chicanos as passive, masochistic vegetables controlled by traditional culture (Romano, 1973).

A very different image of Chicano family life has now emerged. Chicano writers argue that *la familia* is a warm and nurturing institution rather than an unstable, pathological one. The concept of machismo has been redefined in terms of family pride, respect, and honor rather than in terms of male dominance. In fact, the new view asserts that the family is the most important unit in life and the individual is likely to put the needs of the family above his own. The family, then, is depicted as a stable structure where one's place is firmly established, and cooperation among family members is emphasized. An important part of the concept of machismo is seen as the father's using his authority within the family in a fair and just manner. If he misuses his authority, he risks losing respect within the family and the community (Staples & Mirandé, 1980). According to Staples and Mirandé (1980), the older and newer views of the Chicano family agree on four major characteristics: (1) male dominance; (2) age-sex dominance, that is, older dominates younger and male dominates female; (3) clearly established patterns of help and mutual aid among family members; and (4) the precedence of strong family needs over individual needs. The major difference between the two views lies in the interpretation and evaluation of these characteristics. One must decide whether the strong family orientation impedes individual advancement and achievement or whether it is a source of support.

It is important to emphasize, however, that there is no one typical Chicano family, just as there is no one typical Anglo family. Obviously such factors as education, income, age, geographic location, and time of migration to the United States will contribute to a diversity in family types.

Nevertheless, there is little recent evidence to support the patriarchal model as the prototype of the Chicano family. Most studies have not found inflexibility in division of labor or male dominance in decision making. Few important differences have been found between Anglos and Mexican-Americans on marital satisfaction, wife labor-force participation, role expectation, family dynamics, or conjugal power (Vega, Kolody, & Valle, 1988; Vega et al., 1986).

Scholars have described Mexican-American family systems as extended, enmeshed, dense, and self-reliant (Vega et al., 1986). Recent studies have indicated that familism, and hence the availability of social support, increases with each generation living in this country. These findings contradict earlier views that the highest

degrees of familism (the tendency to favor interaction and social support over other alternatives) correlates with "Mexicanness" and Mexican birth and would become weaker in subsequent generations (Vega et al., 1986). Nevertheless, the consequential role of familism among Mexican-Americans, especially with regard to expressive support, cannot be overemphasized. Chicano families have been described as "closed systems" with intense, multiplex relationships and with members who underutilize mental-health services. Perhaps this is due to the stress-buffering qualities of an endogenous support system (Vega, Kolody, & Valle, 1986). Familism is a basic source of emotional support for children. "Family" includes not only parents, but also aunts and uncles, grandparents, cousins, and even friends. In fact, there is little distinction made between relatives and friends—often they are one and the same. The custom of compadres that dates to the colonial times remains intact, with Chicano adults reporting at least one, two, or three such relationships. Often these friends serve as godparents to the children. This kinship web imposes the obligation of mutual aid, respect, and affection. It is interesting to note the results of a study of children who were asked, "Who do you love?" The barrio children did not include anyone but relatives in their responses, but Anglo and black children included many non-family members, with peers being frequently named (Goodman & Beman, 1971).

Vega and his associates (1986) found no major differences between Anglos and Mexican-Americans on dimensions of family functioning, such as cohesion and adaptability. Mexican-American families were well-functioning and resilient. Cohesion has been found to be highest at the early stages of the family life cycle, to decrease as children reach adolescence and thereafter, but to rise again as children leave home. Adaptability also decreases as families move through the child-rearing years and increases again when children leave home.

Value Differences

There is some evidence to suggest that differences still exist between Anglo and Chicano families, partly as a result of value differences that seem to have persisted. For example, Guinn summarized value differences in the following way: Anglos value doing rather than being, whereas Chicanos value being instead of doing; Anglos place greater values on material well-being; Anglos are future-oriented, whereas Chicanos are present-oriented; Chicanos value simple patterns of work organization and group cooperation, whereas Anglos value individual action and reaction; and finally, there is central importance of the family and personal relations among Chicanos, whereas Anglos value impersonal relations (Guinn, 1977).

It appears that few researchers have empirically tested these value differences for their direct effects on children. One interesting study tested the generality that high self-esteem is associated with competitiveness. Since second-generation Mexican-American children display a culture norm of cooperativeness, they might be expected to have poorer self-concepts than Anglo or black children who value competitiveness. The study, however, indicated that non-competitive Mexican-American children were not necessarily deficient in self-concept; in contrast they appeared to be "realizing important cooperative culture values, increasing their self-esteem in the process" (Kagan & Knight, 1979, p. 466). The authors concluded, then, that self-esteem is partly a function of the extent to which children live up to their cultural norms.

Chicano Mothers

Much has been written concerning the Mexican-American mother's care of her children. She has been viewed, both traditionally and recently, as a warm, nurturant person who has the primary responsibility for the children. Luis Laosa has been interested in maternal teaching strategies in Chicano families. His earlier study (1978) found that teaching strategies of Chicano mothers varied considerably as a function of the mother's formal level of eduation. Better-educated mothers used inquiry and praise as teaching strategies, whereas less educated mothers used more modeling, as well as control and physical punishment, with their male children. Moreover, few Chicano mothers, regardless of educational level, used teaching

strategies that involved positive physical contact with the child. A follow-up study (1980) compared Anglo and Chicano mothers on the same dimensions. Again, it was found that while clear differences in teaching strategies were apparent between the two cultural groups, the differences disappeared when the maternal education levels were held constant. However, holding constant the occupational status of mothers and/or fathers did not erase the cultural differences in maternal teaching behavior. The author emphasized that formal education is a powerful force in cultural evolution and hypothesized that when educational equity between the two groups becomes a reality, some of the present differences in child-rearing practices between Anglos and Chicanos will disappear.

Chicano Fathers

Even though the image of the Mexican-American father as all-powerful lord and master has changed, the father is often still deferred to and respected, especially if the family is somewhat traditional. Relationships with children are less warm and affectionate than those of mothers and children. However, several recent studies have indicated a departure from the traditional patriarchal pattern and have found egalitarianism to be far more common than was once believed, especially among younger Chicano families and those with higher incomes. This egalitarianism includes performance of traditional sex-typed tasks (including housework and child care), participation by fathers in social and recreational activities with their wives and children, and shared decision making. However, those families that most often depart from the traditional patriarchal pattern are those in which the wife is employed. It may be that couples are already more egalitarian *before* the wife begins to work rather than that the wife's employment per se creates a more egalitarian arrangement (Staples & Mirandé, 1980; Zinn, 1979).

Rearing Chicano Children

Only a few studies have been conducted on the child-rearing attitudes and practices of Mexican-

American parents, and those that exist fail to provide consistent conclusions. Some researchers have concluded that Mexican-American parents are primarily permissive, whereas others have suggested that traditional values and authoritarian practices are more prevalent. Still others describe Chicano families as nurturing and affectionate within a patriarchal, authoritarian family structure, with unusual respect for males and the elderly (Martinez, 1988).

A recent observational study of predominantly lower-class mothers and their young children found few permissive Mexican-American mothers, and authoritative and authoritarian mothers were about equal in number. Authoritative parents use rational, issue-oriented discipline techniques and set firm limits within a loving context. This style of child rearing is characteristic of Anglo middle-class mothers but is thought to be inconsistent with the communal values of Chicanos. Although these results suggest that at least some Chicana mothers resemble Anglo mothers in their child-rearing patterns, others clearly do not (Martinez, 1988).

The correlation between socioeconomic status and intellectual performance of children has been heavily documented. The parental language dominance and the language dominance and proficiency of Mexican-American children also have been shown to be significant correlates of the child's intellectual performance. Laosa (cited in Valencia, Henderson, & Rankin, 1985) has suggested that parent-child interactions represent the mediating variable between social-status indicators and school performance. Both the home and the school have their own set of specific demand characteristics, and a child's success or failure may depend on the degree to which the competencies required to negotiate the different environments overlap. Giving support to this notion, Valencia, Henderson, and Rankin (1985) found that home environmental process measures showed a strong association with the intellectual development of Chicano children, independent of parental schooling, language, socioeconomic status, and family constellation.

The home environment of Mexican-American children may vary according to their generation status. Shared cultural variables, particularly Spanish-language background and achievement aspirations, vary as a function of generational status. Surprisingly, first- and second-generation children often perform better in school than their third-generation counterparts, suggesting that immigrant parents, particularly mothers, may pass on high aspirations to their children. Further, there is substantial variation in the degree of Spanish retention in each generation. A recent study found that personal aspirations were by far the most potent predictors of first, second, and third generations of Mexican-American students, and that socioeconomic status was unrelated to most measures. These results seem to suggest that the strength of the relationship of socioeconomic status to achievement may be greater for Anglo students than for Chicano students (Buriel & Cardoza, 1988).

As with other ethnic minority groups, there appear to be sex differences in the rearing of Mexican-American children. Mothers seem to be particularly close to their daughters, extending into and beyond puberty. The mother-son relationship is close but not as strong as that of mother and daughter. Fathers appear warm and affectionate when children are young and are playful companions. Some evidence suggests, however, that fathers become more aloof as children approach puberty. Sons often are pampered and indulged more than daughters during childhood, and at adolescence they have far more freedom than girls do.

A recent study suggested that Mexican-American adolescents undergo the identity process somewhat differently than Anglo adolescents do. Specifically, Chicanos have been found to be more "foreclosed" than Anglos are on ideological identity, even when socioeconomic status is held constant; that is, they tend to adopt wholesale the commitments of others, usually their parents, without first testing the fit for themselves. Males were inclined to be more foreclosed and less "identity achieved" than females. This phenomenon may be due to the fact that minority status exposes Chicanos to a narrower range of available occupational and ideological roles and commitments than Anglos, or there may be actual cultural differences in ways the two groups develop identity due to parental socialization techniques. The differences between the two groups in resolving difficulties such as sex roles, dating, friendship, and recreational preferences were less than differences related to issues of political and religious ideology, philosophical life-style, and occupation. Foreclosure is associated with warmth and support, but also a highly controlling parental style is optimal for effectively guiding youth into preconceived roles (Abraham, 1986).

Peers contribute significantly to the socialization of adolescent males, whereas adolescent females are more confined to the home and rely more heavily on mothers and sisters. The value of premarital chastity for females still exists, but its enforcement is more difficult than in the past. Even though strong role differentiation for males and females has persisted, there is evidence that many young Chicanos are challenging their traditional roles, resulting in more equality among males and females, especially among middle-class urban families.

In sum, when attempting to summarize the cultural aspects of parenting in Chicano families, we are struck by several factors: (1) the lack of empirical data to support the stereotyped traditional view of the Chicano family as rigid, patriarchal, and damaging to children; (2) the lack of control in research for socioeconomic status and level of education variables, thereby often confusing cultural values with social conditions; and (3) the tendency to generalize that Chicano families are homogeneous in their family interaction and child-rearing patterns and to ignore the evidence of diversity among these families, taking into account structural family variables.

It does appear that there are some cultural differences in values between Chicanos and other cultural groups that account for differences in parenting. Probably the most important of these are familism (identification with the family) and the normative deference and respect formally accorded to the father. Other differences may well be the result of low socioeconomic status, lower levels of education, and structural components of the family itself. It should be remembered that the Chicano family has experienced change, just as the Anglo family has changed. Much of this change has occurred without rejection of the

cultural heritage or assimilation into mainstream Anglo society (Mirandé, 1977).

Future Research Needs

Because Mexican-Americans seem to be a rapidly growing ethnic group in this country, careful research still needs to be undertaken to give keener insight into these family relationships. Demographic data that differentiates between Hispanics of Mexican and non-Mexican descent would represent a beginning. Convincing empirical evidence, with socioeconomic status and educational variables controlled, would facilitate the elimination of stereotypes. Especially important are data regarding the continued existence of a patriarchal pattern versus a trend toward an egalitarian pattern; attention to the diversity among Chicano families; and the testing of value differences between Chicanos and the majority culture to more clearly determine the effects of these differences on children.

PARENTING IN NATIVE AMERICAN FAMILIES

According to the U.S. Census, Native Americans include American Indians, Eskimos, and Aleutians. Our discussion refers only to the American Indians. It appears that Native Americans currently have few, if any, ties to any particular geographical area. However, the eastern areas of Asia seem to provide the common source for this population, and the majority of American Indians have blood type O, suggesting genetic commonalities (Carpenter, 1980). Unlike other minorities, however, Native Americans are more diverse than they are similar. For example, researchers report more than 200 different languages among Indians in the United States, complicated by phonetic variations. Further, the number of reported tribal groupings ranges from 280 to 334, with many subgroupings. American Indians have been described, then, as "having . . . a complex pattern of diversification that includes sharp differences in ethnic classification and language, as well as a pattern of sociocultural developments that ranges from neolithic to contemporary'' (Carpenter, 1980, p. 456).

Demographics

Contrary to popular belief, Native Americans are not a dying breed. At the present time they number 1.5 million. Between the 1970 census and 1980 census, there was an increase in this group of 72 percent, and the Bureau of Indian Affairs (BIA) estimates that there was a 54 percent increase of Indians living on reservations in that same 10-year period. The BIA further notes that more Indians have recently been returning to the reservations, and fewer are leaving. This phenomenon, combined with fewer infant deaths and better health services, accounts for part of the increase in population. Despite the recent trend of staying on or returning to the reservation, there are currently more Native Americans in cities than on reservations, and as they migrate to the cities, traditions become more difficult to practice (London & Devore,

1988). While American Indians can be found throughout the United States, five states contain 72 percent of all Native Americans residing on reservations: Arizona, New Mexico, South Dakota, Montana, and Washington. American Indians have the longest tenure in this country of all racial minorities (Staples, 1988; Strauss, 1986).

In 1980 there were 210,180 married-couple families with 135,866 children under 18 years of age; 69,902 families were maintained by single females who had 48,834 children under the age of 18. Reservation Indians had 26 percent of all the nation's families headed by females, and the percent for all Indians was slightly lower (Strauss, 1986). Overall, 63 percent of Native American children under 18 lived with two parents. That same year, the average number of persons per family was 3.87. Rural Indian families are larger than urban ones, sometimes having five or more children, and Indian families as a group have more children under the age of 18 than does the general U.S. population.

About half of Indian households include other relatives, and about one fourth include persons unrelated to the family. American Indians resemble blacks in their high fertility rate, out-of-wedlock births, strong roles for women, high rates of unemployment, and high proportion of female-headed households (Miller, 1980).

It is important to emphasize that Native Americans are a diverse group. For example, the high school graduation rate ranges from 63 percent on the Colville Reservation to 17 percent at Ute Mountain. Although the overall poverty rate is close to 25 percent, it reaches nearly 50 percent on the Rosebud Reservation. The overall unemployment rate is approximately 13 percent, but reservation Indians have a 28 percent unemployment rate, and on one reservation it has reached 70 percent. In almost every category reservation Indians, as a whole, are worse off. One exception is the incidence of suicide, which is lower on reservations where traditional practices are maintained. Overall, the suicide rate is far higher than the national average. There are also alarming rates of crime and alcoholism, especially for young males (Strauss, 1986). Alcoholism is viewed by many as the number-one health problem of Native Americans.

More than one third of all American Indians have married non-Indians, with urban Indians having a higher rate of intermarriage than rural. Approximately three fifths of all registered Indian births in 1970 listed both parents as Indians (U.S. Department of Health, Education, and Welfare, 1974; U.S. Bureau of the Census, 1983).

American Indians have the lowest *income* of any group in the United States. In 1980 the median annual income of families with children under 18 was $13,556, and the per-capita income was $4,560. One fourth of all families were living below the poverty level. For Indian women the situation was even worse. For all women the median annual income was $4,268, about half of what males earned. However, for those women who were year-round full-time workers, their median income increased to $9,286. Unfortunately, a female head of household with children under 18 earned an average of $6,596 (U.S. Bureau of the Census, 1983). While income gains have been made over the past

decade, the economic status of the American Indian continues to be far below that of the total population.

The *educational level* of American Indians is slowly improving. In 1980, 56 percent were high school graduates. Only about 17 percent of Native Americans enter college, and just over 40 percent of those actually graduate (U.S. Bureau of the Census, 1983). *Unemployment* among American Indians is exceedingly high. Indians have the lowest rate of male participation in the labor force of any major ethnic group in the United States. In 1983 fifty-nine percent of persons 16 years and older were in the labor force, which included just over two thirds males and 48 percent females. However, only about 53 percent of the males who were employed worked for the full year (U.S. Bureau of the Census, 1983).

Housing, sanitation, and health characteristics are significantly different for American Indians. Conditions of the dwellings of both rural and urban Indians are poor. For example, some urban dwellings are without water, and among Indians lack of toilet facilities is reported 14 times more frequently than among the general U.S. population. Crowding among urban Indian residents was two to three times the norm in 1970, and housing conditions are even worse in rural than in urban areas.

Marginal incomes, crowded housing, poor transportation, and inadequate nutrition make American Indians more vulnerable to health problems such as influenza, pneumonia, tuberculosis, and malnutrition. In 1955 the Indian Health Service assumed responsibility for Indian health care. While death rates due to health problems are considerably higher than for the U.S. population as a whole, there has been a marked decrease since 1955. It could be concluded that, even though conditions are improving for American Indians, as a group they are the most in need of services.

Family Structure

''There is no such institution as the Native American family. There are only tribes, and family structure and values will differ from tribe to tribe'' (Staples & Mirandé, 1980, p. 899).

Polygamy still exists in some tribes; some are matriarchal and others are patriarchal; but Red Horse proposed that tribes define family in terms of three dimensions: the household, the extended family through second cousins, and clan membership (cited in Strauss, 1986).

In one community 92 percent of the elderly population live in independent households but maintain close contact with their children, grandchildren, and great-grandchildren by performing daily family roles (Red Horse, 1979). Further, significant nonkin become family members, either by a formal or informal process. For example, if an individual becomes a namesake for a child (through formal ritual), he then assumes family obligations and responsibilities for role modeling and child rearing (Red Horse, 1980).

Family structure patterns in a small reservation community resemble a village with several households very close together. However, some family systems cover broad geographic regions and in fact represent an interstate family structure, with several households in each of several states. Still other family structures represent a small community in an urban area; for example, several households of the same family may be in close proximity to one another within an urban community. Finally, family households may be spread among several communities or cities of a metropolitan area. All of these types of family structure represent lateral extension, incorporating several households. "[This phenomenon] affects life-long socialization and represents a transactional field that markedly contrasts from that of nuclear family systems common to American culture" (Red Horse, 1980, p. 463). The family is a repository of values and guides behavior through all stages of the life cycle (London & Devore, 1988).

Native Americans view their extended family as a source of strength and perennial support, offering multiple opportunities for the effective socialization of children, but some feel that the extended-family system is greatly misunderstood by human-service professionals (Strauss, 1986). There have been numerous attempts to impose the Western model of the nuclear monogamous family on Native Americans, but they have struggled continuously to maintain their tribal identities and at the same time their special relationships with the federal government (Staples, 1988; Strauss, 1986). Generally, Native Americans have not wanted or acquiesed to acculturation and assimilation into mainstream society. Instead of being viewed as a culturally variant but well-functioning society, they have largely received societal ridicule for their resistance to the norms and models of middle-class American society (Staples, 1988).

Value Orientation

The value systems of Native Americans as a group have consistent themes with tribal-specific expectations. Common among all tribal groups are tribal loyalty, respect for elders, reticence, humility, avoidance of personal glory and gain, giving and sharing with as many as three generations of relatives, and an abiding love for their land (London & Devore, 1988). The value orientation of American Indians has remained relatively constant. In striking contrast to nuclear families, American Indians value collateral relationships in which family involvement, approval, and pride are highlighted as opposed to individualism. In the nuclear system model, there is a linear pattern of increasing independence of the individual. By contrast, the extended system model is curvilinear with periods of self-reliance balanced with mutual interdependence (Red Horse, 1980, p. 464). While competence is a feature of Indian family development, self-reliance is embedded in a combination of interdependent, field-sensitive, relational behavior.

Three major life-span phases of Indian family development have been interestingly described by Red Horse (1980). The first phase, "being cared for," begins with the naming ceremony, which is performed shortly after birth in some tribes or when the child is several years old in other tribes. Naming ceremonies organize an obligatory, supportive network for children, and namesakes may be relatives or other highly trusted and reliable nonfamily members who have been incorporated into the family system. Namesakes are expected to have regular personal contact with the children and to maintain high personal standards of conduct. Namesakes are obligated to care for the child when parents cannot. The particular name given the child sets a path from which the child's life will proceed and provides spiritual sustenance.

Phase 2, "preparing to care for," occurs at about adolescence, when there is considerable self-reliance and personal decision making accompanied by family relational obligations. Even if the adolescent moves out of the parents' home, there usually is close proximity and frequent contact. On a routine basis household members may travel great distances to attend ceremonies and revitalize family relationships.

The final phase, "assuming care for," captures the essence of respect and wisdom. The elderly Indians serve as reminders of heritage, survival, and strength. An elder's role of assuming care for goes beyond the natural family into community situations. There are frequent bonding patterns between old people and children who are not necessarily related to each other. Elders are viewed as wise and bringing order to chaos.

It should be remembered that the term *care* denotes cultural and spiritual maintenance as well as the satisfaction of physical and emotional needs, and care is a continuing thread of family development. It is also important to emphasize that contemporary tribal and situational variations exist among American Indian family systems. Some family systems no longer conduct naming ceremonies, but relational bonding does not seem to be weakened by its absence.

Native Americans value noninterference. Any kind of intervention (for example, by social workers) is contrary to Indians' strict adherence to the principle of self-determination. The less assimilated and acculturated the individual, the more important this principle is to him. This phenomenon characterizes Navajos; the tribes of the northern and southern plains; and, to some extent, other tribes and Pueblo Indians. It is not clear from the literature how much can be generalized based on these values (Strauss, 1986).

Parent-Child Interactions

Perhaps because of the diverse nature of American Indians, there is little systematic knowledge about parenting styles. Further,

because few widely used developmental tests have been standardized for American Indian populations, we have little insight into the development of American Indian children (Fischler, 1980). The most striking difference in child rearing and socialization is the exposure of children to a wide array of persons to whom they can become attached—parents, siblings, aunts, uncles, cousins, and grandparents—thus protecting children and providing them with the assurance of love (London & Devore, 1988; Strauss, 1986). Children are regarded as important to the family—adults rarely hit children; children are included in social activities; and shouting when correcting a child is disapproved. Children are taught that the land is lent to them and therefore is not for private exploitation. Ownership of private property is not highly valued (London & Devore, 1988). There is some evidence to suggest that children are trained for independence at much earlier ages than Anglos and blacks are. This seems especially true with urban Indian populations (Strauss, 1986).

Just as with every other minority group, American Indians have been subjected to criticism and discrimination. It has been asserted that American Indians have had to defend themselves against the stereotype of helplessness, which results in a lack of resources to survive in a wholesome manner (Blanchard & Barsh, 1980). Nevertheless, studies indicate that 25–35 percent of all American Indian children are separated from their families and placed in foster homes, adoptive homes, or institutions. Some have judged the major reason to be neglect. Others have argued that Anglo social workers are ignorant of Indian cultural values and social norms and therefore perceive neglect or abandonment when none exists. The Indian child may be assumed to be deprived by unfamiliarity with the American Indian perspective. The result is that one out of every four American Indian children is not living with his or her family, and 85 percent of these children are living in non-Indian homes without access to their tribal home and relationships (Blanchard & Barsh, 1980).

In 1977, 1.4 percent of reported child abuse and 1.7 percent of reported neglect involved American Indians, although only 0.4 percent of the U.S. population is American Indian. Many of the current-generation American Indian parents were placed in foster homes early in their lives or sent to boarding schools, which is still a common practice. While boarding school experience may actually enhance the success of some Native Americans, those with a history of prior family dysfunction seem to experience failure. Nevertheless, these two types of separation from parents often have been cited as a factor related to poor parenting models and subsequent child abuse and neglect (Fischler, 1980).

Other factors that may affect parent-child interaction are superstition and folklore. Many cultural beliefs (frequently labeled as "old wives' tales" in the majority culture) persist. Some may have detrimental effects on children, for example, the presence of evil spirits or qualities that might result in harsh treatment of children. Certainly these beliefs are not universal among tribes but need to be studied systematically to determine to what extent they might result in harsh treatment of children.

An in-depth description of the American Indian in tribal society and an opposing view of the preceding discussion were recently presented by Blanchard and Barsh (1980). "The American Indian child occupies a central position in tribal life. Children in a very real sense represent the renewal and preservation of life" (p. 350). When a woman is pregnant, every effort is made to keep her in a positive state of mind. She receives support from relatives who will assume responsibility for her child. For example, uncles in some New Mexico pueblos provide the child's crib, and they ultimately assume responsibility for discipline and some types of instruction. Cradleboards are carefully and specifically constructed, and it is believed that tight binding of the cradleboard represents the chlid's first lesson in discipline.

After birth the child is encouraged to view the world from a perspective of protection and security. The emphasis on the connection between everyday activity and the meaning of life may be the most crucial part of an American Indian child's education in the tribal setting throughout her development. American Indians view children as tribal persons, something more than just children. The mutual and interlocking relationship between individuals is quite different from the non-Indian view of relationships. Children are encouraged to develop a sense of community that is complete—to be in touch with their world, to learn from other beings and things, and to allow other beings and things to learn from them. Therefore Native American children are exposed to many people who praise; advise; guide; urge; scold; but, most important, respect children.

Children are expected to meet their share of the obligations of community living. Being responsible results in being highly valued, and meeting community needs enables one to express individuality. Therefore responsible, highly valued adults provide important role models for the children. It is believed that this way of life can only exist within an atmosphere of respect and interdependence.

Blanchard and Barsh seriously questioned Fischler's assertions that folklore and superstition lead to maltreatment of children and instead contended that accounts of early American Indian life evidence a high regard for children. Further, they contended that much is known about parenting styles among American Indians. However, this knowledge is largely limited to American Indians themselves rather than thoroughly catalogued by researchers, who are, in fact, mostly non-Indian. It is unnecessary for data on Native Americans to be researched and interpreted by non-Indians before it can benefit American Indian families. Unfortunately American Indian researchers are not large in number. Only recently have tribal psychologists and tribal social workers been able to conduct tribal research, which probably is less biased than that of non-Indian researchers with little insight into the culture.

School problems for Native American children seem to culminate in the middle-school years, with school dropout patterns and acting-out behavior being most prominent between the fourth and tenth grades. It seems that, as children mature and as they are exposed longer to values of the dominant society, doubts and questions about their true heritage increase, thereby resulting in conflict and confusion for the child. These feelings of inadequacy or negative self-concept may well contribute to the lower educational level of Native Americans and the resulting poverty they experience.

Researchers, however, have reported conflicting evidence regarding self-concept. While some have found Native American children to favor white models over Indian models, others have found no difference between Native Americans and whites in elementary school but decreasing self-concepts for Indians in junior and senior high school. Bruneau (1985), controlling for socioeconomic status, found no overall differences between 4- to 6-year-old whites and Native Americans, except on the variable of Personal-Self. Native Americans scored higher on this variable, which measured self-perception of physical size and emotional state. Indian students need to develop relevant skills and knowledge that result in maximum benefit from both cultures.

The Indian Child Welfare Act

The Indian Child Welfare Act became law in 1978, after 4 years of congressional lobbying. The intent of Congress was to increase the probability that tribal children would grow up in tribal environments. Research has indicated a high correlation between children's removal from tribal cultural settings and subsequent problems with parenting, alcoholism, and suicide (Blanchard & Barsh, 1980). However, passage of the act has caused concern, controversy, and misunderstanding among social workers, particularly between Indians and non-Indians. They cannot agree on how much American Indian children and families benefit by provisions of the act.

American Indians themselves have been gravely concerned about the barriers that have existed to the reunification of American Indian families after separation of a staggering percentage of children from their families. Placing children in non-Indian homes, not allowing parents to visit their children while the children are in substitute care, placing children at great distances from their homes, a series of foster-care placements over a short time, and the disruptive responses of children following visits by their parents have all been viewed as obstacles to family reunification. Thus the Indian Child Welfare

Act was initiated. The law returns to tribes the responsibility for and jurisdiction over American Indian children. Whether the law in the long run will be effective in providing the best life possible for tribal children is much debated and remains to be seen, but clearly the appropriateness of its purposes is not debatable. One issue seems to be the relative emphasis of cultural environment versus household permanency.

In sum, it is difficult to make generalizations about parenting in American Indian families. Because of their diversity, family life-styles cannot be studied easily; and because of their resistance to being studied by non-Indian researchers who are critical and biased, even less data are available. To be sure there are strengths in traditional Native American values and practices that have not been emphasized in the literature by those with little understanding of this minority culture. And further, the status of Native American families is in a state of transition. Nevertheless, it seems imperative that educators, social workers, psychologists, and health personnel make an effort to understand and appreciate the heritage of Native American families so that those children can experience a sense of competence and self-satisfaction in on- or off-reservation situations.

Future Research Needs

There is no doubt that adaptive behavior must be understood within a sociocultural environment. Future research must test treatments that are adaptable to both tribal and nontribal environments. Researchers require deeper insight into the Native American heritage of values and family structure and the role of culture in the child's overall development. Assistance programs must provide support to Native American families in the form of child care, counseling, homemaker services, alcohol- and drug-abuse programs, respite care, foster-care and adoption subsidies, legal counseling, and protective services programs for children. And, finally, Native Americans themselves must be given greater opportunity to prepare for careers as psychologists, health personnel, social workers, and anthropologists so that the body of really insightful data can be enlarged.

SIMILARITIES AND DIFFERENCES AMONG CULTURES

Because there are many subcultures in the United States, we do not have a single identifiable pattern of parent-child interactions or child-rearing techniques. Because we are a democratic society that values freedom of religion, freedom of speech, freedom of the press, and freedom of unique family values, cultural differences in parent-child interactions are evident. Each subculture has unique language patterns, each has traditional rituals, and each has its own perceptions of family structure, roles, and functioning.

In many ways the similarities among cultures are striking. Children are valued and respected, but the outward manifestations may be quite different. Anglo cultures seem to value individualism over familism, whereas both Chicanos and Native Americans demonstrate strong relational bonds with family members. The traditional stereotype of black families as matriarchal and of Chicano families as patriarchal has been replaced by a more contemporary attitude of egalitarianism. Many members of black, Hispanic, and Native American cultures have become "Anglicized" to the degree that they resemble the majority culture more than they do their own minority culture.

Most differences in parenting style are related less to ethnic background than to geographic location, level of education, and socioeconomic status. Recently there has been an attempt to preserve much of the cultural heritage of these minority groups. Surely one's cultural heritage affects his life in many ways, regardless of the effort to become "assimilated" or "acculturated" into mainstream society. Even greater emphasis may need to be put on the preservation of language, values, rituals, and ethnic traditions in our pluralistic society. At the least, greater effort should be made to understand, appreciate, and cultivate the unique characteristics of our minority populations.

SUMMARY

Variations in parenting attitudes and styles are evident among the diverse cultural groups in the United States. This chapter has addressed the characteristics of and similarities and differences among three such groups—blacks, Chicanos, and Native Americans. While many other cultures exist in this country, space prohibits the discussion of additional groups.

A key variable relating to parenting practices in any ethnic or cultural group is the socioeconomic status of the families comprising that group. The literature of the 1960s and the early 1970s identified significant differences among lower- and middle-class parents in the areas of mother-child interaction, value systems, occupational and educational aspirations for children, time devoted to children, and cognitive performance of children. However, these differences were not always consistent, and many observers believe that between-class differences are, in fact, no greater than within-class differences.

The three ethnic groups discussed in this chapter clearly have distinctive characteristics; some derive from the cultural heritage of the group itself, and some are more related to the minority status the group has experienced for an extended period of time. However, those families that have been assimilated into the majority culture and have achieved middle-class status tend to utilize parenting practices that are similar to those of WASP middle-class society.

More objective research and support are needed to emphasize the strengths of culturally diverse groups and to determine how best to preserve these strengths through healthy parent-child relationships. Only then will damaging stereotypes be eliminated.

REFERENCES

ABRAHAM, K. (1986). Ego-identity differences among Anglo-American and Mexican-American adolescents. *Journal of Adolescence, 2,* 151–166.

ALDOUS, J. (1986). Cuts in selected welfare programs: The effects on US families. *Journal of Family Issues, 7*(2), 161–177.

BALL, R., & ROBBINS, L. (1986). Marital status and life satisfaction among black Americans. *Journal of Marriage and the Family, 48*(2), 389–394.

BARTZ, K., & LEVINE, E. (1978). Childrearing by black parents: A description and comparison to Anglo and Chicano parents. *Journal of Marriage and the Family, 40*(4), 709–719.

BEE, H., VAN EGEREN, L., STREISSGUTH, A., NYMAN, B., & LECKIE, M. (1969). Social class differences in maternal strategies and speech patterns. *Developmental Psychology, 1,* 726–734.

BILLINGSLEY, A. (1988). The impact of technology on Afro-American families. *Family Relations, 37*(4), 420–425.

BLANCHARD, E., & BARSH, R. (1980). What is best for tribal children? A response to Fischler. *Social Work, 25,* 350–357.

BROMAN, C. (1988). Satisfaction among blacks: The significance of marriage and parenthood. *Journal of Marriage and the Family, 50*(1), 45–51.

BROPHY, J. (1970). Mothers as teachers of their own preschool children: The influence of SES and task structure on teaching specifity. *Child Development, 41,* 79–94.

BRUNEAU, O. (1985). Self concept: A comparison of Native American and Anglo preschoolers. *Psychology in the Schools, 22*(4), 378–379.

BURIEL, R., & CARDOZA, D. (1988). Sociocultural correlates of achievement among three generations of Mexican-American high school seniors. *American Education Research Journal, 25*(2), 177–192.

CARPENTER, E. (1980). Social services, policies, and issues. *Social Casework, 61*(8), 455–461.

CLARKE-STEWART, A. (1977). *Child care in the family: A review of research and some propositions for policy.* New York: Academic.

CRAWLEY, B. (1988) Black families in a neo-conservative era. *Family Relations, 37*(4), 415–419.

CROMWELL, V., & CROMWELL, D. (1978). Perceived dominance and decision-making and conflict resolution among Anglo, black, and Chicano couples. *Journal of Marriage and the Family, 40*(4), 749–757.

Education of Hispanics sets record. (1988, September). *Albuquerque Journal,* pp. A1, A3.

ELLIS, G., LEE, G., & PETERSEN, L. (1978). Supervision and conformity: A cross-cultural analysis of parental socialization values. *American Journal of Sociology, 84*(2), 386–403.

FISCHLER, R. (1980). Protecting American Indian children. *Social Work, 61*(8), 462–467.

FRAZIER, E. (1939). *The Negro family in the United States.* Chicago: University of Chicago Press.

GOODMAN, M., & BEMAN, A. (1971). Child's eye-view of life in an urban barrio. In N. Wagner & M. Haug (Eds.), *Chicanos: Social and psychological perspectives* (pp. 109–122). St. Louis: Mosby.

GUINN, R. (1977). Value clarification in the bicultural classroom. *Journal of Teacher Education, 28,* 46–47.

HALE, J. (1980). The socialization of black children. *Dimensions, 9*(11), 43–48.

HALE-BENSON, J. (1986). *Black children: Their roots, culture, and learning styles* (rev. ed.). Baltimore: Johns Hopkins University Press.

HARMON, D., & KOGAN, K. (1980). Social class and mother-child interaction. *Psychological Reports, 46,* 1075–1084.

HARRISON, A., & MINOR, J. (1978). Interrole conflict, coping strategies, and satisfaction among black working wives. *Journal of Marriage and the Family, 40*(4), 799–805.

HEFFER, R., & KELLEY, M. (1987, Spring). Mothers' acceptance of behavioral interventions for children: The influence of race and income. *Behavior Therapy, 2,* 153–163.

HENDERSON, R. (1980). Social and emotional needs of culturally diverse children. *Exceptional Children, 46*(8), 598–605.

HESS, R., & SHIPMAN, V. (1965). Early experience and the socialization of cognitive modes in young children. *Child Development, 36,* 869–886.

HESS, R., & SHIPMAN, V. (1967). Cognitive elements in maternal behavior. In J. Hice (Ed.), *Minnesota symposia on child psychology* (pp. 57–81). Minneapolis: University of Minnesota Press.

HILL, C., & STAFFORD, E. (1974, Summer). Allocation of time to preschool children and educational opportunity. *Journal of Human Resources,* pp. 323–343.

HILL, C., & STAFFORD, E. (1980). Parental care of children: Time diary estimates of quantity, predictability, and variety. *Journal of Human Resources, 15*(2), 219–239.

JORGENSEN, S., & ADAMS, R. (1988). Predicting Mexican-American planning intentions: An application and test of a social psychological model. *Journal of Marriage and the Family, 50*(1), 107–120.

KAGAN, J. (1977). The child in the family. *Daedalus, 106*(2), 33–56.

KAGAN, S., & KNIGHT, G. (1979). Cooperation-competition and self-esteem: A case of cultural relativism. *Journal of Cross-Cultural Psychology, 10*(4), 457–467.

LAOSA, L. (1978). Maternal teaching strategies in Chicano families of varied educational and socioeconomic levels. *Child Development, 46,* 1129–1135.

LAOSA, L. (1980). Maternal teaching strategies in Chicano and Anglo-American families: The influence of culture and education on maternal behavior. *Child Development, 51,* 759–765.

LONDON, H., & DEVORE, W. (1988). Layers of understanding: Counseling ethnic minority families. *Family Relations, 37*(30), 310–314.

MARTINEZ, E. (1988). Child behavior in Mexican-American/Chicano families: Maternal teaching and childrearing practices. *Family Relations, 37*(3), 275–280.

MCADOO, H. (1978). Factors related to stability in upward mobile black families. *Journal of Marriage and the Family, 40*(4), 761–776.

MCBROOM, W. (1981). Parental relationships, socioeconomic status, and sex-role expectations. *Sex Roles, 7*(10), 1027–1033.

MCGILLICUDDY-DELISI, A. (1980). The role of parental beliefs in the family as a system of mutual influences. *Family Relations, 29*(3), 317-323.

MCQUEEN, A. (1979). The adaptations of urban black families: Trends, problems, and issues. In D. Reiss & H. Hoffman (Eds.). *The American family* (pp. 79-102). New York: Plenum.

MILLER, A., & COULTER, E. (1984). The world economic crisis and the children: A US case study. *World Development, 12*(3), 339-364.

MILLER, D. (1980). The Native American family: The urban way. In E. Corfman (Ed.), *Families Today* (pp. 441-484). Washington DC: U.S. Government Printing Office.

MIRANDÉ, A. (1977, November). The Chicano family: A reanalysis of conflicting views. *Journal of Marriage and the Family,* pp. 747-756.

MIRANDÉ, A. (1979, October). A reinterpretation of male dominance in the Chicano family. *The Family Coordinator,* pp. 473-479.

MOEN, P. (1983). Unemployment, public policy, and families: Forecasts for the 1980s. *Journal of Marriage and the Family, 45*(4), 751-760.

MOYNIHAN, D. (1965). *The Negro family: The case for national action.* Washington DC: U.S. Government Printing Office.

NORTON, A. (1983). Family life cycle: 1980. *Journal of Marriage and the Family, 45*(2), 267-275.

PETERS, M. (1978). Notes from the great editor. *Journal of Marriage and the Family, 40*(4), 655-658.

PRICE-BONHAM, S., & SKEEN, P. (1979). A comparison of black and white fathers with implications for parent education. *The Family Coordinator, 28*(1), 53-59.

RAINWATER, L. (1966). The crucible of identity: The lower class Negro family. *Daedalus, 95,* 258-264.

RANK, M. (1987). The formation and dissolution of marriages in the welfare population. *Journal of Marriage and the Family, 49*(1), 15-20.

RASHID, H. (1985). Black family research and parent education programs: The need for convergence. *Contemporary Education, 56,* 180-185.

RED HORSE, J. (1979). American Indian elders: Needs and aspiration in institutional and home health care. Unpublished manuscript.

RED HORSE, J. (1980). Family structure and value orientation in American Indians. *Social Casework, 61*(8), 462-467.

RODMAN, H., & VOYDANOFF, P. (1978). Social class and parents' range of aspirations for their children. *Social Problems, 25,* 333-334.

ROGERS, D. (1977). *Issues in child psychology.* Monterey, CA: Brooks/Cole.

ROMANO, O. (1973). The anthropology and sociology of Mexican-Americans: The distortion of Mexican-American history. In O. Romano (Ed.), *Voices: Readings from El Grito, a journal of contemporary Mexican-American thought* (pp. 43-56). Berkeley: Qunto Sal.

RUBIN, R. (1978). Matriarchal themes in black family literature: Implications for family life education. *The Family Coordinator, 27*(1), 33-39.

SCHEIRER, M. (1983). Household structure among welfare families: Correlates and consequences. *Journal of Marriage and the Family, 45*(4), 761-771.

STAPLES, R. (1988). The emerging majority: Resources for nonwhite families in the U.S. *Family Relations, 37*(3), 348-354.

STAPLES, R., & MIRANDÉ, A. (1980). Racial and cultural variations among American families: A decennial review of the literature on minority families. *Journal of Marriage and the Family, 42*(4), 887-903.

STEVENS, J. (1988). Social support, locus of control, and parenting in three low-income groups of mothers: Black teenagers, black adults, and white adults. *Child Development 59*(3), 635-642.

STRAUSS, J. (1986). The study of American Indian families: Implications for applied research. *Family Perspectives, 20*(4), 337-350.

U.S. BUREAU OF THE CENSUS (1980). *Persons of Spanish origin in the United States: March 1979,* Current Population Reports, Series P-20, No. 354. Washington DC: U.S. Government Printing Office.

U.S. BUREAU OF THE CENSUS (1983). *General population characteristics, United States summary,* 1980 Census of Population, Characteristics of the Population, PC801-1-B1. Washington DC: U.S. Government Printing Office.

U.S. BUREAU OF THE CENSUS (1986). *Statistical Abstracts of the United States* (106th ed.). Washington, DC: U.S. Department of Commerce.

U.S. DEPARTMENT OF HEALTH, EDUCATION, AND WELFARE (1974). *A study of selected socioeconomic characteristics of ethnic minorities based on the 1970 census, Vol. III: American Indians,* No. OS 75-122. Washington, DC: U.S. Government Printing Office.

VALENCIA, R., HENDERSON, R., & RANKIN, R. (1985). Family status, family constellation, and home environmental variables as predictors of cognitive performance of Mexican-American children. *Journal of Educational Psychology, 77*(3), 323-331.

VEGA, W., KOLODY, B., & VALLE, R. (1986). The relationship of marital status, confident support, and depression among Mexican immigrant women. *Journal of Marriage and the Family, 48*(3), 597-605.

VEGA, W., KOLODY, B., & VALLE, R. (1988). Marital strain, coping, and depression among Mexican-American women. *Journal of Marriage and the Family, 50*(2), 391-404.

VEGA, W., PATTERSON, T., SALLIS, J., NADER, P., ATKINS, C., & ABRAMSON, I. (1986). Cohesion and adaptability in Mexican-American and Anglo families. *Journal of Marriage and the Family, 48*(4), 857-867.

ZINN, M. (1979). Chicano family research: Conceptual distortions and alternative directions. *Journal of Ethnic Studies, 7*(3), 59-71.

7

Parenting in Nontraditional Families: Structural Variations

Dramatic changes occurred in the marital behavior of American adults during the decade of the 1970s, and some of the trends continued into the 1980s. Specifically, the likelihood of marriage declined or occurred later, divorce increased to a record high, and significant changes occurred in the living arrangements of both adults and children. A majority of households in the United States are not nuclear families with both biological parents living with their offspring. In the 1980s there was a gradual, steady increase in the percentage of adults and children residing in single-parent, blended, or other households that frequently included nonrelated individuals (U.S. Bureau of the Census, 1987).

While the actual number of households composed of married couples increased by 4.9 percent from 1980 to 1987, the proportion of these households compared to households maintained by single parents and other noncouple households declined dramatically. Male-headed households with children under 18 increased by 44.8 percent, and female-headed households with minor children increased by 20 percent (U.S. Bureau of the Census, 1987). Box 7a summarizes households by type in 1970, 1980, and 1987.

Other statistics emphasize the increasing number of nonnuclear families. Box 7b shows the number of divorced persons per 1,000 married persons by sex and race in 1970, 1980, and 1986. As indicated, there was more than a 100 percent increase from 1970 to 1980 in the divorce rate for all groups; the rate increase was steady but not as dramatic for the period of 1980 to 1986. It is interesting to note that the rate of divorce among blacks was twice that of whites. Approximately 75–85 percent of divorced people remarry. The high incidence of divorce and remarriage indicates an increasing number of single- and stepparent families. The number of unmarried couples with children under 15 years of age increased from 196,000 in 1970 to 431,000 in 1980 and to 682,000 in 1986 (U.S. Bureau of the Census, 1987).

This chapter will explore some of the problems experienced by families residing in single-parent and blended households. Parenting styles and suggestions for resources and supports for these nontraditional family structures also will be examined.

SINGLE-PARENT FAMILIES

A single-parent family consists of one parent with dependent children living in the same household.

BOX 7a   HOUSEHOLDS 1970, 1980, 1987

	1970	% Change	1980	% Change	1987
Family	44,728,000	15.7	59,550,000	8.3	64,491,000
Nonfamily	11,945,000	77.7	21,226,000	17.7	24,988,000

FAMILY HOUSEHOLDS 1970, 1980, 1987

	1970	% Change	1980	% Change	1987
Married couples	39,329,000	9.7	49,112,000	4.9	51,537,000
Male maintained	1,239,000	39.9	1,733,000	44.8	2,510,000
Female maintained	5,591,000	55.7	8,705,000	20.0	10,445,000

Source: Adapted from U.S. Bureau of the Census (1987). *Statistical abstract of the U.S.: 1988* (10th ed.). Washington, DC: U.S. Department of Commerce.

The single-parent family also has been referred to as the one-parent, the lone-parent, and the solo-parent family, among other names, to describe family structure (Hanson & Sporakowski, 1986). Since there are a variety of types of single parents, no one label is strictly definitive. A single-parent family implies that a mother or father is parenting singlehandedly; the one-parent label suggests only one parent; and the terms *lone-* and *solo-*parent family also are misleading because the noncustodial parent may be highly involved in child rearing. In the defini-tion we have chosen, single-parent family refers to the living arrangements of this family structure.

Of all households in 1986, 26.3 percent were maintained by single parents with children under 18 years of age. The actual number of single-parent families is even higher when one considers that several groups are omitted from the previously cited statistics: those single-parent families who have children older than 18 years of age living in the same household, those single parents who live with a relative, and those who

BOX 7b   DIVORCED PERSONS PER 1,000 MARRIED PERSONS BY SEX AND RACE, 1970, 1980, 1986

Males	1970	1980	1986
White	32	74	102
Black	62	149	166
Females			
White	56	110	145
Black	104	258	332

Source: Adapted from U.S. Bureau of the Census (1987). *Statistical abstract of the U.S.: 1988* (10th ed.). Washington, DC: U.S. Department of Commerce.

live in homes maintained by unrelated persons. Single parents and their children constitute a rapidly increasing population whose special needs have been insufficiently recognized, infrequently studied, and poorly served.

The life-cycle approach to studying the needs and functioning of families has long been the norm for the traditional family. Only recently has this orientation been extended to single-parent families. Hill (1986) described life-cycle stages for different types of single-parent families and compared life-span careers for intact, divorced, widowed, and twice-married families. He concluded that the principal structural difference between two-parent and single-parent families was that single-parent families lacked the personnel to fill all the normatively expected positions in the family. The different developmental paths for single-parent families are not found in the actual life-cycle stages but in the timing, number, and length of the critical transitions.

Single parents are not a homogeneous group; they exist in all social classes, in all racial and ethnic groups, and in all age groups from 15 to 50. Divorces, separations, desertions, out-of-wedlock births, incarcerations, hospitalizations, military duties, out-of-state employments, and

single-parent adoptions result in single parenthood. However, the rise in the divorce rate is the most significant factor in the increased number of single parents, with one in two marriages now ending in divorce (Norton & Glick, 1986). While the number of never-married parents and single adoptive parents is increasing, these single parents are still few in comparison to divorced single parents. Box 7c depicts the variety of types of single-parent households in 1986.

Researchers have long been interested in the single-parent family. In the 1930s, 1940s, and 1950s, sociological studies of the single parent multiplied. Most of these studies, however, were related to father absence and its resulting effects. In reality these studies were about single mothers and their problems and the effects of father absence on children. Much of the controversy and contradiction regarding single-parent families centers around faulty or questionable conceptualizations and methodological issues in research. Single-parent families headed by males have been largely excluded from research considerations in the past. When single fathers have been studied, sample sizes were almost always small.

In the 1960s and 1970s, considerable data

BOX 7c   HOUSEHOLDS MAINTAINED BY SINGLE PARENTS IN 1986 WITH CHILDREN UNDER 18 YEARS OF AGE

Maintained by Mother	White	Black	% Distribution of All Households
Never married	885,000	1,355,000	6.7
Divorced	2,676,000	581,000	9.7
Widowed	380,000	133,000	1.6
Spouse absent	1,129,000	546,000	5.1
Maintained by Father			
Never married	135,000	60,000	.6
Divorced	513,000	47,000	1.7
Widowed	78,000	7,000	.3
Spouse absent	168,000	40,000	.6

Source: Adapted from U.S. Bureau of the Census (1987). *Statistical abstract of the U.S.: 1988* (10th ed.). Washington, DC: U.S. Department of Commerce.

FIGURE 7–1   TYPES OF SINGLE MOTHERS WITH CHILDREN UNDER 16 YEARS OF AGE, 1986

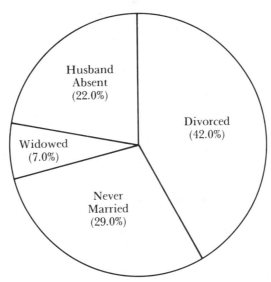

Source: Adapted from U.S. Bureau of the Census (1987). *Statistical abstract of the U.S.: 1988* (10th ed.). Washington, DC: U.S. Department of Commerce.

were collected on unwed teenage mothers. More recently, single fathers, other single parents, and the adjustment processes of single parents and their children have received increased attention (Gasser & Taylor, 1976; Savage, Adair, & Friedman, 1978).

Single parenthood, regardless of its origin, cannot be considered as a single event; rather it is the process or chain of events set into motion that determine the effects on the adults and children involved. Single parents are faced with a number of changes, including decreased financial resources; changes in residence; assumption of new roles and responsibilities; establishment of new patterns of intrafamilial interaction; reorganization of routines and schedules; and, eventually, the introduction of new relationships into the existing family. The nature of these changes demands resources that are most often beyond those immediately accessible to individual family members (Hetherington & Camara, 1984). The following sections will examine some of these changes for mothers, fathers, and children.

Single Mothers

More than 80 percent of single-parent households are maintained by mothers. Mother-child families are disproportionately concentrated among blacks, with approximately one-half of all black families being headed by single mothers. More than one half of all black children live in single-mother families, compared to one sixth of white children. It has been projected that 37 percent of young women in their twenties in the mid-1980s will at some point maintain a single-mother family (Norton & Glick, 1986).

The median age of single mothers has dropped from 37.2 years in 1970 to 34.6 years in 1984 (the same as for intact families). However, there is a greater concentration of very young mothers in one-parent families because of the increased number of never-married teenage mothers. Figure 7–1 indicates the percentage of single mothers with children under 18 years of age who achieved single status because they never married or via divorce, widowhood, or absence of husband. As can be noted, the greatest percentage (about one half) of single mothers has been divorced.

A common assumption has been that the female-headed single-parent household is a pathological family form rather than a viable alternative to the nuclear family. Since the largest percentage of single-parent families are headed by divorced females, this contention has been used on the assumption that the trauma from divorce is likely to result in poorly socialized, cognitively deficient children who experience poor parent-child relationships (Crossman & Adams, 1980).

Problems of single mothers. Previous research has indicated that single mothers share common concerns, including income inadequacy, role overload, parenting and child care, social isolation, and emotional and psychological problems (Hetherington, Cox, & Cox 1976; Wallerstein & Kelly, 1979; White & Bloom, 1981). More recent research has continued to explore the problems of single motherhood.

The economic plight of single mothers has been extensively documented. In fact, the major issue facing single mothers is poverty (Burden, 1986; Norton & Glick, 1986). Partly, the lack of adequate income is the result of a low level of education and inadequate job skills. Single mothers are more likely to have less than a high school education than single fathers and mothers in intact families are. There is evidence, however, that the educational level of single parents improved significantly from 1970 to 1984. Far fewer girls terminated their education short of high school, and more single mothers were college educated. Income figures indicate that the greatest proportion of low-income families are mother-child families. Only about one sixth of single-mother families have incomes higher than $20,000, whereas nearly 60 percent of mother-child families in 1986 lived below poverty level, with one third receiving benefits from Aid to Families with Dependent Children (AFDC) (Norton & Glick, 1986).

Employment is the major source of income for single mothers. Two out of every three are in the work force (approximately 70 percent). More mothers with school-age children work than those with preschool children (85 percent). Black single mothers are less likely than white single mothers to work, especially if they have preschool children. Hispanic single mothers are more likely than black or white single mothers to be unemployed. While employment may not remove a single mother from poverty, it can provide other important benefits. Research has indicated that employment is a major factor increasing the physical, emotional, and financial well-being of women. Overall, the work setting appears to be a vital element in the support network for single parents. Burden (1986) found, however, that single mothers were at significant risk for high levels of job-family role strain and decreased physical and emotional well-being. Despite increased stress, single parents did not report significantly greater numbers of problems with children or more days absent from their jobs than married women did. Further, they expressed equal levels of job motivation and job performance. Pett and Vaughn-Cole (1986) reported that at every socioeconomic level marital dissolution drastically reduced the single-parent family's available income, and that this reduction remained stable over a 5-year period. Lowered socioeconomic status reduces the family's choice of residence, credit availability, choice of friends, and parental self-image. These negative changes are likely to be an impetus for single mothers to prematurely remarry.

Another source of income for single mothers is child support. In 1983, 76.2 percent of divorced women and 40.9 percent of separated women were awarded child-support payments. Of those awarded child-support payments, 76.4 percent of the divorced women and 87.1 percent of the separated women actually received some support, but less than half received the full amount awarded. Support payments were less likely to be received by nonwhite mothers, by those without a college education, and by those with incomes below the poverty level—those who needed it the most (Greif, 1986; Kurdek, 1986).

Reduced income has a direct effect on living conditions of single mothers and their children. They are more likely to live in inner cities and rarely own their own homes. Approximately two out of every three rental houses maintained by single women are in subsidized housing. Single mothers are more mobile, with about 20 percent moving each year as compared to 14 percent of all families.

The amount and source of income significantly affects the custodial parent's sense of fate control. Women who are economically dependent on AFDC, child support, or alimony are likely to feel they have less control over the direction of their lives than economically self-sufficient women do. Those women who must seek public assistance may possess less confidence in themselves and have a more negative self-concept than do those who choose employment in equivalent low-paying jobs. However, the level rather than the source may be a stronger predictor of the mother's belief that her actions are effective in bringing about desirable outcomes. See Figure 7–2 for the sources of income of single mothers and fathers in the Pett and Vaughn-Cole study.

Role overload is another major problem for single mothers. There is little time for doing normal housework in addition to earning a living and rearing children (Sanik & Mauldin, 1986). In a sense, the single mother is committed to two jobs. Burden (1986) found that single mothers spent an average of 75 hours per week trying to balance job and family responsibilities. Theoretically, single parents have the same alternatives as other families to cope with housekeeping demands—reduce them, reallocate them to family members, or hire someone to do them. In reality, financial resources limit the alternatives, such as being able to hire help, eat out, or use convenience foods. Sanik and Mauldin (1986) found that single employed mothers spent the least amount of time (as compared to unemployed two-parent and unemployed single and two-parent mothers) in household tasks, personal care, and recreation. They did not differ from other mothers in time spent with children.

A number of investigators have examined the emotional sequelae of divorce and subsequent single parenthood. Previous research has indicated that especially in the first year following divorce, single mothers feel more anxious, angry, rejected, and incompetent. Most describe their position as burdensome. They report feelings of depression and being less satisfied with their lives as parents. Fine, Donnelly, and Voydanoff (1986) surveyed a group of single, intact, and stepparents and found that single parents reported significantly more feelings of depression than either of the other groups. Females in all groups reported more anxiety than males did, and single parents reported significantly lower levels of family satisfaction, even when socioeconomic status and educational levels were controlled. Box 7d summarizes common problems of single mothers.

Wallerstein (1986) found in her 10-year follow-up study of divorced women that, contrary to past assumptions, the capacity to replace failed relationships is neither a psychological nor a social given. She found that anger associated with divorce can persist for more than 10 years, well into remarriage, and continued to affect interactions with the former spouse in regard to the children. A significant number of women at every age, but especially those married for extended periods of time, had not resolved their feelings of anger that were rooted in feelings of outrage and betrayal.

She found that only about two thirds of the women she studied were able to improve their quality of life after divorce, but those who instigated the divorce were more likely to do so than those who had opposed it. She concluded that divorce leads to a wider range of psychological changes and growth among women than among men. The capacity of women to rebuild intimate

---

BOX 7d PROBLEMS OF SINGLE MOTHERS

Stress and mental illness	Loneliness and isolation
Role overload	Negative view from society
Income inadequacy	Feelings of being "walled-in" or trapped
Lowered standard of living	Difficulties with child rearing

FIGURE 7-2   SOURCES OF INCOME FOR SINGLE MOTHERS

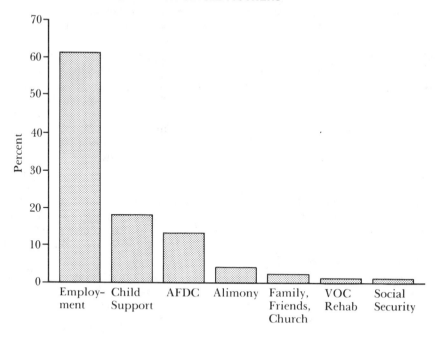

SOURCES OF INCOME FOR SINGLE FATHERS

Source: Adapted from Pett, M. A., & Vaughn-Cole, B. (1986). The impact of income issues and social status on post-divorce adjustment of custodial parents. *Family Relations, 35*(1), 103–111.

adult relationships and to reestablish social and economic stability after divorce is age related. Women more than 40 years of age at the time of divorce appear to be disadvantaged at the re-building task. Many in Wallerstein's study, after 10 years, felt lonely and rejected and lived in economic, social, and psychological conditions well below what they had while married. However, many of the women in their twenties and thirties at the time of divorce showed a resiliency that enabled them to utilize resources within themselves or the environment. As a result they were able to make emotional and economic progress following divorce.

Further, Wallerstein (1986) found that the women who suffered from neurotic problems during the marriage were likely to have impaired functioning following divorce. Loneliness, sometimes found to be associated with over-dependence on adolescent children, emerged as a major psychological issue for women who were divorced in their thirties and forties and who remained unmarried. She also found that insight did not necessarily go hand in hand with psychological change in resolving the divorce crisis. Few seemed, even after 10 years, to recognize their contribution to the marriage failure or to accept any responsibility for the divorce.

While most research on single parents has focused on the problems encountered, Hanson (1986) studied healthy single-parent families. She found, in general, that the physical and mental health of the single parents and their children appeared to be good. Children living with their mothers reported being more healthy than those living with their fathers. Factors that were positively related to mental health were custody arrangements, level of social support, and communication with children. Joint-custody arrangements appeared to contribute to the mental health of mothers. A strong support system and good communication with the children facilitated positive physical and mental health. The level of religiosity and problem solving did not appear to be significant factors in physical and mental-health status. Loveland-Cherry (1986) also found no significant differences for levels of personal health practices between single- and two-parent families. It must be emphasized that the subjects in both studies were from the middle-income level, and different results probably would have been found had low-income mothers been included.

Parenting by custodial mothers. Previous research has indicated that many single mothers report problems with child rearing. The mother may be so overwhelmed by the experience of divorce and single parenthood that she may suffer depression and be unable to care adequately for her child or children. While divorced and separated white mothers report many problems with rearing children, single black mothers report even greater problems. More than 75 percent of single black mothers in one study reported having multiple problems relating to rearing children, with the younger women reporting the most child-rearing problems (Crossman & Adams, 1980; Rohrlick, Rainer, Berg-Cross, & Berg-Cross, 1977; Tucker, 1978).

In the period immediately following divorce, many mothers become punitive and restrictive, unaffectionate, less rational in their attempts to control their children, less supportive of their children, and generally absorbed with their own problems. They make few maturity demands on the children. Poor parenting skills among anxious, depressed parents increase anxiety and

depression, feelings of incompetency, and decreased self-esteem in the mother. Custodial mothers often seem to instigate aggression and noncompliance in sons and have difficulty in terminating their coercive behavior once it has begun (Amato, 1987; Hetherington & Camara, 1984). This appears to stem from the emotional trauma associated with the divorce, stigma of divorce, and role strain. These parental behaviors tend to elicit disobedience and acting-out responses in children, which, in turn, evoke further repressiveness from the mother. A reciprocal aggravation cycle, then, occurs (Peterson & Cleminshaw, 1980). Most of these trends are temporary, however, and parent-child relationships stabilize after the first year or two.

During the initial postdivorce period, single mothers tend to try to control the child by being more restrictive, giving more commands, and utilizing more negative sanctions than do other parents. One study found that poor parenting (for single mothers) was the most marked 1 year after divorce. The single mother gradually decreases the negative sanctions and futile attempts at authoritarian control and becomes more effective in dealing with her child over a 2-year period. After this time the mother seems to demand more autonomous mature behavior of her children, communicates more effectively, uses more explanations and reasoning, and becomes more nurturant and consistent (Amato, 1987; Hetherington, Cox, & Cox, 1976).

The quality of parenting by custodial mothers is closely related to parental adjustment. Factors include the degree of emotional availability of the parent, level of conflict between custodial parent and children as well as conflict with ex-spouse, degree of warmth and affection, home organization, and available economic and social-support system (Johnson, 1986). The style of parenting utilized by the mother is important. Authoritative parenting is associated with social competency in children. Consistency of expectations, enforcement of limits, and rational demands are also factors contributing to positive adjustment of children. Authoritative skills often are absent in parents experiencing great distress following separation. There is a diminished ability to parent, and mothers often turn to an authoritarian approach.

An interesting finding of the Loveland-Cherry (1986) study concerned the relationship of single mothers' child-rearing style to the personal health practices of the family. Not only did mothers who used aversive control methods have lower levels of personal health practices, themselves, but also their child's health was negatively affected. These mothers presented themselves as poor role models to their children in terms of health behavior, were less supportive of their children, and discouraged autonomous behavior.

Amato (1987) studied family processes in single-mother families, stepfamilies, and intact families. He concluded that the effects of divorce appear to be subtle and involve changes in children's relationship with mothers, fathers, siblings, and other family members. Parenting by single custodial mothers was found to differ from parenting in stepfamilies and intact families. He reported that in some single-mother families the condition of "mother absence" exists. Mothers are forced to decrease their time spent in child rearing because of the large number of demands placed on them. Adolescents in mother-headed families often experience less parental supervision than children in two-parent families do.

The level of maternal control reported by primary-aged children in Amato's study did not differ according to family type. However, adolescents reported significantly less maternal control in single-mother families than did those in intact families or stepfamilies. This finding may reflect a lack of supervision, or it may indicate that adolescents in single-mother families are more mature.

Interestingly, children in single, stepparent, and two-parent families did not differ in the perceived levels of support received from their mothers. The children in single-mother families were just as likely as those in intact and stepfamilies to report that their mothers talked to them a lot, were interested in them, provided assistance with homework, and helped with personal problems (Amato, 1987).

Other findings of the family processes in the Amato (1987) study were related to punishment, household responsibilities, sibling relationships, and family cohesion. Punishment by the mothers did not differ significantly in the three family types. Children at both age levels in single-mother families reported more household responsibilities than children in stepfamilies and intact families did.

Children, especially adolescents, in single-mother families rated sibling relationships more negatively than children in stepfamilies and intact families. Children were rarely found to be helpful to each other in coping with the strains of the divorce period. The degree of family cohesion was perceived by children, especially primary-aged, to be significantly lower in single-mother families than in the other family types. Previous research has indicated that life in divorced families tends to be chaotic and stressful during the first year after divorce.

Amato (1987) concluded that the perceived effects by children living in single-mother families occur early and persist over time. Certain factors can mediate the negative parenting of single mothers, such as adequate income, support from noncustodial fathers, and support from other services; over time the parent-child relationship improves in most single-mother families.

Single Fathers

A single-father family is one that consists of an unmarried male and his minor child or children who live in the same household. Single fathers include widowers, divorced or separated fathers, never-married males, and single adoptive fathers who have primary responsibility for care of their children (Lewis, 1978; Mendes, 1976). The phenomenon of single-parent fathers is not new, but the incidence of this family type has increased in recent years. The number of single fathers with custody of their children is about 10 percent of all single-parent families—2,510,000 in 1987. The number of single-father households has more than doubled since 1970, the rate actually increasing more rapidly than single-mother households. Single-mother households, however, are still five times more prevalent than single-father ones (see Box 7a).

In the past, most single fathers were widowers. The maternal mortality rate was 58 deaths per 10,000 live births in 1935, but by the late 1970s it had dropped to 2.5 deaths per 10,000. The number of widowed fathers in recent years has tended to remain constant, just over one-half

million, but single fathers via divorce have increased significantly, and increasing numbers of fathers are being awarded either sole custody or joint custody of their children (Mendes, 1976; Orthner, Brown, & Ferguson, 1976). Child-custody statutes are increasingly being directed toward the concept of the best interests of the child. The implications are that mothers and fathers in the future will be evaluated without obvious sex bias. Boys are twice as likely to live with their fathers as girls are. Boys are more difficult to rear than girls and relate better to their fathers, particularly if they are teenagers (Norton & Glick, 1986).

Presently, adoption is a minor factor in single-parent fatherhood. Typically, single parents can adopt only children who are hard to place, and the few male single parents involved are almost routinely limited to male children (Mendes, 1976; Orthner et al., 1976).

The single-parent family often is a transition life-style lasting from a few months to a few years until remarriage occurs. While the average period for single fatherhood is 2 years, more and more fathers are delaying remarriage, and some plan never to remarry. For these men single fatherhood is not a transition experience. Men in the past who may have hesitated to assume traditionally female roles do not hesitate to do so today (DeFrain & Eirick, 1981; Lewis, 1978; Wallerstein & Kelly, 1979).

The research data concerning single fathers indicate that single fatherhood by adoption and custody remains difficult but possible to obtain; that single fathers are successful at child rearing, both part-time and full-time; and that more research is needed, as single fatherhood is not fully understood. The women's liberation movement, the changing divorce laws, and the general trend toward sexual equality have brought increased attention to single fatherhood. There is a particular need for additional child-centered research. In the past, research has focused on the needs and problems of single fathers. Data are needed to assist judges in custody contests and to help teachers and other child-care providers understand the unique needs of children living in single-father homes. Additional information needs to be gathered about social and academic achievements of the children, father-child relations, and factors contributing to adjustment (Lewis, 1978).

The onset of single fatherhood, whether by death of a spouse or by divorce, produces a psychological crisis for the father and for his children. Many divorced men report that separation trauma exceeds predivorce trauma. Divorced fathers initially tend to suffer a greater loss of self-esteem than divorced women do, although the effects are extended for women. Fathers frequently report feeling rootless, not knowing who they are, and having no structure in their lives. A large percentage of divorced men report sleeping problems because of worry. Others report increased drinking and smoking and the inability to concentrate on work. The separation precipitates feelings of loss, previously unrecognized dependency needs, guilt, anxiety, and depression. Physical and emotional illness appears to be significantly stronger for men than for women, including psychopathology, disease, morbidity and mortality, suicide, and homicide. There are nine times more divorced men who seek psychiatric help than married men (Hetherington et al., 1976; Schlesinger, 1978; White & Bloom, 1981). Single fathers in the study by Fine and his associates (1986) reported greater depression than single mothers, fathers from intact families, or stepparents. Hanson (1986) reported that fathers with sole custody of their male children reported the highest level of overall health.

Time, of course, eases many pains. Nine months after divorce at least half of the men in White and Bloom's (1981) study reported physical and/or emotional separation stress. One third reported dissatisfaction with the progress they were making. By the end of 2 years, however, feelings of loneliness and guilt had decreased markedly, and improvement in social life and sexual integration had occurred. For some, financial stress had increased (Hetherington et al., 1976; White & Bloom, 1981).

The evidence indicates that the experience of separation for men is one that is characterized by social strain, isolation, and poor self-esteem. These stresses relate primarily to external pressures of leaving the social protectiveness of the marital role and the internal pressures of loss. Single fatherhood is reflected in alterations of parent-child relations and changes in life-style. Most men are able to restructure their lives and achieve some degree of stability for the family within a 2-year period (Hetherington et al, 1976; Wallerstein & Kelly, 1979; White & Bloom, 1981).

Problems of single fathers. While single fathers do experience financial problems, they are better able to realize economic security than single mothers are. On the whole they have higher incomes than single mothers do. In fact, the median income for single fathers is twice as high as that for single mothers (Norton & Glick, 1986; White, Brinkerhoff, & Booth, 1985), partly because of the higher educational attainment by fathers. They are almost twice as likely as single mothers to have 13 or more years of schooling. Interestingly, there is a strong inverse relationship between educational attainment and being a single father—the fewer the years of schooling, the greater the likelihood of single parenthood. Single fathers are more likely than intact fathers to have less than a high school education; however, they are more likely to have higher levels of education than single mothers. Another factor related to greater economic security of single fathers is the likelihood of being in the work force. Nearly 90 percent of single fathers are employed, whereas approximately 70 percent of single mothers are.

While single fathers are better off economically than single mothers are, some do experience a decrease in income, and some even experience impoverishment. The decrease is more of an indirect than a direct loss. About 12 percent lose the wife's income, but the hidden contributions made by the wife are far more important—household tasks performed, reduced overtime because of no one to care for children, day-care expenses, and so on (Hill, 1986). Another problem associated with the financial status of single fathers is disagreements with ex-spouses concerning finances, such as alimony and custody payments. Divorced fathers are more likely than married fathers are to increase their workloads in an attempt to increase their incomes, thereby increasing stress. Some fathers report that they are unable to work overtime because of parental responsibilities, and other fathers report difficulties with budgeting. Some studies have indicated that financial status is the key in men's performance and satisfaction as a single father (Amato, 1987). However, Risman's study (1986) did not indicate economic status to be a critical factor.

Although it is unusual, some women pay child support to their custodial ex-husbands. Greif (1986) found that women who pay child support are usually women who (a) earn a higher-than-average income, (b) continue to be involved with their children after divorce, (c) are less likely to be living with any of their children, and (d) do not give financial reasons for not having custody. Reasons given by women for not paying support are related to the financial and societal expectations of women.

Problems concerning employment have been cited by single fathers, especially those that result from conflicts between child-care responsibilities and vocational responsibilities. Business trips, job mobility, working hours, earnings, promotions, and relations with co-workers and supervisors are limited. The problems relating to employment, finances, and child care tend to interact and to impinge on the family at a time when emotional resources are likely to be at the lowest ebb (DeFrain & Eirick, 1981; Gasser & Taylor, 1976; Keshet & Rosenthal, 1978; Schlesinger, 1978). However, Smith and Smith (1981) reported that men in their sample did not view single parenthood as a hindrance to continuing their careers or pursuit of personal goals.

The synchronization of work, supervision of children, and household management seems to be a major problem for most single fathers. For example, they state that they have no chance to shop for bargains, are seldom able to cook economically, and do not have time to perform housekeeping tasks properly. However, divorced fathers especially seem able to perform such homemaking tasks as cooking, cleaning, and shopping without considerable difficulty. In fact, homemaking is a major part of the single-father role. In some studies as many as 90 percent report frequent performance of routine household tasks. This may imply that fathers today are more familiar with roles in home management and child care than men were in the past. The

stress associated with these tasks appears to stem from role overload rather than inability to perform tasks (Keshet & Rosenthal, 1978; Mendes, 1976; Orthner et al, 1976; Schlesinger, 1978; Smith & Smith, 1981). Those men who assumed no household tasks prior to divorce generally experience the most stress in coping with routine household tasks. Divorced fathers are more likely to pick up meals and serve them at irregular times and are less likely to eat at home than married men are (Hetherington et al., 1976).

Single fathers indicate difficulties in establishing a meaningful social life and forming intimate interpersonal relationships. Socializing in our society centers around couples, and being a single parent limits recreational opportunities. Feelings of loneliness for a missing spouse to share companionship and responsibility are common. Humiliation, especially if the wife has deserted, may exist. Divorced men appear to proceed through a predictable sequence in establishing social adjustment. Initially the father tends to disengage himself socially, having little interaction outside the family. Fathers report this curtailment of social activities as due to lack of time, lack of common interests with former friends, a feeling of not belonging, and social ostracism. Many relinquish memberships in clubs and social groups. In fact, a great deal of the role strain experienced is the result of society's negative view of single-parent fathers. Most social activities center around the children, female friends, or themselves. About 1 year following divorce, most fathers are busy dating and have varied casual social encounters. Many have joined ''singles'' organizations and have become involved in self-improvement programs. Friends prior to marriage are replaced by single friends. Contact with the ex-spouse and noncustody children decreases over time. Two years after divorce, the flurry of dating and the many social contacts generally diminish, and a stable social life has been formed. Those men who have not remarried or who have not been able to establish an intimate relationship within 2 years report intense loneliness. Those who have developed an intimate relationship report higher levels of happiness, competency, and satisfaction and have higher self-esteem. Sex is an area of concern because many men feel they should not cohabit and feel a need for sexual discretion (DeFrain & Eirick, 1981; Gasser & Taylor, 1976; Hetherington et al., 1976; Keshet & Rosenthal, 1978; Lewis, 1978; Schlesinger, 1978; Smith & Smith, 1981; White & Bloom, 1981). Widowed single fathers seem to be more concerned with preserving former friendships and ties and appear to be more reluctant to relinquish membership in the organizations to which they belong, which tends to retard social adjustment (Gasser & Taylor, 1976).

Parenting by single fathers.   Relationships with children, child rearing and child care present adjustment problems for single fathers (Gasser & Taylor, 1976; Hetherington et al, 1976; Mendes, 1976; Orthner et al., 1976; Schlesinger, 1978; Smith & Smith, 1981; Tucker, 1978). Both custodial and noncustodial fathers must redefine relationships with their children. The custodial father finds that he is required to make a major shift in life-style and priorities as a result of being the primary caregiver of the child. The bond between father and child becomes a new focal point for self-direction and sets the criteria for organizing the more traditional spheres of male functioning—work and social life. Arrangements for care of young children must be made. Many fathers report that the child-care arrangements they have made are unsatisfactory. These fathers feel that the children are not supervised properly and not well liked by their caretakers. Many school-age children and adolescents are unsupervised after school.

Some single fathers report a lack of patience and time for their children. Other problems include making decisions alone, applying discipline, and having to be away from their children more than desired. A large percentage of single fathers (95 percent in one study) report performing nurturing activities for the children, including discipline and handling emotional upsets. Providing for emotional development of the children seems to present a greater problem for these fathers than the homemaking and entertainment roles. Many men feel unprepared to cope with emotional upsets (Keshet & Rosenthal, 1978). Most single fathers report that they demonstrate love and affection in an open and physical manner to younger children but refrain from

demonstrating affection in the same manner to older children. Affection is demonstrated by performing family roles. A larger percentage of single fathers experience difficulty and insecurity in rearing daughters. Problems primarily relate to discussing sex with their daughters and concern about sexual behaviors (Mendes, 1976; Schlesinger, 1978). Most single fathers share household management with children rather than employing outside assistance. Frequently, democratic procedures are employed in running the household, and children also have to assume more responsibility in taking care of themselves than in two-parent families. These responsibilities tend to foster independence in children (Gasser & Taylor, 1976; Weiss, 1979). There is some evidence to indicate that the degree of involvement in homemaking and child care prior to the divorce is a factor in ease of adjustment. Unfortunately, the extent of many men's involvement is limited to a small amount of physical care and interaction through play. Some have had experience in disciplining children, but few have had classes in child development or have read material on child rearing (Gasser & Taylor, 1976; Smith & Smith, 1981).

Evidence tends to indicate that fathers who seek custody of their children adjust better to child rearing and have more positive feelings about being parents than fathers who do not become single custodial parents by choice. Those who do not want to assume the role of the single father are likely to encounter severe problems with their children (Lewis, 1978).

Noncustodial fathers tend to want contacts with their children to be as happy as possible. Initially after divorce the father tends to be extremely permissive and indulgent with his children. Many noncustodial fathers express difficulty adjusting to reduced involvement in, and control of, their children's lives. These fathers express dissatisfaction with the limited amount of time arranged for them to see their children. Over a 2-year period, the divorced father becomes increasingly less available to his children. But at the end of this period, he tends to make more demands of their maturity, communicates more effectively, is more consistent but less nurturant and more detached (Hetherington et al., 1976; White & Bloom, 1981).

BOX 7e   PROBLEMS OF SINGLE FATHERS

Loss of self-esteem

Feelings of rootlessness, loss, dependency, guilt, anxiety, depression, loneliness

Physical and emotional illness

Difficulty establishing meaningful social life

Redefinition of father-child relationship

Financial problems

Role overload

Child rearing and child care

Single fathers appear to rely on structured recreational activities for their children (Keshet & Rosenthal, 1978). Taking the children swimming, to playgrounds, museums, restaurants, and, less frequently, to the movies are typical activities. Finding activities for children seems to be an important role of the single father. In a study conducted by Keshet and Rosenthal (1978), the fathers reported that they often played with their children, spent half their time at home interacting with them, and frequently invited female companions to accompany the family on outings. However, few of these companions performed any significant child-rearing tasks.

While child rearing clearly requires the single father to adjust his role and redefine the father-child relationship, most single fathers report very positive feelings about this aspect of single parenthood after the period of adjustment has occurred. Most feel that they have developed a closer relationship with their children. Being responsible for children's growth and development and satisfying children's needs bring these fathers in contact with what has commonly been considered a woman's world. As a result the fathers report greater appreciation of responsibility in being a primary parent, more concern about day care, more interest in the education and protection of their children, and less discipline orientation. In response to their children's needs most single fathers successfully restructure their daily lives in order to care directly for their children. More positive feelings about themselves as parents and individuals emerge as a result of this interaction. Those men who achieve positive restructuring generally feel that they are well adjusted and free of problems. Widowed males seem to have more difficulty adjusting and restructuring their families than do divorced men. Even though single fathers do not view the home situation as perfect, most feel that they are in control, that the home is functioning smoothly, and that their children are having similar experiences to other children (Gasser & Taylor, 1976; Keshet & Rosenthal, 1978; Orthner et al., 1976; Smith & Smith, 1981).

Interestingly enough, single-parent fathers report that they feel free to call on the extended family for support, but few actually do. Neither do they rely heavily on female companions to assist with child rearing, although they report the feeling that women are sources of support. It seems that these fathers perceive that they have to prove themselves capable of caring for children alone. In relation to developing an appropriate father-child relationship, support from the ex-

spouse is the most significant support needed. Single-parent organizations, such as Parents Without Partners, also provide a source of support (Hetherington et al., 1976; Lewis, 1978; Orthner et al., 1976; Smith & Smith, 1981).

Noncustodial fathers have a more difficult time redefining their relationships with their children than custodial fathers do. Both young children and adolescents reported less support from noncustodial fathers than children in intact families did (Amato, 1987). In this study only 17 percent of primary children mentioned their noncustodial fathers as people they would go to if they were really worried, as compared to 60 percent who lived in intact families. Comparable percentages for adolescents were 5 percent in single-mother and 20 percent in intact families. On the other hand, 20 percent of children in single-mother families reported a higher level of support than the mean for intact families. Clearly some children experience continued support from noncustodial fathers, while some receive only minimal support from their fathers in intact families.

Amato (1987) also found that noncustodial fathers made virtually no decisions about their children's everyday behavior, which suggests that a major component of the parenting role is no longer exercised by noncustodial fathers. Further, noncustodial fathers were perceived to punish significantly less than fathers in stepfamilies or intact families. Adolescents generally reported less punishment than primary-aged children did. These findings revealed a generally low level of reported punishment by noncustodial fathers— once again a major component of the parenting role is largely absent for these fathers.

Factors Affecting Adjustment to Single Parenthood

Single parents of both sexes report similarities in coping processes, but, regardless of the situation, traditional socialization has not prepared either males or females to be single parents (DeFrain & Eirick, 1981; Wattenburg & Reinhardt, 1979). From the above discussion it is apparent that both single mothers and single fathers report feelings of loneliness, social isolation, and anomie (DeFrain & Eirick, 1981; Hetherington et al.,

1976; Mendes, 1979; Turner & Smith, 1983). In addition, they experience economic depression, conflict with the ex-spouse, and some difficulty in redefining their relationship with their children.

While there is some evidence to suggest that men and women have different experiences in the readjustment process, several common factors seem to exist (Peterson & Cleminshaw, 1980). The *severity of the marital separation crisis* was suggested as one factor affecting the ability of the single parent to adjust to the new role. The degree of emotional stress, despair, separation anxiety, and anger directed toward the ex-spouse is significant. The higher the level of these negative feelings, the more difficult and lengthy the adjustment process is.

The *degree to which the single parent perceives the stigma of divorce as negative* is another factor influencing adjustment. If the single parent has internalized a system of norms that does not include divorce as a deviant life-style, the crisis is moderated. Further, the parent's perception of the new circumstances is a crucial factor. There are added responsibilities for socialization of children, child care, performing domestic tasks, and serving as provider. If the individual views the added role responsibilities as challenging and an opportunity for autonomy and freedom, the role situation is perceived as rewarding as well as obligating. Role overload would not occur, as the demands are offset by rewards.

The *degree of disorganization* in the newly formed family affects the adjustment process. Possession of such qualities as marketable skills, high levels of education, substantial income, and emotional maturity generally facilitate coping with, and may even transcend, the negative consequences of the separation crisis. The *ability to establish and maintain high levels of social participation* provides opportunities for a support network and facilitates reorganization. The *manner in which the family is formed*—through divorce or death— appears to be a major factor in adjustment. A widowed single parent often is given more emotional support, sympathy, and assistance in the single-parent role than is a divorced single parent. But the widowed single parent may be more overwhelmed by role responsibilities than the divorced single parent since the onset of single status is abrupt. The grief over loss of a spouse by death often is heightened by the realization of the roles one must assume. Divorced men, especially, seem to make an easier adjustment than widowers (Gasser & Taylor, 1976; Lewis, 1978).

Children in Single-Parent Families

Approximately 60 percent of all children born in 1986 will spend at least 5 years in a single-mother family and may experience at least two periods of living in a single-parent family during childhood—12 percent because of premarital birth, 40 percent due to divorce, 5 percent because of long-term separation of mother and father, and 2 percent because of death of a parent (Norton & Glick, 1986). Hofferth (1985) suggested that the percentage of black youth who will live with one parent for some time prior to age 18 may be as high as 94 percent.

Effects of divorce on children. The impressive consensus of research on the effects of divorce on children is that divorce results in negative stresses and long-term adjustment of children to continued changes in environment. Widespread behavioral problems of children at the time of separation have been documented. Children of divorce have consistently been found to perform poorly on a wide variety of social, academic, and physical health criteria. Symptoms vary according to the situation and developmental level of children at the time of divorce. Complexities inherent in the adjustment process have been noted (Guidubaldi, Cleminshaw, Perry, Nastasi, & Lightel, 1986). Wallerstein and Kelly (1979) conducted a 10-year study of the effects of divorce on children and described differential outcomes in relation to children's developmental stages at the time of divorce (see Box 7f).

It is now recognized that divorce is not simply a single event—it triggers a chain of events that interact with each other to produce far-reaching effects. The departure of a primary parent is only one of many changes to which a child must adjust. The following studies reflect some of the interrelated factors that affect the adjustment process in children.

Hess and Camara (1979) found that parental harmony was related to the level of stress experienced by the child, and the parent-child relationship was related to children's aggression, social relations, and work effectiveness. Guidubaldi and his associates (1986) also found that parental conflict was related to poor adjustment, especially for boys, and the association was more pronounced at older age levels. Conflict between parents may place the child in a double approach-avoidance conflict in which closeness to one parent introduces the risk of rejection by the other. The child who cannot choose between the two parents, then, is in danger of being disordered (Peterson & Zill, 1986).

Woody, Colley, Schlegelmilch, Maginn, and Balsanek (1984) found six factors to be associated with psychological problems and negative behaviors in children: (1) age of parent, (2) parental use of help in coping with the divorce, (3) stress, (4) parental general symptoms, (5) parental psychosomatic symptoms, and (6) spouse-type relationship. Even when the length of time divorced was controlled, more child symptoms were reported by younger parents, by those who valued and used less help in coping with divorce, by those who had high levels of stress, by those who experienced general or psychosomatic symptoms, and by those who had continuing conflictual communication over spouse-type issues. It was concluded that divorce effects a chain of events that interact and have a far-reaching effect on families.

A large survey of 5-year-old children in England who lived in single-parent families, intact families, and stepfamilies was conducted by Wadsworth, Burnell, Taylor, and Butler (1985). It was found that children in one-parent families had significantly higher antisocial scores than children in two-parent families did. Further, they scored worse on tests of behavior, vocabulary, and visuomotor coordination and were, on the average, more marginally neurotic than children in two-parent families. While children in single-parent families were more likely to live in poor urban neighborhoods and have a young mother with low educational attainment than the other children were, these differences were noted even when social and biological factors were controlled. These researchers concluded that it was

BOX 7f   TYPICAL REACTIONS OF CHILDREN TO DIVORCE

Preschool	School Age	Adolescents
Fear of disruption of nurturance and possible abandonment	May be immobilized by suffering	Becomes either overburdened or encouraged in breaking away from family
Feelings of contributing to divorce	Difficulty obtaining relief	
	Preoccupation with longing for absent parent	Feelings of betrayal
Intense guilt	Inability to use denial as a way of coping	Sorrow
Use of denial as a means of coping		Anxiety about parents' sexuality, loneliness, and regression
	Either avoidance and silence or strong verbal denial of sadness	
Impaired ability to master tasks and secure relief through play		Anger toward parent with whom not allied
	Compulsive behavior	
	Desire for reconciliation	Avoidance
Aggression and acting-out behaviors	Feelings of rejection and abandonment	
Regression to infantile behaviors	Painful loyalty conflicts	
	Displacement of anger to teacher, siblings, peers	
Signs of shock, anger, and depression	Performance in school either suffers or school becomes source of gratification	
	Worry about selves and parents; feelings of shame	
	Demanding and aggressive behaviors	

not the marital status of the mother at the time of birth that made the difference, but rather the situation in which the child lived for the 5 years following birth. These researchers also pointed out that some children in atypical families do well, but many do not. Additional social and educational support could compensate for environmental difficulties.

Stress-producing events (single parenthood, inadequate income, low educational level, conflict with ex-spouse, and others) are cumulative and interactive, producing varying levels of stress for single parents. Single mothers are more likely than single fathers are to experience high stress levels. Hodges, Tierkey, and Buchsbaum (1984) found that cumulative stress was related to the adjustment of children, and that certain stressor events were likely to be related to specific kinds

of adjustment problems. For example, they found that the divorce was predictive of acting out toward parents, distractability, poorer concentration, and aggression in children. Income inadequacy was more predictive of problems than marital status was. Anxiety and depression in children were more pronounced when the mother perceived her income to be inadequate. The researchers concluded that the psychological climate of the home and the economic conditions were more significant in the child's adjustment than was the divorce event itself.

Some research has indicated that the absence of a parent gives single parents an opportunity to develop high-quality interactions with their children; other researchers have found that disruption causes tensions, resentment, and anger for both children and adults, while negatively affecting the parent-child relationship. White, Brinkerhoff, and Booth (1985) studied the effect of marital disruption on children's attachment to parents. They found that children of divorce did not report lower attachment to their custodial parent than respondents from intact families did. Children in single-mother families reported somewhat greater attachment to their mothers than children in intact families did. Those with custodial fathers reported similar attachment to their fathers as did respondents from intact families. But for noncustodial mothers and fathers, child-parent attachment was substantially lower than in intact families. Attachment to noncustodial mothers was about equal to attachment to fathers in intact families. The level of attachment was not found to be related to the age of the child at the time of divorce or to the economic hardship of the family, but it was related to the degree of conflict before and after the divorce, with high levels of conflict reducing the level of attachment. Further, the more frequent the contact with their noncustodial parent, the greater the attachment was.

Research on sex-role development of children in single-parent families has been of interest for some time. Previous studies investigated the effects of father absence with primary concern about an appropriate male model, especially for boys. The absence of a father was seen as an inhibiting factor to appropriate sexual identity and behavior. The importance of a cross-sex model against whom girls can try out their femininity also was emphasized. The importance of surrogate father models was emphasized. Recent research has focused on whether living in a single-parent family stimulates more androgynous attitudes (Richmond-Abbott, 1984). Mothers in Richmond-Abbott's study had relatively liberal sex-role attitudes—more liberal concerning the societal roles for men and women and the assignment of household tasks but less liberal concerning the characteristics of men and women. The pursuit of higher education and occupational choices for women were liberal but political and religious beliefs were more traditional. The higher the education of the mother and the noncustodial father, the more liberal the attitude was. These researchers noted that the children of these mothers followed the same basic patterns as their mothers did. However, boys had more traditional attitudes than did the girls. Further, it was noted that the more liberal attitudes were not necessarily demonstrated in the behaviors of the mothers or the children; the mothers did not interact with their children in a manner that encouraged development of nontraditional skills and actions. Children were likely to receive sex-stereotyped gifts, to perform chores, and to engage in sex-typed activities.

When examining the sex-role development of children in single-parent families, Brenes, Eisenberg, and Helmstadter (1985) predicted that children, especially boys, from single-mother homes as compared to intact homes would be less sex-typed in their toy play but would not differ in gender identity. They found that children from single-mother homes exhibited more knowledge of stereotyped conceptions about sex roles, particularly about the masculine role. These researchers theorized that children without a father may become more sensitive to the dimension of sex appropriateness than children in intact families do. Children in single-mother families tended to be less sex-typed in their choice of toys than the children in two-parent families were. It is important to note, further, that the boys in the single-mother families were not feminized in their play behavior. They were more likely to choose masculine toys and engage in masculine play and only rarely chose feminine toys. It was concluded that the pattern of sex-role adoption of single-parent children is not indicative of gender confusion, and does not differ greatly from that of children from two-parent homes.

Contact with the noncustodial parent has been found to be correlated with better adjustment on social criteria, including productive interaction with peers, less irrelevant talk, less social overinvolvement, and better peer relations. Further, better communication skills, less failure anxiety, higher originality, learning, and academic achievement were found to be associated with contact with noncustodial parents. Better parent-child relationships are facilitated by contact (Guidubaldi et al., 1986; Peterson & Zill, 1986).

As noted earlier, the child-rearing style utilized by parents seems to be related to adjustment. The authoritarian style was found by Guidubaldi and his associates (1986) to be correlated with lower ratings of classroom behavior, including less independent learning, less productive interaction with peers, greater intellectual dependency, more failure anxiety, more negative feelings, more withdrawal and blaming, more inattention, and poorer academic achievement. These adverse effects are especially pronounced for boys. In relation to authoritative parenting, the results were mixed, being associated with some positive behaviors as well as some negative ones. Few significant concurrent relationships between permissive parenting and child adjustment were found. The researchers concluded that child-rearing style is a significant variable in determining postdivorce adjustment. The pattern of relationships varies at different times for boys and girls according to age level.

Parental satisfaction with the parenting of the ex-spouse is related to more indices of adjustment for boys than for girls. Higher IQ, better academic performance, appropriate classroom behavior, better adaptive skills, and fewer problems were facilitated by parental satisfaction with the noncustodial parent. The custodial parent's satisfaction with the parent-child relationship also was important to adequate adjustment. Maternal employment was positively related to the adjustment of girls. It had mixed results for boys—it facilitated peer relations but was negatively related to conduct at school (Guidubaldi et al., 1986).

It was concluded by Guidubaldi and his associates that children from divorced families as a total group performed much more poorly than children from two-parent families on a wide variety of academic, social, and physical health measures. These differences were maintained even when SES was controlled, although family income accounted for much of the academic performance variance. Sex and age level of children in the adjustment process increases the complexity of the situation. Girls, as they develop, tend to function more similarly to children in two-parent families. Males, on the other hand, tend to show an increasing number of differences from

two-parent families, particularly at higher grade levels.

Kinard and Reinherz (1986) examined the effects of marital disruption on academic aptitude and achievement of fourth-grade children. They found that children in recently divorced families were likely to have more problems in certain areas of school performance than those from families who had divorced prior to the child's entrance into school and those from never-divorced families. They had problems with attention, withdrawal, dependency, and hostility. Language, total achievement, and productivity scores were the lowest for the children from recently divorced families. Further, maternal education had a far greater impact on the child's achievement than marital disruption did.

Krein and Biller (1988) examined the relationship of living in a single-parent home to the length of schooling: The more time children spend in one-parent homes, the less schooling they are likely to complete. The largest impact was among white males, with each year spent in a one-parent family reducing eventual education by one-tenth of a year. Thus, with an average of 5.1 years in a single-parent family, a white male would have half a year less schooling than one from an intact family. Black males who spend 8 years on the average in a one-parent family complete .6 years less than those who spend their entire life in a two-parent family. The impact was less significant for girls—none for white girls and only a slight impact on black girls. Child-support payments, the education level of parents (especially the mother), and the amount of reading material in the home were mediating factors among the white subjects but not among the black subjects.

Demo and Acock (1988) reviewed the literature on the impact of divorce on children and isolated these behavioral areas: personal adjustment (self-control, leadership, responsibility, independence, achievement orientation), child's psychological state prior to single-parent status, self-concept, cognitive functioning, interpersonal relationships, and antisocial behavior. They found that the process of adjustment was, indeed, complex, and the empirical evidence on divorce and the effects on children, while inconsistent in places, is punctuated by a number of consistent findings (Demo & Acock, 1988). Most children suffer temporary negative effects in many areas of development, including interpersonal and peer relationships, school performance, and self-esteem, and they exhibit various levels of antisocial behavior. Several mediating factors serve to affect the degree and length of maladjustment: parental harmony, the presence of an additional adult, the sex of the child, and the parents' educational level. Adjustment consistently appears to be adversely affected by continued parental discord—many studies report that children's adjustment is facilitated under conditions of low parental conflict, both prior to and subsequent to divorce. Further, contact with noncustodial parents is important. Research suggests that adjustment problems are more severe and last for longer periods of time among boys. One explanation is that typical postdivorce arrangements are quite different for boys and girls; boys most often have to adjust to living without same-sex parents.

Some studies have found that controlling for SES minimizes differences—when the family has an adequate income, adjustment is facilitated. Parental education seems to be a factor, especially in children's academic achievement, with children whose parents have high levels of education having the advantage. In fact, in some studies maternal education revealed a stronger effect on school performance than marital disruption did. The presence of an additional adult (grandparent, uncle, lover, or friend) in mother-only households has been found to be a factor in reducing antisocial behavior. This suggests that there are some single-mother families who are functionally equivalent to two-parent families. Various family processes change when divorce occurs—daily routines and work schedules are altered, additional demands are imposed on adults and children, and financial conditions may alter living arrangements. The number and kind of changes affect the child's adjustment. While adjustment is affected by the presence or absence of these variables, some psychological problems tend to persist for years, even into adulthood.

Not all the effects on children are negative.

Some researchers view the tendency of children in single-parent families to display more androgynous behavior as a beneficial effect. Skills, competencies, and definitions of gender-appropriate behavior are broadened. Adolescents are frequently characterized as developing greater maturity and feelings of efficacy and an internal locus of control as a result of living in single-parent families.

Many effects of divorce tend to persist for an extended period of time. In Wallerstein's (1985) 10-year follow-up, the preschool children (in their teens at the follow-up) appeared to have fared better than those children who were older at the time of the divorce. Most of these children claimed to have no memories of the intact predivorce family, and the memories they recalled were fragmented and lacked clarity of detail. While at the time many of these children reported being frightened, none mentioned this 10 years later. For 30 percent of the children, the divorce had remained a central aspect of their lives and evoked strong feelings, fears, and profound sadness. They spoke of the loneliness and the continued sense of deprivation within the single-parent or remarried family. At least 25 percent of the children continued to disapprove of the divorce very strongly, but another 25 percent fully approved of the divorce decision. More than half of the children spoke wistfully of life in an intact family.

The diminished protection that children in divorced families experience was expressed in concern for what would happen if their mother died or if their mother and stepfather divorced. Half of the children still had reconciliation fantasies. The children expressed several themes regarding their custodial mothers. At least half indicated closeness, trust, and openness in communication. Many mothers were appreciated for their effort, hard work, and devotion over the years. The children were tuned in to the economic issues, knew about child-support payments, and were aware of financial difficulties. Many of the children expressed concern about the mother's loneliness and emotional well-being and spoke of their desire to rescue her. The concern about growing up and leaving the mother alone, husbandless and childless, was a repeated theme. Some children expressed anger and blame and complained that the mother had not been physically or emotionally available when she was needed. They complained of her selfishness; lack of interest in them; or preoccupation with work, career, or men.

The noncustodial father, regardless of how far away he lived or how often he visited, remained a significant psychological presence in the lives of his children. Relationships to biological fathers and stepfathers were held separate and clearly distinguishable from one another. One third of the children saw their fathers regularly at least once a month, one third visited during extended vacations, and one fourth had contact less than once a year. The frequency of contact was not directly associated with the child's attachment, and it did not predict the child's interest and concern. The need for the absent father seemed to become more intense as children neared adolescence. A powerful impulse to make contact with the absent father, frequently to confide their innermost feelings, was evident, especially with girls. Some children expressed anger toward fathers who had not maintained contact with them or had failed to provide economic support for them. Many worried about the fragile relationship with their noncustodial father and tried to shape their behavior to avoid distressing or offending him. Some worried about their unstable or troubled fathers, and others expressed satisfaction as well as concern about how visits were sandwiched into crowded schedules. Most of the children were performing adequately in school. Many expressed optimism about the future and looked forward to an enduring marriage and children of their own.

The outcomes for the children who were 9 years or older at the time of the divorce were different from those of the younger children (Wallerstein, 1985). These children, at the 10-year follow-up, were between 19 and 29 years of age. Of the 40 interviewed almost half of the young adults were in school full-time. The lack of a high level of schooling, degree of unemployment, and low-level jobs of those employed are striking in that most of the families in the study were middle class. The burden of postsecondary education for the children represented a grave issue.

Sixty-eight percent of the group had engaged in mild to serious illegal activities during adolescence or young adulthood—half were alcohol- or drug-related and 30 percent included assault; burglary; arson; drug dealing; theft; or serious traffic violations, such as drunk driving. Of the 40 young adults, 6 women and 3 men had married. Three of the women married as teenagers, and 3 were pregnant out of wedlock. One quarter of the women had had abortions, and one woman had had two.

The availability of strong feelings, particularly sadness, was evident. The predominant mood attached to looking back was one of regret, restrained sadness, and yearning. There was agreement of a sustained loss. About two-thirds felt that their childhood and adolescence had been significantly burdened by the divorce. They felt that they had missed the protection and nurturance of an intact family and felt needy. They expressed sorrow over their loss. Eighty percent indicated that the divorce continued to hold a central position in their psychological functioning. A small subgroup, about 30 percent, reported feelings of relief about being separated from a tyrannical parent.

Most of the group expressed a desire to avoid their parents' mistakes and to have a lasting marriage. About 30 percent of the young women, although they were attractive and intelligent, were worried about, even despairing and fearful of, being rejected in their search for a man and had great concern about marriage relationships. However, many of these young adults described themselves as having emerged stronger and more independent as a consequence of the divorce. They affirmed they had been placed into positions of responsibility as a result of the divorce and benefitted from it. They reported contributing to the care of household, taking care of younger children, and taking responsibility for themselves at a very young age. Despite the pride of accomplishment, many perceived that the price was too high and that they had been pushed or exploited. They felt that a significant amount of play and school time had been sacrificed. Some of the subjects reported feelings of solidarity and closeness to their siblings and felt that this helped them get through the rough times.

Wallerstein concluded that some psychologi-

BOX 7g   HOW TO HELP CHILDREN ADJUST TO DIVORCE

Discuss family problems with the child. Use simple, honest explanations on the child's level.

Tell the child in advance that a divorce will occur.

Assure the child that he is loved and will continue to be loved by both parents.

Tell the child the primary issues and reasons for the divorce at the level he can understand. Be truthful.

Avoid placing blame for the divorce.

Express positive feelings and confidence about the future.

Do not ask a young child to make the decision concerning which parent will assume custody.

Avoid disrupting the child's routine as much as possible.

Encourage the child to express his feelings and concerns.

Expect the child to feel and express negative emotions.

Avoid arguments concerning money, custody, visitations, and so forth.

Plan for continuous contact with the absent parent and the extended family.

---

cal effects of divorce are long-lasting. Those children who are the youngest at the time of divorce seem to fare better as a result of the fading memories associated with the divorce. Thus they are more likely than older children to be optimistic about the future, and, depending on the mediating factors after divorce, they experience a healthy and happy childhood. It must be emphasized, however, that the children involved in this study were from middle-class backgrounds. The chances that children from poor minority homes will experience positive mediating circumstances are, indeed, rare.

There are a variety of ways that parents and professionals can assist children in adjusting to divorce. Suggestions can be found in Box 7g.

Services and Support for Single-Parent Families

It has been suggested that professionals who work with single-parent families need to help them adopt a "single-parent family model" (Mendes, 1979). In this model the single parent is perceived as a "contributing coordinator" where he or she does for the child what can be managed without undue stress. The remainder of parental functions should be assigned to other competent persons within or outside the family. In this model children, too, are perceived as "contributing coordinators" instead of reactors or recipients. Children should assume some responsibility for contributing resources based on their ability. Parents should be helped to see that they cannot be both father and mother. These single parents need help in weighing the consequences of overburdening themselves by trying to carry out the impossible role of two parents. Family members need assistance in understanding the value of their individual and collective contributions.

It has been suggested that children in single-parent families can be helped by helping their parents (Black, 1979). Parents need help in coping with their own emotions, in feeling worthy again, in working out acceptable relationships with former spouses, and in developing understanding of their children's reactions. The children, then, benefit as the parents become better adjusted. Parents often need training in child management and help in organizing the household.

The development of an adequate and appropriate support system is crucial to single-parent families. This system may be composed of extended family; friends; employment and child-care resources; and community resources such as schools, churches, clinics, or social-service agencies. Families may need help in identifying, contacting, and developing relationships with an appropriate support network. Neighborhood resources would be beneficial and convenient. This kind of support system facilitates the parenting role and is associated with life satisfaction, personal growth, and less distress for both men and women (Hetherington & Camara, 1984). Further, the formation of a new intimate relationship for divorced men and women is a source of support and is particularly important in life satisfaction. The relationship with kin is a complex one. The interaction between the newly singled parent and his or her parents continues, with contact often increasing. Parents are frequently a source of financial and emotional support for the single parent, especially the single mother. The relationship with in-laws usually subsides, at least for the adult, and perhaps even for the children.

Many single parents find that joining organizations, such as Parents Without Partners, Inc., offers an opportunity to share similar concerns, problems, and interests with other single parents. Membership can help to alleviate loneliness and social isolation. Parents Without Partners, founded in 1957, is an international, nonprofit, nonsectarian, educational organization that focuses on children. About 150,000 parents and their children in 1,000 chapters come together to share social, educational, and recreational activities. Emotional stress is often eased by opportunities for companionship. A sense of belonging may be satisfied through involvement in this organization (Parks, 1977).

Several types of services for single parents have been suggested (see Box 7h). In addition, individuals need information about single parenthood and knowledge about rearing children without a co-parent before experiencing this life-style. High school students, both male and female, need to be taught home-making, including budgeting and marketing. Knowledge about child development and criteria for quality alternative child care is of critical importance (Mendes, 1976; Turner & Smith, 1983).

The resources available for children in cop-

ing with divorce and adjusting to a single-parent family have been studied less than those for adults. Resources available to children vary with the sex of the child and his or her developmental level. Older children have access to more out-of-home resources than do younger ones. The peer group can serve as a source of support and gratification. The school, neighborhood, and the workplace (for working adolescents) can help to counter the deleterious effects of an adverse home situation. Boys may not receive as much support as girls do—generally because boys are viewed more negatively by parents, peers, and teachers. Boys confront more negative sanctions, inconsistency, and opposition and less responsiveness to their needs, particularly from divorced mothers. Grandparents offer support to their grandchildren, and where there is a grandmother available, children have shown better adjustment (Hetherington & Camara, 1984).

Professionals developing programs for recently singled parents should have the following goals for these families: to resolve conflict, to reduce the psychological stress felt by family members, to improve parenting skills in managing and setting limits for children's behavior, to establish new coping strategies and methods for adapting to new roles of family members, to provide a network of resources available for continual support, and to help families cope with specific issues (Hetherington & Camara, 1984).

In sum, divorce clearly has an impact on children and requires moderate to significant adjustment. Research has indicated that the first year following divorce seems to be particularly stressful for both children and their parents, with parent-child relationships being less than optimal. However, over time the majority of children become socially and psychologically better-adjusted, depending on their age and sex at the time of the divorce and on family characteristics such as parental harmony, the parents' educational level and SES, the family processes, and the presence or absence of another adult in the home. While some negative effects have been seen in children's personal adjustment, their self-concepts, their cognitive functioning, their social behaviors, and their interpersonal relationships, some positive effects also have been found.

BOX 7h   SERVICES NEEDED BY SINGLE PARENTS

More part-time work for mothers and fathers who wish to combine parenting and work or who desire to supplement their income.

Adequate child-care services that are affordable, convenient to either work or home, have an extended day, provide drop-in care, and have after-school care for school-age children.

Programs that are supportive of single-parent families can be beneficial to both parents and children.

Transportation for chidren to child-care centers.

Child care in shopping centers.

Babysitting cooperatives.

Organized, registered housekeeper services to provide quality help when needed.

Increased tax deductions for child care and housekeepers.

Greater acceptance of single fathers in public housing.

"Big Sister" programs for fathers rearing daughters.

School holiday programs by public schools and child-care centers.

Increased counseling services for parents and children.

Flex-time by employers to allow more flexible hours for work and family sick leave benefits. It is clear that the demands of work and family must be integrated more successfully for single-parent families to survive.

Additional supportive organizations, especially for low-income families.

Additional research on needs of single parents and how institutions and policies can be altered to meet these needs.

Sources: Crossman & Adams, 1980; DeFrain & Eirick, 1981; Orthner, Brown, & Ferguson, 1976; Schlesinger, 1978; Turner & Smith, 1983; Wattenberg & Reinhardt, 1979. For the complete bibliographic citations, see the References at the end of this chapter.

Various methodological problems with the research have been cited that impose limitations on conclusions and provide the basis for inconsistent findings. Failure to use representative samples, to control for variations in the single-parent structures (military, death, or permanent separation) and for income or social class, committing the "ecological fallacy" (assuming that relationships at the aggregate level apply at the individual level), and failure to use longitudinal designs are methodological problems that need to be corrected in future research.

CHILD CUSTODY

Child-custody laws have undergone a variety of changes throughout history. Prior to the 1800s fathers were given custody because they were better able to support children, and when they were denied custody, their financial responsibility to support the children terminated. In the early 1900s, however, it was recognized that fathers were responsible for their children even if they did not have custody. As the women's movement progressed and more women entered the labor force, greater attention was given to the mother's role in caring for her children. This gave rise to the "tender years" philosophy—when children are young, the mother is the preferred custodial parent; but for older children equal rights of mothers and fathers are considered. More recently the trend has shifted from favoring mothers (Howell & Toepke, 1984), and several courts have found the "tender years" presumption to violate fathers' constitutional rights of equal protection (Derdeyn & Scott, 1984).

BOX 7i · SUMMARY OF CHILD-CUSTODY PROVISIONS

Provision

Child's welfare and best interests are prime factors in determining custody

Passed the Uniform Child Custody Jurisdiction Act (Texas and Massachusetts are the exceptions)—an attempt to encourage cooperation between courts of different states

Neither parent preferred over other by custody

Wishes of child considered

Parental wishes, parent-child relationships, child's relationship with other significant persons, child's social adjustment, mental and physical health of all involved are considered

Consideration of which parent is most likely to promote child's relationship with noncustodial parent

Visitation rights of grandparents

Visitation of other relatives in addition to grandparents

Joint custody

Access to child's school, health, or other personal records

After reaching a certain age child allowed to choose parent with whom she lives

Psychological investigation may be ordered by court

Parental conduct not affecting relationship with child not considered

Source: Adapted from Howell, R. J., & Toepke, K. E. (1984). Summary of the child custody laws for the fifty states. *American Journal of Family Therapy, 12*(2), 56–60.

Equality in custody adjudication has emerged in the form of the concept of acting in the "best interests" of the child.

The notion of "best interests" of the child is included in all state codes but is often difficult to determine. It is considered to be the most important consideration in a custody suit. It has been interpreted to mean that a child has a right to a loving, stable home with adequate provision for her maintenance, education, and continued contact with the noncustodial parent. The same standard is applied when determining the frequency and circumstances with which the noncustodial parent will be permitted to exercise visitation privileges with the child (Howell & Toepke, 1984; Jones, 1984).

In the absence of national standards for custody arrangements, individual states have developed a variety of child-custody options. Box 7i shows the range of provisions considered by the courts in awarding custody.

In general the custody of children involves both physical custody—the actual day-to-day care and control of children—and legal custody—the arrangements regarding the child's education, religious training, and medical care (Hagen, 1987). These two elements of custody may be the responsibility of one or both parents. *Sole* custody, the most prevalent option, awards the child to one parent, usually the mother, who maintains both physical and legal custody. *Divided* custody, also referred to as *alternating* custody, divides control and responsibility between the two parents, who each have ultimate control when the child is in his or her physical custody. Each parent has the child for part of the year or on alternating years, with the noncustodial parent having visitation rights. *Split* custody apportions the children between the parents with each having ultimate control over the children in his or her sole custody. The other parent has visitation rights with noncustodial children. The most recent custody option is *joint* custody (Hagen, 1987).

Contacts with Noncustodial Parents

Most noncustodial parents are fathers because in 80 percent of divorce cases the mother is awarded custody of minor children, and in 10 percent the father is awarded custody. Frequent paternal contact seems to be important for successful adjustment of the child to divorce and for continued optimal development. However, frequent contact is beneficial only if it is in the context of low interparental conflict, if the father continues to provide financial resources to the mother, if the father can serve as a buffer against the effects of a pathogenic mother-child relationship, or if visitation mitigates some of the mother's stress due to single parenting. Other factors positively related to father's frequency of contact are nonminority status, a higher level of education and income, residential propinquity, the assurance of children's acceptance of them, not remarrying, the mother's positive attitude toward the father, and the ability to adapt to the logistics of visitation scheduling. Those fathers who have invested in their children prior to the divorce are likely to visit frequently as a means of continuing this relationship or to visit infrequently because of the discomfort involved when contact is reestablished (Kurdek, 1986).

Kurdek (1986) found that noncustodial fathers who rated high in preseparation conflict, as compared to low conflict, visited their children less regularly and were less regular in their payment of child support. Regardless of the preseparation conflict, however, paternal involvement was related to the degree of investment in the child but not to the child's age, gender, or length of separation. In low-conflict families, higher paternal involvement was evident when there was low environmental change and the child had well-developed interpersonal understanding skills.

Perhaps the least studied and least understood single parents are mothers without custody, an estimated population of 1,200,000. These mothers are the object of curiosity and, frequently, of disdain. To many it is odd that a mother is not rearing her child after a marriage dissolves, and the assumption is that she is unfit. Greif (1987) conducted a national survey of noncustodial mothers and found that adjustment to the role varied greatly, and few generalizations could be made. One third of the mothers seemed to be satisfied or comfortable with their status, one third had mixed reactions, and one third were dissatisfied and uncomfortable. Those mothers comfortable in their role reported the most satisfaction with their children and believed the children were better off living with their fathers. Further, those mothers comfortable with noncustody were likely to have a satisfactory social life, were less lonely, were more satisfied with their children's progress, were satisfied with their careers, and were likely to give their ex-husbands high ratings as fathers. Factors that significantly related to the mothers' feelings of comfort with noncustody included voluntarily giving up custody, sharing the blame for the divorce, reluctance about moving children, a low level of stress during the divorce process and custody division, lack of religious affiliation, and the ability to alter her financial status. In other words, acceptance and comfort of the role of non-custodial mother is related to a variety of other positive aspects of her life. The most important factor, however, was a positive relationship with her children.

Custodial Parents

Ambert (1986) investigated differences in children's behavior toward custodial mothers and fathers. She found that custodial fathers reported better child behavior toward them than custodial mothers did. The children of custodial fathers verbalized their appreciation for the father, but those with custodial mothers did so only rarely. The socioeconomic status of the mothers was an important factor, with the higher SES mothers perceiving significantly fewer problems with their children than the lower SES mothers. The author concluded that there is interaction and feedback between social resources and children's behavior and parental behavior in single-parent families. The feedback is mediated by the sex and the socioeconomic status of the custodial parent.

In Turner's (1984) study of fathers with custody, it was found that there were differences in fathers who sought custody at the time of the divorce and those who waited for an average of 2 years after the breakup. Specifically, those fathers seeking custody at the time of divorce were more likely than other fathers to have been involved with their children from birth and continued to maintain close relationships with their children. Further, they were more likely to have

felt that the marriage was initially good and were remorseful about the breakup.

There is no consensus among state legislatures, as well as among the legal and mental health professions, regarding the definition of joint custody. The distinguishing element of legal joint custody is that both parents are empowered by the court to retain equal rights, authority, and responsibility for the care and control of children. Neither parent's rights or authority is superior. Joint custody does not determine physical custody, but it allows parents to plan creatively the residential arrangements that will best meet the child's needs (Elkin, 1987). Joint custody does not mean a rigid 50/50 division of residence. While the actual physical arrangements are varied, joint custody has been defined as any form of custody or visitation arrangement that allows both parents to have adequate and normal day-to-day interaction with the children and provides that each adult participate in both the responsibilities and the rewards of child rearing. Time-sharing arrangements have been found to vary according to the particular needs of children and parents. Some children alternate between parents' homes on an equal-time basis. Other families have a more traditional arrangement, in which children spend the week with one parent and weekends with the other parent. The children's ages and school situations, as well as the parents' employment and availability, must be considered when planning an appropriate physical custody arrangement. The concept of joint custody has been referred to by other names, including shared parenting, dual parenting, co-parenting, shared custody, joint parenting, and co-custody.

Joint custody has become increasingly more popular since the mid-1970s. The advantages and disadvantages of joint custody are identified in Box 7j.

Initially, joint custody was viewed by judges as an option only when both parents were stable, desired the arrangement, and were willing to cooperate. As the enthusiasm for this alternative has increased, these criteria are receiving less attention. Many states now permit a judge to order joint custody when only one parent desires it or even when neither has sought the arrangement. Some states require that joint custody be the first

BOX 7j ADVANTAGES AND DISADVANTAGES OF JOINT CUSTODY

Advantages   **Disadvantages**

For the Parents

Allows judges to escape the difficult application of a sex-neutral "best interest" standard

Possible negative criticism from society

Neither parent is a winner or a loser—there is equal power and authority between the parents

Personal sacrifices necessary—considerable effort must be expended to make arrangement work

The self-esteem of neither parent suffers

Must tolerate differences in values and the child-rearing styles of ex-spouse

There is no discrimination between the sexes

Must be geographically close to ex-spouse

Promises that both parents will maintain contact with the child—and eliminates the demeaning, alienating, and artificial concept of "visitation"

Discourages adjudication of the custody issue

Decreases the burden of single parenthood

Provides for self-determination—parents make the decisions about their lives and their children's lives

Both parents have more time for themselves and feelings of being overburdened or trapped are decreased

For the Child

Promises that the child will continue significant contact with both parents—he will have two functioning homes rather than one home and a visitor to the other

Discontinuity of parent-child relationships and surroundings

Reduces conflict over divided loyalties

Difficulty relating to and profiting from two psychological parents

May feel less rejected and abandoned and fear of losing a parent is diminished

Relating to two authority figures

Reduces risk of losing contact with kin network, particularly grandparents

Possible difficulty in maintaining peer contacts and making school arrangements; having cherished possessions accessible

Reduces child's fantasies about each parent

consideration in every case involving minor children. Some experts view this trend as troubling. Since only about 10 percent of custody cases involve parents who are so antagonistic that they cannot resolve their conflicts short of litigation, encouraging the court to impose joint custody on one or both such parents might perpetuate conflict. A parent might approve joint custody even if he does not desire it for fear of appearing uncooperative, thereby chancing the loss of sole custody (Derdeyn & Scott, 1984).

While joint custody has enjoyed rather rapid acceptance, research on the arrangement remains limited. Early investigations relied on personal accounts and case histories. More recently, data have revealed a wide variety of parenting arrangements and relationships among joint-custody parents. The myth that all joint-custody parents are amicable or that they share responsibility equally for their children has been destroyed. Some evidence indicates that children are more satisfied, at least for a while, with joint-custody than with sole-custody arrangements, even though they find it burdensome to divide their time between two homes. Bowman and Akrons (1985) found that joint-custody fathers were significantly more involved in parenting than noncustodial fathers were. Joint-custody fathers had significantly more contact with their children; they rated themselves as more highly involved in activities with their children; and they reported greater sharing of parental responsibilities with their former wives than noncustodial fathers did. It was not known, however, whether those fathers who were more involved prior to divorce chose joint custody, whether the joint-custody arrangement encouraged more involvement, or whether the involvement was a result of a combination of the two factors.

Ilfeld, Ilfeld, and Alexander (1982) found that the relitigation rates for joint-custody families was one half that of exclusive custody families, suggesting that joint custody may be a more beneficial arrangement in terms of reduced parental conflict. Some research has indicated that boys, particularly school-age and adolescent boys, have fewer behavior problems when there is a joint-custody arrangement versus maternal custody (Shiller, 1986). Further, joint-custody

parents had a higher level of self-esteem than did maternal physical-custody parents.

Guidelines for joint custody should be based on child-development theory and research. Two important factors influencing the arrangements are the ages of the children and the general geographic location of parents. The younger the child, the more predictable and frequent the contact with both parents should be. During the infancy and toddlerhood stages, time away from the primary home should be short. A predictable and consistent schedule for preschoolers is important also. As children move into the school-age years, more contact with the noncustodial parent seems beneficial, but the contact must be determined around the child's school activities. Adolescents want more time to be with peers, but supervision and guidance must be provided as the child is allowed to separate from the family. Equitable time-sharing is more difficult when parents do not reside in the same community. If at all possible, both parents should reside in the same general community during the child's early years (birth to school age). When parents live in different communities, maintaining frequent phone contact, exchanging letters and photos, and a general willingness to share in the inconvenience of transportation are recommended.

Elkin (1987) provided the criteria for making joint custody work and identified some negative factors that prevent it from being a viable alternative for some divorcing families (see Box 7k).

The limited empirical data available suggest that, for those parents who choose the option of joint custody, it appears to be a workable and satisfactory arrangement that permits both parents to continue their parenting roles and relationships after divorce. It involves, however, commitment, cooperation, and trust from parents. The vast majority of empirical investigations on joint custody have been conducted with middle- or upper-middle-class families. Little research has been conducted concerning the cost of joint custody. Since joint custody requires the maintenance of two separate homes or apartments, the cost is not insignificant and potentially represents a major barrier to joint custody. In some states joint custody has been found to

---

BOX 7k   PARENTAL CHARACTERISTICS FOR JOINT CUSTODY

Criteria

Commitment to making joint custody work because of love for child and desire to be involved in his life

A clear understanding of their role in the joint custody plan and a willingness to negotiate differences

Ability to give priority to children's needs and arrange their life-styles to accommodate these needs

Ability to separate spousal and parental roles

Possession of a reasonable level of communication and willingness to cooperate

Negative Characteristics

History of addiction in one or both parents

Family violence (spousal and/or child abuse)

Child neglect

Mental pathology

History of parental conflict, particularly concerning child rearing

Inability to differentiate parental needs from the child's needs

Children who are unresponsive toward joint custody

History of family disorganization

Opposition of both parents to joint custody

Logistics mitigating against a joint custody plan

Source: Adapted from Elkin, M. (1987). Joint custody: Affirming that parents and families are forever. *Social Work, 32*(1), 18–24.

---

conflict with the AFDC eligibility requirements—namely, that a dependent child must be deprived of parental support or care. The issue of child support becomes a complex one for joint custody because the tax code is not designed for joint-custody arrangements.

Future research must document the effects of joint custody on parenting practices and on children, and longitudinal data are essential. Further, more research is needed on joint custody in low-income and minority families. What may be a positive arrangement for white middle-class parents may not be for other families (Hagen, 1987). Until further information about joint custody and its viability for a variety of families is available, these arrangements must be thoroughly explored with caution by the courts and other professionals working with families.

BLENDED FAMILIES

THE STEPDAUGHTER

Tension in the air,
*   unease,*
I'm on my toes.
My stepdaughter is visiting.
I like her—
*   that's not the issue.*
It's this tension in the air.
After all these years
*   we still test each other.*
We evaluate.
We are judgmental.
Does it ever stop?
Will we someday
*   take each other for granted,*

accept one another
as women of the same family?
I hope so,
    but I don't know
    how to make it happen
    now.

Natasha Josefowitz*

The blended family is one in which either or both parents bring with them children from a previous marriage (Hetherington & Camara, 1984). By definition a blended family cannot exist without children (Knaub & Hanna, 1984). A common name for this type of family structure is stepfamily. The term *stepfamily* does not appear in the dictionary, but terms for individual family members do. The terms *stepmother* and *stepfather* merely imply the occupation of the mother's or father's position by virtue of marriage. There is no explanation of the roles or responsibilities that either is to perform. The old English term *steop,* from which the present prefix *step-* is probably derived, means "bereaved" or "orphaned" (*American College Dictionary,* 1966; *World Book Dictionary,* 1976). Therefore the term *stepparent* may be appropriate when the death of a parent occurs, but in the case of divorce, the adult is an additional parent rather than a replacement.

The phenomenon of stepfamilies is certainly not new, but a quantitative increase and qualitative changes have in the last decade taken place in this family system (Ambert, 1986; Teachman & Heckert, 1985). As children we enjoyed such stories as "Hansel and Gretel," "Snow White and the Seven Dwarfs," and "Cinderella," all of which depicted a wicked and cruel stepmother. The stepfamily concept dates at least to Greek mythology, and stories about this family structure are found worldwide (Visher & Visher, 1978).

In order to avoid the negative connotations of the label *stepfamily,* this family form has been referred to as the reconstituted, blended, merged, remarried, multimarried, sequential, recoupled, or combined family (Jenkins, 1978;

Kent, 1980; Visher & Visher, 1978). We have chosen to use the term *blended family* in our discussion concerning parenting in this family structure.

Blended families vary both in composition and in the manner in which they are formed. The most frequent combination is a mother, her children, and a stepfather. But the family may be composed of a stepmother, father, and his children; or a mother and father may bring together two sets of children. Thus the many variations of blended families provide complex family environments—structurally, interpersonally, and emotionally. This complexity distinguishes blended families from other family forms and is a major cause of difficulty for its members' adjustment and adaptation. Previous research has tended to ignore this complexity. It has been estimated that there are three times more stepfathers than stepmothers. In the past most blended families were formed because of the death of a spouse. Today, however, the primary reasons are the high rate of divorce, increasing numbers of children affected by divorce, and the large percentage of people who remarry. The rate of remarriage has almost matched the divorce rate, with 83 percent of divorced men and 80 percent of divorced women remarrying, most within 5 years after divorce (Clingempeel, Brand, & Ievoli, 1984). In the case of divorce, more mothers receive custody of their children than fathers do. This accounts for the predominance of blended households composed of mothers, their children, and stepfathers (Ambert, 1986; Buehler, Hogan, Robinson, & Levy, 1986). One study found that the biological mother was present in 92 percent of the households (Wadsworth, Burnell, Taylor, & Butler, 1985).

Blended families represent the most common alternative family structure, about one in every five households (Clingempeel et al., 1984). One in every six children in two-parent households lives with one biological parent and a stepparent (Norton & Glick, 1986). Approximately 16 percent of all children in the United States, or about 7 million, are living with a stepparent (Fine, 1986; Knaub & Hanna, 1984). Further, an unknown number of the 20 percent of American children residing in single-parent households

*Josefowitz, N. *Is this where I was going?* New York: Warner Books, 1983, p. 102. Reprinted by permission.

BOX 71 MYTHS REGARDING THE BLENDED FAMILY

1. The blended family is a nuclear family that has been recreated and functions in the same manner as a nuclear family. Since a separation has occurred in one or both original nuclear families, the newly merged family becomes the nuclear family with a mother, father, and children.

2. The blended family is a deviant or pathological family. This myth has persisted because of a general tendency by society to recognize only the nuclear family as the acceptable family form, due in part to philosophical or religious beliefs concerning divorce and remarriage. In the past, persons who divorced were considered deviants, and divorce is the predominant cause in forming blended families.

3. The stepparent instantly adjusts to and loves his or her stepchildren and will love all children in the family equally.

4. When the blended family is formed as a result of death of a spouse, rather than divorce, stepparenting is easier.

5. Stepchildren are easier to get along with when they are not living in the home.

Sources: Jacobson, D. S. (1979, May). Stepfamilies: Myths and realities. *Social Work*, pp. 230–233; Kent, M. O. (1980). Remarriage: A family systems perspective. *Journal of Contemporary Social Work, 61*(3), 146–153; Visher, E. B., & Visher, J. S. (1978). Common problems of stepparents and their spouses. *American Journal of Orthopsychiatry, 48*(2), 252–262.

---

have a stepparent who is married to their non-custodial parent. In the 1990s estimates are that 25–35 percent of all children will be a part of a stepfamily before their 18th birthdays (Ganong & Coleman, 1987).

Myths

In the 1970s much of the literature emphasized the myths that were commonly held regarding blended families (see Box 71). There has been ample evidence to refute most of these myths. The blended family is a unique family with different organization and integration processes. Further, it has been concluded that blended families differ from other family forms in their structure, boundaries, roles, mythology, negotiation processes, member autonomy, and family affect. Blended families, unlike nuclear households, have more ''permeable'' boundaries, representing an open system (see Figure 7–3). There is an absence of common household locus of parental authority and economic subsistence, creating divided affections and loyalties of the children. Many of the shared experiences, symbols, and rituals that helped maintain the psychological boundaries of the first marriage are missing in the new family (Cherlin, 1978; Kent, 1980; Visher & Visher, 1978, 1979). Amato (1987), investigating family processes in stepparent, single-parent and nuclear families, found that family cohesion was notably lower in stepfamilies than in intact families. This may reflect lingering sources of tension in the family, or it may be that children in stepfamilies have more outside interests and social contacts than do children in intact families. Dahl, Cowgill, and Asmundsson (1987) also reported differences in family cohesion and a sense of belonging between intact and blended families. She found that while attachments may be warm, they are less intense than in intact families. Boundaries in stepfamilies overlapped with families of other parents whether the noncustodial parent was deceased, remarried, or single. It was concluded that it takes 3 to 5 years for family members to develop a sense of belonging. In those families with adolescents, it takes longer because their normal developmental separation tasks take precedence over the need to integrate.

There is at least twice as much clinical literature about blended families as there is evidence

FIGURE 7-3 Boundaries of Nuclear and Blended Families

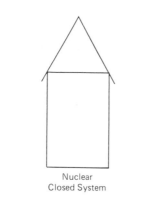

Nuclear
Closed System

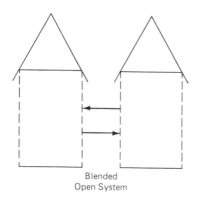

Blended
Open System

indicated that there is a greater acceptance and understanding of blended families than in the past, and present research focuses on testing conclusions and expanding concepts of previous studies (Ganong & Coleman, 1986). Some experts contend that the breadth of research on stepparenting is yet to be undertaken (Ambert, 1986).

Roles of Stepparents

Earlier research indicated that the absence of well-defined, appropriate, and acceptable roles for stepparents clearly distinguishes blended families from nuclear families. The role definitions of stepparents in this society are both poorly articulated and imply contradictory functions of "parents," "stepparents," and "nonparents." A stepparent cannot totally assume the role of father or mother; he or she is a nonparent. Some of the most obvious roles of natural fathers are those that are biological, financial, and educational. Stepfathers cannot assume a biological role; they frequently share the financial responsibilities with the natural father; and they certainly share socialization of the child simultaneously or temporally. The three roles (parent, stepparent, and nonparent) in most cases are interwoven, and the question "How much should I parent?" seems to persist (Cherlin, 1978; Fast & Cain, 1966; Kompora, 1980; Visher & Visher, 1978; Walker & Messinger, 1979).

In nuclear families, roles are more or less assigned to the individual without reference to differences or abilities, but in blended families roles are left open to be filled through competition and individual effort. When the roles are assigned, they usually are roles that are more appropriate for natural parents than for stepparents—a parent is supposed to love, support, and protect the child, and a parent has the right to expect love and respect in return. The role of stepparent, then, is likely to be incongruent with actual sentiments (Walker & Messinger, 1979). The lack of appropriate labels for the stepparenting role has negative consequences for family functioning and is an indication of lack of institutional support for the role (Cherlin, 1978; Kompora, 1980; Walker & Messinger, 1979). The complex and contradictory functions

from empirical studies. This fact has contributed to common negative stereotypic beliefs that blended families are fraught with problems and need assistance (Ganong & Coleman, 1986). Much of the earlier literature compared stepfamily processes and relationships to those in nuclear families, with the implicit belief that stepparent-child relations should be similar to those in intact families; and if they were not, they were negative. Some of the earlier studies used self-report perceptions, and significant differences in processes and relationships were found between blended and nuclear families. Other research was merely descriptive. More recent research has led experts to conclude that comparisons of blended and intact families are nonproductive and inappropriate since the blended family functions entirely differently from nuclear families. The research in the 1980s has

of the stepparent role can be illustrated by such proposed labels as "nonparent," "co-parent," "acquired parent," "Mom II," or "Dad II."

In their study of stepfamilies, Dahl and her associates (1987) found that stepparents were usually referred to by their first names by older children. When kinship terms were used they were varied, and family members expressed uncertainty of what label to use and felt awkward with most labels. Children used the label *step* more than the adults did.

In general, previous research has pointed out the lack of information on how stepfamilies organize and define parental and stepparental roles, the lack of institutionalized norms, and stress resulting from this ambiguity. Individuals lack opportunities for learning the role of stepparent, and there has not been a clear course of action indicating when stepparents do or do not perform a certain role (Giles-Sims, 1984).

Remarriage, as does divorce, represents a period of transition in which family roles, rules, and relationships are redefined and new patterns of resource allocations are established. The first year or so following remarriage tends to be the most difficult (Buehler et al., 1986; Dahl et al., 1987). Recent research indicates that there is still confusion about the role stepparents should assume. It is clear that the stepparent role is distinct from the parent role in some respects. The role must be developed over a period of time and, to a degree, earned. There are no societal norms to assist stepparents in this development. It appears that stepparent roles and responsibilities vary widely and seem to take longer to work out than do stepsibling roles. Months of trial and error by most stepparents are needed when many roles, such as consultant, coach, mediator, and friend, are tried (Dahl et al., 1987).

Giles-Sims (1984) investigated three aspects of parent roles in blended families, expectations of members, typical or modal behaviors, and sanctions associated with nonperformance of role expectations. Of the respondents in the study, 96 percent felt that husband and wife should share equally in caring for and rearing children from the present marriage, whereas only 59 percent said that they should share equally for children of the wife's prior marriage, and 52 percent desired equal responsibility for children of the husband's prior marriage. When asked who actually made decisions, 70 percent of husbands and wives made decisions together for the "ours" children, and 27 percent reported that the wife made more decisions. Only 20 percent shared decisions concerning children from the husband's prior marriage and 29 percent from the wife's prior marriage. These findings indicate that there is an important gap between expectations and actual parental role performance. More than 70 percent of the sample in the Giles-Sims (1984) study stated that stepparents should be sanctioned for refusing to bring up stepchildren. However, the sanction for this role was not as strong as for the parental role (93 percent).

The inconsistency among these three dimensions of the stepparent role indicates that role ambiguity remains a problem. Whether or not stepparent roles are becoming more institutionalized or in what particular ways they are changing is not known. It appears that further research is needed before roles of stepparents become clearly defined. See Box 7m for suggestions stepparents can use when developing the stepparent role.

Legal issues relating to stepparent roles. Because of the increase in the number of blended families, it is likely that new laws explicitly related to these families will be adopted. Unfortunately, there is little empirical evidence to assist policy makers at the present time. The research that has been conducted on blended families, for the most part, has not addressed questions relevant to the development of law. Traditionally, laws governing domestic relations have been left to the states. Most of the states do not require stepparents to support stepchildren financially. Only 14 states have statutes that directly obligate stepparents to support stepchildren, and typically the obligation imposed is more limited than that imposed on a biological parent (Ramsey, 1986). For example, the stepparent may not be liable for support unless the child is living with the stepparent or unless the child will become a public charge.

The majority of states also have the common-law doctrine of *in loco parentis* which can be a source of financial support, although it is not permanent. The stepparent relationship alone

---

BOX 7m   SUGGESTIONS FOR DEVELOPING STEPPARENT ROLE

Allow ample time to work out grieving for old relationships and restructuring new ones

Know yourself and family members

Work to help each family member find his or her place in new family

Develop a distant but cordial relationship with each partner's ex-spouse and their new partners

If possible, move to a new household, or renovate the old, so new spouse and stepchildren have opportunity to establish own territory

Communication, negotiation, compromise, joint decision making, respect, and acceptance of what cannot be changed is essential

Understand the legal obligations involved with the new marriage—wills, child support, and/or alimony

Attempt mutual courtesy but do not expect stepchild's love

Respect special biological bond between biological parent and child

Source: Adapted from Dahl, A., Cowgill, K., & Asmundsson, R. (1987). Life in remarriage families. *Social Work, 32*(1), 40–44.

---

does not establish an *in loco parentis* relationship, but one can be established if the stepparent assumes parental responsibilities. Since this relationship is voluntary, it can be terminated at any time. Although the general common-law rule is that the stepparent's income should not be taken into account when making a child-support award, a number of states have begun to allow the stepparent's income to be considered. Except for the broad reach of the policy toward AFDC children, stepfamilies, for the most part, have not been singled out for special treatment by the federal government or by the states. As stepparents receive greater recognition as financial resources for children, and as a group who needs formal recognition for their position, statutes explicitly related to them will be developed.

Ramsey and Masson (1985) identified four major issues that should be considered when defining the scope of the stepparent financial obligation: (1) the apportionment of resources between natural and stepparent and between natural and stepchildren; (2) the amount of contact between stepparents and stepchild; (3) the financial obligation of the stepparent when the marriage to the natural parent ends; and (4) whether a stepparent should be obligated to sup-

port a stepchild only if the child would become a public charge without the support. It is clear that the financial role of stepparents is an intricate part of other aspects of the stepparent role. How does financial support relate to contact with the stepparent and with the natural parent? How does it affect the psychological boundaries of the new family? How does financial support by the stepparent affect the relationship of the natural parent and his or her ex-spouse? It appears, then, that research that explores the relationship between stepfamily processes and support could be beneficial in developing support requirements and in setting support standards. Further, measuring perceptions of stepfamilies regarding support and stepfamilies' attitudes toward stepparent rights are needed (Ramsey, 1986).

Spousal Relationships

Remarriage reduces many of the stresses experienced by custodial parents following divorce. Concerns about finances, task overload, and household disorganization may diminish when single parents, especially mothers, remarry (Hetherington & Camara, 1984). In their study of stepfamilies, Dahl and her associates (1987) found that both men and women reported many positive feelings, as well as some problems, associated with the remarriage. Husbands and wives reported that sharing feelings and experiences about their previous marriages and divorces during their courtship was important to the sense of having common bonds. Good parenting ability was mentioned as a reason for selecting the partner, because having someone who could understand and assist in the care of the children was important. Day-to-day care of the children was shared by both parents, but major issues tended to be handled by biological parents. A major factor in marital satisfaction was the way in which the spouse related to the children.

Reports of what was positive in the marriage indicated that women felt less lonely, were better off financially, and enjoyed sharing their lives, whereas the men reported liking the intimate communication in the remarriage and feeling understood. Women felt they were more independent, freer, and more trusting than they were in the previous marriage. They also felt a greater sense of closeness and mutuality with their mates than they did with their previous husbands. Being with a caring mate, working as a team, and having a home were also cited as positive factors in the remarriage. Amato (1987) reported that remarriage often increases the standard of living, promotes greater feelings of self-esteem and well-being in the parents, and provides compensatory emotional support and companionship for stepchildren when noncustodial parents fail to maintain contact with them.

Stepmothers

Previous research has indicated stepmothering to be more difficult than stepfathering and greater acceptance by children of stepfathers than of stepmothers. Historically the stepmother has had negative press, and she has had to combat the wicked and cruel stepmother myth. Subsequent research indicated, however, that only a small percentage of stepmothers actually rejected their stepchildren. These attitudes toward stepmothering have been explained partly by the fact that stepmothers spend more time with the children, thus incurring more opportunity for disharmony

because of proximity and the nature of the role. In addition it has been assumed that children in our society have been closer to their mothers, and therefore no one could follow in the steps of a natural mother easily (Bernard, 1956; Duberman, 1973; Kompora, 1980; Visher & Visher, 1978).

Another problem emphasized in earlier literature on stepmothers was the failure of stepchildren and society in general to accept their performance as substitute mothers. It was reported that behavior often accepted in a natural mother is criticized in a stepmother. She has to be better than a natural mother in order to be considered good. The existence of the wicked stepmother myth puts her on the defensive, and people are looking for evidence to corroborate it (Bernard, 1956). Sometimes the stepmother is viewed by her stepchildren and others as the person responsible for the breakup of the first marriage. Frequently, problems during children's adjustments to the blended family are attributed to her rather than to the divorce and the readjustment to a new family life-style. She is not accepted; not trusted; and, at times, considered "armed and dangerous" (Wagner, 1980). Box 7n identifies the predictable stages of stepmothering.

If a woman becomes a stepmother and she has sufficient ego strength and the genuine support of her husband, the relationship with the stepchildren can grow into a mutually satisfying and enriching one. If, on the other hand, she has a shaky self-esteem and is in need of support and her husband consciously or unconsciously chooses her to "mother" him rather than his children, the relationship is sure to become problematic. In addition, if he has unrealistic expectations of her ability to love his children instantly, mother them, or discipline them, her difficulties in developing an appropriate relationship are increased (McClenaghan & Most, 1978; Shulman, 1972).

Any mother's ability to give and relate to her child is at least partially dependent on the nurturing she receives from her spouse. A stepmother is even more dependent on, and in need of, her husband's support. She is a newcomer to an already formed relationship between father and child and may be seen as both rescuer and in-

---

BOX 7n   PREDICTABLE STAGES OF STEPMOTHERING

Enthusiastic. We're all going to live happily ever after.

Sadder but wiser. This isn't a cinch after all. But anything worth doing takes time. It's all going to work out just fine.

Hopeful: If I just keep on smiling, they'll love me.

Wary: Something is really wrong. Is it just me? Am I crazy?

Hurt: I have been treating this child as if he were my own, and I don't even get a "thank you."

Confused: I don't really hate him, do I? I'd love to see him, but does it have to be this weekend?

Ambivalent: If that child says one more word to me, I'll kill him. But first I think I'll bake his favorite cookies.

Angry: I'm sick and tired of this.

Hostile: It's me or that child. My spouse will have to decide.

Source: Goldenberg, I. (1978, September). Instant parent: How to deal with stepchildren. *Harper's Bazaar*, pp. 230–233. (Cited by Kalter, 1978, p. 330.)

---

truder. The stepmother may feel she has to make up for past hurts. Because the stepmother's role and status are so dependent on the support of her husband, the level of his self-confidence is important. If he is a passive, weak, and exclusively dependent man, he often betrays his wife. By virtue of passivity he avoids the areas of significant interaction with the child. This position allows him to criticize his wife no matter what she does. Thus the stepmother is cast into the role of disciplinarian, and the father—by default—becomes the softer, kinder person. The stepmother's predicament makes her feel worthless and angry. The anger is usually turned against the child, and a vicious circle begins (Schulman, 1972).

No doubt, being a stepmother is difficult and requires a lot of work. Some stepmothers report that being a full-time working mother is not nearly as difficult as being a part-time stepmother (Dodson, 1977). However, more recent research has indicated that the wicked stepmother myth is not nearly as visible as it was earlier. The research emphases have been on examining the variables affecting the stepmother-stepchild relationship. These include age and sex of children, past experiences of mother and stepchildren, contact of stepchildren with non-

custodial parents, marital satisfaction, and others.

In the study by Dahl and her associates (1987), girls expressed more overt hostility toward stepmothers than boys did. This was true whether or not they lived together. Expressions of mixed feelings and concern about the permanence of the remarriage were expressed by the children, as well. However, Amato (1987) found no differences in children's perceptions of the mother in stepfamilies when compared to perceptions in intact and single-parent families. Children reported that stepmothers were just as likely to talk to them a lot, were interested in them, provided assistance with homework, and helped them with personal problems as did biological mothers. Finally, in the Gonong and Coleman (1987) study, stepchildren did not feel more distant from stepmothers than from stepfathers. In general, children perceived themselves to be at least moderately close to their stepmothers.

In summary, stepmothers have a harder time adjusting to their roles than stepfathers do. They appear to make a better adjustment if they are under 40 years of age, have been married before, bring any children they may have with them into the remarriage, inherit stepchildren who are under 13 years of age, have sufficient ego strength and self-esteem, have the nurturance and support of their husbands, and have a willingness to accept not being loved for a while.

Stepfathers

There are more stepfathers than stepmothers because most blended families are formed because of divorce rather than death, and most mothers retain custody of their children. Adjustment to the role of stepfathering is easier than that of stepmothering. Stepfathers have their problems, too, but they are not perpetuated in mythology and fairy tales, as with stepmothers. Therefore stepfathers do not have to overcome a negative press. Society is more likely to give assistance to stepfathers than stepmothers and to provide social acceptance for their role (Duberman, 1973; Visher & Visher, 1978). Being a stepfather does not entail the same expectation as being a stepmother, largely because our culture expects less love and nurturing from a man than from a woman (Shulman, 1972).

The limited research on stepfathering is shocking since there are such large numbers of families with stepfathers, and these numbers are increasing each year (Bohannan & Erickson, 1978). The research relating to the stepfather's effectiveness has been contradictory. For example, Perkins and Kahan (1979) found some evidence to indicate that families with stepfathers functioned less effectively than families with natural fathers. They found that all members of the family perceived the stepfather as less well adjusted, less understanding, and less powerful than the natural father. On the other hand, other research indicates that stepchildren, in general, are equally as happy and successful as children in natural families. Stepfathers, however, do not perceive this phenomenon and tend to see themselves as less effective than natural fathers (Bohannan & Erickson, 1978).

The stepfathers in Bernard's (1956) study had more affectionate relationships with their stepchildren than did stepmothers. Stepfathers are introduced to the children under more favorable conditions than stepmothers are, since a woman often will give children greater preparation for a new parent than a man will. Perhaps the new fathers faced children who were themselves more

friendly so that it was easier to be affectionate toward them; or perhaps men are better stepparents than women because they are less possessive in their love and spend less time with the children. Further, the man is more apt to remarry for love of the woman and her children than is the woman, who may marry for support or prestige.

Some of the difficulties stepfathers experience are intensified because they feel they are taking on an awesome task and are eager to do a good job. They spend more time thinking about their roles and responsibilities. They are more self-conscious about effectiveness and more critical of themselves. They tend to measure themselves against some ideal-father model more so than natural fathers do (Bohannan & Erickson, 1978).

In any case it can be concluded that the role of father and the role of stepfather are not identical (Bohannan & Erickson, 1978). Many stepfathers, however, are performing roles simultaneously. They often are concerned about the quality of their fathering roles, as their children usually are living with their ex-spouses. Being a weekend or holiday father is difficult. However, it is possible and desirable to continue a significant parental role and still give recognition and support to the authority and relationship of the adult who lives with the child on a daily basis (Messinger, Walker, & Freeman, 1978).

Many stepfathers wish to adopt their stepchildren legally, particularly if the children are young. Legal adoption gives the new family emotional as well as legal solidarity. It also gives the child a certain security in knowing that he is a full family member in good standing (Bernard, 1956). On the other hand, adoption does not assure affection, trust, or respect between stepfathers and stepchildren (Walker & Messinger, 1979).

Areas of difficulty for stepfathers primarily center around discipline and finances. These problems are compounded by guilt and loyalty conflicts. The area of discipline creates problems for first families, too, but they are more intensified in stepfamilies. Discipline for the stepfather is more of a problem today than in the past. At the beginning of the century, stepfathers usually married widows, and the role as father was clear.

Today the role is poorly defined, and often serious problems in the area of discipline emerge. In stepfamilies, difficulties are intensified as the stepfather tries to discipline children with whom he has a very short relationship. Natural fathers have had many months to work together on establishing family patterns and methods of discipline. Unless there is agreement between the parents concerning the occasions for, and the nature of, disciplinary action, difficulties will surely arise. Measures a parent might apply to his own children without self-consciousness may produce deep conflict when they are applied to the children of a spouse. The stepfather may experience this conflict more acutely than the biological parent or the child (Visher & Visher, 1978).

Frequently double messages are sent by the mother, creating problems for the stepfather in disciplining the stepchildren. The mother may be delighted to have someone share parenting and financial obligations, but she often protects her children and overrides the stepfather's authority. This behavior leaves him feeling helpless, frustrated, and without any real role in the family (Messinger et al., 1978). In the face of such difficulties, the stepfather may retreat into passivity and relinquish all the discipline to his wife. She, then, may feel resentful that she is not receiving the help that she expects and needs (Visher & Visher, 1978).

A mother of an adolescent girl may unconsciously fear that the stepfather will find her daughter more attractive than she is. This fear is often expressed in vague anxieties and illusions and is projected onto others and the outside. At best, the stepfather often finds himself caught between the wife's wanting him to show interest in her daughter and his fear that such interest will be misconstrued or that his impulses will not stand the strain of closeness (Schulman, 1972).

The hazards of favoritism in disciplining children are pronounced, especially in families where both parents have children. Frequently the stepparent, in an effort to be fair, overcompensates and neglects his own children. The overcompensation in favor of the stepchild may be viewed by that child as evidence of not belonging. The parent who sees that his own child is being discriminated against may also develop resentments and even antagonisms that can breach the solidarity of the family. Unless the children are rewarded and punished based on merit rather than on ancestry, a sense of injustice may deveolp (Bernard, 1956).

It has been suggested that the stepparent move slowly in taking a co-management role. Moving too quickly can not only alienate the child but also drive a wedge between the couple. Even discussing discipline and the role each adult is to assume prior to remarriage does not eliminate all the problems (Visher & Visher, 1979).

Conflicts concerning money present problems for blended families. The problems are more acute for the stepfather, as the male is generally viewed as the primary economic supporter. In most cases payments are being made by the absent parent for child support. Such payments may invoke feelings of concern, anger, or guilt in stepparents. Bitterness over money issues can be very deep and may produce enough friction to thwart integration of the new family. Children often feel that one child or another is the favorite based on expenditures. As children get older and need larger amounts of money for education and other needs, these feelings may become intensified. Sometimes the standard of living has to be lowered as money is divided among two households. Stepfathers' children may resent whatever is spent on stepsiblings (Visher & Visher, 1978, 1979).

Remarried fathers without custody frequently feel a deep sense of guilt at having brought pain to their children at the expense of their search for happiness. Many wish to show that their love for their children has not diminished and therefore cannot refuse the financial demands of a former wife. Late child support incites anger, and each time a payment is made it is a reminder of the former marriage. Tensions may develop, and arguments over monetary arrangements become a major issue. Often this tension is the result of the realization that there has been a former intimate relationship (Visher & Visher, 1979).

A lack of control over the spending of support payments causes many difficulties. Guilt, helplessness, and frustration about receiving no appreciation plague many relationships. Some spouses without custody fear that if they do not comply with the ex-spouses' requests for money, they will not be able to see their children. Money often is equated with love. Spouses may perceive extra payments to ex-spouses as symbols of affection; wives may feel that material things lavished on natural children by stepfathers is a sign that they do not care for the stepchildren. Children may perceive that their fathers do not care because their standard of living has been lowered. Wishing to test the parent's love, children may make unreasonable demands for material objects. In families where adults and children are unsure of their roles and relationships, money is more apt to be considered a tangible evidence of caring (Visher & Visher, 1979).

These problems appear to be continuing issues with stepfamilies, as 50 percent of the stepparents in the study by Dahl and her associates (1987) reported problems with matters relating to children, especially discipline and difficulties managing adolescents. Further, financial issues, especially resentments about alimony and child-support payments, were cited as problem areas.

In the Ganong and Coleman study (1987), 40 percent of children in stepfamilies felt that both parents favored other children. Of the stepfathers with female children, 44 percent of the stepdaughters indicated that they were not close to their stepfathers and half indicated that they did not get enough love and attention from them. In the Amato (1987) study, school-age children in stepfamilies reported less support from their stepfathers than did children from intact families with biological fathers. However, children felt that their stepfathers had as much control over them as their noncustodial fathers did. Stepfathers were unlikely to play the role of disciplinarian, at least as far as the children were concerned. The stereotype of a harsh and punitive stepfather who alienates his stepchildren by asserting his status as boss of the family was not borne out by this research.

Coping with guilt feelings about leaving the children of the previous family to become the stepfather of another is one of the most difficult problems that stepfathers face. Sometimes these guilt feelings are so strong that the stepfather is unable to enjoy his stepchildren. He cannot give freely and openly because he feels guilty about depriving his own children of affection and concern (Visher & Visher, 1978).

Guilt also makes it difficult for him to deal with rivalry between his children and his new spouse for his affection and attention. He wants to give much to his children and tries to make up for the pain he has caused them. At the same time, he realizes that his wife may feel threatened and rejected when he does so. Guilt is also a factor as he tries to placate his ex-wife, extending himself to avoid offending her and permitting frequent contacts to demonstrate his continued interest in the welfare of his children (Visher & Visher, 1978).

Anger and guilt associated with the divorce make it difficult to separate from the past and to make clear choices in the present. The stepfather also feels guilty about the tension his children create for his wife. Sometimes he tries to resolve this situation by reassuring her that his children do not really mean what they say, which usually makes her feel worse rather than better about her role (Visher & Visher, 1978).

In summary, stepfathers generally have an easier time establishing a relationship with their stepchildren than stepmothers do. However, they do experience stress because they often are uncertain about how much discipline to exercise and how much affection to show stepchildren. Stepfathers and stepchildren may be accustomed to different household rules, activities, and ways of doing things; children may be jealous of stepfathers and see them as rivals for attention of their mothers. Further, children may feel loyal to their noncustodial fathers and experience guilt and a sense of betrayal if they like their stepfathers (Amato, 1987). Other adjustments stepfathers must make include the resolution of guilt concerning finances and not being a full-time father to his own children. Most of these adjustments can be made over a period of time, and after about 3 years it is likely that relationships with stepchildren will be positive.

Problems of Blended Families

Much of the earlier research on blended families was based on clinical reports and impressions of professionals working with these families in counseling situations. Thus there was considerable emphasis on problems they encountered. Many studies were plagued by methodological problems—failing to account for the effects of the timing of remarriage or the number of years elapsed since the divorce of one or both partners, the experiences prior to marriage, and the age and developmental stages of the children. Entry into a second marriage is unlike that of a first marriage since both adults and children carry their own previous marriage and family histories into the second. The first few years following remarriage represent a transitional stage for the new family, requiring individuals to revise their definitions of marriage, redefine their roles, and negotiate new relationships. The residual effects of a previous marriage, especially when children are involved, present a complex set of adjustments for family members (Hetherington & Camara, 1984). The first year following remarriage tends to be quite difficult. Dahl and her associates (1987) found that during the first year after remarriage, one third of the families in their study moved twice in order to avoid living in someone else's home or to have enough space for the children. Thus many children were forced to change schools or communities, contributing additional adjustment problems.

Problems cited in earlier research with which blended families had to cope included resolving residual conflicts within the first family, redefining physical and psychological boundaries and developing a workable family structure from a network of relationships, formulating a comfortable solution of complementary marital status while at the same time working out parental interactions, and establishing a parental relationship between stepparent and child (Visher & Visher, 1978; Walker & Messinger, 1979; Whiteside & Auerbach, 1978). See Box 7o for a summary of the problems cited in earlier research.

Factors Related to Adjustment

While recent research has failed to refute the problems identified in earlier research, it has emphasized the necessity for considering the many mediating factors affecting the ability of individual families to resolve these issues (Hetherington & Camara, 1984). In the study by Dahl and her associates (1987), the problems reported by stepfamilies included matters relating to the children, especially discipline; spouses feeling left out because of strong bonds within biological parents' relationship with own children; not enough time to be alone together or to socialize with friends; financial problems, including resentments, about alimony and/or child-support payments.

Remarriage of the resident parent requires a reallocation of the personal resources of family members, a reassignment of roles, and a redistribution of parent-child boundaries. Some of the time and affection previously given to children are reallocated to the new spouses. The stepparent may assume some of the adultlike roles

---

BOX 7o   PROBLEMS OF BLENDED FAMILIES

Resolving residual conflicts regarding first family—mourning process over the loss of the primary relationship

Resolving problems relating to continued association with "other" household

Redefining roles

Redefining physical and psychological boundaries of family

Formulating a spousal relationship simultaneously with assumption of parental role

Formulating relationship with stepchildren—coping with negative feelings such as rejection and hostility of stepchildren

Having unrealistic expectations regarding affection for stepchildren

Lowering self-esteem and lack of confidence regarding ability to sustain relationship

and responsibilities assumed by children after the divorce. Thus the power and status of the child built during the single-parent structure may diminish and an adult-headed power structure reestablished (Brand & Clingempeel, 1987). Both Amato (1987) and Brand and Clingempeel (1987) found that adolescents had a more difficult time accepting the remarriage of their parents and adjusting to the new family structure than preschool and school-age children did.

The interrelationship of the age and sex of the stepchild and the sex of the stepparent seems to affect the stepparent-stepchild relationship. Brand and Clingempeel (1987) conducted an interesting study of the role of the marital relationship in the stepparent-stepchild adjustment. They studied stepmothers with male and female stepchildren and stepfathers with male and female stepchildren. The children were between the ages of 9 and 12, and all parents had been married less than 3 years. They found that the effects of marital quality on stepparent-stepchild relationships and children's psychological adjustments differed across the four sets of resident stepparents. In stepmother families, striking differences were found for male and female stepchildren. For stepmothers, the more positive the marital relationship, the poorer the adjustment of stepdaughters.

The negative effects of marital quality in stepmother families with stepdaughters may be due to unique characteristics of this group. Girls are rarely awarded to fathers after divorce, usually only if there is a problematic mother-child relationship. Further, there are fewer institutional guidelines for stepmother-stepdaughter relationships than for other stepparent relationships, since mother replacements for girls may be especially alien to societal norms. As a result of these differences and the greater socialization of females toward nurturing and parenting roles, girls may acquire an almost "wifelike" relationship with fathers following divorce. Girls may enjoy this confidant, household manager role, and the new status that it accrues. Fathers may come to depend on daughters for emotional support. After remarriage the stepmother may be viewed as a competitor for the father's time and affection. The more positive the remarriage, the

more likely there are to be reallocations of the father's time and affection.

Stepmothers may try harder and earlier than stepfathers to become parent-figures to girls, and this effort may exacerbate loyalty conflicts for stepdaughters who perceive that positive responses to stepmothers represent disloyalty to biologial mothers. Patterns of stepmother-stepdaughter interactions may be circular rather than linear processes. Unrewarding interactions and adjustment problems of stepdaughters may lead to stepmothers investing more energy into the marital relationship. This, in turn, may lead stepdaughters to withdraw even further from stepmothers.

For stepmothers of males, more positive marital relationships were associated with better psychological adjustment of stepsons and positive stepmother-stepson relationships. Boys with stepmothers may perceive higher marital quality as supporting rather than detracting from previously positive parent-child relationships. During single-parent status boys may develop a "buddy" type of father-son relationship that centers on companionship and joint activities. Consequently a more positive marital relationship is seen as additional support rather than as an encroachment on the father-son relationship.

Stepfathers with stepchildren of both sexes behaved toward and perceived their stepchildren more positively to the extent that their marital relationships were more positive. The stepfather, as a newcomer to the household, may recognize the importance of a good marriage and relationship with stepchildren. Being more positive toward stepchildren brings greater rewards from wives.

Thus in this study stepmothers with female children had a difficult time establishing positive relationships. Over time these patterns change, and the family establishes equilibrium, and relationships become more positive and stable (Brand & Clingempeel, 1987).

Ganong and Coleman (1987) did not find adolescents' attitudes toward stepparents to differ according to the sex of the child or the stepparent, and they did not perceive their stepparents particularly negatively. Some of the adolescents were high school students and some were college students, the majority being older than 18 years of age. Some, or most, may not have been living at home with the stepparents at the time of the study. These factors could have affected the perceptions of the children.

These researchers did find that most of the children in stepfamilies favored the biological parent over the stepparent. There was a tendency for same-sex pairings to be perceived as closer than cross-sexed pairings—89 percent of stepdaughters felt at least moderately close to their stepmothers, and 73 percent of stepsons felt this way toward their stepfathers. However, their relationships to the biological parents were even closer, with 92 percent who had stepmothers feeling close to their fathers and 89 percent with stepfathers feeling close to their mothers.

When examining 9- to 12-year-old children's relationships with stepparents, Clingempeel, Brand, and Ievoli (1984) found that stepparent-stepdaughter relationships in both stepmother and stepfather families were more problematic than stepfather-stepson relationships were. The expectation that both boys and girls would have greater difficulties relating to stepmothers than to stepfathers was not supported.

Fine (1986) compared college students' perceptions of stepparents and biological parents according to the family structure in which they lived (intact, single-parent, or stepparent families). The findings confirmed that students from all three family types held stereotyped perceptions of stepparents, both of stepmothers and of stepfathers. However, stronger stereotypes of stepmothers existed. The data did not suggest, however, that these views were extremely negative or pathological but essentially average as noted by semantic differential ratings. Ratings of natural parents were considerably above average. Students from single-parent and stepparent families generally had less stereotyped perceptions of stepmothers than their counterparts from nuclear families did.

Thus there appears to be a complex interaction between the sex and the age of the stepchildren and the sex of the stepparents. Further, the degree of contact and relationship with noncustodial parents also is a factor. It seems that additional research is needed to examine these relationships in greater depth.

Ambert (1986) found stepchildren's place of residence to be significantly related to the marital relationship for stepmothers. Stepmothers who lived with their stepchildren reported a very high level of marital happiness and were totally satisfied with their spouses after 2 years of remarriage. Stepmothers with stepchildren from 2 to 12 years old who were not in residence were less happy in their marriages and had more conflict with their husbands. Stepfathers were not affected by stepchildren's place of residence. For them the ideal situation was when stepchildren were on their own.

Both stepmothers and stepfathers developed a closer relationship with their live-in stepchildren than with stepchildren living elsewhere. This relationship was facilitated if their own children lived with them. When a man's children lived with their mother but his stepchildren lived with him, he was drawn to his stepchildren when he had no access to his own children or when they disappointed him. But when he maintained contact with his own children, he kept a certain distance with his live-in stepchildren. It was as if he feared being unfair to his own children by giving affection to his wife's children.

Those couples with the "ours" children rated their marriages the happiest of all. These stepfathers also had the warmest feelings toward their stepchildren. Conclusions by Ambert (1986) were that the stepparenting experience is a more positive one with live-in stepchildren. However, even with live-in stepchildren, there was significant ambivalence about stepparenting expressed by stepmothers. Greater marital happiness was expressed when stepchildren lived with the stepparent, but 20–60 percent of both stepmothers and stepfathers indicated that their marriage would be happier and more harmonious without stepchildren.

Previous research has focused on the difficulties children of remarriage are likely to experience—dealing with the loss of a primary parent, divided loyalties, confusion in terms of belonging, membership in two households, unreasonable expectations, fantasies of natural parents' reuniting, guilt over causing the divorce, identity and sexuality issues among adolescents' relationships with noncustodial parents, and others. Whether children in step-

families suffer and have greater problems than children from intact families is still being debated. It does appear that it is a disservice to continue to focus on the negative aspects of stepchild adjustment, and comparisons between stepfamilies and biological families should be avoided (Knaub & Hanna, 1984).

Knaub and Hanna (1984) investigated children's (ages 9–12) perceptions of family strengths in stepfamilies and found that, in general, they perceived their families as relatively high in strength. This was especially true of their perceptions of happiness with the remarriage, feelings of closeness within the stepfamily, and their own sense of self-worth. Furthermore, 70 percent rated their families as successful in their adjustment to one another. The mean age of the children in the study was 8 years. The children reported that they were familiar with the stepparent prior to remarriage, many reporting that they knew the stepparent very well. The gender of the children did not appear to make a difference in the perception of family strength; however, boys did score significantly higher on four of the eight family strength components.

The age of the child was found to be related to the child's perceptions. The older children in the sample, as compared to the younger, scored lower on family strength components, reported more conflict with both parents, and were significantly more likely to wish their natural parents would get back together. Some support was found for the contention that positive relations between stepparent and child is easier if the child is living in the home than if he visits. It appears that children adjust easier in a continuing home environment and prefer stability and the opportunity to spend longer periods of time with a new parent before accepting him. Adolescents in stepfamilies are more likely to rate sibling relationships more negatively than those in intact families (Amato, 1987).

Children in stepfamilies also reported having more household responsibilities than children in intact families did. This may be due to the fact that they began these responsibilities during the single-parent family status and continued them after the parent remarried (Amato, 1987).

Most of the problems relating to stepparent-stepchild relationships are temporary, being the most evident the first year after remarriage (Dahl et al., 1987) and diminishing with succeeding years. Most adjustments have been made within a 3-year period. Dahl and her associates found that those children with the most positive attitudes toward their stepfamily were those who had been in the family for more than 3 years.

Further Research

The breadth of research on stepparenting is yet to be undertaken (Ambert, 1986). Because of the complexity of stepfamilies, researchers should focus on specific subgroups. A more consistent use of theory would decrease the need for large sampling procedures. Consideration for changes within stepfamilies over time would greatly enhance the understanding of development of stepfamily systems and the effects of transitions on children in stepfamilies. Further, future research needs to focus on the hundreds of questions already generated by clinicians regarding the family dynamics, transitional adjustments, incomplete institution, emotional responses, and expectations in stepfamilies (Ganong & Coleman, 1986).

Support for Blended Families

Empirical studies on the dynamics of stepfamily functioning and factors affecting family reorganization have been limited. The variability of these families have posed significant problems in designing systematic studies and in providing services for them.

In the 1970s and 1980s books written especially for blended families appeared. Various community agencies have instituted self-help groups for stepfamilies so that comfort and support from sharing common problems and feelings might be provided. In one aspect the support by the extended family may be greater for stepfamilies than that experienced by single parents since the possibility exists for an additional set of parents. Friends and co-workers often are additional sources of support for blended families.

It has been suggested that programs for adults who are planning to form a blended family would assist in the process of structuring a new family. Knowing what to expect of the new spouse, typical reactions of children to the stepparent, and areas likely to produce conflict would assist in developing more realistic expectations. The essential ingredient in such programs should be the process by which couples are encouraged and taught to discuss specific problems of remarriage openly and constructively (see Box 7p).

Einstein and Albert (1986) developed a commercial parenting program for stepfamilies. It includes five workshop sessions on the following topics: the pitfalls and potentials of stepfamily living; dealing with anger and guilt; major decisions about money, more children, and living arrangements; discipline and rules; and sexuality. Materials in the complete kit include a leader's guide, three audio cassettes describing vignettes to stimulate discussion, a participant's packet (a handbook and 30 at-home activities to involve the entire stepfamily), wall charts, blackline masters of activities and assessment forms, publicity aids, and certificates of participation. The goal is to help stepfamily members learn to communicate better, resolve conflicts, and structure their home life to improve their relationships.

In sum, the phenomenon of blended families is increasing in frequency and importance and with such rapidity that it is essential for both the social sciences and the helping professions to focus significant effort on its problems and many ramifications. There is a need to provide continuing services to these families. It appears that providing opportunities to share experiences with others who have the same feelings and problems is helpful (Jacobson, 1979; Visher & Visher, 1978). Professionals who work with blended families need to know as much as possible about the individual history of each family member. It is important for the professional to understand the stresses related to the new situation and to help each family member identify and understand them. The needs of each individual should be recognized, and efforts aimed at effective adjustment must take into account what is tolerable for all, so that no one is the object of attack. The professional's task is to help free family members emotionally so that they can direct their energies to the new family situation.

It is apparent from the preceding discussion that blended families are more dissimilar than similar to nuclear families. Because they possess unique strengths and weaknesses, they are in need of understanding and support.

The evidence suggests that the stepparent role may be one of the most difficult assumed by adults in today's society, and children in blended

---

**BOX 7p   GROUP DISCUSSION TOPICS
FOR COUPLES PLANNING TO REMARRY**

1. Feelings related to the previous marriage and divorce. Discussion should allow for expression of feelings about the first marriage and the legal settlement, involving custody, visitation, and financial arrangements.
2. Remarriage adjustment, including adjustments between the children and the parent's new spouse, between the parent's new spouse and children, to a new lifestyle, to a new family group, to different expectations for household management, to new kin, and to a new individual position in family.
3. Division of labor in present marital household.
4. Perception of role relations, including those of the new partner to the children and the children to the new partner.
5. Responsibilities of the new partner to the children (financial, disciplinary).
6. Exchange of views between the present couple on child rearing.
7. Perceptions of what constitutes a "happy family life" and perceptions of ways the second marriage's family life is viewed as different from the first.
8. Feelings about financial arrangements.
9. Feelings about continued relations between the ex-spouse and/or the ex-spouse's kin; and between the children and the absent parent and kin.
10. Feelings about the partner's children living with ex-spouse who visit regularly in the present household.
11. Discussion allowing for recognition of difficulties of acquiring an "instant family" and the time factor for privacy for a couple relationship.

Source: Messinger, L. (1976, April). Remarriage between divorced people with children from previous marriages: A proposal for preparation for remarriage. *Journal of Marriage and Family Counseling,* pp. 193–200.

---

families experience considerable confusion during the readjustment process. Recognizing the stresses may help prepare family members for the realities of their new family structure.

Adults in the new blended family need time alone to develop a positive spousal relationship. Building other relationships takes time. Instant love should not be expected. Divided loyalties, different histories of values and life-styles, and the expanded network of new relationships are factors that may interfere with rapid adjustment.

It seems important for children in blended families to continue relationships with the noncustodial biological parent. If stepparents do not compete with natural parents but attempt to establish their own roles with stepchildren, stepparenting will be more effective and more rewarding.

SUMMARY

Dramatic structural changes in families occurred in this country during the decade of the 1970s, and some of these trends continued into the 1980s. Most of these changes were due to the increase in single-parent and blended families. The high divorce rate and the growing number of people who remarry account for the increase in these family structures.

While the stereotypical image of the single-parent family as deviant and pathological is being replaced by a healthier image, single parents generally experience problems of adjustment, such as finances, mobility, feelings of loneliness and isolation, difficulties with child care and child rearing, and synchronization of family and work responsibilities. Recent research on the effects of divorce on children has provided information about the complex process of adjustment following divorce. Most children suffer temporary negative effects in many areas of development, including interpersonal and peer relationships, school performance, and self-esteem, and exhibit various levels of antisocial behavior. Several factors mediate the degree of stress and length of the adjustment period. These include parental harmony, the sex of the child, and the parents' educational and income levels. Further, contact with noncustodial parents is important. Problems tend to be more severe and long-lasting for boys. While adjustment is affected by the presence or the absence of these variables, some psychological problems may continue for years.

The phenomenon of stepfamilies is not new, but the quantitative increase and the qualitative changes in functioning have brought more attention to the needs of parents and children residing in these families. Blended families have become the most common alternative family structure, occurring about one in every five households. In the 1990s estimates are that about 25 to 35 percent of all children will be a part of a stepfamily before their 18th birthdays.

Research in the 1980s has indicated that there is better understanding and greater acceptance of blended families than in the past. Blended families function very differently from nuclear families, utilizing different organizational and integration processes. Further, it has been concluded that the blended family differs from other family forms in its structure, boundaries, roles, mythology, negotiation processes, member autonomy, and family affect. Remarriage, as does divorce, represents a period of transition in which family roles, rules, and relationships are redefined and new patterns of resource allocations are established. All family members are faced with a period of adjustment, with the first year after remarriage being the most difficult and effective family functioning is achieved in about 3 years.

Clearly single-parent and blended families represent unique problems and needs for the parents and children involved. This does not, however, imply that these family structures are weaker than the traditional nuclear family. It does suggest that understanding and support may be needed. Undoubtedly these families possess unique strengths, as well, most of which are yet to be documented by research.

REFERENCES

AMATO, P. (1987). Family processes in one-parent, stepparent, and intact families: The child's point of view. *Journal of Marriage and the Family, 49*(2), 327–337.

AMBERT, A. (1986). Being a stepparent: Live-in and visiting stepchildren. *Journal of Marriage and the Family, 48*(4), 795–804.

American college dictionary (1966). C. L. Barnhart (Ed.). New York: Random House.

BERNARD, J. (1956). *Remarriage: A study of marriage.* New York: Dryden.

BLACK, K. (1979, January). What about the child from a one-parent home? *Teacher,* pp. 24–28.

BOHANNAN, P., & ERICKSON, R. (1978, January). Stepping in. *Psychology Today,* pp. 53–59.

BOWMAN, M., & AKRONS, C. (1985). Impact of legal custody status on fathers' parenting post-divorce. *Journal of Marriage and the Family, 47*(2), 481–488.

BRAND, E., & CLINGEMPEEL, W. (1987). Interdependencies of marital and stepparent-stepchild relationships and children's psychological adjustment: Research findings and clinical implications. *Family Relations, 36*(2), 140–145.

BRENES, M., EISENBERG, N., & HELMSTADTER, G. (1985). Sex role development of preschoolers from two-parent and one-parent families. *Merrill-Palmer Quarterly, 31*(1), 33–46.

BUEHLER, C., HOGAN, M., ROBINSON, B., & LEVY, R. (1986). Remarriage following divorce. *Journal of Family Issues, 7*(4), 405–420.

BURDEN, D. (1986). Single parents and the work setting: The impact of multiple job and homelife responsibilities. *Family Relations, 35*(1), 37–43.

CHERLIN, A. (1978). Remarriage as an incomplete institution. *American Journal of Sociology, 84*(8), 634–648.

CLINGEMPEEL, W., BRAND, E., & IEVOLI, R. (1984). Stepparent-stepchild relationships in stepmother and stepfather families: A multimethod study. *Family Relations, 33*(3), 465–473.

CROSSMAN, M., & ADAMS, R. (1980, November). Divorce, single parenting, and child development. *Journal of Psychology, 106,* 205–217.

DAHL, A., COWGILL, K., & ASMUNDSSON, R. (1987). Life in remarriage families. *Social Work, 32*(1), 40–44.

DeFRAIN, J., & EIRICK, R. (1981). Coping as divorced single parents: A comparative study of fathers and mothers. *Family Relations, 30*(2), 265–273.

DEMO, D., & ACOCK, A. (1988). The impact of divorce on

children. *Journal of Marriage and the Family, 50*(3), 619-648.

DERDEYN, A., & SCOTT, E. (1984). Joint custody: A critical analysis and appraisal. *American Journal of Orthopsychiatry, 54*(2), 199-209.

DODSON, F. (1977, September). Weaving together two families into one. *Family Health/Today's Health,* pp. 44-52.

DUBERMAN, L. (1973). Step-kin relationships. *Journal of Marriage and the Family, 35*(2), 283-292.

EINSTEIN, E., & ALBERT L. (1986). *Strengthening stepfamilies.* Circle Pines, MN: American Guidance Service.

ELKIN, M. (1987). Joint custody: Affirming that parents and families are forever. *Social Work, 32*(1), 18-24.

FAST, R., & CAIN, A. (1966). The stepparent role: Potential for disturbances in family functioning. *American Journal of Orthopsychiatry, 36*(3), 485-491.

FINE, M. (1986). Perceptions of stepparents: Variation in stereotypes as a function of current family structure. *Journal of Marriage and the Family, 48*(3), 537-543.

FINE, M., DONNELLY, B., & VOYDANOFF, P. (1986). Adjustment and satisfaction of parents. *Journal of Family Issues, 7*(4), 391-404.

GANONG, L., & COLEMAN, M. (1986). A comparison of clinical and empirical literature on children in stepfamilies. *Journal of Marriage and the Family, 48*(2), 309-318.

GANONG, L., & COLEMAN, M. (1987). Stepchildren's perceptions of their parents. *Journal of Genetic Psychology, 148*(1), 5-17.

GASSER, R., & TAYLOR, C. (1976). Role adjustment of single parent fathers with dependent children. *Family Coordinator, 25*(4), 397-402.

GILES-SIMS, J. (1984). The stepparent role. *Journal of Family Issues, 5*(1), 116-130.

GREIF, G. (1987). Mothers without custody. *Social Work, 32*(1), 11-15.

GUIDUBALDI, J., CLEMINSHAW, H., PERRY, J., NASTASI, B., & LIGHTEL, J. (1986). The role of selected family environment factors in children's post-divorce adjustment. *Family Relations, 35*(1), 141-151.

HAGEN, J. (1987). Proceed with caution: Advocating joint custody. *Social Work, 32*(1), 26-30.

HANSON, S. (1986). Healthy single families. *Family Relations, 35*(1), 125-132.

HANSON, S., & SPORAKOWSKI, M. (1986). Single parent families. *Family Relations, 35*(1), 3-8.

HILL, R. (1986). Life cycle stages for types of single parent families: Of family development theory. *Family Relations, 35*(1), 19-29.

HESS, R., & CAMARA, K. (1979). Post-divorce family relationships as mediating factors in the consequences of divorce for children. *Journal of Social Issues, 35*(4), 79-98.

HETHERINGTON, E., & CAMARA, K. (1984). Families in transition: The process of dissolution and reconstruction. In R. Parke (Ed.), *Review of Child Development Research 7: The Family* (pp. 398-431). Chicago: University of Chicago Press.

HETHERINGTON, E., COX, M., & COX, R. (1976). Divorced fathers. *Family Coordinator, 25*(4), 417-427.

HODGES, W., TIERKEY, C., & BUCHSBAUM, H. (1984, August). The cumulative effect of stress on preschool children of divorced and intact families. *Journal of Marriage and the Family, 46*(3), 611-617.

HOFFERTH, S. (1985). Updating children's life course. *Journal of Marriage and the Family, 47*(1), 93-115.

HOWELL, R., & TOEPKE, K. (1984). Summary of the child custody laws for the fifty states. *American Journal of Family Therapy, 12*(2), 56-60.

ILFELD, F., ILFELD, H., & ALEXANDER, J. (1982). Does joint custody work? A first look at outcome data of relitigation. *American Journal of Psychiatry, 139*(1), 62-66.

JACOBSON, D. (1979). Stepfamilies: Myths and realities. *Social Work, 24*(3), 202-207.

JENKINS, S. (1978, March-April). Children of divorce. *Children Today,* pp. 16-48.

JOHNSON, B. (1986). Single mothers following separation and divorce: Making it on your own. *Family Relations, 35*(1), 189-197.

JONES, C. (1984). Judicial questioning of children in custody and visitation proceedings. *Family Law Quarterly, 18*(1), 43-91.

KALTER, S. (1978, September). Instant parent: How to deal with stepchildren. *Harper's Bazaar,* pp. 230-233.

KENT, M. (1980). Remarriage: A family systems perspective. *Journal of Contemporary Social Work, 61*(3), 146-153.

KESHET, H., & ROSENTHAL, K. (1978, May-June). Fathers: A new study. *Children Today,* pp. 13-17.

KINARD, E., & REINHERZ, H. (1986). Effects of marital disruption on children's school aptitude and achievement. *Journal of Marriage and the Family, 48*(2), 85-293.

KNAUB, P., & HANNA, S. (1984). Children of remarriage: Perceptions of family strengths. *Journal of Divorce, 7*(4), 73-90.

KOMPORA, D. (1980). Process of stepparenting. *Family Relations, 29*(1), 69-73.

KREIN, S., & BILLER, A. (1988, July 17). Single-parent home affects boys' schooling. *Albuquerque Journal,* p. B-1.

KURDEK, L. (1986). Custodial mothers' perceptions of visitation and payment of child support by noncustodial fathers in families with low and high levels of preseparation inter-parent conflict. *Journal of Applied Developmental Psychology, 7*(4), 307-323.

LEWIS, K. (1978). Single father families: Who they are and how they fare. *Child Welfare, 57*(10), 642-651.

LOVELAND-CHERRY, C. (1986). Personal health practices in single parent and two parent families. *Family Relations, 35*(1), 133-139.

McCLENAGHAN, J., & MOST, B. (1978). How to make his stepchild love you. *Saturday Evening Post, 250,* pp. 34, 96-99.

MENDES, H. (1976). Single fathers. *Family Coordinator, 25*(4), 439–444.

MENDES, H. (1979). Single parent families: A topology of lifestyles. *Social Work, 24*(3), 193–200.

MESSINGER, L., WALKER, K., & FREEMAN, S. (1978). Preparation for remarriage following divorce: The use of group techniques. *American Journal of Orthopsychiatry, 48*(2), 263–272.

MESSINGER, L. (1976, April). Remarriage between divorced people with children from previous marriages: A proposal for preparation for remarriage. *Journal of Marriage and Family Counseling,* pp. 193–200.

NORTON, A., & GLICK, P. (1986). One-parent families: A social and economic profile. *Family Relations, 35*(1), 9–17.

ORTHNER, D., BROWN, T., & FERGUSON, D. (1976). Single-parent fatherhood: An emerging family life style, *Family Coordinator, 26*(4), 429–437.

PARKS, A. (1977, Summer). Children and youth of divorce in Parents Without Partners, Inc. *Journal of Clinical Child Psychology,* pp. 44–48.

PERKINS, T., & KAHAN, J. (1979). An empirical comparison of natural-father and step-father family systems. *Family Process, 18,* 175–183.

PETERSON, G., & CLEMINSHAW, H. (1980). The strength of single-parent families during the divorce crisis: An integrative review with clinical implications. In N. Stinnett, B. Chesser, J. DeFrain, & P. Knaub (Eds.), *Family strengths, positive models for family life* (pp. 431–443). Lincoln, NE: University of Nebraska Press.

PETERSON, J., & ZILL, N. (1986). Marital disruption, parent-child relationships, and behavior problems in children. *Journal of Marriage and the Family, 48*(2), 295–307.

PETT, M., & VAUGHN-COLE, B. (1986). The impact of income issues and social status on post-divorce adjustment of custodial parents. *Family Relations, 35*(1), 103–111.

RAMSEY, S. (1986). Stepparent support of stepchildren: The changing legal context and the need for empirical policy research. *Family Relations, 35*(3), 363–369.

RAMSEY, S., & MASSON, J. (1985). Stepparent support of stepchildren: A comparative analysis of policies and problems in the American and English experience. *Syracuse Law Review, 38,* 659–714.

RICHMOND-ABBOTT, M. (1984). Sex-role attitudes of mothers and children in divorced, single-parent families. *Journal of Divorce, 8*(1), 61–81.

RISMAN, B. (1986). Can men "mother"? Life as a single father. *Family Relations, 35*(1), 95–102.

ROHRLICK, J., RAINER, R., BERG-CROSS, L., & BERG-CROSS, G. (1977, Summer). The effects of divorce: A research review with a developmental perspective. *Journal of Clinical Child Psychology, 6,* 15–20.

SANIK, M., & MAULDIN, T. (1986). Single versus two parent families: A comparison of mothers' time. *Family Relations, 35*(1), 53–56.

SAVAGE, J., ADAIR, A., & FRIEDMAN, P. (1978). Community-social variables related to black parent-absent families. *Journal of Marriage and the Family, 40*(4), 779–785.

SCHLESINGER, B. (1978, May–June). Single parents: A research review. *Children Today, 12,* pp. 18–20.

SCHULMAN, G. (1972). Myths that intrude on the adaptation of the stepfamily. *Social Casework, 53*(3), pp. 131–139.

SHILLER, V. (1986). Joint versus maternal custody for families with latency age boys: Parent characteristics and child adjustment. *American Journal of Orthopsychiatry, 56*(3), 486–489.

SMITH, R., & SMITH, C. (1981). Childrearing and single parent fathers. *Family Relations, 30*(3), 411–417.

TEACHMAN, J., & HECKERT, A. (1985). The impact of age and children on remarriage. *Journal of Family Issues, 6*(2), 185–203.

TUCKER, C. (1978). Parental perceptions of child-rearing problems. *Child Psychiatry and Human Development, 8*(3), 145–161.

TURNER, J. (1984). Divorced fathers who win contested custody of their children: An exploratory study. *American Journal of Orthopsychiatry, 54*(3), 498–501.

TURNER, P., & SMITH, R. (1983). Single parents and day care. *Family Relations, 32*(2), 215–226.

U.S. BUREAU OF THE CENSUS (1987). *Statistical abstract of the U.S.: 1988* (10th ed.). Washington, DC: U.S. Department of Commerce.

VISHER, E., & VISHER, J. (1978). Common problems of stepparents and their spouses. *American Journal of Orthopsychiatry, 48*(2), 252–262.

VISHER, E., & VISHER, J. (1979). *Stepfamilies: A guide to working with stepparents and stepchildren.* New York: Brunner/Mazel.

WADSWORTH, J., BURNELL, I., TAYLOR, B., & BUTLER, N. (1985). The influence of family type on children's behavior and development at five years. *Journal of Child Psychiatry and Applied Discipline, 26*(2), 245–254.

WAGNER, R. (1980). Hansel and Gretel revisited: A parable about stepfamilies. *School Social Work Journal, 4*(2), 73–79.

WALKER, K., & MESSINGER, L. (1979). Remarriage after divorce: Dissolution and reconstruction of family boundaries. *Family Process, 18*(2), 185–192.

WALLERSTEIN, J., & KELLY, J. (1979). Children and divorce: A review. *Social Work, 24*(6), 468–475.

WALLERSTEIN, J. (1985). Children of divorce: Preliminary report of a ten-year follow-up of young children. *American Journal of Orthopsychiatry, 54*(3), 444–458.

WALLERSTEIN, J. (1986). Women after divorce: Preliminary report from a ten-year follow-up. *American Journal of Orthopsychiatry, 56*(1), 65–76.

WATTENBERG, E., & REINHARDT, H. (1979). Female-headed families: Trends and implications. *Social Work, 24*(6), 460–466.

WEISS, R. (1979). Growing up a little faster: The experience of growing up in a single parent household. *Journal of Social Issues, 35*(4), 97-111.

WHITE, L., BRINKERHOFF, D., & BOOTH, A. (1985). The effect of marital disruption on child's attachment to parents. *Journal of Family Issues, 6*(1), 5-22.

WHITE, S., & BLOOM, B. (1981). Factors related to the adjustment of divorcing men. *Family Relations, 30*(3), 349-359.

WHITESIDE, M., & AUERBACH, L. (1978). Can the daughter of my father's new wife be my sister? *Journal of Divorce, 1*(3), 271-283.

WOODY, J., COLLEY, P., SCHLEGELMILCH, J., MAGINN, P., & BALSANEK, J. (1984). Child adjustment to parental stress following divorce. *Social Casework, 65*(7), 405-412.

World book dictionary (1976). C. Barnart & R. Barnart (Eds.). Chicago: Field Enterprises Educational Corp.

8

Parenting in Nontraditional Families: Life-Style Variations

It is difficult to accurately conceptualize a prototype of a nontraditional family life-style. Actually life-styles among families in the United States are more diverse than they are similar. Within each family structure—nuclear, extended, single-parent, or blended—exists a variety of life-styles, and the freedom to choose among this variety is one of the strengths of our nation.

This chapter will explore only a few family life-style variations. These include dual-career families, mobile families (military, corporate, and migrant), families with a cohabiting parent, and families with a homosexual parent. These are far from exhaustive but represent ones that have been researched to some extent and ones that, in some way, have an impact on the parent-child relationships. While they are all labeled as *nontraditional life-styles,* in fact they may be more common than they are rare. However, each life-style departs from the traditional stereotype of a family consisting of a breadwinner father, a homemaker mother, and two or more children.

DUAL-CAREER FAMILIES

DUAL-CAREER FAMILY

*When he brings home the bacon,
    she fries it.
When she brings home the bacon, too,
    they eat out.*

Natasha Josefowitz*

There is a widely held belief, especially among upper-middle-class individuals, that educated, bright, and talented women should not bury their talents in domestic and child-rearing concerns. Instead, these women should ardently pursue careers and compete with men in the world of work. At the same time, however, these career women are expected to maintain their

*Josefowitz, N. *Is this where I was going?* New York: Warner Books, 1983, p. 20. Reprinted by permission.

FIGURE 8-1   WORKING WOMEN WITH CHILDREN UNDER 16 YEARS OF AGE

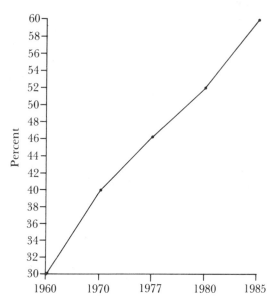

Source: Adapted from data in Nadelson, C., & Nadelson, T. (1980). Dual career marriages: Benefits and costs. In F. Pepitone-Rockwell (Ed.), *Dual career couples* (pp. 91–109). Beverly Hills: Sage; Nelson-Horchler, J. (1986, February 3). Super moms: Mixing business careers and motherhood. *Industry Week,* pp. 32–36; Chapman, F. (1987, February 16). Executive guilt: Who's taking care of the children? *Fortune,* pp. 30–37.

femininity, get married, have children, and manage households. In response to these incongruent and impossible cultural expectations, many families are attempting a relatively new life-style where both partners are engaged in dual roles (Johnson & Johnson, 1980). These families have been labeled dual-career. This family form has become relatively common in recent years. Nearly 60 percent of the women in the labor force in 1982 were married, and approximately 18 percent of these were engaged in professional or technical work (White, Mascalo, Thomas, & Shoun, 1986).

The dual-career family was first defined by Rhonda and Robert Rapoport as one in which both partners pursue careers and, at the same time, maintain a family life together. The concept of dual career is different from that of dual work in that a high degree of commitment and continuous development characterize a career. Work, on the other hand, may involve any kind of gainful employment. The practice of women working outside the home has been accepted for some time, but the focus on couples where each is committed to a career is fairly recent. Dual-worker families considerably outnumber dual-career families (Rapoport & Rapoport, 1971, 1976).

Although it is difficult to ascertain the number of dual-career families in the United States, it is reasonable to assume that the percentage has increased significantly along with the general labor-force participation rates of women (Hopkins & White, 1978).

Figure 8-1 shows the increase of working women with children under 16 years of age from 1960 to 1985. A large percentage of these women have young children. Of the mothers with children under 3 years of age, 45 percent have jobs; 60 percent have children under 6 years of age (Chapman, 1987; Nelson-Horchler, 1986).

Thus it may be concluded that the dual-earner family is the norm rather than the exceptional life-style. A number of factors have contributed to the increase in career-oriented women, including increased numbers of women who have college degrees or technical training, greater demand for skilled labor, increased awareness of sex-role equality, the women's movement, and federal legislation prohibiting discrimination (Skinner, 1980).

Evidence indicates that greater numbers of young collegiates are planning for a dual-career life-style. In 1971, 81 percent of the college women surveyed by Nadelson and Nadelson (1980) indicated that a career coupled with marriage and motherhood was important. Contrary to mythology 91 percent of the males in the sample expressed interest in wives with careers. Of this group 60 percent felt that fathers and mothers should spend equal time with children; 44 percent believed that men and women should share household responsibility equally; and 70 percent of the females and 40 percent of the males felt that each spouse should contribute equally to financing the family. By 1977 these investigators noted that three fourths of the college men indicated that they expected to spend as much time as their wives in bringing up children.

Leslie (1986) surveyed more than 500 eleventh- and twelfth-grade females concerning their future work and fertility plans, characteristics of their family life at present, and their assessments of how rewarding and costly the roles of employee and parent would be to them. A large percentage of these girls planned to combine work and parenthood throughout their lives. Support was found for the "do it all" attitude in many young women. Of those planning a career requiring a college education, 26 percent desired four or more children. Knaub (1986) found that approximately 70 percent of the adolescents and young adults in dual-career families she surveyed intended to choose the combination of marriage, career, and parenthood as their own family life-style.

Characteristics of Dual-Career Families

While there is great diversity among dual-career couples, some generalizations can be made. When the characteristics of dual-career and traditional families were compared, both spouses in dual-career families tended to be highly qualified persons and to share similar values; they seemed to have fewer needs for affection, inclusion, and control; and they appeared to be more self-reliant than single-career couples are (Price-Bonham & Murphy, 1980). Dual-career couples tend to have only one or two children and to delay childbirth until wives are well established in their careers. On the other hand, traditional couples generally have their children before wives enter the work force. Recently, considerable interest in delaying parenthood has been exerted by the media. More women are having their first child in their thirties and early forties. In the 1970s there were 7.3 first births per 1,000 for women aged 30–34, and in 1979 this figure had escalated to 12.1, an increase of 66 percent. A recent article cited a Census Bureau report that indicated that one third of the babies born in 1988 were to mothers 30 and older (Schmid, 1989). Advantages cited by these couples include greater financial security and a lack of concern about advancement in their already established careers. Further, they reported the likelihood of flexibility in work schedules.

Since dual-career couples are more educated, they tend to have higher incomes. Wives in this life-style are likely to be employed full-time and to come from higher social-class backgrounds than their husbands. Career-oriented women, as compared to women in traditional families, have more likely had employed mothers and few siblings, and have been the first or only child. Further, career women usually come from families with significant elements of tension but not necessarily deviant families. In childhood, dual-career women have frequently had warm relationships with a conspicuous figure of strength—an older brother, father, or a grandparent.

Less empirical information is available about men in the dual-career life-style. Some evidence indicates that they can be differentiated from traditional males by having had warm relationships with their mothers. In addition, dual-career husbands have been found to facilitate their wives' careers by believing that the integration of family and work is crucial to the success of the wives' careers. It is likely that dual-career couples seek out marriage partners who complement their personalities and talents. Therefore

---

BOX 8a CHARACTERISTICS OF DUAL-CAREER COUPLES

Both husband and wife possess highly qualified job skills
Share similar values
Have fewer needs for affection, inclusion, and control
Are self-reliant
Have small number of children (one or two)
Delay childbearing
Have higher incomes than other couples

---

the dual-career husband responds to his wife's need for support and approval. In addition husbands of career women usually respect competence and achievement in women (Nadelson & Nadelson, 1980; Price-Bonham & Murphy, 1980). Box 8a summarizes characteristics of dual-career couples.

Dilemmas of Dual-Career Families

Considerable interest in the stresses experienced by dual-career couples has been generated. The Rapoports (1971, 1976) found that dual-career couples experienced stress from dilemmas arising from five different areas—role overload, normative dilemmas, identity, social network, and role cycling. These dilemmas provide tensions that contain excitement as well as difficulty; they provide zest to life as well as create problems. Resolution of the dilemmas seems to result in feelings of accomplishment and creativity as well as relief.

Role overload.   The sheer amount of work involved with a career, household supervision, child care, and social arrangements leads to overload. The work must be redistributed or left undone. Families vary in the manner in which they cope with this problem. Many hire outside help, but because of standards for housework the quality of help is rarely satisfactory. Outside help also intrudes on the family's privacy. In varying degrees the husband and the wife perform the necessary household tasks. This solution, however, usually involves considerable strain as each tries to sustain a demanding occupational

role. Sometimes children are pressed into assuming responsibility for themselves and for some household tasks. Studies of domestic time allocations have shown that the male's participation has increased little (Hopkins & White, 1978; Johnson & Johnson, 1980; Rapoport & Rapoport, 1976). The total workload of employed women is greater than that of their husbands, regardless of the number and ages of children present.

The goals of egalitarianism of domestic responsibilities and career advancement are unrealistic expectations for most dual-career couples. Studies have shown that, although these goals may be shared by the couple, behaviorally the actual performance of home-care responsibilities is largely assumed by the female. Research has indicated that, in general, the wife's career is secondary to the husband's—an attitude shared by both spouses. In fact, many women feel fortunate that their husbands allow them to pursue their career activities (Hopkins & White, 1978). Explanations for these attitudes and behavior are complex. Women are susceptible to conscious and unconscious motives to satisfy the nurturant needs of others; men are not. When these motives are compounded with the sex-linked normative restrictions of the female role, the result is often an unbalanced dependency on the wife in the dual-career family, despite the best intentions of the couple to distribute the workload. Women continue to bear the primary responsibility for child rearing at the same time they are engaged in careers. A major problem encountered is the guilt and anxiety about perceived failure to be an effective parent (Johnson & Johnson, 1980).

Normative dilemmas. Although working women are more acceptable to society than ever before, continuous work at a highly demanding occupation in competition with men is quite another matter. In the work field the career woman must contend with prejudice, discrimination, and delayed career advancement. It is no wonder, then, that the problems of dual-career families are largely problems encountered by women (Johnson & Johnson, 1980). Society has expected a married woman to have children and to enjoy mothering. Career mothers have the challenge of providing for stable, reliable care for the child and performing quality mothering. Many dual-career couples go to great lengths to assure quality care for the child. Particularly problematic is the lack of available quality care, a problem that will be discussed more fully in Chapter 12.

Some recent evidence indicates that executive fathers are sharing not only the family responsibilities but also the worry, stress, and guilt associated with leaving the child in someone else's care. Chapman (1987) found that fathers were almost as likely as mothers to say that the job interferes with family life. And 30 percent had sacrificed career opportunities (refused a new job, promotion, or transfer) because it meant less family time.

Identity dilemmas. Internal doubt and anxiety about whether the female is being an effective wife and mother and whether the husband is losing some of his manliness as he takes on more domestic roles are common among dual-career couples. While many of these couples intellectually accept egalitarian roles, socially they have internalized some of society's sex-role stereotyping. Although lip service may be given to equality between the sexes, the assumption remains that maximizing the male's opportunities is more important. Resulting behaviors from these feelings of ambivalence, concern, and guilt may take many forms—overindulging the child, being defensive or sensitive to criticism, or experiencing periods of self-doubt and/or depression.

Social network dilemmas. In dual-career families the wife's associates tend to be drawn into the social circle more than in traditional families, probably in response to the need for environmental supports to sustain the dual-career pattern. Her associates are more likely to provide this support than the extended family or the husband's associates. The extended family may hold a traditional gender-based division of labor viewpoint, or the couples themselves are mobile and geographically separated from the extended family. Dual-career couples often help to resolve their guilt by excluding kin who do not share their viewpoints (Johnson & Johnson, 1980; Rapoport & Rapoport, 1971, 1976).

Role cycling. Dual-career couples tend to establish themselves in their careers before they have children. Conventional families, however, normally establish the husband's career simultaneously with the bearing of children, and the wife's career is not established until motherhood has been assumed. After the couple establishes themselves occupationally, they tend to have all their children in a compressed period. Thus the wives can minimally interrupt their work. Dovetailing and planning for these multiple roles often create problems.

Marital Relationships in Dual-Career Families

The balancing of societal, familial, and professional roles creates stress for dual-career parents. It has been concluded that stress is an inherent attribute of the dual-career family, but it is accepted by both spouses as long as it remains manageable. White and her associates (1986) reported research on marital relationships in dual-career families and sources of stress for the couple. Moderate degrees of stress resulting from actively juggling the numerous roles may be less tension-producing than the stress of boredom and dissatisfaction that might result from the wife's lack of involvement in meaningful work. Further, wives' employment seems to have little effect on the amount of marital discord or stress reported by husbands. In fact, husbands of working wives seem to be happier and less stressed than those of nonworking women. Thus it can be concluded that the stress characteristic of the dual-career marriage may at times be positive in nature.

However, when levels of stress become unmanageable, marital problems often emerge. Usually both partners in a dual-career dyad have strong needs for self-esteem enhancement. Marital conflict is likely to emerge when a spouse fails or is unable to attend to the ego needs of the other. Further, incongruent perceptions of each other, their relationship, and their goals can lead to conflict and resentment between spouses. The differences between the husband's perceptions of his wife's role obligations increase the difficulty she feels in fulfilling her numerous role functions.

White and her associates (1986) found that wives perceive themselves as experiencing more stress than their husbands do, and that the sources of their stress are related to family roles rather than to work roles. They further found that dual-career wives perceive less emotional intimacy in their relationships than do husbands. They concluded that dual-career couples must move from a process of role expansion to one of role redefinition. Women must modify the demands of their family roles if they are to have the resources for addressing the demands of their careers. The goal for the dual-career couple should not be to remove stress but rather to reduce it, particularly for the wife.

Children in Dual-Career Families

While dual-career parents have a number of concerns regarding the care of their children, according to a survey conducted by *Fortune* magazine (Chapman, 1987), most were very satisfied with the child-care solutions they had found. These parents were convinced that the children of dual-career couples are more independent, are more socially adept, and have interesting role models as parents. But they admitted to many anxieties. Box 8b illustrates the child-care concerns that emerged from the study.

Knaub (1986) surveyed adolescents and young adults to determine their perceptions about growing up in a dual-career family. They found, in general, that these young people rated their families relatively high on the components of family strength—appreciation, concern, respect, support, esteem, commitment, positive communication, and conflict management. The mother was indicated by nearly 73 percent of the sample as the most influential parent. These young adults reported that they were satisfied with their experience in a dual-career family. The benefits they cited as a result of their family life-style were having positive role models and financial security. They felt their families were drawn closer by planning activities, such as travel and vacations, in order to be together. These youngsters expressed pride in their parents and felt that their parents respected each other's work. They were sensitive to the problems in dual-career family living. Time-related issues were identified as the greatest problems. More than 50 percent felt that their mothers took primary responsibility for managing the household and for child care.

Dual-career parents probably utilize indirect discipline and emotional support more often than conventional parents. Techniques such as reasoning and isolation are frequently utilized. Parents tend to train children to be self-reliant and independent. The development of consideration, self-control, and curiosity also seems to be valued by dual-career parents. These values contrast with those of working-class mothers, who emphasize behavioral conformity such as obedience, respect, and neatness. Mothers who work

BOX 8b   CONCERNS ABOUT CHILD CARE

	Fathers (%)	Mothers (%)
Both spouses share equally in child-care responsibility	55.1	51.9
Job interferes with family life	37.2	40.9
Sought less-demanding job to have more family time	20.5	26.5
Refused a job, promotion, or transfer because it would mean less family time	29.6	25.7
Felt nervous or under stress in past 3 months	49.2	70.2
Missed at least one workday in the past 3 months due to family obligations	37.8	58.6
Think children of working parents benefit by having interesting role models as parents	77.5	86.3
Think children of working parents suffer by not being given enough time and attention	55.4	58.2
Would like their companies to provide a subsidized child-care center	38.5	54.1
Would like their companies to offer flexible working hours	34.8	54.1
Think companies can do more to help manage work/family responsibilities	34.5	30.9

Source: Adapted from Chapman, F. (1987, February 16). Executive guilt: Who's taking care of the children? *Fortune,* pp. 30–37.

use coercive discipline less often and feel less hostility and more empathy for their children, but tend to be overindulgent. Professional women also seem to experience pleasure in their children's growing independence, to be less overprotective and less self-sacrificing (Gilbert, Holahan, & Manning, 1981; Johnson & Johnson, 1980; Nadelson & Nadelson, 1980). In fact, in this life-style there is less chance that the child will be a primary source of maternal dissatisfaction.

Dual-career parents appear to be more concerned about the quality of the parent-child relationship than with the child's objective behavior. Thus parents devise activities that are directed toward enhancing the environment of the children both at home and in educational settings. They develop hobbies and activities in which the entire family can participate. Dual-career mothers participate in the school-age child's activities by supervising the child's progress and being involved in school activities,

---

BOX 8c   CHARACTERISTICS OF CHILDREN IN DUAL-CAREER FAMILIES

Develop independence and resourcefulness

Share in household tasks

Show pride in the accomplishments of their parents

Demonstrate a wider range of interests

Have a greater variety of role models available

Enjoy expanded occupational life and experience

Boys develop a more egalitarian viewpoint

---

which can be coordinated with their work. These parents also set a high priority on achievement and psychological adjustment of the child (Johnson & Johnson, 1980).

Studies of daughters' academic achievements provide additional evidence of the positive effects of a career mother. Achieving women and career women more often had educated and employed mothers than did women whose mothers did not have such accomplishments (Nadelson & Nadelson, 1980).

Of course, the child in a dual-career family can manifest pathological behavior just as a child in any other life-style, depending on how the situations are managed and what social pressures are operating on the family. Leaving children to ''fend for themselves'' could fail to produce resourcefulness and, instead, arouse greater dependency. Guilt on the part of the parent(s) could lead to overprotectiveness or indulgence. A lack of appropriate child-care arrangements could confuse the child and create anxiety (Rapoport & Rapoport, 1976). Box 8c lists some of the characteristics of children in dual-career families.

It appears that children receive more positive benefits than negative effects. Some evidence (Trimberger & MacLean, 1982) indicates that the child's age, sex, and ordinal position influence her perception of maternal employment. Further, communication patterns between mother and child influence the child's perception of having a working mother. Since these findings indicate that demographic, psychological, and social variables influence children's perceptions, future research should focus on these variables.

Support for Dual-Career Parents

Neither partner is prepared fully for the potential conflict, competition, and stress accompanying a dual-career life-style. Research indicates that conflicts between professional and parental roles are especially stressful for the female spouse. Women appear to be able to handle conflicts arising from the professional role more easily than those arising from family roles. Therefore support for families in this life-style should be from the preventive as well as the crisis intervention standpoint. Effective parenting appears to depend on both parents having a positive attitude about the mother's working, her job situation, appropriate child-care arrangements, and effective resolution of the dilemmas experienced. Several approaches have been suggested to assist dual-career families.

Group experiences. Provision for group experiences where dual-career parents can share common problems could facilitate a sense of community with similar families, thus decreasing feelings of guilt and alienation. Sharing ideas with similar families can serve to increase coping skills. Knowledge and information regarding available quality child-care facilities and/or domestic help could be shared.

Groups composed of families in different stages of the life cycle can help orient younger couples as to what to expect. Discussions that help couples understand the concept of equitable, rather than equal, opportunities and constraints would facilitate understanding and acceptance among spouses. Families need help in learning the process of negotiating and implementing time-limited behavior contracts. When pressures and obligations are especially acute for a particular family member, another member gives assistance, which helps to develop feelings of fairness. Development of management skills can assist families with planning and organizing all tasks associated with the dual-career role. More effective use of time can help facilitate time for leisure activities in which the entire family can participate. Developing communication skills in all family members would enhance the sharing of feelings and thoughts with one another, thereby reducing hostility.

Avis (1986) described an enrichment program, Working Together, to assist dual-career couples deal with stress and to function more effectively in this life-style. Couples are helped to renegotiate roles and responsibilities, structure and manage time, meet emotional needs, deal with competition, and share control and power. The program consists of seven 2½-hour weekly sessions.

The "family meeting" approach is a means of working toward the goal of equity for all family members. In this approach each member is allowed his or her chance to speak and has a part in the development of rules that govern the family. This concept also provides the opportunity for families to grow and change as the family moves through the life cycle (Hopkins & White, 1978).

Preparing young unmarried persons for a dual-career life-style appears to be warranted. Recognizing the likelihood that both parents will probably work, developing insight into the stresses and strains they might experience, and appropriate techniques for resolution, seems to be an important preventive approach. Further, educating young people, as well as those who are already parents, in the benefits of shared parenting would be important (Russell, 1986).

Environmental changes. Several environmental changes have been proposed that would support the dual-career life-style (Bonfield, 1986; Magid, 1986; Nelson-Horchler, 1986; Simon, 1984). While more and more men are performing household tasks and parenting roles, there is still a widely held belief that the mother can perform these more effectively and should do so. The attitude that men are being helpful to their wives when they perform child-rearing and household tasks is prevalent. Continued *change in society's attitude* toward promoting a more equitable reorganization of domestic responsibilities appears important. Children could then benefit by having fathers who participate in the full range of parenting responsibilities.

An upgrading in the domestic-helper occupations and improvement in the whole range of services available to the dual-career family are necessary. Providing additional quality child-care alternatives and upgrading child-care occupations are important sources of support for the dual-career family.

Construction of family housing units that meet the varied needs of families and that are located conveniently to support services and the workplace would facilitate this life-style. Families in different stages of the life cycle who live in close proximity can provide some of the same benefits that extended families have provided in the past—provision of models, assisting with child care, encouragement, and the like.

Many *changes in the world of work* are emerging, but progress should continue. A few pioneering employers have found that strengthening working parents' abilities to help themselves through family-responsive work policies and programs is the most effective support they can provide. Flexible career paths, parent-tailored benefits, financial assistance, and on-site child-care centers are ways that organizations can help employees with career/family conflict (Magid, 1986).

Flexible career paths, for both men and women, allow working parents to take "time-outs" or work on a "temporary plateau" without leading to a career setback. When appropriate, the linear path or an ascending pattern can later be resumed. In addition to promoting flexible career paths, parent-responsive benefits packages would support dual-career parents; these include flexible work times for full-time employees, permanent part-time employment with benefits, job sharing, work-at-home options, cafeteria-style plans that allow employees to select benefits most helpful to their family situation, and family-oriented sick-leave policies (Magid, 1986). Currently only 18 percent of the nation's employees have some flex-time programs. Flex-time allows employees, male and female, to have an input into when they begin and end the workday (Bonfield, 1986). Greater flexibility in work hours would allow parents to more effectively combine the two careers—work and parenthood.

In August 1984 the city of Philadelphia passed a law that gave adoptive fathers the same right as natural fathers to have up to 6 months unpaid leave with a guarantee of returning to their old jobs. Philadelphia was the first city to grant paternal leave for all municipal employees. One survey indicated that 1,500 companies have implemented some form of paternal-leave policy (Simon, 1984).

Education and support programs sponsored by industry could include seminars at the work site and/or in-house referral services. Financial-assistance programs provide a variety of options for assisting parents with child care (Magid, 1986). Vendor programs, vouchers, flexible spending accounts, or on-site child-care facilities are examples. However, corporate America still views child care as a "women's" issue not as an economic one. Child care as a part of an employee benefits program is not currently a high priority for most companies (Bonfield, 1986). In 1986 only about 2,000 out of 6 million employers had an on-site child-care center for their employees (Nelson-Horchler, 1986). This number, however, was triple the number in 1982. Not all parents want on-site centers, but employers need to assess employee needs and provide options for parents.

Although progress has been made in these areas, many of the necessary changes have not occurred because of the inflexibility of social systems and internalized resistance to change on the part of individuals. While some social systems can be altered by legislation, attitudinal changes are more difficult. Obviously, sex roles are learned early. Values and attitudes that affect one's ability to function effectively in a dual-career life-style are being formed during the preschool years. Throughout the child's development, appropriate concepts regarding this and other life-styles should be taught so that individuals can make wise decisions concerning options available.

In summary, dual-worker and dual-career families are increasing at a rapid pace, out of both economic necessity and a desire by women to fulfill personal goals. It is true that dual-career couples have more financial resources with which to seek necessary assistance—child care, maintenance of the home, and so on. However, they face the dilemmas of role overload, normative and identity dilemmas, social network dilemmas, and role cycling. While children of dual-career families seem to manifest more positive than negative characteristics, career couples may need help in resolving the potential conflicts between their professions and their families.

Commuter Marriages

The commuter marriage is one type of a dual-career life-style. These marriages have been defined as those couples who commute between two households that are usually considerable distances apart. It has been estimated that there are about one million couples around the country who maintain this life-style, the number increasing in tandem with the number of dual-career couples (Kantrowitz, Namuth, Karagia, & Burgower, 1985). Couples maintaining this life-style usually are in the middle- or upper-income brackets and are frequently found in the academic world, where tenure track positions have become too rare to give up. Most view this arrangement as temporary, necessary, but inconvenient. Most commute for an average of 2 years.

Obviously, there are advantages and disadvantages to this life-style. The advantage is that neither spouse has to sacrifice career for marriage. The disadvantages are real emotional and financial costs. Loneliness is a major problem, and the telephone becomes a very important mode of communication. This, along with frequent travel and maintaining two residences, is very expensive. When the couple is together, time is very precious. Social life is reduced, and friendships suffer. If the couple has children, then many of the disadvantages relating to parent-child relationships of single parents would be applicable. However, for some couples commuter marriage may be the most feasible solution for the present.

MOBILE FAMILIES

One of the descriptors frequently used in relation to current society is *mobile*. It has been estimated that each American will move an average of 14 times in her lifetime (Constable, 1978). In one five-year period, 49 percent of the population in this country relocated. Of this 49 percent, 41.3 percent moved within the United States and 7.7 percent to another country. Moving to another location within the same *county* was most common. About 17 percent moved to a different county within the same state, whereas only 8.6 percent moved to another state (U.S. Department of Commerce, 1977). However, more recent data indicated that the rate of moving is declining. During this 2-year period approximately 17 percent of the population changed residence. Consistent with earlier patterns, most of the moves were for short distances (U.S. Bureau of the Census, 1983b). The decline in mobility has been attributed to a weak economy and high inflation ("America's new immobile society," 1981). Certain groups of the population move more frequently than others due to occupational demands, socioeconomic conditions, or environmental changes. Families are required to relocate by private industry, public programs, urban renewal, highway construction, and the military (Carter, 1981).

The most frequently stated reasons for moving are search for employment or increased job opportunities in a new area, dislike of current community, and the desire to improve housing conditions (Marsh, 1976). Other reasons include the desire to be closer to relatives, health considerations, separation, and divorce (Levine, 1976). Many occupations in government and private industry require relocation for training and/or advancement purposes. Transfers are most prevalent among white-collar workers, especially those in managerial or sales positions. Blue-collar workers traditionally have not been highly mobile. They are seldom offered transfers, and those who move independently take the risk of dropping to the bottom of union seniority lists ("America's new immobile society," 1981). Local moves often are related to forced circumstances in the original neighborhood—for example, urban renewal or neighborhood changes—or a difficult interpersonal or school situation (Constable, 1978). Relocation frequently has a significant bearing on the present and future socioeconomic status and thus affects adjustments made by individual family members.

It has been estimated that about 12 million school-age children change residence each year, and the largest percentage of these change schools as well. In a 5-year period, 50 percent of all school-age children are likely to experience at least one relocation. Although children become mobile for different reasons, children in military, corporate, and migrant families are the most likely to experience mobility. Children in low-income families are likely to experience greater mobility than upper-income children. In a low-income-area school it was found that 49 percent of the children moved in a year, compared to 16.7 percent of the children in an upper-income school (Levine, 1976). The military moved 59.5 percent of its personnel in a year, resulting in the relocation of 878,659 male personnel, of whom 42.8 percent had one or more dependents (Marsh, 1976). It has been estimated that among military families are 120,000 adolescents whose development is particularly vulnerable to certain aspects of geographic and social change (Carter, 1981).

Effects of Relocation and Factors Affecting Adjustment

Much of the literature on relocation has focused on the loss of social and geographic familiarity as well as on the long-term relationships and values. In addition to loss of personal relationships, the family experiences the loss of community and kinship (Richards, Donohue, & Gullotta, 1985). It cannot be concluded, however, that all geographic relocation represents a crisis or a hardship for the family. Often the family is excited by the new opportunities afforded by relocation but is threatened by the unknown. The type of adjustments needed depend on the style of the family and position of individuals in that family.

It is reasonable to assume, however, that the family does experience a degree of disruption of previously maintained social and interpersonal relationships, and a series of interactions between the family and its environment must take over as the family seeks to establish equilibrium in the new environment. Whatever the situation, individuals will probably attempt to adjust to their new environment, and this adjustment takes time. There is always a period of accommodation, adjustment, and integration that must occur. Regardless of the reason for the move and the attitudes of family members toward it, relocation presents complex tasks to be accomplished. The family is simultaneously trying to accomplish all the tasks associated with physically moving household and personal belongings from one residence to another; severing the relationships and ties to the former community; forming relationships and becoming involved in the new community; establishing, in some cases, new relationships among its own family members (especially if the move is in conjunction with change in the family structure); carrying on routine affairs of the family; and functioning as a family unit (Constable, 1978; Marsh, 1976).

Research has indicated that the effects of relocation on family members can be both positive and negative. For example, frequent relocation may cause interfamilial dependence as the family provides the only refuge for its members. Individuals may not have enough time to develop friendships or a support system. In some cases it may cause a child to become a loner. On the other hand, moving to another location may serve as an adaptive function, contributing to cognitive complexity, flexibility, and academic performance. A sense of social isolation may be experienced by the family, created by the loss of established relationships and the deficit of new ones. Further, in most cases (when the relocation is related to the father's employment), the identity of the wife and mother is diminished. But the identity of the husband may be enhanced because he can transfer credentials from one job to another.

Various factors have been found to affect the adjustment process. The *individual's perception* determines the difficulty and length of the adjustment process. Obviously some family members may have a more positive or negative attitude than other members. The reason for the move has a significant bearing on the attitudes toward the move. If the relocation is a result of a promotion and increased income, the attitudes of the father, and perhaps the other family members, are likely to be positive. In like manner an improvement in housing, a better neighborhood, or a more prestigious school would probably promote positive feelings in most family members. Individuals who have had deep commitments to and involvement in a community may experience extended grief reactions upon leaving it. However, those individuals who become integrated into the new community tend to make adjustments more quickly and easily, while those who continue to feel and experience alienation have problems (McKain, 1976).

The *distance of the move* is another factor. The greater the distance and the more dissimilar the new environment is to the old, the greater the difficulty of adjustment will be. Some families experience greater and more abrupt disruption in their patterns and habits of integration than other families do. A military family, for example, moving across the country from one military base to another may actually experience less change than a family moving from a middle- to an upper-class or a lower-class neighborhood in the same city (Tooley, 1970). It cannot be assumed, then, that the distance a family moves is the major factor in environmental change for the family; rather it is the *degree of disruption* that occurs. *How the family views the relocation* determines whether or not it is a crisis for the family. The military, despite creating family hardships by requiring frequent moves of great distance, provides a fairly stable environment with minimal place-to-place changes in social and economic structure. Both the physical and social aspects of the new environment are important in adjustment.

The *ages of the family members* seem to be a factor also in the length and degree of adjustment. Younger families tend to make more satisfactory adjustments than older, more settled adults do. Further, younger children tend to adjust more easily than older children do.

It appears, then, that the effect of a move varies depending on the age of the children, the career stage of the husband, the meaning given to the move by each family member, the social supports in the community, the coping resources of the family, and the support provided by employers (Richards et al., 1985). There appears to be a temporary period of disruption and disorganization in the family as a result of relocation. In this transition period major changes in life space must be made. Learning new tasks in a new environment, becoming an integral part of the community, adapting to a new school, and developing new relationships create stress, but they can be accomplished after a period of time by most families.

Military Families

Military families are clearly different from traditional nuclear families in that they are exposed to pressures of frequent parent absence and geographic mobility. Some research indicates the fallacy of grouping all military families into one kind of life-style. Those families who live on military bases rather than in the community have more similarities in attitudes and activities than do military families living off-base (McCubbin, Dahl, & Hunter, 1976).

Military fathers. Military parents must perform several roles simultaneously—soldier, spouse, and parent. The military considers its personnel to be on 24-hour duty. Duty first, family second has been the predominant attitude (Darnauer, 1976). Historically the military was interested only in single men. There was an old military saying: "If Uncle Sam had wanted you to have a wife, he'd have issued you one." The number of married military personnel has increased, and thus there are more dependents. The average enlisted family has 1.5 children, whereas the average officer family has 1.7 children (Ott, 1978). Only recently has the military recognized the correlation between the quality of service personnel's family life and performance of duties (*Cofo Memo,* 1981; McCubbin et al., 1976). Even though the military has

recently changed programs and policies that provide greater consideration to families of personnel, the military system rewards behavior that serves the system and punishes behavior that threatens it. If the military system conflicts with the family system, tension results and changes occur. Scapegoating is a frequent result of conflict between the soldier and family roles.

Information from families whose children were referred to a military mental-health clinic revealed some common problems resulting from the relationships of the families to the military system. Reported were feelings of their lives being managed by someone else, resulting in a sense of loss of control. Thus a tension-producing environment existed. Forced compliance, authoritative hierarchy, discouraged confrontation, and channeling of problems through the chain of command contributed to these feelings. The family felt it existed only as an extension of the father. Rights and privileges existed through him and only as long as he lived (Lagrone, 1978).

Military wives. The civilian mother in the military family may be viewed as weak and dependent, and the father strong and independent. Wives frequently find that husbands are compliant, tightly bound to the military system, and unsupportive of their needs. Women married to military personnel find it particularly hard to pursue a career or to continue their schooling. The dual-career family, particularly, encounters difficulties. The disadvantages associated with wives' employment center around the loss of benefits (salary, fringe, and seniority) caused by transfers; difficulties in establishing a career; lack of uniformity from state to state in credentialing, such as teacher certification; and discrimination by employers because of transitory existence of military families (Finlayson, 1976).

Mothers in military families are likely to function differently when fathers are present than when they are away on military assignments. When the father leaves, roles have to be reassigned. There is a "closing of the ranks" as the mother assumes some of the father's role. The mother's perception of separation is particularly important, as are resources utilized and hardship of separation. Learning to cope and "make

do" are tasks that military wives and mothers must accomplish. Even though the mother becomes more independent when the father is away, she often feels rejected. With succeeding separations, these women become more effective in adjustment (McCubbin et al., 1976; Ott, 1978). When the father returns, he must be reintegrated into the family. This process takes time and produces stress.

Mothers in the military. The number of women in the military services has increased in the last 10 years. As of December 1987 there were 32,207 women officers, or 10.5 percent of all officers, and 189,315 enlisted women, or 10.2 percent of all enlistees. These trends reflect the changing attitudes of the military services toward women's roles. While approximately 90 percent of all military personnel are still male, many women are proving themselves as valued military persons. A recent film clip on television depicted a female as second in command of a battleship. Many of these women are married to military men. About half of all military personnel in 1987 were married. Of the 2,160,727 people in the military 1,152,821 were married and these families had 1,625,111 children (U.S. Department of Defense, 1988).

Obviously, military mothers encounter some unique problems. They may be separated from their children for lengthy periods of time. Role overload, child care, and spousal relationships are other areas that may cause stress. Little research has been conducted concerning the issues of military mothers. As the number increases, this appears to be a fruitful area for research.

Discipline. While military families use a variety of approaches in guiding and disciplining children, the authoritarian approach is most common. Discipline and a sense of orderliness often are learned quicker in a military home than in a civilian one (Ott, 1978). In a study of children referred to a military mental-health clinic, it was found that the greatest number (93 percent) of behavioral problems were from homes in which the authoritarian approach was used. In most instances the fathers themselves had come from authoritarian homes, and most of these authoritarian fathers were career men. It is probable that this background was a factor in the choice of the military as a career.

Children of career military men often follow their fathers into a military profession. In 1976, 75 percent of the active-duty soldiers had at least one other family member who had been in the military. Of the West Point cadets, 25 percent are former military dependents (Ott, 1978).

Advantages of military dependency.   There are a number of studies portraying the positive aspects of being a military child (McCubbin et al., 1976; Ott, 1978). There is relative homogeneity among the children of military families. There is little income differential, free medical care, and parents are average or above in intelligence. These conditions make for a relatively select group. As a group these children have higher IQs, better school achievement, and less juvenile delinquency than the U.S. child population as a whole. Travel has been mentioned frequently as a major benefit for military children. Many of these children have seen at least one-half of the United States and one or more foreign countries. Through extensive travel they have been exposed to different life-styles, which serves to broaden their perspective, and development of sophistication and worldliness at a younger age is possible. Military children may learn more about the workings of government than civilian children. Extensive relocation allows for a broader perspective toward other people. Intermingling with persons from diverse cultures allows children to grow up with nondiscriminatory attitudes. Some military children learn to enjoy moving from place to place and may become bored if they stay too long in one place. Military life is viewed by some parents as helpful in preparing children for a mobile society. Out of necessity the military child learns to become adaptable and flexible.

Disadvantages of military dependency.   The major disadvantages for children of military parents center around the transitory life and relationships that are necessary because of the frequent relocation and periodic absence of a parent. Children must leave friends behind and change schools with each relocation. Because a military child has no consistent peer group when growing up, she often turns to the family. The family becomes the stabilizing factor in the child's life. Leaving friends behind is never easy, but it is a fact of life that military adults and children quickly learn to accept, although often grudgingly. They learn to form temporary relationships since they know they will be moving again in a couple of years. The temporary nature of these relationships eases the trauma when the move occurs. Military children adapt to their parents' impermanent way of life out of necessity, but some would prefer a life of fewer disruptions (Ott, 1978).

Adolescents, particularly, appear to be vulnerable to relocation. They decry giving up old relationships and establishing new ones. Some adolescents also feel that the requirement for compliance with military policy concerning rank differentials, racial equality, and personal behavior is troublesome, and they feel hampered in their desire to express themselves and to experiment. Having to be concerned about how their behavior will affect the parent's career is viewed negatively. Parents who pressure adolescents "not to get into trouble" tend to enforce rigid rules that may lead to family conflict. Some adolescents feel that the restrictions of the military environment are "good" for them. Other military youth perceive themselves as second-class citizens because concern for the parent's image and advancement takes priority over the interests and desires of family members (Darnauer, 1976).

Effects of military life on children.   Studies relating to effects of frequent relocation on academic adjustment and performance of children have yielded inconclusive results. Some research has found that the number of moves is associated with behavior problems in school; other research has found no relationship. It appears that those children who have problems prior to the move are likely to continue to have them, but mobility in and of itself does not alter the academic and school adjustment of children. Mobility, then, can have positive or negative effects or none at all (Caron, 1975). Young children seem to make adjustments to school more easily than older ones. Teenagers seem to make the poorest adjustment to a change of school. Making new friends and being accepted by the peer group is quite important and sometimes difficult. Some children prefer to attend all-military schools because other children have the same outlook and problems (Ott, 1978).

Frequent parent absence is another factor that affects parenting in military families. Adjusting to wartime assignments, unaccompanied tours, and repeated temporary duty assignments are likely to have a profound effect on family members. Adjustment to separation during wartime may be more difficult than in peacetime, as fear for the father's safety may be a factor. The degree of adjustment appears to be related to the ability of the family to reorganize roles and whether the family continues to meet the needs of its members. The mother's perception of the separation is particularly important. Stress nearly always accompanies the father's separation. Sometimes young children feel that they have led to the father's leaving. Extreme guilt may be felt, and severe problems may result. For example, grief, depression, anxiety, and feelings of being deprived of their sources of comfort, pleasure, and security are often experienced. The effects of the father's absence tend to be related to the prior father-child relationship. When this relationship has been sound, the adjustment process is easier. Boys of absent military fathers have been found to have increased masculine striving and poorer peer adjustment than boys of fathers present in the home. Extended father absence during the critical stages of sex-role and moral development can deter these processes. This phenomenon is true for both boys and girls. Children may be viewed by the mother in two ways. She may see the children as a source of support and comfort, or she may see them as restricting her participation in the outside world (McCubbin et al., 1976).

Reuniting the father into the family after his absence also is a complex process that creates stress. The family's history, the characteristics of the family members, the family's adjustment during his absence, and the interactions of the family at the time of reentry affect reunification. The process involves the reestablishment of coherence and family unity—including the husband-wife relationship, the revitalization of

the father-child relationship, the division of labor within the home, and the reallocation of roles. The father may fail to recognize the changes that have occurred in the family while he was away, and on return he may expect to resume the position of power. Emotional struggles, particularly feelings of rejection, and reestablishment of affection between father and family members are extremely difficult and complex (McCubbin et al., 1976). The advantages and disadvantages of military life are found in Box 8d.

Single military parents. Single military parents have all the problems of other single parents and more. They are expected to meet the same duty requirements as other personnel, and they are frequently assigned with little notice to guard duty, CQ (in charge of quarters), TDY (temporary duty), field exercises, and overseas assignments. Special assignments that require long absences from home present particularly pressing problems.

The military often provides child-care centers, and some consideration is given when making assignments. Single parents, as well as families in which both parents are military, are required to file a Dependent Care Plan. This plan specifies who will care for the children during any absence, where they will be cared for, and how they will be cared for. This plan is signed by the parent(s), one copy filed with the military, one with the parent, and one with the person named in the plan.

Support for military families. Recently all branches of the military have recognized the importance of family-policy offices and family-services programs both in this country and abroad in promoting the family life of military personnel. In addition to the establishment of these offices and a variety of programs, the Military Resource Center has been developed to support and link these family programs and to facilitate improved liaison with the civilian community. By 1985, 360 armed forces family programs were in operation. Most of these programs include information services, referral and coordination of family-service providers and resources, relocation aid, spouse employment, consultation and job information, family financial

---

BOX 8d   ADVANTAGES AND DISADVANTAGES OF MILITARY LIFE

Advantages	Disadvantages
Free services	Frequent parent absence
Travel	Increased mobility
Development of a broader perspective toward people	Multiple roles for parents
	Sense of loss of control
Increased adaptability and flexibility	Possible impaired identity for family members
Relating to people with similar interests, income, and circumstances	Difficulty for civilian wives in completing their education or in pursuing a career
Greater exposure to the functioning of government	Frequent reassignment of family roles
	Transitory relationships

---

management education, and aid to families in crisis (Voydanoff, 1987).

The higher the rank, the more likely the family is to know about the available resources and services as well as about the perception of social cost. There is a widespread belief that family conflict that comes to official attention will be dealt with in a punitive way by the commanding officer. Many families prefer to utilize informal problem-solving resources, such as friends and relatives, rather than military-provided ones (McCubbin et al., 1976). In a study of children and adolescents referred to a military mental-health clinic, Lagrone (1978) found that 94 percent were the children of enlisted personnel and only 6 percent were the children of officers. Marsh (1976), who studied hardships experienced by military families, found that those families with the most hardships utilized community resources more than military-provided ones.

Suggested ways that the military can assist families were provided by Lagrone (1978). These included educating family members about what to expect from the military system; detecting problems early; using appropriate referral; conducting parenting classes; keeping records confidential; stabilizing tours of duty; reintegrating family sessions when the father returns from an isolated tour; and continuing already existing programs to improve race relations, to help abusive parents, and to work with drug and alcohol abusers.

Corporate Families

More than one half of the individuals (approximately 22 million people) who moved during the 1970s moved for job-related reasons. The young, upwardly mobile executive moves more frequently than others do. Corporate families, however, are increasingly resisting relocation. Among the factors contributing to the resistance to mobility in corporate families are the disruption of family life, the increase in dual-occupation families, home ownership and increased housing costs, and the escalating interest rates required to purchase another home. The high cost of transfers to companies also has been identified as a primary factor in the declining trend of labor mobility ("For lots of reasons," 1977).

Problems of corporate life. Although the number of corporate families who relocate each year may be declining, there are still large numbers of families and children experiencing the stresses of this life-style. Even though the process of relocation may favorably affect the attainment of career and financial goals of one parent, usually the father, it is experienced as a stressful situation by many corporate families and may create trauma for individual family members. Several sources of stress for the corporate family were enumerated by Voydanoff (1980): routine parent absence; work-related stress associated with time pressure and mobility aspirations; and stress associated with status changes relative to employer, geographic mobility, and job or career transfer.

The stress created by relocation in corporate families is similar to that in military families. The corporate family is likely to move across state lines. Therefore the loss of kin and extended family is added to the loss of friends and other community ties. It may be difficult for corporate families to integrate into the new community. Members of the community do not reach out to them because they realize that many of them will move again in a short period of time (Tiger, 1974). Unlike military families, they do not experience a "steady-made" social community.

The corporate father. In a number of ways the corporate father is similar to the military father. Corporations have expected managerial personnel to be totally committed to the company—in effect, to be a company man. Geographic mobility has been viewed as the employee's commitment to the company. Moves are expected to be perceived as opportunities for advancement, and refusing to move has been assumed to be a form of career suicide.

Father absence is frequent in corporate families, as in military families. Even though the corporate father may be in town, he may be absent from family activities because he is at the office or emotionally absent when at home due to preoccupation with the demands of the job. The effects of father absence in corporate families are the same as in other families. Many corporate husbands utilize the "in-and-out" mode of parenting. The frequent entrances and exits of the work-involved father make parenting difficult and upset both parental and spousal relationships (Richards et al., 1985).

Of all family members the corporate father is the least affected by relocation. He does not suffer as much from the loss of friends, community ties, or extended family as do other family members. Despite the fact that he finds himself in a new office, his business situation typically remains familiar. He is generally accepted by his peers at work because of his skills and credentials as an executive. He is not totally without stress, however, as he may have to prove himself in a new position and establish relationships with co-workers. His self-esteem may be at risk until he has performed to his and others' satisfaction.

The effects of relocation are significantly different for husbands and wives (Ammons, Nelson, & Wodarski, 1982; Richards et al., 1985). Men are considerably more enthusiastic about the relocation than their wives are. Wives frequently experience significantly more depression, boredom, and sense of loss than their husbands do. Corporate wives often adopt a self-sacrificial attitude. They tend to minimize relocation problems and direct complaints inward. They may internalize and define problems as personal failings. The corporate wife and mother may pay the greatest price for the family's relocation, not only in terms of community ties and friendships but also in terms of a sense of identity and self-worth ("Why moving day comes," 1975). While her husband is provided the stimulation and challenge through his new job, she is placed in the position of maintaining balance and continuity of the family, often to the detriment of her own career development. Although this attitude is still prevalent, it does appear to be changing to a degree (Duncan & Perucci, 1976). In the past the wife's employment, no matter how successful, has been secondary to the husband's and inconsequential to the decision to move.

The noncareer wife of the corporate employee may find that the social credentials she has built through community activities, volunteer work, and social organizations do not transfer to the new location (Voydanoff, 1980). There are growing numbers of educated homemakers who have been excluded from the professional socialization process because they have not been in one location long enough (Gaylord, 1979).

Obviously the wife's feelings about her role as corporate wife, frequent relocation, and absence of her husband affect her ability to adjust. Her attitudes primarily determine the adjustment of the children. Three factors have been found to be associated with the ability of the corporate executive's wife to adapt to routine job-related absence by her husband: her ability and desire to fit into the corporate life-style; her desire and ability to develop her own interests, talents, and interpersonal relationships; and her ability to establish independence and self-sufficiency (Bass, McCubbin, & Lester, 1979).

The following changes in life-style have been listed by wives of corporate men when relocation was experienced: personal adjustment, finding a suitable neighborhood, higher mortgages, new recreational patterns, fewer family get-togethers, and altered financial states. Change, even change perceived as positive, is stressful (Ammons et al., 1982).

There is some evidence to indicate that the factors of age, education, income, and participation in prerelocation site visitations affect the wives' adjustments. The younger and more educated the wife and the higher the income, the more likely it is that a satisfactory adjustment is made. Participation in prerelocation site visitations also correlates with happiness in the new community (Richards et al., 1985).

Husbands and wives report different variables as being important in making a smooth transition to the new community. Husbands focus more on work-related conditions, such as knowledge of what the new job will entail, the scope of their new responsibilities, contact with the new boss before the job begins, and early success experiences on the new job. Wives report family and community issues as important, including having a part in the decision to move, feeling that the community is a desirable place to live, and feeling that children are making a satisfactory adjustment (Richards et al., 1985).

The corporate mother. Many societal changes, including changing attitudes toward women's roles, increasing numbers of highly educated women, and policies prohibiting discrimination, have led to more women in managerial positions in business and industry. In the last 20 years, the percentage of managerial positions held by women increased by 150 percent (Crouse, 1987). By 1984 women were holding an estimated 33 percent of all administrative and managerial positions in business. However, of the top 50 companies in the United States, only 2 percent of the boardroom executives were women. Thus the majority of corporate women hold lower-level managerial positions. Many of these women are mothers, which adds another dimension to the problems they encounter. A number of these problems have been discussed in the section on dual-career families.

The focus of books written for women managers reflects changing societal attitudes. In the 1970s the books were how-to-do-it in approach, focusing on looking and acting like managers. There was little concern for performance or quality. In the 1980s there was a shift from image to survival techniques and performance or quality. Few women have survived the corporate world, but those who made significant advances did so with enormous sacrifices in their personal lives. Some women are calculating the costs and are deciding the costs are too high. A large percentage work long hours and still are responsible for routine management of the household, personal care, and child care (Crouse, 1987).

There is some indication that men's attitudes toward women administrators are changing. In one study men's favorable attitudes toward women executives rose from 35 percent in 1965 to 73 percent in 1985 (Crouse, 1987). Many men in subordinate positions to women are comfortable interacting with them, but some are not. Today's corporate woman wants to be able to reach her potential, matching her abilities and interests with demands of the job. She wants to be a vital part of the organization or corporation, and often this means she is in competition with a male for an aspired position.

There has been limited research focusing on issues of corporate women. Most of the research on corporate families has utilized male samples. However, considerable research has focused on working women in general (Voydanoff, 1987). It is likely that increased research will focus on women executives as their numbers continue to increase. When reviewing the literature on the effects of work on the family, some generalizations may be made regarding family functioning in corporate families (see Box 8e).

Clearly child care is an issue with corporate mothers. Early studies indicated that highly

BOX 8e EFFECTS OF CORPORATE LIFE ON FAMILY FUNCTIONING

For Both Spouses	Routine absence of spouse/parent
	Work-related stress, such as time pressure and mobility aspirations
	Loss of contact with extended family, friends, and other community ties when relocating
	Difficulty in fulfilling some aspects of family roles, such as companionship with spouse and children, attending family and school functions, and participating in household maintenance
	Possible lower quality of home life and higher level of work/family conflict and strain—the more hours spent in work activities, the greater the likelihood of these effects
For Corporate Mothers	Possible lower marital satisfaction of husband due to necessary life-style routines, demands to participate in household work, or a relative loss of power and status
	Greater power in family, especially in financial decision making
	Time spent in family work reduced by half as compared to full-time homemakers—accounted for by lower standards, increased efficiency, and outside assistance with child care
For Corporate Fathers	Difficulty in parenting and spousal relationships due to frequent entrances and exits to household
	Less affected by relocation than other family members
	Transferability of skills and credentials result in greater acceptance by peers
	Self-esteem dependent on proven competency in new position
For Noncorporate Spouses	Possible boredom, depression, and extreme loss when relocating
	Interference with ability to pursue own career
	Nontransferable credentials from one community to another
	Possible difficulty adjusting to new life-style

educated women were more constrained in employment by the presence of young children. More recent studies, however, indicate that this pattern has reversed. This may be due to these mothers changing their minds about the quality of child care available or because they spend as much time with children as do other mothers, at the expense of their own leisure or sleep (Spitze, 1988). While it is not known how corporate mothers resolve their child care needs, it is likely that a wide variety of options are utilized, including nannies or other hired personnel who come into the home to care for the child, child-care centers, husbands who have full or partial responsibility for care, and flex-time or other family-oriented workplace policies.

Various coping strategies have been found to be utilized by corporate families: maintaining family integrity, fitting into corporate life-style, believing in spouse's profession, developing interpersonal relationships and social support, managing psychological tension and strain, and developing self-reliance and self-esteem (Voydanoff, 1987).

Research indicates that most successful women executives have a strong support system, which includes a husband and children who approve of and support her commitment and involvement in her career. An expanded support system composed of friends, extended family, colleagues, church, clubs, and neighbors also seems to be important (Crouse, 1987). Future research should focus on the conditions under which positive work and family outcomes can occur for corporate mothers.

Effects of corporate life-style on children. As with all mobile children, corporate children experience problems related to loss of friendships and change of schools. A period of adjustment is required after each relocation to establish new peer and authority relationships as well as to familiarize themselves with physical and social resources of their new communities. Children can suffer considerably, too, from the emotional absence of a corporate parent. Feelings of rejection may lead to serious emotional problems (Pederson & Sullivan, 1964).

It has been suggested that corporate managers tend to deny or otherwise trivialize problems experienced by their children (Margolis, 1979). Parental attitudes toward relocation and toward parental absence are critical to the children's adjustment. Children also can benefit from being in corporate families. Many of the benefits discussed in the section on dual-career families apply to children in corporate families. In these families, a higher income provides for an elevated standard of living, daughters are likely to be independent and aspire to a career, and both sons and daughters have more egalitarian sex-role attitudes and view women as more competent.

Support for corporate families. The corporate family can be assisted in adjustment by communities *offering collective group support activities,* during which spouses can freely discuss their feelings of loneliness, depression, boredom, and loss. Such groups could be sponsored by a local fam-

ily-service agency, mental-health clinic, church, or newcomer's club (Ammons et al., 1982).

Corporations also can *provide positive intervention* that could affect the employee's adjustment to the job and community. The relationship between corporate provision of a social support network and family adjustment to geographic location was studied by Carter (1981). He found that corporate social-support policy made a difference in the number of contacts a family received. Increased adjustment and satisfaction was found for the families receiving the greater number of social support contacts. Those families who made more adequate adjustment to their new communities demonstrated less family conflict, fewer reports of symptomatic behavior, and greater overall life satisfaction than the less adequate adjustors. It was concluded by the investigator that company policy, social network supports, and attitudinal factors all directly or indirectly affected family social adjustment following relocation. There were no differences between the adequate and less adequate adjustors in their perceptions of child behavior problems.

Companies might *offer relocation services* for families of transferred employees. Seminars to discuss social, logistical, emotional, and financial implications of relocation could be provided for employees and their spouses. Companies might offer their own support group activities or work cooperatively with community agencies in developing such activities. Further, corporations could *provide assistance to spouses* in employment searches (Ammons et al., 1982).

Family-life specialists could serve as consultants to community agencies or corporations in designing seminars, workshops, or mutual-help groups for corporate families. Problems of mobility and suggested strategies for successful coping should be included in *parenting programs for high school students.* Knowing what to expect can serve as a preventive measure for future corporate families.

Many large corporations are already aware of the increased productivity of their employees and lower absenteeism when they offer support services that enhance family life. Benefits programs are frequently including *subsidies for child care,* paternity as well as maternity leave, and sick leave policies that allow employees to stay home and care for children who are ill. Still other companies offer *child-care centers on site* or contract with nearby child-care facilities to enroll children of their employees. Other companies are providing *parent-education* workshops, classes, or seminars for their employees on site. Doubtless these activities will continue to expand as evidence mounts on their relationship to stress reduction.

Migrant Families

The definition of a migrant family is a family that has moved across a state or county line at least once every 12 months. While military and corporate families could be considered migrant, the term has been associated with that segment of the population that moves from one geographic location to another to secure seasonal employment, usually associated with agriculture. A large portion of these families are Mexican-American, black, or Puerto Rican. Concentrations of these groups are found in Texas, Florida, and California.

Most migrant families live in poverty and experience the deprived existence associated with being poor. Families often are large, with six to eight children, grandparents, aunts, cousins, and friends living together. Life is characterized by continual change, rejection by people who live in the area, lack of health care or proper nutrition, and lack of routine. One-room shacks with no heat, poor lighting, and no plumbing often constitute the living quarters. Since life is so temporary, few belongings are accumulated.

Migrant children. Most migrant children are not born in hospitals, do not see their mothers often as they are working in the fields, and begin to assume responsibility very early. It is not unusual for 5- to 6-year-old children to work in the fields, care for younger siblings, or to prepare meals. Few limits are imposed on these children as they are unsupervised, and learning experiences are restricted. Some do not attend public schools, and those who do move from one to another. Children are not provided with toys or games. There are no routines, and children sleep wherever they can find a place. They have very little that they can call their own, either in space or in possessions.

Children of Mexican-American migrant workers were compared to two groups of black children with similar characteristics. One group of clinical black children had been referred for consultation, and the other group of black children had not been referred. Intellectual, academic, and emotional strengths and weaknesses of each group were assessed and compared. The nonreferred black children performed significantly better than clinical blacks and migrants on several intellectual measures. Migrant children scored significantly lower than the clinical blacks on verbal abilities. However, the migrant children did not score below either group on nonverbal measures. Perceptual organization skills were significantly higher than for the clinical blacks. Therefore vulnerability seemed to be specific to verbal ability.

The migrant children showed achievement deficits significantly below the nonreferred group. This was probably due to the lack of verbal skills. Without an understanding of the language of the dominant culture, the Spanish-speaking child is at a disadvantage educationally, and hence vocationally and socioeconomically, even though he might possess significant nonverbal intellectual skills.

Self-concept scores of the migrant children were significantly below the nonreferred group and were lower than those of the clinical group. These results are probably a fairly accurate reflection of the life migrant children lead (Henggeler & Tavormina, 1978).

Discipline in migrant families is most often harsh, administered by the father who shouts, slaps, or whips the child. Children learn to fear authority, fear hunger, and fear separation from parents. They are often shy, insecure, easily frustrated, frightened of school situations, and have negative self-concepts.

Support for migrant families. It is crucial that migrant families have a supportive network. Children need intervention programs to ameliorate verbal deficiencies. Preschool and early elementary school-age children need programs to develop English vocabulary and verbal comprehension skills. These children need greater academic consistency and continuity. Mobile classrooms that travel with children, rather than

---

BOX 8f   PRINCIPLES FOR WORKING WITH MIGRANT CHILDREN

Provide early assessment. Be sensitive to the child's difficulties.
Plan for the child's placement in a group in which he or she can be successful.
Avoid negative stereotyping.
Utilize staff collaboration in assessing and planning for the child's school experience.

Source: Constable, R. (1978). Mobile families and the school. *Social Casework, 59,* pp. 421–423.

---

having children adjust to a new classroom with each move, could help to provide this continuity (Henggeler & Tavormina, 1978).

Four principles in working with migrant children as they experience new school environments were proposed by Constable (1978). These are summarized in Box 8f. Unfortunately, however, current research provides no solutions to the psychosocial problems of migrant children (Henggeler & Tavormina, 1978). Until solutions can be found to provide some stability for the migrant child, she is likely to suffer from all of the consequences of poverty as well as the deleterious effects of mobility.

COHABITING PARENTS

During the period from 1970 to 1982, the number of unmarried-couple households more than tripled. An unmarried-couple household is defined by the Bureau of the Census as a household with exactly two unrelated adults of the opposite sex. These living arrangements may include an elderly man with a live-in nurse or an elderly widowed woman who rents a room to a male college student. However, the data indicate that these situations account for only a small proportion, with 63 percent of all couples in these households being under 35 years of age and the largest proportion being divorced or never married. A cohabiting couple has been defined as a heterosexual couple living together for at least 5 days per week for 3 or more months who are not legally or religiously married, are sexually intimate, and may or may not have marriage as a goal. At the last census date there

were nearly two million such couples in the United States (Newcomb, 1979; U.S. Bureau of the Census, 1983a).

Even though the number of couples practicing this family life-style is still small, it is continuing to increase at a rapid rate. Couples who cohabit represent a wide age range, from college students to elderly persons. Some research indicates that at least 50 percent of today's married couples have cohabited prior to marriage. A recent study found that 60 percent of people who remarried between 1980 and 1987 had set up housekeeping with someone, usually the eventual spouse, beforehand (Barringer, 1989). However, cohabitation for most couples is a temporary arrangement—ending either in termination or in marriage. In fact, about 40 percent of the unmarried cohabiting unions end within a year either because the couple gets married or because they split up. Only one-third of these relationships continue 2 years without marriage or a split; only 1 in 10 lasts 5 years or more without marriage or a split (Barringer, 1989). Some cohabiting homosexual couples continue a long-term committed relationship similar to marriage for heterosexual couples.

Three quarters of cohabiting households have no children. Several studies have shown a relationship between cohabitation and the number of children produced. For example, it has been found that couples who cohabit are less interested in producing children once married and are likely to have smaller families. Significantly more couples who had not cohabited before marriage bore children during the first 4 years of marriage than did couples with prior cohabitation. Further, the length of cohabitation before marriage was related to childbearing. Thirty-five percent of those who cohabited for 10 months or less had children, whereas only 6 percent who had cohabited for 11 months or longer had children. Thus it appears that most cohabitors do not decide to marry to provide a basis for having children. However, for both male and female cohabitors, having children from a previous marriage was a predictor of positive outcome of the cohabiting relationship and subsequent marriage (Bower & Christopherson, 1977; Newcomb, 1979; Newcomb & Bentler, 1980).

If children are born of a cohabiting union, there are legal complications. While there is a trend toward increased legal protection of these children, most states have not adequately defined their rights. Some researchers have contended that these children are penalized to a greater extent than their parents are, particularly when their parents separate. An uncertain child-custody situation may result, including a significant economic loss due to lack of mandated child support. When a cohabiting partner has custody of a child by a prior marriage, there is a clear risk that the former spouse may successfully maintain action to secure custody, especially if he or she is remarried and resides in a traditional family life-style (Bernstein, 1977; Newcomb, 1979). However, little research exists on other effects of cohabitation on children conceived from that union or on children brought to a cohabiting household from previous marriages.

The studies comparing cohabiting and married couples have examined factors such as reported satisfaction, commitment, decision making, emotional stability, division of labor, sexual satisfaction, and communication, but not relationships with, or effects on, children. Few differences have been found to exist between the two groups except in commitment. Comparisons of married couples on these variables who have and have not cohabited before marriage have yielded few significant differences between the two groups. Cohabiting couples perceive the rewards of the arrangement to outweigh the costs (Macklin, 1980; Newcomb, 1979). However, most researchers have expected these "trial marriages" to result in increased marital stability. Surprisingly, a recent study revealed the opposite. Couples were surveyed 10 years after

marriage; 38 percent of those who had cohabited prior to marriage were divorced, whereas 27 percent of those who had not cohabited were divorced (Barringer, 1989).

In one study in-depth interviews were conducted with lesbian and heterosexual single mothers with custody of their children. Those respondents who had live-in lovers indicated that often lovers were expected to provide on-the-spot child care, to step in under emergency conditions as a substitute parent, and to share financial resources. In fact many of these mothers indicated that cohabitation reduced financial disaster for the family or at least reduced financial dependency on their own families. Therefore one might conclude that an advantage of cohabitation could be increased financial security for parents and children (Lewin & Lyons, 1982).

Both sets of cohabiting mothers in the Lewin and Lyons' study reported some conflicts between children and lovers, as well as periodic conflict between their perceptions of their roles as mothers and as lovers. Both expressed fear that intimate relationships might harm their children. Both groups of mothers were firm believers in the importance of male models and encouraged children's continued relationships with their fathers.

Studies specifically examining the relationship of children to parents' homosexual lovers have indicated that children form close relationships with these adults and suffer from a sense of grief and loss when the relationship is terminated. It can be assumed also that children of single heterosexual parents, either never married or multi-married, form love relationships with other adults in the household, given enough time to do so. Thus how parental serial relationships affect children's development is of concern. Recovery from the loss of a primary relationship takes time. Children who are continually developing new relationships or recovering from lost ones are hampered in their development. For those cohabiting couples whose relationship is long-term and stable, the nonparent may function in ways similar to a stepparent, and the child's relationship with that person may be more like those relationships in blended families. However, heterosexual relationships that appear to be successful and in which a satisfactory co-parenting role has been assumed by the lovers have been found to be more likely to move in the direction of legal marriage after a relatively short period of co-residence (Lewin & Lyons, 1982; Macklin, 1980).

HOMOSEXUAL PARENTS

While homosexuality has always existed and the gay movement has a long history, only in the past 10 to 15 years has this phenomenon been discussed openly by the lay public and emphasized in research. Position statements by the American Psychiatric and Psychological Associations in the 1970s led to the removal of homosexuality from the list of mental illnesses. The affirmation of the rights of gay people by these professional and other groups have helped to promote considerable change in societal attitudes. The once firmly held cultural stereotypes and myths regarding homosexuality have been reexamined. However, many issues of homosexuality are still highly emotionally charged and debated. Among these issues are whether these individuals should be allowed to rear their own children or, in the case of women, be allowed to be artificially inseminated, to adopt, or to provide foster care to children.

Some authors define *gay* and *homosexual* differently—with *homosexual* being defined as "one with an erotic preference for a member of the same gender," whereas a gay person, in addition, has managed to reject the negative stereotype associated with being homosexual (Morin & Schultz, 1978). Thus the term *gay* connotes a value system as well as designating group membership. This term indicates a positive identification, but the term *homosexual* has neutral or even negative connotations.

It has been estimated that approximately 10 percent of the population, or 23 million people, are predominately homosexual, and a great many more have had sexual experiences with an individual of the same sex. The actual number of homosexual, or gay, parents is not known. Part of the reason is that a large percentage of homosexuals have not "come out of the closet," or established their identity as gay persons. Some

are reflected in the data on unrelated adults living together (less than 4 percent of households); others are counted in the single-parents category, and many are still residing in nuclear households.

Estimates of the total population of lesbian mothers range from 400,000 to 3 million. It has been concluded that about one out of every five male homosexuals in the United States has been married, resulting in one to three million gay men as natural fathers. Therefore it appears that the number of homosexual mothers and fathers is substantial. One estimate claims that 1.5 million lesbian mothers reside with their children as a family unit. The number of households headed by gay fathers is probably much smaller. The combined number of children of gays and lesbians is somewhere between 6 and 14 million. However, many homosexual parents are still married, and their family members do not know that they are homosexual. Whatever the accurate figure, one cannot assume that these parents or their children are insignificant in number (Bozett, 1980, 1987a; Hoeffer, 1981; Hotvedt & Mandel, 1982; Pennington, 1987).

Reasons Homosexuals Marry and Become Parents

Research studies have suggested a number of reasons why homosexuals marry and become parents. These include the desire to conceal one's true sexual orientation, testing the ability to respond heterosexually, denying homosexuality and/or eliminating homosexual impulses, yielding to social pressure, escaping an intolerable relationship with one's immediate family, fleeing from disappointing heterosexual relationships, the desire to have children, genuine affection for the prospective spouse, and believing one is bisexual (Bozett, 1980, 1987a). However, it was reported that most of the gay fathers in one study did not identify themselves as homosexuals when they had their children. The process of self-identity and finally public identity apparently takes time for many homosexuals. A number enter marriage expecting and desiring contentment within the traditional nuclear context. Children, then, result from this attempt.

Gay Fathers

". . .the desire to parent is not the sole preserve of heterosexuals" (Bozett, 1987a, p. 3). Homosexual fathers have two diametrically opposed roles—one that is fatherhood, which is a culturally accepted role, and the other that is a gay identity. These conflicting roles present a complex set of problems relating to self and to social acceptance that heterosexual fathers do not encounter. Thus, homosexual fathers have all the problems other fathers have plus the problem of handling the cognitive dissonance associated with the dual roles.

Most of the recent research conducted on gay fathers to date has been carried out on men who were married, although now alternative routes to fatherhood are available (donation of sperm to surrogate mothers, adoption, and foster care). The primary mode of adjustment to the father's homosexuality is separation and/or divorce, but homosexuality may or may not be the major cause for divorce (Bozett, 1987a).

Four types of life-styles of homosexual fathers were described by Miller (1979a). The *trade father* is one who engages in clandestine sexual behavior with men but does not accept his behavior as anything more than a genital urge. Considering himself a heterosexual, he lives with his wife and children, who are unaware of his sexual behavior. Most trade fathers contend that children are the major reasons for staying with their wives.

The *homosexual father* has a self-identity but not a public identity that is consistent with his sexual behavior. Because he believes that outward heterosexual identity is necessary to maintain his public or professional credibility, he maintains a conventional heterosexual life-style and keeps his two worlds separate. Excessive gifts to his wife and children to assuage his guilt are common.

The *gay father*'s self-identity, and to some extent his public identity, reflect acceptance of his sexual behavior. He normally does not live with his wife and children but has a regular visitation schedule with his children. Normally everyone except his employer and his children know he is gay, and he is frequently susceptible to blackmail by his ex-wife. Most gay fathers report an enhanced self-image after leaving their wives.

The *publicly gay father* not only has a self-identity consistent with his homosexuality but also proudly acknowledges his life-style, often in the face of abuse. These men organize their lives around the gay culture. Their children are aware of their sexual preference, and a number have custody of their children and live with a lover.

Establishing a gay identity. Support has been found to indicate that fathers who are homosexually active prior to marriage and who have already established themselves in the gay world have the easiest time reconciling their gay and father identities. Those who begin to act on their homosexual desires after marriage have a difficult time resolving the identity conflict. Many men perceive the two roles as hopelessly incompatible. Thus inner turmoil is likely to be high. Gay fathers have had no role models to follow; they have been reared in heterosexual and nuclear family orientations. Most have no one in whom they can confide (Bozett, 1981, 1987a).

For some homosexual men resolution of the two conflicting roles and acceptance of self come only after extended therapy. Essential factors contributing to the resolution include engaging in a variety of social and sexual experiences in the gay world over a period of time, disclosing his homosexuality to his intimate and significant others (referred to as "coming out of the closet"), and receiving positive sanctions in these endeavors. Self-acceptance almost always demands disclosure of sexual orientation. This is a hard decision for a homosexual father because the outcome cannot be predicted. He loves his children and, in many cases, his spouse. Giving up a secure and known relationship in exchange for an unknown future in the gay world is difficult. Being able to predict how his children will respond to the knowledge of his homosexuality and the fear of rejection by them are risks many homosexual fathers are too reluctant to take. These uncertainties contribute to many homosexual men's continuing their secret life in a nuclear family situation.

Bozett (1987a) has pointed out that parenting

by gay fathers who remain married and do not disclose their homosexuality to their children is frequently of lesser quality than those who do because of the tension in the relationship; the time involved in clandestine gay activities; and the tendency to be workaholics, thereby resulting in spending minimal time at home. On the other hand, gay fathers who come out to their children frequently live in stable, domestic relationships, often with a permanent partner. They tend to be dependable and to spend quality time with their children. Although many gay fathers do not reveal their homosexuality to their children, many do. Many men feel it important to do because they want to be able to share with their children and they wish to be honest. Further, many gay fathers feel it is important for their children to have an opportunity as they grow up to become acquainted with competent and accomplished gay men and lesbian women. In this way children will have contact with role models they can respect (Bozett, 1980, 1987a).

The establishment of a gay identity in the gay world is difficult because many aspects of the father role conflict with the gay life. For example, the gay world is one that is single-oriented, with few long-term commitments in time, finances, or responsibilities. It is a transient world and a very difficult one for fathers to participate in unless they have abandoned all parental responsibilities. In addition, the gay world is youth-dominated. Most gay fathers are older than other males in the group.

Many gay men are intolerant of children, and gay fathers with custody of their children may find it difficult to establish relationships with other gay men. All these factors minimize the chances of the gay father's social success of an identity in the gay world (Bozett, 1981).

Parenting by gay fathers. "It is sometimes assumed that gays . . . molest and pervert children entrusted to their care. Consequently, many people are surprised to learn that there are gay fathers with healthy children, fathers who have achieved their unpromised paternity" (Miller, 1979a, p. 239). Traditionally homosexuality has been believed to be incompatible with effective parenting. However, evidence to date fails to support such a belief.

The notion that homosexual men are more effeminate is a myth. In fact, it has been reported that the chances are 20 to 1 that an effeminate man one meets on the street is heterosexual (Voeller & Walters, 1978).

Several studies have compared parenting by gay and heterosexual fathers. One such study found no differences between the two groups in problem solving, in providing recreation for children, and in encouraging autonomy. The gay fathers demonstrated greater emphasis on nurturance, less emphasis on the role of economic provision, were less traditional in their overall paternal attitudes, and assessed themselves significantly more positively in the paternal role than the heterosexual fathers did. The investigator concluded that gay fathers had a substantial psychological investment in their father roles (Scallen, 1982).

The Miller (1979a) study cited earlier revealed that publicly gay fathers were least likely of the four types studied to favor corporal punishment. These fathers were less authoritarian in general and expressed strong desires to rear their children with nonsexist egalitarian values. He found, like Bozett, that homosexual men still living with their wives tended to spend less time with their children than those living apart (Miller, 1979b). Those fathers with custody appeared to have no more problems with child rearing than single heterosexual fathers with custody. Turner, Scadden, and Harris (1986) concluded that most of the gay fathers in their study had positive relationships with their children, that fathers' sexual orientation was of little importance in the overall relationship, and that gay fathers may try harder to create stable home lives for and positive relationships with their children than one might expect. Harris and Turner (1986) found no significant differences between gay and nongay parents except that heterosexual parents made a greater effort to provide an opposite sex role model for their children. Finally, Skeen and Robinson (1984) found that when gay men were asked what things were more important to them in their lives, the recurring responses were their children and their lovers. Gay fathers seemed to value stability of family relationships from childhood into their adult lives. Bozett (1987a), too, stressed the primacy

of bonds to children over the bonds to lovers, especially for custodial gay parents.

Lesbian Mothers

The lesbian-mother family is one of the most stigmatized and least studied types of single-parent families. According to McCandlish (1987), "Lesbian mothers raise their families in a larger society that is hostile and uncomprehending and that fails to provide role models and adequate protection" (p. 23). However, lesbian mothers now win 15 percent of contested custody cases, as opposed to 1 percent in 1970. Fertility alternatives for lesbians that bypass custody disputes are likely to increase significantly the number of lesbian mothers rearing children. These alternatives are discussed later in this section. The lesbian mother tries to fulfill several roles. The normal problems associated with the maternal role, whether as a single mother or as a mother in a nuclear family, are compounded by lesbianism. Single mothers, regardless of their sexual orientation, can be expected to face many of the same kind of problems, especially those related to economics and social isolation.

Unique problems of lesbian mothers. One of the major problems faced by single lesbian mothers is obtaining and maintaining custody of their children. Though lesbianism per se is not grounds for denial or loss of child custody, it frequently is the real reason thinly disguised by judges' concerns for the "best interests of the child" (Hall, 1978). The biggest percentage of lesbian mothers always live with the fear that a bid for custody can be made by the child's father or his extended family. This ever-present threat creates a unique problem for them (Pennington, 1987). As in the case of gay fathers, decisions of the court concerning lesbians rearing their own children, foster children, or adoptive children are based on commonly accepted myths. There is concern that children reared by lesbians may be sexually molested, grow up to be lesbians themselves, and suffer from the stigmatizing process surrounding culturally labeled deviants. In spite of the evidence to the contrary, these myths are still widely believed. Currently, lesbians have a better chance of securing and maintaining custody of their children if they lead conventional lives in other respects and if the child is female and under five years of age. Many judges stipulate that, if the mother wants to retain custody, she must not have a live-in lover and must not see the lover in the presence of the child (Hall, 1978).

The lesbian mother must also contend with problems associated with the relationship of the lover and her children. Many of these adults view themselves as instant parents, and thus conflicts often emerge relating to child rearing, especially discipline. The child, perhaps suffering from loss of the father, may feel threatened by the attention the mother gives to her lover (Hall, 1978). Some research has found that in those lesbian mothers' homes where there are live-in lovers, the children relate to them in similar ways that children in blended heterosexual homes do. "Stepparenting" in gay and lesbian families will be discussed more fully later in this section.

These lovers are viewed as an additional mother, sister, aunt, but not as a father. Close relationships are formed, and reactions of loss, grief, guilt, and depression may follow the dissolution of the relationship (Kirkpatrick, Smith, & Roy, 1981). A recent study by Harris and Turner (1986) indicated that both gay fathers and lesbian mothers were more likely to have a live-in lover than single heterosexual parents. Serial relations of gay parents would thus present problems for children and be similar to those that children experience in serial marriages or cohabitation by heterosexual parents.

Lesbian mothers may experience difficulty "coming out of the closet" and revealing their sexual orientation to their children. The unpredictability of the child's acceptance of the mother's sexual orientation and the fear that the child will experience difficulty being accepted by her peers and/or others once this is known are inhibiting factors for making this disclosure. Lesbian mothers appear to be discrete in efforts to protect their children (Pennington, 1987).

Parenting by lesbian mothers. Lesbian mothers have been found to be more similar to single heterosexual mothers than different from them. The area of greatest commonality appears to be the salience of motherhood in their lives. Both groups of mothers reported that motherhood influenced the conduct of their lives in ways that overshadowed the influence of other factors. Lesbian mothers did, however, report fears of possible harassment of their children (Lewin & Lyons, 1982).

A study comparing lesbian and heterosexual single mothers and their children between 6 and 9 years of age found no differences between the sets of mothers on encouragement for children's sex-role traits and behaviors and no differences between children's contacts with adult males (Hoeffer, 1981). A comparison of black lesbian and single heterosexual mothers found lesbians to be more tolerant, especially of the child's sexuality, more permissive about modesty, and more open about accepting and sharing sexual information. Lesbians used fewer rules of conduct for both sexes and rated their perceptions of boys and girls as more similar than dissimilar (Hill, 1981). On the other hand, Rees (1980) found no differences in parenting styles when mother-child pairs of lesbian and single-parent heterosexual mothers were compared.

Taken together the evidence seems to suggest that lesbians differ from other mothers largely in their sexual preference. They experience problems in childrearing that are similar to those experienced by other single mothers or to those experienced in blended families.

Effects of Homosexuality on Children

During the past 10 years researchers have shown increasing interest in the area of homosexuality. The major focus has been on the acceptance of the homosexual by the family. The effects of children growing up with a homosexual parent have received little attention. Several recent studies, however, have been concerned with whether the children of gay parents are any different in their behavior, their orientation, and their adjustment when compared to children of heterosexual parents (Hoeffer, 1981; Kirkpatrick et al., 1981).

Of primary concern have been the reactions of children to first learning that a parent was gay. Most parents felt initially that children would reject them if they knew of their homosexuality. Even though children differ in their reactions, overall, children have accepted the news better than expected, and in almost all cases better than spouses (Maddox, 1982; Miller, 1979a, 1979b). Interviews with gay fathers indicated that candor and honesty had helped to strengthen the father-child relationship. "Coming out" tended to relieve family tensions, especially in situations when children might have blamed themselves for family difficulties. Two types of negative reactions emerged. Those children who had previously suspected their father's homosexuality felt that their fathers did not trust them and should have told them earlier. Some children felt "replaced" by lovers. Others manifested ambivalence (Miller, 1979b).

Bozett (1987a) reported that the overriding concern of children when told that their fathers were gay was that others would think they, too, were gay. However, Pennington (1987) stated that females, more than males, worry that people will think they, too, are gay. Her study of 32 children of 28 lesbian mothers noted that children under 7 years of age seemed to be more concerned with their parents' separation or divorce than with their mothers' lesbianism, and similar conclusions were reached by Hotvedt and Mandel (1982). Fear of others discovering that their mothers were lesbians increased after 7 years of age and intensified during pubescence, only to subside with the establishment of their own identities and independence from their mothers.

There is conflicting data on whether the gender of the child is a factor related to the acceptance of and adjustment to a parent's homosexuality. One study claimed that it is more difficult for sons than for daughters of lesbians because of limited or nonexistent male role models and less support for sons from the lesbian community. The situation intensifies when the son reaches adolescence, when peer approval and self-identity become so important (Hall, 1978). The literature review of children of lesbian mothers by Hotvedt and Mandel (1982) noted that older adolescent boys reacted most negatively of all to their mothers' lesbianism.

On the other hand, Pennington (1987) noted that it has been surmised (but with little supportive data) that female children have more difficulty accepting a lesbian mother than males do, especially teenagers. Sons are believed to be able to distance themselves more from their mothers

than daughters are. Further, she noted that boys generally do not react with the kind of intrusiveness and negativity more characteristic of girls. Boys occasionally feel left out and invalidated by the mother and her lover, whereas daughters will compete more overtly than sons with a lover for the mother's attention. The author emphasized that, regardless of gender, the more open and relaxed the mother is concerning her sexual orientation, the more accepting the child will be.

Since lesbian mothers are more likely to have custody of their children than gay fathers are, the children of the latter have received less attention. It has been reported (Wyers, 1984) that approximately 40 percent of children with gay fathers reacted positively when they were initially told of their fathers' homosexuality; 35 percent were uncertain; and 25 percent were negative. When fathers were asked to report how their children felt *now*, approximately 50 percent were reported as feeling positive; 45 percent were uncertain; and 5 percent were currently negative. It is important to emphasize that fathers were *reporting* reactions of children.

Bozett (1987b) described three kinds of social-control strategies used by children of gay fathers: *boundary control* (controlling their fathers' behavior, controlling their own behavior, and controlling others' behavior in efforts to be discrete), *nondisclosure* (avoiding telling others that their father is gay), and *disclosure* (the opposite of the above—"preparing" their friends for their fathers' homosexuality but choosing very carefully whom they will tell). There appear to be four influencing factors that determine the use of these strategies: *mutuality* (the degree of the child's identification with the father), *obtrusiveness* (how discernible the child perceives the father's homosexuality to be), the *age of the child* (older children are more able to select and use social-control strategies), and *living arrangements* (whether the father has a live-in lover).

The evidence, then, does not support the commonly accepted reactions of trauma by children on disclosure of their parents' homosexuality. However, it is important to recognize that the samples studied were small, voluntary, and represent a highly select population of gay parents and their children. For this reason it would be erroneous to imply that the news of a homosexual parent is met with indifference by the majority of children.

Several studies have compared children of a homosexual parent to children of a single heterosexual parent of the same sex. For example, both male and female children of lesbian and single heterosexual mothers were examined by Kirkpatrick and her associates (1981). It was found that neither the children's responses nor the type or the frequency of pathology differed as a function of the mother's sexual orientation. The gender development of the two groups of children was evaluated by historical data on favorite toys, characters chosen in fantasy play, special interests, sex of favored playmate, sex play, questions and reported relationships with adults of the opposite sex, and reports of cross-dressing or interests in cross-sex play roles. It was found that those children who had gender problems were more likely to have had a history of physical difficulty rather than a mother with a particular sex orientation. Children in both groups clearly mourned the loss of their fathers.

Children's acquisition of sex-role behavior in lesbian-mother families was examined by Hoeffer (1981). Again, these children were compared to those of single heterosexual mothers. Results showed no significant differences between the groups of children as a function of mothers' sexual orientations. Boys and girls in both groups scored significantly higher on appropriate sex-typed toy preferences. Girls of both groups selected more neutral toys than did the boys. The lesbian mothers seemed to prefer a more equal mixture of sex-typed masculine and feminine toys than did the heterosexual mothers. Both groups of mothers were more willing to encourage neutral toys than opposite sex-typed toys. The author concluded that the two groups of children were markedly similar in acquisition of sex-role behavior.

Other studies have failed to show significant differences between children of homosexual and heterosexual parents. For example, blind testing of children, aged 5–12 years, of lesbian and heterosexual single mothers revealed no differences in degree of emotional maladjustment. In fact, the investigators, using projective techniques with the children, could not distinguish the sexual preferences of the mothers (Smith,

1982). Further, no differences could be found between lesbian- and nonlesbian-reared children between the ages of 10 and 20 years on moral maturity and patterns of socialization (Rees, 1980).

When gay and lesbian parents were asked to indicate on a four-point scale (from "none" to "extensively") the extent to which their homosexuality had caused any of the following problems for their children, the majority responded "none" to all problems: making and keeping friends, doubting their own sexuality, being teased, academic performance, discrimination by teachers and other adults, obtaining a job, and tension due to keeping a secret. On the other hand, gay and lesbian parents were likely to see the following benefits of their homosexuality for their children: facilitating the acceptance of their own sexuality, showing tolerance and empathy for others, getting exposure to new points of view, and making new friends (Harris & Turner, 1986). In effect, no studies have found any significant differences between children of lesbian mothers and heterosexual mothers. The body of research supports the normalcy of children reared by lesbians, who do not differ from their counterparts in sex-role socialization, gender identity, achievement of developmental tasks, intelligence, reaction to father absence, parental separation and divorce, and general adjustment and development (Pennington, 1987).

Finally, studies point out that one of the greatest fears of society—that homosexual parents are more likely to produce homosexual children—is not confirmed. In fact, second-generation homosexuals are rare (Maddox, 1982; Miller, 1979a, 1979b). Twenty-seven female and 21 male children who had reached an age where sexual orientation could be assessed were interviewed by Miller (1979b) in his gay fathers study. Only three sons and one daughter were gay. The notion that children, especially boys, will "catch" homosexuality was not supported. Apparently sexual preference is much more related to a warm, nurturing relationship with parents than to parents' sexual behavior.

Bruce Voeller, Executive Director of the National Gay Task Force and a father of three children, suggested that homosexuality is determined early in life. Some believe the potentiality is established as early as the embryonic stage of development. This theory suggests that the patterns of male bondings found in our culture and in others have little to do with the development of homosexual attraction (Voeller & Walters, 1978). Given the fact that infants and young children are powerful forces in creating their own environment, there is the possibility that the resulting parent-child relationships are quite different for the eventual homosexual and heterosexual child.

Alternative Routes to Parenthood for Gays and Lesbians

The norm of two-parent heterosexual families is being increasingly challenged by the following alternative routes to parenthood: lesbians parenting alone through fertilization by artificial insemination by donor (AID); a gay couple hiring a surrogate mother to be fertilized by one or both partners through AID; a lesbian and a gay both becoming biological parents, through fertilization by intercourse or AID; a lesbian and her partner contracting with a gay man to parent together—the gay man not always being the biological parent (donor); and one partner from a lesbian couple and one from a gay couple conceiving, with the agreement that all four partners have equal responsibility in parenting the child. These alternative routes may sound implausible, but they are all very real, with the first alternative currently being the most common.

Little data exists on the number of children conceived by these methods and reared by their gay parents. However, a chapter in a recent book about gay parents (Pies, 1987) raised some extremely provocative issues, including the following: who the biological parents will be; whether a surrogate mother will be used; whether the donor will be known or unknown; whether the child will know both biological parents; whether the donor or surrogate will participate in parenting the child; how many parents the child will have; the kind of relationship the biological parent's lover will have with the child; and whether there will be a legal contract with the parenting parties.

Of course there are no norms and few role models to assist in making these decisions. For lesbians, deciding whether to use a known or an unknown donor seems to be the most difficult initial task, and this decision is complicated by the growing concern about the transmission of AIDS through donor sperm (Pies, 1987).

Even after initial decisions regarding the conception, pregnancy, and birthing have been made, more difficult ones remain. What inherent right do children have to know their biological parents? With unknown donors as biological fathers, children will never be able to exercise that right. How will children perceive the lover in relationship to the parenting role? Because gays have biologically assymetrical relationships with children, the co-parenting relationship can become strained.

Clearly there are many questions and few answers surrounding these alternative approaches. Choices made now will have long-term impact on children's lives, but it will be years before researchers are able to determine just what the impact will be.

"Stepparenting" in Gay and Lesbian Families

Because legal marriages between gays and lesbians are not recognized, partners of gays who have children are not recognized as stepparents. In most research, gay and lesbian parents are compared to same-sex single heterosexual parents. However, in the case of heterosexual cohabitation as well as in gay and lesbian relationships a stepfamily-like structure may exist, where the partner assumes a role not unlike a stepparent. In fact, in many cases the partner shares equally in a co-parenting arrangement.

Baptiste (1987) defined a gay stepfamily as a cohabitive living arrangement involving two same-sex adults and their children—biological, adoptive, or conceived through artificial insemination. He noted that observations of gay and lesbian stepfamilies have overwhelmingly shown that when sexual preference of the adults is controlled for, the bahaviors of gay and lesbian stepfamilies tend to be indistinguishable from those of heterosexual stepfamilies. However, heterosexual stepparents may legally adopt their stepchildren under certain conditions, but gay stepparents are rarely able to do so.

Nevertheless, these families experience problems similar to other stepfamilies. There is the tentative nature of the stepparent's role, his or her rights and responsibilities. There may be initial confusion of the children, especially if they are young, as they piece together the unique nature of their familial relationships. Later, understanding just who the stepparent is may be difficult for some children. In most cases, gay and lesbian stepfamilies remain fairly invisible to neighbors; that is, they are perceived to be same-sex friends, one who is a parent, sharing living quarters (Baptiste, 1987). In the event of a dissolved relationship, the stepparent has no legal claim to the child, unless a legal agreement stipulating such rights is in effect. Children who have experienced a stable stepfamily relationship feel a significant loss if the relationship ends, much the same as in divorce.

The notion that particular sex roles are assumed in gay relationships (for example, "dyke" and "butch") is clearly inaccurate. In fact, these relationships, for both men and women, appear to be largely egalitarian. Therefore the process of maintaining an egalitarian relationship in a gay stepfamily is no different from that in a heterosexual stepfamily.

Clearly children reared alone by a gay or a lesbian parent have different experiences than children reared in gay couple relationships (stepfamilies). Research in the future should focus on these differences.

Gay Adoption and Foster Care

When seeking to adopt or become foster parents, most gays and lesbians make no mention of their sexual preference. It was not until 1979 that it was reported that an openly gay couple had adopted an infant. However, hundreds of gays and lesbians have adopted and have been licensed as foster parents without their sexual orientations being public. Now a growing number of public and private agencies across the country are beginning to see lesbian and gay homes as appropriate foster-care placements for homosexually identified youth (Ricketts & Achtenberg, 1987).

At the time of this writing, all states allowed adoption by unmarried persons, but only two states explicitly regulated the ability of homosexuals to become foster or adoptive parents. Twenty-six states at the present time continue to have antisodomy laws on the books, and licensing of openly gay foster and adoptive parents is unlikely in these states. Even when openly homosexual men and women succeed in adopting, with few exceptions they must do so as single individuals, even if they are in couples and even if their partners are co-parenting on an equal basis (Ricketts & Achtenberg, 1987).

Screening out gay men as prospective adoptive or foster parents has been partly based on the fear of child molestation. Yet this fear has not been substantiated by research. Rather, national police data confirm that more than 90 percent of all sexual abuse to minors involves an adult male and a female child—a heterosexual crime rather than a homosexual one.

Support for Homosexual Parents

Since many homosexuals have undergone years of turmoil relating to the negative sanctions of the family and the larger society, socialization as a heterosexual when feelings and desires were homosexual, the need to "come out of the closet," and other problems relating to this sexual orientation, extensive counseling and/or psychotherapy may be needed. Obviously, support groups of gay fathers and lesbian mothers would be helpful as a means of exploring common problems and solutions, and a number of these exist today.

The changes in society and its institutions that are needed to provide support for persons engaging in this life-style were proposed by Morin and Schultz (1978). These authors contended that society and its institutions must stop trying to stamp out homosexuality through intervention programs. They contended that these programs promote a negative identity relating to homosexuality rather than a positive one and, in addition, have a high rate of failure. Intervention programs communicate that homosexuals are sick and ought to be cured. The failure, then, compounds the damage by implying that the individual is sick and cannot get better despite all that has been done.

It was further suggested by these authors that social systems must provide support and facilitate the development of a gay identity and life-style by informing children about the existence of this sexual orientation and providing opportunities for children to observe competent gay models. Exploring this as an optional life-style should help young people grow up with a greater openness and sense of freedom to be whoever they are.

It is likely then that this life-style will become more visible to the lay public, and greater numbers of professionals will be called on to render services to these families. It was pointed out by Hall (1978) that gay parents are a unique group with a special identity and special needs. They need assistance with parenting, self-disclosure, handling stigma, and with formation and maintenance of the family unit.

In conclusion, gay parents seem to be more similar to than different from other single parents and/or stepparents and their children resemble children from heterosexual single-parent and stepparent families. While being gay is incompatible with traditional marriage, it does not seem to be incompatible with parenting. In fact gay fathers and mothers, especially those who have resolved their identity problems, seem to be very concerned and involved with their children. Clearly this population of families is difficult to study, and much more research needs to be conducted.

SUMMARY

Life-style variations that depart from the traditional prototype include dual-career families, highly mobile families (military, corporate, and migrant), cohabiting families, and homosexual families. Dual-career families constitute the largest percentage of this group and, when combined with dual-worker families, outnumber single-career families with children. Even so, the societal stigma of mothers working, especially when their children are young, has not been entirely overcome. Both mothers and fathers in dual-career families may feel guilty about spend-

ing too little time with their children. In any case they face dilemmas as they combine their family and professional roles. However, there is a little evidence to support the notion that maternal employment is, in and of itself, detrimental to children.

Highly mobile families have decreased in number during the past few years. However, military families, corporate families, and migrant families continue to experience frequent mobility. These families experience the stresses of temporary relationships and frequent social and academic adjustments. Migrant families are further plagued by the effects of poverty. Although mobility per se does not necessarily cause emotional maladjustment in children, it is important to recognize the unique problems that mobility creates.

Cohabitation, at least openly, is one of the most recent and rapidly increasing nontraditional life-styles. Many cohabiting couples with children present become legally married, so this life-style is often temporary. Research on cohabitation and its effects on children is severely limited. However, it is believed that parental serial relationships may have detrimental effects, and in some cases the losses children experience may be similar to the effects of divorce. Readjustments to parents' new lovers may be similar to readjustment in blended families.

Homosexual parents and their children experience considerable stigma and discrimination. The gay rights movement has reduced discrimination to some extent, and more and more gay parents are obtaining custody of children and are producing children in a variety of nontraditional ways. Homosexual parents without a live-in lover are similar to single parents with custody. They experience, however, not only the same problems as other single parents but also the problems associated with being gay. Likewise, those parents with live-in lovers experience problems similar to those in blended families, plus the problems of being gay.

Little research has been conducted on children in gay and lesbian families. Existing studies have utilized small samples most often restricted to a particular geographic area. Therefore few generalizations can be made. However, the evidence to date suggests that children reared by homosexual parents are little different from children reared by heterosexual parents and are no more likely than other children to become gay or lesbian themselves.

REFERENCES

America's new immobile society (1981, July 27). *Business Week*, pp. 58–62.

AMMONS, P., NELSON, J., & WODARSKI, J. (1982). Surviving corporate moves: Sources of stress and adaptation among corporate executive families. *Family Relations, 3*(2), 207–212.

AVIS, J. (1986). Working together: An enrichment program for dual-career couples. *Journal of Psychotherapy and the Family, 2*(1), 29–44.

BAPTISTE, D. (1987). The gay and lesbian stepfamily. In F. Bozett (Ed.), *Gay and lesbian parents* (pp. 112–137). New York: Praegar.

BARRINGER, F. (1989, June 9). Couples who live together first divorce more. *New York Times*, pp. 1, 23.

BASS, P., MCCUBBIN, H., & LESTER, G. (1979). The corporate executive wife's coping patterns in response to routine husband-father absence. *Family Process, 18*(1), 79–86.

BERNSTEIN, B. (1977). Legal problems of cohabitation. *Family Coordinator, 26*(4), 361–366.

BONFIELD, P. (1986). Working solutions for working parents. *Management World, 15*, 8–10.

BOWER, D., & CHRISTOPHERSON, V. (1977). University student cohabitation: A regional comparison of selected attitudes and behavior. *Journal of Marriage and the Family, 39*(3), 447–452.

BOZETT, F. (1980). Gay fathers: How and why they disclose their homosexuality to their children. *Family Relations, 29*(2), 173–179.

BOZETT, F. (1981). Gay fathers: Evolution of the gay-father identity. *American Journal of Orthopsychiatry, 51*(3), 552–559.

BOZETT, F. (1987a). Gay fathers. In F. Bozett (Ed.), *Gay and lesbian parents* (pp. 3–19). New York: Praegar.

BOZETT, F. (1987b). Children of gay fathers. In F. Bozett (Ed.), *Gay and lesbian parents* (pp. 39–57). New York: Praegar.

CARON, M. (1975). The relationship between geographic mobility, adjustment, and personality (Doctoral dissertation, McGill University, 1974). *Dissertation Abstracts International, 35*, 5101–5102B.

CARTER, B. (1981). Family stress and social adjustment following geographic relocation: A study of the function of organizational policy and social network supports. An unpublished doctoral dissertation, University of Virginia.

CHAPMAN, F. (1987, February 16). Executive guilt: Who's taking care of the children? *Fortune*, pp. 30–37.

Cofo Memo (1981, Summer/Fall). Newsletter *3*(3), 1–8. Washington, DC: Coalition of Family Organizations.

CONSTABLE, R. (1978). Mobile families and the school. *Social Casework, 59*(7), 421–423.

CROUSE, J. (1987). The managerial woman. *Vital Speeches, LIII*(1), 57–60.

DARNAUER, P. (1976). The adolescent experience in career military families. In H. McCubbin, B. Dahl, & E. Hunter (Eds.), *Families in the military system* (pp. 42–66). Beverly Hills: Sage.

DUNCAN, R., & PERUCCI, C. (1976). Dual occupation families and migration. *American Sociological Review, 41*(2), 252–261.

FINLAYSON, E. (1976). A study of the wife of the army officer: Her academic and career preparations, her current employment and volunteer services. In H. McCubbin, B. Dahl, & E. Hunter (Eds.), *Families in the military system* (pp. 19–41). Beverly Hills: Sage.

For lots of reasons, more workers are saying "no" to job transfers (1977, February 14). *U.S. News and World Report*, pp. 73–74.

GAYLORD, M. (1979). Relocation and the corporate family: Unexplored issues. *Social Work, 24*(3), 186–191.

GILBERT, L., HOLAHAN, C., & MANNING, L. (1981). Coping with conflict between professional and maternal roles. *Family Relations, 30*(3), 419–426.

HALL, M. (1978). Lesbian families: Cultural and clinical issues. *Social Work, 23*(5), 380–385.

HARRIS, M., & TURNER, P. (1986). Gay and lesbian parents. *Journal of Homosexuality, 12*(2), 101–113.

HENGGELER, S., & TAVORMINA, J. (1978). The children of Mexican-American migrant workers: A population at risk? *Journal of Abnormal Child Psychology, 61*(1), 97–106.

HILL, M. (1981). Effects of conscious and unconscious factors on child-rearing attitudes by lesbian mothers. (Doctoral dissertation, Adelphi University, 1981). *Dissertation Abstracts International, 42*(4), 1608–B.

HOEFFER, B. (1981). Children's acquisition of sex role behavior in lesbian-mother families. *American Journal of Orthopsychiatry, 51*(3), 536–543.

HOPKINS, J., & WHITE, P. (1978). The dual-career couple: Constraints and supports. *Family Coordinator, 27*(3), 253–259.

HOTVEDT, M., & MANDEL, J. (1982). Children of lesbian mothers. In W. Paul, J. Weinrich, J. Gonsiorek, & M. Hotvedt (Eds.), *Homosexuality: Social, psychological, and biological issues* (pp. 275–285). Beverly Hills: Sage.

JOHNSON, C., & JOHNSON, F. (1980). Parenthood, marriage, and careers: Situational constraints and role strain. In F. Pepitone-Rockwell (Ed.), *Dual career couples* (pp. 143–161). Beverly Hills: Sage.

JOSEFOWITZ, N. (1983). *Is this where I was going?* New York: Warner Books.

KANTROWITZ, B., NAMUTH, T., KARAGIA, E., & BURGOWER, B. (1985, November 18). Love on the run. *Newsweek*, pp. 111–113.

KIRKPATRICK, M., SMITH, C., & ROY, R. (1981). Lesbian mothers and their children: A comparative survey. *American Journal of Orthopsychiatry, 51*(3), 545–551.

KNAUB, P. (1986). Growing up in a dual-career family: The children's perceptions. *Family Relations, 36*(3), 431–437.

LAGRONE, D. (1978). The military family syndrome. *American Journal of Psychiatry, 135*(9), 1040–1043.

LESLIE, L. (1986). The impact of adolescent females' assessments of parenthood and employment on plans for the future. *Journal of Youth and Adolescence, 15*(1), 29–49.

LEVINE, M. (1976). Residential change and school adjustment. In R. Moos (Ed.), *Human adaptation: Coping with life crises* (pp. 239–252). Lexington, MA: D. C. Heath.

LEWIN, E., & LYONS, T. (1982). Everything in its place: The coexistence of lesbianism and motherhood. In W. Paul, J. Weinrich, J. Gonsiorek, & M. Hotvedt (Eds.), *Homosexuality: Social, psychological, and biological issues* (249–252). Beverly Hills: Sage.

MACKLIN, E. (1980). Nontraditional family forms: A decade of research. *Journal of Marriage and the Family, 42*(4), 905–922.

MADDOX, B. (1982, February). Homosexual parents. *Psychology Today*, pp. 62–69.

MAGID, R. (1986, December). When mothers and fathers work: How employers can help. *Personnel*, pp. 50–56.

MARGOLIS, D. (1979). *The managers.* New York: Morrow.

MARSH, R. (1976). Mobility in the military: Its effect upon the family system. In H. McCubbin, B. Dahl, & E. Hunter (Eds.), *Families in the military system* (pp. 92–111). Beverly Hills: Sage.

MCCANDLISH, B. (1987). Against all odds: Lesbian mother and family dynamics. In F. Bozett (Ed.), *Gay and lesbian parents* (pp. 23–36). New York: Praeger.

MCCUBBIN, H., DAHL, B., & HUNTER, E. (1976). The legacy of family research in the military. In H. McCubbin, B. Dahl, & E. Hunter (Eds.), *Families in the military system* (pp. 291–319). Beverly Hills: Sage.

MCKAIN, J. (1976). Alienation: A function of geographic mobility. In H. McCubbin, B. Dahl, & E. Hunter (Eds.), *Families in the Military System* (pp. 112–121). Beverly Hills: Sage.

MILLER, B. (1979a). Unpromised paternity: The lifestyles of gay fathers. In M. Levine (Ed.), *Gay men: The sociology of male homosexuality* (pp. 239–252). New York: Harper & Row.

MILLER, B. (1979b). Gay fathers and their children. *Family Coordinator, 28*(4), 544–552.

MORIN, S., & SCHULTZ, S. (1978). The gay movement and the rights of children. *Journal of Social Issues, 34*(2), 137–147.

NADELSON, C., & NADELSON, T. (1980). Dual-career marriages: Benefits and costs. In F. Pepitone-Rockwell (Ed.), *Dual-career couples* (pp. 91–109). Beverly Hills: Sage.

NELSON-HORCHLER, J. (1986, February 3). Super moms:

Mixing business careers and motherhood. *Industry Week*, pp. 32–36.

NEWCOMB, M., & BENTLER, P. (1980). Assessment of personality and demographic aspects of cohabitation and marital success. *Journal of Personality Assessment, 44*(1), 11–24.

NEWCOMB, P. (1979). Cohabitation in America: An assessment of the consequences. *Journal of Marriage and the Family, 41*(3), 597–603.

OTT, L. (1978). Army brats: Growing up army style. *Soldiers, 33*(11), 33–36.

PEDERSON, F., & SULLIVAN, E. (1964). Relationship among geographical mobility, parental attitudes and emotional disturbances in children. *American Journal of Orthopsychiatry, 34*(3), 575–580.

PENNINGTON, S. (1987). Children of lesbian mothers. In F. Bozett (Ed.), *Gay and lesbian parents* (pp. 58–74). New York: Praeger.

PIES, C. (1987). Considering parenthood: Psychosocial issues for gay men and lesbians choosing alternative fertilization. In F. Bozett (Ed.), *Gay and lesbian parents* (pp. 165–174). New York: Praeger.

PRICE-BONHAM, S., & MURPHY, D. (1980, April). Dual career marriages: Implications for the clinician. *Journal of Marital and Family Therapy*, pp. 181–188.

RAPOPORT, R., & RAPOPORT, R. N. (1971). *Dual-career families.* Harmondsworth, England: Penguin Books.

RAPOPORT, R., & RAPOPORT, R. N. (1976). *Dual-career families re-examined.* New York: Harper & Row.

REES, R. (1980). A comparison of children of lesbian and single heterosexual mothers on three measures of socialization. (Doctoral dissertation, California School of Professional Psychology, Berkeley, 1979). *Dissertation Abstracts International, 40*, 3418–3419B.

RICHARDS, S., DONOHUE, K., & GULLOTTA, T. (1985). Corporate families and mobility: A review of the literature. *Family Therapy, XII*(1), 59–73.

RICKETTS, W., & ACHTENBERG, R. (1987). The adoptive and foster gay and lesbian parent. In F. Bozett (Ed.), *Gay and lesbian parents* (pp. 89–111). New York: Praeger.

RUSSELL, G. (1986). Shared parenting: A new childrearing trend? *Early Child Development and Care, 24*, 139–153.

SCALLEN, R. (1982). An investigation of paternal attitudes and behavior in homosexual and heterosexual fathers (Doctoral dissertation, California School of Professional Psychology, Los Angeles, 1981). *Dissertation Abstracts International, 42*(9), 3809-B.

SCHMID, R. (1989, July 24). More moms are over 30; College, career come first. *Albuquerque Journal*, p. B1.

SIMON, F. (1984). Parental leave: A step toward equality. *Essence Magazine, 15*, p. 46.

SKEEN, P., & ROBINSON, B. (1984). Family backgrounds of gay fathers: A Descriptive study. *Psychological Reports, 54*, 999–1005.

SKINNER, D. (1980). Dual-career family stress and coping: A literature review. *Family Relations, 29*(4), 473–481.

SMITH, K. (1982). Children raised by lesbian mothers (Doctoral dissertation, University of California, 1981). *Dissertation Abstracts International, 42*(8), 3444-B.

SPITZE, G. (1988). Women's employment and family relations. *Journal of Marriage and the Family, 50*(3), 595–611.

TIGER, L. (1974, September). Is this trip necessary? The heavy human cost of moving executives around. *Fortune,* pp. 139–141, 182.

TRIMBERGER, R., & MACLEAN, M. (1982). Maternal employment: The child's perspective. *Family Relations, 44*(2), 469–475.

TOOLEY, R. (1970). The role of geographic mobility in some adjustment problems of children and families. *Journal of the American Academy of Child Psychiatry, 9*(2), 366–378.

TURNER, P., SCADDEN, L., & HARRIS, M. (1986). Parent-child relations in gay and lesbian families. Paper presented at the International Parenting Conference, Chicago.

U.S. BUREAU OF THE CENSUS (1983a). *Marital status and living arrangements—March 1982,* Current Population Reports, Series P-20, No. 381. Washington, DC: U.S. Government Printing Office.

U.S. BUREAU OF THE CENSUS (1983b). *Geographical mobility: March 1980 to March 1981,* Current Population Reports, Population Characteristics, Series P-20, No. 377. Washington, DC: U.S. Government Printing Office.

U.S. DEPARTMENT OF COMMERCE (1977). *Statistical abstract of the United States for 1977.* Washington, DC: U.S. Government Printing Office.

U.S. DEPARTMENT OF DEFENSE (1988, September/October). Guide to military careers. *Profile,* pp. 30–31.

VOELLER, B., & WALTERS, J. (1978). Gay fathers. *Family Coordinator, 27*(2), 149–157.

VOYDANOFF, P. (1980). Work roles as stressors in corporate families. *Family Relations, 29*(4), 489–494.

VOYDANOFF, P. (1987). *Work and family life.* Newbury Park, CA: Sage.

WHITE, P., MASCALO, A., THOMAS, S., & SHOUN, S. (1986). Husbands' and wives' perceptions of marital intimacy and wives' stresses in dual-career marriages. *Family Perspectives, 20*(1), 27–35.

Why moving day comes less often for executives (1975, January 13). *U.S. News and World Report,* pp. 51, 53.

WYERS, N. (1984). *Lesbian and gay spouses and parents: Homosexuality in the family.* Portland: School of Social Work, Portland State University.

9

Parenting in High-Risk Families

There are numerous factors that influence the degree of risk that might be involved in parenting for any particular family or any specific group of families. Risk factors may be related to health, medical, psychological, structural, economic, developmental, or social aspects of family life, or to any combination thereof. It is probably accurate to say that some risks exist in every family situation. Many families are able to minimize the risk factors by a network of support systems, but others are unable to do so with any degree of success.

There are certain groups of families that exist and attempt to function in relatively high-risk situations. Therefore they are in greater need of support services than other families. Two such family situations—teenage parents and abusive or neglectful parents—will be discussed in this chapter. In the discussion of adolescent parents we do not mean to imply that these family types are pathological. We do mean to emphasize, however, that the degree of risk for optimal parenting is considerable. Abusive parents, on the other hand, represent a risk situation for children and their parents that is clearly serious— and often deadly, at least for the children involved. Both of these types of families have unique needs and require special kinds of support and intervention services.

ADOLESCENT PARENTS

Teenage parenthood is not a new social phenomenon, but only in recent years has public concern been expressed about the extent of adolescent childbearing and the problems associated with it. Adolescent sexuality, pregnancy, and parenthood have generated intense debate for the last 10 years (Polit, 1987). A teenage pregnancy is clearly an event that has considerable personal consequences and costs for individual adolescents and their families. Families headed by teenage mothers are especially likely to be on public welfare. It has been estimated that more than one third of all women who become AFDC recipients when they are 21 years of age or younger will have more than 9 years of dependency. Nationally more than half of all AFDC expenditures are for households in which the mother was a teenager when her first child was born; this amounts to more than $15 billion annually. It is estimated that $150 million could be saved in a year if AFDC teenagers would postpone childbearing by a single year (Polit, 1987).

The Problem

Looking at the statistics, one can hardly disagree that teenage childbearing raises serious social, economic, and health concerns. Teenage pregnancy rates in the United States are more than two times higher than in Canada, England, and France; almost three times higher than they are in Sweden; and seven times higher than they are in the Netherlands. Further, the U.S. rates, particularly for younger teenagers, are considerably higher than those found in a number of less-developed countries, such as Rumania and Hungary (Jones et al., 1985).

These higher rates occur despite the fact that the United States reports higher levels of religiosity, weaker pronatalist fertility policies, fewer maternity benefits, and a higher minimum age for marriage than other countries do. In addition, government subsidy of abortions does not appear to be associated with teenage fertility (Jones et al., 1985). Several factors have been associated with higher teenage fertility rates in the United States, the first of which is low socioeconomic status. Although the United States is considered to be a wealthy nation, a relatively small proportion of its income is distributed to families on the bottom rungs of the economic ladder. Further, Jones and her associates (1985) pointed out that U.S. teenagers receive less information about contraceptives in schools and are less likely to get free or low-cost contraceptive services than in countries such as Canada, England, Sweden, France, and the Netherlands.

In this country more than 3,000 teenage girls become pregnant each day, with 2,300 of these pregnancies being unintentional. Teen mothers give birth to 1,300 babies; of these mothers 800 have not completed high school and 100 have not even completed the ninth grade. Five hundred school-age teens have abortions. Twenty-six 13- and 14-year-olds have their second child. Each year, 1 American teen in 10 becomes pregnant. Of the more than 1 million teen pregnancies that occur, 125,000 are to girls 15 years and younger. Of these, 3 out of 4 are unintended, and about 1 in 2 ends in abortion (Children's Defense Fund, 1986). These facts are obviously cause for concern. Box 9a shows the live births to all unmarried teenage girls in 1975, 1980, and 1982.

As may be noted, the percentage distribution of all live births attributed to teenagers has declined. Adolescent fertility reached its peak in 1975 and has gradually declined since that time.

The ratio of births to unwed black females is approximately four times that of whites (see Box 9b.) The birthrate does not tell the entire story, however. While the birthrate may have declined in recent years, the pregnancy rate for all females 15–19 years increased by 8.2 percent from 1974 to 1980; and for females 12–14 years it rose from 3.9 per 1,000 in 1974 to 4.3 in 1980, a 10.3 percent increase (U.S. Department of Health and Human Services, 1986).

While adoption may be a viable option for unmarried adolescents who are unwilling or

---

BOX 9a   LIVE BIRTHS TO ALL UNMARRIED TEENAGE GIRLS (1975, 1980, 1982)

Year	Under 15* Years Old	Distribution of All Live Births (%)	15–19* Years Old	Distribution of All Live Births (%)
1975	11.0	2.5	222.5	49.7
1980	9.5	1.4	262.8	39.5
1982	8.7	1.2	260.6	36.4

*Per 1,000 population.
Source: U.S. Department of Health and Human Services/Public Health Service. (1986, May 2). *Morbidity and Mortality Weekly Report, 35,* 271.

BOX 9b BIRTHS TO UNMARRIED FEMALES, 15–19 YEARS OF AGE, BY RACE

Year	White (%)	Black (%)
1975	11.0	48.8
1980	11.6	55.2
1982	12.1	56.7

*Per 1,000 population.
Source: U.S. Department of Health and Human Services/Public Health Service. (1986, May 2). *Morbidity and Mortality Weekly Report, 35,* 271.

unable to care for their babies, only about 4 percent who carry their babies to term enter into an adoption plan or arrange for their babies to be cared for by relatives or friends. There is an increasing percentage of teens who also are choosing not to marry to resolve their pregnancies. These young women, then, are keeping their babies and rearing them with or without the help of a mate or their parents and with whatever support services they can secure (Leibowitz, Eisen, & Chow, 1986).

In October 1978 the first federal legislation especially targeted to this problem was passed: Titles VI, VII, and VIII of the Health Services and Centers Amendments, PL 85-626 (Chilman, 1979). But in October 1981 these titles were repealed when the U.S. Congress passed the Adolescent Family Life Bill, an amendment to the Public Health Service Act. Thirty million dollars was appropriated for the 1981–1984 years to help reduce teenage pregnancy and deal with the strains of adolescent parenting by requiring greater family involvement; to provide care services for pregnant adolescents and adolescent parents with emphasis on adoption as a positive alternative for adolescents who do not choose to parent their children; to develop prevention services relating to problems associated with adolescent premarital sexual relations; to provide for research concerning the causes and consequences of adolescent premarital sexual relations, contraceptive use, pregnancy, and child rearing; to

evaluate the relative effectiveness and efficiency of different means of service delivery; and to disseminate results of programs and research projects relating to adolescent premarital sexual behavior, pregnancy, and parenthood.

During each year since 1981, millions of dollars have been appropriated for projects to examine these issues. So far few solutions have been found to reduce the teenage pregnancy rate. Weed and Olsen (1986) found that teenage involvement in family-planning programs is associated with a reduction in the birthrate of teenagers but not with a reduction in abortions or the overall pregnancy rates.

Factors Associated with Adolescent Pregnancy

Hamner and Ladewig (1987) conducted an extensive review of the literature on teenage pregnancy and parenthood. They found the factors listed in Box 9c to be associated with the incidence of teenage fertility.

Outcomes

The adverse consequences of teenage childbearing have been well documented and include risks for both the health and development of the child and the diminished educational and vocational achievement for the teenage mother (Campbell, Breitmayer, & Ramey, 1986). These consequences are summarized in Boxes 9d and 9e.

Research emphasizes the need for continued education of teen parents. Klerman (1986) pointed out that although teen mothers who marry men employed at reasonable wages usually have higher incomes than those who remain single, early marriage often leads to large family size and to leaving school, both of which have negative economic impact. In addition, early parenting negatively affects the father's educa-

---

BOX 9c FACTORS ASSOCIATED WITH TEENAGE FERTILITY

Lowered Age of Reproductive Maturation

12.8 years compared to 17 years in 1800s; due to improvements in diet and health

Social Extension of Adolescent Stage of Development

Culturally, adolescence extended at both ends
Major period in life cycle
Few societally approved meaningful activities except school and athletics

Changing Attitudes Toward Sexuality

More liberalized attitudes toward premarital intercourse, cohabitation and other alternative life-styles
Publication and wide dissemination of literature on sexual practices and inadequacies
Federal funding of family-planning clinics
Legalized abortion
Laws prohibiting pregnant girls in public schools
Gaining strength of feminist movement

Increased Sexual Activity

50 percent of all unmarried females have had sexual intercourse once
69 percent of white and 89 percent of black 19-year-olds are sexually active
25 percent of white and 50 percent of black 15-year-olds have had intercourse
Because the proportion of adolescents who are sexually active is so substantial, sexually active teenagers are not considered socially deviant

Failure to Use Contraceptives

Many fail to use any method of birth control until a year after initiating activity

When birth control is used, it is often sporadic and ineffectual

Teens from higher SES use more birth control than those from lower SES

Blacks and Hispanics use contraceptives less often than whites do; may be due to the fact that they value motherhood more highly

Social Situations

Link between sexual activity, contraceptive use, pregnancy, and parenthood

Low levels of achievement, aspirations, religiosity, poverty, lack of supervision at initiation of dating associated with pregnancy

Parent/Adolescent Communication

Some research indicates level of communication unrelated to pregnancy; other research indicates that even minimal sex education has significant implications

Parents are never cited as major source of information about sex

Psychological Factors

Influence of drug and alcohol use unclear—perhaps same cluster of psychological factors influences both

Desire for affection may lead to early coitus for some girls

Belief in equality of sexes

Critical attitude toward societal norms

Peer pressure (especially for boys)

Risk-taking (especially for boys)

Source: Hamner, T., & Ladewig, B. (1987). Teenage pregnancy: Social and psychological considerations. *School and Food Service Journal, 11,* 7–13.

BOX 9d OUTCOMES OF TEENAGE PREGNANCY FOR THE CHILD

Infant Health

25–50 percent increased risk of prematurity and low birth weight

Risk greatest for those 15 years and under; declines through mid-twenties

Risks more related to poor prenatal care than age

Congenital malformations, neurological defects, perinatal mortality, growth failure more common, especially among poor nonwhite babies

Black infants suffer neonatal and postnatal mortality rates twice as frequently as whites

Development of Infant

Teen parents less knowledgeable about child development than adults

Punitive attitudes toward childrearing are likely

Social stimulation may be inappropriate

Difficulty in securing quality care for infant

Skills and knowledge for securing appropriate support services may be inadequate

---

BOX 9e   OUTCOMES OF TEENAGE PREGNANCY FOR MOTHERS

Maternal Health

Poor nutrition

Less mature reproductive system

Failure to seek early and continuous prenatal care (50 percent seek no prenatal care in first trimester, 16 percent in second trimester)

Improper weight gain with more weight going to other products of conception than to baby

Greater incidence of toxemia

"Teen" effects most evident in youngest (15 years and under)—effects decline with age

Maternal Stress

Related to school, peer group, parents—may result in alcohol and drug use, depression

Major transition to pregnancy

Child abuse—may become abusive after reaching adulthood

Premature Decision Making

Immature cognitive skills

Perceive narrow range of alternatives

Long-term consequences overlooked

Outcomes distorted

Egocentric, belief in "here and now"

Inability to improvise or make balanced, effective decisions

Decisions likely to be based on own needs rather than on baby's

Economic Consequences

Direct effect on educational attainment, impacting labor-force participation and wages

Continued schooling unlikely if deliver before age 18 (only 50 percent who become parents prior to 18 graduate from high school)

Likelihood of larger families, which affects ability to seek and maintain employment

Likelihood of welfare dependency (⅔ families headed by women 14–25 years of age live below poverty level)

Likelihood of lifetime of economic stress and limited opportunities

---

tional and vocational advancement. Card and Wise (1978) reported that men who became fathers at 18 years of age or younger were over-represented in blue-collar jobs and under-represented in the professions. Further, the high probability of separation and divorce among those who marry during adolescence makes it unlikely that marriage can be considered a general solution for the economic difficulties faced by teen mothers.

Continued education of adolescent mothers has been associated with improved socio-economic outcomes and better behavioral and academic outcomes for their children (Schilmoeller & Baranowski, 1985). Although enhanced opportunities often are related to the continued assistance of family members, it is important to note that teen parents cannot be considered a homogeneous group with similar educational aspirations and needs.

Roosa (1986) distinguished three types of pregnant adolescent school drop-outs. One type includes girls whose pregnancy and parenthood can be viewed as a manifestation of subcultural norms and expectations as well as limited success in school. Among this group adolescent parenthood may be viewed by the subculture simply as a stage in the transition to adulthood. A second type identified by Roosa consists of girls who intend to complete school but are forced to drop out because of such problems as inflexible school attendance policies, difficulty in finding or affording child care, and lack of transportation. The third group consists of a relatively small number of girls who have both high educational aspirations and strong support systems. Roosa concluded that this group typically survives quite well unless and until they are faced with a second pregnancy that overwhelms the capacities of the mother and her support network.

Gray and Ramsey (1986) compared adolescent parents who had completed high school with those who had not. All girls had participated in a preschool intervention program earlier in their lives. These investigators found that those who completed high school had a better home situation—a father or a stepfather in the home and a mother who provided an achieving role model. Not only had the graduates entered high school with greater aptitudes, but also they were more responsive to teachers and had higher grades. The home benefits produced a spiraling effect. At the birth of the baby, family members cared for the infant so that the mother could continue her schooling. The opposite was noted for those girls who had dropped out—a less favored home situation existed, and they were relatively disadvantaged intellectually. While they may have returned to school following the birth of the first baby, they dropped out after their second baby because the support from the home and school had diminished. These researchers concluded that adolescent pregnancy in and of itself was not an important determinant of women's school careers; rather the home situation, personal resources, and supportive school officials and policies were the factors that affected the adolescent parents' continued schooling.

Parenting by Adolescents

Adolescents who become parents face the demands of parenting concurrently with the developmental tasks of adolescence. Most research in the 1970s and 1980s indicated that teenage mothers may show less desirable child-rearing attitudes, are unprepared for parenting in terms of their limited understanding of infant capacities and developmental norms, that they may offer less verbal stimulation to the infant, and are likely to be irritable and to use physical punishment (Klein & Cordell, 1987; Reis, Barbera-Stein, & Bennett, 1986). More recent research has pointed out that adolescent parenting is very complex, determined by the interrelationships of socioeconomic status, age, personal characteristics, and support services available. Some research has even focused on the strengths of teenage motherhood.

Reis and her associates (1986) examined the interrelationships between factors predicting parenting (knowledge of child development, age, psychological resources, and type and amount of perceived social support) as well as the contribution of each to parenting behaviors. Using low-income adolescent parents, they found that those who were punitive in their perspectives on childrearing practices also were less knowledgeable of children's developmental milestones, had less social support, and were more depressed. Further, they tended to be younger, although age was not a significant predictor of parenting skills. Contrary to predictions these parents reported high levels of social support. The authors concluded that the analyses did not give an indication of the cause-and-effect relationship between depression, knowledge, expectations, attitudes, and perceived social support, but that they should be interpreted as a set of factors that contribute to the quality of family functioning and the potential well-being of the child.

Roosa, Fitzgerald, and Carlson (1982) found that the negative effects of adolescent childbearing were not due to maternal age per se but to the correlates of early childbearing—truncated education, limited job opportunities, and reduced earning power for the mother and her male companion. While teenage mothers (more than 15 years of age) may have more optimal reproductive status, greater energy, and more enthusiasm than older mothers do, these traits are offset by low socioeconomic status. The effect of socioeconomic status was found to be several times greater than the influence of age in association with negative effects of early parenthood.

Some researchers (Barth, Schinke, & Maxwell, 1983a) have found that teenage pregnancy and motherhood (at least in the first year) are not in and of themselves as psychologically incapacitating as previous research has indicated; rather contextual factors (socioeconomic status, age, and social supports) affect the degree of distress and impairment. The poor and isolated adolescents seem most psychologically impaired.

An interesting study by Klein and Cordell (1987) examined maternal characteristics that were assessed immediately after the birth of a baby, and again when the baby was 2 months old. The young mothers demonstrated significant stability over the first 2 months of parenting for several important affective characteristics. High stability was found for resentment toward parenting, role satisfaction, anxiety concerning the infant, and anticipated use of physical punishment. The experiences of interacting with the infant did not change these affective characteristics. The investigators also found that specific knowledge and understanding of infants' needs for contact and stimulation were positively related to adjustment to parenthood. Further, they assessed the manner in which mothers held their babies and found that holding the babies at the appropriate distance for social interaction was positively related to satisfactory adjustment.

Women who were unmarried and living with their parents as opposed to those married and living with their husbands showed lower levels of adjustment in terms of feelings toward the parenting role and in meeting infants' needs. In addition, those mothers with well-defined career and educational aspirations showed greater strains in adjustment to parenting.

The coping strategies preferred by school-age mothers were investigated by Barth, Schinke, and Maxwell (1983b). The analyses revealed that school-age mothers preferred indirect coping strategies, such as avoiding the situation, changing the meaning of the event, and calming via distraction—all strategies more highly associated with distress. These researchers also found that nonwhite adolescent mothers were strongly reluctant to use negotiation or assertion for managing the offensive behavior of others. They concluded that avoidance responses, very popular with nonwhite adolescent mothers, may reflect cultural, generational, and environmental exigencies.

The need for social support of teen parents has been underscored repeatedly. Support from family, school, agencies, and the partners of the mother has been determined as critical for appropriate development of mother and child. Social support reduces pre- and postpartum complications, thus lowering medical costs, mortality, and morbidity; mediates the strain of pregnancy and motherhood, thus promoting better mental health; and improves the chances of the mother's and father's completing an educational program, thus enhancing opportunities for economic self-sufficiency (Barth & Schinke, 1984).

Research relating to various aspects of support has been conducted. Campbell, Breitmayer, and Ramey (1986) explored the benefits of providing free educational child care from birth to children of single teenage mothers. These mothers and children were followed for 4½ years. They found that high-quality free child care increased the rate of success (mother reared the child by herself or with the help of her family, she completed high school, and the family became economically self-supporting by the time the child was school age). Three fourths of the mothers who received child care as opposed to fewer than half of the control group (did not receive free child care) achieved this successful status. The children of the successful status teenagers benefited intellectually from the educational child care. They scored significantly higher on general cognitive indices than the children from the control group of mothers did. These researchers concluded that a good child-care program can make the difference between success or failure for single teenage mothers.

Although social supports provide numerous advantages for teenage parents and their children, many young mothers lack the skills and knowledge necessary to seek and use support services effectively. Research has identified some of the factors associated with the use of support services (Colletta, 1987). The degree of achievement motivation, the perceived inadequacy, and the feelings of indebtedness are attitudinal predictors of help seeking. Further, there is a strong association between positive attitude toward professional help and using professional services. A positive network orientation, then, is developed out of a past history of success in arranging for and utilizing support. Adolescent parents, particularly poor nonwhite ones, lack this successful past history. Barth and Schinke (1984) found that a program designed for high school parents to teach skills for enlisting social supports was effective. Students enrolled in the program as opposed to those not enrolled showed better interpersonal skills (assertion, requesting help, and negotiating difficult situations) and cognitive skills (self-talk, interpersonal problem solving, and awareness of a variety of social supports) following the program.

Colletta (1987) found that network orientation was related to the mothers' past support history, to personality characteristics, and to current stress. A positive orientation was related to higher self-esteem and frequent contact with potential support providers, whereas membership in a highly stressed network was related to negative network orientation. The actual amount of support received was most strongly related to accessibility of support followed by a past history of having found help and having a family with a positive orientation toward help seeking.

Teenage Fathers

Despite the increased emphasis on the needs of unmarried pregnant adolescent females, adolescent fathers have received less than adequate attention (Gershenson, 1983; Lamb, Elster, Peters, Kahn, & Tavare, 1986; Westney, Cole, & Munford, 1986). Most people believe that teenage fathers' first impulse is to walk away from their parental responsibilities. In the popular media they are likely to be pictured as self-centered ''ne'er-do-wells,'' the ''macho'' type interested only in sexual gratification, who

have fleeting, casual relationships with their girlfriends and leave town at the first hint of pregnancy. In reality many young men experience the same emotional confusion and struggles that young mothers do. Most have had relationships with their girlfriends for more than a year and report feelings of affection and love. Most often they are not consulted when decisions are made about their babies—decisions usually made by the mother and her parents (Robinson & Barret, 1985).

A group of unwed prospective fathers was surveyed by Westney and his associates (1986) to determine their readiness for fatherhood, their behavioral interactions after birth, and projected future behaviors with their partners and with the infants. Initially 75 percent reported that they were definitely not ready for fatherhood. However, as pregnancy advanced during the second trimester, only 57 percent did not want to become parents. To a significant extent those who did not were the least likely to engage in supportive behavior of their mate's health after birth or to indicate a desire to care for and interact with the expected infant. In addition, they projected lower levels of postnatal involvement with the mothers than the fathers did who were accepting of impending fatherhood. Males who had maintained long pre-pregnancy relationships with their mates tended to be more supportive of them prenatally and perceived themselves as maintaining close relationships with the mothers and infants after delivery. Finally, 86 percent of the adolescent fathers planned to contribute to the support of their infants.

Elster and Lamb (1986) reported that the parental behavior of adolescent fathers is remarkably similar to that of adult fathers, and that adult and adolescent fathers do not differ on measures of personality and psychopathology. Despite the common misconception that adolescent fathers have little contact with their infants, Parke, Power, and Fisher (1980) concluded that many unmarried fathers show a surprising amount of paternal involvement for extended periods following the birth. However, such involvement is often limited by attitudes of healthcare providers, social-service workers, and the girl's parents, which may result in the total exclusion of teen fathers from opportunities to par-

ticipate in prenatal care or even to see their female partners or children.

Adolescent mothers and their male partners interacting with the mothers' 6-month-old babies were observed by Lamb and Elster (1985). They found that the mothers engaged in more interaction of all types with their infants than their partners did. Play was the preferred interactive mode of the father figure. The quality of the father-infant interaction was significantly correlated with almost all measures of the mother-father interaction. Further, the paternal involvement was related to the amount of financial/material help available. The age of the father did not appear to have an impact on the early social experiences of the infants and their mothers.

The characteristics of married and unmarried adolescent mothers and their partners were examined by Lamb and his associates (1986). They found that different types of young couples faced different types of problems. Those who were already married received more positive responses from their own parents than those who were not married. Married fathers-to-be earned more than the nonmarried fathers-to-be. The already married fathers were more likely to have terminated their education prematurely. They were more likely to be present at delivery than the nonmarried groups; however, they were no more likely to be viewed by the mothers as sources of emotional support than the nonmarried partners

were. Those fathers who married after conception were more responsible and committed than the dating fathers were. In fact, the psychosocial situation of the couples who married during pregnancy appeared substantially better than that of the initially married or the dating couples.

It is obvious from the research that there are significant differences in the attitudes of teenage fathers and the degree to which they function as parents. Clearly they can provide effective support for the mother and can contribute to the development of the child. Like teen mothers, young fathers must deal with the stressful demands of adolescence and parenthood simultaneously rather than sequentially. Therefore they are in great need of support and services.

Programs for Teen Pregnancy and Parenthood

Programs relating to teen pregnancy and parenthood are aimed at three target groups, with the focus and content differing for each group. The first group are those youngsters who are not pregnant but desire to be parents in the future. The focus for these children, who may range in age from 5 years through the teens, should be on the challenges and responsibilities of parenthood, the maturity required for effective parenting (physically, socially, psychologically, and economically), decision-making and problem-solving skills, and the effects of socioeconomic status on both mothers and children. Further, information on parental and child development and family relationships is appropriate. In effect, the goal is to help youngsters delay parenthood. The concepts and approaches for providing information should vary depending on the age level of the participant. We advocate training for parenthood beginning in kindergarten. Most of the present programs of this nature are being conducted in public schools. However, they often are fragmented and do not provide in-depth knowledge about parenting.

The second target group consists of pregnant teens and, hopefully, the prospective fathers. These teens, for the most part, have not planned to be parents and are not ready to assume the impending role. While it is not possible during the pregnancy period to prepare teenagers ade-

---

**BOX 9f   COMPONENTS OF COMPREHENSIVE PROGRAMS
FOR TEEN PARENTS**

Comprehensive services involving extensive interagency coordination

Provisions for child care, transportation, personal counseling to alleviate problems associated with pregnancy

Sympathetic and supportive atmosphere

Mechanism for peer group support

Provisions for continuation of schooling and/or training for employment

Services offered for extended period of time

Sensitive, caring, nonjudgmental staff

Involvement of teen's parents and father of baby or father figure

Information on nutrition, child growth and development

Development of effective parenting skills

Diversified funding sources

Source: Polit, D. (1987, February). Routes to self-sufficiency: Teenage mothers and employment. *Children Today, 16,* 6–11.

---

quately for parenthood, the focus should be on providing services so that both the mother and the father can remain in school. The content should include prenatal development, nutrition and its relationship to the health of the mother and the developing baby, appropriate prenatal care, medical facilities, labor and delivery procedures, care of the newborn, development during infancy, goal setting for parents' and child's development, counseling to solve psychosocial problems that may have led to the pregnancy, and available social services. Many programs for pregnant teens are conducted by community agencies and often are focused only on the medical care of the mother. Creative and innovative approaches are needed to secure the involvement of the prospective fathers.

The third group for whom programs should be provided is teen parents. The primary emphasis of these programs should be on the continued educational development of both fathers and mothers. See Box 9f for the components of a comprehensive program for teen parents.

In summary, substantial research has documented the problems associated with early childbearing. Most of the research on teen pregnancy and motherhood has emphasized the negative outcomes for both mother and child. Bucholz

and Gol (1986) pointed out, however, that teen pregnancy can stimulate positive change in the adolescent's life. They suggested that the developmental level interacts with the psychological, sociocultural, economic, family, and health variables to create a context in which teenage pregnancy can be either an inhibitor or an enhancer of maturation. Current research is examining these various interrelationships in order to increase the understanding of the effects of teen parenthood and to provide information to alleviate some of the negative effects. It is clear that the issues of teen pregnancy are complex and that adolescent parents are not a homogeneous group.

Treatment programs will be effective only if they are geared to the individual differences of target groups, if premature pregnancies are prevented, and if adequate support services are provided, including quality child care and enhancement of parenting skills once parenthood occurs. Programs must take into account the parents' developmental level, their socioeconomic status, their race/ethnicity, and the available support systems. Meeting the needs of pregnant teens and parents probably presents the greatest challenge to professionals involved in the development of parent-education programs.

BOX 9g   RELATIONSHIP OF ABUSIVE OR NEGLECTFUL ADULT TO CHILD

Relationship	Cases (%)
Natural parent	86.9
Stepparent	7.1
Other relative	1.8
Other	1.5
Grandparent	.8
Adopted parent	.6
Sibling	.6
Foster parent	.3
Preschool caregiver	.3
Teacher	.3
Institutional staff	.3

Source: The American Humane Association (1982). *National analysis of official child neglect and abuse reporting.* Denver: The Center for Social Research and Development, Denver Research Institute.

ABUSIVE PARENTS

The maltreatment or abuse of children by their parents is not a new phenomenon. Today one would certainly consider infanticide, allowing or requiring young children to work for long hours in factories, and even "treating young children as miniature adults" as child abuse. Yet in previous years these were common practices. Only since the 1960s has child abuse been of such public concern that reporting statutes have been enacted. Currently all 50 states and the District of Columbia have passed statutory provisions for mandatory reporting of nonaccidental injury or neglect of children (Education Commission of the States, 1977). Child maltreatment has come into public focus because of both the seriousness of the acts and the widespread extent of the problem (Bousha & Twentyman, 1984). Concern for abused and neglected children has never been more intense in the United States than it is today. It is now recognized that abuse not only is a tragedy for the child and his abusive family but also is a community problem (Garanzini, 1984).

While the national Child Abuse Prevention and Treatment Act, as well as most state laws, prohibits child abuse by any person who is re-

sponsible for the child's welfare, there are more parents than caregivers or other adults who abuse children. More than 85 percent of child abuse and neglect cases involve natural parents. Some statistics indicate that approximately 61 percent of the abusive and neglectful parents are natural mothers or stepmothers and 30 percent are fathers or stepfathers. Sometimes both parents abuse the child. This preponderance of female perpetrators is due mainly to the greater number of neglect cases. In validated cases of abuse only, females are the perpetrator in 45 percent of the cases. It has been concluded that fewer than 10 percent of all child abusers are persons other than parents (The American Humane Association, 1982) (see Box 9g).

The national Child Abuse Prevention and Treatment Act (PL 93-247, passed in 1974) defined child abuse and neglect as "the physical or mental injury, sexual abuse, negligent treatment, or maltreatment of a child under the age of eighteen by a person who is responsible for the child's welfare under circumstances which indicate that the child's health or welfare is harmed or threatened thereby" (U.S. Department of Health, Education, and Welfare, 1975, p. 3). Thus it can be seen that the spectrum of maltreatment of children has a wide range. Both acts of commission and acts of omission are included, so that physical abuse, sexual abuse, emotional abuse, as well as neglect, are considered as maltreatment. Abuse may appear as emotional or nutritional deprivation without any evident physical signs—acts of omission (neglect)—or abuse may be incipient or insidious maltreatment, mild deprivation with verbal abuse, and/or premeditated trauma with permanent injury or death—acts of commission.

Types of Child Abuse/Neglect

Child abuse is an active, hostile, deliberate, and aggressive act carried out by the child's caregiver with the intent of willfully injuring the child. Child neglect, on the other hand, is a more passive type of treatment characterized by a lack of interest in the welfare of the child (Chase, 1975). Categorizing the various types of abuse is only beneficial from a diagnostician's point of view. From the child's standpoint it does not make any difference; it is all maltreatment (Fontana, 1973).

Physical abuse or neglect is the easiest to detect and the most often reported. In this case the parent (or caregiver) inflicts physical injury to the child through beating, whipping, branding, scalding, shaking, or even torture. Common weapons are hairbrushes, belts, sticks, light cords, or whatever is at hand. Frequently cigarette burns or burns caused by scalding water or open flames are inflicted. Gouges in the skin caused by belt buckles, sticks, or other implements are common evidences of physical abuse, as are welts, lesions, and severe bruises. X-rays frequently reveal bone scars where previously unattended breaks have occurred.

Physical neglect may also be relatively easily detected. Parents just simply and completely ignore the child or do not allow the child to have adequate food, clothing, shelter, or sanitation. These children frequently are unclean, unkempt, inappropriately dressed, underweight, and in need of medical attention.

Sexual abuse occurs when someone known to the child, who is usually female, attempts to have sexual relations through force or seduction. Concern for the victims of sexual abuse has become a national issue only during the last 5 years. In-

creased attention has been paid to sexual abuse both in the home and by other adults caring for children (Hodson & Skeen, 1987). This interest has been stimulated by the increase in reported cases and by the attention of the media. No one knows the actual extent of the problem, but a conservative estimate is that by 18 years of age, 19 percent of girls and 9 percent of boys have been sexually abused. A larger percentage of sexually abused children are girls, with perpetrators most likely being a male known to the child (40 percent are related in some way—father, stepfather, uncle, sibling, and so on).

The outbreak of highly publicized cases of sexual abuse of children in child care led to a recent study (*Child Protection Report,* April 1, 1988). Although the number of children abused by child-care providers is disturbing, children actually are at less risk of sexual abuse in the child-care setting than in the home. Approximate calculations of children abused in child care are 5.5 per 10,000 enrolled. This compares to a risk of 8.9 per 10,000 for children under 6 years of age in the home. Further, the study indicated that 40 percent of the abusers were women, most of whom were operators of the center or the staff, and that the abuse was most frequently committed in conjunction with other abusers. Frequently the abuse involved a number of children over an extended period of time. These women were usually well educated, were highly regarded in their communities, and did not have a history of deviant behavior, leading one to conclude that criminal record checks were of little use as an employment screening device.

Emotional abuse occurs when the parent (or adult caregiver) inflicts damage to the child through behaviors other than physical or sexual. These behaviors include systematically ignoring the child; continually shaming, ridiculing, teasing, or shouting at the child; and isolating or scapegoating the child. This type of abuse or neglect is difficult to detect and is rarely reported.

Incidence.   No one really knows the accurate incidence of child abuse. What is known is the number of cases reported. In 1986 a study of the national incidence and prevalence of child abuse and neglect was financed by the National Center on Child Abuse. At the time of this writing, the report of findings had not been released to the public. In the new study the definition of maltreatment was broadened to include children whose health and safety were "endangered" through abusive or neglectful treatment, whereas previous incidence studies had been restricted to cases where the child suffered "demonstrable harm" (*Child Protection Report,* June 10, 1988). See Box 9h for the number of reported cases.

It is apparent from these figures that between 1980 and 1986, the incidence of moderate abuse increased dramatically; there was a five-fold increase in neglect; the number of sexually-abused children tripled; and a four-fold increase of emotional abuse occurred. Overall female children suffered more abuse than males, particularly sexual abuse. Fatalitites were more numerous among younger children, whereas moderate injuries were more common among older children. Higher rates of maltreatment were found among families with four or more children (*Child Protection Report*, June 10, 1988).

The broader definition of maltreatment no doubt accounted for a substantial part of the increase, but even when the 1980 standard was applied, there was still a 64 percent increase over the 6-year period. Included in these numbers were only those cases reported to child-protection agencies and community agencies, including public schools, hospitals, and police. Children enrolled in private schools, seen by private physicians or clinicians in private practice were not included. Therefore the numbers represent conservative estimates.

The original child-protection laws were received by the public with mixed reactions. Often people were opposed on the grounds of intrusion into the private domain of the family.

BOX 9h   INCIDENCE OF CHILD MALTREATMENT (1980 AND 1986)

Category	Original Definition 1980	Original Definition 1986	Revised Definition 1986
Fatal	1,000	1,100	1,000
Serious	131,200	157,100	160,000
Moderate	393,400	740,000	952,600
Probable	97,500	127,800	173,700
Endangered	(Not included)		297,200
Unknown	2,000	—	—
Total	625,100	1,025,900	1,584,700

Source: *Child Protection Report* (1988, June 10). Child abuse and neglect rocketed 150 percent in Reagan years. *XIV* (12), pp. 1, 4–5 (newsletter).

The problems faced by agencies today, however, are quite different. Workers are not facing a lack of clout, inadequate laws, or community resistance, or even difficulty in diagnosing the maltreatment; rather the obstacle is the sheer magnitude of the problem. There are too many cases for too few trained and qualified case workers and inadequate services for the victims and their parents. Nationwide the average caseload is between 40 and 50, twice that considered reasonable. More than half of the reported cases are dismissed after the case worker's first visit; agencies must focus on the most serious cases. The 1986 study (*Child Protection Report,* June 10, 1988) attributed the lack of treatment of reported cases to inadequate resources so that more stringent screening standards for investigation need to be applied. Although the reported cases of child abuse and neglect rose nearly 55 percent from 1981 to 1985, the resources for abused children increased by only 19 percent, a fraction of the increase in incidence. The shortage of resources was due largely to federal budget cutbacks ("Reports of Child," 1987).

Characteristics of Abusive Parents

Why do parents abuse their children? The answer to this question is not simple. Early research sought to identify the personality characteristics of abusive parents, the social/environmental factors, the child characteristics, and the parent-child interaction patterns in an attempt to identify the risk factors of abuse. Methodological problems with these studies have been cited as a severe limitation to generalizing the characteristics of abusive parents and children. Failure to use representative samples, comparison subjects, observers who were blind to subjects' maltreatment status, inadequate definition of terms, and/or descriptive or inferential statistics in reporting findings all have been cited as weaknesses (Kaufman & Zigler, 1987). Recent theories emphasize abuse as complex and multidetermined. Interactions between environmental, interpersonal, parental, and child factors are the focus of current research. Box 9i summarizes the general characteristics of abusive parents that have been identified in the literature.

Abusive parents may respond in one of two ways: They either cry out for help or do not care. Oddly enough, frequently only one child within the family is singled out to be abused. Abuse becomes a pattern and continues until intervention occurs or until the child is killed. One half of abused children who are returned to their parents' homes die of renewed abuse. A parent typically abuses the child, takes him to the emergency room, receives support from the spouse in a fictitious story, and then later repeats the abuse. The most common precipitating factor of child abuse and neglect is the unemployment of the father. Unemployment increases crime, alcohol intake, drug addiction, and family breakdown and results in poor physical and mental health. With poor self-images, these parents are desperate, experience failure repeatedly, and see no hope for the future (Chase, 1975).

An interesting study comparing family interactions of abusive and neglectful families and normal families was conducted by Burgess and Conger (1977). These investigators, when observing patterns of day-to-day interactions of families, found that abusive and neglectful families have lower overall rates of interaction and are much more likely to emphasize the negative and eliminate the positive in their relationships with one another. The study recorded more than 20,000 verbalizations for each of 17 abusive, 16 neglectful, and 19 normal families. Abusive mothers were found to direct 24 percent fewer verbal contacts to other family members and 27 percent fewer to their children than did the normal mothers. Interestingly enough, the children reciprocated by addressing their mothers 25 percent less often than the control children did. Similarly, abusive mothers exhibited 40 percent fewer positive interactions with their children than the control mothers did. The children in the abusive families indicated that they were adopting some of the same patterns of interactions, as they responded negatively to one another considerably more often than the children in the control families did.

The neglectful families demonstrated many of the same interactive patterns, except that the differences between neglectful and control families were more sharply delineated. Parents in neglectful families displayed rates of negative contacts with other family members more than

BOX 9i CHARACTERISTICS OF PARENTS WHO ABUSE CHILDREN

Physical Abuse

Intrapsychic disorders such as marital discord, drinking problems, mental illness

Family discord

Modeling of aggressive behavior preferred mode of interaction

Low self-esteem, low family satisfaction (mothers)

Low family interaction—emphasis on negative aspects

Intolerance

Aversive behavior (mothers)

High in life stresses

Likelihood of emotional problems

Neglect

Social disorganization

Low family interaction; emphasis on negative aspects

Related to environmental factors and parental inadequacies—unemployment, low income, poor housing, separation, and divorce

Usually a relative

Psychic disorders

Withdrawal from environment (mothers)

Intellectual inadequacies

Larger families

Resistance to rehabilitation

Sexual Abuse

Home situation similar to physical abuse

Perpetrators commonly males who live with and/or related to child (stepfathers living in home five times more likely to abuse stepdaughters than biological fathers)

Child placed in adult role early in life

Likelihood of promiscuity and alcoholism (fathers)

Intellectual inadequacies

Sources: Hodson, D., & Skeen, P. (1987). Child sexual abuse: A review of research and theory with implications for family life educators. *Family Relations, 36*(2), 215–221; Martin, M., & Walters, J. (1982). Familial correlates of selected types of child abuse and neglect. *Journal of Marriage and the Family, 44*(2), 267–276; Perry, M., Wells, E., & Doran, L. (1983). Parent characteristics in abusing and nonabusing families. *Journal of Clinical Psychology, 12*(3), 329–336.

twice as high as the control parents. Mothers interacted negatively with their children more than two and one half times more often than did control mothers.

In a later similar study, Bousha and Twentyman (1984) essentially found the same results: Neglectful mothers interacted least with their children and demonstrated depressed verbal instruction; abusive mothers interacted less than the control mothers but more than the neglectful mothers. Again, the children's rates of interaction followed a similar pattern to that of the

mothers. Abusive mothers demonstrated substantially higher rates of physical and verbal aggression than did the other mothers, and their children obviously modeled their behavior as they, too, showed higher levels of physical and verbal aggression.

Using carefully matched control samples for socioeconomic status and other variables, Perry, Wells, and Doran (1983) compared abusive and nonabusive families. Abusive mothers exhibited higher anxiety, experienced less cohesion and expression and more conflict in their families, and expected slower than normal development from their children than did the control mothers. Abusive males and females showed greater impact of life stress than did their control counterparts. Fewer differences were found between abusive and nonabusive fathers than between the two groups of mothers. Fathers' patterns of abuse were different from mothers; they had different perceptions of their families and expectations for their children's development. They reported less family cohesion and moral/religious emphasis, expected slower development of their children, and demonstrated more family conflict. Interestingly, male abusers did not exhibit lower self-esteem or higher anxiety than their controls. It was suggested that the factors contributing to abuse for fathers may be more situational or family related than for mothers.

When the effect of mother's education was removed, the difference between abusive and nonabusive mothers was not maintained for self-esteem, which has been repeatedly mentioned in the child abuse literature as a factor related to abuse. The findings of Perry, Wells, and Doran (1983) in relation to self-esteem emphasize the importance of carefully matched control studies. That abusive parents expect their children to develop skills at later ages than normal was interesting. Previous studies have found that abusive parents often have unrealistic expectations of children, and they frequently look to their children to meet their own needs. This has led to the role-reversal concept and to the conclusion that parents expect more adult behavior from their children. The results of the present study did not reject the role-reversal hypothesis. Abusive parents in the study may have expected their children to meet their needs and, at the same time, resisted their attempts for greater independence and responsibility.

Several implications may be drawn based on the previously cited research. First, children obviously use the same coercive and negative approach patterns of interacting with each other that parents use with them. Thus the pattern of abuse is learned early and continues. Second, different factors seem to contribute to abuse for mothers and for fathers. Future research should explore these differences more fully. Finally, one can see how the child is a powerful force in the creation of her own environment by the low response rates of neglected children to their parents and their siblings.

Characteristics of Abused Children

To what extent the children themselves play a role in their own abuse is not clear. We do know that children are powerful forces in creating their own environments. Abused children often are described by their parents as being different, strange, or bad. Since one child in the family is frequently singled out to be abused, that child usually is one who disrupts or interferes with the family life cycle. She may have problems sleeping, cry a lot, or respond poorly when attempts are made to comfort her. Whether these behaviors are in response to parent behaviors or the result of them is impossible to discern. In any case abuse is precipitated by the interaction of the parent and child.

Abused children have been reported to be more aggressive, less mature, less self-confident, less responsive to positive overtures by peers and teachers, and less responsive to adult modeling than nonabused children are. Camras, Grow, and Ribordy (1983) investigated the differences between abused and nonabused children in the ability to identify the facial expressions of adults. They found that abused children were not only less socially competent but also were significantly less able to judge the emotional expressions of adults. Fear, surprise, and disgust were recognized less easily than happiness, sadness, and anger. These investigators concluded that abused children's social difficulties may be due in part to inaccurate perceptions of others' emotions.

Giblin, Starr, and Agronow (1984) investigated the affective behavior of abused children. They found that home environment was a mediating factor in the expression of positive and negative behaviors. Those abused children with favored home environments (mothers who served as sources of social stimulation and appropriate play materials) displayed more positive affective behaviors than did the nonfavored control group. The abused less-favored group on home environmental variables demonstrated more negative affective behaviors than the less-favored control group did. The

---

BOX 9j   CHARACTERISTICS OF ABUSED CHILDREN

Physically Abused

Frequent conflict with parent

Self-manipulative, overt, negative communication with peers

Cringing, withdrawal when adult makes overtures

Demonstration of behaviors irritating to parents

High physical and verbal aggression in peer relationships

Neglected

Large family
Underweight
Inappropriate dress
Possible physical or other defects
Withdrawal and lack of social competence

Unkempt
Unattended health problems and illness
Low peer interaction
Low curiosity and exploratory behavior
Aggressive, attention-seeking behavior

Sexually Abused

Emotional/psychological problems
Likelihood of physical or mental disability

Lonely, hungry for affection
More commonly female—stepdaughters and daughters of single, dating women at high risk

---

heightened positive affective responses of some of the children were interpreted to be the result of the vigilant monitoring and rapid adjustment by abused children to adapt to a threatening environment. It has been proposed that abuse sensitizes children to their environment and to the behavior of others. This adaptive strategy is thought to be necessary and possible when the child has some resources within the environment on which he can draw. See Box 9j for characteristics of abused children.

Child misbehavior and parental discipline strategies in abusive and nonabusive families were investigated by Trickett and Kuczynski (1986). Abusive and nonabusive parents were trained to report their children's misbehaviors, their disciplinary and affective reactions, and their children's responses. They found that abused children committed more aggressive transactions and were more likely to oppose parental intervention than were nonabused children. Abusive parents used punitive disciplinary practices more frequently than did control parents, who used more reasoning techniques and simple commands. Abusive parents

reported more often feeling angry and disgusted after disciplinary interventions. The type of discipline used by control parents varied with the type of misbehavior. For abusive parents, physical punishment was the predominant type of discipline regardless of the misbehavior.

Browne and Finkelhor (1986) reviewed the literature on the effects of child sexual abuse. With regard to the initial effects, empirical studies have indicated—in at least some portion of the victim population—reactions of fear, anxiety, depression, anger, hostility, aggression, and sexually inappropriate behavior. Frequently reported long-term effects include depression and self-destructive behavior, anxiety, feelings of isolation and stigma, poor self-esteem, difficulty in trusting others, tendency toward revictimization, substance abuse, and sexual maladjustment. The kinds of abuse that appear to be most damaging are experiences involving father figures, genital contact, and force.

There is some evidence to suggest that children who witness family violence have adjustment problems that resemble the problems exhibited by abused children. Jaffe, Wolfe,

Wilson, and Zak (1986) examined the impact of the exposure to family violence on school-age boys. They found that abused boys demonstrated more externalizing and internalizing problems than the witnesses or the control group. However, the boys who witnessed family violence had significantly higher incidences of problems than the control group did. Internalizing problems included clinging to adults; complaining of loneliness; and feeling unloved, unhappy, sad, jealous, and worried. Major externalizing problems included disobeying at home and school, lying and cheating, destroying things belonging to self and others, being cruel to others, associating with undesirable friends, and fighting. They found 90 percent of the abused and 70 percent of the exposed children to exhibit behavior problems. These researchers concluded that boys who are exposed to family violence have adjustment difficulties that resemble the problems shown by abused children. Further, they underscored the importance of exposure to family violence as a critical factor in assessing children's problem behavior.

The belief that abused children become abusive parents has been widespread. Kaufman and Zigler (1987) proposed that unqualified acceptance of this hypothesis is unfounded. They reported that mediating factors affect the rate of intergenerational transmission of abuse and estimated it to be about 30 percent. Some studies have indicated that environmental factors (poverty, stress, and isolation), family structure, available social supports, and feelings about their abuse as children are related to the intergenerational transmission of abuse. Those who are poor, isolated, and have fewer social supports are more likely to repeat the abuse with their children. Those nonrepeaters more often reported a supportive relationship with one parent when growing up, had greater awareness of their history of being abused and vowed not to repeat the pattern, and had fewer current stressful life events. Perry, Wells, and Doran (1983) did not find that a history of child abuse differentiated between abusive and nonabusive parents when level of education was controlled.

Approximately one third of all individuals who are physically abused, sexually abused, or extremely neglected are projected to subject their offspring to one of these forms of maltreatment, whereas two thirds are not. This rate, however, is approximately six times higher than the base rate for abuse in the general population (5 percent). Although being maltreated as a child puts one at risk in the etiology of abuse, the path between these two points is far from direct or inevitable. It is of critical importance to assess the multiple factors and their relationships and to use comparison groups when examining intergenerational transmission of abuse (Kaufman & Zigler, 1987).

In summary, recent research highlights the importance of careful selection of abusing populations and use of adequately matched control groups in the examination of factors contributing to child abuse. Further, it is important to evaluate characteristics of mothers and fathers separately, and studying the interactions of environmental, interpersonal, parental, and child factors is warranted.

Reporting Abuse

The child abuse and protection laws in all 50 states require certain professionals to report known and suspected incidents of child abuse and neglect. Included are teachers, child-care workers, doctors, nurses, social workers, and anyone who renders services to children under 18 years of age. These laws are aimed at protecting children and are not meant to punish those who neglect or abuse them but to rehabilitate them. To ensure the protection of children, reporters do not have to be certain that the child is abused or neglected, rather one "has cause to believe" or is "reasonably suspect" that it is occurring. The use of these terms affords legal protection to those who do report suspected cases. A review of all state statutes clearly indicates that reporters are immune from civil or criminal liability, as long as the report is made in good faith (Breezer, 1985).

Reports of suspected abuse and neglect should be made to the local departments of human services or to the police. It is the local child-protection services division that ultimately receives and investigates reported cases. Persons who work with children should make themselves aware of the symptoms of abuse so that they have reasonable bases for reporting. Evidence might be the nature of the child's injury, a variance between the explanation of the injury and the actual injury, or statements made by a reliable person. For example, the presence of a cigarette burn on the child's back would be considered at variance with the parent's explanation that the child was playing with a cigarette.

Many people fail to report suspected cases because they are not sure what constitutes abuse and neglect, do not know how or to whom to make a report, are reluctant to get involved for fear of prosecution by the child's parents, and lack confidence that a report will ultimately do any good. Recently, a concerted effort has been made to educate professionals in these areas. With the significant increase in the number of reported cases, apparently more professionals are following through with their responsibilities in the battle against child abuse.

Support for Abusive Parents

Each reported case is investigated, and decisions are made concerning the most appropriate way to assist the family. Since many abusive parents can be rehabilitated, it is important that a plan for this rehabilitation be developed as soon as possible. Some parents seek help on their own.

Various organizations are available to assist the abusive family. Parents Anonymous is a nationwide organization that provides group therapy, ego-building sessions, and a 24-hour "hotline." The aim of the organization is to change behavior through modification. Local groups of this organization are found nationwide.

Most organized services have been established to help the child and family after the abuse pattern has been established and the parent has been reported to the authorities—tertiary intervention. These services include supportive, supplementary, substitutive, and protective approaches. The best interventionist approach includes education in parenting, counseling, and social services.

Most programs have focused on rehabilitating parents, with few aimed at the abused child. Recent research emphasizes the need for treatment programs for abusive parents to be directed toward a specific homogeneous group—the type of maltreatment (abusive, neglectful), the sex of the perpetrator, and the socioeconomic status. Further, it has been suggested that emphases also

include the development of effective communication and parenting skills.

There has been considerable emphasis on the prevention of child abuse. Previous prevention approaches have focused primarily on helping children learn the dangers of advances made by strangers, yet only 15–20 percent of sexual abusers are not known to the child. Prevention programs aimed at known offenders are becoming more common in public schools. Saslawsky and Wurtele (1986) evaluated the effectiveness of a commercially produced film, *Touch*, designed to teach children self-protection skills. They found that children who viewed the film demonstrated enhanced knowledge about sexual abuse. Findings suggested that the film was effective in encouraging children to tell an adult when inappropriate touching had occurred, a critical first step in breaking the secrecy surrounding sexual abuse.

An evaluation of preschool sexual abuse "good touch/bad touch" prevention programs, funded by the National Center on Child Abuse and Neglect, has indicated that preschool children are too young to grasp the intent of adults (*Child Protection Report*, May 27, 1988). These children are not developmentally ready to act on the concepts taught in the programs. They find it difficult to understand that someone they love and depend on might do something harmful to them. It was recommended that money spent on these programs be spent on older children or on parent-teacher awareness programs.

Much more research needs to be done regarding programs for children victimized by all kinds of abuse. Obviously the child's cognitive level must be considered. The kind of abuse also must be considered since children are affected in different ways by different types of abuse. It appears that the entire family must be involved if rehabilitation programs are to succeed.

Obviously the number of reported cases of child abuse and neglect is increasing. The problem is one with which parents, teachers, family-services personnel, and researchers need assistance. Additional information concerning family processes in abusive and neglectful families, effective approaches to rehabilitating parents, and methods of assisting the abused children themselves are clearly needed. It is difficult to determine the extent to which child abuse has long-term effects on children, but the pattern is learned early and may continue.

SUMMARY

Teenaged parents and abusive parents represent families in high-risk situations, but the type and degree of risk are vastly different for each group. Teenagers are immature, both physically and psychologically, and represent, in reality, children rearing children. From a physical standpoint very young mothers are likely to have inadequate nutrition, poor prenatal care, and labor and delivery complications. From a psychological perspective most are still in the process of developing their own sense of identity and therefore are unable to experience a positive sense of generativity. A large percentage are single parents. These conditions make effective parenting more difficult than for other parents.

The lack of preparation for parenthood and the limited knowledge and skills of child care that most teenage parents possess frequently cause unrealistic expectations to be made of children. On the other hand, spontaneity, flexibility, and a high energy level may be seen as strengths in the parenting process. The assistance of other adults, such as the teenager's own parents, seems to mitigate some of the deleterious effects on children of teenage parents.

Abusive parents pose considerable threat to the health, safety, and welfare of children. However, the majority of parents who abuse or neglect their children are hurt, lonely, and guilt-ridden. Many are young, impoverished, socially isolated, unemployed, and/or were abused themselves as children. Considerable evidence supports the fact the abuse may be perpetuated from one generation to the next. Often abusive parents make unrealistic demands on their children, and children try to comply to avoid being harmed. Our society has yet to find an effective system for the prevention of child abuse and neglect or for the rehabilitation of abusers. Clearly these issues need to be high priorities.

REFERENCES

AMERICAN HUMANE ASSOCIATION (1982). *National analysis of official child neglect and abuse reporting.* Denver: The Center for Social Research and Development, Denver Research Institute.

BARTH, R., & SCHINKE, S. (1984). Enhancing the social supports of teenage mothers. *Social Casework: Journal of Contemporary Social Work, 65*(9), 523–531.

BARTH, R., SCHINKE, S., & MAXWELL, J. (1983a). Psychological correlates of teenage motherhood. *Journal of Youth and Adolescence, 12*(6), 471–487.

BARTH, R., SCHINKE, S., & MAXWELL, J. (1983b). Coping strategies of counselors and school-age mothers. *Journal of Counseling Psychology, 30*(3), 346–354.

BOUSHA, D., & TWENTYMAN, C. (1984). Mother-child interactional style in abuse, neglect, and control groups: Naturalistic observations in the home. *Journal of Abnormal Psychology, 93*(1), 106–114.

BREEZER, B. (1985, February). Reporting child abuse: Your responsibility and your protection. *Phi Delta Kappan, 66,* 434–436.

BROWNE, A., & FINKELHOR, D. (1986). Impact of child sexual abuse: A review of the research. *Psychological Bulletin, 99*(1), 100–117.

BUCHHOLZ, E., & GOL, B. (1986). More than playing house: A developmental perspective on the strengths in teenage motherhood. *American Journal of Orthopsychiatry, 56*(3), 347–357.

BURGESS, R., & CONGER, R. (1977, March). Family interaction in abusive, neglectful and normal families. Paper presented at biennial meeting of The Society for Research in Child Development, New Orleans.

CAMPBELL, F., BREITMAYER, B., & RAMEY, C. (1986). Disadvantaged single teenage mothers and their children: Consequences of free educational day care. *Family Relations, 35*(1), 63–68.

CAMRAS, L., GROW, J., & RIBORDY, S. (1983). Recognition of emotional expression by abused children. *Journal of Clinical Child Psychology, 12*(3), 325–328.

CARD, J., & WISE, L. (1978, July/August). Teenage mothers and teenage fathers: The impact of early childbearing on the parents' personal and professional lives. *Family Planning Perspective, 10,* 199–205.

CHASE, N. (1975). *A child is being beaten.* New York: Holt, Rinehart & Winston.

Child Protection Report, (1988, April 1). Sexual abuse in day care: A national study. Newsletter, *XIV*(7), 4, 5.

Child Protection Report, (1988, June 10). Child abuse and neglect rocketed 150% in Reagan years. Newsletter, *XIV*(12), 1, 4–5.

Child Protection Report, (1988, May 27). Phaseout of preschool sexual abuse prevention urged as ineffective. Newsletter, *XIV*(11), 3.

Children's Defense Fund (1986). Children having children. (Pamphlet available from Children's Defense Fund, Washington, DC).

CHILMAN, C. (1979). Teenage pregnancy: A research review. *Journal of the National Association of Social Workers, 24*(6), 492–497.

COLLETTA, N. D. (1987, April). Correlates of young mothers' network orientations. *Journal of Community Psychology, 15,* 149–159.

Education Commission of the States (1977, January). *Trends in child abuse and neglect reporting statutes.* Report No. 95.

ELSTER, A., & LAMB, M. (1986). Adolescent fathers: The understudied side of adolescent pregnancy. In J. Lancaster & B. Hamburg (Eds.) *School-age pregnancy and parenthood* (pp. 177–190). New York: Aldine De Gruyter.

FONTANA, V. (1973). *Somewhere a child is crying.* New York: Macmillian.

GARANZINI, M. (1984, October). Child abuse and neglect: A system in trouble. *America,* pp. 221–223.

GERSHENSON, H. (1983). Redefining fatherhood in families with white adolescent mothers. *Journal of Marriage and the Family, 45*(3), 591–599.

GIBLIN, P., STARR, R., & AGRONOW, S. (1984). Affective behavior of abused and control children: Comparisons of parent-child interactions and the influence of home environment variables. *Journal of Genetic Psychology, 144,* 69–82.

GRAY, S., & RAMSEY, B. (1986). Adolescent childbearing and high school completion. *Journal of Applied Developmental Psychology, 7*(3), 167–179.

HAMNER, T., & LADEWIG, B. (1987). Teenage pregnancy: Social and psychological considerations. *School Food Service Journal, 11*(1), 7–13.

HODSON, D., & SKEEN, P. (1987). Child sexual abuse: A review of research and theory with implications for family life educators. *Family Relations, 36*(2), 215–221.

JAFFE, P., WOLFE, D., WILSON, S., & ZAK, L. (1986). Similarities in behavioral and social maladjustment among child victims and witnesses to family violence. *American Journal of Orthopsychiatry, 56*(1), 142–145.

JONES, E., FORREST, J., GOLDMAN, N., HENSHAW, S., LINCOLN, R., ROSOFF, J., WESTOFF, C., & WOLF, D. (1985). Teenage pregnancy in developed countries: Determinants and policy implications. *Family Planning Perspective, 17*(2), 53–63.

KAUFMAN, J., & ZIGLER, E. (1987). Do abused children become abusive parents? *American Journal of Orthopsychiatry, 57*(2), 186–191.

KLEIN, H., & CORDELL, A. (1987). The adolescent as mother: Early risk identification. *Journal of Youth and Adolescence, 16*(1), 47–57.

KLERMAN, L. (1986). The economic impact of school age childrearing. In J. Lancaster & B. Hamburg (Eds.) *School-age pregnancy and parenthood* (pp. 361–378). New York: Aldine De Gruyter.

LAMB, M., & ELSTER, A. (1985). Adolescent mother-infant-father relationships. *Developmental Psychology, 21*(5), 768–773.

LAMB, M., ELSTER, A., PETERS, L., KAHN, J., & TAVARE, J. (1986). Characteristics of married and unmarried adolescent mothers and their partners. *Journal of Youth and Adolescence, 15*(6), 487–495.

LEIBOWITZ, A., EISEN, M., & CHOW, W. (1986, February). An economic model of teenage pregnancy decision-making. *Demography, 23,* 67–77.

MARTIN, M., & WALTERS, J. (1982). Familial correlates of selected types of child abuse and neglect. *Journal of Marriage and the Family, 44*(2), 267–276.

PARKE, R., POWER, T., & FISHER, T. (1980, December). The adolescent father's impact on the mother and child. *Journal of Social Issues,* pp. 88–105.

PERRY, M., WELLS, E., & DORAN, L. (1983). Parent characteristics in abusing and nonabusing families. *Journal of Clinical Child Psychology, 12*(3), 329–336.

POLIT, P. (1987, February). Routes to self sufficiency: Teenage mothers and employment. *Children Today, 16,* 6–11.

REIS, J., BARBERA-STEIN, L., & BENNETT, S. (1986). Ecological determinants of parenting. *Family Relations, 35*(4), 547–554.

Reports of child abuse rise 55%, study says. (1987, March 5). *New York Times,* p. A17.

ROBINSON, B., & BARRET, R. (1985, December). Teenage fathers: Many care about their babies. *Psychology Today, 66,* 66–70.

ROOSA, M. (1986). Adolescent mothers, school drop-outs and school based intervention programs. *Family Relations, 35*(2), 313–317.

ROOSA, M., FITZGERALD, H., & CARLSON, N. (1982). A comparison of teenage and older mothers: A systems analysis. *Journal of Marriage and the Family, 44*(2), 367–377.

SASLAWSKY, D., & WURTELE, S. (1986). Educating children about sexual abuse: Implications for pediatric intervention and possible prevention. *Journal of Pediatric Psychology, 11*(2), 235–244.

SCHILMOELLER, G., & BARANOWSKI, M. (1985). Adolescent mother-infant-father relationships. *Developmental Psychology, 21*(5), 768–773.

TRICKETT, P., & KUCZYNSKI, L. (1986). Children's misbehaviors and parental discipline strategies in abusive and nonabusive families. *Developmental Psychology, 22*(1), 115–123.

U.S. DEPARTMENT OF HEALTH AND HUMAN SERVICES/PUBLIC HEALTH SERVICE (1986, May 2). *Morbidity and Mortality Weekly Report, 35,* 271.

U.S. DEPARTMENT OF HEALTH, EDUCATION, AND WELFARE, OFFICE OF HUMAN DEVELOPMENT/OFFICE OF CHILD DEVELOPMENT, CHILDREN'S BUREAU/NATIONAL CENTER ON CHILD ABUSE AND NEGLECT (1975). *Child abuse and neglect: The problem and its management.* (DHEW Publication No. OHD 75-30073).

WEED, S., & OLSEN, J. (1986). Effects of family planning programs on teenage pregnancy—replication and extension. *Family Planning Perspective, 20*(3), 173–195.

WESTNEY, O., COLE, O., & MUNFORD, T. (1986). Adolescent unwed prospective fathers: Readiness for fatherhood and behaviors toward the mother and the unexpected infant. *Adolescence, XXI,* (84), 901–911.

10

Parenting an Exceptional Child

An exceptional child is one who is different in some way from the "normal" or "average" child. The term *exceptional children* includes those with special problems related to physical handicaps, sensory impairments, emotional disturbances, learning disabilities, and mental retardation, as well as those who have special talents, that is, the gifted. Most exceptional children require special education and related services if they are to reach their full potential of development.

It is estimated that 1 out of every 10 children in the United States is an exceptional child, representing a total of nearly 8 million children. However, it is difficult to determine the number of exceptional children in a given category for the following reasons: The definitions of handicapping conditions often are ambiguous; the diagnosis of a condition may overlap with another condition or diagnoses may change over time; many exceptional children remain undetected; and often parents resist having their children identified as exceptional because of the stigma attached to labeling (Hallahan & Kauffman, 1982).

REACTIONS OF PARENTS AT BIRTH

The birth of a handicapped child into a family no doubt requires considerable adjustment on the part of family members. Most parents plan for and expect healthy, happy babies. When an impairment is immediately obvious, the acknowledgment of it is traumatic. The initial reaction of parents may be one of disbelief, and the degree of disbelief is related to the degree of the visibility of the handicap. Disbelief and shock may shortly be followed by a period of denial, or a wish to be rid of the situation (Drotar, Baskiewicz, Irvin, Kennell, & Klaus, 1975). One must consider that childbirth is already accompanied by physical and emotional fatigue and a disturbance of the family routine. The birth of a handicapped child marks the transition to a period of prolonged indecision and problems, further compounding the existing natural stresses (Christensen & DeBlassie, 1980). A period of denial, however, may offer parents additional time to become accustomed to the pain and disappointment that changes in family expectations and self-concept bring (Bloch, 1978).

Denial may be followed by sadness, accompanied by intense anxiety and a fear that the baby might die. Parents may express anger toward themselves, their spouses, or doctors and hospital staff. When parents begin to search for a reason for the impairment, they often blame themselves or the other parent, which results in guilt, manifested in a number of ways. Guilt, however, often is related to a lack of accurate information about the nature and cause of the child's disability (Christensen & DeBlassie, 1980; Drotar et al., 1975).

Some parents report difficulties in the bonding process with infants who are handicapped. There may be a number of reasons for this phenomenon: The parents may be "turned off" by the child's appearance; if the child is unresponsive, parents may give up trying to interact; if the child is at risk and is physically separated from the parents after birth, the opportunities to bond are diminished; and/or the parents may fear the child will die, and for that reason they resist bonding (Drotar et al., 1975; Klaus & Kennell, 1976).

Coupled with the reactions described above may be the process of mourning by parents of a handicapped child—grief over the death of the dreams and expectations they held for their child and over the loss of a healthy child (Hinderliter, 1988). Some parents may even carry this grief and sorrow with them for the rest of their lives. Most parents, however, eventually begin a period of gradual adaptation and reorganization in which they gain confidence in their ability to care positively for the child in a rewarding way. Five steps in the acceptance stage have been described by Ehlers, Krishef, and Protero (1973): the awareness that the child is different, the recognition of a problem to be dealt with, the search for the cause of the problem, the search for a cure, and the recognition of the child's limitations while being able to accept him.

Several factors affect the degree of stress that families experience with the birth of a handicapped child: cultural attitudes; social class; religious beliefs; the number, sex, and age of siblings; the nature and visibility of the handicap; the coping strategies of family members; and the degree of marital stability (Barsch, 1968; Drotar et al., 1975; Dunlap & Hollingsworth, 1977). It is safe to assume, then, that parents will experience at least some degree of stress and reorganization with the birth of a handicapped child, and that these parents will need psychological as well as medical support services to enable them to fulfill their parenting roles. The following sections will describe the broad categories of handicapping conditions as well as the category of gifted and talented and the similarities and differences among them in parent-child relationships.

THE PHYSICALLY HANDICAPPED

Physical handicaps cover a broad range and include a variety of types. Most are congenital, but others may be acquired after birth by accidents or diseases. The following medically based categories describe the various physically handicapping conditions: neurological impairments, such as cerebral palsy, epilepsy, spina bifida, polio, and multiple sclerosis; muscular dystrophy, rheumatoid arthritis, clubfoot, scoliosis, osteomyelitis, and congenital malformation of the hip, extremities, and heart; and accidents, diseases, and other conditions such as asthma, diabetes, rheumatic fever, tuberculosis, and hemophilia (Hallahan & Kauffman, 1982).

When physical handicaps are congenital, the intensity of denial on the part of parents may depend upon the degree of obvious visibility of the handicap (Drotar et al., 1975). Helplessness, shock, grief, and guilt also may occur. As mentioned earlier, the separation of infant and mother and the fear of infant's dying may interfere with the bonding process of parent to infant. However, it has been reported that most mothers do seem to bond to their infants eventually, with only a few experiencing overt rejection (Walker, Tomas, & Russell, 1971). On the other hand, it has been asserted that the trauma of having a physically handicapped child is in a sense ongoing because the physical presence of the child is a constant reminder of grief and loss (Poznanski, 1973). If the child becomes handicapped later in life due to accident or disease, the parents have probably formed a strong attachment to the child, and the trauma may be lessened.

Problems of Parents

One of the biggest problems that parents of the physically handicapped have is the difficulty in caring for the child. For example, some children with neurological problems may never acquire locomotion and will remain dependent on others for meeting their needs long after the infancy stage. Prolonged and incessant crying may become a problem due to the infant's faulty sucking and swallowing (Battle, 1977). As the child gets older, lifting and transporting may become difficult. Toilet training may be achieved later than usual, and incontinence may become a problem to the parent. In short, physical handicaps often result in excessive demands made on the parents' physical and psychological strength.

Another problem that exists for many parents of physically handicapped children is social isolation. Often parents refuse to take their children to public places because they feel ashamed under public scrutiny, especially if the handicap is extremely visible. In addition, mothers may refuse to work for fear that handicapped children will not receive the best of care in their absence. Parents tend to retreat from their neighbors and friends and to discourage or diminish socializing on the part of the child. In fact, parents may even be isolated from their own families by being totally silent about the child's handicap and shielding her from normal interactions (Poznanski, 1973).

Parent-Child Relationships

Positive parent-child interaction often is difficult for parents and their physically handicapped children. An interesting study involved videotaping the free play of mothers and their 2-year-olds, who were physically handicapped, premature, or normal. Mothers of handicapped toddlers withdrew and ignored their children significantly more than did mothers of normal toddlers. Children with facial anomalies were more likely than any other to be ignored (Wasserman & Allen, 1984).

Because of the increased demands by children and fewer rewards to the parents, angry feelings toward the child and subsequent guilt over this anger may result in a vicious circle of resentment, guilt, and overprotection. Several researchers have indicated that parents of the handicapped encourage unnecessary dependence in their children (Battle, 1977; Kogan & Tyler, 1973; Poznanski, 1973). While this probably is related to the mother's guilt and ambivalence about having a handicapped child, it could also be related to limitations of the child's abilities. Overprotection allows parents to deny their feelings of guilt and anger and to "make up" to the child for his disability. One hospital's physicians and physical therapists reported that often the child could not reach a new level of motor functioning without hospitalization for, in effect, a "parentectomy" (Poznanski, 1973).

However, there is not complete agreement on the degree and extent of overprotectiveness and intrusiveness by parents of handicapped children. Some studies have indicated that parents of cerebral palsied school-age and adolescent children are not significantly more controlling than parents of nonhandicapped children of the same age (Harper, 1977), while parents of preschool cerebral palsied children do demonstrate overprotective behavior (Kogan & Tyler, 1973). Perhaps intrusiveness and overprotection at younger ages serve a useful purpose since the children are less advanced developmentally and need more attention and care from parents at that time.

When physically handicapped children enter school, parents are often faced with the difficult situation of finding adequate arrangements for the child's education. Although most school systems have special education resources and attempt to mainstream the handicapped child whenever possible, the child and the family may experience stress by the labeling of the child or by her placement into a special education program. Overprotective parents of handicapped children may have more difficulty "letting go" at this time than parents of normal children. Further, because the child has physical limitations, she is often prohibited from entering into extracurricular activities with peers and may be unduly concerned about her body image. Because of these factors the self-concepts of both the child and the parents are likely to be threatened. Parents should seek psychological as well as support services to enable them to alleviate their own

guilt and to help their children achieve in areas where they are capable. If handicapped children are to be rehabilitated physically and emotionally, the parents must focus their attention on the normal aspects of the child's development rather than on the physical handicap.

Effects on Families

Obviously a physical handicap affects not only a given child but also the parents and siblings. There is not complete agreement on the extent to which marital stability is threatened. Some researchers have contended that the shock and grief of having a physically handicapped child can cause irreparable damage to the marriage (Kolin, Scherzer, New, & Garfield, 1971), while others have reported that the handicap did not affect marital relationships (Walker et al., 1971). In some instances, however, the mother may isolate herself with her children to such an extent that the father isolates himself from the home. Certainly in marriages already under stress, the addition of a physically handicapped member to the family will result in marital disruption.

Since most parents of handicapped children have normal children as well, one must consider the effects the presence of a handicapped child has on siblings. Since this area deserves much

attention and since generalizations may be made about siblings of children with a variety of types of handicaps, the final section of this chapter will include a discussion of sibling relationships.

While having a physically handicapped child surely results in some degree of stress and logistical problems for parents, it is unlikely to cause major malfunctions in families unless they are already at risk. If parents are helped through their stages of shock, denial, grief, and guilt; if they are able to accept the child's physical limitations and focus on his strengths; and if they are able to foster a positive self-image in themselves and the child, most will adapt and reach a stable equilibrium.

THE MENTALLY HANDICAPPED

The American Association on Mental Deficiency has defined mental retardation as "significantly subaverage general intellectual functioning existing concurrently with deficits in adaptive behavior, and manifested during the developmental period" (Grossman, 1977, p. 11). However, it has been pointed out that most of the individuals who have been defined as mentally retarded by IQ test performance are capable of functioning adequately in society with little or no assistance.

The dividing point between the mentally retarded and the normally functioning is fairly arbitrary. Most authorities now use an IQ score of 70 to differentiate the two groups (Harris, 1986). Hence, an individual scoring below 70 is usually classified as retarded, but one obviously must ask what the difference is between an individual with an IQ of 69 and one with an IQ of 71. Within the classification of mental retardation there are three levels: mildly retarded (an IQ range of approximately 50 to 70); moderately retarded (an IQ range of approximately 36 to 49); and severely and profoundly retarded (an IQ of under approximately 35). Those who are mildly retarded, approximately 85 percent of the retarded population, are classified as "educable" and reach a mental age of somewhere between 8 and 12 years. The moderately retarded are classified as "trainable" and achieve a mental age of between 3 and 7 years. The severely and profoundly retarded reach a mental age of 0 to 2 years.

The prevalence of mental retardation is difficult to ascertain, partly because of discrepancies in definition and methods of gathering data. However, the estimated percentage of the population under age 19 in the United States that is mentally retarded approximates 2–3 percent (Hallahan & Kauffman, 1982). There are approximately 250 different causes of mental retardation, and only in a small percentage of the cases can the cause be determined with any degree of certainty. It has been said, however, that Down's syndrome and fetal alcohol syndrome currently constitute the two leading causes (K. Hymbaugh, personal communication, April 2, 1982). Other causes include metabolic disorders, infections, malnutrition, brain damage, radiation, or cultural-familial factors.

One of the major differences for parents of physically handicapped children and parents of mentally handicapped children is the time at which they become aware of the handicapping condition. Unless an infant is born with an obvious birth defect associated with mental retardation—such as Down's syndrome or hydrocephalus (characterized by an enlarged head caused by increased fluid in the brain)—mental retardation may remain undiagnosed for months or even years. The less severe the retardation, the longer it is undiagnosed. Mild retardation is virtually impossible to diagnose during the first year of life (Apgar & Beck, 1972).

However, beginning in early infancy, infants with Down's syndrome may offer fewer rewards to parents who naturally look for sociability with their infants. Temperament differences may contribute to a fussy or exceptionally drowsy appearance. The development of early gaze, vocalization, and whole body response to parents' voices may appear extremely limited in the first few months of life. It is, then, extremely important that parents respond contingently to the infant's sounds (Richard, 1986).

When retardation is not manifested visibly at birth, parents typically first suspect that their child may be retarded when she is delayed in reaching such milestones as crawling, walking, or talking. However, since there is a wide age range considered "normal" for most skills and since many parents are only mildly aware of such age-level expectations, delays often go unnoticed. The delayed diagnosis of mental retardation could have both positive and negative effects. During the early days and months of a child's life, parents will be able to get off to a good start with the infant without the trauma associated with learning of a handicap. These positive patterns of behavior may provide parents with strength to cope with their grief at a later time. On the other hand, if retardation is not diagnosed until several years after birth, and the child has no obvious physical handicap, parents may not be clearly aware of what is wrong or why. Their prediction for the child's future course of development is difficult, and the family's role with the child may be more ambiguous than with a physically handicapped child. Often because of their uncertainty, parents may not abandon unrealistic expectations for the child and may perceive her to be "lazy" or "faking" (Grossman, 1972).

Reactions of Parents and Peers

The largest percentage of identified mentally retarded children are in the 10–14 age range and the smallest percentage in the 0–5 years range. This partly reflects the fact that IQ test scores are less reliable under the age of 5 and minimal social demands are made on young children. However, by the age of 10, children have been in school and thus have been faced with more demanding academic and intellectual tasks. Further, IQ scores are much more predictive of the child's functioning. Whenever the diagnosis is made, parents will then experience many of the feelings discussed at the beginning of this chapter—disbelief, shock, denial, and grief. A typical reaction is to "shop around" for a more satisfying diagnosis. In fact, some believe that the impact of the retarded child in a family can be a massive threat to the family structure (Love, 1973).

The extent to which a mentally retarded child in the family is viewed as a crisis will depend upon the degree to which other members of the family perceive that their lives will change undesirably and irreversibly. Crisis, then, is a function of the family's reaction to the event rather than the event itself (Turner, 1980).

Most of the literature suggests that children respond negatively to retarded peers because they are seen as different. Bak and Siperstein (1987) tested whether information viewed by nonretarded children that highlighted the similarities between them and their retarded peers would bring about more positive attitudes. The nonretarded children viewed video vignettes of a retarded child reading (which made differences between them apparent) and a retarded child talking about his or her interests and activities (which made similarities between them apparent). Results indicated that children were able to see themselves as similar to their retarded peers and did, indeed, demonstrate more positive attitudes toward them after their exposure to this information.

Impact on Families

A number of studies have examined the impact of mental retardation on families. For example, mothers and fathers of retarded children have been found to be more depressed, to have more problems handling their anger, to be more preoccupied with their retarded children while enjoying them less, and to display less of a sense of parental competence than mothers and fathers of normal children (Cummings, 1976). Others have indicated that parents of retarded children were less sociable, had less child-centered homes, were less understanding and sensitive to the retarded child, and were more apt to criticize the child. These studies seem to suggest that parents are affected by the stress of rearing a mentally retarded child. There are, however, a number of other studies that report remarkably good adjustment in families of the mentally retarded (Stanhope & Bell, 1981). Adaptation to a mentally retarded child seems to be influenced by the factors depicted in Box 10a.

Because the existence of a mentally retarded child is seen as a family problem, therapy with families has been a useful tool in facilitating adaptation. Therapy has focused on helping families deal with the following: accepting the diagnosis of the child's handicap and setting realistic expectations; moving from crisis intervention to long-range goal setting; dispelling misconceptions and increasing knowledge about mental retardation; expressing feelings about the child's handicap and family situation in an appropriate manner and developing ways of coping with future emotions; identifying the roles of the family members and the extended family; relating as a family to the problems of the child; improv-

---

BOX 10a   FACTORS AFFECTING FAMILIAL ADAPTATION TO A RETARDED CHILD

Degree of retardation: The more severe, the more difficult the adjustment.

Socioeconomic class: Upper-socioeconomic-status families experience most difficulty when child's care is minimal, but lower-socioeconomic-status families have more difficulty coping with children requiring extensive care.

Size of family: The larger the family, the less negative the impact.

Sex of the child: Initially, mothers are more disturbed by the birth of a retarded female and fathers more by a retarded male child. In lower-socioeconomic-status families where cultural sex-role expectations are more pronounced, difficulties of adjustment are greater.

Religious affiliation: Catholics are more effective in using religion to come to terms with a child's handicap than are Protestants and Jews. Protestants are more accepting than Jews are.

Source: Grossman, F. K. (1972). *Brothers and sisters of retarded children.* Syracuse, NY: Syracuse University Press.

ing parenting skills; and promoting family involvement and sharing responsibility for meeting the needs of the handicapped and other children in the family, and parents' needs as well (Miezio, 1983; Turner, 1980). The degree to which a family adapts to a mentally retarded child seems to be dependent on a number of demographic and situational factors; and adaptation, obviously, will influence the care and training that families are able to provide. Obviously a mentally retarded child is limited in the degree of his intellectual functioning. As we have already pointed out, there is wide variation in the intellectual performance of retardates. Educable retardates are considered to be those who can be taught the basic academic subjects. In fact, learning characteristics of educable retardates are similar to those of normal children of the same mental age. In other words, educable mentally retarded children go through the same stages of learning but at a slower rate. However, there is a belief that educable mental retardates may have different learning styles than normal children do. Nevertheless, retarded children tend to be underachievers relative to the expectation of their mental ages, and this underachievement is most pronounced in reading (Hallahan & Kauffman, 1982).

. It has been asserted that the social adjustment of the mildly retarded is influenced as much by personality factors as by the individual's IQ, and these personality factors may explain the failure of retarded children to do as well on cognitive tasks as one would expect from their intellectual level. It seems that retarded children develop maladaptive motives, attitudes, and styles of problem solving that inhibit optimal functioning. These patterns are based on their expectancy of failure, deriving from their greater amount of failure in past experiences. In other words, mild retardates are characterized by "outer-directedness"—that is, the child distrusts her own solutions to problems and looks for guidance in the immediate environment. They seem to be more motivated to avoid failure than to achieve success and demonstrate a high degree of suggestibility. In addition, they demonstrate a strong need for attention and support (Kimble, Garmezy, & Zigler, 1974). These characteristics seem to suggest a need for more success experiences and reward for independent thinking in retarded children.

Home Environment

The same kind of home environment that facilitates optimal development of normal children applies to children with below-normal learning abilities. Because of the increased burden of care, many families may have to modify their activities outside of the home. Activities such as shopping and entertaining may be more difficult. However, most families do not report total social isolation as a result of having a retarded child (Stanhope & Bell, 1981). For most families, warmth, nurturance, and acceptance, with a focus on the total developing child, rather than on her handicap, will result in positive functioning of the child. During the preschool years the retarded child needs an environment where she has increased opportunities for sensory stimulation—touching, listening, exploring, looking, moving about; experimenting; language stimulation; and other types of mental nourishment. Often appropriate group-learning experiences are helpful at this time (Apgar & Beck, 1972). Preschool classes usually place a major emphasis on readiness skills. The retarded child may take 2 or 3 years to acquire the same readiness skills that a normal child acquires in 1.

Some general suggestions have been made for working with retarded children in a school setting, and these seem to be applicable to parents as well (see Box 10b).

In summary, there seems to be no simple description of the impact of mental retardation on family life. A subject of considerable recent interest has been the effects of a mentally retarded child on her siblings. This aspect of family life will be discussed in the last section of this chapter. While discipline seems to be a problem for many parents of retarded children (Stanhope & Bell, 1981) and while some evidence suggests that marital relationships may deteriorate, the success with which families face their increased difficulties appears to involve a number of factors, in combination with their resources and coping styles. Positive parenting skills may be somewhat threatened by the demands of a retarded child, but, with patience and realistic

---

BOX 10b   SUGGESTIONS FOR WORKING WITH RETARDED CHILDREN

Sequence learning tasks; teach relatively complex tasks one step at a time.

Expose the child to the same materials repeatedly.

Have the child verbally rehearse what he is to learn.

Provide structure and familiarity along with moderate novelty to increase motivation.

Provide consistent reinforcement for skills associated with learning to learn.

Provide continuous and immediate feedback for learning activities.

Source: Hallahan, D. P., & Kauffman, J. M. (1982). *Exeptional children: An introduction to special education* (2d ed.). Englewood Cliffs, NJ: Prentice-Hall.

---

expectations, mentally retarded children can become self-sufficient individuals.

THE LEARNING DISABLED

Of all the categories of exceptional children, that of the learning disabled is the most ambiguous. Until the mid-1960s there was a confusing variety of labels used to describe children with particular types of learning problems. These labels included minimally brain-injured, dyslexic, slow learners, and perceptually disabled. In 1966, 99 characteristics were attributed to children labeled as learning disabled. It has been noted that this figure allows for 4,851 possible pairings of any 2 characteristics—a possibility that emphasizes the heterogeneity of the learning disabled population (Smith, 1985).

Learning disabilities constitute the single largest category of special-education services as well as the fastest growing area. It is estimated that at least 4 percent of all school children are learning disabled, and that this number represents 40 percent of children receiving special-education services. In addition, male learning disableds outnumber female learning disableds by five to one (Wojnilower & Gross, 1988). The historical roots of learning disability were biological, in that it was equated with brain dysfunction or neurological impairment. It is likely that a subset of learning disabled children do represent specific neurologically based syndromes, but

diagnostic practices have changed, and the focus is now on both child and extra-child influences (Keogh, 1986).

The most accepted criterion of learning disability is an ability-achievement discrepancy, but this merely identifies a pool of potential learning disabled individuals, and the range of characteristics within the pool is broad. There is, then, no single prototypic learning disabled child; rather they are characterized as much by their differences as by their similarities. But most experts agree that learning disability represents multiple disabilities as opposed to a single one. Further, learning disability is not merely a learning problem, as manifested by the high number of learning disabled children who have behavioral, social, and affective problems (Keogh, 1986).

Nevertheless, some generalizations can be made about children who fall into this category: (1) the child is usually not physically handicapped or sensory-impaired; (2) the learning problems are not due to mental retardation, but the child demonstrates academic retardation—he does not achieve up to his potential, as measured; (3) the learning problems are not related to environmental or cultural disadvantage; (4) there may or may not be central nervous system dysfunction, but the child fails to accurately receive, process, and/or integrate sensory stimuli; and (5) an uneven pattern of development exists—the child may be very low in some areas of development and high in others (Hallahan & Kauffman, 1982; Harwell, 1982).

BOX 10c TEN MOST FREQUENT CHARACTERISTICS OF LEARNING DISABLED CHILDREN

Hyperactivity

Perceptual-motor impairments

Frequent shifts in emotional mood

Coordination defects

Attention disorders

Impulsivity

Memory and thinking disorders

Academic problems

Speech and hearing disorders

Equivocal neurological signs and irregular EEGs

Source: Hallahan, D. P., & Kauffman, J. M. (1982). *Exceptional children: An introduction to special education* (2d ed.). Englewood Cliffs, NJ: Prentice-Hall.

Characteristics

Diagnosing and defining learning disabilities continues to be a problem. Identification varies so widely from state to state that continuity in criteria is suspect (Keogh, 1986). However, the ten most frequently found symptoms of learning disabled children are cited in Box 10c. It should be emphasized once again that not all learning disabled children demonstrate all these characteristics.

Parents and teachers often describe learning disabled children as clumsy or awkward and showing lack of control in fine motor activities, such as cutting with scissors and printing or writing. They may also demonstrate difficulty in sequencing symbols and may continue to reverse letters and numbers long after it is developmentally "normal" to do so. These visual perceptual problems may result in a decreased ability to read. It should be emphasized, however, that all children with reading problems do not have perceptual deficits and some children with perceptual deficits can read adequately (Hallahan & Kauffman, 1982).

Some learning disabled children have been described as being hyporesponsive, or slow to respond, but most are hyperactive, that is, they display rates of motor activity that are too high for their age group. Coupled with these behaviors may be frequent mood changes. Because of learning disabled children's on-again, off-again behavior, it is often difficult to differentiate them from emotionally disturbed or behaviorally disordered children. They may appear to be sullen, depressed, and withdrawn and may demonstrate unusual aggression.

It has been estimated that as many as 85 percent of learning disabled children are not identified until they are 9 or 10 years of age, when they are placed in a learning situation that creates demands incompatible with abilities (Beers & Beers, 1982). Many of these children may, however, have experienced numerous failures (teacher rejection, grade repetition, and parental hostility) before being diagnosed. But because diagnosis of learning disabled school-age children is difficult, diagnosis of preschool children is virtually impossible. Difficulties with early diagnosis stem from several sources: "immaturity" or a slower rate of maturation and behavior problems make it difficult to obtain valid test results; planners who develop identification procedures do not fully understand the wide variability of normal development and tend to label any deviancy or lag as a problem; and predicting learning problems at an early age may act as a self-fulfilling prophecy (Beers & Beers, 1982).

Obviously the earlier the identification of learning disabilities, the earlier the intervention is. Parents tend to be more concerned about the consequences of learning disabilities for academic achievement than about the other behavioral aspects of the learning disabled child. Achievement may be inhibited by receptive or expressive language disorders, memory deficits for both auditory and visual stimuli, deficient concept development and problem-solving strategies, and impulsivity. Reading disabilities seem to be the most prevalent of all academic problems.

Impact on Families

There is little available information on the effects of a learning disabled child on the family. One might surmise, however, that since the child has no obvious handicap, parents are more likely to attribute behavior and poor performance to laziness, stubbornness, or lack of motivation. The fact that behavior and performance vary from time to time seems only to compound the problem, giving the parent the idea that when the child tries, he succeeds or "behaves." Parents, then, may be in a dilemma as to how much to push the child. Once parents know of the learning disability, they may tend toward intrusive behavior, although the data in this respect are inconclusive.

It has been documented, however, that many learning disabled children develop emotional and behavioral problems, partly due to their repeated failures and learning problems (Hallahan & Kauffman, 1982; Stanhope & Bell, 1981). Differences between parents on how to handle these problems often can lead to increased marital tension. It has been suggested that learning disabled children should be actively involved in either conjoint or concurrent family therapy, with the child assuming a positive role in the recognition and reeducation of family unison and dysfunctional family patterns (Turner, 1980).

Parent-Child Relationships

Parental and sibling perceptions of learning disabled children and their degree of understanding and acceptance have an impact for the learning disabled child's self-concept and motivation. An interesting study by McLoughlin, Clark, Mauck, and Petrosko (1987) found that parents perceived greater adverse effects of learning disability in all academic and cognitive areas than the learning disabled adolescent themselves did. In fact, the adolescents rated their academic, social, and vocational/career skills as similar to those of most people, but parents rated their performance as lower, especially in reading, writing,

school content areas, and socialization. Learning disabled students expressed more ambitious postsecondary plans than parents did. Finally, the learning disableds reported having many friends; parents reported their children as having few friends. It is difficult to know whose perceptions were more nearly accurate or what impact the discrepancy had on parent-child relationships. In any event the results suggest the need for communication between parents and their learning disabled children.

How can parents help the learning disabled child? First, these children often seek inordinate amounts of *affection, praise, and approval* from both adults and peers. If parents can meet these needs, the child will function with fewer behavioral problems, although parents should not be surprised at signs of emotional disturbance. Second, parents need to *provide a number of success experiences.* A series of small accomplishments is more likely to result in long-term improvement than allowing the child to always have her way. Third, *expectations of conformity should be reasonable and flexible.* Because of the child's distractibility and hyperactivity, she may conform less well than normal children. Fourth, in conversations *parents need to enunciate well and look directly at the child.* Fifth, *clear instructions should be provided* for the child with an awareness that she may not understand them even if she appears to. Finally, parents should *be liberal and honest with praise* and other types of reinforcement at frequent intervals (Hallahan & Kauffman, 1982; Harwell, 1982).

In summary, learning disabled children display no obvious handicapping condition. They are not normally diagnosed until some time during the school-age years. Because their problems are generally less serious than those of mentally retarded children and of some physically handicapped children, they may have a less negative impact on family members. However, because the specific nature of their problem may not be readily apparent, parent-child interaction, as well as marital interaction, may deteriorate because the parent mistakenly attributes the child's behavior to personality characteristics. Therefore it is important for parents to look for symptoms of learning disabilities and to seek diagnosis before undue disruptions occur in family functioning.

THE SENSORY IMPAIRED

Children rely heavily on their senses to take in information about their surroundings and to utilize such information in organizing their environments. When one of the sensory modes is impaired, children are likely to have a more difficult time progressing normally in several areas of their development. The most common types of sensory impairment involve vision and hearing, with impairment existing in either or both of these sensory modes.

The Visually Impaired

Visual impairments tend to create a greater degree of discomfort by observers of the impaired than almost any other disability, partly because the effects of impairment are quite visible. Blindness may be determined legally or educationally; for example, a person is declared legally blind if visual acuity of the better eye is 20/200 or less with correction. A person may be declared educationally blind if his impairment is severe enough to require learning to read by braille. The partially sighted are those individuals who, by legal terms, have visual acuity in the better eye of between 20/70 and 20/200 with correction, or who, educationally, can read print with magnifying devices. Legal blindness affects less than 1 percent of the population, and it is ten times more common in adults than in children (Hallahan & Kauffman, 1982).

Visual impairments may be caused by a number of conditions, but the most common impairments of partially sighted children are nearsightedness and farsightedness. Total blindness in children is usually a result of a congenital disability due to genetic or environmental conditions. In fact, it has been estimated that 64 percent of the visual impairments of children are due to prenatal causes.

Most of the research on visually handicapped children has focused on blindness rather than on the broader category. Therefore our discussion emphasizes the effects of blindness. It can be assumed, however, that visual handicaps of any degree might cause special problems for the child and her family but to a lesser extent than more severe visual impairment.

Problems of blind children. One of the most significant problems of parents with blind infants is the inability to establish eye contact. The infant's gaze appears to be one important cue in sustaining reciprocal interactions with a caregiver and thus promoting positive social and emotional behaviors. It has been emphasized (Fraiberg, 1974, 1977) that these harmonious exchanges can be disturbed by the nature of the infant's handicap. In addition to lack of eye contact, blind babies do not display the clearly differentiated facial expressions of sighted babies, for example, alertness, distrust, and coyness. Further, they smile less and often fail to smile even at the sound of the mother's voice. They do not reach for things they want. Therefore the signals they give to their caregivers are more subtle and motorically related. Box 10d summarizes problems of blind infants.

BOX 10d　PROBLEMS OF BLIND INFANTS

Inability to establish eye contact
Absence of clearly differentiated facial expressions
Inability to detect mother's presence unless there is physical contact or language
Delayed prehension skills
Delayed representational intelligence

Sources: Fraiberg, S. (1974). Blind infants and their mothers: An examination of the sign system. In M. Lewis, & L. Rosenblum (Eds.). *The effect of the infant on its caregiver,* (pp. 215–232). New York: Wiley; and Fraiberg, S. (1977). *Insights from the blind.* New York: Basic.

The failure of caregivers to interpret these signals may lead to serious disruption in the bonding and attachment process. The blind infants studied by Fraiberg (1977), however, discriminated the mother from a stranger and reacted negatively to a stranger at about the same age as sighted infants. Further, during the second year they followed the mother and returned to her as a secure base. Fraiberg noted that qualitative differences between the attachment behaviors of blind and sighted children were seen chiefly in the high level of distress when the mother left the blind child's perceptual field and could not be found, or when the child was separated from the mother for a few hours or longer. Fraiberg concluded that the blind child during the second year does not yet have a mental representation of the mother that can sustain him in her absence.

Related to this phenomenon is the infant's inability to detect the mother's presence unless she is in physical contact or is speaking to the child. The sighted child relies heavily on her visual sense to remain assured of the mother's presence over a distance. Without a secure sense of the mother's presence, the blind child may be inhibited in exploration of the environment and might feel a sense of desertion or rejection (Tait, 1972).

One of the notable impediments of blindness can be found in the infant's prehension skills. When sighted infants are achieving proficiency in the coordination of reaching and obtaining an object within reach, blind babies are making no gesture to reach for persons or toys, even when a voice provides cues. Even with intervention blind babies do not achieve the coordination of ear and hand within ranges that correspond to eye-hand coordination in sighted children. On the other hand, postural attainments of blind children appear to be within the ranges for sighted children, while mobility attainments are considerably delayed. Blindness does not seem to interfere with acquisition of language during the first 2 years of life if the child has a language-enriched environment. However, the blind child is significantly delayed in development related to representational intelligence, which leads the sighted child into the organization of an object world (Fraiberg, 1977). It appears that the earlier

the parents get help for the blind child, the better the chances for normal development.

Reactions of parents.   It is difficult to ascertain the extent to which early disruptions negatively affect the later mother-child relationship (Stanhope & Bell, 1981). Mothers, however, may display any one of a number of characteristics. A common one is overprotectiveness, which frequently results in unrealistically low expectations for the child, thereby limiting the experiences to which he is exposed. These mothers may be non-rejecting and in fact may display devotion or dedication to the child. The result is an underestimation of the child's abilities. Other parents may display disguised or overt rejection, often resulting in ignoring the child and failing to stimulate his development. And, then, of course, there are parents who are truly accepting of the blind child's handicap and whose children turn out to be developmentally normal, well-adjusted children. How parents and significant others behave toward the child will determine to a great extent the personality characteristics he will develop. Since blind children usually experience some degree of social isolation and since they depend on verbalization of experience as a substitute for visual integration, they may experience emotional problems (Cohen, 1974). If the child is not made to feel inferior, if parents emphasize what the child can do rather than the handicap, and if parents provide optimal social experiences, most of the impediments of blindness can be overcome with appropriate intervention.

Of course, parents of blind children are concerned that their children develop positive self-concepts. Since self-concept is strongly affected by the attitudes of others toward oneself and since blind children tend to be more affected by other people's attitudes toward them than are sighted children (Cohen, 1974), parental attitudes toward the child become more crucial. Therefore either overprotection or unrealistic expectations can inhibit the blind child's process of developing a positive image of himself. Even as the child begins to rely less on the opinions of others and bases his self-concept on actual inner abilities, interests, and strivings, the blind child is still more vulnerable than the sighted child. This is due to the fact that vision inherently presents the outside world as external and as such is instrumental in the development of ego differentiation. The blind child, then, must verify externality by the interaction of his remaining senses, often with difficulty (Cohen, 1974).

We have focused largely on the child blind from birth and some of the possible consequences for those children and their parents. While some of these may be serious, children blinded from birth do not have to adjust to blindness per se and therefore never have to accommodate themselves to the *loss* of vision as do children blinded by illness or accidents. The latter may have feelings of hopelessness and despair that can cause chronic anxiety and depression (Cohen, 1974).

Role of parents. What can parents do, then, to enhance the lives of their blind children? First, they can accept the child's handicap realistically without overprotecting or conversely setting expectations too high. Achieving this balance may necessitate counseling, along with an accurate appraisal of the child's capabilities. Second, they can provide the child with many experiences that stimulate the development of other senses—hearing, touch, taste, smell, and vestibular. Third, they can seek intervention from medical, educational, and psychological resources as early as possible to provide necessary training and treatment. And, finally, they can emphasize the child's strengths rather than the handicap and provide adequate success experiences so that the child will develop a positive self-concept.

The Hearing Impaired

It has been said that hearing impairment remains one of the most difficult disabilities to research and one of the most controversial to manage (Warren & Hasenstab, 1986). Children with hearing impairments can be classified into two major groups: the deaf and the hard-of-hearing. The deaf child is one whose sense of hearing is nonfunctional for the ordinary purpose of life or one whose hearing disability precludes successful processing of linguistic information through audition (Hallahan & Kauffman, 1982). As with blindness, children may be born deaf or acquire deafness through accident or illness. For those children in the latter category, the prognosis is considerably better if deafness occurs after the development of speech and language. A hard-of-hearing child is one who generally, with the use of a hearing aid, has sufficient residual hearing so that she can process linguistic information through audition. However, it is interesting to note that many professionals categorize hearing-impaired children largely on the basis of their language abilities so that a child who does not acquire language naturally may be considered deaf, and one who has understandable speech may be considered hard of hearing. The estimates of numbers of hearing-impaired children vary considerably, but it is believed that roughly 5 percent of all school-age children have hearing outside the range of normal (Hallahan & Kauffman, 1982).

Hearing impairments may involve the outer ear, the middle ear, or the inner ear. Most outer ear problems result in the child's being hard of hearing rather than deaf. Although abnormalities of the middle ear are more serious than those of the outer ear, most do not result in deafness and many are correctable with surgery or treatment. The most severe hearing impairments and deafness are associated with abnormalities of the inner ear. The majority of these abnormalities are caused by hereditary and prenatal influences, including Rh incompatibility, viral infections (rubella and mumps), bacterial infections (meningitis and encephalitis), and anoxia (Hallahan & Kauffman, 1982).

Problems of deaf children. The most severely affected area of development in the hearing-impaired child is the ability to learn speech and language. Because our society is language-oriented, these children suffer extreme disadvantages. However, it is now believed that there are few, if any, deaf children who cannot be taught to use some language, but without extensive training this goal is not usually achieved. There are three critical disadvantages of deaf children: (1) they receive inadequate auditory feedback when they, themselves, make sounds; (2) they receive inadequate verbal reinforcement from adults; and (3) they are unable to hear adequately an adult language model (Hallahan & Kauffman, 1982).

During the early weeks and months, there often is a circular relationship between the mother and her deaf baby. The child is unable to communicate, and the mother becomes discouraged and frustrated and subsequently diminishes her efforts. Some experts believe that limited interaction with and negative feedback from family members account for much of the impact of the deaf child's development of self-identity (Loeb & Sarigiani, 1986). Box 10e summarizes problems of deaf children.

The deaf child begins to fall behind in development at about 9 months of age, when she does not respond to the voices of others. She can only imitate gestures. Severely deaf children tend to sit and walk later than normal children and have a tendency to drag their feet and appear clumsy (Love, 1970).

The question of whether deaf children are intellectually inferior to hearing children is one that has not been neatly resolved. Since the influence of hearing loss on language development is profound, indeed, and since language facilitates conceptual development, many have assumed that deaf children are handicapped in their cognitive abilities. To complicate matters further, most IQ tests rely heavily on language skills, and a deaf child's performance on such tests is inhibited by his language handicaps.

Matey and Kretschmer (1985) compared maternal speech patterns in a play situation with hearing-impaired, Down's syndrome, and normal children. They found that the speech patterns of mothers of hearing-impaired and mothers of Down's syndrome children were

identical. Presumably the level of cognitive development of hearing-impaired children would exceed that of Down's syndrome children of the same chronological age, yet in both cases the mothers adjusted their speech patterns to the language level of the child, which was similar for both types of children. What impact this has on challenging the deaf child's cognitive capacity is not known.

Several researchers, however, have insisted that deaf children are not necessarily slower than normal children and that the thinking processes among these groups of children are similar. When deaf children do perform more poorly than normal children on intellectual tasks, it may be because of inadequate parental stimulation or educational instruction (Blank, 1974; Furth, 1964, 1971, 1973).

One of the major concerns regarding deaf children is developing a healthy self-concept. A recent study compared hearing-impaired children 8 to 15 years old with normal children of the same age. The hearing-impaired children perceived themselves as not popular, as having a hard time making friends, as infrequently chosen as playmates, as the cause of trouble in the family, and as unimportant and disappointing. They exhibited shyness and low expectations with regard to their ability to perform. Communication deficits may well pave the way for isolation, and consequent isolation, in turn, fosters shyness, thus creating a vicious circle.

Warren and Hasenstab (1986) identified three categories of variables that relate to self-concept in hearing-impaired children: demographics (age, sex, and socioeconomic status), variables directly related to the hearing impairment (com-

---

BOX 10e   PROBLEMS OF DEAF CHILDREN

Inadequate auditory feedback and verbal reinforcement

Lack of adult language model

Developmental lag

Sensitive self-concept

Source: Hallahan, D. P., & Kauffman, J. M. (1982). *Exeptional children: An introduction to special education* (2d ed.). Englewood Cliffs, NJ: Prentice-Hall.

munication method, hearing status of parents, etiology of impairment, and communication development prior to impairment), and parental child-rearing attitudes and practices. Their results indicated that the last category of variables was by far the most important predictor of the child's self-concept. Indulgence, protection, and rejection led to a more negative self-concept, and appropriate discipline led to a better self-concept.

Although a number of studies suggest maladjustment for many deaf children, Aplin (1987) found that the 12-year-old hearing-impaired children in her study demonstrated lower levels of maladjustment than have been previously reported. Further, she found that those children attending regular schools were better adjusted than those attending private schools.

Parent-child relationships. There is some evidence to suggest that deaf children are more impulsive than hearing children and are often rated by their mothers as being overly dependent, restless, fussy, and disobedient. In terms of attachment, contradictory evidence exists. While some studies have indicated that attachment bonds may be weaker between deaf children and their mothers than they are between hearing children and their mothers, other studies show these patterns of attachment to be similar (Greenberg, 1978; Love, 1970; Stanhope & Bell, 1981). Let us explore these behaviors a bit further. Of course, the major problem for parents of hearing-impaired children is being able to communicate effectively with them. If the parents themselves are deaf, they are more likely to rely on manual communication with the child, thus being able to communicate with her at an earlier age. On the other hand, hearing parents must decide whether to communicate manually, orally, or in combination. If a parent relies only on oral communication, of course the young child cannot respond to questions or statements. Since parents are likely to feel frustrated in their attempts to reach the deaf child, they may become tense and antagonistic, using unusual intonations when speaking to the child (Goss, 1970). These behaviors, in conjunction with the fussy, impulsive, and dependent behaviors exhibited by the child, may create a vicious circle of more frustration and tension.

Parents may also be more protective of the deaf child than they are of the hearing child in their efforts to keep the child out of danger. Since hearing-impaired children cannot be called to, parents must use some other method of helping the child anticipate potential dangers. These efforts could result in what some call overprotectiveness.

It does seem that deaf parents are better able to establish a more positive relationship with their deaf children than hearing parents. Most certainly this phenomenon is partly due to their earlier more effective communication with them. However, other factors seem to be involved, too. For example, deaf parents are less likely to view their child's handicap as a crisis. Since early communication seems to have a positive impact on the child's development, the overall parent-child relationship is enhanced. Deaf children of deaf parents have shown higher self-evaluations and better performance on a number of measures of social and intellectual functioning than deaf children of hearing parents (Meadow, 1968, 1969). Furthermore, these children are less impulsive than those of hearing parents (Harris, 1978).

The relationship that hearing parents establish with their children appears to be at least partly dependent on the type of communication they use with them. One study indicated that mothers and their children who used total communication (manual and oral) had relationships that involved more positive affect, more play, less restrictive interactions, and more compliance. These mothers also felt more in control of their children's behavior, even though they did not differ in discipline style from mothers who used oral communication only (Greenberg, 1978).

The preceding discussion clearly indicates the central role that communication plays in the parent-child relationship and in the deaf child's social and intellectual development. There is not complete agreement between those who favor oralism and those who favor manualism, but it does appear that a combination of the two methods of communicating with deaf children produces positive results.

Another recent study found that parents of preadolescent hearing-impaired children who were in high reading and math groups showed early acceptance of their children's handicap, had permissive rather than overprotective child-rearing orientations, set high standards for school performance, had high occupational aspirations for their children, and used praise to reinforce behavior (Bodner-Johnson, 1985). The parents' adaptation to the child's hearing impairment and their press for achievement seemed to be more influential in the child's reading and math performance than was family involvement/interaction.

It is important to obtain early detection and diagnosis of hearing loss, training of the child at home as early as possible, active participation of the family at all stages of the educational process, maximum use of residual hearing with hearing aids, constant exposure to normal patterns of speech behavior, and skilled teachers once the child enters school (Ling, 1975).

Mild hearing losses. We have primarily focused on the child with a profound hearing loss. It is not unusual for a child with a mild hearing loss to remain undetected for several years. If children have learned to compensate for this loss, it may not be readily detectable to parents or teachers. Symptoms of mild hearing loss were described by Hallahan and Kauffman (1982) and appear in Box 10f. Often mild hearing losses are temporary, but those that are permanent may be corrected with hearing aids, if necessary. If they remain undetected and uncorrected, the child's social and academic adjustment may be unduly disturbed.

In summary, parents of hearing-impaired children may feel relief on discovering that the child's handicap is deafness, not mental retardation. However, these parents may need help in avoiding the strains of being either overly conscientious or self-conscious concerning their responsibilities as parents. If the child can be treated as normally as possible—talked to with animated facial expressions, not isolated from the mainstream of society, and encouraged to communicate—then she will probably have a desire to communicate and will develop in an optimal fashion (Love, 1970).

Deaf-Blind Children

The multihandicap of deafness and blindness is a severe one because the physical disabilities create serious problems of mobility and communication. Deaf-blind people can be classified into three groups: those who are born deaf and educated as deaf and later lose their sight; those who are born blind and who have learned speech before becoming deaf; and finally those children who are born deaf-blind or become so during their formative years before they develop any useful means for self-expression (Smithdas, 1970).

Sight and hearing are the two major faculties by which a normal child observes the world and gathers experience and understanding of life situations. Being deprived of both, the deaf-blind child is severely limited in his scope of ex-

---

BOX 10f SYMPTOMS OF MILD HEARING LOSS

Frequent ear infections, sinus congestion, or severe seasonal allergies
Difficulties in speaking and understanding language
Inability to follow directions, inattentiveness, daydreaming
Confusion, disorientation, or distraction
Behaviors that might be associated with learning disabilities, mental retardation, or emotional disturbances

Source: Hallahan, D. P., & Kauffman, J. M. (1982). *Exceptional children: An introduction to special education* (2d ed.). Englewood Cliffs, NJ: Prentice-Hall.

perience, and the learning process is necessarily slower than it would be under normal conditions. Therefore these children rely to a greater degree than normal on their remaining senses of taste, touch, and smell for direct information about the world in which they live.

The deaf-blind child gets most information indirectly; he is dependent on others for assistance in traveling; if he lacks intelligible speech, the problem of communication is intensified. In short all the disadvantages of blindness and all of those of deafness are combined, magnifying the problems for both the child and the parents.

The method of teaching a deaf-blind child is essentially the same technique of association used by Anne Sullivan in teaching Helen Keller. The child is shown an object or action, and the word associated with it is either spelled out in the manual alphabet or pronounced orally by the teacher. Today the Tadoma method of vibration is widely used in schools teaching deaf-blind children. The thumb is placed over the lips of the speaker and the fingers are held along the side of the face and throat so that the child can feel the vibration of the teacher's voice; the thumb picks up the shape of the lips and the passage of breath as individual sounds are made. Obviously this process is slow and requires a great deal of patience and dedication (Smithdas, 1970).

One of the typical characteristics of deaf-blind children is their "touch-me-not" or "affectionless" behavior. Yet they depend almost exclusively on their mothers or other primary caregivers for their survival and development since they lack visual and hearing input from the environment. The lack of positive feedback from the child can lead a mother to become frustrated and despondent, especially in view of the considerable time and energy she must devote to her handicapped child (Yu, 1972).

The stresses for families with deaf-blind children were categorized by Yu (1972) (see Box 10g). In addition, it has been pointed out that there are particular situations in the child's life when readjustment is called for on the part of the parents—at birth, at diagnosis and treatment, at age for school placement, at puberty, at the time for vocational planning, and as parents approach old age (Hammer, 1972). Therefore adjustment is not an absolute; parents face a series of particular crises and unique adjustments that are necessary to keep the family unit intact.

In summary, the combined handicaps of visual and hearing impairments create serious difficulties for both the child and his family. Of course the issue of communication is central to these difficulties. However, with appropriate intervention and support services, often continuing throughout the life of the child, adjustment can be achieved. The development of specialized programs for education and rehabilitation and the assimilation of deaf-blind children into the social life of their communities are of comparatively recent origin. However, these efforts toward education and training for employment have produced encouraging results.

The effects of a sensory-impaired child on family functioning appear to be quite variable. While some parents report that their marriages have been strained, others report that the presence of a sensory-impaired child improved their marriages. But the majority report a neutral impact. Apparently the initial shock and disbelief gradually give way to acceptance and adjustment (Stanhope & Bell, 1981).

THE GIFTED AND TALENTED

Unlike the other exceptionalities already discussed, giftedness and talent are characteristics to be nurtured not eliminated. However, because the moral obligation to provide assistance to those children who have some disadvantage seems greater than that to provide assistance to those children who already have an advantage,

special-education programs for the gifted are more recent and less prevalent than programs for the handicapped (Hallahan & Kauffman, 1982).

Perhaps the greatest problem associated with giftedness is that of definition. One educator listed 113 definitions of giftedness (Love, 1970). In general gifted children are ''those whose performance, in a potentially valuable line of human activity, is consistently remarkable'' (Love, 1970, p. 94) or are ''[those who] are in some way superior to a comparison group of other children of the same age'' (Hallahan & Kauffman, 1982, p. 375). A more precise, multiple-criteria definition was suggested by Hallahan & Kauffman (1982): Gifted children are those who have demonstrated high ability, high creativity, and high task commitment. According to these authors, if a child has demonstrated that he is better than 85 percent of his peers on all three of these criteria and better than 98 percent of his peers on one, then he may be classified as gifted. Ability is measured by standardized IQ and achievement tests, and creativity and task commitment are measured by tests of creativity, rating scales, and/or judgments of teachers and parents. Using

---

BOX 10g CATEGORIES OF STRESS FOR FAMILIES WITH DEAF-BLIND CHILDREN

Medical factors
    Frequent hospitalizations, creating environmental deprivation
Economic factors
    Extensive medical care
    Frequent hospitalizations
    Purchase of corrective devices
    Educational and remedial programs
    Loss of mother's income if she chooses to remain at home with the child
Emotional factors
    Parents' lack of feedback from child
    Parents' lack of time alone
    Concern about safety of the child
Professional factors
    Lack of philosophical agreement among professionals
    Lack of professional understanding and support of parents

Source: Yu, M. (1972). The causes of stresses to families with deaf-blind children. Paper presented at the Southwest Regional Meeting of the American Orthopsychiatric Association, Galveston, Texas.

this definition, it can be estimated that 3–5 percent of the school-age population is gifted.

An interesting study that examined the ability of parents to identify giftedness in their children utilized a parental checklist consisting of 16 items (Silverman, Chitwood, & Waters, 1986 [see Box 10h]). The comparison of these results to children's IQ scores on the Stanford-Binet revealed that 90 percent of the parents had correctly identified their children as mildly, moderately, or extremely gifted, with the biggest majority of children scoring in the moderate range (IQ of 132–147). The authors noted that despite the common assumption that all parents think their children are gifted, research has consistently shown that parents are much better able than teachers to identify giftedness in their children. One study reported 61 percent accuracy of parents of gifted kindergarteners as opposed to 4.3 percent accuracy of teachers (Silverman et al., 1986).

The measurement of giftedness is nevertheless complicated. Clearly IQ tests have many limitations. However, many studies have indicated that the most effective and efficient way of screening and identifying high ability is to first use group IQ test scores, followed by individual IQ tests. These may be augmented by achievement tests, teacher ratings, and honor roll listings.

Measuring creativity is even more thorny than measuring intelligence. Again the problem is associated with the definition of creativity itself. Although there is no agreed-on simple definition of creativity, all definitions seem to imply components of divergent thinking, specifically novelty or inventiveness. However, the measurement of these aspects is limited to responses along certain dimensions of specified tasks. While there are a number of tests of creativity that seek to identify the divergent thinker who may be overlooked in IQ tests, these tests have many limitations (Hallahan & Kauffman, 1982).

Task commitment usually is measured by parent and/or teacher ratings. However, some

---

BOX 10h PARENTS' CHECKLIST FOR IDENTIFYING GIFTEDNESS

Good problem-solving abilities
Rapid learning ability
Extensive vocabulary
Good memory
Long attention span
Sensitivity
Compassion for others
Perfectionism
High degree of energy
Preference for older companions
Wide range of interests
Excellent sense of humor
Early or avid reading abilities
Ability in puzzles, mazes, or numbers
Seems mature for age at times
Perseverance in areas of interest

Source: Silverman, L., Chitwood, D., & Waters, J. (1986). Young gifted children: Can parents identify giftedness? *Topics in Early Childhood Special Education, 6*(1), 23–33.

children may be underachievers, may be belligerent or apathetic about school, or may have some other motivational problem. The rating scales by parents and/or teachers could overlook some children, then, who are gifted. It has been suggested, however, that the mother is probably the very first to notice giftedness in her child. Teacher judgment continues to be used as a screening technique even though there are opposing points of view as to the effectiveness of these judgments. Love (1970) contended that teacher judgment is 90 percent accurate. On the other hand, some researchers have contended that teacher judgment is poor because teachers are not trained in what to look for and their judgments are not structured in any way. Recent efforts have been made to develop rating scales that structure teacher judgments and make them more objective. Obviously these techniques should be combined with others to identify gifted children accurately (Hallahan & Kauffman, 1982).

Characteristics of Gifted Children

The traditional stereotype of the gifted child as being maladjusted, weak and puny, emotionally unstable, and generally eccentric is just beginning to be dispelled. In fact it now appears that, in general, gifted children tend to be superior in every way—in intelligence, physique, achievement, social attributes, physical health, emotional stability, and moral character (Hallahan & Kauffman, 1982; Love, 1970; Terman & Oden, 1951).

Other studies have found gifted children to perceive themselves as more competent in the cognitive domain than their peers are. Gifted children have been found to use less hedonistic reasoning and significantly more needs reasoning; less frequent reciprocity and stereotypic reasoning; and more frequent abstract, internalized reasoning (Simmons & Zumpf, 1986). These authors concluded that although, in general, gifted children behave more prosocially than nongifted, no underlying factor relating these variables has been identified.

It should be remembered, however, that gifted children can and do have physical or personality problems or can deviate from the norms

of their group, just as average children do. Therefore it would be a mistake to assume that all gifted children are superior in every way, just as it would be a mistake to assume that all average children are average in every way. In general, however, gifted children tend to be happy and well liked by their peers, to have high self-concepts, and to have wide and varied interests. However, children with extremely high IQs (180 and above) may have more social problems and emotional difficulties than those children with IQs in the 130–150 range, especially if they are subjected to social conditions that interfere with positive mental health (Hallahan & Kauffman, 1982).

Usually gifted children are ahead of their peers in academic achievement, particularly in reading. However, many gifted children remain unrecognized by teachers because they ask many annoying questions, they may be bored with unchallenging school work, or they possess unusual knowledge or wit (Hallahan & Kauffman, 1982). If these children are "turned off" early, they may lack motivation and perform less well academically.

Factors Related to Giftedness

There are several factors that seem to be related to giftedness. First, parents with high intelligence are more likely to produce gifted children than parents with average or below-average intelligence. To what extent *genetic* factors influence intelligence is an issue that has been clearly debatable for many years. Further, some gifted children are identified whose parents are not necessarily bright. However, statistically speaking, gifted children have parents who are better than average in intelligence.

Social and cultural factors seem to play a significant role in giftedness. Research has repeatedly indicated that gifted children are more likely to come from homes in which the parents are above average in income and education (Fisch, Bilek, Harrobin, & Chang, 1976; Terman, 1926). However, again this does not mean that gifted children are never found in lower-income homes. The numbers are simply smaller. One could assume that the enrichment and stimulation, the emphasis placed on achievement, the amount of reading materials in the home, and the better educational opportunities available in privileged homes are factors that contribute to giftedness in children who grow up in these homes.

Finally, *parental characteristics* of gifted children seem to have an impact. Fathers have been found to be more independent, aloof, assertive, and tense, whereas mothers were found to be more independent, but more conscientious and persistent and to demonstrate a more calculated and controlled approach to life (Fell, Dahlstrom, & Winter, 1984). On the other hand, Karnes and Shwedel (1987) found fathers of gifted preschool children to have longer or more frequent instances of involvement with their children, to read an average of three times longer per day to their children, to report more sharing of activities with their children, to place more emphasis on reading, and to encourage oral language and independence.

A recent study by Cornell and Grossberg (1987) found that families of gifted children scored higher in the following areas than did families of normal children: cohesion and expressiveness (they valued mutually supporting relationships and open expression of thoughts and feelings); active-recreational (they valued recreational pursuits but not in a competitive framework); and intellectual-cultural (they valued intellectual pursuits). On the other hand, these families scored surprisingly lower in achievement motivation as well as in control (they did not emphasize set rules and regulations).

Parent-Child Relationships

While gifted children do not usually present the same set of problems to their parents as handicapped children do, it is safe to assume that their parents may experience some degree of stress in interacting with and providing appropriate experiences for these children. It has been pointed out that parents seem to take one of two extremes in handling a bright child: they either neglect or belittle her, failing to understand why she is different from other children, or they exploit her exceptional traits and push her beyond normal limits (Love, 1970). Of course either of these extreme positions fails to provide an atmosphere

that is conducive to fostering giftedness and adequate adjustment.

The "better baby" movement that claims that parents can produce superior minds is not based on secure, consistent demonstrations but on anecdotal accounts: ". . . parents, themselves, rather than artificial devices, are the key to opening the doors for the gifted preschooler" (Chamrad & Robinson, 1986, p. 76).

Parents may become frustrated by a gifted child's innumerable questions and continuous curiosity, the inferior feelings she may arouse in her siblings, and/or the belief that schools are not adequately challenging the child. Again, the parent may be faced with the problem of shopping around for schools (Stanhope & Bell, 1981).

Another source of frustration and disappointment for parents is the underachieving gifted child. The sources of underachievement are not clear, but achieving gifted children seem to come from homes where the parents neither overprotect their children nor subject them to excessive pressure to achieve. Parents seem to be approving, trusting, affectionate, and somewhat permissive, encouraging initiative and independence (Stanhope & Bell, 1981).

Gifted underachievers are characterized as having low self-concepts, being unable to persevere, lacking a sense of purpose, feeling inferior, and experiencing family conflicts (Callahan, 1981). Clearly the fostering of giftedness and positive adjustment are tasks of both the home and the school. Parents need to encourage original thinking, questioning, and experimentation without being overly demanding, treating the child as a normal member of the family without exploiting her superiority. Providing a variety of reading materials, not interfering with the child's work, and avoiding dictating or dominating the child's activities are ways in which parents can contribute to healthy development.

Schools can provide for the gifted in several ways. The three most common ways are enrichment, ability grouping, and acceleration. There are proponents and opponents of each of these methods. Even though more evidence supports the effectiveness of acceleration than of enrichment or ability grouping, it is the least frequently used method of educating gifted children

(Hallahan & Kauffman, 1982). The lack of agreement on how best to meet the needs of gifted children and the fear of excessive pressure or of discrimination have probably prevented public education from developing adequate programs for the gifted, both in number and content.

In summary, parents of gifted children face special challenges. They must ascertain the potential their children possess, create a home environment that is conducive to the facilitation of their children's potential, and at the same time allow their children to function as children who are not different from their peers or siblings. Further, they must utilize community services and seek appropriate educational programs to assist their exceptionally capable children in developing to their fullest potential.

THE BEHAVIORALLY DISORDERED

Children whose behavior causes adults serious concern have been labeled as behaviorally disturbed, maladjusted, or emotionally and/or socially handicapped. These labels reflect both the extreme variation in the types of behavior described and the conceptual confusion about the problems themselves (Kauffman & Kneedler, 1981).

There is no consensus regarding an acceptable definition of behavior disorders or emotional disturbance. An emotionally disturbed child may be described as one who has emotional problems that are serious enough to affect adversely his relationship to some aspect of his environment (Love, 1970), or disturbed children are those whose behavior may be at odds with others' expectations or with their own expectations for themselves (Kauffman, 1977). Nearly all definitions emphasize that disordered or disturbed behavior is extreme, chronic, and unacceptable because of social or cultural expectations (Hallahan & Kauffman, 1982).

Federal regulations governing the implementation of PL 94-142, an act requiring school systems receiving federal funds to provide education for all handicapped children, include a definition of emotionally disturbed children. The definition states that a child is emotionally disturbed if he exhibits one or more of the following five characteristics to a marked extent over a period of time: (1) an inability to learn that cannot be explained by intellectual, sensory, or health factors; (2) an inability to build or maintain satisfactory interpersonal relationships with peers and teachers; (3) inappropriate types of behavior or feelings under normal conditions; (4) a general, pervasive mood of unhappiness or depression; and (5) a tendency to develop physical symptoms, pains, or fears associated with personal or school problems (Hallahan & Kauffman, 1982).

While this definition may be useful in guiding the delivery of services to behaviorally disordered children, its ambiguity has been criticized. In fact, children are "disturbed" or "behaviorally disordered" if they are considered so based on clinical assessments of an acceptable authority. Obviously there is a problem in defining behavior disorders as a distinct category of exceptionality and as a set of problems distinct from environmental circumstances (Kauffman & Kneedler, 1981).

Because of the lack of consensus over the definition and because it is common for children to exhibit behavior disorders and other characteristics of behavior disorders, the prevalence of behaviorally disordered children has not been clearly established. However, based on a number of studies, it is safe to assume that between 7.5 percent and 10 percent of school-age children exhibit behaviors consistently perceived by teachers as serious enough to require special attention or intervention. On the other hand, the Bureau of Education for the Handicapped for many years estimated a prevalence of 2 percent for the category of "seriously emotionally disturbed," and more recent data showed only about 0.5 percent of school children being identified as such (Hallahan & Kauffman, 1982; Kauffman & Kneedler, 1981).

Causes of Behavioral Disorders

Determining the causal factors of behavior disorders is even more complex than arriving at a definition. Clearly behavior problems exist be-

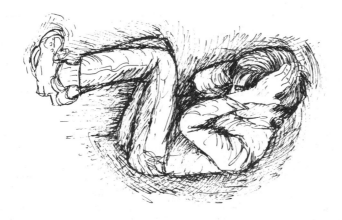

cause the social interaction between the child and his environment is inappropriate and must be attributed to the interdependency of multiple contributing factors. However, three major categories of factors seem to be frequently cited: biological, family, and school (Hallahan & Kauffman, 1982). The first includes genetic, neurological, and biochemical factors. There is, however, little evidence to support the notion that any of these contributes significantly to emotional disturbance, except that autistic and schizophrenic children often show signs of neurological defects.

The second category, family relationships, is the one that has received the most emphasis in the literature. However, as we have emphasized throughout this text, parent-child relationships are not always simple, and the nature of the relationship is always reciprocal. Especially with behaviorally disordered children, it is often not clear whether children are disturbed because parents behave the way they do toward their children, or if parents behave the way they do because their children are disturbed. The literature cites the following parental characteristics that seem to be associated with evidence of behavior disorders in children: unreasonable or punitive discipline; emotional deprivation or rejection; marital conflict; ambivalence or inconsistency; perfectionism, especially in fathers; overindulgence; domination; authoritarianism; overpossessiveness; detachment; excessively high morals; and unsociability (Love, 1970; Marion, 1981).

The third category, school experiences, probably operates in a secondary fashion to one or both of the first two categories. For those children who develop emotional disorders during their school years, it is likely that traumatic school experiences are interacting with a difficult temperamental disposition or unstable family relationships. Certainly, though, inconsistent behavior by the teacher, repeated failure at school tasks, rejection by peers, and inappropriate expectations can all contribute to pushing a tenuous emotional condition into a full-blown emotional disturbance.

It should be apparent at this point that there are a number of theories regarding the origin, nature, and treatment of behavior disorders in children. These conceptual models are summarized in Box 10i. The point in describing these models is to emphasize to the reader that because so many conceptual frameworks exist for behavior disorders, this category of exceptionality may be particularly difficult and confusing for parents. They will receive conflicting diagnoses, conflicting explanations of causes, and conflicting types of treatment. And to complicate the problem even more, society often holds the parents of a behaviorally disordered child either partially or totally responsible for the child's condition. Clinicians probe the parent-child relationship in attempting to solve the child's problem. Any other handicap—physical, sensory, or mental—can hardly be blamed on parent-child interactions (Love, 1970). These factors suggest that parents of behaviorally disordered children

---

BOX 10i CONCEPTUAL MODELS OF BEHAVIORAL DISORDERS

Biogenic/Biological Model: Behavior disorders represent genetic, biological, or neurological disorders. Medication is utilized for treatment.

Psychodynamic/Psychoanalytic Model: Behavior is the result of a pathological imbalance of the id, ego, and superego. Traditional psychoanalytic approaches are used to search for the underlying cause.

Psychoeducational Model: Based on psychoanalytic theory, this model deals therapeutically with surface behavior by stressing acquisition of academic and life skills.

Humanistic Model: Based on Rogers and Maslow, this model views behavior as symptomatic of the child's being out of touch with self and feelings. The child operates in an open, free, nontraditional atmosphere, utilizing adults as resources.

Ecological Model: This model views the child as part of the social system. Behavior is seen as the result of poor interaction with elements of the system. The target for intervention is the ecological system—home, school, and community.

Behavioral Model: This model views all behavior as learned, and therefore maladaptive behavior represents inappropriate learning; it uses operant conditioning to alter behavior.

Social Learning Model: This model is based on the behavioral model and extends consideration to cognitive and affective variables. It views behavior as interacting with both environment events and "person" variables.

Sources: Hallahan, D. P., & Kauffman, J. M. (1982). *Exceptional children: An introduction to special education* (2d ed.). Englewood Cliffs, NJ: Prentice-Hall; Kauffman, J. M., & Kneedler, R. D. (1981). Behavior disorders. In J. M. Kauffman & D. P. Hallahan (Eds.), *Handbook of special education* (pp. 165–194) Englewood Cliffs, NJ: Prentice-Hall; and Marion, R. (1981). *Educators, parents, and exceptional children.* Rockville, MD: Aspen Systems Corp.

---

may need even more support than parents of children with other handicaps.

Characteristics of Behaviorally Disordered Children

There is as much variation in the behavior of behaviorally disordered children as there is in the conceptual framework of the handicap. However, some generalizations can be made. First, very few disturbed children score above the bright normal IQ range, and most mildly or moderately disturbed score in the dull normal range. Even allowing for their below-normal IQ scores, most disturbed children are under-achievers in school (Hallahan & Kauffman, 1982).

Second, the social-emotional characteristics of the behaviorally disordered may range from mild or moderate immature or withdrawn behavior to severe acting-out or aggressive behavior. The severely withdrawn child may be referred to as autistic or schizophrenic. These children have been described as "helplessly withdrawn from the realities of the world and [living] in an inner world not entered frequently by parents and strangers" (Marion, 1981, p. 157). An extremely aggressive child may be labeled as hyperactive, hyperkinetic, or even sociopathic, destroying property through frantic and uncontrollable physical activity and/or engaging in hostile/aggressive acts toward other children and adults. And, of course, there are mild and moderate forms of both withdrawn and aggressive behavior. The withdrawn children have few friends, lack social skills, and often retreat to fantasy or daydreaming. Overly aggressive children are not popular with their peers and respond poorly to helpful adults, and their behavior is resistant to change by usual disciplinary methods.

Severely disturbed children may lack self-help skills, display perceptual deviations (such as appearing to be deaf or blind), lack cognitive skills, fail to relate or react to other people, demonstrate language and speech deviation, and engage in self-stimulation and self-injurious behaviors. These children are likely to function at a retarded level and require continued supervision and care (Hallahan & Kauffman, 1982).

Parent-Child Interactions

Parents of some behaviorally disordered children are faced with handling difficult behavior problems as early as the first year. This seems to be particularly true with those children who are extremely hyperactive or extremely withdrawn. When children do not respond well to punishment or to other usual disciplinary techniques, parents are likely to become angry, frustrated, or ineffective. Conversely, when severely withdrawn children do not react or respond to parents' attempts to communicate and interact with them, parents may feel helpless, hurt, resentful, and guilty. The negative feedback from the child is likely to result in even more negative behaviors on the part of the parent, especially rejection and guilt because the parent feels less "love" for the child than she feels she should. The problems, then, are compounded by the reciprocal nature of the relationship. When the child enters school, parents are afraid of rejection of the child by teachers, and particularly concerned that others will think that they are "bad" parents.

It is apparent that behaviorally disordered children and their parents experience considerable stress. Perhaps more than any other handicapping condition, the prognosis for the child and her family is poor because of the sensitive nature of the handicap. Counseling, special-education resources, and ongoing support, however, can help families to adjust.

SIBLING RELATIONSHIPS IN FAMILIES WITH EXCEPTIONAL CHILDREN

The dominant conception of the birth of a handicapped child is that it always has tragic implications, not only for the exceptional child but also for other family members. The evidence to support this conception, however, is far from conclusive. Until recently, little emphasis has been placed on the effects on normal siblings of having a handicapped child in the family. However, in the past few years researchers and clinicians have conducted surveys of parents, interviews with normal siblings, and even workshops or training programs for siblings to act as therapists with their handicapped brothers and sisters.

It probably is true, nevertheless, that siblings of handicapped children have questions and concerns, sometimes unspoken, about their brothers and sisters. Examples of such concerns appear in Box 10j.

Effects on Siblings and Factors Related to Adjustment

Since brothers and sisters often spend considerable time with the handicapped child, one must be aware of the concerns they may have and their potential for emotional and behavioral problems. The degree to which siblings will be affected negatively obviously depends on a number of factors. It has been assumed that the severity and visibility of the handicap is an important factor in the degree to which family members are affected and their subsequent ability to adjust. However, in her study of siblings of retarded children, Frances Grossman (1972) found that it was the family's definition of the problem that most directly affected the ability of members of the family to adjust. In other words the normal child's development and adjustment depended on the meanings and explanations the family provided regarding the handicap rather than the severity of the handicap itself.

In an effort to determine the long-range effects of having a mentally retarded sibling, Cleveland and Miller (1977) surveyed 90 men and women concerning their recollections of childhood and adolescent experiences involving their younger retarded brother or sister. They found interesting sex differences; for example, the male siblings revealed a lack of information about the retarded child that continued into adulthood. The authors hypothesized that the lack of information was a function of his role in the family; his role demanded less involvement

---

BOX 10j CONCERNS OF SIBLINGS OF HANDICAPPED CHILDREN

What caused Mary's blindness?

Is there something wrong with me?

Caring for my brother interferes with my activities.

I'd like to talk to my mother about Alice's problems, but I don't know how.

Mother spends all her time with Mark and not enough with me.

I have to work extra hard in school to make up for my sister's deficiencies.

I don't want to tell my friends about my retarded brother; they'll think we're all stupid.

Maybe if I get married and have children, they'll be retarded, too.

When my parents die, I'll probably have to take care of Aaron.

I wish I knew how to help Kathy and get along better with her.

---

with the retarded child and hence evoked less information.

Female siblings' responses, on the other hand, indicated a closer relationship with the retarded child, extending into adulthood. Since she was assigned more surrogate-parent responsibilities, she learned more about the handicapped child's condition. The demands on the female sibling were greatest when she was the eldest and was thus held responsible in place of the parents. Other studies have supported the notion that older female children are at greater risk to parental censure for adverse developments than other siblings.

The same study revealed that family size may also be a factor in adjustment. Those siblings who were the only normal siblings were much more likely to be oriented toward educational achievement than other siblings in the study. This phenomenon may represent extra stress on the normal sibling to "make up" for the deficits of the retarded child. In general, the literature suggests that retarded children have less of an impact on larger families than on smaller ones (Grossman, 1972). This is probably because there are more siblings to share the burdens of care for the handicapped child and the pressure on normal children to achieve is less because it is "shared." However, some studies have reported more adverse effects on normal siblings in larger families, especially if they are lower

class (Gath, 1974). One might surmise that in families where parents are financially burdened, poorly educated, and inept at coping with the burden of a retarded child, little energy is left for intense, positive family involvement. Those families in Grossman's study (1972) who were in this category appeared to be loosely knit, with members uninvolved with one another. Thus, the presence of a handicapped child simply interacted with other factors that might interfere with family functioning.

Finally, it appears that birth order has some relationship to the degree of adjustment by siblings of handicapped children. Older children seem to suffer most, especially if they are girls, and younger siblings seem to suffer least, partly because the family has already had time to make adjustments. Of course this factor cannot be considered in isolation from other factors such as sex, family size, and income. Apparently, older children are most affected by the demands for care giving placed upon them. However, if younger children are severely deprived of necessary nurturance and attention because of the burdens of an older handicapped sibling, they, too, can suffer.

The extent to which children are held responsible for their handicapped siblings is highly related to feelings and perceptions about themselves, their siblings, and their parents. It has been assumed that excessive responsibility may lead to anxiety, depression, and anger. However, in her comparison of adolescents with normal younger siblings and those with hearing-impaired younger siblings, Israeli (1986) found no differences between the two groups in family responsibility, depression, or anxiety. Further, there were no differences in overall self-esteem, but the family circumstances of those with handicapped siblings influenced the subtle aspects of their psychological function, such as identity and social self.

Another study, by McHale, Sloan, and Simeonsson (1986), concluded that young children had positive things to say about their siblings whether they were handicapped or not, and that sibling relationships of children with handicaps were similar to those of children without handicaps. They noted, however, that siblings of handicapped children reported highly variable relationships, depending on other factors. Worries about the handicapped child's future, perception of parental favoritism, and feelings of rejection toward the child were all associated with more negative sibling relationships. On the other hand, when children perceived their parents and peers as reacting positively to the handicapped sibling and when they had an accurate understanding of the handicapped child's condition, the sibling relationship tended to be more positive.

In spite of the concern for normal children, the vast majority of research indicates then that their adjustment is positive. Parents have reported that, in spite of certain occasional resentments (the belief that the handicapped child is loved more, given more attention, or given more material things), normal siblings seem to accept and adjust to their handicapped brothers and sisters, and the general course of everyday living among all siblings is pleasant (Barsch, 1968).

Similarly older normal siblings of retarded children indicated that their parents were quite adaptive in raising a family with a handicapped child—they attended to the needs of the normal children and provided them with appropriate information regarding the handicapped child's condition. Therefore the respondents felt that they had led relatively normal, successful lives as children and adolescents (Cleveland & Miller, 1977).

Other studies have been somewhat less conclusive. For example, Grossman's (1972) extensive study revealed what she considered harm to approximately half of the siblings of retarded children that she studied. Mostly these individuals, who were then college students, felt shamed by the association with the retarded child and anger and bitterness at their fate. Guilt and hatred also were expressed. Another 45 percent of the sample, however, were perceived by the researchers to have benefited in some way from the experience—they displayed greater tolerance for deviant individuals, more awareness of the harmful effects of prejudice, unusual understanding or compassion for others, or a sense of family closeness.

It has been noted that research on siblings of handicapped children has tended to involve effects from a unidirectional model; that is, it has focused on the impact of handicapped children on normal siblings with the assumption that handicapped children have specific influences on nonhandicapped siblings, and it has emphasized negative effects rather than processes. Further, most research has used questionnaires, recollections, maternal reports, teacher ratings, and few naturalistic observations. On the other hand, research on siblings of normal children has been bidirectional (reciprocal) in its approach, considers both positive and negative effects, and uses naturalistic observations (Senapati & Hayes, 1988). Perhaps different approaches and methodologies would yield more accurate results with respect to siblings of handicapped children.

One area that has been neglected in research is relationships between gifted and nongifted siblings. Clearly the perception of being gifted or not affects parental treatment and attitudes. Grenier (1985) found that labeled gifted children reacted positively to the competitive aspects of sibling relationships and were encouraged to cooperate and communicate more with nonlabeled siblings. However, competition had a negative impact on unlabeled siblings, who avoided situations of cooperation when competition was involved; that is, they reduced closeness and identification with the sibling. Instances of friction were greater when the gifted sibling was older, but an age gap of more than three years was beneficial to the sibling relationship. There was a strong positive correlation between parental treatment and self-image of both siblings. The author concluded that how parents are perceived as feeling about the child is highly influential in shaping how siblings feel about themselves.

Programs for Siblings

Clearly generalizing about the effects of exceptional children on normal children is difficult because of the interaction of a multitude of factors. There appear to be wide variations among families. What is encouraging, however, is the attempt nowadays to direct programs toward siblings as well as to counsel parents. An interesting program, the Sibling Training Program, was conducted by Weinroot (1974) at a camp where both the retarded and their siblings were present. The normal children first observed the handicapped children in their activities and classes and were gradually trained to participate as teachers themselves. These children were taught methods of dealing with aggression, resistance, and failure as well as content in speech, reading, creative dramatics, and the like. The author reported that 2 months after completion of camp the normal siblings were reported by parents to have vastly improved the quality of their interactions with their handicapped brothers or sisters. Specifically they showed a greater tendency to focus atten-

tion on the child's adaptive behaviors, and they performed more ''teaching'' as opposed to custodial tasks with the child.

The Sibling Training Program and others similar to it seem to be accomplishing several goals that might alleviate some of the potential risk for siblings of handicapped children. First, these programs *provide normal children with accurate information regarding handicapping conditions.* Second, they *help normal children develop realistic expectations for behavior of their siblings,* and finally, they *give children opportunities to develop specific skills in interacting with and teaching handicapped children.* Obviously, these benefits assist in the formation of a constructive sibling relationship.

Many of our comments in this section have been related to siblings of retarded children. That is because most of the literature concerns this particular population. A few studies have been conducted with siblings of hearing-impaired children, and a few training programs have been developed for siblings of deaf-blind children. While the literature in this area is sparse, the results appear to be consistent with those cited above, and the techniques for training are similar.

In summary, it seems clear that siblings of exceptional children are affected by their experiences. These effects are varied and may be positive or negative, depending upon a number

of situational factors. The research emphasis on this population and the development of therapeutic programs designed especially for them are predictive of even better adjustment in the future.

SUPPORT FOR PARENTS OF EXCEPTIONAL CHILDREN

While the reaction of parents and their adjustment to the integration of an exceptional child into the family vary considerably, these families are in need of special support. First, there is the matter of accepting a child that is less than normal and that differs from parents' initial expectations. Many parents will need professional counseling to ease the pain of disappointment. This counseling may be provided by both health and mental-health personnel.

Second is the problem of diagnosis. The nature and extent of the handicap will determine the ease, accuracy, and timing of diagnosis. Both physicians and special education professionals, including diagnosticians, can be resource persons in assisting parents at arriving at an accurate diagnosis and a realistic prognosis. The National Foundation of the March of Dimes currently has more than 100 centers throughout the United States that assist families in the prevention, diagnosis, and adjustment to birth defects. Many other specialized agencies provide these services, as well. Nearby medical schools may have departments of dysmorphology where professionals would have the most up-to-date information on the causes and treatment of specific handicapping conditions.

The third step is to develop a plan for appropriate intervention and/or treatment and support services to families that are necessary for promoting optimal development of exceptional children. These services include those that are medical, educational, and psychological in nature. In most instances the sooner a plan can be devised, the better the prognosis for both the child and the family will be. Often very young children suffer the most because of the difficulty of diagnosis, the fear of labeling, and the reluctance of parents to accept the child's handicapping conditions. Individualized Educational

Programs (IEPs) are required for all exceptional children to whom PL 94–142 applies, and Individual Family Service Plans (IFSPs) are required for all children to whom PL 99–457 applies. IEPs must be developed with an educational official (teacher or other official) in conjuction with the parent and child if appropriate. There is great diversity in the content and length of IEPs, but they must be written, signed by a parent or guardian, and include statements regarding present level of educational performance, annual goals to be accomplished, short-term objectives, specific educational services to be provided, the extent to which the child will participate in regular classrooms, projected date for length of institutionalization if necessary, and procedures for annual evaluation of objectives achieved. Thus, at least superficially, parents must be involved in the educational development of their handicapped children. The value of IEPs has been debated. Obviously, the use of IEPs could become routine and merely be prepared in order to meet federal guidelines. On the other hand, they could serve as an important promoter of teacher-parent relationships and facilitate not only the child's educational development but other aspects of development as well (Hallahan & Kauffman, 1982).

IFSPs are developed and written for children birth to 3 years of age by a multidisciplinary team and the parents. They must contain the following: (1) a statement of the child's present level of development; (2) a statement of the family's strengths and needs related to enhancing the child's development; (3) a statement of expected outcomes; (4) the criteria, procedures, and time-lines for determining progress; (5) the specific early intervention services that will be necessary; (6) the projected dates for initiation of services and duration; (7) the name of the case manager; and (8) the procedures for transition from early intervention into the preschool program. The IFSP must be evaluated at least once a year and reviewed every 6 months, or more often when appropriate. Because PL 99–457, at the time of this writing, was only beginning to be implemented, the success of IFSPs is untested.

Professional and self-help parent organizations can also be extremely helpful to parents in adjusting to a handicapped child in the family and in gaining information concerning the particular handicapping condition. While professional organizations having some bearing on the handicapped were first founded in this country in the 1800s, the first organization devoted to special education was the Council for Exceptional Children, established in 1922. This council has 12 divisions relating to various aspects of exceptionality and more than 40,000 members. Perhaps the most important parent organization is the National Association for Retarded Citizens (NARC), which was created in 1950. This organization provides for informal groups of parents who get together to share common problems and needs. In addition, it gives help to members in handling frustrations and anxieties and provides information concerning services and resources for their children.

SUMMARY

An exceptional child is one that is different in some way from the norm. Approximately 10 percent of all children are exceptional, and the category includes those with physical handicaps, sensory impairments, learning disabilities, behavioral disorders, and unusual abilities. Some handicaps are more obvious than others and are therefore easier to diagnose.

Whatever the handicap, mainstreaming an exceptional child into both home and school life requires understanding and patience. The degree of impact on parents and other children in the family is controversial. Nevertheless, it seems clear that both parents and siblings of exceptional children need support systems to help them adapt to the day-to-day process of interaction with the child and one another. PLs 94–142 and 99–457 have helped to assure that exceptional children receive appropriate intervention from birth to age 3 and appropriate academic instruction from ages 3 to 21.

Numerous organizations exist that serve as support groups to parents with exceptional children. These organizations help to educate parents about behaviors they can expect from their children and to develop appropriate parenting skills. Nevertheless, parents of exceptional children are still in need of services that would support them in their parenting roles.

REFERENCES

APGAR, V., & BECK, J. (1972). *Is my baby allright?* New York: Pocket Books.

APLIN, D. (1987). Social and emotional adjustment of hearing impared children in ordinary and special schools. *Educational Research, 29*(1), 56–64.

BAK, J., & SIPERSTEIN, G. (1987). Similarity as a factor affecting change in children's attitudes toward mentally retarded peers. *American Journal of Mental Deficiency, 91*(5), 524–531.

BARSCH, R. (1968). *The parent of the handicapped child: The study of child-rearing practices.* Springfield, IL: Charles C. Thomas.

BATTLE, C. (1977). Disruptions in the socialization of a young, severely handicapped child. In R. Marinell & A. Dell Orto (Eds.), *The psychological and social impact of physical disability.* New York: Springer.

BEERS, C., & BEERS, J. (1982). Early identification of learning disabilities: Facts and fallacies. In J. McKee (Ed.), *Annual editions: Early childhood education 1982/83* (pp. 150–156). Guilford, CT: Dushkin.

BLANK, M. Cognitive functions of language in the preschool years. *Developmental Psychology, 10,* 229–245.

BLOCH, J. (1978, November–December). Impaired children: Helping families through the critical period of first identification. *Children Today,* pp. 2–6.

BODNER-JOHNSON, B. (1985). Families that work for the hearing-impaired child. *Volta Review, 87*(3), 131–137.

CALLAHAN, C. (1981). Superior abilities. In J. Kauffman & D. Hallahan (Eds.), *Handbook of special education* (pp. 49–86). Englewood Cliffs, NJ: Prentice-Hall.

CHAMRAD, D., & ROBINSON, N. (1986). Parenting the intellectually gifted preschool child. *Topics in Early Childhood Special Education, 6*(1), 74–85.

CHRISTENSEN, B., & DEBLASSIE, R. (1980). Counseling with parents of handicapped adolescents. *Adolescence, 15*(58), 397–407.

CLEVELAND, D., & MILLER, N. (1977, June). Attitudes and life commitments of older siblings of mentally retarded adults: An exploratory study. *Mental Retardation,* pp. 38–41.

COHEN, J. (1974). Effects of blindness on children's development. In S. Kirk & F. Lord (Eds.), *Exceptional children: Educational resources and perspectives* (pp. 320–326). Boston: Houghton Mifflin.

CORNELL, D., & GROSSBERG, I. (1987). Family environment and personality adjustment in gifted program children. *Gifted Child Quarterly, 31*(2), 59–64.

CUMMINGS, S. (1976). The impact of the child's deficiency on the father: A study of fathers of mentally retarded and of chronically ill children. *American Journal of Orthopsychiatry, 46,* 246–255.

DROTAR, D., BASKIEWICZ, A., IRVIN, N., KENNELL, J., & KLAUS, M. (1975). The adaptation of parents to the birth of an infant with a congenital malformation: A hypothetical model. *Pediatrics, 56,* 710–717.

DUNLAP, W., & HOLLINGSWORTH, J. (1977). How does a handicapped child affect the family? Implications for practitioners. *The Family Coordinator, 26,* 286–293.

EHLERS, W., KRISHEF, H., & PROTERO, J. (1973). *An introduction to MR: A programmed text.* Columbus, OH: Merrill.

FELL, L., DAHLSTROM, M., & WINTER, D. (1984). Personality traits of parents of gifted children. *Psychological Reports, 54,* 383–387.

FISCH, R., BILEK, M., HARROBIN, J., & CHANG, P. (1976). Children with superior intelligence at 7 years of age. *American Journal of Diseases of Children, 130,* 481–487.

FRAIBERG, S. (1974). Blind infants and their mothers: An examination of the sign system. In M. Lewis & L. Rosenblum (Eds.), *The effect of the infant on its caregiver* (pp. 215–232). New York: Wiley.

FRAIBERG, S. (1977). *Insights from the blind.* New York: Basic.

FURTH, H. (1964). Research with the deaf: Implications for language and cognition. *Psychological Bulletin, 62,* 145–164.

FURTH, H. (1971). Linguistic deficiency and thinking: Research with deaf subjects 1964–1969. *Psychological Bulletin, 76,* 58–72.

FURTH, H. (1973). *Deafness and learning: A psychosocial approach.* Belmont, CA: Wadsworth.

GATH, A. (1974). Sibling reactions of mental handicap: A comparison of the brothers and sisters of Mongol children. *Journal of Child Psychology and Psychiatry, 15,* 187–198.

GOSS, R. (1970). Language used by mothers of deaf children and mothers of hearing children. *American Annals of the Deaf, 115,* 93–96.

GRENIER, M. (1985). Gifted children and other siblings. *Gifted Child Quarterly, 29*(4), 164–167.

GREENBERG, M. (1978). Attachment behavior, communicative competence, and parental attitudes in preschool deaf children. Unpublished doctoral dissertation, University of Virginia, Charlottesville.

GROSSMAN, H. (1972). *Brothers and sisters of retarded children.* Syracuse: Syracuse University Press.

GROSSMAN, H. (1977). *Manual on terminology and classification in mental retardation.* Washington, DC: American Association on Mental Deficiency.

HALLAHAN, D., & KAUFFMAN, J. (1982). *Exceptional children: Introduction to special education.* (2d ed.). Englewood Cliffs, NJ: Prentice-Hall.

HAMMER, E. (1972). Families of deaf-blind children: Case studies of stress. Paper presented at the southwest regional meeting of the American Orthopsychiatric Association, Galveston.

HARPER, D. (1977). Perceived maternal childrearing behavior among disabled and non-disabled adolescents. *Perceptual and Motor Skills, 44,* 1095–1105.

HARRIS, C. (1986). *Child development.* St. Paul, MN: West.

HARWELL, J. (1982). The LD syndrome: How to recognize and deal with it. In J. McKee (Ed.), *Annual editions: Early childhood education 82/83* (pp. 146–149). Guilford, Ct: Dushkin.

HINDERLITER, K. (1988, Jan./Feb.). Death of a dream. *Exceptional Parent, 1,* 48–49.

ISRAELI, N. (1986). Hearing-impaired children and the psychological functioning of their normal-hearing siblings. *Volta Review, 88*(1), 47–53.

KARNES, M., & SHWEDEL, A. (1987). Differences in attitudes and practices between fathers of young gifted and fathers of non-gifted children: A pilot study. *Gifted Child Quarterly, 31*(2), 79–82.

KAUFFMAN, J. (1977). *Characteristics of children's behavior disorders.* Columbus, OH: Merrill.

KAUFFMAN, J., & NEEDLER, R. (1981). Behavior disorders. In J. Kauffman & D. Hallahan (Eds.), *Handbook of special education* (pp. 165–194). Englewood Cliffs, NJ: Prentice-Hall.

KEOGH, B. (1986). Future of the learning disabilities field: Research and practice. *Journal of Learning Disabilities, 18*(8), 455–460.

KIMBLE, G., GARMEZY, N., & ZIGLER, E. (1974). *Principles of general psychology.* New York: Ronald Press.

KLAUS, M., & KENNELL, J. (1976). *Maternal-infant bonding.* St. Louis: Mosby.

KOGAN, K., & TYLER, N. (1973). Mother-child interactions in young physically handicapped children. *American Journal of Mental Deficiency, 77,* 492–497.

KOLIN, I., SCHERZER, A., NEW, B., & GARFIELD, M. (1971). Studies of the school-age child with meningomyelocele: Social and emotional adaptation. *Journal of Pediatrics, 78,* 103–1019.

LING, D. (1975). Recent developments affecting the education of hearing impaired children. *Public Health Reviews, 4,* 117–152.

LOEB, R., & SARIGIANI, P. (1986). The impact of hearing impairment on self-perceptions of children. *Volta Review, 88*(1), 89–99.

LOVE, H. (1970). *Parental attitudes toward exceptional children.* Springfield, IL: Charles Thomas.

LOVE, H. (1973). *The mentally retarded child and his family.* Springfield, IL: Charles Thomas.

MCHALE, S., SLOAN, J., & SIMEONSSON, R. (1986). Sibling relationships of children with autistic, mentally retarded, and non-handicapped brothers and sisters. *Journal of Autism and Developmental Disorders, 16*(4), 399–413.

MCLOUGHLIN, J., CLARK, F., MAUCK, A., & PETROSKO, J. (1987). A comparison of parent-child perceptions of student learning disabilities. *Journal of Learning Disabilities, 20*(6), 357–360.

MARION, R. (1981). *Educators, parents, and exceptional children.* Rockville, MD: Aspen Systems.

MATEY, C., & KRETSCHMER, R. (1985). A comparison of mother speech to Down's syndrome, hearing-impaired, and normal-hearing children. *Volta Review, 88*(3), 205–212.

MEADOW, K. (1968). Early manual communication in relation to the deaf child's intellectual, social, and communicative functioning. *American Annals of the Deaf, 113,* 29–41.

MEADOW, K. (1969). Self-image, family climate, and deafness. *Social Forces, 47,* 428–483.

MIEZIO, P. (1983). *Parenting children with disabilities.* New York: Marcel Dekker.

POZNANSKI, E. (1973). Emotional issues in raising handicapped children. *Rehabilitation Literature, 34*(11), 322–326.

RICHARD, N. (1986). Interaction between mothers and infants with Down's syndrome: Infant characteristics. *Topics in Early Childhood Special Education, 6*(3), 54–70.

SENAPATI, R., & HAYES, A. (1988). Sibling relationships of handicapped children: A review of conceptual and methodological issues. *International Journal of Behavioral Development, 11*(1), 89–115.

SILVERMAN, L., CHITWOOD, D., & WATERS, J. (1986). Young gifted children: Can parents identify giftedness? *Topics in Early Childhood Special Education, 6*(1), 23–33.

SIMMONS, C., & ZUMPF, C. (1986). The gifted child: Perceived competence, prosocial and moral reasoning, and charitable donations. *Journal of Genetic Psychology, 147*(1), 97–105.

SMITH, C. (1985). Learning disabilities: Past and present. *Journal of Learning Disabilities, 18*(9), 513–517.

SMITHDAS, R. (1970). The deaf-blind child in society. In *Educational counseling for parents of the deaf-blind child: Proceedings of a special institute,* Montgomery, AL: State Department of Education.

STANHOPE, L., & BELL, R. (1981). Parents and families. In J. Kauffman & D. Hallahan (Eds.), *Handbook of special education* (pp. 688–713). Englewood Cliffs, NJ: Prentice-Hall.

TAIT, P. (1972). The effect of circumstantial rejection on infant behavior. *New Outlook for the Blind, 66,* 139–151.

TERMAN, L. (1926). *Genetic studies of genius, Vol. 1: Mental and physical traits of a thousand gifted children* (2d ed.). Stanford, CA: Stanford University Press.

TERMAN, L., & ODEN, M. (1951). The Stanford studies of the gifted. In P. Witty (Ed.), *The Gifted Child* (pp. 20–45). Boston: Heath.

TURNER, A. (1980, April). Therapy with families of a mentally retarded child. *Journal of Marital and Family Therapy,* pp. 167–170.

WALKER, J., TOMAS, M., & RUSSELL, I. (1971). Spina bifida and the parents. *Developmental Medicine and Child Neurology, 13,* 462–476.

WARREN, C., & HASENSTAB, S. (1986). Self-concept of severely to profoundly hearing-impaired children. *Volta Review, 88*(6), 289–295.

WASSERMAN, G., & ALLEN, R. (1984). Maternal withdrawal from handicapped toddlers. *Journal of Child Psychology and Psychiatry and Applied Disciplines, 26*(3), 381–387.

WEINROOT, M. (1974). A training program in behavior modification for siblings of the retarded. *American Journal of Orthopsychiatry, 44*(3), 362–375.

WOJNILOWER, D., & GROSS, A. (1988). Knowledge, perception, and performance of assertive behavior in children with learning disabilities. *Journal of Learning Disabilities, 21*(2), 109–114.

YU, M. (1972). The causes for stresses to families with deaf-blind children. Paper presented at the southwest regional meeting of the American Orthopsychiatric Association, Galveston.

11

Alternatives to Biological Parenthood

Most people become parents by biologically bearing children. However, a small percentage of individuals, for various reasons, do not wish to or cannot achieve parenthood through the ordinary methods of reproduction. Adopting children is a desirable option for some; others may wish to utilize one of the embryo technology approaches; and some may elect to become foster parents. Further, biological parents often want to add additional children to the family and choose one of these alternatives for that purpose. Each alternative has its appealing as well as its risky characteristics. There are legal, social, economic, and moral issues associated with each, many of which are yet to be satisfactorily resolved. Especially in the case of embryo technology, the resolution of these issues has lagged behind the technology itself. This chapter explores these alternatives to ordinary biological parenthood.

ADOPTIVE PARENTHOOD

Adoption touches the lives of few people directly (1–2 percent of married couples) but has profound significance for the lives of those it does

affect. It offers a means of providing a pregnant woman with an alternative home for her child; offers a solution for a couple who cannot have children of their own; and provides an adopted child with a family that is presumably better equipped to rear the child than the one to which he was born. Despite the significance of adoption, statistical information about it is sparse (Bachrach, 1986).

Incidence

The incidence of adoption rose dramatically between 1951 and 1970 but fell substantially in the 1970s and leveled off in the 1980s (see Box 11a).

Two factors seem to indicate that the demand for adoptive babies will continue to increase in the future: parity and sterility (Bachrach, 1983). Many women are choosing to delay parenthood. Because the ability to bear healthy children decreases with advancing age, some women will delay parenthood until they find it difficult or impossible to conceive. The prevalence of sterility and infertility among American men and women also point to an increased demand for adoption. Sterility for women, which increased

---

BOX 11a   LIVING ARRANGEMENTS OF BABIES OF ALL RACES

	Year		
Place	1971 (%)	1976 (%)	1982 (%)
In mother's household	85.6	93.3	92.6
With relatives or friends	4.7	1.0	2.5
In adoptive household	7.6	2.6	4.6
No longer living	2.1	3.1	0.3

Source: Adapted from Bachrach, C. A. (1986). Adoption plans, adopted children, and adoptive mothers. *Journal of Marriage and the Family, 48*(2), 243–253.

---

dramatically in the last decade, is due to increased numbers of vaginal infections and surgical sterilization.

Regardless of the demand for adoptive children, adoption itself is limited by the supply available. Historically the major source of babies for adoption has been births to unmarried women. Even though the number of babies born out of wedlock has increased dramatically in recent years, the percentage placed for adoption has decreased equally as dramatically. This decrease is due to the greater accessibility of abortion and the wider acceptance of premarital pregnancy and out-of-wedlock births. Fewer than 3 percent of out-of-wedlock babies are relinquished for adoption (Bachrach, 1983). Babies born to white mothers are more likely to be placed for adoption than babies born to black mothers. Compared to women who give birth premaritally and rear their babies themselves, women who place their babies for adoption are less likely to be poor and have received public assistance and are more likely to have completed high school.

Characteristics of Adoptive Parents

Complete data on who adopts children are not available since the federal collection of national adoption statistics has been discontinued. Data in the past were collected only for women in the childbearing years (15–44 years) and did not include adoptions by never-married men and women. These adoptions, however, are still relatively rare, although the number has increased dramatically in recent years. More than 50 percent of legal adoptions are granted to step-parents, and four out of five of the remaining are placed with persons unrelated to the child (Bachrach, 1983). There are many children informally adopted, particularly by relatives, but there is no record of these adoptions.

Until recently the traditional adoptive parents were middle-class established white couples who had difficulty conceiving a child of their own (Hailstock, 1984). Studies indicated that married, older (over 30 years of age), childless, and sterile women were the most likely persons to adopt (Bachrach, 1983, 1986). These studies also suggested that women of higher educational and income levels were more likely to adopt than women of lower educational and income levels. In recent years the differences in income and educational levels have not been as great as in previous years. In the past, black, poor, and less-educated women were relatively unlikely to adopt unrelated children. Hailstock (1984) pointed out that black people have historically been strong proponents of the extended family, and children who needed guardians were embraced within the family or the community. Black couples who were interested in formal adoption often were reluctant to undergo the

stringent procedures conducted by public and private welfare agencies. Being a foster parent was more attractive. These barriers are now being eliminated, and courts and agencies are more responsive so that more black families are utilizing formal adoption.

The transition to adoptive parenthood and its problematic nature has received attention by a number of researchers (Singer, Brodzinsky, Ramsay, Steir, & Waters, 1985). Infertile couples who have not resolved their feelings about sterility may begin to resent one another or the adopted child and thus create a family atmosphere that hinders the emergence of basic trust and security for the child. Further, the anxiety and uncertainty surrounding the timing of the adoptive process presents problems. Unlike birthparents, who have approximately 9 months to adjust to the idea of parenthood, adoptive parents sometimes wait for years for a child. If sanctioned agencies are used for adoption, a rather extensive evaluation by agency personnel is viewed as highly intrusive and anxiety-arousing for many prospective adoptive parents. It has been further suggested that adoptive parents have fewer appropriate role models for parenthood than biological parents do and are less likely to receive wholehearted support for adoption from significant others. These experiences often make the transition to parenthood somewhat more difficult for adoptive parents by undermining their competence to handle the normal problems associated with adoption.

Another factor affecting the parent-child relationship is the child's preplacement history. When a child is older and has spent considerable time with the birthparents or with foster parents, the development of a warm and secure socioemotional relationship with the adoptive parents may be jeopardized. The identity with a child of a racial/ethnic group different from that of the parents is more difficult, and less social support is received for the adoption. Mothers of interracial adopted infants reported being less comfortable than mothers of nonadopted or intraracial adopted infants in having extended family members, as well as family members, care for their babies (Singer et al., 1985).

Few studies have assessed the differences between adoptive mothers and fathers; rather the adoptive parent has remained undifferentiated and genderless. In light of recent evidence that biological mothers and fathers begin immediately after birth to relate to the baby in unique ways, it appears that the differences in adoptive mothers and fathers are worthy of empirical inquiry (Singer et al., 1985).

Of interest, too, has been research relating to

the experience and adaptation of birthparents. Most research has focused on the birthmother because birthfathers historically did not necessarily have contact with the adoption agency. This is consistent with the general trend in developmental psychology to minimize, until recently, the role of the father in child development. Birthmothers who surrender their children experience pervasive feelings of guilt; a recurring sense of loss, pain, and mourning; but also feelings of comfort about the decision to relinquish the child so that he would experience a more positive child rearing than she could provide. Birthmothers also experience fears of disgrace related to the child's anticipated resentment of abandonment. The research that has been conducted on birthfathers indicates that they have similar feelings. Most research relating to birthparents has been limited to the experience of relinquishing the child, as they most often do not have postplacement contact with the agency. As more and more adult adoptees press for full information related to their adoption, studies of birthparents may increase.

Adopted Children

In the past, and perhaps still in the present, the most wanted child for adoption has been a healthy white infant. Yet the greatest numbers of children available for adoption have been older, nonwhite youngsters who may have been mentally or physically handicapped or were part of sibling groups. The decreasing number of available babies, plus a more concerted effort to place special needs children, has led recently to greater numbers of these children being adopted. Further, the availability of foreign children and the changing attitudes toward inter- and intraracial adoptions have altered adoption practices.

A significant amount of research has focused on the outcomes of adoption, for both parents and children. Some studies have focused on the child's conception of adoption (Demick & Wapner, 1988). Utilizing a constructivist framework, six stages of the child's cognitive understanding of adoption can be delineated, ranging from no understanding whatsoever (preoperational) to an understanding of adoption as a permanent relationship involving legal transfer of rights and responsibilities (formal operational). These same developmental stages are common to all children whether or not they are adopted. Using this framework a preoperational child (2–7 years) typically shows little understanding of adoption and does not differentiate the processes of birth and adoption. Preschoolers may be puzzled by the differences in appearance between themselves and their adoptive parents. Children 6 to 7 years old not only recognize the basic differences between adoption and birth, but also are aware of the existence of a third party (the agency) that is involved in the process. Children at this age, however, are likely to view adoption as temporary and to believe that biological parents may in the future reclaim their parental rights. Children 8 to 11 years old are beginning to understand the differences between adoptive and biological families. It is not until the child reaches 12 to 14 years of age that adoptive status is seen as stable and permanent and that a legal transfer of parental rights and responsibilities has occurred. Children are then able to understand the motivational bases for adoption and see it in complex, abstract, and future-oriented terms (Demick & Wapner, 1988).

What and how adoptive parents should tell their children about their births should be based on children's conceptual abilities. A generation ago parents were urged to do the following: (1) tell the child early of her adoption using only simple facts, and as the child matures, the number and complexity of facts should increase; (2) minimize the differences between adopted and biologically related children; (3) give minimal and generally positive information about biological parents; and (4) emphasize that the child was "chosen" (Kowal & Schilling, 1985). It was assumed that these procedures would automatically lead to an understanding of adoptive status. Some of this professional advice has been challenged. Studies of adult adoptees indicate that a large percentage felt that the information provided to them about their birthparents and the reasons for the parents giving them up was insufficient (Kowal & Schilling, 1985). It was further revealed by these investigators that individuals view the "chosen child" response very differently. Only about one third of the adult adoptees in their study reported that they felt chosen or special, and some of these also reported feelings of worry and anxiety. Katz (1987) stated that there are two problems with the "chosen child" approach. One is that if the matter of choice and selection is emphasized too strongly, it may cause a feeling that deep down there is something tragic about the condition of being adopted and that being with one's natural parents is really best. The other problem is what this approach says about the natural children of the adoptive parents. Are they "stuck" with what they got? All children, biological or adopted, need to be made to feel they are wanted.

When questions are raised about why the child is not living with the birthmother, a simple and frank answer, without casting any undesirable shadows on the natural mother's character or motives, should be given. It could be pointed out that most children *do* live with their biological mothers, but others are adopted, reared, and loved by other women. If the reason the child was placed for adoption is not known, the parent can speculate on some possible reasons, presenting a sympathetic view of the possibilities. The birthmother should be referred to as simply that, without hesitation.

It is important, then, to use the child's conceptual level as a basis for what to tell the child about adoption. For younger children it is best to answer questions in an honest, straightforward manner and to indicate that it will become clearer later on (Katz, 1987). For older children the aspects of adoption revelation should be continually tailored to the child's cognitive-developmental status. As children reach adolescence, the chances that they will want full information, and even desire to contact their birthparents, is likely.

Considerable research has focused on the psychosocial adjustment of adopted children. Until recently the traditional, closed adoption practice, where no communication occurred between the biological parents and the adoptive parents, was the usual procedure. These studies (Demick & Wapner, 1988) have indicated that adopted children, when compared to nonadopted children, are referred for psychological treatment two to five times more frequently, with impulsive, provocative, aggressive, and antisocial behaviors toward others as the reasons for referral. However, the generalizability of findings from clinical samples is suspect. Further, studies have shown that the adoptee experiences decreased self-esteem, identity confusion, and academic problems more frequently than nonadoptees. Interest in the effects of disruption of the bonding process also have been studied. The assumption has been that early disruption would deter, if not prevent, the reestablishment of a significant connection with the adopted parent. However, Singer and his associates (1985) found that the quality of mother-infant attachment in middle-class adoptive families was similar to that found in nonadoptive families. This was especially true for families who adopted infants of the same racial/ethnic background as themselves. It must be pointed out that these infants were 13–18 months of age at the time of the study, and all were adopted by the time they were 6 months of age. Numerous investigators (Fanshel, 1972; Feigelman & Silverman, 1983; Jewett, 1978) have all found that the older the child at the time of placement, the more likely he or she will display behavioral and school-related problems. Most research indicates that children of transracial, intercountry, and single-parent adoptions are more likely to have greater adjustment problems than children of traditional adoptive parents are. Parents have greater difficulty identifying with a child from a different racial/ethnic group, and they receive less social support from significant others (Demick & Wapner, 1988; Singer et al., 1985).

Methodological problems have been cited as problematic with the research relating to the impact of adoption (Demick & Wapner, 1988; Singer et al., 1985). Most studies have failed to account for the individual differences of adoptive parents and of the children; it has been assumed that adoption is a monolithic event that affects all the participants in the same negative ways. Further, some studies have had sampling problems, and most have not taken a systems approach to conceptualizing the problem. Finally, most studies have been cross-sectional rather than longitudinal. There is a lack of empirical evidence regarding whether adoptive families develop in similar or dissimilar ways to biological families. What does seem to be important is the emergence of caretaking confidence and competence on the part of the parents and an atmosphere of warmth and consistency, based on the developmental needs of the child (Singer et al., 1985).

One program that has been developed to assist in the adjustment of school-age children to adoption is that developed by the Children's Home Society of Virginia. Group sessions are planned for the children to explain the adoption process, clarify the roles of significant adults in the lives of children (birthparent, adoptive parent, and caseworker), examine the children's concerns about adoption, and ease inhibitions they may have about sharing their experiences. Music, poetry, and role-playing are used to stimulate discussion by the children (Pufki, 1983).

Adoption Procedures

In recent years there has been considerable controversy over the traditional policies and practices of the closed adoption system. The increasing number of adult adoptees who have requested and even demanded access to confidential information about themselves and their birthparents has been a significant factor in revising laws and practices. Other factors that have contributed to a more open system are a decrease in the number of infants available for adoption, a greater emphasis on rights of both adoptees and birthparents for more information when the child becomes an adult, research that indicates that adoptive parents are generally not afraid of allowing children more information about their birthparents, and the popularization by the media of the theme of the adoptive child's search for and reunion with her birthparents (Demick & Wapner, 1988).

Several researchers have cited reasons for adoptees' need to seek out information about their natural parents (see Box 11b). These studies have focused on adult adoptees and their searches for additional information about aspects of their adoption (Gessinger, 1984; Kowal & Schilling, 1985; Sobol & Cardiff, 1983). See Box 11c for the characteristics of adult adoptees who have searched for adoption information.

The proponents of open adoptions claim that many of the problems faced by adoptive parents and children can be eliminated or at least medi-

ated by this system. It has been suggested that an open adoption policy would alleviate considerable concern about the child's genetic background, may facilitate the child's integration of various aspects of his dual identities, and adoptive parents may be able to integrate the different aspects of the adoptee's identity so as to avoid blaming "bad blood in the background" for any of their difficulties (Demick & Wapner, 1988). Further research needs to be conducted not only on open adoption but also on the degree of involvement and support of various aspects of network members, the congruence in how adoption was originally viewed and continually viewed, the impact of adoption on network members, and the development of adoptive family relationships. Further, longitudinal research needs to be conducted.

In summary, adoption has long been a socially acceptable way of achieving parenthood. Recent changes in society not only have been an impetus for increasing the demand for adoptive babies but also have made the number of young infants less accessible. In the past the largest percentage of adoptive parents were middle-class established white couples who had difficulty conceiving a child, and white infants were preferred. Now more single men and women are adopting children. Older children, children of various races and minority groups, and handicapped children are being placed. A growing trend is for adult adoptees to seek out and contact biological parents. This process has been facilitated by changing laws and policies. Many experts feel that additional changes in adoption policies and procedures are needed. More research is needed regarding adoptive children and families in order to resolve some of the issues surrounding this approach to parenthood.

PARENTING VIA EMBRYO TECHNOLOGY

When the first "test-tube baby," Louise Brown, was born in England in 1978, the event was acclaimed as a revolutionary new way to become parents. More than 10 years have since passed, and great strides have been made. Artificial insemination by donor (AID or DI), in-vitro fertilization, embryo transfer, and surrogate

BOX 11b REASONS ADULT ADOPTEES SEEK INFORMATION ABOUT NATURAL PARENTS

Medical necessity or other practical reasons, such as pregnancy or birth of a child

Genealogical curiosity

Fantasy of being reunited with ideal parent

Late revelation of adoption and resulting bewilderment and confusion

To fill a void in their lives

To understand themselves better

To obtain a sense of belonging

Need for a love object to counter feelings of loneliness and depression and desire to replace love object lost through illness or death

Source: Adapted from Anderson, W. (1977, March). The sealed record of adoption controversy. *Social Service Review*, pp. 141–152; and Kowal, K., & Schilling, K. (1985). Adoption through the eyes of adult adoptees. *American Journal of Orthopsychiatry, 55*(3), 354–361.

BOX 11c CHARACTERISTICS OF ADULT ADOPTEES WHO HAVE SEARCHED FOR INFORMATION ON ASPECTS OF ADOPTION

Initial Revelation and Feelings—The more information about initial revelation and the more negative the feelings about being adopted, the more likely to search.

Sex—Some studies indicate more women than men search; other studies have found no differences between the sexes.

Age at Time of Search—No differences based on age. (*Note:* searches are not undertaken until young adulthood.)

Age at Time of Placement—The older the child is when adopted, the more likely to undertake search.

Socioeconomic Status—People with higher incomes are more likely to search than people with low incomes.

Parent-Child Relationships—Some studies have indicated that the more negative the adoptee perceives childhood relationships, the more likely to search. Other studies have found the opposite.

Self-esteem—Adoptees with low self-esteem are more likely to search than those with higher levels of self-esteem.

Failure of Parent to Discuss Adoptive Status—The lack of freedom of discussion in home concerning adoptive status tends to be positively related to searching.

Fantasy About Birthparents—The greater the degree of fantasy, particularly during adolescence, the greater the tendency to search.

Source: Adapted from Geissinger, S. (1984). Adoptive parents' attitudes toward open birth records. *Family Relations, 33*(4), 579–585; Kowal, K., & Schilling, K. (1985). Adoption through the eyes of adult adoptees. *American Journal of Orthopsychiatry, 55*(3), 354–362; Sobol, M., & Cardiff, J. (1983). A sociopsychological investigation of adult adoptees' search for birthparents. *Family Relations, 32*(4), 477–483.

BOX 11d   EMBRYO TECHNOLOGY DEVELOPMENTS

Artificial insemination by donor (AID)   Embryo transfer

In-vitro fertilization   Frozen embryos

Surrogate mothers   Gamete intrafallopian transfer

---

motherhood are occurring with increasing frequency. Numerous variations in noncoital reproductive techniques were perfected in the 1980s: nonsurgical ovum transfer in 1983, surrogate embryo transfer in 1984, frozen embryo transfer into a surrogate mother in 1984, and gamete intrafallopian transfer in 1985 (see Box 11d). It is now possible for a child to have five "parents": a genetic and a rearing father and a genetic, a gestational, and a rearing mother (Sokoloff, 1987).

Parenthood in the laboratory rather than in the bedroom has increased for several reasons, the first of which is infertility, which has risen dramatically for both males and females. Sterility has tripled in the last 20 years, 40 percent for males and 20 percent for females. Sperm count in American males has decreased more than 30 percent in the last 50 years. Approximately one fourth of all men now have sperm counts so low that they are considered functionally sterile, partially due to environmental pollutants. More women, too, are having difficulty conceiving. The proportion of women unable to conceive a child increases with age—from 9 percent at ages 25 to 29, to 15 percent at ages 30 to 34, to 30 percent at ages 35 to 39, and to 64 percent at 40 to 44. Since delayed parenthood is on the rise, the biological clock is running out for many women. Some sterility in women is due to increased untreated gynecological infections, due in part to women having sex with a variety of partners. Involuntary sterility now affects one of six married couples (Andrews, 1982; Hubbard, 1982).

In addition to infertility as a reason for increased demand for alternative parenting techniques, fewer babies are available for adoption. Historically adoption has been the only culturally accepted way for infertile couples to achieve parenthood. In addition, scientists face an unprecedented opportunity to shape human life.

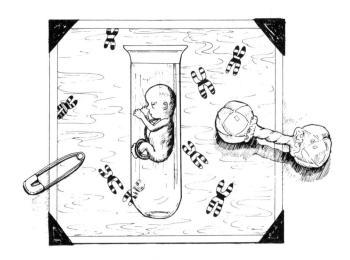

Artificial Insemination by Donor

Artificial insemination by donor (AID or DI) is the most commonly used alternative to parenthood, probably because it is the most frequently offered and is inexpensive and successful. Further, it has a short waiting period and usually offers anonymity to the donor as well as to the inseminated female (Sokoloff, 1987). In this method, semen (fresh or frozen) from a donor (known or unknown) is injected into the uterus of a fertile female. Conception then takes place in the usual manner. The use of fresh versus frozen semen is a highly debated issue with medical personnel utilizing alternative reproductive techniques. There are advantages and disadvantages of both. The success rate with fresh semen is higher (93 percent versus 45 percent) than with frozen. Several more treatment cycles are necessary when frozen semen is used. However, using frozen semen reduces the risk of transmitting infectious diseases, is more convenient because there is always an available supply (also from the same source), and allows a better possibility for matching patients' desires for phenotype characteristics. There is the possibility, however, that the fertility potential of frozen semen may be reduced. The freezing/thawing procedure damages many sperm, and therefore it should be analyzed prior to insemination.

AID usually is chosen when the husband is functionally sterile, or if the possibility exists that he might transmit a gene for a heritable disease, such as Huntington's chorea or Tay-Sachs. While it is not known how many children are conceived by AID, it is thought to be considerably more than 20,000 yearly. In fact recent reports have indicated that California alone has 20,000 annual conceptions by AID. Donor inseminations are being performed for single women who want to conceive without sexual relations and without potential problems that might arise if a woman knew the biological father. Lesbians who desire a child most often use AID. Conservative estimates are that more than 1,500 single women each year are artificially inseminated, with 500 of these being lesbians. Recent surveys suggest that as many as 10 percent of women in the United States receiving donor inseminations are single (Alexander & Ackerman, 1987).

Most of the donors are unknown to the recipients. In fact many clinics initially mixed sperm from two or more donors so that anonymity for all concerned could be maintained. Further, this procedure alleviated some of the legal problems that might have resulted. Any change in custom or practice relating to reproduction and parenthood has always elicited emotionally charged responses. In the 1950s and 1960s, when legislation became necessary, there was at first horrified negation; then negation without horror; then slow but gradual curiosity, study, and evaluation; and, finally, a very slow steady acceptance. While some prohibitory laws were proposed, none were passed. Now approximately 30 states have laws that facilitate AID, declaring the husband of the sperm recipient as the legal father, even though he may not have adopted the child (Andrews, 1987). In some cases written permission from the husband of a married woman must be filed before AID can be performed. Nonetheless, legal and social problems associated with this type of parenthood have yet to be resolved, and the debate continues. In fact, some states are currently reviewing their laws relating to AID as they consider legislation on surrogate motherhood.

Schenker and Frenkel (1987) proposed the following problems that statutes need to address: (1) the legal status of children born as a consequence; (2) the rights of the donor; (3) the rights and obligations of the social father; (4) the responsibilities of the physician with regard to the selection of donors, the limitation of the use of a single donor, the liability of the donor, the recipients, and any resulting child; and (5) the licensing of sperm banks, centers, and physicians allowed to perform AID.

Issues related to AID. Issues surrounding AID that are currently being debated include the procedures for screening and accepting donors, the records of donors, the psychological effects on parents, and the well-being of children conceived in this manner. A survey of physicians who were members of the American Fertility Society or who were associated with medical schools revealed some startling practices regarding screening selected donors (Sokoloff, 1987). The selection of donors has been based entirely on the involved physician's choice for what he or she believes to be superior genes. Donors tend to be of above-average intelligence and health. Medical or college students are commonly paid $25 or more for their sperm. Screening techniques have varied considerably among physicians. Most donors have been screened for family medical histories merely by being asked if any genetic illness exists and by completing a checklist of familial diseases. Minimal laboratory testing for chromosomal translocation, trisomy, or hereditary and infectious diseases have been performed. Further, only about 30 percent of physicians kept records of the donors. More than half of the mothers who became pregnant were referred to another physician's care during pregnancy. The anonymity of the donor and his genetic history has thus been assured. There was no substantial method or effort to limit the number of pregnancies produced by a single donor. Six percent of the physicians used the same donor for more than 15 pregnancies, and one even used a single donor for 50 pregnancies. With increased interest in the role of genetics, concern about the transmission of diseases, such as AIDS; the individual's right to knowledge of genetic parents; the demand for guidelines; and more complex laws have substantially increased. The chance for incest is another suggested reason for the limitation of the number of children born of the same donor's sperm. Ten to 15 per donor has been suggested as the maximum. However, because of the strong genetic component of personality, it is certainly reasonable to use the same donor for the second child of a family (Alexander & Ackerman, 1987).

The following recommendations have been proposed relating to the selection and screening of donors (Alexander & Ackerman, 1987; Sokoloff, 1987):

1. Develop uniform standards for donor selection and screening. Exclude men who have ever had sexual intercourse with a male, who have had a blood transfusion in the last year, whose sex partner in the last year was a prostitute, and who have used intravenous drugs. Select men who are monogamous or who use condoms.
2. Obtain and maintain records of nonidentifying information, including complete medical and genetic history, as well as a profile of family members' ages, interests, occupations, and levels of schooling. Inform donors that the offspring might (at maturity) have access to these records.
3. Limit the number of pregnancies per donor.
4. Eliminate the practice of mixing sperm from more than one donor and the donor's and the father's sperm.
5. Require genetic and psychological counseling for the infertile couple during a mandatory waiting period.
6. Establish and disseminate general guidelines to ensure quality control in all aspects of alternative reproduction.
7. Introduce legislation that is uniform and adequately protective of all members of the infertile family. Assure the legal rights of the child should death or divorce of parents occur.
8. Open the subject of alternative reproductive techniques to the public so that they will become more accepted.
9. Eliminate the need for secrecy in families who use alternative methods for parenting.
10. Establish a research program for the psychological development of these families and children.
11. Use the experience gained in the field of adoption as a guideline for serving the best interests of the child.

There continues to be a paucity of information about the well-being of children produced by alternative reproductive techniques. The highly advocated secrecy among these families precludes adequate follow-up. Questions have been raised concerning both the physical and the psychological effects of alternative methods. With the present available data, normal pregnancies seem to result. Therefore only the normal medical problems associated with any pregnancy should result. The psychological effects, however, are another matter. Without available data one can only speculate on some of the problems that might occur. Are children from these unions appearing, as are adoptees, in disproportionately high numbers for psychological therapy? There is no way of knowing. There are a few cases reported in the literature describing emotional problems among AID families (Sokoloff, 1987), but the data are far from convincing.

An infertile stigma can induce traumatic feelings of inadequacy and alienation. Both partners may experience emotional stress related to their inability, as a team, to procreate. The strain may result in psychological or marital instability. It has been suggested that a couple be encouraged to take their time (about a year) to mourn and accept their sterility. Feelings involved in the complex crises of infertility include, at first, surprise and then denial, anger, isolation, grief, relief, and hopefully resolution (Sokoloff, 1987). Therapeutic treatments for infertility and the ultimate decision to utilize AID can substantially complicate the situation. Subconscious impressions of infidelity may occur. Family, friends, and especially the husband may experience difficulties in fully accepting the child conceived in this manner. Anxious periods of hopeful anticipation during the treatment phase, followed by significant depression when conception does not occur, are typical. Patients undergoing several cycles of treatment may experience an emotional "roller coaster" (Alexander & Ackerman, 1987).

Obviously, feelings surrounding infertility and infidelity must be resolved if the couple are to be effective parents. Counseling should be received prior to, during, and after the child is born. It is known that the father feels deeply about his loss of genetic input. Subsequently, and perhaps forever, the father may feel that he is a fraud. The growing child may serve as a constant reminder of his infertility. Particularly if the child is male and as he enters puberty, the father may be threatened by the child's emerging sexuality because of the subconscious association of his own sterility with lack of virility. If a boy surpasses his father in physical, athletic, or mental capacities, the feelings of failure may arise again. A significant number of fathers have displayed discipline problems in dealing with their nonbiological children (Sokoloff, 1987).

Some women who have been denied the emotional experience of motherhood as a result of their husbands' infertility may develop special reactions and attitudes toward their husbands. Some feel selfish, knowing that the husband is not the genetic father. Near the time of delivery, some women become preoccupied with the donor's looks and personality. Dealing with the "family secret," thinking and fantasizing about the donor, and too closely observing the husband's reactions to the child constitute some of the problems the mother might experience. The balance of power, too, is tipped in favor of the mother—the baby is genetically hers.

Presently, with the identities of donors unknown, children are not entitled to the identity of their genetic fathers. The present trend is for professionals to recommend to parents that the child be informed of his conception by AID, following the principle that an adopted child should be in possession of this knowledge. Further, some countries are providing for the child at 18 years of age to have access to hospital records to obtain information concerning the ethnic origin and genetic health of his biological father. It has been previously thought that donor participation would be greatly reduced unless anonymity was maintained. This has not proved to be true in other countries. Eliminating the "family secret" seems to have great advantages. It will enable the entire family unit to seek outside counseling, and communication will no longer be strained.

Only when adequate samples of children born via AID are available for study can the effects on the child be assessed. Presently, the anonymity of donors precludes this possibility. The issues involving unknown donors must be resolved. In addition, longitudinal data on the children and their parents would be of great value when assessing parent-child relationships.

In-vitro Fertilization

In-vitro fertilization may be chosen when a woman is unable to become pregnant because of tubal blockage and/or scarring. In this method a mature egg is fertilized outside the woman's body, most often by the husband's sperm. Pa-

tients are given fertility drugs to develop more than one egg at a time. Normally about 5 or 6 eggs are retrieved per patient. One woman produced 17. Blood tests and ultrasound indicate when ova are ripe. Then the eggs are extracted in a delicate operation performed under general anesthesia. Ultrasound or a laparoscope is used to guide the needle into the follicles. Eggs, which are only $\frac{1}{4,000}$ of an inch in diameter, and the surrounding fluids are gently suctioned out. Ova are carefully washed and placed in a petri dish and incubated for 4 to 8 hours. The sperm is prepared in a solution and then added to the petri dish. When the embryo is at least two to eight cells (about 24 hours), it is placed in the woman's uterus. There is a 20 percent chance of success with the implementation of one fertilized egg, 28 percent with two, and 38 percent with three. Since several fertilized eggs are implanted in the uterus to increase the chances of success, multiple births can occur. It is known at the time of this writing that 56 sets of twins, 8 sets of triplets, 2 sets of quads, and 1 set of quintuplets have occurred as a result of this technique.

The business of in-vitro fertilization is booming. While no data exist on the number of couples who have tried the procedure, experts estimate that more than 5,000 babies conceived this way have been born worldwide. Couples may spend $4,500 to $6,500 for a single attempt at conception. The potential market has been estimated at $30 to $40 million per year. The American Fertility Society and the American College of Obstetricians and Gynecologists have established minimum standards for clinics, but they cannot compel their members to adhere to the guidelines. It has been estimated that half of the 200 clinics performing the procedure in the United States have yet to produce a baby. The establishment of a registry of clinics that would record their success rates and other pertinent statistics has been proposed ("Pressure to regulate," 1988).

The chances of a successful pregnancy from in-vitro fertilization depend on the age of the woman, the nature of her fertility problem, and the skill and expertise of those performing the procedure. A key moment is the implantation of a fertilized egg into the womb. Some data suggest that the best candidates are women in their twenties or early thirties whose only reproductive problem is blocked fallopian tubes. Even the best candidates have a mere 25 percent chance of a successful pregnancy on one attempt and close to 50 percent chance with three attempts. Some experts contend that the success rate for some clinics ranges from 9 to 12 pregnancies per 100 candidates. About half of the 3,000 babies born through in-vitro fertilization in this country have taken place in just three centers—the Jones Institute for Reproductive Medicine in Norfolk, Virginia; the Nevada Fertility Center in Reno, Nevada; and the Institute for Reproductive Medicine in Los Angeles.

Issues relating to in-vitro fertilization. In-vitro fertilization is the most socially accepted alternative reproductive technique, probably because both the parents contribute to the conception of the child. The problems arising from parenthood using this approach are not moral and legal ones resulting from the involvement of a third party; rather this technique has been questioned because it has not been perfected. Also, surgical procedures always incur some element of risk. Congressional efforts to regulate this technology have received support because some experts fear that the medical profession will not police itself, and infertile couples will be exploited. The insurance industry standards may preempt government regulation. Five states have recently mandated insurance coverage for infertility treatment, prompting insurance companies to begin discussing with doctors the minimum standards of performance. Insurers have resisted providing coverage for in-vitro fertilization because of the low success rates and uncertain outcomes ("Pressure to regulate," 1988).

Until recently the in-vitro technique had been limited primarily to women with blocked fallopian tubes. Now embryo transfer is occurring in a variety of forms. A woman who has ovulation problems can secure a donated oocyte and have it fertilized with her husband's sperm, or a single woman may have the egg fertilized with sperm from a known or unknown donor. A woman might even secure her own oocyte from a relative or friend. Since many women planning in-vitro fertilization may choose to have their own oocytes frozen for later use should they have difficulties with implantation, fewer oocytes are available for use with other women who need them or for research purposes. The technique of embryo transfer is no different from the usual embryo transfer in in-vitro fertilization, except that it is performed in another clinic to maintain anonymity of the donors and the recipients.

Many of the ethical and legal questions surrounding oocyte donation remain controversial and are yet to be addressed by statutes in most countries. The following questions have emerged that need to be resolved: Should the government and/or the public be involved in oocyte donation? What is the status of the child born as a result of donor oocyte procedures? How can the risk of incest be prevented? How can donors be legally protected if anonymity is not preserved? What screening procedures need to be developed? What kind of counseling is necessary and can it be assured? Obviously technology is far ahead of the resolution of the social and legal issues associated with embryo transfer.

Surrogate Mothers

The most controversial alternative reproductive technique thus far under public scrutiny is the use of surrogate mothers. The most prevalent use of this method occurs when a couple whose wife is infertile, who has a disease that might be passed on through heredity, or for some reason is unable to carry a baby to term contracts with another woman to be artificially inseminated with the husband's sperm. The chosen surrogate carries the baby until she is born and then relinquishes her to the couple who contracted with the surrogate. The wife of the couple, then, according to some state laws, must adopt the child in order to become the legal mother. This situation is the reverse of AID—the child has the father's genes but not the mother's. The concept of surrogate motherhood is not new. Even the Bible offers an example. When Sarah was unable to give her husband, Abraham, a child, she told him to visit her handmaiden Hagar. The process, obviously, has been refined since then. With artificial insemination the mother and father need not meet. However, in some cases a friendly relationship is formed between the couple and the surrogate mother during the pregnancy; and in some cases, the couple is present in the delivery room during the birthing.

In another type of surrogate motherhood, a woman might have her own eggs fertilized by her husband in the laboratory and then have them implanted in another woman. While no cases thus far have been reported, a busy career woman could decide to "rent the womb" of another woman by having one of her fertilized eggs implanted in the other woman. The "genetic" mother could, then, continue her work while the baby developed. After birth, the husband and wife could claim their 100 percent genetic child. Various other combinations of the use of surrogate mothers could occur—for example, with single women.

An estimated 500 to 600 babies have been born to surrogate mothers. The usual fee is between $10,000 and $13,000. However, most contracts hold the father responsible for all the medical costs incurred. With lawyer's fees, screening tests, and other costs, the total bill is between $25,000 to $45,000. Obviously these services are available only to the financially privileged. However, it has been reported that there are not enough women willing to be surrogates to satisfy the demand. Approximately a dozen agencies handle surrogate parenting cases in this country at the present time (Kantrowitz, Killop, Joseph, Gordon, & Turque, 1987).

Reasons women become surrogates. Many people wonder what kind of women become surrogates. More attention has been given to the selection of surrogates than to the couples contracting for their services. Women who choose to be surrogates have motivations ranging from selflessness to egocentricity, and from guilt to joy. No single motive explains why a given woman would seek to bear a child for another couple. Normally there are mixed desires and needs, with some more predominant than others. Clearly money is a significant factor, with 9 out of 10 surrogate mothers citing money as a major reason. One study indicated that 40 percent of surrogate mothers are unemployed and/or on welfare (Sokoloff, 1987).

Psychological factors also seem to be important. The women who adjust best to surrogate mothering are those who enjoy being pregnant, viewing pregnancy as a positive experience. Ninety percent of the women selected thus far have been pregnant before. Apart from the pleasures of pregnancy, compassion for the childless couple (a very high level of empathy and altruism) is evident. About 10 percent have been adopted and feel that surrogate mothering is a way to express gratitude for their adoptive homes. About one third have some lingering guilt resulting from a previous abortion or from giving up a child for adoption. One of the major psychological traits that would disqualify a

potential surrogate is an inability to adjust well to separation and loss. Most of the surrogates are high school graduates, but many have been unable to fulfill their career goals. Prospective women are given a battery of psychological tests to identify the risks. A woman who is a poor risk might fail to secure adequate prenatal care or fail to surrender the child after birth ("Surrogate mothers," 1987).

Most surrogate mothers, while feeling joy and fulfillment at being able to bear children for others, do not find it easy to relinquish the child. Many experience long periods of grief. One study indicated that 10 percent of the mothers in their sample were so distraught after giving up their babies that counseling was necessary. Several have indicated problems with their own children as a result of surrendering the baby, being unable to understand why their mother would give the baby away and fear that she might also give them away ("Surrogate mothers," 1987). Some surrogates report experiencing hostility from parents, in-laws, friends, and the community.

Although surrogate motherhood has been practiced for nearly 10 years in this country, it was only in 1987 that it received significant publicity, stirring national debate and controversy. In the "Baby M" case, the surrogate mother refused to honor her contract to surrender the baby and was sued by the participating father. The court trial was highly publicized, and the final outcome has been the impetus for the development of national guidelines and state laws regarding surrogate mothering. The issues surrounding surrogate parenting are legal, moral, and social. Some religious groups, Roman Catholics and Orthodox Jews, have condemned it. The Vatican issued a rather lengthy document calling for all governments to curb birth technology and to outlaw surrogates ("Vatican asks," 1987).

Legal issues relating to surrogate motherhood. The legal issues are obviously numerous. Is surrogate mothering "baby selling"? All states in the United States have laws that prohibit trading children for money. Others contend that surrogate motherhood does not fall in that category, but rather the fee is for services rendered. Many lawyers and judges feel that the right to procreate through a surrogate or other means is constitutionally protected. Is the contract between the commissioning couple and the surrogate enforceable in a court of law? If the contract is unenforceable, then who obtains custody of the child if it is challenged? What rights do the commissioner, the surrogate, and the child have? Until the "Baby M" case, these questions were not debated. They are far from settled even now. The decision by the New Jersey judge in the case—custody was awarded to the father with visitation rights awarded to the surrogate—was based on the constitutional right to procreate by noncoital means and what he deemed was the "best interests of the child" (Rust, 1987).

Andrews (1987) reviewed the proposed state laws relating to surrogacy. She pointed out that legislative responses range from horrified prohibition to cautious facilitation. However, less than one third of those statutes proposed have clear provisions establishing the legal parents after the birth of a baby conceived pursuant to a surrogate agreement. Under the remaining proposals, recourse to the courts is still the only way for the biological father or biological mother to gain legal custody of the child when there is conflict. At the time of this writing, five states had banned commercial surrogacy, one announced that it will not uphold commercial surrogacy contracts in court, and one had decided that they are permissible ("A Jersey panel," 1989). Lawmakers are grappling with such issues as whether or not surrogates should be paid; what types of screening participants should undergo; what safeguards are necessary to insure that participants have given voluntary, informed consent; whether the commissioning couple should be recognized as the legal parents; whether the surrogate should have a certain period of time after the birth to assert her parental rights; and whether the child later in life will be able to obtain medical information about the surrogate or learn of her identity. Some states are also reviewing, at the same time, their laws regarding other alternative reproductive techniques.

The surrogate mother is in reality a donor. The same concerns relating to the transmission of infectious and hereditary anomalies are factors that need to be considered. The kind of prenatal care to be required also is an important consideration.

People interested in women's issues are torn between the woman's right to use her body as she chooses and opposing the elements of exploitation. The idea that women are breeding machines is offensive. Some individuals have voiced concern that the adults involved have focused on only their own needs and wishes and have given no thought to the effects on the child. The psychological effects on children if the situation is known to them are exceedingly important (Sokoloff, 1987). Only time will tell how some of the legal and social issues will be resolved. The knowledge of the effects on the child also awaits the future.

FOSTER PARENTHOOD

Another alternative to biological parenting is to assume the role of a foster parent. Most foster parents, however, are those who have already parented their own children for a certain period of time. Foster care does not exist primarily for the benefits of adults who are seeking children but to substitute for, or supplement, families who ostensibly do not, or cannot, adequately care for their children (Hubbell, 1981). As the following discussion indicates, there are a number of rewards for parenting a foster child but also unique problems, concerns, and social issues surrounding this alternative to parenthood.

The removal of a child from his biological parents is a serious step. One can hardly imagine a greater intrusion on the lives of families by the government or society than that of separating children from their biological parents. When such separation is effected by no fault of the child, the question arises as to what conditions would warrant this extreme action. Since the 1900s, there has existed in this country a strong commitment and policy toward maintaining children in their families of origin whenever possible. A statement was made at the first White House Conference on children in 1909 that home life was the highest and finest product of civilization and that children should not be deprived of it except for urgent and compelling reasons (Pelton, 1987).

In the 1800s family poverty was a primary reason for removing children from their parents. It was believed that poverty was synonymous with unworthiness of character. But in the early 1900s a shift toward maintaining children in their own homes occurred. The federal Adoption Assistance and Child Welfare Act of 1980 (PL 96–272) provides that reasonable efforts be made to prevent or eliminate the need for removal of the child from his home and to make it possible for the child to return to his home. However, there has always been a considerable number of children living in foster homes, and while the rationale and motives for separating children from their parents have changed, these children by and large have continued to be poor children from impoverished families. Figure 11-1 shows the rate of placement of children in foster care from 1910 to 1985.

As noted in Figure 11-1, there was a significant increase in the placement of children in foster care during the 1960s and 1970s. Several explanations account for the explosion of child placement during that time. One was the public and professional awareness and concern for child abuse and neglect that emerged. This movement encouraged further intervention into the lives of families. In 1963 about 75,000 abused or neglected children were placed in foster care. In 1980 more than 300,000 were placed for the same reasons. Besharov (1986) pointed out that more than half of the abused children placed in foster care are not in immediate danger of serious physical injury. Even more are placed because of low-quality physical care. Besharov contended that these placements are a misuse of foster care and advocated compensatory services for families.

Title IV of the Social Security Act was amended in 1961 to make federal money available to states for court-ordered placement of children from families receiving ADC funds. More important, the Public Welfare Amendments of 1962 provided grants-in-aid to the states for social services. Public welfare agencies greatly expanded during this time, allowing case workers to investigate increasing numbers of cases. Although the intent of the amendments was to strengthen family life, more and more children have been removed from their homes. If these agencies had used the federal funds to develop

FIGURE 11-1   CHILDREN PLACED IN FOSTER CARE (1910 to 1985)

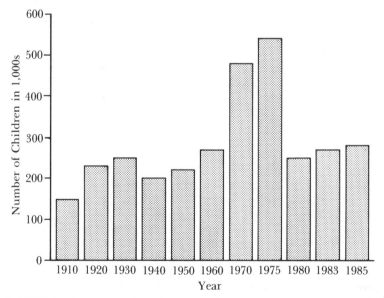

Source: Pelton, L. (1987). Not for poverty alone: Foster care population trends in the twentieth century. *Journal of Sociology and Social Welfare, 14*(2), 37–62.

concrete supportive services for families rather than increasing the number of workers, fewer children might have been placed in foster care.

As noted in Figure 11–1, the rate of placement began to rise again in 1983. It could be an indication of the failure to prevent foster-care placement in the first instance. The permanency planning philosophy, because it is aimed at children already in foster care and because it has spurred a push toward adoption as well as returning children to their homes, may lead to increasing numbers of displaced children remaining where they are. It is as though the system wants it both ways: The child-abuse crusade continues unabated so that children are placed in foster care almost as readily as before, and attempts are made to keep the foster-care population down by getting children out of foster care more quickly. Prevention continues to take a back seat. More than 500,000 children are in the foster-care system, living in foster homes or in institutions (Hampson & Tavormina, 1980; Hubbell, 1981). Many children spend their entire childhood in foster homes, and many more move in and out of foster care, either returning to their own homes for periods of time or moving from one foster family to another (Fein, Davies, & Knight, 1980).

Overstay in foster care is a problem well documented in the literature. Large numbers of children spend 5 years or longer in foster care, and the average length of stay may be as many as 3 years. Milner (1987) investigated the factors affecting the length of time a child spends in foster care. He found that the differences in duration of foster care were not distinguishable by the characteristics of the children, the circumstances of the parent-child separation, the characteristics of the social workers and their supervisors, the quality of the foster-care placement, or the cultural conflicts that may have been present. A strong statistical relationship was found, however, between the child's relationship with the biological family members while in their care and the length of the placement. Those children who spent less time in foster care were those who were visited by their parents frequently with affectionate and enjoyable interactions.

There were other mediating factors found by Milner (1987) regarding length of placement.

One was the number of social stressors for the family, including economics, parents' mental health, housing, marital relationship, and parent-child relationship. This finding emphasized the multiple problems of many families whose children were in foster care. The greater the number and intensity of stress factors, the longer the child was in foster care. The support systems available to parents were also found to be significantly related to length of foster-care placement. Thus the more isolated or alienated the family, the more likely the child would have an extended stay. The agency's responsiveness to the child and his parents also is a factor. Social workers who see the parents regularly and consistently over the course of the placement, who continually evaluate and recognize progress made by the parents, who offer encouragement to parents who visit their children, and who provide needed support services can facilitate parent-child contact.

How a Family Enters Foster Care

A family may enter the foster-care system in several ways: The family may already be receiving social services through Aid to Families with Dependent Children, and it is deemed necessary by the agency that the child be placed in foster care; the family is brought to the attention of protective services as being neglectful or abusive to the child; or the family seeks placement because of inability to cope with the problems it faces. Unmarried mothers or parents with severe emotional or physical illnesses often find that they cannot adequately care for their children (Hubbell, 1981). Foster children are products of all social, economic, ethnic, and cultural groups, but there is a difference in how these various socioeconomic groups cope. Among the more affluent groups, the family lawyer or physician may be the first to become aware of the child's need. For the poor, social-service agencies, law-enforcement personnel, or schools may be the first diagnosticians (Finkelstein, 1980).

The Role of the Foster Parent

The foster-parent role is one that is voluntarily assumed. The assumption of any role implies evaluation of one's performance by others. The foster-parenting role is viewed positively by some people in society and negatively by others. Some segments of the community define foster parents as virtuous; others look on these role performers with suspicion. Birenbaum and Re (1983) examined the perceptions foster parents held regarding their sources of stress and role performance. They found that foster parents defined their role as one serving a worthy social purpose that provided them with increased self-esteem. Religious motivations also were evident.

These researchers discussed the uncertainty or ambiguity when determining what constitutes adequate foster-parent role performance. The required levels of effort, commitment, and investment to fulfill successfully the duties and responsibilities toward the foster child are ambiguous. Both the foster parent's and the agency's definition of success contribute to this confusion. Most foster parents have little or no opportunity for encountering role models prior to certification and have no chances to interact with other foster parents once they assume the role. Further, foster parents have little or no training for the role. Agencies typically have no formal requirements for role performance, with the exception of those related to minimal health and safety standards; only general guidelines exist.

Foster parents, for the most part, conceptualize their role as analogous to that of a natural parent. Most foster mothers, when asked what they have to offer clients, mention giving love. They feel that they have been certified for this role primarily because they have been successful in rearing their own natural families. Even though these parents see their role as analogous to that of natural parents, this does not resolve the problem of role ambiguity. Since the role is viewed as analogous to the natural-parent role, reciprocal relationships are implied. This is the point at which the natural parenting analogy breaks down, for as much as the tasks associated with the two roles may have in common, the relationships they imply do not. If the natural parenting analogy is embraced too fully, various types of role strain situations will develop. These sources of role strain appear in Box 11e.

Obviously, in order to reduce stress associated with the role, foster parents must be able to effectively resolve these problems. The cooperation of all the family members is required if the foster child is to be integrated into the family. One technique to avoid such conflicts involves the individual's organization of her role by priority into hierarchies, favoring the roles that provide greater satisfaction or are subject to severe negative sanctions if neglected. Of course there is strong cultural pressure to favor one's spouse and natural-parent roles; therefore the entire family must be involved in decisions and choices made.

The ever-present prospect of having the foster child removed either by the natural parents or by the agency is a strong deterrent to the complete adoption of the natural-parent analogy.

BOX 11e POTENTIAL SOURCES OF ROLE STRAIN FOR THE FOSTER-PARENT/FOSTER-CHILD RELATIONSHIP

Conflicts between foster-parent role and role of natural parent and spouse
Possible (or real) loss of foster child
Relying on foster child to provide "rewards" and satisfaction
Conflicts with natural parent of the foster child
Receiving payment for being a foster parent (being paid for what is considered to be the greatest contribution one has to offer—love)
Relationship with agency

Source: Birenbaum, A., & Re, M. (1983). Family care providers. *Journal of Family Issues, 4*(4), 633–658.

The foster parent is naturally suspended in the child's life. Avoidance of the development of intimate relationships is not the solution to this problem. One remedy does entail the acceptance of additional placements, but also shifting the emphasis from the child to the agency helps the foster parent, to a degree, conceptualize her role, not as caretaker of an individual child, but as an agent of an organization caring for a needy child.

Foster parents can expect only limited reciprocity from the foster child and must be able to gain supplemental satisfaction from positive feedback provided by the agency and the community at large. When seeking to resolve the conflicts that arise, foster parents must be able to redefine their role in ways that differentiate it from the natural-parent role. Substituting the agency as the reciprocal role partner and emphasizing its professional or therapeutic functions apart from, or in addition to, their roles as surrogate parents is recommended. Some experts suggest that shifting the label of "foster parent" to that of "child-care worker" also might help eliminate some ambiguity toward this role. However, a shift toward an occupational role definition would eliminate a great source of satisfaction—the intrinsic pleasure derived from the relationship with a child. Further, it would imply some level of training in addition to the criterion of being able to rear one's own children effectively.

Children's Reactions to Foster Care

Rice and McFadden (1988) found that although most children expressed positive feelings about their foster-care experiences, they reacted differently according to developmental level. The 5- to 10-year-olds seemed to parrot caseworker explanations by stating that a foster home was where one could stay while parents solved their problems, was where one could get needed love and attention, was a place to get help, and was a place to go when parents cannot take care of you. Some used denial by stating that they were being babysat temporarily. Considerable anxiety was noted in the behaviors of this age group. In addition, depression, anger, low self-esteem and pain were expressed. Generally the children

seemed confused about their foster-care placement and situation.

The younger adolescents, 11 to 14 years of age, expressed positive feelings about their foster families. They believed that a foster home was a place to give you love when your mother does not have a house, when your parents die, or when you need a place to help solve your problems. Their expressions of feelings indicated that this age group, particularly the boys, is characterized by denial and repressed rage.

The older adolescents were positive about foster families as well but felt that they were considered to be different from other adolescents by their peers and adults. These adolescents had experienced a number of school problems and displayed rage and worry about themselves. They were very vocal and expressed deep feelings of inferiority and worthlessness and perceived themselves as being treated as second-class citizens. They hated the system that made them different. In general they were very anxious and angry and lacked confidence in themselves. They viewed adults as intrusive; they sought guidance but resented direction.

Effects of Foster Care

There are, nevertheless, some benefits to the children placed in foster care. For those who are physically abused, foster care is undeniably successful. Moreover, available research indicates that foster care meets the emotional needs of many children. Many maltreated children do very well in foster care. Some studies have shown that the physical development of foster children improved after placement, as did IQ and school performance. Most foster children do not exhibit serious emotional or behavior problems associated with placement. However, there are significant differences according to the age of the child at placement and the length of placement. The younger children adjust better than older ones (Besharov, 1986). Several studies have documented that children in foster care experience higher rates of chronic illness and poorer health status than children living in their natural homes (Moffatt, Peddic, Stulginskas, Pless, & Steinmetz, 1985). These researchers assessed the health status of 900 children in foster care. They

found that although major handicapping conditions among the children were well cared for, prevention, care of minor conditions and emotional problems, and overall coordination of care were found to be lacking. The data indicated that almost half the children had failed at least one grade, 35 percent were below the second percentile on a normal academic progress scale, and 44 percent admitted having school problems. Of the sample, 35 percent were suspected to have potential emotional problems and 39 percent scored below the second percentile on a measure of social competence. Other research has indicated that many foster children are from poverty families. It could be that these problems would have been evident regardless of whether they were in foster care.

Moffatt and his associates (1985) concluded that providing health care for foster children requires a planned, systematic approach with clearly designated responsibilities for all concerned. They suggested that the agency designate a central source of specialized care and establish a close working relationship with it.

The dark side of foster care is that a large subset of children cannot be quickly returned home or freed for adoption. More than 50 percent of children in foster care on a "temporary" basis are there for more than 6 years and often are lost in the "limbo" of the foster-care system.

Further, many are moved from one foster home to another. One study found that 29 percent of the foster children studied had been in four or more homes in less than 5 years. Moreover, treatment services for parents of children in foster care are largely nonexistent. In fact, the child's placement usually reduces the level of services that their biological families receive—reduction of public assistance grants, food stamps, homemaker services, and even caseworker visits are reduced or suspended. Only parents who wish to be relieved of obligations of parenthood gain anything from their child's placement. As a result the children are trapped in a vicious circle. The parents cannot care for their children; the children are removed; existing services do not improve parents' functioning; children cannot be returned home; they cannot be placed for adoption; and they continue in "limbo" in the system for years (Besharov, 1986).

Very little attention has been given to the experiences of the foster child's siblings, yet it is known that children are influenced by what happens to them (Hegar, 1988). Approximately three-fourths of children in foster care have siblings who are also placed in substitute care. Despite the evidence of family groups of children in the foster-care population, most literature focuses on foster children as individuals. Greater professional interest has been recently demonstrated in sibling relationships. This is due to several factors—the broadening focus on attachment to significant persons other than parents and the effects of separation from them, the number of adoptees who search for existent siblings, and the political and professional emphasis on the family unit. In addition, the legal emphasis on "best interests of the child" frequently includes consideration of ties to siblings when making placement decisions.

There has been some evidence of efforts to place siblings together and to facilitate contact between them, even when they are separated. However, there has been greater emphasis placed on sibling rivalry as a reason for separation rather than focusing on sibling support. The issues, legal and social, relating to sibling relationships of foster children demand serious attention by the court and placement professionals.

Children placed in foster homes do, however, fare better than those placed in residential settings. Colton (1988) compared children, 12 years and older, in 12 foster homes and in 12 residential children's homes. The foster homes were found, overall, to be significantly more child-oriented than the children's residential homes in terms of the dimensions of care. Caretakers in the foster-care homes as contrasted to residential staff played more games with the children, watched TV with them, talked to them, and took an everyday interest in them. The focal point of activities was the living room or kitchen. In contrast, the staff in the residential children's homes seemed to focus on supervision and control. Contact with the children was primarily in the offices of staff or other locations where supervision and surveillance could be facilitated.

Foster parents were found to use proportionately more informative and approving speech than did residential staff during interactions with children. The residential staff often used negative speech, such as criticism and censure, and the tone was more controlling in nature. The duration of contact between residential staff and children was significantly shorter than was the foster parent/child contact.

Some research has indicated that continuing relationships with the biological family are basic to the foster children's adjustment and growth (Tiddy, 1986). Persons who are emotionally cut off from significant others are psychologically at risk. Symptoms include self-destructive behavior patterns and an inability to sustain intimate relationships. These children have trouble trusting and opening up to other persons. They do not resolve this feeling of alienation by remaining cut-off. In order to finish this unresolved business, some form of contact must be established. This is even more important for children in long-term foster care. If children are unable to maintain contact with biological parents, they often establish fantasy parents, a natural defense mechanism to deal with separation trauma.

A basic ingredient in the child's process of achieving integration into the foster family is to experience two (or more) family systems, not denying the existence of one or the other. The imprint of the biological family is basic to the child's identity. Continued association with the biological family reduces the loyalty conflicts experienced by the child. Placed children also experience a tremendous sense of loss, which they frequently interpret as abandonment or rejection. They feel, then, devalued and guilty, and internalize the loss. Contact with, and discussion about, family of origin can bring these feelings to the surface and reduce the sense of guilt and abandonment. Foster children carry much anger at their parents over the injustices that life has dealt them. The source of this anger is frequently beyond their awareness because it is too powerful to admit or to handle. To admit that they are angry with their parents also jeopardizes their position with parents and frustrates their efforts to remain loyal. This anger, thus, is displaced onto others or is deeply internalized. To varying degrees, the children become dysfunctional as a result. On the one hand, their love for the biological parents is difficult or impossible to express because of the anger. For some children this love becomes obsessive. Many foster children find these powerful conflicting emotions too difficult to manage.

To work through these feelings, involving the biological family, the child, and perhaps the foster parents in therapy sessions is the best solution. In order for this to work, certain conditions must exist—all concerned have to trust the therapist to select the appropriate persons to meet together and to follow appropriate procedures.

All need to be aware of what is likely to happen in the process, and each must recognize the importance of his contribution.

Selection of Foster Homes

The selection and securing of appropriate foster homes present continuous problems for foster-placement agencies. It is increasingly difficult to find qualified foster families due to increased numbers of working women and inflation. Most state policies provide for careful selection of a foster home, but frequently these policies are not followed. There is simply no guarantee that foster care will be better for an individual child's development than his or her natural home. Foster homes theoretically are selected based on the extent to which the interests, strengths, abilities, and needs of the foster family enable them to understand, accept, and provide for the needs of the child to be placed. The age of the child, her interests, intelligence, religion, cultural background, parental relationships, educational status, social adjustment, individual problems, and plans for future care all should be considered. Most natural parents are not involved in the selection of a foster home for their child even though they know the child better than the case worker (Hubbell, 1981).

Continuity of care for foster children is enhanced if the foster family is as similar as possible to the natural family. The home of a relative, for example, may be a good choice since this family is more likely to know the background of the child and to be of the same ethnic group and social class. The family life-style and child-rearing approaches are more likely to be similar. But, more important, there is a preexisting relationship between the family and the child. When the child cannot be placed in the home of a relative, the foster family should be matched as closely as possible with the natural family. To ensure appropriate development of the child, it has been suggested that more rigorous screening of potential foster parents be done. This screening should include direct observation of interactions between the foster parents and the child, assessment of the foster parents' attitudes and motivations, and more accurate matching of the foster child to the foster home based on the therapeutic abilities of the parents to handle the problems of the child (Hampson & Tavormina, 1980; Hubbell, 1981).

Obviously placement agencies consider particular family characteristics in their search for foster homes. Several researchers have been interested in identifying the general characteristics of families who qualify for and accept foster children. These characteristics are summarized in Box 11f.

It was interesting to note that the foster mothers who had foster placements for 2 years or longer gave significantly more ''social'' motivators for becoming foster parents, whereas the majority of others reported ''private'' motives, for example, wanting a child to care for or desiring a playmate for her own child. Further, approximately 80 percent of all foster mothers

---

BOX 11f CHARACTERISTICS OF FOSTER PARENTS

Family of origin is larger than average
Have fewer children than average
Tend to marry early
Have brief education
Mother is the central caregiver

Love children, interested in child's well-being
Display desire to help someone else
Show capacity for understanding and acceptance
Are nonjudgmental in relation to values

Sources: Davies, J. L., & Bland, D. C. (1978). The use of foster parents as role models for parents. *Child Welfare, 57*(3), 175–179; and Hampson, R. B., & Tavormina, J. B. (1980, March). Feedback from the experts: A study of foster care mothers. *Social Work,* pp. 108–113.

studied indicated that they would be foster parents even if they received no payment (Hampson & Tavormina, 1980).

Nevertheless, it seems that predicting successful placements is difficult. Determination of the following factors assists in accurate prediction: motivations for foster parenthood, styles of discipline, affective style, degree of cooperation with agency and social worker, physical health, marital stability, and flexibility (Davies & Bland, 1978; Hampson & Tavormina, 1980).

Solutions and/or Recommendations for Solving Problems

Training programs. Various suggestions and/or recommendations have been made to improve the foster-care system and thus ensure more effective care of children while in the system. The need for additional and more qualified foster homes, more effective screening of foster families, and better matches between foster families and children already have been discussed. Training for foster parents has been advocated by a host of investigators (Davies & Bland, 1978; Edwards, 1980; Gross, Schuman, & Magid, 1978; Hampson & Tavormina, 1980; Penn, 1978), and several approaches to training have been utilized: (1) using foster parents as role models for natural parents (Davies & Bland, 1978); (2) using behavior modification to alter the foster child's behavior (Penn, 1978); (3) emphasizing child growth and development for foster parents caring for children under 3 years of age (Gross et al., 1978); (4) training foster parents to provide care for foster children with physical, emotional, and/or mental handicaps (Smith, 1981); and (5) using peers as foster parents for adolescents (Edwards, 1980). Positive outcomes have been reported for each of these programs.

Rice and McFadden (1988) reported the results of a workshop attended by social workers, foster parents, and foster children aged 5 to 20 years. The purpose was to give foster children an opportunity to express pent-up emotions regarding foster placement, to learn that they were not alone in these feelings, and to share experiences. Further, feedback was provided to the system, and foster parents were able to have a greater understanding of their foster children. The children, according to age level, met in groups with a consultant. Their feelings about foster care and case workers were expressed. Later, the children's feelings were shared with the foster parents, who expressed concern about what the foster children had said, felt overwhelmed and overburdened and aware of their formidable task, and expressed a sense of urgency to find ways of helping their child. These authors felt that group sessions such as these are excellent avenues for helping both foster children and foster parents to express their feelings and concerns. They recommended a series of such meetings for greater effectiveness.

Compensatory services for families has been suggested as a preventive measure for foster care. In-home services should be provided to the parents, and placing children in quality preschool programs should be an alternative to foster care. The key to using preschool programs as an alternative to foster care rests with juvenile judges. They must be reoriented to view the importance of preschool programs. Presently there is considerable inconsistency in placement decisions, with some children who really need it not being placed and others who could benefit from an alternative approach being removed from the home. The compensatory approach to families and children is cost effective. While it might not reduce the amount of money spent by states and the federal government, it would be promoting the development of children and preventing circumstances for families that make foster care necessary (Besharov, 1986).

Government's role. Public Law 96-272, passed by Congress in 1980, provided mechanisms that limited funding to states unless they implemented certain safeguards and requirements regarding maintenance payments, and this law further established federal participation in adoption subsidies. It also provided fiscal incentives to states that organized listings of children in foster care for 6 months or more and implemented statewide information systems on children in foster care, case review systems, and services designated to reunite families and to prevent placements. The old fiscal incentives to keep children in care would have been reduced by limits on foster-care maintenance payments available to each state. The increase in funding was allocated to provide the preventive and re-unification services needed to reduce the need for foster care. States were to develop coordinated plans that described services provided and the steps to be undertaken to achieve goals. This law was viewed as an important step in the re-vamping of the nation's foster-care system and legislation that was highly supportive of families. It provided families with important services, safeguards, and recognized parents' crucial roles in planning for their own children (Hubbell, 1981). Unfortunately the block grant system of the Reagan administration in allotting federal funding to states did not provide the incentives and funding that are so sorely needed. At the time of this writing, then, it is doubtful that the procedures provided for in Public Law 96–272 are being consistently implemented.

Future Research Needs

To help ensure that foster children are provided with the best environments, additional research is needed. More information on the effects of foster care on children, on their biological families, and on the foster families is warranted. There is currently meager information on the mechanics of the foster care system. Effective screening devices and procedures for selecting foster families need to be developed and tested. The entire area of foster care appears to be a fruitful one for research.

Some foster children have such serious problems that they are in need of therapy and specialized services. Specialized foster-care programs have been developed to provide services to this group. Two thirds of SFC programs serve emotionally or behaviorally disturbed children, but other types of special needs children are served (delinquents, drug abusers, retarded, and handicapped). SFC parents are trained to provide a therapeutic milieu; professionals direct and monitor the therapeutic regimen based on multi-disciplinary input; and comprehensive supportive services are provided. The biological family may be involved, and therapeutic utilization of the local community and aftercare services may be provided (Webb, 1988).

Obviously foster parents and children need a variety of support services. Creative ways to meet the needs of foster families need to be developed. Preventive programs must be a priority.

SUMMARY

Adoption, various forms of embryo technology, and foster parenthood are alternatives to traditional biological childbearing. Adoption has long been a socially acceptable alternative, but with the number of available babies for adoption continuing to decline, parents are seeking other ways to achieve parenthood. With increased technology and acceptance of alternative life-styles, in-vitro fertilization, artificial insemination, and other forms of embryo technology have become more popular. Foster parenthood has long been an alternative, and some couples choose either to initially become parents in this manner or to add additional children to the family by this approach.

Each approach presents specific social and legal issues that must be resolved. A recent trend regarding adoption is for adult adoptees to seek and contact their birthparents. Policies are being changed to accommodate this desire. Open adoption policies are still being debated.

The legal issues surrounding some forms of embryo technology have yet to be resolved. Some states are in the process of banning surrogate parenting. There are lingering medical risks and cost factors associated with embryo technology that prohibit many couples from choosing this approach.

The foster-care system has many disadvantages for both the parents and the children involved. Research has indicated that foster children have many psychological and other problems that make parenting extremely difficult. The lack of permanence in placement precludes development of the usual parent-child lasting relationships and attachment. Yet for many parents and children the relationship can be extremely positive, and development of children can be facilitated.

More research is needed on each of these alternatives to parenthood, and particularly on the outcomes for children. Legal and social issues must be resolved so that both parents and children can benefit from these family situations.

REFERENCES

A Jersey panel backs limits on surrogacy pacts (1989, March 13). *New York Times*, p. A14.

ALEXANDER, N., & ACKERMAN, S. (1987). Therapeutic insemination. *Obstetrics and Gynecology Clinics of North America, 14*(4), 905–929.

ANDERSON, W. (1977, March). The sealed record in adoption controversy. *Social Service Review*, pp. 141–152.

ANDREWS, L. (1982). Embryo technology. In H. Fitzgerald & T. Carr (Eds.), *Human Development, Annual Editions.* (pp. 50–52). Guilford, CT: Dushkin Publishing Group.

ANDREWS, L. (1987, October/November). The aftermath of Baby M: Proposed state laws on surrogate motherhood. *Hastings Center Report*, pp. 31–40.

BACHRACH, C. (1983). Adoption as a means of family formation: Data from the national survey of family growth. *Journal of Marriage and the Family, 45*(4), 859–865.

BACHRACH, C. (1986). Adoption plans, adopted children, and adoptive mothers. *Journal of Marriage and the Family, 48*(2), 243–253.

BESHAROV, D. (1986). The misuse of foster care: When the desire to help children outruns the ability to improve parental functioning. *Family Law Quarterly, XX*(2), 213–231.

BIRENBAUM, A., & RE, M. (1983). Family care providers. *Journal of Family Issues, 4*(4), 633–658.

COLTON, M. (1988). Foster and residential care practices compared. *British Journal of Social Workers, 18*(1), 25–42.

DAVIES, L., & BLAND, D. (1978). The use of foster parents as role models for parents. *Child Welfare, 57*(3), 175–179.

DEMICK, J., & WAPNER, S. (1988). Open and closed adoption: A developmental conceptualization. *Family Process, 27*(2), 229–249.

EDWARDS, K. (1980). A new alternative: Adolescent foster peer program. In N. Stinnett, B. Chesser, J. DeFrain, & P. Knaub (Eds.), *Positive models for family life.* (pp. 393–404). Lincoln: University of Nebraska Press.

FANSHEL, D. (1972). *Far from the reservation.* Metuchen, NJ: Scarecrow.

FEIGELMAN, W., & SILVERMAN, A. (1983). *Chosen children: New patterns of adoptive relationships.* New York: Praeger.

FEIN, E., DAVIES, L., & KNIGHT, G. (1980, March). Placement stability in foster care. *Social Work*, pp. 156–157.

FINKELSTEIN, N. (1980, March). Children in limbo, *Social Work*, pp. 100–105.

GEISSINGER, S. (1984). Adoptive parents' attitudes toward open birth records. *Family Relations, 33*(4), 579–585.

GROSS, B., SHUMAN, B., & MAGID, D. (1978). Using the one-way mirror to train foster parents in child development. *Child Welfare, 57*(10), 685–687.

HAILSTOCK, G. (1984, December). Sharing your love with a child. *Black Enterprise, 15,* pp. 105–106, 112.

HAMPSON, R., & TAVORMINA, J. (1980). Feedback from the experts: A study of foster care mothers. *Social Work, 25*(2), 108–113.

HEGAR, R. (1988). Legal and social work approaches to sibling separation in foster care. *Child Welfare, LXVII*(2), 113–121.

HUBBARD, R. (1982). Test tube babies: Solution or problem. In H. Fitzgerald & T. Carr (Eds.), *Human Development, Annual Editions.* (pp. 53–54). Guilford, CT: Dushkin Publishing Group.

HUBBELL, R. (1981). *Foster care and families' conflicting values and policies.* Family Impact Seminar Series. Philadelphia: Temple University Press.

JEWETT, C. (1978). *Adopting the older child.* Cambridge, MA: Harvard Common Press.

KANTROWITZ, B., KILLOP, P., JOSEPH, B., GORDON, J., & TURQUE, B. (1987). Who keeps ''Baby M''? *Newsweek*, pp. 44–49.

KATZ, L. (1987, January). Adopted children. *Parents*, p. 116.

KOWAL, K., & SCHILLING, K. (1985). Adoption through the eyes of adult adoptees. *American Journal of Orthopsychiatry, 55*(3), 354–362.

MILNER, J. (1987). An ecological perspective on duration of foster care. *Child Welfare, LXVI*(2), 113–123.

MOFFATT, M., PEDDIC, M., STULGINSKAS, J., PLESS, B., & STEINMETZ, N. (1985). Health care delivery to foster children: A study. *Health and Social Work, 10*(2), 129–134.

PELTON, L. (1987). Not for poverty alone: Foster care population trends in the twentieth century. *Journal of Sociology and Social Welfare, 14*(2), 37–62.

PENN, J. (1978). A model for training foster parents in behavior modification techniques. *Child Welfare, 57*(3), 175–179.

Pressure to regulate in-vitro fertilization grows as demand rises. (1988, July 28). *The New York Times*, p. 19.

PUFKI, P. (1983, July–August). Silly questions and straight answers about adoption. *Children Today*, pp. 11–14.

RICE, D., & MCFADDEN, E. (1988). A forum for foster children. *Child Welfare LXVII*(3), 231–243.

RUST, M. (1987, June). Whose baby is it? *American Bar Association Journal*, pp. 52–56.

SCHENKER, J., & FRENKEL, D. (1987). Medico-legal aspects of in-vitro fertilization and embryo transfer. *Obstetrical and Gynecological Survey, 41*(7), 405–413.

SINGER, L., BRODZINSKY, D., RAMSAY, D., STEIR, M., & WATERS, E. (1985). Mother-infant attachment in adoptive families. *Child Development, 56*(6), 1543–1551.

SMITH, R. (1981, January). Specialized foster parent training project: A proposal. Unpublished manuscript.

SOBOL, M., & CARDIFF, J. (1983). A sociopsychological investigation of adult adoptees' search for birth parents. *Family Relations, 32*(4), 477–483.

SOKOLOFF, B. (1987, January). Alternative methods of re-production. *Clinical Pediatrics,* pp. 11–17.

Surrogate mothers. (1987, January 27). *Albuquerque Journal,* pp. C1, 2.

TIDDY, S. (1986). Creative cooperation: Involving biological parents in long-term foster care. *Child Welfare, LXV*(1), 53–62.

Vatican asks governments to curb birth technology and to outlaw surrogates. (1987, March 11). *New York Times,* pp. 1, 10–12.

WEBB, D. (1988). Specialized foster care as an alternative therapeutic out-of-home placement model. *Journal of Clinical Child Psychology, 17*(1), 34–43.

12

Alternatives
for Child Care

Increasing numbers of parents are seeking part-time or full-time alternatives for assistance with parenting and child care. Parents are turning to individual caregivers who come into the home, family day-care homes, center-based child care, nursery schools, parent cooperatives, play schools, drop-in child-care centers, Head Start, and after-school programs for child-care assistance.

Programs for young children may be sponsored by public agencies, private nonprofit organizations, or individuals for profit. Reports of what parents themselves pay for child care have been conflicting. According to hearings in the House Select Committee on Children, Youth, and Families in 1985, fees for preschool children in center child care ranged from $45–$75 per week. However, another 1985 study of the cost of child care in four major cities indicated costs for a preschooler to be from $50 per week (in Dallas) to $110 per week (in San Francisco) ("Second thoughts . . . ," 1985). Costs are even higher for infant care. Accounting for inflation, that would put the average yearly cost of preschool care in 1989 at just over $4,000. In addition, both the federal and the state governments, and a few local governments, subsidize child care. Charitable organizations, such as United Way, and churches also provide support for child care. Some employers and unions sponsor or support on-site or community child-care centers, provide vouchers to parents to assist in paying for care, arrange flextime, allow shared jobs, give sick-child leave, and/or provide child-care information and referral. All told, a considerable investment is made annually in child care, and the need is still largely unmet.

The services offered by programs range from care and protection of the child for part of the day while the child is entrusted to the caregiver; child care for parents who work full-time, day, evening, or night; to a full range of services to the child, family, and community, based on the needs of families. The efficacy of the care depends on the commitment, skill, and spirit of the providers. In privately owned centers specific provision is usually not made for social services, but centers receiving federal funds may provide some health-care and social services and/or family-support services.

Parents enroll their children in these programs for a variety of reasons, including their need for temporary relief from continual responsibility for child rearing, the desire to provide opportunities for the child to interact with peers and other authority figures, and/or so that the child can receive cognitive stimulation. However, the primary reason that increasing numbers of parents seek alternative child care is that mothers are working.

NEED FOR CARE

There has been a continuing trend toward increasing numbers of women working outside the home, including mothers of very young children. At the last report, between 55 percent and 60 percent of parents with children under the age of 6 were employed, and the numbers are growing each year. The fastest-growing segment of employed mothers is the one with infants between 3 weeks and 3 months of age (Clarke-Stewart, 1988). In fact, about 50 percent of all new mothers now return to work before their babies are 1 year old. The greater the increase of time and money invested in education, the more rapid the return to work after childbirth ("Second thoughts . . . ," 1987). It is projected that by 1990, 75 percent of all mothers will work (Gamble & Zigler, 1986) and that there will be 10.5 million young children in need of child care (Schindler, Moely, & Frank, 1987).

The need for child care is not limited to particular ethnic groups or social-class levels. For many years child care was viewed primarily as a welfare service, only for those mothers who were forced to work out of economic necessity. Because of greater educational and career opportunities for women, the battle for equal rights, and the current difficulty or impossibility for young families to live on one income, child care has become a widespread necessity for a diversity of families. The United States is nearly alone among industrialized nations in the absence of a national family and child-care policy. However, for the first time ever, child care was a public issue in the 1988 presidential campaign.

SELECTING ALTERNATIVE CARE

The kind of alternative care arrangements families select depends on several factors. Obviously if a mother is working full-time, all-day care is likely to be needed unless part of the child's care is assumed by other family members. During the last several years there has been a move away from in-home care and toward out-of-home care among all socioeconomic groups. Factors affecting choice of arrangements include the family income, the size of the family and the age of the children, the availability of service,

---

BOX 12a   TYPES OF ALTERNATIVE CARE OF PRESCHOOL CHILDREN UTILIZED BY FULL-TIME WORKING PARENTS IN 1982

Percentage	Type of Care
15	Relative in another home
23	Father or other relative in the child's home
6	Nonrelative in the child's home
22	Nonrelative in another home
19	Group care center
9	Mother cares for child while working
6	All other arrangements

Source: Corsini, D., Wisensale, S., & Caruso, G. (1988). Family day care: System issues and regulatory models. *Young Children, 43*(6), 17–22; O'Connell, M., & Bloom, D. (1987). *Juggling jobs and babies: America's child care challenge.* Washington, DC: Population Reference Bureau.

and the family life-style. The current trend is for better-educated mothers to select child care centers and care in another home by nonrelatives, whereas less-educated mothers are more likely to use care in another home by a relative (O'Connell & Bloom, 1987). Box 12a shows the percentage of families using different types of child care in 1982.

If center-based care is chosen, the selection is frequently based on the adequacy and dependability of caregivers, the location, and the cost, as well as the developmental or educational nature of the program. If every parent who needed child care were to seek a licensed center, there would simply not be enough facilities available. Most parents use unlicensed centers or family day-care homes but, ironically, appear to be satisfied with them.

In their study of the child-care needs of single parents, Turner and Smith (1983) found the following factors, in rank order, to be considered as important in choosing a child-care center for infants and preschool children: the personal qualities of the caregivers, cleanliness of the center, program activities, location, training of the staff, cost, number of children enrolled (size of group), hours of operation, and space available. A somewhat different order of factors considered to be important was found when parents were selecting after-school care for older children: In order of importance, it was location, program activities, personal qualities of the caregivers, training of the staff, hours of operation, cleanliness, cost, space available, and transportation provided.

TYPES OF CHILD CARE

Parents have a number of alternatives in arranging for child care. Each alternative has its advantages as well as its disadvantages. The range of available alternatives is affected by geographic factors, family income, and personal belief system.

Caregiver in the Home

More than one fourth of families with young children find that a single caregiver who comes into the home can best meet their needs for the care of the child. These caregivers consist of both relatives (including fathers) and nonrelatives. As the number of two-parent professional families grows, the number of persons seeking full-time, often live-in, care in their own home increases. In fact, over the last 5 years, several nanny-training programs have been established throughout the United States. It should be emphasized, however, that a very small percentage of families are economically able to employ a full-time nonrelative as a caregiver. Other advantages and disadvantages of this type of alternative care are enumerated in Box 12b.

Family Day-Care Homes

Family day-care homes are utilized by approximately 37 percent of parents with young children as alternatives for child care. Approximately 15 percent of children are cared for by grandparents or other relatives. Securing relatives to care for the child outside the child's home may have several advantages: the preexisting relationship between the child and the caregiver; the greater likelihood of a relative being loving to the child, thus providing a higher quality of emotional care; and the possibility of less expense for the parents. The other 22 percent are cared for by nonrelatives in a situation where a caregiver provides care for a few children in his or her home (Corsini, Wisensale, & Caruso, 1988).

Most states require that family day-care homes be licensed, certified, registered, or approved. Regulations relate to the maximum number of children, by age, who may be cared for, as well as health and safety standards; and some states have regulations relating to the activities provided for the children, equipment, nutrition, discipline, and so on. The specified adult-child ratio and maximum number of children vary from state to state, but the ratio is approximately 6 children to 1 adult. This number may or may not include the caregiver's own children. A variation of the family day-care home that may be found in some states is the mini-center or group day-care home. In this arrangement approximately 12 children compose the group, but the center is located in a caregiver's

---

BOX 12b   ADVANTAGES AND DISADVANTAGES OF CAREGIVER IN HOME

Advantages

Parent can choose caregiver

Child can remain in familiar home environment

Opportunities for adult-child interactions are greater than in center-based care

Children can continue to play with familiar peers in own neighborhood

Disadvantages

Finding alternative care when caregiver is ill

Minimum or no supervision of caregiver

Potential loneliness and isolation of caregiver

Lack of planned group experiences

Limited toys and equipment

Limited educational experience

More expensive than other types of care

Source: Snell, E., & Turner, P. (1981). *Education for parenthood: A curriculum for secondary students.* Santa Fe, NM: Department of Education, Vocational Division.

---

home, and at least 2 adults must supervise the group (U.S. Department of Health & Human Services, 1980).

In spite of the prevalence of family day care and its potential for meeting the growing needs for child care, family day-care homes have been largely invisible to public scrutiny. Despite state regulations, the majority of family day-care homes operate outside the formal regulatory system. For example, in 1975 only 6 percent of children cared for in someone else's home were in homes that were licensed or registered. It has

been said that even though the number of regulated homes in 1985 was equal to twice the number 10 years earlier, the percentage of children in regulated homes changed little during that time (Corsini et al., 1988).

Not surprisingly, the conditions in these homes range from quality care to inadequate or intolerable care. Very little is known about the kinds of experiences that are provided for the children and the consequences of these experiences on the child's development. The difficulties in locating family day homes, the reluctance of caregivers to be observed, the self-selection of caregivers and day-care families, the high turnover, and the changing composition of homes have contributed to the problems of research on family day care (Wandersman, 1981). Obviously, responsibility falls on the parent for selecting a quality family day-care home. When parents are considering family day care, both the advantages and the disadvantages should be considered (see Box 12c).

Research on family day care. As previously stated, research relating to family day care has been minimal. The research that has been conducted suggests that children in center-based care outperform their family day-care counterparts on measures of intellectual functioning. But family day-care environments have been found to be superior to center care on a variety of seemingly important social dimensions, such as the caregiver/child ratio, social interaction, individual attention, and positive socioemotional stimulation. Further, sophisticated vocalization has been found to be more characteristic of children cared for in family day care than children in child-care centers, probably due to a greater amount of adult-child interactions in family day-care homes. Families utilizing family day care have reported positive changes in family finances, probably as a result of lower cost for this type of care. These family-care users also reported less change in marital relationships as a result of using day care than did those families using child-care centers. Those families using babysitters, however, were more likely to see positive changes in their marital relationships (Belsky & Steinberg, 1978; Etaugh, 1980).

In a study of the ecological relationships of family day care, it was found that the age and sex of the children were related to the number of children served in the day-care homes. Those homes who served more children had older children and more females. It was also found that in homes with more children, five to eight versus two to four, the children experienced more intellectual pursuits, interacted more with peers, received encouragement from them, and engaged in fewer negative emotional activities. The caregivers' attitudes were also related to the activities of the children in their homes. Feelings of high emotional drain were related to a lower incidence of intellectual activity, less encouragement, less participation, and less affection/reinforcement among the children; caregiver burnout was related to fewer highly intellectual activities, fewer continuing activities, and less affection/reinforcement among the children. Caregivers in homes with five to eight children were also found to have more relevant educational backgrounds than those caregivers who cared for two to four children. These results suggest that caregivers with more training cared for more children and planned and administered their programs more like child-care centers (Wandersman, 1981).

There appears to be a need for parents to select a family day-care home carefully. The considerations should include the background and experience of the caregiver; the attitudes of the caregiver; and the number, age, and sex of the children served since these factors seem to influence the quality of the program provided. The implications are that caregivers who care for infants and toddlers have fewer children and seem to model the family aspect. Less time is spent with the children, and housekeeping and other tasks are performed simultaneously with the care of the children. It is likely that these caregivers are not sufficiently trained to provide a stimulating environment. If family day-care homes are to provide a rich and stimulating environment for young children, caregivers need training, a relatively high adult/child ratio should be maintained, wages should approach the professional level, and models and supports should be provided. Caregivers need assistance in utilizing everyday interactions, basic care, and household

---

BOX 12c ADVANTAGES AND DISADVANTAGES OF FAMILY DAY CARE

Advantages

A greater likelihood that:
The homelike atmosphere will be less threatening to the child

The child will interact with a single caregiver

The child will interact with children of varying ages, thereby learning from older children and helping to teach responsibility to younger ones

The child will have to adjust to fewer children

Through a warm, "child-centered" home environment, the child will receive stimulation and learn through daily home chores and activities

The home will be based on life-styles and values similar to those of the child's family

The facility will be closer to the parents' home and thus more convenient

Disadvantages

A chance that:
The provider will be unsupervised and have less training

Alternate care will have to be arranged when the caregiver is ill

The home will be unlicensed or unregistered

There will be less variety in equipment, materials, and activities

The nutrition program will be inferior to that of a center

Field trips will not be a part of the program

Sources: Snell, E., & Turner, P. (1981). *Education for parenthood: A curriculum for secondary students.* Santa Fe, NM: Department of Education, Vocational Division; and Wandersman, L. P. (1981). Ecological relationships in family day care. *Child Care Quarterly, 10*(2), 89–102.

---

routines as opportunities to facilitate the child's development. Parents need to be educated to select those family day-care homes that are licensed or approved and those where the strengths of caregivers and programs offered match objectives that parents have for the child's care.

Center-Based Care

Historical perspective. Child-care centers in this country have been associated historically with social services for the poor. It was not until the late 1970s that middle-class parents began to demonstrate the need for alternative care, as well. Recently, child-care policy and programs have been involved in political and philosophical controversy and confusion. While the role of

child care has been debated, the need for alternative-care arrangements for working parents continues to increase. Through the last several centuries children have been cared for in facilities outside the home, but no commitment has been made to develop or expand programs to provide adequate care, much less quality care. Society sanctioned child care during the world wars and during the Depression but withdrew the sanction when the crises were over. Until recently the role of the mother in the home as the primary caregiver has prevailed, and efforts to resolve child-care problems by working mothers have been largely discouraged.

The historical conception of child care as a welfare service has changed, at least from the perspective of child development and family life specialists, and child care is presently viewed as a social utility needed by large numbers of non-problematic families to supplement the family's responsibilities in the provision of child development and early education experiences for their children. The collaborative arrangement between the child-care provider and the family is just beginning to be understood by researchers and the general public. The relationships between child-care programs and parents are seen as dynamic, multidimensional, and developmental, and have the potential for serving many functions formerly provided by the extended family. In this sense child care represents a social support for, rather than the replacement of, the responsibilities of the family (Peters & Benn, 1980).

Although the number of families who select center-based day care for their children is small in comparison to those who choose other forms of care, the numbers are increasing and represent a substantial population. Single-parent families and low-income families constitute a high proportion of the families using center-based care. A preschool child with a single employed parent is about 30 times more likely to be enrolled in a child-care center than a child in a two-parent family in which only one parent is employed. Hispanic-Americans are four times more likely to have a child cared for by relatives than by nonrelatives, while whites are slightly more likely to use relatives instead of nonrelatives in a private home setting (U.S. Department of Health & Human Services, 1980). While single working parents may need the full-time care that is offered by child-care centers more than nonworking married mothers, more and more families are choosing this arrangement as a means of promoting the child's growth and development. When parents are considering center-based care as an alternative, both advantages and disadvantages need to be considered (see Box 12d).

INFANT CARE

Prior to the mid-1960s it was believed harmful to separate an infant from her mother, and few

---

BOX 12d   ADVANTAGES AND DISADVANTAGES OF CENTER-BASED CARE

Advantages

A greater likelihood that:
The center will be licensed or regulated

The child will receive constant supervision

The staff will be trained

The caregiver will not experience isolation

The caregivers will always be available

The child will experience stability of place and routine

A wider variety of equipment, materials, activities and programs will be available

An educational component will be provided

Disadvantages

A chance that:
There will be less flexibility in schedules for individual differences in children

There will be less adult-child interaction

There will be multiple caregivers rather than a single, primary one

The children will be exposed to caregiver's and other children's diseases and/or infections

There will be larger groups of children

The child will have less space

Source: Snell, E., & Turner, P. (1981). *Education for parenthood: A curriculum for secondary students.* Santa Fe, NM: Department of Education, Vocational Division.

infants were placed in child-care centers. A number of studies in the 1970s supported the contention that the separation of the mother and infant as a result of child care did not impede mother-infant attachment. For example, Caldwell, Wright, Honig, and Tannebaum (1970) found no differences in mother-infant attachment between center-based and home-reared infants. Subsequent research by Moskowitz, Schwarz, and Corsini (1977) supported the contention that child care does not impair children's attachment to their mothers. The research by Kagan, Kearsley, and Zelazo (1978) was probably the most comprehensive and best controlled. These investigators compared 32 pairs of children aged 30–42 months and matched the sex, ethnicity, and social class. Half of the sample were in child-care centers and half were being reared at home. Again, as in many other studies, the child-care children were in a high-quality, university-sponsored, research-oriented center. There was an optimum caregiver/child ratio. It was found that the crying behavior of infants when separated from their mothers did not differ from those being reared in the home. Further, when the crying behavior of child-care children, home-reared children, and children of the same ages from other cultures were plotted, striking similarities emerged. These investigators concluded that separation anxiety may be more a function of maturational than experiential processes and thus it is inappropriate to study the effects of child-care on the child-mother attachment relationship.

Other researchers compared a group of 3-year-old children who had been in an infant treatment program to a matched sample of children who were entering regular child care for the first time at age 3 to evaluate the effects of early child-care intervention. All children in both groups were from minority groups, and the neighborhood of residence, socioeconomic level, race, and ethnic origin were constant in each population. All children were assessed on general pathology, play, and socialization behaviors and were observed in the naturalistic setting of the child-care center. No significant differences between the two groups were found on any of the variables (Resch, Lilleskov, Schur, & Mihalov, 1977).

The coping patterns of the two groups were found to be somewhat different. The children who had not been in infant care interacted more with other children on arrival at the center, showed more general play effectiveness, were healthier, and showed less immediate separation distress than those children who had been in infant care. The child-care children showed a more variable range of activities, from solitary play to social interaction, in their organization of play after arrival. This suggested that those children who had child-care experience did not rely as heavily on social interaction as a play organizer or as an organizer of separation distress. This may mean that experience in a child-care program that is oriented toward individual emotional needs could be a significant moderator in enabling children to utilize a variety of social modalities in their play and in dealing with distress.

In another study a variety of behaviors of a group of 3- and 4-year-old children who had been in a high-quality child-care program continuously from nine months of age were compared with those of a matched group of subjects who had no previous child care prior to the age of 3. The infant child-care group was found to be significantly more physically and verbally aggressive, more motorically active, and less cooperative with adults. There was a tendency for the infant child-care group to be less tolerant of frustration. No differences were found between the two groups on ability to get along with peers, on spontaneity, or intellectual competence as determined by success at problem solving, ability to abstract, and playfulness. Conclusions were that early entry into child care may not adversely affect adjustment with peers but may slow acquisition of some adult cultural values (Schwarz, Strickland, & Krolick, 1974).

These and other research studies have been interpreted as providing evidence that quality infant care is not harmful to the child's development. In fact, it is believed to promote development in many ways. The issue of infant care resurfaced in 1988, and at the present time the effects of infant care are being hotly debated among professionals nationwide. The crucial issue, once again, is whether infants with extensive early nonmaternal care are more likely to be less securely attached to their parents than other infants are. The debate was sparked by an analysis of data from two longitudinal studies by Belsky and Rovine (1988). Children's attachment was measured by utilizing Ainsworth's strange situation at 12–13 months of age. The investigators claimed that the data revealed that infants who experienced more than 20 hours of nonmaternal care per week displayed more avoidance of their mothers on reunion and were more likely to be classified as "insecurely attached" than infants with fewer than 20 hours of nonmaternal care. Sons in extensive child care, particularly, were more insecurely attached to both mother and father. However, Belsky and Rovine pointed out that half of the male children with extensive nonmaternal care established secure relationships with their fathers and two thirds established secure relationships with at least one parent. They concluded that certain factors contribute to the development of insecurity: being male, being "fussy" or "difficult" (as described by mothers), having mothers with limited interpersonal sensitivity, having mothers with less satisfaction with certain aspects of their marriages, and having mothers with a strong career orientation.

Since the publication of Belsky's interpretations, many researchers have conducted studies and have found evidence to refute his conclusions. Richters and Zahn-Waxler (1988) criticized Belsky's work because the research question was too simplistic; further, they were critical of the methodology, the design, and the data interpretation. They believe we still know painfully little about this question: "Under what conditions are what outcomes associated with what patterns of early nonmaternal care, to what extent, and why?"

Another group of researchers (Field, Masi, Goldstein, Perry, & Parl, 1988) studied 71 preschool children entering child care at different ages (earlier than 6 months and later than 6 months) who were observed on reunion with their parents, in a play situation, and who received ratings from their teachers. They found that age of entry into child care had no significant effects on attachment to mothers or on play and social skills.

Another project that took a slightly different approach was actually two studies conducted by Howes, Rodning, Galluzzo, and Myers (1988). Overall the results of both studies suggested that middle-class children in child care were no more likely to be insecurely attached than those cared for by their mothers. They emphasized the importance of examining children's relationships both with their mothers and with their caregivers when explaining influences of child care and maternal employment on child behaviors. Further, their data suggested that one secure attachment relationship may at least partly compensate for an insecure attachment relationship. However, children categorized as insecure with their mothers engaged in lower levels of play with caregivers regardless of their rating of attachment security to the caregiver. The security of attachments to caregivers was more predictive of engagement with peers than was the security of attachment to mothers. Further, children were less likely to form attachments to caregivers when they were frequently ignored and when the number of children per adult increased.

Clearly the issue of nonmaternal care for infants is a complex one. While recent studies have begun to consider the quality of the caregiving environment as a variable and while more longitudinal studies are being conducted, there still exists a need for sophisticated, well-designed, and tightly controlled research. It is nonproductive to focus on whether it is good or bad for infants to be in child care; the real issue is how we can improve the quality of care so that it enhances optimal development.

SCHOOL-AGE CHILDREN IN SELF CARE

Recent studies have pointed to the increasing number of school-age children who are without direct adult supervision for some portion of the day (Cole & Rodman, 1987). These children have for years been referred to as latchkey children. The term *latchkey* was based on the practice of children wearing housekeys on chains around their necks. More recently, in order to avoid the negative connotations with latchkey and unsupervised children, the label *self care* has emerged (Powell, 1987). There are many complex situations that complicate the description of

children who are labeled as those under self care. However, it seems appropriate to refer to latchkey or self-care children as those school-age children who are old enough to care for themselves for limited periods of time and yet young enough to require adult supervision most of the time. Although an absolute age range cannot be established, it has been suggested that these are children between the ages of 6 and 13 who spend time alone or with a younger sibling on a regular basis (Cole & Rodman, 1987). While this phenomenon has created considerable anxiety for professionals and parents, there is a lack of evidence regarding the outcomes of this arrangement.

Children under self care not only are children of working parents, but also are those left in charge of themselves while parents are away from home engaged in other activities. Further, all children are not under their own care after school in the afternoons. One study found that 15 percent of self-care children are home alone in the mornings, 76 percent in the afternoons after school, and 9 percent at night (Rodman & Pratto, 1980). Two demographic factors, increasing numbers of mothers in the labor force and single parents, contribute to the growing numbers of children under their own supervision. In 1985, 68 percent of all mothers and 83 percent of divorced women with children between the ages of 6 and 17 were in the labor force. Estimates of the numbers of children in self care are between 20,000 to 10 million. It ap-

pears that 6 million is a conservative estimate. Studies have indicated that some children 7 years and younger are under self care, but about 40 percent begin this arrangement between 8 and 10 years of age (Powell, 1987).

Readiness for Self Care

Although all parents expect their children to accept increasing responsibilities as they develop, the decision to use a self-care arrangement involves a considerable increase in responsibility. When are children ready to care for themselves? The decision is obviously not an easy one for parents to make. A particular age is certainly not the criterion. Some children develop faster than others and can assume responsibility for themselves earlier than others. Family and community circumstances, the diversity of experiences that the child has had as he develops, parental attitudes toward protecting the child, and the state's legal requirements for child supervision must be considered. Cole and Rodman (1987) offered suggestions for parents to use in determining when children are ready to assume the responsibility for self care (see Boxes 12e, 12f, and 12g).

Effects of Self Care

Several viewpoints currently exist in relation to children under their own supervision. Some view self-care arrangements as expecting children to assume adult-like responsibilities too soon. The pressure on children to grow up too soon can lead to unnecessary stress with negative outcomes in such areas as achievement and socioemotional development. Yet, increasingly, families must face limited choices regarding child-care options. It is questionable whether some families can afford the luxury of childhood (Powell, 1987).

What are the effects of adult-supervised situations versus children under their own supervision? Are latchkey children at risk? The research has not kept pace with the growing public use of this arrangement and parents' and professionals' concerns about it. There is limited research, most of which compares children in unsupervised versus adult-supervised child-care arrangements. Conclusions cannot be drawn from

---

BOX 12e   DETERMINING CHILD'S READINESS FOR SELF CARE

Physically

The child must be able to:

Control her body to the degree that she will not injure herself as she moves through the house.

Manipulate the locks on the doors.

Safely operate any accessible equipment to which she has access.

Emotionally

The child must be able to:

Be comfortable enough to be alone for the required period of time without undue fear.

Follow important established rules without testing them.

Handle the usual and the unexpected events without excessive fear or anxiety.

Not exhibit a pattern of withdrawn, hostile, or self-destructive behavior.

Socially

The child should:

Be able to solicit, if needed, help from friends, neighbors, or other designated persons.

Understand the role of, and call on when needed, the appropriate community resources— police, fire department, rescue squads, and so forth.

Be able to maintain friendships with peers and adults.

Source: Cole, C., & Rodman, H. (1987). When school-age children care for themselves: Issues for family life educators and parents. *Family Relations, 36*(1), 92–96.

BOX 12f   PARENT'S ROLE IN CHILD'S SELF CARE

The parent must:

Maintain appropriate communication with the child and exercise some supervision even though not physically present.

Be available, or designate other persons, for contact when emergencies occur.

Be stable enough to provide emotional security to the child.

Train the child in the special issues of self care.

Source: Cole, C., & Rodman, H. (1987). When school-age children care for themselves: Issues for family life educators and parents. *Family Relations, 36*(1), 92–96.

---

these studies because of the methodological problems and the limited sample sizes.

Some research conducted in urban areas has reported fear and loneliness associated with the experience of staying home alone (Long & Long, 1982). The Longs reported that 30 percent of the latchkey children they interviewed had unusually high fears, including someone breaking into the house, noises, outdoor darkness, and animal cries and barking. Loneliness and boredom were

---

**BOX 12g NECESSARY COMMUNITY CHARACTERISTICS
IN PROMOTING SELF CARE**

The community must:

Be reasonably safe and perceived as so by the child and parent.

Have a variety of child-care options so that the family has choices as the child develops
and family needs change.

Source: Cole, C., & Rodman, H. (1987). When school-age children care for themselves: Issues for
family life educators and parents. *Family Relations, 36*(1), 92–96.

---

the chief complaints of these children. The results of this study must be viewed with caution because it lacked precision, and interviewer bias was associated with the procedures. Further, the study was conducted with children living in an inner-city ghetto area. Zill (1983) found 32 percent of boys and 41 percent of girls between the ages of 7 and 11 years worried when they were at home without an adult. Their primary concern was "someone bad" getting into the house.

Rodman, Pratto, and Nelson (1985) examined the differences between self-care children and adult-supervised children who were in the fourth and seventh grades in Piedmont, North Carolina. Twenty-six pairs of children in each grade level were matched on age, sex, race, family composition, and social status. They found no significant differences between self-care and adult-supervised children in self-esteem, locus of control, and teacher ratings of social adjustment and interpersonal relations. A study of third-, fifth-, and seventh-graders in rural Pennsylvania found no differences in school adjustment, academic achievement, orientation to the classroom, and fear of going outdoors between children in self care and those under adult supervision (Galambos & Garbarino, 1983).

Not all latchkey children go home after school. Some go to friends' houses where there is no adult supervision; some "hang out" at shopping malls or other retail areas. These after-school experiences are obviously quite different from those experienced by children alone at home. Some evidence indicates there is a need for concern about those who "hang out" (Steinberg, 1986). Steinberg studied 865 children in fifth grade

through ninth grade in Madison, Wisconsin. He found that both boys and girls were more susceptible to peer pressure when they were in after-school situations removed from consistent adult control. Children on their own were more susceptible than those in their own homes. A hierarchy of susceptibility appeared to be operating. Children who were "hanging out" were more susceptible than those who went to unsupervised friends' houses, and the latter were more susceptible than those who went home. There was no difference in susceptibility between those who were alone at home and those who were supervised by an adult or older sibling. A key factor seemed to be what Steinberg referred to as "distal supervision"—whether or not the parent knew the location of the child.

Another important finding of the Steinberg (1986) study was that children reared in an authoritative parenting style were less susceptible to peer influence, even when they were under their own care and susceptibility to peer pressure was quite high. Authoritative style was defined as the parents conferring with the child on matters of spending money, leisure activities, and so forth but still maintaining control over the decision. The less distal supervision exercised, the more important the authoritative parenting style is.

Vandell and Corasaniti (1988) examined the outcome differences associated with types of after-school care among 150 white, predominantly middle-class third-graders from a suburban school district in Texas. The care arrangements included children who returned home to their mothers, attended child-care centers, stayed with sitters, or returned home alone or with siblings. No significant differences were found between latchkey and mother-care children in terms of their classroom sociometric nominations, academic grades, standardized test scores, conduct grades, self-reports of self-competence, or parent and teacher ratings of the children. Significant differences were found for children who attended child-care centers after school. These children received more negative peer nominations, made lower academic grades, and had lower standardized test scores than the mother-care or the latchkey children. The children who stayed with sitters received more negative peer nominations than did the latchkey and the mother-care children but resembled these groups in other areas. These outcome differences were apparent in both divorced and intact families.

From these few studies it can be noted that a number of factors potentially influence the effects of the self-care arrangement—the age level of the child and his unique strengths and weaknesses, the context of the setting in which self care takes place, the patterns of child rearing and whether or not parents maintain distal control, and the geographic location (rural versus urban or inner city). Future research must focus on how the character of the parent-child relationship might mediate the effects, the important quality-of-life indicators in the neighborhood and community, the developmental processes of children and the indicators of readiness for self care, and the child's need for and conception of privacy. Further, evaluations of different approaches to supporting children in self care should be conducted. Longitudinal designs would provide developmental outcomes for children and families over time (Powell, 1987; Robinson, Rowland, & Coleman, 1986).

Parents' Viewpoints

Some studies have examined parents' viewpoints regarding self-care arrangements (Robinson, Rowland, & Coleman, 1986). Despite the fact that parents often report positive benefits their children receive from the latchkey experience, most choose self care for their children with concern, guilt, ambivalence, and uncertainty. Several factors have been found to affect the parental

satisfaction with self care: whether or not the arrangement is voluntarily undertaken, whether the child is a boy or a girl, and whether the amount of time the child has to spend alone is excessive. When self care is involuntary, involves girls more than boys, and occurs for long periods of time, parents tend to be more dissatisfied with the arrangement. The reasons cited by some parents for using self care varies—transportation problems, the expense of child care, and the belief that the child is old enough to care for herself. Other research (Powell, 1987) has not found the cost of after-school programs to be the major barrier to their use. In fact, some of the better-educated parents who could well afford to pay for after-school programs do not use them. Low-income parents do, however, seem to be more sensitive to cost factors. The factors that Powell (1987) has found to affect the choices of parents include the convenience of the location of an available program and the parental values relating to self help and independence of children.

After-School Programs

It is projected that more and more parents will be making a decision regarding after-school child care. Being able to assess the available options is important for parents. Some practices are questionable. For example, staff-child ratios of 1:100, where children are herded into a gymnasium to do homework for 3 hours, can be as harmful as, or more so than, children alone at home (Powell, 1987). Powell proposed several possible support programs for children and parents considering self care. Phone-in hotlines where children can get help with homework and personal concerns and training programs for parents and children on the best ways to handle self-care issues were mentioned. He suggested that whatever the environmental setting, it should allow the child to experience autonomy, control, and mastery of the activities included.

Guerney and Moore (1983) described a prevention-oriented service for latchkey children—PhoneFriend. This after-school telephone service was staffed by trained volunteers to be a "friend in need" to provide social contact for any child who sought it. In a 6-month period, callers ranged from 4 to 16 years of age, and the average call was 4½ minutes in length. In a large percentage of calls, the child was lonely or bored and just wanted to talk. Other children reported being scared or worried; being curious about the service; having difficulty with a sibling or a schoolmate; or having a variety of lesser concerns relating to heterosexual relationships, household maintenance, use of the phone, minor medical problems, homework, or pets. A total of 1,266 calls were received within this time frame.

Kids Check-in programs were described by McKnight and Shelsby (1984). These programs are designed for older elementary and junior high school children and provide flexible care and supervision by a trained neighborhood-based family day-care provider. With parental permission, children can spend time in their own homes, visit friends, play in their neighborhoods, or attend after-school and community activities. Under a special contract, parents designate exactly how much freedom and responsibility they want their child to have. The contract also specifies the role of the provider in the supervision and care. An individual plan is made for the child that involves the parent, provider, and the child. This individual plan allows for the unique needs and interests of the child. The check-in programs provide flexible care and supervision for children who are almost, but not quite, ready for total self care.

The overriding question with regard to programs for school-age children should not be whether harm or risk has been prevented, but whether the child's development has been enhanced. The energies and commitment of program designers should be toward this end (Powell, 1987).

In summary, more and more parents are faced with a decision regarding after-school care for their school-age children. A growing number of children are left at home in their own care or "hang out" on their own. Parents and professionals have ambivalent feelings about self care, and research has yielded conflicting results about its effects. Future efforts need to be directed toward investigating the mediating variables that affect the outcomes. Attention should be focused also on providing a variety of quality options from which parents can choose.

QUALITY CHILD CARE

The issue of what constitutes quality child care is a complex one, and the difficulty of defining quality is compounded by the diverse opinions of parents, policy makers, providers, and advocacy groups. Each group has a distinct philosophy about what child care should accomplish for children and families. Quality may be defined in relation to the services offered and the educational, social, health, and physical activities provided for the children. The climate of the classroom—such as caregiver behavior, the social structure, and the interaction patterns of the adults and the children—is of primary concern to others. Some experts and parents are concerned about the developmental changes in children as a result of child-care experience, and others combine several or all of these factors in describing quality programs.

Parents have few, if any, resources available to assist them in selecting quality child-care programs. One of the first criteria that parents can apply in their search for quality child care is that of licensing. States have assumed the responsibility for licensing, certifying, or registering family day-care homes, mini-centers, and child-care centers. This licensing requirement is designed to protect children in group situations. Legally, states pass laws to provide for minimum standards that programs or homes must meet in order to exist. A licensing law assigns a state agency to be responsible for developing and enforcing these minimum standards. In most cases the agency is the human services department; the state department of pensions and security; the department of public welfare; and, in some cases, the departments of health and environment and education. Licensing has been an important influence since World War II, and all states have some kind of regulation of child-care programs. Most states require licensing of child-care centers and family day-care homes. States continually revise their regulations, and the minimum requirements, the types of care covered, and the enforcement practices vary from state to state. States generally agree on the need for child-care regulations, but the agreement ends there.

Most states have minimum standards that

relate to the building and grounds, the personnel and staffing, and the services and care of the children. Before a center is approved for licensing and begins operation, the facility usually is inspected by the licensing agency and is reinspected from time to time thereafter in order to renew the license. In most states licensers are not allowed to provide parents with information on the quality of specific child-care centers unless this information is directly related to licensure. These agencies can disclose whether or not a center is licensed, what its licensed capacity is, the number of hours it operates each day, and the training and experience of the caregivers. Evaluation of the quality of the program is not allowed, and agency personnel cannot recommend one center over another. A list of licensed centers can be provided, as can a copy of licensing guidelines, and some states have developed simplified checklists for parents to use. Many states encourage agency personnel to suggest to parents that they visit and observe in a variety of centers to determine which one best meets their needs. Sometimes parents are encouraged to contact a local child-care association for information. These procedures, however, are not very helpful to parents. It cannot be assumed

that parents will visit a center prior to the child's enrollment; many make arrangements over the phone. Further, licensing guidelines probably would not be helpful even if parents visited. Not only are the guidelines complex, but also generally they are not designed to differentiate between programs that barely meet guidelines and those of quality. It is much easier to evaluate the plumbing, the heating, and the temperature of the refrigerator than to discover the attitudes of teachers and curriculum.

The National Day Care Study, initiated in 1974 and completed in 1978, was undertaken to determine the impact of variations in the staff-child ratio, the number of caregivers, the group size, and the staff qualifications on both the development of preschool children and the costs of center care. The effects of other center characteristics such as the educational program and the physical environment on the quality and cost of child care were investigated. While the findings of this study were extensive, we will mention only a few. First, small groups of children provide the best care situation. Groups of 15 or fewer children versus 25 or more children (3 to 6 years of age), with correspondingly small numbers of (but at least 2) caregivers, were associated

with higher frequencies of desirable child and caregiver behaviors and with higher gains by the children on the Preschool Inventory and Peabody Picture Vocabulary Test. Lead teachers in smaller groups engaged in more social interaction with the children, such as questioning, responding, instructing, praising, and comforting, than did teachers in larger groups. Children in smaller groups showed higher frequencies of such behaviors as considering/contemplating, contributing ideas, giving opinions, persisting at tasks, and cooperating than did children in larger groups (U.S. Department of Health, Education, and Welfare, 1978).

Second, staff specialization in child-related fields, not necessarily formal education, is linked to quality care. Teachers who had training in child development and early childhood education engaged in more social interactions with the children than did teachers without training. Finally, some determinants of quality in center care for infants are different from those for 3- to 5-year-old children. High staff/child ratios, not just small groups, are associated with less stress on infants and staff. One adult per four or five children appeared to be the most effective. Greater education and specialization of caregivers was associated with higher staff interaction with children, more teaching of language, and more touching of children (U.S. Department of Health, Education, and Welfare, 1978).

With the increase of federal dollars allocated for the purchase of child care in the late 1960s and 1970s attention was focused on quality of purchased care. In 1968 the Federal Interagency Day Care Requirements (FIDCRS) were developed as a response to this concern. Proposals for changes were made in 1972, and in 1975 a modified version of FIDCRS was attached to Title XX of the Social Security Act. Title XX funds were allowed only for centers that met FIDCRS. At one point the requirements were changed to HEWDCRS (Health, Education, and Welfare Day Care Requirements). Considerable controversy emerged over these federal regulations, especially in relation to adult/child ratios. No federal money was legislated to enforce these regulations or to assist centers in meeting them. In actuality, they were never enforced, and at the time of this writing no attempt is being made

to enforce these regulations. However, current legislation pending in Congress—the Act for Better Child Care—provides, once again, for the development and implementation of national standards for child care, as well as an effort to upgrade state minimum standards, but its passage is far from assured.

In the absence of national standards, the National Association for the Education of Young Children has developed a set of standards as well as "Developmentally Appropriate Practices" for children from birth through age 8. Centers may seek to become accredited voluntarily by first undergoing an extensive self-study and finally submitting to evaluation by a national team. If the program meets all the requirements, then it may become accredited. More and more centers are undergoing the accreditation process, which, at the time of this writing, is the only recognized mechanism for distinguishing high-quality centers.

Only recently have the effects of child care been examined within the context of quality. The researchers conducting one longitudinal study examined the long-term consequences of child-care quality by observing 20 white middle-class 4-year-olds during free play at good- and poor-quality centers and again at 8 years of age as they participated in triadic play sessions. Maternal, peer, and researcher observational ratings were obtained. In the analysis, when the effects of socioeconomic status were removed, children from high-quality centers had more friendly interactions and fewer unfriendly interactions with peers, were rated as more socially competent, were happier, and received fewer "shy" ratings from peers. Significant continuity was found between the 4-year-olds' behavior and the children's functioning at 8 years. Specifically, positive interactions with adults at age 4 were positively correlated to ratings of empathy, social competence, and peer acceptability at 8 years, and unoccupied behavior at 4 was negatively related to ratings of empathy, social competence, and conflict negotiation at 8 years. These results argue that behavior at 4 years old is not short-term but is reflected in the child's behavior 4 years later (Vandell, Henderson, & Wilson, 1988).

In another study, by Holloway and Reichhart-Erickson (1988), 55 children in 15 child-care centers of varying quality were observed. The ratings of quality were significant predictors of the children's behavior. The children were more prosocial in knowledge of social problem solving in centers where teachers demonstrated a style of respect, engagement, responsivity, and democracy. Further, when there was adequate space and fewer children per adult, children spent more time engaging in focused solitary play; in crowded conditions they spent more time observing others. Finally, social reasoning skills were related to the opportunity for interaction with others and to smaller group size.

Peterson and Peterson (1986) selected 3- to 5-year-olds in two high-quality and two low-quality centers, as well as a group of home-care controls. Children were observed interacting with their mothers in three episodes: while being ignored, while being attended to, and while being required to do a difficult task. Several differences were observed. Children in poor-quality centers were the least compliant—they spent less time doing the task and more time running around. Home-care children and those in high-quality centers were more willing to comply with their mothers' wishes. Home-care children carried on more sustained dialogues; children in good-quality centers were intermediate in their verbal behavior, but children in poor-quality centers were more likely to limit verbal interaction to single statements (less dyadic exchange). The most important overall conclusion was that the type of center affects how the children interact with their mothers.

In summary, more research on the effects of quality versus minimal child care is just beginning to surface. The preliminary data strongly suggest that quality does make a difference, clearly in the short-term and perhaps in the long-term. These findings underscore the need for widespread advocacy for quality care.

Help for Parents

Most parents believe that they are equipped to select quality care for their children, despite some evidence that suggests that parents actually do little observation and investigation of centers prior to enrolling their children (Turner & Smith, 1983; Turner & Gallegos, 1984). An attempt has been made by a number of individuals, organizations, and agencies to provide checklists that parents may use in evaluating a child-care or early childhood program. A Parent's Guide to Quality Day Care was developed by Bradbard and Endsley (1978). This guide consists of 65 items that relate to health, safety, adult-child-peer interactions, program activities, home-center coordination, and other components of high-quality care. The items are descriptively clear, and parents can use a nine-point rating scale in their evaluations. This evaluation is designed to be completed in 20–30 minutes. The U.S. Department of Health and Human Services published a lengthy as well as short evaluation form that may be used in selecting quality child care. The Metropolitan Life Insurance Company, the League of Women Voters, and the National Association for the Education of Young Children have all distributed information relating to criteria for quality programs. The problem seems to be that of educating parents about the need for selecting quality programs, providing them with guidelines for evaluation, and following through with evaluations.

EFFECTS OF CHILD CARE

Parents and experts have been concerned for years with the effects of child care on children. Prior to the 1970s few answers could be provided with any degree of assurance. However, during that decade research on child care increased substantially. The research was by no means flawless. For example, most of the research was conducted in high-quality centers that were not representative of most substitute care arrangements; most studies were limited to the direct effects on an individual child and have consequently ignored important questions concerning the broader impact of child care on parents, the family, and social institutions; there was nearly exclusive reliance on standardized tests to evaluate the intellectual and social development of children; some studies failed to control such variables as the caregiver/child ratios at different ages, the stability and the continuity of the caregivers, the nature of the child's daily experience, the provision of adequate conditions of nutrition and health, and the quality of the child-care experience. In addition, the long-term follow-up of children was neglected (Belsky & Steinberg, 1978; Etaugh, 1980). From a rather extensive review of research relating to the effects of child care on children by Belsky and Steinberg (1978), Etaugh (1980), and other studies the following conclusions may be reached.

Effects on Cognitive Development

For most middle-class children who attend centers that meet legal guidelines for quality, child care has neither salutory nor adverse effects on intellectual development as measured by standardized tests. For economically disadvantaged children, however, child care may have enduring positive effects, for it appears that quality child-care experience may attenuate the decline in test scores typically associated with high-risk populations after 18 months of age.

For example, the effects of 11 high-quality preschool intervention programs were documented by Lazar, Darlington, Murray, Royce, and Snipper (1982). They found positive effects on intellectual development in all the programs, and the typical decline at 18 months was much less pronounced.

Most of the research on child care and cognitive development has taken place in university-based programs rather than in community programs. A longitudinal study conducted by Burchinal, Lee, and Ramey (1989) used the random assignment of low-SES children to a university-based child-care program, to a community-based program, and to a no-intervention control group. The first two groups had experienced at least 1 year of quality child care. The results indicated that quality care (in both the university and the community centers) enhanced intellectual development—for example, higher preschool IQs, even after adjusting for the effects of maternal and home characteristics. The investigators further concluded that quality is more important to cognitive development than the age of the child at entry or the amount of child care.

For children from relatively advantaged homes, exposure to even high-quality, cognitively enriched programs does not appear to result in any long-term gains or declines in test performance. However, some evidence indicates that the child's prolonged involvement in child care tends to reduce maternal involvement with the child, thereby undermining any positive effects the program may have had on the child's IQ. Turnover in personnel also tends to be related to a washout of gains. Some observational data indicate that child care is associated with problem solving, abstraction abilities, and ability to plan in children. It appears that additional research that measures cognitive ability through observation rather than standardized tests would provide information on whether children in child care are learning functional skills applicable to everyday life.

Effects on Emotional Development

In the earlier section on infant care, the question of the quality of attachment of infants in child care to their mothers was discussed. While there appears to be evidence on both sides of the issue, firm conclusions are premature. Part of the difficulty lies with the assessment of attachment. The most common type of measurement is the Strange Situation, in which a mother and her child are together in a strange room with toys; a stranger enters, the mother leaves, and finally the mother returns. The child's behavior, toward both the mother and the environment, is rated in each condition. Several studies utilizing this approach have found that children were more likely to interact with their mother than with the caregiver, and when confronted with a problem-solving task all children who requested help turned to their mothers. Neither the age of entry into day care nor the length of time in day care appeared to affect the mother-child attachment bond. Additional evidence indicates that infants can develop a discriminating attachment-like relationship toward a familiar caregiver. However, this relationship does not supersede the child's emotional bond with his mother. Children continue to express preference for their mothers.

However, some researchers question the validity of the Strange Situation, and others criticize those who utilize it at the improper period of development. In short, interpretations of evidence on both sides should be viewed with caution. Nevertheless, at this time there is little reason to conclude that the participation of infants in high-quality child care leads to "insecure" attachment to mother and replacement of her by the caregiver as the primary object of attachment.

Effects on Social Development

As early as the late 1970s, some evidence suggested that children who entered child care before the age of 2 years were more likely than children who entered later to interact with peers in both positive and negative ways. Children in child care tended to exceed home-reared children in both physical and verbal aggression toward peers and adults. Child-care children also were less cooperative with adults and engaged in more activity (running about) as opposed to sitting in one place. And, once the child entered school,

child-care experienced children tended to be less involved in educational activities. Home-reared children appeared to have greater tolerance for frustration, as reflected in their ability to accept failure and to be interrupted. Child-care children tended to interact with peers more than with adults, were more self-assertive, less conforming, less impressed by punishment, less aversive to dirt, and more prone to toilet lapses than home-reared children. (Belsky & Steinberg, 1978; Etaugh, 1980).

An interesting study by Rubenstein and Howes (1979) examined social interaction and play behavior of community-based child-care infants and matched home-reared infants. Adult-infant, infant-peer, and infant-toy interactions were observed for the two groups. The results indicated that more infant verbal responsiveness to maternal talking, more infant crying, and more maternal restrictiveness were found in the home. While infants responded more to the mother's voice than to the caregiver's, mothers gave four times more directions and commands than the caregivers did. More adult-infant play, tactile content, and reciprocal smiling were found

in child care. About 50 percent of infants' time in each setting was spent in positive interactions with adults (53 percent in center and 47 percent in the home). The developmental level of play with toys by infants was higher in child care, suggesting that competence in dealing with in-animate objects may be facilitated by child care. In addition, child-care infants tended to interact more with peers than did home-reared infants. The differences in adult-child interactions were found to be related to differences in infants as well as in adults. These findings supported the hypothesis that infants shape their own environments. No adverse effects of daily mother-infant separation were noted in the social and play behaviors of the child-care group. Peers contributed to high levels of play noted in the child-care group, and peers also seemed to facilitate separation from the adult caregiver. The authors concluded that caregiving in a social context that includes peers for both infants and caregivers appears to facilitate a more harmonious caregiver-infant relationship. In the isolated setting of the home, the infant makes more social demands on the caregiver than in centers. Further, the infant's needs compete with needs of the household and with the mother's needs for adult social contact. Long hours of exclusive infant care in the home can contribute to maternal irritation and restrictiveness. Peers seem to offer an alternative source of social stimulation and seem to reduce the infant's exclusive dependence on an adult caregiver. As early as 2 years of age, infants seem to profit from a stable group of peers. Both maturity of play and positive emotional responses were highest when the infant was engaged in positive peer interaction.

Another study found that extended time in child care was positively related to increased social participation, increased associative interaction with peers, and decreased unoccupied and onlooker behavior. Other differences among children varied by the type of child-care center—university-based, community-based (high quality), or private center. In the university center extended care was related to increased constructive play activity by children. However, children in the private center showed no positive nor negative behaviors as a function of time in care. Overall there were three differences

between the two high-quality centers and the private center: children in the first two centers were in mixed-age groups, there were fewer children per adult, and there was more emphasis on social development than on cognitive development. This study underscores the importance of examining center characteristics when assessing the effects of child care (Schindler, Moely, & Frank, 1987).

Another recent study found that middle-class children with more hours of child care engaged in less watching, less solitary play, and less teacher comfort-seeking behavior and showed more cooperative play, positive affect, and peer interaction, but teachers rated them as more assertive-aggressive (Field et al., 1988). These researchers concluded that the more child-care experience children have, the more socially interactive they are. However, they emphasize the importance of stability and quality in child-care arrangements.

PARENTAL SATISFACTION WITH CHILD CARE

Numerous studies have found high parental satisfaction with child care. For example, Roopnarine and Hempel (1988) found high satisfaction by both mothers and fathers with both the caregiving environment and the effects of child care. Whether children entered child care early (before 6 months) or later (during the second year) had no relationship to the perceptions of parents about the effects of child care on parent-child interactions. A similar study by Roopnarine, Mounts, and Castro (1986) reported favorable maternal ratings of child care, but mothers with children in centers perceived greater benefits for their children and had more positive perceptions of care than did mothers with children in home-based programs. The perceptions of the child's care experiences were positively correlated with perceived relationships with spouses. Further, another interesting study found that employed mothers' satisfaction with child care, plus frequent social contacts, predicted security in mother-child attachment (Weinraub, Jaeger, and Hoffman, 1988).

An earlier study comparing the child-care

needs, attitudes, and practices of single-parent and intact families included a rating of 14 features of child-care centers or family day-care homes. Parents with infants and preschool children were asked to rate on a scale of poor to excellent each feature of their current child-care arrangement. The quality of care, the cleanliness, and the nutrition program received good to excellent ratings by both sets of parents. All the other features (space, equipment, program activities, and so on) received average to good ratings. Those features rated lowest were cost, discipline methods, and support to parents. The authors were surprised, however, at the relatively high level of satisfaction with child care that the respondents expressed (Turner & Gallegos, 1984). It may be that parents overinflate their satisfaction responses because they cannot consciously accept that their children may be spending considerable amounts of time in a less-than-adequate environment.

IN THE FUTURE

If the nation works to meet the need for child-care services, several considerations should be taken into account. Quality child care cannot be conceived as the panacea for a troubled society. Overpromise can breed resentment and bitterness. Child care appears to be a viable option as: substitute care while parents work or participate in vocational or educational programs; substitute care for children whose parents are physically or mentally disabled; a provider of enriching, stimulating, and developmental activities for children, especially children from less-than-adequate homes; and as an alternative to institutionalization for children living in dangerous home situations. Further, providing child care in isolation from comprehensive services to families must be avoided. The involvement of the entire family must be achieved. In addition, quality programs must be ensured. Regulating and monitoring for warmth, patience, understanding, and enjoyment of children by caregivers is difficult but must be implemented.

Parents seem to provide the best key for qual-

ity control and must be involved in the decision-making process. Educating parents must be an ongoing process accomplished by community and professional groups. There is a need for diversity of models and creative approaches to child care. Standardized equipment, buildings, and curricula are not necessary. Standardized children are not what society needs.

Credentialing of child-care personnel is seen by many as a way of increasing professionalism in the field and one way to contribute to quality programs. Thus far few incentives for child-care workers exist in most states. Low wages are paid, and only a small percentage of child-care agencies have agreed to include credentials as a recognition of achievement. Head Start has attempted through the Child Development Associate program (CDA) to recognize achievement of caregivers through training and credentialing. Difficulties with administering and funding CDA have persisted, and currently, with few exceptions, funds for CDA training and credentialing are available for only Head Start employees.

A nationally recognized voice for children is needed. Child-care personnel have begun to join with professional organizations such as the Coalition for Children and Youth, the National Association for the Education of Young Children, the Children's Defense Fund, and many others to form the Alliance for Better Child Care so that common needs can be articulated. There is a need for cooperation between child-care groups and other youth groups such as residential child care, probation personnel, hospital child-care workers, foster parents, group home workers, 4-H, "Y" boys' and girls' clubs, and Scouts. Current evidence indicates that the best treatment for most youngsters is successful, developmentally oriented life experiences to prevent the need for therapeutic approaches.

Research Needs

Continued research on child care from an ecological perspective is needed. Research is needed that focuses on the broader effects of child care rather than on the consequences of child care and its direct effects on the child. Few studies have examined effects on parents or parent-child relationships. One exception is a study conducted by Roopnarine and Hempel (1988) that surveyed parents of two groups of children: those who entered child care before the age of 6 months and those who entered during the second year. The parents' perceptions of parent-child interactions were related to their perceptions of the effects of child care on social and cognitive skills. The perceived effects of child care also were related to the parents' assessments of personal well-being, companionship in marriage, marital stress, job satisfaction, and social supports. There were fewer associations for fathers than for mothers.

More needs to be known about the differential consequences of center-based care, family day care, and care in the home; and information is needed about specific influences of the child-care environment on child outcomes, such as the extent of exposure to adult models other than the major caregiver. Questions such as the following need to be answered: What are the long-term effects of a child-centered environment that has few restrictions or off-limits areas? How are children affected by age segregation? How are parental perceptions of, attitudes toward, and interaction with the child influenced by alternative care arrangements and by access to child-care professionals? Does child care encourage parents to abdicate their roles as child-rearers? Does child care affect child-care responsibilities at home, and how does this influence parental roles? How does inconsistency of socialization in child care and the home affect the child's development? What effects does child care have on marital relationships, work pursuits, or functioning in the neighborhood? What effects does child care have on society's attitude toward children, the function of the family, and the role of women in our culture (Belsky & Steinberg, 1978)?

Some progress has been made in child-care research. For example, prior to 1980 most research was conducted in high-quality centers only; now we have moved beyond research centers to include all types of community child care and varying levels of quality, and longitudinal studies are being initiated. Despite this progress, high-quality research, as a whole, is limited.

OTHER PRESCHOOL PROGRAMS

Head Start programs, nursery schools, play schools, parent-cooperative programs, and drop-in centers also provide alternatives for care for young children. Nursery schools, as opposed to day-care centers, are normally open for half a day from 2 to 5 days per week. Most nursery schools are closed during the summer months and do not meet the needs of working mothers. Children from 3 to 5 years of age are served, and opportunities for social interaction with peers and educational activities are provided. Emphasis is placed on the child's total growth and development, and particular attention is given to meeting the child's early learning needs.

For parents whose preschool children can function effectively away from them, nursery school may prove to be a valuable experience for both parents and children. The same criteria for educational activities, facilities and equipment, and teachers that denote quality for child care are appropriate for nursery school programs. Nursery schools rarely provide lunch but do offer nutritious snacks; they do not have separate facilities for sleeping. Parents can benefit by having some relief from parenting for part of the day and may gain greater understanding about their child's growth and development through the parent education and involvement aspects of the program. A nursery school provides many experiences, equipment and toys, and activities that supplement those offered by most parents. Children benefit from interacting with peers and another authority figure. All aspects of development can be promoted through the program offerings.

Most of the research relating to the effects of preschool programs on the child's development since the late 1960s has focused on intervention programs for disadvantaged children. Perhaps the best evidence of the positive contributions of preschool education to the development of low-income children has been the longitudinal research conducted by Schweinhart and Weikart (1980) and other longitudinal studies summarized by the Consortium for Longitudinal Studies (U.S. Department of Health, Education, and Welfare, 1979). The Perry Preschool project, an intervention program for low-income, 3-

and 4-year-old high-risk children, was begun in 1962. The 123 children have been followed since that time. Data indicate that children in the project have been significantly better school achievers than the control children; they have been perceived by their teachers to be better students than the control children; they have had less need of special education services; they have had a significantly lower crime rate; there has been a trend toward less use of welfare by the group that participated in the project; and there appears to be a trend toward greater college attendance by the preschool participants.

These investigators concluded that quality preschool education, especially for low-income high-risk children, should receive high priority for federal, state, and local funding, as the results of these programs clearly point to a favorable cost-benefit analysis. Individual states can save millions of dollars by intervening during the preschool years. Earlier estimates were for every $1 million invested, $4.5 million in later expenditure could be saved (Schweinhart & Weikart, 1980), and more recent estimates are closer to $7 million.

The Consortium for Longitudinal Studies examined research data for experimental preschool programs throughout the country during the 1960s and 1970s. Center-based, home-based, and combination home-center programs were reviewed for long-term effects on children's development. Several significant findings emerged: (1) early-education programs significantly reduced the number of children assigned to special education classes; (2) early-education programs significantly reduced the number of children retained in grade; (3) early education significantly increased children's scores on fourth-grade mathematics achievement tests, with a suggestive trend toward increased scores on fourth-grade reading tests; (4) low-income children who attended preschools surpassed their controls on the Standford-Binet IQ test for up to 3 years after the preschool programs ended; and (5) children who attended preschool were more likely than control children to give achievement-related reasons for being proud of themselves, and mothers of children who attended preschools had higher vocational aspirations for themselves and their children

(U.S. Department of Health, Education, & Welfare, 1979).

These longitudinal studies have been carefully controlled. Taken together, the results strongly suggest that quality preschool programs, at least for low-income children, result in favorable long-term effects on participating children, their families, and society.

Drop-In Child-Care Centers

The need for occasional care for young children not regularly enrolled in a preschool program is still prevalent in our society due to the mobility and social isolation of many young families. More and more commercial child-care centers are accepting children on a drop-in basis, along with regularly enrolled children. However, specialized drop-in centers are being established and more are needed. These centers are located primarily in shopping areas, bowling alleys, and even in prisons and are becoming more prevalent. Occasional part-time care of preschool children is available for the convenience of the customers. Moms' Morning Out, sponsored by churches, is another form of drop-in child care. Sometimes health clinics or community centers provide similar services. Fees may or may not be charged. When charged, parents usually pay by the hour. An interesting drop-in center was developed outside the state prison in New Mexico. One portion of the Visitor Hospitality Center was converted into a playroom for visitors' children. A trained early childhood specialist supervises the children as they play. The teacher also plans various educational activities for the children. The center is open during the days inmates can have visitors. Children may stay all or part of the day, and no fees are charged. Since these children and their parents have unusual needs, the director of the program faces quite a challenge.

Parent Cooperatives and Play Groups

Some nursery schools and child-care programs are parent cooperatives. In these programs parents are actively involved in all aspects of the program. Among the duties performed and roles assumed by parents are serving on advisory committees, interviewing and hiring personnel, paying tuition to support the educational program, and volunteering to work during the preschool sessions. Parents also may serve on a board of directors; organize fund-raising activites; and assist with general maintenance such as repair equipment, yard work, and housekeeping.

A modified approach to parent cooperatives is utilized in play groups, which primarily provide opportunities for children to play together with a group of peers under the supervision of an adult. Most often, mothers of the children involved alternate supervision responsibilities. Some groups are more formalized and meet at the same location, supervised by the same adults rather than on a rotating basis. These may be referred to as play schools. The development of social skills is the primary focus for both play groups and play schools. Appropriate indoor and outdoor equipment, toys, and planned activities are provided. Many play schools and groups operate only part of the day, 1 to 5 days per week. These programs can be a valuable resource for parents who are seeking part-time care and who are primarily interested in the child's developing skills in peer interaction. Parents would want to be sure that equipment, activities, and caregiver attitudes and behavior are of quality.

Head Start

Head Start has provided alternative care for millions of low-income children for nearly 25 years and has provided much-needed health services, nutrition, and educational benefits. Further, parents have had opportunities to become involved in the educational programs themselves. Federally funded, Head Start programs are free to participants. However, only a fraction of the eligible population is served, primarily due to budget cutbacks during the 1980s. Head Start, from its inception, has sought to promote the social, physical, and intellectual development of the child, has emphasized parent participation, and has responded to local needs. It has mainstreamed thousands of handicapped children. The program has fostered long-lasting gains in children's school performance and in the well-being of their families.

While the quality of Head Start programs varies considerably from one community to another and from classroom to classroom, it still remains an attractive option for low-income parents. Hopefully the U.S. Congress will continue to fund a proven successful program.

SUMMARY

Clearly our contemporary complex society requires a variety of alternatives for child care that support and supplement parents' roles and responsibilities. An "Aunt Jane" or Grandma who helps with child care or who intervenes in a crisis situation is no longer available for many American families during their child-rearing years. We have presented several options in the present chapter for parents who need part-time or full-time care for their children or for those parents who simply wish to provide peer interaction for their children. Alternatives include in-home care by a relative or nonrelative, family day care, center care, preschool programs, latch-key programs, and Head Start.

While alternatives for child care clearly exist in this country, we have by no means fully met the needs of America's families. At the time of this writing, fewer and fewer federal dollars are being allocated for care, and only the more affluent can afford quality care for their children. Preschool programs, excluding those few federally funded child-care programs, consist largely of children from middle- and upper-class families. In fact, child care in the United States is put to shame by comprehensive systems in many other nations. We still have a long way to go before all parents are truly provided with viable alternatives for child care that are acceptable and affordable.

REFERENCES

BELSKY, J., & ROVINE, M. (1988). Nonmaternal care in the first year of life and the security of infant-parent attachment. *Child Development, 59*(1), 157–167.

BELSKY, J., & STEINBERG, L. (1978). The effects of day care: A critical review. *Child Development, 49*, 929–949.

BRADBARD, M., & ENDSLEY, R. Special report: Identifying quality day care centers. *Child Care Quarterly, 7*(4), 279–288.

BURCHINAL, M., LEE, M., & RAMEY, C. (1989). Type of day care and preschool intellectual development in disadvantaged children. *Child Development, 60*(1), 128–137.

CALDWELL, B., WRIGHT, A., HONIG, A., & TANNEBAUM, J. (1970). Infant day care and attachment. *American Journal of Orthopsychiatry, 40*, 397–412.

CLARKE-STEWART, A. (1988). Evolving issues in early childhood education: A personal perspective. *Early Childhood Research Quarterly, 3*(2), 139–150.

COLE, C., & RODMAN, H. (1987). When schoolage children care for themselves: Issues for family life educators and parents. *Family Relations, 36*(1), 92–96.

CORSINI, D., WISENSALE, S., & CARUSO, G. (1988). Family day care: System issues and regulatory models. *Young Children, 43*(6), 17–22.

ETAUGH, C. (1980). Effects of nonmaternal care on children, research evidence and popular views. *American Psychologist, 35*(4), 309–319.

FIELD, T., MASI, W., GOLDSTEIN, S., PERRY, S., & PARL, S. (1988). Infant day care facilitates preschool social behavior. *Early Childhood Research Quarterly, 3*(4), 341–359.

GALAMBOS, N., & GARBARINO, J. (1983). Identifying the missing links in the study of latchkey children. *Children Today 12*(4), pp. 2–4, 40–41.

GAMBLE, T., & ZIGLER, E. (1986). Effects of infant day care: Another look at the evidence. *American Journal of Orthopsychiatry 56*(1), 26–42.

GUERNEY, L., & MOORE, L. (1983). PhoneFriend: A prevention-oriented service for latchkey children. *Children Today, 12*(4), 5–10.

HOLLOWAY, S., & REICHHART-ERICKSON, M. (1988). The relationship of day care quality to children's free-play behavior and social problem solving skills. *Early Childhood Research Quarterly, 3*(1), 39–54.

HOWES, C., RODNING, C., GALLUZZO, D., & MYERS, L. (1988). Attachment and child care: Relationships with mother and caregiver. *Early Childhood Research Quarterly, 3*(4), 403–416.

KAGAN, J., KEARSLEY, R., & ZELAZO, P. (1978). *Infancy, its place in human development*. Cambridge, MA: Harvard University Press.

LAZAR, I., DARLINGTON, R., MURRAY, H., ROYCE, J., & SNIPPER, A. (1982). Lasting effects of early childhood education: A report from the Consortium of Longitudinal Studies. *Monographs of the Society for Research in Child Development, 47* (2–30, Serial No. 195).

LONG, T., & LONG, L. (1982). Latchkey children: The child's view of self care. (ERIC Document Reproduction Service No. ED 211–229).

MCKNIGHT, J., & SHELSBY, B. (1984). Checking in: An Alternative for latchkey kids. *Children Today, 13*(3), 23–25.

MOSKOWITZ, D., SCHWARZ, J., & CORSINI, D. (1977). Initiating day care at three years of age: Effects on attachment. *Child Development, 48*, 1271–1276.

O'CONNELL, M., & BLOOM, D. A. (1987). *Juggling jobs and babies: America's child care challenge*. Washington, DC: Population Reference Bureau.

PETERS, D., & BENN, J. (1980). Day care: Support for the family. *Dimensions, 9*(11), 78–82.

PETERSON, C., & PETERSON, R. (1986). Parent/child interaction and day care: Does quality of day care matter? *Journal of Applied Developmental Psychology, 7*(1), 1–16.

POWELL, D. (1987). After-school care. *Young Children, 42*(3), 62–66.

RESCH, R., LILLESKOV, R., SCHUR, H., & MIHALOV, T. (1977). Infant day care as a treatment intervention: A follow-up comparison study. *Child Psychiatry and Human Development, 7*(3), 147–165.

RICHTERS, J., & ZAHN-WAXLER, C. (1988). The infant day care controversy: Current status and future directions. *Early Childhood Research Quarterly, 3*(3), 319–336.

ROBINSON, B., ROWLAND, B., & COLEMAN, M. (1986). Taking action for latchkey children and their families. *Family Relations, 35*(4), 473–478.

RODMAN, H., & PRATTO, D. (1980). How children take care of themselves: Preliminary statement on magazine survey. Unpublished report submitted to Ford Foundation.

RODMAN, H., PRATTO, D., & NELSON, R. (1985). Child care arrangements and children's functioning: A comparison of self-care and adult-care children. *Developmental Psychology, 21*(3), 413–418.

ROOPNARINE, J., & HEMPEL, L. (1988). Day care and family dynamics. *Early Childhood Research Quarterly, 3*(4), 427–438.

ROOPNARINE, J., MOUNTS, N., & CASTO, G. (1986). Mothers' perceptions of their children's supplementary care experience: Correlation with spousal relationships. *American Journal of Orthopsychiatry, 56*(4), 581–587.

RUBENSTEIN, J., & HOWES, C. (1979). Caregiving and infant behavior in day care and in homes. *Developmental Psychology, 15*(1), 1–24.

Second thoughts about infant day care (1987, May). *U.S. News and World Report*, pp. 73–74.

SCHINDLER, P., MOELY, B., & FRANK, A. (1987). Time in day care and social participation of young children. *Developmental Psychology, 23*(2), 255–261.

SCHWARZ, J., STRICKLAND, R., & KROLICK, G. (1974). Infant day care: Behavioral effects at preschool age. *Developmental Psychology, 10*(4), 502–506.

SCHWEINHART, L., & WEIKART, D. (1980). Young children grow up: The effects of the Perry Preschool Program on youth through age 15. *Monograph of the High Scope Education Research Foundation*. No. 7. Ypsilanti, MI: High Scope Press.

SNELL, E., & TURNER, P. (1981). *Education for parenthood: A curriculum for secondary students*. Santa Fe, NM: Department of Education, Vocational Division.

STEINBERG, L. (1986). Latchkey children and susceptibility to peer pressure: An ecological analysis. *Developmental Psychology, 22*(4), 433–439.

TURNER, P., & GALLEGOS, B. (1984). A comparison of the day care needs, attitudes, and practices of intact and single-parent families. *Journal of Employment Counseling, 21*(1), 19–30.

TURNER, P., & SMITH, R. (1983). Single parents and day care. *Family Relations, 32*, 215–226.

U.S. DEPARTMENT OF HEALTH, EDUCATION, & WELFARE, OFFICE OF HUMAN DEVELOPMENT SERVICES, ADMINISTRATION FOR CHILDREN, YOUTH, AND FAMILIES (1978). *National day care study: Preliminary findings and their implications.* Cambridge, MA: Abt Associates.

U.S. DEPARTMENT OF HEALTH, EDUCATION, & WELFARE, OFFICE OF HUMAN DEVELOPMENT SERVICES, ADMINISTRATION FOR CHILDREN, YOUTH, AND FAMILIES (1979). *Lasting effects after preschool* (DHEW Publication No. OHDS 79-30179). Washington, DC: Government Printing Office.

U.S. DEPARTMENT OF HEALTH & HUMAN SERVICES, OFFICE OF HUMAN DEVELOPMENT SERVICES, ADMINISTRATION FOR CHILDREN, YOUTH, AND FAMILIES. (1980). *The status of children, youth, and families* (DHHS Publication No. OHDS 80-30274). Washington, DC: Government Printing Office.

VANDELL, D., & CORASANITI, M. (1988). The relation between third graders' after-school care and social, academic, and emotional functioning. *Child Development, 59*(4), 868–875.

VANDELL, D., HENDERSON, V., & WILSON, K. (1988). A longitudinal study of children with day care experiences of varying quality. *Child Development, 59*(5), 1286–1292.

WANDERSMAN, L. (1981). Ecological relationships in family day care. *Child Care Quarterly, 10*(2), 89–102.

WEINRAUB, M., JAEGER, E., & HOFFMAN, L. (1988). Predicting infant outcomes of employed and unemployed mothers. *Early Childhood Research Quarterly, 3*(4), 361–378.

ZILL, N. (1983). *American children: Happy, healthy, and insecure.* New York: Doubleday/Anchor Press.

Indexes

Author Index

Subject Index